SOUTHERN BIOGRAPHY SERIES

Titles in the SOUTHERN BIOGRAPHY SERIES

Edited by Fred C. Cole and Wendell H. Stephenson

Felix Grundy, by Joseph Howard Parks
Thomas Spalding of Sapelo, by E. Merton Coulter
Edward Livingston, by William B. Hatcher
Fightin' Joe Wheeler, by John P. Dyer
John Sharp Williams, by George Coleman Osborn
George Fitzhugh, by Harvey Wish
Pitchfork Ben Tillman, by Francis Butler Simkins
Seargent S. Prentiss, by Dallas C. Dickey
Zachary Taylor, by Brainerd Dyer

Edited by T. Harry Williams

John Bell of Tennessee, by Joseph Howard Parks
James Harrod of Kentucky, by Kathryn Harrod Mason
Arthur Pue Gorman, by John R. Lambert
General Edmund Kirby Smith, by Joseph Howard Parks
William Blount, by William H. Masterson
P. G. T. Beauregard, by T. Harry Williams
Hoke Smith and the Politics of the New South, by Dewey W. Grantham, Jr.
General Leonidas Polk, by Joseph Howard Parks
Mr. Crump of Memphis, by William D. Miller
General William J. Hardee, by Nathaniel Chearis Hughes, Jr.
Montague of Virginia, by William E. Larsen
Thomas Mann Randolph, by William H. Gaines, Jr.
James Lusk Alcorn, by Lillian A. Pereyra
Robert Toombs of Georgia, by William Y. Thompson
The White Chief: James Kimble Vardaman, by William F. Holmes
Louis T. Wigfall, by Alvy L. King
L. Q. C. Lamar, by James B. Murphy
Breckinridge: Statesman, Soldier, Symbol, by William C. Davis
Joseph E. Brown of Georgia, by Joseph Howard Parks

JOSEPH E. BROWN OF GEORGIA

JOSEPH E. BROWN
of Georgia

JOSEPH H. PARKS

Louisiana State University Press
BATON ROUGE

Designer: Dwight Agner
Type face: Linotype Monticello
Typesetter and printer: Heritage Printers, Inc., Charlotte, N.C.
Binder: Delmar Company, Charlotte, N.C.

LIBRARY OF CONGRESS CATALOGING IN PUBLICATION DATA

Parks, Joseph Howard.
   Joseph E. Brown of Georgia.
   (Southern biography series)
   Bibliography: p.
   Includes index.
   1. Brown, Joseph Emerson, 1821–1894. 2. Legislators—
United States—Biography. 3. Georgia—Governors—Biogra-
phy. 4. Georgia—Politics and government—1775–1865. 5.
Reconstruction. I. Title. II. Series.
E664.B8613P37   975.8′03′0924   74–27192
ISBN 0–8071–0189–3

To the memory of Mary B., Taylor, and Claude

Contents

Acknowledgments *xiii*

I — Out of the Mountains — *1*

II — Into the Statehouse — *19*

III — He Defied Them All — *40*

IV — Politics of Patronage — *53*

V — Little Dogs Must Bark — *70*

VI — Stephens, Not Cobb — *90*

VII — Delay Is Full of Danger — *110*

VIII — Would That I Could Accompany You — *129*

IX — If You Refuse, You Will Regret It — *150*

X — Regiments but No Brigades — *170*

XI — Bold and Dangerous Usurpation — *198*

XII — The Question Is One of Bread — *220*

XIII — A Wicked Act — *253*

XIV — Let the States Decide — *273*

XV — I Therefore Decline — *301*

XVI — Private Citizen Again — *324*

XVII — Agree with Thine Adversary Quickly — *350*

XVIII — In Support of Congressional Reconstruction — *373*

XIX	Full-fledged Republican	406
XX	Action, Action, Action	434
XXI	Democrat Again	475
XXII	New South Versus the Old	507
XXIII	End of the Line	534
	Bibliographical Essay	579
	Index	595

Illustrations

Following page 272

Joseph E. Brown as a young man
Joseph E. Brown, governor of Georgia
The home of eight Georgia governors, 1838–1868
The Georgia Statehouse where the Ordinance of Secession was passed
Joseph E. Brown about 1870
Joseph E. Brown's home in Atlanta
The "Buzz Saw Politician"
The Brown family, *circa* 1890

Acknowledgments

THANKS ARE owed to many for their assistance and interest in the writing of this volume. Through the exercise of their collector's instinct Felix Hargrett and Charles Brockman, Jr., made available materials without which no reasonably complete biography of Joseph E. Brown could have been written. The courteous and efficient staffs of the special collections and manuscript divisions of the libraries of the University of Georgia, Emory University, Duke University, University of North Carolina, Georgia State Archives, and Atlanta Historical Society made research a pleasure. Deborah McCain, Yvonne Crumpler, and Alan Pitts gave valuable assistance in preparing the manuscript for publication. Research grants were provided by the University of Georgia and the University of Alabama in Birmingham. My sincere appreciation to all.

J. H. Parks

JOSEPH E. BROWN OF GEORGIA

Chapter I

Out of the Mountains

AMONG THE THOUSANDS of Scotch-Irish who migrated from Ireland to the American colonies in the eighteenth century were William and Margaret Fleming Brown. They arrived with their family in the Phila- delphia area in 1745, leaving behind the hardships of Londonderry life. Soon the Browns and their children, who eventually increased to seven —David, Fanny, Elizabeth, Joseph, James, William, and Jane—were moving along the Shenandoah Valley to Culpeper County, Virginia, thence to Guilford County, North Carolina, where William died in 1757. In 1785, when Margaret was eighty-four, she migrated with her youngest daughter, Jane, and her husband Reese Porter to Middle Tennessee. She died there in 1801 at the age of one hundred.

William and Margaret Brown's second son, Joseph, born in Ireland in 1731, married Mary Porter, daughter of Hugh and Violet Mackey Porter, also Irish immigrants. To Joseph and Mary Brown were born six sons and six daughters—William, Hugh, Joseph, James, Margaret, Violet, Elizabeth, David, Mary, Jamie, George, and Frances.

Members of two generations of the Brown clan were ardent and active American Revolutionary patriots. However, according to family stories, the elder Joseph was disqualified for military service because of injuries sustained when he fell out of a second-story window while sleepwalking.

After the Revolution, Joseph, Sr., accompanied by his sons Wil- liam, Hugh, James, and Joseph, moved to Washington County, East

Tennessee, then to Pendleton District, South Carolina, where he settled on Big Mouth Creek. He died near Belton in 1815. Brown's elder sons had remained in East Tennessee, where Joseph, Jr., married Jemima Broyles, and Hugh married her sister Anna. They were the daughters of Adam Broyles, formerly of Culpeper County, Virginia. Hugh subsequently moved to Middle Tennessee and Joseph to Panther Creek, Habersham County, Georgia, where his fourth son, Mackey, was born on February 11, 1797.[1]

While still a teenager Mackey Brown decided to join relatives in Middle Tennessee. He fought with the Tennessee militia in the Battle of New Orleans with Captain Andrew Patterson's company in General William Carroll's brigade. He returned to Tennessee in 1815 and on February 22, 1816, married Sally Rice, daughter of Dangerfield and Margaret Looney Rice of Bedford County.[2] Soon the Mackey Browns moved to South Carolina, where their first son, Joseph Emerson, was born on Long Creek, Pickens District, on April 15, 1821.[3]

While Joseph Emerson was young, the family returned to Georgia, settling in the Gaddistown area, Union County. Until he was nineteen Joseph worked on the farm and peddled produce and firewood in nearby Dahlonega. This was "gold rush" country, but in after years Brown

---

1 Other children were Elizabeth, who married Joseph Williams; William married Ruth Smith; Hugh married Elizabeth Smith; Aaron married Mary Leden; Mary married Abram Duff; Ebenezer never married; Edna married Job Arrowood.

2 Dangerfield Rice's second wife was the daughter of Hugh Brown, uncle of Mackey.

3 Other children born to this union were Emeline and Prudence, both of whom died in early childhood; Mary Elizabeth, who married Joseph Watkins; Edna Elija married Berryman Turner; James Rice married (1) Harriet France Lewis (2) Mary Reynolds Walker; William Carroll married Anna Louisa Dean; Aaron Pleasant married Carrie Peers; Nancy Verlinda married (1) Charles Lay (2) Reuben Latimer; Sally Melissa married John Houser; Jemima Ann; John Mackey; George Washington.

The above information on genealogy is taken from numerous items in the Mary Connally Spalding and Elizabeth Grisham Spalding Sheffield Collection of Brown papers, University of Georgia Library, hereinafter cited as Spalding Collection; Correspondence of Joseph E. Brown and the Reverend Joseph Brown (Giles County, Tenn.), April 22, 1858, to May 14, 1859, copy in the Felix Hargrett Collection, University of Georgia Library; Joseph E. Brown to Mrs. Sarah A. Williams (Greeneville, Tenn.), July 5, 1877, Spalding Collection; Brown-Grisham Papers in private possession of Charles Brockman, Jr., Athens, Georgia, hereinafter cited as Brockman Collection.

made no mention of ever attempting to follow this path to riches.

In 1840, when Joseph decided to leave the farm and seek an education, he could read and write and do arithmetic "as far as the rule of three." Taking with him his younger brother, James, and his father's plow horse, he drove a yoke of oxen before him on the 125-mile trek to Professor Pleasant Jordan's Academy in Anderson District, South Carolina. The oxen were exchanged for eight months' board and lodging, and James returned to Georgia with the horse. Professor Jordan extended credit for eight months' tuition, and Joseph E. Brown began his formal education. At the close of the term he returned to Georgia where he taught an "old field" school for three months and paid his debt.[4]

Brown later related that "under the encouragement of Dr. O. R. Broyles of Pendleton, South Carolina, and the doctor's father, Mayor Aaron Broyles of Calhoun, and the late Judge J. P. Reed," he returned to Anderson Calhoun Academy, then operated by Professor Wesley Leverett.[5] When Leverett moved to Anderson Court House at the close of the year, Brown followed for a second year on credit.[6]

In January, 1844, he took charge of the academy at Canton in Cherokee County, Georgia, and in a letter dated October, 1843, Professor Leverett recommended him as "a gentleman of great moral worth and reputable attainments, of much energy and decision of character, all combining to constitute him a judicious and efficient Instructor of youth."[7]

Brown apparently remained at the academy only long enough to earn the money to pay his debts. During the winter of 1844–1845 he tutored the children of Dr. John W. Lewis of Canton and read law in his spare time. On August 20, 1845, the Honorable Augustus R. Wright issued him an admission to the bar;[8] but Brown did not immediately

---

4 Herbert Fielder, *A Sketch of the Life and Times of Joseph E. Brown* (Springfield, Mass., 1883), 94 ff. See also speech delivered by Brown at Macon, Ga., October ?, 1890, quoted in Cherokee (Ga.), *Advocate*, December 4, 1894.
5 Cherokee *Advocate*, December 4, 1894.
6 Atlanta *Daily Examiner*, July 8, 1857. Professor Jordan had apparently moved to Arkansas, where he later became attorney general.
7 Cora Brown McLeod Collection of Brown family papers, University of Georgia Library, hereinafter cited as McLeod Collection.
8 Original in McLeod Collection.

begin practice. Instead, he secured a loan from Dr. Lewis and, in October, entered Yale law school.[9]

Little is known of Brown's experiences at Yale. He did not remain to receive his diploma at the end of the one-year course, and in after years he seldom referred to his experiences there.[10] He hurried home to open a law office and secure clients for the fall term of court. On March 22, 1847, he was admitted to practice before the Georgia Supreme Court.[11]

In December, 1846, on a visit to relatives on Long Creek, Brown was forced to seek a night's lodging in the home of the Reverend Joseph Grisham, near West Union, several miles from his destination. A part-time Baptist minister and strong supporter of the temperance movement, Grisham was the owner of considerable property, consisting at times of hotels, mills, and lands. He also had a twenty-year-old daughter, Elizabeth, whom Brown liked immediately, and within a few days he returned to the Grisham home and apparently remained during the Christmas holidays. He was back for another visit in April and still another in June, traveling 125 miles each way on horseback. The wedding was set for Tuesday, July 13, 1847, Elizabeth's twenty-first birthday, the Reverend B. F. Mauldin officiating.[12]

Theirs must have been the most elaborate wedding celebration West Union had ever witnessed. Invitations went out to many persons at a distance, and all who lived within a radius of "six or seven miles" were requested to attend.

For weeks in advance the Grisham household was astir with prepa-

9 Fielder, *Brown*, 98.
10 Other young men from the South who were his classmates were R. W. Johnson, Arkansas; A. T. Hawthorne, Camden, Ala.; J. R. Nolan, Madison, Ga.; Charles B. Buckholts, Jackson, Miss., Daniel Fisher, Bladen Springs, Ala. See Oliver F. Case (New Haven, Conn.) to Brown, July 15, 1846, enclosing a list of classmates, McLeod Collection.
11 Original license in McLeod Collection.
12 Pendleton (S.C.) *Messenger*, July 16, 1847. Joseph Grisham first married Nancy Watts who bore him three children—Jane, James Denton, and Nancy Frances. According to a family account, shortly before her death in 1821 Nancy Grisham chose her friend Mary Steele to be a mother to her children and requested her husband to marry Mary. This he did, and to the union were born Elizabeth, William Steele, and Susan Melinda. Much information on the Grisham and Steele families is found in the Brockman Collection.

rations for the feast. Mrs. Melinda Watson, aunt of the bride, supervised operations. Cakes were baked by the dozens—"pound cakes, sponge cakes, fruit cakes" and "three large steeple cakes over two feet high with ornaments on top"—cookies by the bushels, pies by the scores, "nuts, candies syllabub, boiled custard." There were "chickens, turkeys, hams, bacon, roast beef in abundance," and four fat shoats, two of which were roasted whole. The guests ate far into the night. Those from afar either bedded down on the floor or sat up the remainder of the night. Local families, who returned home to do their chores and care for the livestock, were back again by dawn. But even then twenty-seven cakes remained uncut.

The newlyweds began their long trip at midday following the wedding, stopping for successive nights at Devereux Jarrett's, Tallulah Falls, Nash Hotel in Clarkesville, Choice Hotel in Dahlonega, and finally at the bride's Uncle William Grisham's home in Canton, where they boarded until their new home on Marietta Road was completed. Canton, the county seat, had been incorporated in 1833, but it remained only a frontier farming community with Cherokees roaming the roads and trading with the settlers. By 1847 the Indians were gone, but the slow-growing settlement did not appear in the census reports until 1870, and then it had only 214 residents.[13]

In October, 1847, the Browns returned to South Carolina to attend the wedding of her brother William to Martha Josephine Knox, daughter of Samuel Knox. Mrs. Brown remained until after the Christmas holidays, and when Brown returned for her, their home in Canton was completed. The Grishams loaded up a six-horse wagon and a single vehicle with household goods "consisting of kitchen furniture, two feather beds, pillows, mattresses, crockery, preserves, lard, soap, etc." They also sent a slave, Celia, and her children, Lewis, fifteen, and Emma, twelve. With "Old York" as chief teamster, the caravan set out for Canton. Because of Old York's liking for strong drink, Grisham did not trust him to return all the wagons; so he gave the horse and single wagon to his daughter. Brown later exchanged the horse for four hundred fence rails. On January 2, 1848, the Browns moved into

13 Lloyd G. Marlin, *The History of Cherokee County* (Atlanta, 1932), 102 ff.

the house that would remain their family home until it was destroyed by Federal troops during the Civil War.[14]

The Joseph Grisham family soon followed their daughter to Georgia, settling near Canton, where Grisham continued to prosper. On September 12, 1849, he advertised for sale as many as twenty thousand acres of "good land well improved and on reasonable terms to approved purchasers. My object is to improve society, by promoting honest industry and the cause of Religion and Temperance." Lands not sold would be leased to "honest, industrious temperance men . . . and Baptists of the right sort will be preferred."[15] Grisham died in 1857.

Joseph Brown, plain, practical, conscientious, thorough, and willing to give his best efforts, became the common man's lawyer. One admirer later recalled that his speeches to juries were "marvels of effect," exhausting "practical sense and reason."[16] He quickly developed a town-country legal practice, investing his surplus funds in real estate. In November, 1847, he paid one thousand dollars for eight lots in Canton, and a few months later his friend Dr. Lewis, "in consideration of the friendship, good will and esteem" which he bore for "the said Brown," gave him another lot.[17] Soon Brown was reaching into the county, acquiring agricultural lands, some of which later proved to contain minerals deposits.

Although his practice prospered, it was a dull business. A politician by nature, Brown was eager to test his abilities in that field. In 1849 he was elected to the state Senate, representing Cherokee and Cobb counties. Not interested in any special legislation, he wanted to see and be seen; consequently, the next months in the capital town of Milledgeville would prove valuable. The great Georgia "triumvirate"—Robert Toombs, Alexander H. Stephens, and Howell Cobb—were in Washington, but many others who would be important in Brown's future were in the state capital during the legislative session.

Brown never considered his lack of experience a disability, and from the beginning of the session he was prominent. Soon he would

---

14 Account written by Elizabeth Grisham Brown for her daughter Sally. Copy in Spalding Collection.
15 Circular in Spalding Collection.
16 Isaac W. Avery, *The History of the State of Georgia from 1850 to 1881* (New York, 1881), 15.
17 Original deeds in Hargrett Collection.

clash with Andrew J. Miller, the Whig leader from Augusta; before the close of the session he was the acknowledged Democratic leader in the Senate, demonstrating what remained true throughout his life—in whatever he did, he would be conspicuous.

Public issues within the state were of minor interest, but on the national scene there was much agitation and excitement. The Mexican War had ended, leaving more problems than it solved, most of them closely related to the slavery controversy. What was to be done with the territory acquired from Mexico? Pennsylvania Congressman David Wilmot's proposed prohibition of slavery in that territory was not approved by Congress, yet the principles upon which it was based remained much alive. Further, free states of the North refused to cooperate in the capture and return of fugitive slaves. And there were demands for the abolition of slavery in the District of Columbia.

The new president, Zachary Taylor, strictly a military man, thought that the best solution of a problem was a quick one. The question of slavery in the territories, he thought, could be solved by immediate statehood for California and New Mexico. To promote this plan he dispatched Congressman Thomas Butler King of Georgia to California as a special agent to assist local leaders in the preparation for statehood.[18] The news of King's departure for the west created considerable excitement in his home state.

The Georgia General Assembly convened on November 5, 1849. On the following day Governor George W. Towns delivered his biennial message. "In view of the present excited state of the public upon the subject of slavery," he suggested that the Assembly review all existing laws on the subject and make such modifications as seemed desirable. He wished the world to know that although Georgia was guided by a "humane and Christian policy" it would be as rigorous as necessary in enforcing "perfect subordination" and in punishing those who sought "to interfere with our domestic policy. . . . Let our policy be marked with kindness to the slave, but with terror to him who dares invade the citizen's right in property in them."

He further urged "constant vigilance and great moral firmness" to protect against "Federal encroachments." The consuming "spirit of

18 Holman Hamilton, *Zachary Taylor: Soldier in the White House* (Indianapolis, 1951), 178 ff.

blind and infuriating fanaticism" so prevalent in the nonslaveholding states he feared might soon control a majority of their votes and gain control in Washington. Therefore, he requested the legislature to authorize the governor to convoke a state convention should the Wilmot Proviso or any other similar measure be approved by Congress.[19]

That portion of the governor's message relating to the slavery controversy and all bills proposed on that subject were referred to the Senate Committee on the State of the Republic. The committee reported a set of resolutions denying that Congress possessed power to prohibit slavery in a territory or to interfere with the institution in the District of Columbia; denouncing the Wilmot Proviso as unconstitutional and all action retarding the capture and return of fugitive slaves as "a plain and palpable violation of the letter of the Constitution, and an intolerable outrage upon Southern rights." The eighth resolution provided "That in the event of the passage of the Wilmot Proviso by Congress, the abolition of slavery in the District of Columbia, or the continued refusal of the non-slaveholding states to deliver up fugitive slaves as provided in the constitution, it will become the immediate and imperative duty of the people of this state to meet in convention to take into consideration the mode and manner of redress."[20]

Brown vigorously supported these resolutions in one of the few speeches reported. Had slavery proved profitable in New England, he charged, it would have become firmly rooted there. But because it was not profitable, New England owners and importers sold their sable cargoes to the South "with as much cool effrontery as they now peddle among us with wooden clocks." And they were now eating bread bought with the profits of this slave trade. Yet the legislatures of Connecticut and Vermont had recently passed resolutions "of a character the most insulting to the South and to Georgia as a slaveholding state."

As to the morality or immorality of slavery, Brown would say that it had been in existence since the beginning of recorded time. Noah, Abraham, David, and Solomon were slaveholders. "Moses in his law received from the Creator himself made provisions for relations be-

19 Milledgeville *Federal Union*, November 6, 1849; Georgia *Senate Journal*, 1849, pp. 37 ff.
20 Milledgeville *Federal Union*, November 16, 1849.

tween master and servant. Paul speaks without the slightest disapprobation of the relations of master and servant. I am not ashamed to be found doing that which was countenanced and practiced by such men as these, more especially when they were acting under divine inspiration."

As to the territory under discussion in Washington, Brown declared it had been acquired as a result of a war to which the South provided three-fifths of the fighting men. Yet it was proposed that the southern slaveholder be excluded from it.[21] There was nothing new in Brown's remarks but they were just what Georgians wanted to hear.

When Andrew J. Miller attempted to modify the Eighth Resolution by amendment, he and Brown engaged in heated argument. In the end Brown voted with thirty-four other senators in favor of the measure; Miller was one of three who voted *no*.[22]

Brown was much concerned. Although he owned few slaves himself and lived in an area where slaves were not numerous, he was a staunch defender of the "peculiar institution." The exact nature of Congressman King's mission to California was not yet known in Georgia, but the knowledge that he had gone was sufficient to arouse excitement. On December 18, 1849, the Milledgeville *Federal Union* carried notice that King had resigned his seat in Congress and a special election had been called to fill the vacancy. King, a wealthy gentleman planter from Glynn County, had once been a strong states' rights man but had recently become "one of the most nationalistic of Southern Whigs."[23]

Brown became aroused by the news and offered to the Senate a set of resolutions denouncing King. It was reported, he explained, that in California, King was making public speeches in favor of the admission of that territory into the Union as a free state and that he represented the "views and feeling of the Cabinet at Washington." It also appeared that he was "busily seeking a seat in the United States Senate" from the proposed state, which would be "under a constitution which excludes the South from equal participation of the privileges of a Territory purchased in part by her blood and treasure." Therefore

21 *Ibid.*, February 19, 1850.
22 *Senate Journal*, 1849–50, pp. 274–79.
23 See Edward M. Steel, Jr., *T. Butler King of Georgia* (Athens, Ga., 1964), for account of King's California activities.

Be it resolved:

That in the estimation of this general assembly, it is derogatory to the character of a Southern man, and especially of a Southern Representative in Congress, to advocate upon her own soil the admission of California into the Union as a free state, and still more derogatory to such an individual to accept a seat in the National Council, purchased by moral treason to that portion of the Union that has hitherto fostered him and extended to him her confidence.

That the conduct of Mr. King in his reported speeches in California and in offering himself as a candidate to represent her in the Senate of the Union after she had adopted a constitution inhibiting slavery, meets the unqualified disapprobation of this General Assembly.[24]

No final action was taken on Brown's resolutions; knowledge of King's activities was based entirely upon "reports." Legislators preferred to wait for further developments. In line with the governor's recommendations the legislators reviewed the laws relative to slavery and decided to tighten up on restrictions. Brown voted in favor of preventing religious assemblies of Negroes unless supervised by whites, and opposed the licensing of Negro preachers.[25]

Turning from slavery to the subject of strong drink, Brown opposed mixing politics and temperance. When a measure was introduced providing for the incorporation of the Sons of Temperance, it was referred to a special committee of which Brown was made chairman. The committee made a negative report, and Brown in "an eloquent speech" explained that although a majority of committee members were temperance men, they considered the measure ill-advised. The Sons were already making considerable progress and had a right to enjoy corporate privileges; however, there was considerable public prejudice against the organization. The proposed legislative action might further "inflame the public mind." Success of the order must depend upon "its inherent moral influence," Brown explained; therefore attempts to legislate on the subject of temperance should be avoided.[26]

Brown was no more favorable to rights for women than privileges for slaves. He voted *no* on Andrew J. Miller's "Woman Bill" for the

24 Milledgeville *Federal Union*, December 25, 1849; *Senate Journal*, 1849–50, pp. 281–82.
25 *Senate Journal*, 1849–50, pp. 44, 93, 101, 214, 263, 270.
26 Milledgeville *Federal Union*, December 11, 1849; Senate Journal, 1849–50, pp. 234–35.

preservation and protection of the rights of married women and the distribution of their estates. This measure would have given women the right to own and transfer property independent of their husbands. Brown expressed fear that it would result in lawsuits between wives and husbands, destroying affection, confidence, and peace "in marriage relations."[27] He also voted *no* on a suggestion that the proposal be submitted to popular vote, permitting women between the ages of sixteen and fifty to participate in the voting. Again he voted *no* on a proposal to limit the liability of husbands as to debts contracted by wives before marriage. And finally he opposed efforts to liberalize the divorce laws.[28]

Brown certainly subscribed to the theory that women should keep house, rear children, and be completely submissive to their husbands. In his own home, although usually kind and considerate, he was sometimes harsh, even abusive. And Mrs. Brown's tolerance of his words and actions did nothing to soften them. "Mr. Brown called me a liar, a fool and a great many other hard things because I could not find a bundle of papers that he thought he had brought to the house," she confided to her diary.[29] "I know I come far short of doing my duty but if God knows my heart I intend and try to do my duty. I forgive him & pray God to forgive him—he has very many things to vex him." Again: "Mr. Brown whipped Emma [slave] for nothing to show me he was master. I sometimes think if I was under ground, he would have no cause to get mad. I know I am not his equal. I am quick tempered and he is unwilling to yield anything. I pray God to *make* me submissive to Mr. Brown. I know he is right, if I can please him every wish is gratified."[30]

Intelligent, cultured, mild mannered, physically weak, never weighing more than one hundred pounds, Mrs. Brown supervised the household, bore children, and often worked late at night copying her husband's briefs and speeches. Julius was born May 31, 1848, and Mary Virginia on January 5, 1850. Approaching the birth of her third child in 1851 and fearing she might not survive the ordeal, Mrs. Brown secretly recorded a simple statement of her philosophy and wishes:

27 Milledgeville *Federal Union*, December 14, 1849.
28 *Senate Journal*, 1849–50, pp. 78, 94, 134, 150, 157.
29 Elizabeth Grisham Brown Diary, 1853–57 (MS in Brockman Collection), August 5, 1854.
30 *Ibid.*, January 5, 1856.

"My confidence in my God is strong that he will do all things right. . . . If I should have a son and I should die I want his name to be Joseph Grisham."[31] She did survive the birth of her second son on December 28, 1851, and she named him Joseph Mackey, not Joseph Grisham. Then came Franklin Pierce on April 15, 1853. On March 25, 1854, she confided to her diary that she had "learned how to prevent children." Either the method was not applied or it was ineffective. She bore four more children.

Following the close of the legislative session at Milledgeville, Brown returned to his law practice at Canton. Meanwhile, in Washington, Congress had been working out a compromise based upon Henry Clay's resolutions, which became known as the Compromise of 1850. In Georgia there was much opposition to some of the proposed measures. Brown's precise position on the compromise principles is not a matter of record, but Governor Towns issued a call for a convention to meet on December 10, 1850. The Georgia Triumvirate at Washington rushed home to convince voters of the soundness of the Compromise and to promote the cause of Unionists as opposed to Southern Rightists. Since a few within the Southern Rights group were outspoken secessionists, it was inevitable that the entire group would be denounced as disunionists.

Brown was not a candidate for a seat in the convention, and there is no evidence that he was an active participant in the spirited campaign. The Unionist victory was impressive, assuring acceptance of the Compromise by the convention. Union spirit ran high and those who even suggested secession were soundly denounced. Yet when the convention settled down to work, a spirit of moderation prevailed, and both Whigs and Democrats joined efforts in working out the "Georgia Platform."

Georgia's loyalty to the Union was reaffirmed, and the principles of the Compromise of 1850 were accepted "as a permanent adjustment of the sectional controversy." But this acceptance was accompanied by a warning that disunion would be inevitable should Congress take steps

31 Original in Hargrett Collection. Mrs. Brown further recorded: "I want my children raised in the nurture and admonition of the Lord—I have every confidence in my husband's good judgment—I want them to learn to work I do not want them to have many negroes about them, as they (negroes) corrupt the morals of the young."

to interfere with the interstate slave trade, abolish slavery in the District of Columbia, refuse to permit the introduction of slaves into the territories of Utah and New Mexico, unfavorably modify the fugitive slave law, or refuse to admit additional slave states into the Union.

Riding the crest of Unionism as opposed to Southern Rights, leaders from both the Democratic and Whig parties joined in the formation of a new Constitutional Union party and the election of Howell Cobb as governor in 1851. Cobb's opponent was Charles J. McDonald, whose Southern Rights platform, although not advocating secession, proclaimed secession as a right. But few persons were interested in discussing the abstract right of secession; consequently, it did not develop as a major issue. It is likely that Brown supported McDonald for governor; the two became good friends, and in 1859 Brown named his fifth son Charles McDonald.

Whatever plans Toombs and Stephens might have had for developing the new national organization were soon abandoned; in Washington the two major parties had no idea of abandoning their fight against each other. Neither was there need for continuing a Unionist organization in Georgia; there was no longer serious threat of disunion. By midsummer 1852 the Constitutional Union party of Georgia was no more and the political situation was one of confusion. The Southern Rightists, labeling themselves Regular Democrats, under the leadership of Herschel V. Johnson, approved the nomination of Franklin Pierce for president, and eventually Cobb's Union Democrats had no choice but to join them, although each group presented its own electoral ticket. Many Georgia Whigs refused to support Winfield Scott, the national nominee, and cast their votes for Daniel Webster.

Brown, who played a minor role in the Pierce victory by permitting the use of his name as an electoral candidate, soon became a great admirer of the new president. When Howell Cobb decided to become an active supporter of Herschel V. Johnson, the Democratic candidate for governor in 1853, Brown became an interested observer, if not a participant. When Cobb spoke at Kingston on September 8, urging Union Democrats to return to their old party, Brown was present. Following a Democratic rally at Marietta, he took Cobb home with him for the night. On the following day Alexander H. Stephens and Cobb opposed each other in a three-hour debate at the Canton courthouse. Brown then took Cobb back to Marietta.[32]

The passage of the Kansas-Nebraska Act in 1854 and the rise of the Republican party completed the destruction of the Whig party as a national organization. Although some southern Whigs thought the Act unnecessary, not even they advocated political fellowship with northern free-soilers and abolitionists. Georgia Whigs who wished to remain in public life were forced to seek new political affiliations. Some joined the Democrats immediately. Others found a temporary home in the American party.

While Congress was debating the Kansas-Nebraska bill, councils of the American party were being established in Georgia.[33] This party, popularly known as Know-Nothings, was an outgrowth of the nativistic movement that was spreading over the country. Originally pledged to secrecy and avowedly hostile to foreigners and Catholics, it proved attractive to "joiners," the curious, and those seeking a new political home, as well as those who were actually fearful of the growing power and influence of foreigners and Catholics.

Brown did not fit any of these categories. His wife probably expressed his views when she recorded in her diary: "I went to hear Milner at the Presbyterian church . . . he made a regular set stump speech in favor of the Know Nothings, denounced the Catholics, appealed to protestants to keep the enemy from our free country; not to let Baal rear his altars among us. I felt disgusted to hear such stuff from the Sacred desk as he gave us today."[34]

By 1855 the Know-Nothings felt strong enough to challenge the Democrats on the state level, but their candidate for governor, Garnett Andrews, was decisively defeated by Governor Johnson, who now had the support of former Whigs Toombs and Stephens. Also disastrously defeated was the new Temperance party which had nominated Basil H. Overby.[35] Brown, still much opposed to making temperance a political question, quietly withdrew from the Sons of Temperance.[36]

32 Brown Diary, September 8, 26, 27, 1853.
33 For a detailed account of the activities of this party see W. Darrell Overdyke, *The Know-Nothing Party in the South* (Baton Rouge, 1850).
34 Brown Diary, June 17, 1855.
35 See Allen P. Tankersley, "Basil Hallman Overby, Champion of Prohibition in Ante-Bellum Georgia," *Georgia Historical Quarterly*, XXXI (1947).
36 Brown Diary, November 27, 1854.

During the period 1850 to 1855 Brown's principal interests were his legal practice and the expansion of his real estate holdings. He did a small amount of work for the state. In 1851 he and Augustus R. Wright represented the state in a suit against contractors who were building a road across Lookout Mountain.[37] But most of his practice was confined to his home district. Sometimes absent from home as long as three weeks, he attended court wherever it met. Then upon returning home he assigned to his wife the task of copying his legal papers. She worked until late hours but never complained. "My old man is one of the smartest men in Georgia; more than I think so," she proudly confided to her diary. She also recorded that Brown "collected $2,200 during the year 1853." For her services he sometimes rewarded her with "a fancy silk dress," "a chain $25," "a bonnet and headdress $15.00" and a sash pin $2.00, "a locket and ring $12.50."[38]

Whether Brown was home or away, Mrs. Brown spent much time with family matters. There were many Browns and Grishams and they were not always contented and happy. Brown's brothers James and Carroll both proposed marriage to Mrs. Brown's sister, Susan Melinda, who rejected both.[39] Mrs. Brown approved the rejections and recorded in her diary that "1 of a family is sufficient." James Brown, a recent graduate of Yale Law School, then married Dr. Lewis' daughter, Harriett. William Carroll Brown graduated from the Medical College in Philadelphia and opened practice in South Carolina. He later gave up medicine and became a planter.

Occasionally the Joseph E. Brown family had guests from a distance. "Ex-Governor McDonald took dinner with us." "Judge Newton of Athens took supper and sat til bed time," recorded Mrs. Brown.[40] But contacts outside their home district were not numerous.

Brown's interests in lands developed rapidly. On June 10, 1853, he "cut wheat on our Earle place"; took possession of "his Holloway place" in January, 1854; bought the James Maddox land for $3,000 in

37 See letter from John T. Smith, November 1, 1851, in McLeod Collection.
38 Brown Diary, November 15, 1853, January 4, June 2, 1854, December 5, 6, 1855.
39 Susan Melinda later married Patrick Henry Brewster whom the Browns did not like. "I would prefer to see Sister Sue dead & buried than to have her marry Patrick H. Brewster," Mrs. Brown confided to her Diary, September 18, 1853. She considered the Brewsters of "crabbed & perverse disposition."
40 Brown Diary, May 5, 1854, June 5, 1855.

December, 1854; owned the "little river farm" by January, 1855; and bought "pa's" river farm for $10,000 in August, 1855. Lands in the Cherokee area were not suited for large-scale production.[41]

With the purchase of land it became necessary for Brown to acquire field hands. In January, 1853, he and Robert J. Cowart bought, from William Bell, "Dock" and "Willis," one black, one light, for $1,400; in February, 1854 he purchased "Jane" and her three children from the Keith estate; and on March 2, 1855, he bought "Allen" from "Pa" for $1,000.[42] Apparently the Brown place was sometimes used as an assembly ground for slaves of other masters. "Plenty of negroes to eat with us today," Mrs. Brown recorded on Christmas Day, 1853. Later: "A crowd of negroes to dinner, a negro frolic in town last night."[43]

Brown also had extensive mineral interests. The North Georgia gold mines did not extend to the Cherokee area but there was much speculation in copper. Brown bought, sold, and leased copper lands with regularity and at considerable profit. "Mr. Brown and I went to see the shaft that Harris is sinking for copper," Mrs. Brown wrote in November, 1854. The next day, in disgust, she recorded, "Pa" had sold to Sufords & Hoyle the "copper interests" he had promised to sell her husband. Three weeks later: "Mr. Brown sold 3 copper interests today."[44] A few months earlier Brown had leased copper interests on a tract in Gilmer County to Andrew J. May. A month later he bought up the lease. In January, 1855, he reported that valuable copper had been struck on his land at seventy to eighty feet and he had sold one

41 *Ibid.*, June 10, 1853, January 14, December 22, 1854, January 12, August 15, 1855.
42 *Ibid.*, February 7, 1854, March 2, 1855; bill of sale, dated January 29, 1853, in McLeod Collection.
43 Brown Diary, December 25, 1853, April 21, 1855.
    On August 13, 1855, slave girl Jane gave birth to a baby girl, "half white," the first slave child born within the Brown family, Mrs. Brown did not speculate as to the identity of the father but recorded "I do not like a mixed breed." Again Mrs. Brown recorded: "Celia gave me some insolent jaw for which her master whipped her and she ran away." She was back before bedtime. Meanwhile, Brown searched the quarters of the female slaves. In Emma's (Celia's daughter) trunk he found $7.10, a gold button, a deck of cards, a bottle of whiskey, a bottle of cologne, and many other articles which Mrs. Brown thought no "virtuous person" would be able to purchase. Diary, January 31, 1856.
44 Brown Diary, November 2, 3, December 22, 1854.

fourth of the mineral rights for $4,000.[45] A friend later reported that Brown sold for $25,000 one half the copper interests on a tract of land that cost him only $450. He invested the profits in more land.[46]

Why a successful lawyer, farmer, and speculator in mineral rights should want to become a circuit judge is difficult to understand. Nevertheless, in 1855 Brown became a candidate for judge of the Blue Ridge Circuit which included eleven counties, beginning with Polk on the Alabama line, extending inward through Paulding, Campbell, and Cobb, and thence northward to Fannin and Union on the Tennessee line.[47] The incumbent, David Irwin, held office by legislative appointment, but since his appointment a new law had provided for popular election.

There was no bad feeling between Brown and Irwin; at times the judge had been entertained in the Brown home while holding court in Canton.[48] But being methodical and orderly in everything he undertook, Brown joined many citizens, including some lawyers, in strongly disapproving the manner in which Judge Irwin conducted court—often in wild disorder and delay. Irwin's moral character was "entirely free from reproach," announced a Brown supporter, but Brown was a man of piety. It was admitted that Irwin possessed "a mind of no ordinary cast," yet Brown also possessed "superior natural endowments." Here the concessions ended.

Brown's supporters were not impressed by the fact that few of Irwin's decisions had been reversed by a higher court; only a few had ever been "carried up." But they emphasized that he could not clear his present docket within two years, for he either did nothing or permitted his courtroom to become a scene of confusion with frequent violations of rules of practice and decorum, "a place of disgust to persons of good taste." Even when a case was heard, the judge would often send for a lawbook and in hopes of impressing the bar and courtroom audience with his "learning" would read aloud the "law in the case." And as

45 Lease and purchase contracts in McLeod Collection, May 10, June 7, 1854; Brown to John B. Brown, January 30, 1855, in McLeod Collection.
46 Avery, *History of Georgia*, 14.
47 Other counties included were Cherokee, Pickens, Gilmer, Lumpkin, and Floyd.
48 Brown Diary, April 7, 1854.

election day drew nearer, observers noted an increase in the judge's concern about the rights, convenience, and comfort of the people.[49]

It was reported by Irwin's enemies that a Know-Nothing convention in Marietta had unanimously endorsed the judge and that all members were secretly pledged to his support.[50] Perhaps the few Know-Nothings in the circuit did prefer Irwin, for he had long been a member of the late Whig party. There is no evidence, however, that he was ever affiliated with the Know-Nothings.

How active Brown himself was in this rough and tumble campaign is unknown, but his friends carried him through. Judge Irwin won in only three counties and that by a total of only 68 votes. Cobb, his home county, gave him only a 2-vote majority. Brown carried eight counties with a majority of 2,898 votes.[51]

In celebration of victory the Browns made a trip to Milledgeville. Presumably, this was Mrs. Brown's first trip to the Georgia capital; Brown himself had not been a frequent visitor. They saw the penitentiary, asylum, and a cotton factory. They visited the office of the *Federal Union* and the Statehouse and attended a levee at the Governor's Mansion. They shopped extensively and as a souvenir had their pictures made for Mrs. Brown's locket. On the return trip they stopped for a night at the Atlanta Hotel "kept by Hester and miserably done."[52]

49 Atlanta *Daily Examiner*, July 26, 1855; unidentified newspaper clipping in Spalding Collection.
50 Circular in Spalding Collection.
51 Avery, *History of Georgia*, 27–28.
52 Brown Diary, November 27–30, December 1–12, 1855.

Chapter II

Into the Statehouse

JUDGE BROWN no doubt brought order to the courtrooms of the Blue
Ridge Circuit. One friend observed that if the new judge had a fault
it was a "leaning toward severity." It was reported that Brown fined a
drunk who created a disturbance in the courtroom, and when he made
considerable noise leaving, Brown had him brought back and added
another fine. The man then crawled out of the room.[1] On another
occasion Brown inquired of a juror if he was drunk. The juror replied
"'No siree Bob.'" "'Well,'" said Brown, "'I fine you $5 for the *re* and
$10 for the *bob*.'"[2]

An observer at the Ellijay court thought the youthful Brown presided with "dignity and ability." "He has won golden opinions from the
bar and from people generally. He is a terror to gamblers, dram-
drinkers and sellers, and is ridding the county of such characters as
fast as Georgia law will permit." The five groggeries in Ellijay would
no doubt furnish plenty of material for the judge to work on.[3] Those
who felt the sting of Judge Brown's alleged severity grumbled, but he
built a reputation for being without prejudice.[4]

Judge Brown impressed many people throughout the Blue Ridge
region, and some marked him as a potential political leader on the state
level. But he did little to promote his own interests. Although he made

1 Avery, *History of Georgia*, 29.
2 Macon *Georgia Citizen*, June 27, 1857.
3 Unidentified newspaper clipping in Spalding Collection.
4 Avery, *History of Georgia*, 29.

some valuable friends in the state Senate, he did not stand for a second term; neither is there evidence that he visited Milledgeville during legislative sessions. He attended some rallies in his home section, and made contact with a few important political leaders, but if he made any political speeches the fact was not reported. Neither is there a record of his having attended a state party convention.

The Democratic convention for selecting a candidate for governor met in Milledgeville on June 24, 1857. Tenant Lomax, editor of the Columbus *Times*, was selected as presiding officer, and Judge Thomas W. Thomas of Elberton was chosen chairman of the committee on resolutions. There were no state issues of great importance, but there was much concern over the situation in the Kansas Territory. The Kansas-Nebraska Act of 1854 had repealed the Compromise of 1820 and opened the territories to the introduction of slavery. The struggle between free-soilers and proslavery men for control in Kansas began immediately. James Buchanan had been elected president in 1856 on a platform which opposed further agitation on the subject of slavery and recognized "the right of people of all the Territories . . . to form a constitution with or without domestic slavery, and be admitted into the Union."[5]

Georgia Democrats had endorsed this platform and carried their state for Buchanan. Howell Cobb journeyed to Pennsylvania and made "ten speeches in ten days to huge audiences from Philadelphia to Erie" in support of the candidate and was later rewarded with a cabinet post. Since the new president was known to have southern sympathies, his Georgia supporters expected him to offer no obstacle to proslavery activities in the Kansas Territory.[6]

Buchanan appointed Robert J. Walker, a resident of Mississippi, as governor of the Kansas Territory. A native of Pennsylvania, Walker accepted slavery as sanctioned by law, but he showed no sympathy for the proslavery cause in Kansas. In his inaugural address in Kansas he declared that Congress should and would refuse to admit Kansas as a state unless the entire proposed constitution should be submitted to the people for approval. Furthermore, as to slavery, there was no need for

5 Philip S. Klein, *President James Buchanan* (University Park, Pa., 1962), 255 ff.
6 *Ibid.*, 259–60.

controversy; nature had already decided the question. In other words, Kansas would eventually be admitted as a free state.[7] This was not what southern proslavery men had in mind; consequently, Walker was vigorously denounced, and since Buchanan appointed him many held the president responsible for the governor's policies. *"We are Betrayed,"* exclaimed Thomas W. Thomas of Elberton to Alexander H. Stephens, ". . . if Kansas is admitted as a free state we are ruined . . . . With my present views I can never vote in the democratic convention for a resolution approving this vile treachery of Buchanan."[8]

From Washington, Secretary of the Treasury Howell Cobb tried to reassure his friends and the coming Democratic convention that Walker did not truly represent the administration. He wrote Stephens that the president did not wish any official of his administration to use his position to affect the decision on slavery. The president was indifferent as long as the people of Kansas were permitted to make an honest and fair decision.[9]

No one was convinced, and feeling was running high when the Georgia Democratic convention assembled. The Thomas committee on resolutions offered a set of five. Numbers one and two approved of the principles set forth in the Cincinnati Convention of 1856. Numbers four and five expressed appreciation to Senators Robert Toombs and Alfred Iverson and Governor Johnson for their services to Georgia and the nation. No opposition was offered to these harmless expressions, but resolution number three would produce serious party division:

Resolved, That the inaugural address of Governor Walker, in prescribing the terms on which Congress should admit Kansas into the Union, and in attempting to dictate the submission of their Constitution for ratification, and to what class of persons, constitutes a presumptuous interference in matters over which he has no legitimate control, and that the same address in expressing the official opinion that Kansas would become a free State, and in presenting arguments to support that side of the question, is a gross departure from the principle of non-intervention and neutrality which were

7 Roy F. Nichols, *The Disruption of American Democracy* (New York, 1948), 108.
8 June 15, 1857, in Ulrich B. Phillips (ed.), *The Correspondence of Robert Toombs, Alexander H. Stephens, and Howell Cobb. Annual Report,* American Historical Association for 1911, II (Washington, 1913), 400–401.
9 *Ibid.,* June 18, 1857, p. 402.

established by the Kansas bill; and this Convention has full confidence that Mr. Buchanan will manifest his fidelity to the principles which carried him into office by recalling Gov. Walker.

Thomas made a strong speech in favor of the resolutions, but Augustus R. Wright of Rome submitted a minority report that criticized Walker but did not demand his removal. All attempts to amend the majority report, however, failed and all five resolutions passed with "great unanimity."[10]

Governor Herschel V. Johnson, completing his second term, would not be a candidate to succeed himself. His administration had been popular; and the overall strength of the Democratic party throughout the State was not in question. Yet there were signs of trouble. Numerous aspirants had their own group of hard-core supporters, and there was resentment over the dominant influence in party affairs exercised by Cobb, Toombs, and Stephens. Preconvention speculation centered on Hiram Warner of Merriwether County, Supreme Court justice, 1846–1853, and member of the Thirty-fourth Congress; William H. Stiles of Savannah, several times a state legislator, member of the Twenty-eighth Congress, and chargé d'affaires to Austria, 1845–1849; Henry G. Lamar of Macon, sometime judge and legislator and member of the Thirty-first and Thirty-second Congresses; James Gardner, until recently editor and still proprietor of the Augusta *Constitutionalist*; and John Henry Lumpkin of Rome, nephew of ex-Governor Wilson Lumpkin and four-term member of Congress, but not a candidate to succeed himself. This was indeed an impressive array of talent. Then there were at least two members of the convention who had still another possible candidate in mind. As Leander N. Trammel of Union County and Sumner J. Smith of Towns drove toward Milledgeville in their buggy, they had discussed the possibility of placing the name of Judge Joseph E. Brown before the convention.[11]

It was generally known that Cobb, Toombs, and possibly Stephens wished the nomination of John H. Lumpkin. Two months before the convention, Toombs wrote Cobb: "Lumpkin is undoubtedly ahead of the crowd, but he has great reason to fear strong combination from that fact. If Gardner were out of the way it could be easily managed

10 Milledgeville *Federal Union*, June 30, 1857.
11 Avery, *History of Georgia*, 32.

I think & that *may* happen before the convention."[12] Gardner did not withdraw; the names of all five prominent contenders were placed in nomination.

On the first ballot Lumpkin received 112 votes, Gardner 100, Lamar 97, Warner 53, and Stiles 35. Five ballots later Gardner stood at 141, Lumpkin 124, Warner 56, and Lamar 46. On the eighth Lamar dropped to 35, Gardner moved up to 152, and Lumpkin fell to 122. Lamar's name was then withdrawn, and on the next ballot Gardner picked up 20 votes and Lumpkin 5, but Warner received 64. Two ballots later Gardner fell to 151, and following the thirteenth, his name was withdrawn. But on the fourteenth Lamar was again in nomination and received 137 votes while Lumpkin moved up to 179, Warner 56, Stiles 4, and Alfred H. Colquitt 10. Further balloting brought no substantial change. Several other names were submitted but received little support. The only change of note was that on the twentieth ballot three votes were cast for Joseph E. Brown.[13] The deadlock was complete: the supporters of neither Gardner nor Lamar would shift to Lumpkin.[14] A hard core of Lumpkin supporters remained faithful; no one could get the required two-thirds majority.

In private it was conceded by many who were not supporters of Lumpkin that it was time for the upcountry, commonly known as the Cherokee country, to be awarded the governorship. Yet they were determined that it should not be Lumpkin. This pointed in the direction of a compromise candidate from that area. Taking the suggestion, Richard H. Clark of Bibb proposed to a group of friends that Joseph E. Brown be the man. Clark later related, "The opinions were varied; some said it would do, while some said not & even ridicules it." It was Hope Hull of Clark, however, who moved to break the deadlock by proposing that the district delegation from each congressional district appoint three men for the purpose of working out a solution. The few known friends of Brown saw their opportunity. L. N. Trammell, described by a contemporary as "a quick-witted and unequaled political manager,"[15] maneuvered the Sixth District into selecting Sumner Smith of Towns, J. E. Roberts of Hall, and Hope Hull of Clarke as

12 April 17, 1857, in Cobb Family Papers, University of Georgia.
13 Milledgeville *Federal Union*, June 30, 1857.
14 Cobb to J. B. Lamar, July 10, 1857, in Cobb Papers.
15 Avery, *History of Georgia*, 36.

their members of the committee. All three were known to be friendly
toward Brown. The Fifth, the other Cherokee district, named three
strong Lumpkin men, including Augustus R. Wright and John W. H.
Underwood. Clark of Bibb later stated that he himself prevailed upon
his district delegation to name him one of its committee members.

The special committee went to work immediately, with I. T. Irwin
of Wilkes presiding. Numerous names were suggested as possible
candidates, including some of those already before the convention, yet
it was generally conceded that the compromise candidate must come
from the Cherokee region, and that man could not be John H. Lumpkin,
the strong friend of Howell Cobb and President James Buchanan. It
was agreed that each committee member should write down the name
of the candidate of his preference. This would of course result in the
proposal of several names. At this point Linton Stephens, half-brother
of Alexander Stephens, now proposed to Clark that if there was no
winner after the third ballot a process of elimination be resorted to,
dropping the lowest man after each ballot. Clark pointed out that this
method would result in the nomination of Lumpkin, which action would
certainly not be acceptable to the convention. Stephens then changed
his plan and, before the first ballot was counted, proposed that Brown
be chosen as a compromise candidate. Underwood and Wright objected but Underwood gave in. Wright never did, either in the committee or subsequently in the convention. He knew Brown well; he had
admitted the young attorney to the bar; yet he was strongly committed
to Lumpkin and had his eye on Lumpkin's seat in Congress. The committee selected Brown by voice vote. A subsequent count of the written
ballot revealed that Alfred H. Colquitt had received a majority of one![16]

Chairman Irwin submitted Brown's name to the convention and
Richard H. Clark of Bibb made a short nominating speech. He had
known Brown since their service in the state Senate and had found him
"a man of sound principles, clear head, unquestioned ability, and speaking power of the first order ... a man of exceptional character, in every
respect, private and public ... young enough for the services of the
campaign, and for a long career of usefulness, and not too young for

16 *Ibid.*, 36. Richard H. Clark's account is enclosed in letter to Brown, April 21,
1877, in Hargrett Collection.

mature judgment, and prudent counsels."[17] The vote was unanimous. A "dark horse" had won a race that he had not knowingly entered.

While the Democratic Convention at Milledgeville was selecting him as candidate for governor, Joseph E. Brown was harvesting wheat. Upon going to the field after lunch he had found too many men using cradles and too few tying bundles, so he pitched in and worked until almost dark. As he was washing up for supper, his Canton friend Samuel Weil rode up, and in an excited manner inquired if Brown knew who had been nominated for governor. Brown guessed John E. Ward, for he had heard that Ward of Chatham would be a prominent candidate. "No" Weil replied, "it is Joseph E. Brown of Cherokee." Weil had been at Marietta when the telegraph brought the news. Ward's name had been presented to the convention, but he appears never to have received more than three votes.[18] A prominent Savannah attorney, Ward had been of sufficient political importance to be chosen chairman of the National Democratic Convention of 1856 which had nominated Buchanan.[19]

The people of Georgia were surprised; so was Brown. Senator Robert Toombs, in Texas at the time, was reported to have asked, "And who in the Devil is Joe Brown?"[20] If he asked this question, it was in jest; he knew very well who Joe Brown was, for they had certainly met in Milledgeville while Brown was a state senator and Toombs a member of Congress.[21] But there were many people in other parts of Georgia who honestly did not know Brown.

Many persons also questioned "Why Joe Brown?" and there was no clear explanation. Linton Stephens, who proposed Brown to the special committee, was not an original Brown man, although he had known Brown since they served together in the legislature. When Stephens learned that Lumpkin placed upon him much of the blame for defeat, he wrote Lumpkin a long letter of explanation. He claimed to have gone to the convention with no hostility toward either of the prominent candi-

17 Quoted in Avery, *History of Georgia*, 38.
18 Avery, *History of Georgia*, 36.
19 Klein, *Buchanan*, 255.
20 Pleasant A. Stovall, *Robert Toombs, Statesman, Soldier, Sage* (New York, 1892), 154.
21 Avery, *History of Georgia*, 54.

dates, but since Unionists Cobb and Toombs were secretary of the treasury and United States senator, he felt that the governor should be a Southern Rightist; consequently, he had supported Gardner before proposing Brown as a compromise candidate.[22] Others thought the motives for Brown's nomination were less laudable. The elimination of Lumpkin was a "deep played game," declared a writer in the Cassville *Standard*. "They think Lumpkin is not only 'killed off' for the present but for the future."[23]

Lumpkin was bitter. When Cobb suggested that this temporary defeat need not set him back politically, he agreed; but then he launched a sharp denunciation. He was pleased to retire to private life and had begun "to esteem the baseness & treachery of pretended friends an act of kindness. . . . McDonald was my bitter and uncompromising enemy, and was the master spirit in the intrigue to effect my defeat." Toombs, he thought, stood by him until placed under pressure. "But my honest opinion is that A. H. Stephens was opposed to my nomination, and influenced Toombs, Thomas & Linton Stephens to support Gardner and any other Southern Rights man over me." Lumpkin further charged that the resolutions relative to Walker and Kansas were drawn up at Alexander Stephens' Crawfordsville home by Toombs, Thomas, and the Stephens brothers, and their aim was either to control the Buchanan administration or take issue with it by demanding the removal of Walker.[24] Lumpkin was not entirely correct.

To his brother Alexander, Linton Stephens explained "I was pleased with the action of the convention. The Kansas part of the platform was drawn by me. . . . Brown is a man that I know to have decided ability; as a debater, he is far superior to any of those who were before the convention. Indeed, without being an orator, he is a very effective stump-speaker. He is quick, clear-headed, and a close reasoner, with considerable turn for sharp, witty remark. He was a firm Southern rights man, and one of the most prudent among them. Besides all this, he is a man of fine personal character, and self made. . . . He stands high in the upcountry, and deserves it. I served in the Legislature with him

22 This letter has not been found but it is paraphrased in Lumpkin to Cobb, July 14, 1857, in Cobb Papers.
23 Quoted in Savannah *Republican*, July 21, 1857.
24 Lumpkin to Cobb, July 14, 1857, in Cobb Papers.

in the session of 1849 and 1850. The man, and the section from which he comes, are also a lick for Toombs."[25]

Howell Cobb, secretary of treasury in President Buchanan's cabinet and with eyes on the Democratic nomination for president in 1860, wrote his wife, "I have just heard of the action of the convention at Milledgeville, and I am out of all patience with the democracy of Ga so far as that convention represented their views & feelings—The course of the party in Ga is to me inexplicable. They have lost all good sense & seem bent on self destruction—In the history of politics I have never witnessed any thing like it—I am thoroughly disgusted and should give five hundred dollars this night for the privilege of making an hour speech to the good people *the honest people* the only reliable men at last—I grow weary & restless at the idea that good men are thus to be deluded hoodwinked & imposed upon."[26]

Before receiving this letter Mrs. Cobb wrote inquiring how her husband liked the nomination of Brown. "I have never heard of him— but he may be a wise & learned man for all that. I feel as if *we* shall have no governor since Judge Lumpkin was set aside." This "old nullifying—Southern rights" group would not do. They would ruin the Democratic party.[27] A few days later she told her husband that the reason for taking a man from Cherokee was to "kill all Judge L. aspirations." Had her husband been there it would not have happened. However, since he would not withdraw himself from politics he "must take patiently what the leaders of the So Rights Democracy choose to serve up to you and the honest *union* men at home."[28]

Writing to J. B. Lamar, Cobb stressed the fact that Brown got the nomination only when it became impossible for anyone else to get the required majority. He then added: "If it had stopped here—it could have been borne with but the convention denounced Gov. Walker for his course in Kansas and demanded his removal—thus making an issue with the administration."[29] Cobb wanted his good friend Lumpkin to

25 Linton Stephens to Alexander Stephens, June 29, 1857, quoted in James D. Waddell (ed.), *Biographical Sketch of Linton Stephens* (Atlanta, 1877), 127.
26 June 27, 1857, in Cobb Papers.
27 July 1, 5, 1857, *ibid.*
28 July 5, 1857, *ibid.*
29 July 10, 1857, *ibid.*

be governor, but most of all he wanted peace with the Buchanan administration. In 1860 he would need support from both Georgia and the Buchanan administration. Brown, though a Southern Rights man, was not pledged, and the platform was certain to irritate the national administration.

After a few more days of reflection Cobb wrote Alexander Stephens, "I know Judge Brown very well and he will conform to the judgment of his friends, but if left to his own may blunder. The canvass is deep water and it requires prudence sagacity and [reason?] to conduct it successfully."[30] In short, the young inexperienced Democratic candidate for governor must be given supervision.

Brown moved quickly to placate disappointed aspirants for the nomination. Within a few days he drove to Rome to confer with Lumpkin and his long-time friend Augustus R. Wright, carrying with him his letter of acceptance which had not yet been made public. Lumpkin was friendly but not enthusiastic. According to Lumpkin's version of the meeting, Brown assured him that he had "no agency either directly or indirectly," in his own nomination; he was as much surprised as anyone in Georgia. Brown pledged full support of the Buchanan administration and requested Lumpkin's support in the coming campaign. Lumpkin explained that he had "no cause of complaint against him personally" and would give him cordial support if his political position was acceptable. But privately Lumpkin told Cobb that he considered Brown's letter of acceptance "non-committal" and he prophesied that it would not please either division of the party. He sensed much apathy following the nomination and thought victory would be by a small vote, if at all.[31]

Indeed, Brown's letter was rather noncommittal. He stood for the Constitution and its protection against "assault of fanaticism and error," and for the preservation of the reserved rights of the states. The Constitution provided the best government and if properly administered would guarantee "the blessings of civil, religious, and political liberty." He pledged support of the principles adopted by the state convention and praised the Democratic party for its past attainments. On a final point, however, he did make himself quite clear. "The circumstances of

30 July 23, 1857, in Alexander Stephens Papers, Emory University.
31 Lumpkin to Cobb, July 14, 1857, in Cobb Papers.

my nomination preclude the idea that I have made any promise either expressed or implied, and I shall neither make nor intimate any to any one, as to the distribution of Executive patronage in the event of my election." In making appointments "I shall have regard to the capacity, integrity and industry of the persons appointed as I consider the union of these three qualities essential to the just and efficient execution of public duties."[32]

Brown made an acceptance speech to his friends in Canton, and the ladies of Cherokee County presented him with a calico bedspread. His opponents would make many gleeful remarks about the incident during the campaign. His friends also had some fun. The Democratic Milledgeville *Federal Union* made merry: "All we have to say is—go ahead gals—give Joe Brown as many calico bedquilts as you please— it will be a compliment to the *Mountain Boy*, and save the state hundreds besides. Hurrah for the girls of Cherokee, the ploughboy judge and the calico bed-quilt."[33]

Many newspapers, Democratic and opposition, ran columns headed, "Who is Joe Brown?" the former papers to enlighten and the latter to ridicule. A number of Brown's friends, both old and new, thought it their duty to inform Georgia voters just who and what the Democratic candidate was. A contributor to the Savannah *Morning News*, who claimed to have been intimately acquainted with the candidate for the past thirteen years, described him as being five feet ten inches in height and weighing 145 pounds. When walking, his position was erect, his step "rather slow and measured." His chest was flattened, "indicating a consumptive tendency," and his complexion, though not sallow, did not have "that florid hue one would expect of a man accustomed to mountain air." Yet a black beard beneath the chin and heavy black hair atop a forehead "broad and high," blue eyes, and a wide mouth made him appear as "one of nature's real noblemen."[34]

The Augusta *Evening Dispatch* observed that Brown's friends were loudly singing the praises of the "Mountain Boy," even though opposition papers pronounced him "a third rate lawyer, an unscrupulous demagogue and little more than a conceited upstart." The editor, claim-

32 Milledgeville *Federal Union*, July 21, 1857.
33 Avery, *History of Georgia*, 42; Milledgeville *Federal Union*, July 21, 1857.
34 June 30, 1857.

ing to hold no bias, declared that, as a judge, Brown had shown considerable ability. Although "not a brilliant speaker or writer," he possessed "a logical, well-balanced mind, and in his moral character exhibits adherence to elevated principles of temperance and morality quite refreshing to find among our professional politicians. . . . But at the same time we consider him a 'lucky dog' to get the nomination." There were probably fifty Democrats in Georgia who were better speakers or writers and a hundred with "superior claim to having fought, bled, and died in the service of their party." Yet since "*availability*" made presidents of Polk, Taylor, and Pierce and the country prospered under their administrations, "We should not despair when such men as Warner, Ward, Gardner, Lamar, Lumpkin, and other veterans of the party, are set aside under the dictates of this modern idea of policy." Except for Brown's "political bitterness—for he is a most intense partisan—he is a good man, and we have no doubt will make a competent Governor."[35]

"We know Judge Brown well," announced the editor of the Milledgeville *Federal Union*, "and a better man does not walk the soil of Georgia. He is emphatically a man of the people. . . . We believe both his moral and political character are without spot or blemish; such a man cannot fail to make a good Governor."[36]

The Democrats, though decisive victors in every election since 1853, were not to have the field to themselves. The American party, though a loser in the past two elections, was not dead. It assembled in convention on July 8 and nominated Benjamin H. Hill by acclamation. None of the old Whigs who had drifted into the American party actively sought the nomination. The platform denounced the Democratic policies in Kansas, opposed squatter sovereignty and any further agitation on the subject of slavery, and endorsed the Georgia platform.[37]

It was uncertain whether Hill was the first choice of the Know-Nothings, commented the editor of the Democratic *Federal Union*, but he certainly was the choice of his Democratic opponents. Ben Hill was the very man they wanted to beat. He thought that the real reason why Hill was "settled upon" was that "he had no laurels to lose, having been

35 *Ibid.*
36 *Ibid.*
37 Savannah *Republican*, July 14, 1857; Haywood J. Pearce, Jr., *Benjamin H. Hill: Secession and Reconstruction* (Chicago, 1928), 22–23.

defeated for Congress, and then defeated as a Fillmore elector by over fourteen thousand votes."[38]

Like the American party platform, Hill's letter of acceptance was devoted almost entirely to Kansas. He declared that the Federal government had no right "to open its mouth, directly or indirectly, for or against" the manner in which the people of Kansas exercised their rights. "When therefore Gov. Walker objected to or officially uttered one word concerning the plan which the qualified voters were pursuing, he *intervened*; when he prescribed a different plan (as he did), he *dictated*; and when he went further and declared his plan must be adopted, or the constitution would and ought to be rejected by Congress, he *threatened*; and when he declared that, if his plan was not adopted, he and the President would join the Republicans in opposition to what he admitted to be legal constituted authority in Kansas, he *hectored*, and that most insolently." Furthermore, since the president, with full knowledge of the facts, had not repudiated and recalled Walker, but instead had explained that he had "acted with wisdom and justice, he became no better than Walker himself and is solely responsible."[39]

If the purpose of a political campaign is to enlighten voters, then the Georgia gubernatorial campaign of 1857 might well have ended with the publication of the platforms and letters of acceptance. Kansas was the only issue of importance. Both parties denounced Walker. The Americans also denounced Buchanan, but the Democrats approved his administration and were willing to give him sufficient time to act wisely.

While other newspapers were extolling the virtues of their respective candidates, the Bainbridge *Argus* made a comparison of the two. Brown was a Baptist, an advocate of temperance and sobriety. In politics he was "an uncompromising fire eater," a Southern Rights man. As a man, politically and morally, he was "pure, spotless and incorruptible."

Hill was a Methodist. Socially he had no superior. He was "loved and respected by all who knew him." In politics he was originally a Democrat, then a Unionist, and finally turned Know-Nothing or American. A gentleman and a Christian, he deserved "the respect of every lover of virtue in the State." Being a Democrat, the editor of the *Argus*

38 July 14, 1857.
39 Savannah *Republican*, July 25, 1857.

explained, he would vote for Brown, yet he warned that "no one shall attack Mr. Hill in our columns." Gentlemanly argument and fair discussion would be permitted.[40]

When those who disliked the prospects of losing their free drinks on election day began chiding Judge Brown about his temperance views, the editor of the temperance *Crusade* made further comparison of the two candidates. Judge Brown had "never been ashamed" of being a temperance man, and Hill was "equally as ardent an advocate. . . . The jeers and taunts heaped upon the temperance cause are only strong evidence of the baseness, imbecility, and degradation of those who are guilty of the habit," exclaimed the editor. "The drunken rabble, sports-hunting demagogues, and sottish mole-eyed political Editor may point the finger of scorn at the candidate who claims to be a lover of temperance, but that will not swerve sober, sensible man from his conviction of duty and path of rectitude."[41]

At the beginning of the campaign Senator Toombs appeared as somewhat of a supervisor of the inexperienced Democratic nominee. He alone of the Big Three canvassed the state in the interest of the party. At times he and Brown were together, but it soon became evident that the young candidate needed no supervision. Howell Cobb was in Washington, and Alexander Stephens limited his activities to his home district, but on strategy they agreed with Toombs: Governor Walker might be denounced for his activities in Kansas but there should be "strong and active adherence" to the Buchanan administration.[42] "Apart from this Walker business," Stephens told the voters of his district, "no administration has ever in my day so fully met my cordial approval." He felt that the president must have his reasons for not immediately removing Walker; therefore, he was not willing to condemn without a hearing. However, in the end the president could not escape responsibility for the "consequences attending his retention."[43]

The great concern was that Brown might not adhere to this formula devised by party leaders. "If Brown writes a foolish letter denouncing the Administration he will be beat," declared a friend of Cobb.[44] An-

40 Quoted in Savannah *Morning News*, July 25, 1857.
41 July ?, September 24, 1857.
42 Toombs to Stephens, August 15, 1857, Phillips, *Correspondence*, 420–21.
43 Phillips, *Correspondence*, 409ff.
44 W. R. de Graffenried to Cobb, July 14, 1857, in Cobb Papers.

other Cobb friend was more optimistic after conversing "very freely" with Judge Brown. "He feels the delicacy of his position, some urging him to denounce Mr. Buchanan & others requiring him to endorse Walker." But the Judge would under no circumstances abandon the administration.[45]

Cobb was not convinced that Brown could be depended upon, and he was much concerned about party division regarding the Buchanan administration. Writing from Washington, he urged Stephens to assemble a caucus of party leaders in Athens during the university's summer commencement exercises for the purpose of promoting party harmony. Although a number of prominent persons, including Judge Brown, did journey to Athens, there is no evidence that any organized caucus was held. However, Ben Hill, in a speech at Newnan, declared that there was a caucus of leaders of the State Rights and Union wings of the Democratic party to determine what course Judge Brown should follow with regard to answering questions propounded by the opposition. It was decided, Hill explained, that the judge should adopt a "non-committal policy."

"I pronounce the statement a *falsehood*," declared Brown; "I care not by whom it is made." In Athens, members of both wings of the party were frequently in his room, he explained, but he knew of no caucus. No one advised him not to answer questions and he had always answered fully. "When I accepted the nomination I endorsed every resolution and word of the platform laid down by the convention which nominated me. I have changed no opinion then expressed. I still endorse and stand upon the platform, the *whole platform* of that convention. The principles contained in it still command the approbation of my judgment, and will continue to receive my cordial support."[46]

Not all Democrats were as willing as Brown was to accept the Walker Resolution and Buchanan's conduct. Opinions varied from one extreme to the other. The Cassville *Standard* defended Walker's efforts to restore peace in Kansas. It did not matter whether the territory became a free or slave state, the editor explained. "All we ask is that the people be allowed to decide for themselves." The *Standard* would

45 P. Clayton to Cobb, August 7, 1857, *ibid.*
46 Brown to editor of Augusta *Constitutionalist*, September 21, 1857, *Constitutionalist*, September 23, 1857.

support Brown but wanted no part of "any line of policy" that would foment strife.[47]

The Rome *Southerner*, a Lumpkin paper, explained that the movement against Walker was not "a movement *generally* based upon political feelings or devotion to principles." It was "a plan to roll the administration of Buchanan out of power on the *Cobb* of Georgia." The "action of the convention in passing the third resolution was hasty and inconsiderate." Many members, not well informed on the subject, placed too much trust in leaders. Were that convention in session again no such resolution would be passed.[48]

On the other extreme was Thomas W. Thomas, influential political leader of Elberton, who had served as chairman of the committee that reported the "third resolution" in the recent Democratic convention. He still supported the "resolution," but he was very bitter toward Buchanan for failure to repudiate Walker. By the president's failure to act, Thomas declared, he had exhibited a want of "fidelity to the principles which carried him into office." In short, the president was a "traitor."[49]

Thomas was denounced by those Democrats who did not wish to involve the president, and it was rumored that he might bolt the party. In reply to his critics he observed: "Like monkeys they will bite anybody for the one who holds them. Mr. Buchanan holds them now and they bite me; if I held them, I could as easily make them bite him."[50]

But even Thomas fell in line to support Brown when insulted by a suggestion that he join the American party and run for Congress against his friend Alexander Stephens. "Why should I not support Judge Brown?" he asked, ". . . When I voted for the third resolution I did not doubt Walker would be removed. Now would it be just or sensible in me to desert Judge Brown because he cherishes this hope longer than I find myself able to do?"[51]

Brown made an extensive campaign. At Rome he was introduced by John H. Lumpkin, who spent more time praising President Buchanan then he did Brown. As in all of his other speeches, Brown's

---

47 Quoted in Savannah *Republican*, July 14, 1857.
48 Savannah *Republican*, July 4, 1857.
49 Thomas to editor, Augusta *Constitutionalist*, July 23, 1857.
50 Thomas to James Sledge, August 10, 1857, Athens *Southern Banner*, August 20, 1857; Augusta *Constitutionalist*, August 18, 1857.
51 Augusta *Constitutionalist*, August 18, 1857.

principal topic of discussion was Governor Walker and Kansas. He denounced Walker for his "climate argument against slavery in Kansas"; condemned him for dictation relative to the submission of the constitution to the people, and for threatening its rejection by Congress. He had no idea that Buchanan approved of such interference and was willing to wait for the president's annual message to Congress. To the extent that Buchanan failed to disapprove Walker, Brown would disapprove Buchanan. But even should Buchanan fail in his performance there was no need to desert the party. In such an eventuality the Democrats should do what the Whigs had done in the Tyler administration—desert the president but adhere to party principles.[52]

After hearing Brown speak in Savannah an opposition editor was less than complimentary. "He is a plain common-sensed man, of ordinary abilities, wholly without pretention to oratory, and but limited information on the public affairs of the country." If this speech was a sample of the Democratic candidate's ability, the editor thought it ridiculous to suppose he could triumph over Ben Hill in any contest.[53]

Hill was as active as Brown. Even his opponents were impressed with his ability. He was truly "adept at picking flaws," declared the Atlanta *Daily Intelligencer*. "He is emphatically the embodiment of dexterous pleading. 'To make the worse appear the better reason,' seems to have been the study of his life, and we grant to him considerable success. He is a sophist—a dangerous one—but still nothing but a sophist. He will insidiously capture your judgment temporarily with a spacious view of the cause. He will then pick up disconnected positions of an opponent and torture them into something like he would have you believe.... Mr. Hill's speech meant this much, reduced and compressed: Buchanan is wrong—so is Walker—elect me, Ben Hill, and it will all be made right."[54] The only statement by Hill that angered the Atlanta editor was an insinuation that Alexander Stephens had made remarks in Congress as unwise as those made by Walker.

The editor of the Milledgeville *Federal Union* also denied this charge against Stephens and declared, "He is far more culpable than Walker." While Walker was trying to prevent civil war in Kansas,

52 *Ibid.*, September 20, 1957.
53 Savannah *Republican*, August 12, 1857.
54 Atlanta *Intelligencer*, July 20, 1857.

Hill was trying to keep southern slaveholders from going there.[55]

A few weeks later, the *Federal Union* declared Hill's greatest fault was that he could not "endure to wait . . . it almost throws him into spasms." He wanted action now before it is too late to help him, but he would just have to wait, even though the delay might be fatal to him and his party. "The Democrats will not quarrel and divide for their benefit."[56]

As a result of pressure from those who enjoyed spirited political combat, the two candidates agreed to a series of joint meetings. At Carrollton, according to the editor of the *Southern Democrat*, Brown "performed in a noble and dignified manner," proving himself an "able and eloquent advocate of the principles of Southern Rights Democracy." Though small of stature, he was "a giant in talent," and "he completely 'wound up' the great K. N. stump orator." He was not too severe in his denunciation of Walker and Buchanan but was "sufficiently plain and pointed."[57]

Both at Carrollton and at Franklin in Heard County the speakers engaged in a question and answer session. Hill asked if Brown approved Buchanan's failure to remove Walker from office. Brown replied that he would not condemn the president "until I am satisfied that he has betrayed the trust reposed in him." He would not "pronounce hasty judgment," but would "give ample time for considerate action." How long was Brown willing to wait? Brown replied, "I will allow a reasonable time having due regard to all circumstances by which Mr. Buchanan is surrounded." As things now stood, did Brown "sustain the administration of Buchanan?" Brown replied, "I do."

Brown then asked Hill some equally petty questions. Did Hill approve the Know-Nothing platform adopted in Philadelphia in 1855? Hill did. Would Hill permit any expression of opinion as to whether or not Congress had the power to establish or prevent slavery in a territory? Hill replied that he would not, for Congress had no such power. In answer to further questioning, Hill declared his approval of the recently adopted American platform "with all my heart." Brown inquired what change would he suggest in the naturalization laws. Hill would

---

55 August 4, 1857.
56 September 1, 1857.
57 Carrollton *Southern Democrat*, August 5, 1857.

fix the minimum residence requirement at twenty-one years. Did he approve the failure of the American convention that nominated him to disapprove of and condemn Governor Walker's action? Hill shot back "I approve the course taken by that convention and that convention did condemn Walker." Finally, was Hill in favor of selling the state-owned Western and Atlantic Railroad? "I answer emphatically, I am."[58]

Under an Act passed by the General Assembly in 1836, the state of Georgia had constructed the Western and Atlantic Railroad connecting the Chattahoochee River with the Tennessee River at Chattanooga. From the beginning, there was much opposition to the state undertaking such a project. But the determination of promoters finally triumphed over financial and engineering obstacles, and the road was opened to traffic in 1851. It was not an immediate financial success, but under control of the governor it had furnished numerous jobs for loyal members of the party in power. During the spring of 1857 there had been lively newspaper debate on proposals to sell or lease the road.[59]

The road, under the management of the governor, had not yielded the profits expected. Many considered it a financial liability. The opposition charged that the Democratic party was reaping as many as 20,000 votes each election through use of railroad patronage. It was reported that in a speech at Cool Springs, Wilkinson County, Ben Hill charged that all who pledged to vote for Joe Brown were given passes to ride the Western and Atlantic trains without charge. All persons who so pledged were given an emblem in the form of a cross to wear on their hats. Hill claimed that he himself had seen these crosses, and all who wore them were identified as Brown supporters. According to reports, Hill also claimed that while on the road he was propositioned: If upon election he would promise to retain the present employees in office, he could pick up 10,000 votes.[60] Of course Hill spurned the suggestion!

In other speeches Hill did not hesitate to advocate the sale of the road to private citizens. Brown was not so definite. Yet in a public letter to W. H. Burton of the Carrollton *Democrat* he discussed the possibilities. The road belonged to the people, and they should so instruct their

---

58 Savannah *Morning News*, August 14, 1857, quoting Atlanta *Examiner*.
59 James H. Johnston, *Western and Atlantic Railroad of the State of Georgia* (Atlanta, 1931), Chaps. I, II; Ulrich B. Phillips, *A History of Transportation in the Eastern Cotton Belt* (New York, 1908), Chap. VII.
60 Augusta *Constitutionalist*, September 27, 1857.

legislators should they wish to sell or lease it. If they wished to do neither, he would suggest that management of the road be taken out of the hands of the governor. Should he himself be elected governor he would sign any bill on the subject passed by the legislature, provided it protected the interest of the people. No decision should be made to sell solely to get rid of this improvement. If the decision should be to sell, then the general public should have the first opportunity to purchase stock in it. No capitalist should be permitted to buy a large block of stock until the people in all counties had had the opportunity.

Further, should the road pass under private control the contract for transfer should contain definite restrictions as to freight and passenger rates to be charged, for there was no competing line. There should also be caution against waste of the money realized from such a sale. One omnibus bill "effecting different local interests" might have sufficient legislative support "to appropriate the whole find." Instead of squandering it on local interests, Brown suggested that the money be used to pay the state debt and establish a public school fund. If there was a remainder it might be invested in stocks of other railroads under construction.[61]

According to "B," reporting to the Savannah *Republican* from Athens, Hill and Brown, while attending the university commencement exercises agreed to two joint meetings in that area. At Lexington, on August 7, the reporter "heard" that the discussion "terminated most gloriously" for the American party. But a reporter to the *Wilkes Republican* had a different view—all Hill did was repeat false statements made at Newnan.[62]

The two candidates also met at a barbecue near Athens on August 9. Here Hill was reported to have charged that in 1856 the Democrats had promised to the voters "Buck, Breck and Kansas." They got Buck and Breck, but where was Kansas? When Hill continued to press the Kansas issue, Brown attempted to dodge it. It was further reported that while Judge Brown was performing so poorly, a disgusted "Democrat" standing nearby suggested that someone take the judge out and

61 Dated September 11, 1857. Copy in Athens *Southern Banner*, October 1, 1857.
62 Quoted in Athens *Southern Banner*, August 27, 1957; Savannah *Republican*, August 15, 1857.

"liquor him, as he certainly required some stimulus."[63] Apparently Brown's friends failed to report this meeting.

Hill's friends claimed that Brown's managers put an end to the joint meetings of the two candidates, that both sides might have grown tired of listening to each other. Speeches became repetitious, and Kansas was worn to shreds. Yet those were the days when oratory was an art, and Ben Hill had the ability to say the same thing in many different ways. Who won the oratorical contest depended upon who did the judging; biased judges rendered biased decisions.

Ben Hill and Joe Brown differed greatly in their stump performances. One contemporary likened Brown to Socrates rather than Cicero. What he said resulted from reasoning power of the highest order, but listeners who craved excitement were not impressed. Brown was not a scholar; his illustrations never reflected a knowledge of history or literary classics. They were usually drawn from his knowledge of country life. This gave him some advantage when addressing country people, but it did not help his standing with the more elite, and many unkind remarks were made about his manner of speaking and his pronunciation. He became a political and financial success, but the need for formal education remained with him.

A contemporary, in reviewing the campaign of 1857, recorded: "Mr. Hill was an orator. Mr. Brown was a talker. Bold denunciations, bitter invective, relentless irony and passionate appeal were the weapons of the former. Homely speech, keen observation, apt retort and sagacious comment were the tools of the latter. The former was the embodiment of fiery zeal. The latter was the incarnation of philosophic repose. . . . The former was the Athenian eloquent whose fiery fulminations shook the forum. The latter was the Athenian wise, whose sober teachings solemnized the market-place. But Greece needed both her orator and her philosopher; and Georgia in the trying ordeal which was now before her could spare neither her Brown nor her Hill."[64] The vote was Brown 57,568 and Hill 46,826. Each had improved upon the showing made by his party during the recent presidential election.[65]

---

63 Savannah *Republican*, August 15, 1857.
64 Lucian Lamar Knight, *Reminiscences of Famous Georgians* (Atlanta, 1907), I, 239 ff.
65 Milledgeville *Federal Union*, November 10, 1857.

Chapter III

He Defied Them All

THE ELECTION of Joseph E. Brown to the governorship was something of a revolution in Georgia. His humble origin, meagre education, and limited political experience did not fit the mold in which recent governors and the more prominent political leaders had been cast. It was not so much a question of his ability to govern as it was his right to be there. The old establishment considered him an upstart, even though they refrained from so declaring in public, and worse still, the voters appeared to relish the change.

Those leaders who supported him dared not do otherwise, for Hill and the American party were not acceptable alternatives. Now that they had elected Brown, however, they were uneasy. He was pledged only to a conditional support of the Buchanan administration, and he exhibited an intellectual shrewdness and determination that marked him as a man who might be difficult to handle.

Letters of congratulation began to arrive at the Brown home even before the official results of the election had been made known. Some offered unsolicited advice. "Accept my cordial congratulation on your election," wrote Howell Cobb from Washington. "But for the unfortunate and ill-advised Third resolution, I am satisfied your majority would have been double what it is. In view of the embarrassments thrown around you by that resolution, I think you have cause to be proud of the result. . . . The people of Georgia are a conservative, national people in their feelings, & it is a blunder to mistake the wild ultraism of a few for the political sentiment of the mass. . . . A wise statesman should always be ready *to meet issues boldly and never to make them unnecessarily.*"[1] In a note of the same date to his friend Alexander H. Stephens, Cobb suggested "Gov. Brown and our friends in the legislature ought to be warned not to make *hasty and unnecessary issues.* They should remember the fate of Gov. Towns and the democratic party in 1850."[2]

To his brother Howell, Thomas R. R. Cobb reported a conference with Senator Toombs. The Senator was convinced that Brown would not "put himself in the hands of the fireaters. . . . I asked him to beg Brown not to commit himself to ultraism in his Inaugural—He said he would see to that."[3] Truly the subject of Kansas and its probable effect upon the Democratic convention of 1860 was weighing heavily upon the minds of the Cobb brothers.

"I . . . send you my sincere congratulations at the glorious result for so I consider it," wrote Stephens to Brown. "It is one of the greatest victories ever achieved by any party in this state.[4]

John Henry Lumpkin, having recovered from disappointment and chagrin and no longer entertaining political ambitions, was much impressed by Brown's campaign performance. "I congratulate you upon this result not only here but throughout the state, and tender you my thanks for the gallant manner [in which] you have conducted this canvass. There are few men in Georgia who could have conducted this canvass with more judgment and ability, and none with more indefatigable zeal and industry. I frankly confess that I could not have performed the labor that you have performed, and if our success was dependent upon these extraordinary efforts, the convention made the proper selection. . . . I am your friend personally and politically, now as at all times heretofore, and I expect to give your administration my cordial support to the extent of my influence."[5]

Senator Toombs, the only one of the Big Three who had been active statewide during the campaign, sent no letter of congratulation, but he and Brown understood each other. The battle just won was also

1 October 8, 1857, in Spalding Collection.
2 Cobb to Stephens, October 9, 1857, Phillips, *Correspondence*, 424–25.
3 October 12, 1857, in Cobb Papers.
4 October 17, 1857, in Hargrett Collection.
5 October 10, 1857, in Hargrett Collection.

a Toombs victory; he must stand for reelection by the next General Assembly.

The Browns moved to Milledgeville early in November, 1857. During ten years of their married life they had lived in their modest Canton home where their five children had been born. Milledgeville was no city, but life there would be much more gay and not so simple, especially for a governor's family. And the Governor's Mansion was a palace compared to their Canton dwelling. Mrs. Brown was a bit awed. "This place has a great many gay persons here at this time," she wrote her mother, "and the Mansion is a very large house and well furnished with most things. . . . But with all these things surrounding me I am lonesome and could enjoy more at my dear old home. I often yearn to be there." With lard and hams twenty-five cents per pound, butter forty, pork ten, beef eight, and eggs twenty-five cents per dozen, she further commented, "I hardly see how we can afford to live here."[6]

Mrs. Brown spoke of the beautiful weather and the large crowd at the inaugural, but she made no mention of a reception or ball at the Mansion. Indeed, functions at the Mansion during the Brown administration would be few and dignified. Those who did dine did so without stimulation from strong drink. Governors Towns, Cobb, and Johnson had permitted "disgraceful" mob festivities although their better tastes were offended. Brown would tolerate no repetition. There would be no magnificent feeds at heavy cost, no "festivity of mash and gluttony, and plunder," no gorging of stomachs and filling pockets with what remained, no broken dishes and tables. Regardless of custom or democratic principles involved, these things must go. In their place would be orderly, dignified Friday night receptions.[7] Brown believed that with the rights of the common man went an obligation to be decent. Residents of other sections of the state might have expected the "plow boy Governor" to continue this "practical incarnation of equality religiously cherished," but those who knew him as neighbor, lawyer, and judge in the Cherokee region expected him to do exactly what he did.

Brown took the oath of office on November 6, 1857. The legislature was already in session, and, on the previous day, retiring Governor

6 Elizabeth Brown to Mary L. Grisham, November 8, 1857, in Hargrett Collection.
7 Avery, *History of Georgia*, 68.

Herschel V. Johnson had delivered to that body his final report and recommendations. He had recently received from James M. Spullock, superintendent of the Western and Atlantic Railroad, the annual report for the year ending September 30.[8] The net income from operation had been $464,981. Of this amount $383,661 had been paid for continued construction and equipment; $100,000 had been paid into the state treasury. Business during the past year had not been as good as hoped for owing to "decline in prices of grain and want of commercial confidence." However, Spullock concluded, "I can safely and do confidently assert, that even with the same amount of business in 1858 that the road has done the past year, it can and should with proper management, pay into the State Treasury $350,000."

After elaborating on this very optimistic report, Governor Johnson declared that the Western and Atlantic Railroad was on the "eve of realizing the expectations in which it originated. . . . I fully concur with the Superintendent, that, henceforth, under proper management, it will pay into the State Treasury $350,000 annually."

Of much more immediate concern to the people of Georgia than the condition of the Western and Atlantic Railroad was the action recently taken by most of the banks. Under a law dating from December 18, 1840, if a bank suspended specie payment on its notes, the governor was to begin legal action leading to an annulment of its charter. As the economic distress commonly known as the Panic of 1857 moved into Georgia there developed a serious financial crisis. Fearing a drain on their limited amount of specie, banks began ignoring the law and suspending specie payment, thus further intensifying the panic. Governor Johnson, undecided what should be done, did nothing. When a committee representing "merchants and citizens of Savannah" urged him to withhold action against suspending banks until the legislature should meet, he replied, "I should have done as you suggest if no request had been made."[9]

In his last message to the Legislature the governor explained why he had taken no action against the banks. He admitted that these banks had ignored the law, causing "panic, broken confidence, and general

8 Milledgeville *Federal Union*, November 5, 24, 1857.
9 Savannah *Republican*, October 22, 1857; Augusta *Constitutionalist*, October 24, 1857.

stagnation in commerce." However, since another session of the General Assembly was so near at hand and suspension appeared necessary, he had decided to leave the decision to the Assembly, and he suggested that it seemed wise to tolerate the suspension by those banks that "proved to be sound and solvent."

It is presumed that Brown listened to Governor Johnson's message. If not, he certainly read it in the newspapers the same day it was delivered. He took the oath of office and delivered before the General Assembly his inaugural message the following day, November 6. He rejoiced that in a race for public office in Georgia "all are alike eligible; industry, integrity, virtue and ability being the principal qualifications looked to by an enlightened public opinion."

Brown then issued the customary appeal for an end to "party strife and party prejudice" and the substitution of "calm and dignified deliberations." The state was truly rich in soil, minerals, and commercial and manufacturing potential but its greatest wealth was "the energy, intelligence and patriotism of her people." This energy and enterprise had recently united the sections by railroads and telegraph.

He thought the "proudest monument of Georgia enterprise" was the Western and Atlantic Railroad. It "unlocked to our Atlantic coast the rich treasures of the great West." It had converted the Cherokee section from a "wild, uncivilized region, into one of the most interesting and prosperous sections of our State." The legislature might well consider the desirability of extending aid to the development of other sections. "What Georgians would not feel proud to see our beautiful commercial emporium connected by rail-road with our South-Western border and the Gulf of Mexico," thus causing the wilderness to "bloom like the rose."

But while developing physical resources, the development of the mind should not be neglected. All progress depended upon the "virtue and intelligence" of the people. This required a more liberal endorsement of colleges and the establishment of a common school system, thus placing education within the reach of "every son and daughter" within the state. Many a "bright-eyed" boy with ability but humble in circumstance was denied even a common school education. Given an opportunity these boys would become leaders in business, government, and the army.

After this burst of oratory, Brown returned to the subject of the Western and Atlantic and repeated what he had proposed during the campaign. The road belonged to the people; they should decide whether to sell, lease, or continue it under public operation. Whatever disposition was made of this valuable asset, the net income should be used to reduce taxes.

Finally the new governor came to the subject of greatest immediate concern—the banks and their suspension of specie payment. He exhibited none of the tolerance proposed by his predecessor. In "the midst of a high state of commercial prosperity, with abundant crops, and a bright prospect for the future," he explained, "the country is suddenly shocked by an almost general bank suspension, causing distress and depression in all our commercial affairs." This situation had resulted from wild speculation by banks and the extension of their paper in violation of principles which required them to redeem their notes in specie. This being true, these banks were "certainly not the proper objects of public sympathy." The law provided a penalty, and it was the duty of the governor to apply it. "I consider the law imperative," said Brown, and when he received legal evidence of a bank's violation "I shall order proceedings for the forfeiture of its charter."[10]

Smiles produced by Governor Johnson's message were turned to frowns by Governor Brown, and state bankers and their lobbyists headed for Milledgeville. "The lobbies were thronged with bank men and their friends." The governor was warned that he would "ruin the state and shock irreparably the public weal" by warring upon the banks. "He defied them all."[11]

The governor's charge against the banks was "uncalled for, wrong and ruinous, unenlightened and unjust," declared the Savannah *Republican*. "It affords another instance of the danger of the elevation of small men to great places."[12] "Whatever may be said against our banking system," decared the Savannah *News*, "—and we are certainly no advocate of its abuses—the present is, in our judgment, not the proper time for the adoption of 'desperate remedies'" which would destroy business and do nothing to improve the banking system.[13]

10 Milledgeville *Federal Union*, November 10, 1857.
11 Avery, *History of Georgia*, 60.
12 November 11, 1857.
13 November 9, 1857.

Threatened by the governor, the banks turned to the legislature for relief. A bill was quickly introduced changing the penalty from loss of charter to a 10 percent penalty for failure to redeem bank notes in specie. Also, this penalty was not to be applied prior to November 15, 1858. Further, no bank might charge interest in excess of 7 percent or purchase notes or debts at more than 7 percent discount.[14]

Press support of this proposed relief for banks ranged from mild to enthusiastic in the cities. Small town newspapers were generally opposed. "We are not the champion of the banks," explained the Augusta *Daily Constitutionalist*. "We owe them nothing, nor do we ask any favors at their hands, but we believe their suspension was justified by the extraordinary circumstances of the times and ought to be legalized by the present legislature."[15]

To a friend, Brown wrote in confidence: "The bank question still lies on the table in the House. Neither side seems anxious to move. I find the House the soundest on that question and am looking mostly to it. There will probably be a motion when it comes up again to lay the whole matter on the table for the balance of the session. The bank men dread the issue, I think. Whether the House will do this I think quite uncertain. Their disposition however is to put pretty hard terms on the banks. Whether hard *enough* is the question which I shall have to consider."[16]

The governor also observed with some satisfaction the reported reaction to his recent veto of a joint resolution of the two houses urging the discharge of two female convicts. "The bank men are said to have been a little alarmed at this. They said it was a sort of Jackson like stubbornness, telling the Legislature to mind its own business & I would attend to mine."[17]

The governor was wrong in his predictions; the bank bill passed the House by sixty-four to fifty, and the Senate by fifty-eight to twenty-seven. The House vote was much less than the two-thirds majority that would be required to override a possible veto by the governor. And since forty House members and thirty senators had refrained from

---

14 Milledgeville *Federal Union*, December 8, 1857.
15 December 1, 1857.
16 Brown to Dr. [Lewis?], December 9, 1857, in Hargrett Collection.
17 Brown to Lewis, December 9, 1857, *ibid.*

voting, the outcome would be very uncertain.[18] However, it was reasonable to expect that a young politician from the mountains, who had limited knowledge of high finance, would refrain from arraying himself against the money powers. Yet the governor had spoken with much firmness in his message, and to many he was already known as a determined man. Still others would soon learn that he had his own ideas of right and wrong. His reasoning might be faulty as a result of insufficient knowledge, but if he thought he was right, he kept driving. Attempts at persuasion failed, and the governor vetoed the bank bill.

All capital is a result of labor, he told the legislature, which created a favored class and conferred upon it privileges denied to others, enabling it to enrich itself "by taking from the laboring masses the income of their labor." This was not only unjust, but contrary to the genius and spirit of our government. The banks had acquired favored class status through legislation permitting them to issue three dollars in notes for each dollar of paid-in capital; to make loans for periods as short as thirty days, deducting interest in advance; and still to use the original dollar for speculative purposes rather than holding it in the vault as security for notes. Indeed, such favoritism permitted banks to make 35 to 50 percent profit on each dollar of paid-in capital. At the same time, a laboring man with a few dollars to lend was forbidden by law to charge more than 7 percent. "I deny that it is right to give a bank, or to any other corporation, such unreasonable and almost unlimited privileges," said Brown.

What promises had the banks made to the people in return for these exclusive privileges? They had promised to furnish at all times a sound currency, "convertible into specie *on demand*, regardless of cost or sacrifice necessary." In times of prosperity these privileges had brought the banks great fortunes. Were they not in times of adversity obligated to fulfill their promises "to redeem their bills at par, and therefore afford relief to the people, no matter what it may cost them?"

Specie could be obtained at a small premium in northern markets, the governor explained. And by this small sacrifice Georgia banks could resume specie payment immediately, restore confidence, check the decline in the price of cotton, and bring back prosperity and happiness to the people. But this the banks refused to do, for it was to their selfish

18 *House Journal*, 1857, pp. 416–17; *Senate Journal*, 1857, p. 169.

interest "to keep up the panic," thus driving prices lower, and then grab property and become still richer.

Banks guided themselves by their own interests only, Brown charged. "They demand Gold and Silver or its equivalent from those in debt to them, and sell their property, no matter how great a sacrifice if it is not paid. And if the property goes at a ruinous sacrifice, they will increase speculation by appointing an agent to buy it for them." All the while, they refused to redeem their own bills. When a business man expanded beyond his ability to pay, he was forced to close up. He neither asked for nor received much public sympathy, but was condemned for his "extravagance and folly." Yet banks claimed their action was necessary and expected sympathy and also relief from their charter obligations.

Framers of the Act of 1840 had expected the banks to comply. They never expected the day when banks would possess power "to violate the law with impunity, and to dictate the terms of their own pardon." But banks had increased in numbers, wealth, and influence since 1840, and when their interests were at stake they applied great pressure upon lawmakers. In the present crisis they demanded "unconditional pardon in the form of an act to legalize their illegal act of suspension, till such time as it may suit their convenience to resume." The question now was "shall the banks govern the people or shall the people govern the banks. . . . While I have the responsibility of its execution, I am determined to know no man or association of men, and that all shall bow to the authority of the law without regard to wealth, power or influence which they may possess. . . . I shall order proceedings against the wealthiest bank, or chartered monopoly in Georgia, as soon as I will against the humblest individual who has disregarded and violated the law."[19]

These were the words debt-ridden Georgians could understand and like; the Jacksonian distrust of banks was still strong. But in Milledgeville the pressure was great, and before members could consult with their constituents, they were asked to override the governor's veto. As soon as the message was read in the Senate, where the bill had originated, John E. Ward came down from the president's chair to deliver the principal speech in favor of overriding the veto. It was

19 *Senate Journal*, 1857, pp. 558 ff.

reported that, expecting a veto, he had spent the entire previous night in preparation. An admiring bank supporter declared: "Never did I hear a more thrilling speech, courteous in tone and manner, delivered in a voice whose tremulousness betrayed the emotion of the speaker, but added to the effect; every word fell clearly and distinctly on the ears of a silent and attentive audience. I compared it at the time to a Damascus scimitar, as keen as it was polished." This was the type of speech that should have been expected from a bank attorney. The bank lobby was effective; the veto was overridden. A total of seventy-six members abstained.[20]

Brown's veto of the bank bill created a sensation even though he was immediately overriden. For one of so little training and experience to take such a bold stand was scarcely expected. To those who were still not reconciled to having a man from the mountains in the governor's chair his action was more than imprudent; it was impudent. But to the common man who had so enthusiastically voted for him, he was another Andrew Jackson, doing battle against financial monopoly. Brown agreed with the Jacksonian belief in the need for a broader metalic basis to sustain the paper issues, explained the editor of the *Constitutionalist*,[21] but as for a "strictly hard money currency we put that down as the impractical dream of enthusiasts." Brown could not subscribe to the injustice done by the denunciations hurled at the suspending banks; there was no need to engender strife between the banks and the people. "It is not true that the interests of the banks and the people are antagonistic, and that the former can thrive best when pecuniary embarrassment and distress come on the latter." The editor later added that the columns of the *Constitutionalist* would be open to discussion of the merits of the bank question, but, "Vituperation and abuse of the Governor we shall not copy."[22] The veto message was a strange document, observed the Savannah *News*, "which will reflect no credit on the liberality or intelligence of Governor Brown."[23]

The Savannah *Georgian* thought some expressions used by the governor were "out of keeping with a State paper," and would only

20 Savannah *Morning News*, December 25, 1857; *House Journal*, 1857, pp. 499–500; *Senate Journal*, 1857, p. 577.
21 December 27, 1857.
22 December 31, 1857.
23 December 25, 1857.

"furnish an excuse for vituperation and abuse by his enemies," and thus "warp the judgment of men by exciting their passions and prejudices." Neither would the editor agree that bankers as a group were "dishonest and corrupt or unmindful of their obligations to the community at large."

Yet the governor's message exhibited much sound reasoning. He had "clearly demonstrated the injustice of granting such extended privileges . . . and the necessity of withdrawing them when the banks fail in the discharge of their obligations to the people." The banks had been guilty of unwise expansion, giving a "temporary inflation to all species of property and branches of trade," and creating a "delusive appearance of prosperity and wealth," which must inevitably be followed by "the most fearful revulsions, prostrating the energies of the country, and destroying the happiness and prosperity of the people."

The governor, the editor concluded, believing the bill failed to provide the proper remedies, had acted with "remarkable determination of character" in discharging his duty even in the face of formidable moneyed influence. In so doing, he "stands acquitted today of any blame for future troubles." To those journalists who had denounced the governor in so unjust and distasteful a manner he would like to quote the homely adage: "Crises, like chickens, always come home to roost."[24]

The Columbus *Times and Sentinel* agreed with the sentiments expressed in the governor's message but did not think the veto "wise and judicious" in the present crisis. The extension granted was designed as temporary relief. Was it relief for the banks or their customers? "The people were in debt to the banks more than the banks to the people. . . . The banks could not pay if they could not collect, and if compelled to pay they would be compelled to collect. The Albany *Argus* also agreed with Brown's views, yet in view of the existing situation, it feared that any measure which crippled or destroyed the banks would "re-act with destructive effect upon the interests of the people."[25]

When the small towns were heard from they expressed strong approval of the governor's action. The people would sustain him, announced the Clarksville *Georgian*. They knew that the banks had been guilty of gross outrage against their interests, and merited the treat-

24 Quoted in Augusta *Daily Constitutionalist*, January 1, 1858.
25 *Ibid.*, January 5, 10, 1858.

ment received at the hands of the governor. "Governor Brown is right," announced the Newnan *Banner*. "We are proud . . . that the able Senator and Representatives of Coweta firmly stood by the Governor until the last," added the Newnan *Blade*.[26]

Before the bank crisis reached its height, Brown was also clashing with the legislature over the use of the pardoning power. Early in December the two houses passed a joint resolution recommending the pardoning of two female prisoners, one convicted of manslaughter and the other of rioting. Brown rejected the resolution and sent to the two houses his reason. The pardoning power, he explained, must be used with caution "in the exercise of a sound judgment after a thorough investigation of the whole case." Should the pardoning power be used upon almost every application, the law would cease to be "a terror to evil-doers." So-called mercy to a criminal might not be mercy to his community. Those who exercised the pardoning power should not be influenced by false sympathy "lest in their attempt to mitigate the sufferings of the guilty, they greatly exercise the suffering of the innocent." If favorable action should be taken on this resolution, others would soon follow.

Under the Constitution, the governor further explained, the legislature had no power to pardon except in cases of treason or murder. He recognized the right of individuals to request the pardon of a convict, but he considered legislative action as interference with executive functions. "As a general rule, in my opinion, it would be better to leave all these cases where the courts and juries have left them." There were undoubtedly a few exceptions where evidence and circumstances of the trial should be investigated. But the power to do such investigating was constitutionally assigned to the Executive "without dividing the responsibility with the General Assembly." Consequently, legislative investigation would consume time that could be spent more profitably in considering "such matters as the constitution has confided to that branch of the government." He would therefore respectfully suggest that each department of government "be content to confine itself within the sphere of action assigned to it by the constitution."[27] The

---

26 Quoted, *Ibid.*, January 10, 1858.
27 *Senate Journal*, 1857, p. 205; Atlanta *Intelligencer and Examiner*, December 13, 1857.

governor's reasoning was clear and convincing to most persons other than legislators. Legislative interference with the exercise of the pardoning power was an old practice which previous governors had accepted.

Two weeks later the governor received a bill commuting the sentence of one John Black from death to life imprisonment. Black had been convicted of murder in Habersham County and sentenced to be hanged. Governor Brown immediately vetoed the bill. At the time of Black's conviction, he explained, the only penalty prescribed for a convicted murderer was death. A legislative attempt to substitute life imprisonment would be the application of a law that did not exist at the time of the crime. This would be an *ex post facto* law which was specifically forbidden by the Constitution. Black had been convicted in a fair trial and given the only penalty possible. The legislature could not assume jurisdiction in the case and set aside the conviction. In support of his position the governor entered into a lengthy legal and constitutional argument which, when printed, filled two newspaper columns.[28] In short, Governor Brown maintained that there must be either a pardon or a hanging; there could be no life imprisonment. An attempt to override the governor's veto failed by an overwhelming majority.

The governor strongly believed that the wages of sin should be collected from the transgressor. When a prominent citizen of Calhoun requested a reprieve for one N. S. Hawkins, who had been sentenced to death for murder, Brown replied: "I deeply regret his unfortunate condition and I join you in prayer to Almighty God that the prisoner may receive at his gracious hand a full and free pardon for all his guilt." He hoped the prisoner would fully realize the fact that time was short and that he would "spend it pleading for pardon through the merits of Jesus Christ alone."[29]

28 *House Journal*, 1857, pp. 117, 457–66; Milledgeville *Federal Union*, January 5, 1858.
29 Brown to H. C. Carter, May 17, 1858, in Brown Papers, Georgia State Archives.

Chapter IV

Politics of Patronage

SOON THE dismissed officeholders and the disappointed office seekers joined the bank group in opposition to the Brown administration. The greatest source of political patronage at the state level was the Western and Atlantic Railroad. Only recently had the road ceased to be a financial liability; it had always been a political plum for the party in power. Its present management appeared efficient, and retiring Governor Johnson and Superintendent Spullock predicted an exceedingly bright future for the enterprise. Yet some critics still maintained that the state government should not be in business; others, who had not shared the patronage, offered political opposition; and still others charged corruption in management.

During his campaign Brown had suggested that management of the road be taken out of the hands of the governor; he did not repeat this in his message to the legislature. The legislature, which considered proposals to sell, lease, or place control in the hands of a commission, did nothing more than appoint a Senate investigating committee, leaving management in the hands of the governor. Brown interposed no objection.

State employees had noted with concern Brown's assertion in his letter accepting the nomination that he had made no patronage promises, "expressed or implied." It was at least disturbing to those who knew how they had secured their appointments. Then when he set up his own standards for measuring qualifications for office many persons no doubt thought of President Andrew Jackson and the "spoils system."

Those who held the more important positions with the Western and Atlantic were well aware that during the past two administrations Howell Cobb and his close associates, particularly Congressman John H. Lumpkin, had dispensed the patronage; the governor went along without opposition. This same Cobb group was now uneasy, for their avowed support of the Democratic nominee had been lukewarm. Their chief was away in Washington, and the second in command, John Henry Lumpkin, had decided to retire from active politics.

Cobb did not trust Brown; yet he realized the necessity of moving with the tide, assisting in its direction when possible. On the same day that he received the election results, Cobb rushed off to Governor-elect Brown a recommendation for two friends. Anderson Reese of Athens wanted to be one of the governor's secretaries, and Wiley Pope a messenger.[1] Neither was appointed. Cobb next joined Lumpkin in trying to save their friend James M. Spullock, superintendent of the Western and Atlantic Railroad. "I have no favor to ask for myself," Lumpkin told Brown, but he did "feel a deep solicitation for some of my personal and political friends who are now in positions of trust and honor" and wished to continue in office. Judge Spullock had been appointed by Governor Herschel V. Johnson. He had proved to be an efficient railroad official, Lumpkin insisted, very acceptable to the Cherokee Democracy, and a very active supporter of the Democratic candidate in the recent campaign. "This matter I have greatly at heart."

In his travels along the road, Lumpkin said he had found the employees "for the most part solid, moral and industrious men, entitled to the confidence of the public." Lumpkin would also appreciate his brother-in-law, M. D. McComb, being retained in his present position as one of the governor's secretaries.

Howell Cobb also "most cheerfully" united with other friends of Spullock in requesting his retention,[2] but Brown was only partly convinced. McComb was retained, but effective January 1, 1858, Spullock was replaced by Dr. John W. Lewis. The appointment in this case was almost as irritating to Lumpkin as the dismissal, for he and Lewis were bitter enemies.

1 October 8, 1857, Hargrett Collection.
2 October 16, 1857, *ibid.*

This change was but the beginning. Soon came announcements that Edward R. Harden of Whitfield County had been named agent at Dalton and N. J. Camden of Cherokee agent at Chattanooga. Benjamin May of Stewart became treasurer, Dr. George Phillips of Habersham auditor, and Elijah W. Chastain of Fannin attorney.[3] One by one all remaining important positions were filled by close friends of Brown and Dr. Lewis. All replaced men had been at least indirectly recommended by Lumpkin.

Governor Brown sent to Superintendent Lewis definite written instructions. He was to cut all unnecessary expenses, but keep the railroad in good repair; dismiss all employees who were supernumeraries or not absolutely necessary to the operation of the road. Where salaries were found to be higher than those paid for similar service on other railroads they were to be reduced. He was to require "absolute subordination, and prompt obedience to orders." All employees, regardless of position, who were known to use "intoxicating liquors of any kind" as a beverage or who engaged in "gaming" or "any other dissipation or immorality" were to be dismissed. Strict economy was to be required in even small transactions. Conductors were to make financial settlement at the end of each run and depot agents report once each week. The superintendent was to pay all profits into the state treasury at the end of each month. "Prompt obedience to these orders will be required. That they may not be misunderstood by any, you will have them printed and a copy delivered to each officer and employee on the road."[4]

Brown made no charges against those removed. He had a job to do and could do it best with the assistance of those in whom he had the greatest confidence. If a change was to be made in the superintendency of the Western and Atlantic, Dr. Lewis was a logical choice. From the days when Brown was a struggling law student until his candidacy for governor, Dr. Lewis had been ever at his side with finances, friendship, and advice. And the doctor's business ability was well known throughout north Georgia. Camden, the new agent at Chattanooga, was also a special friend of Brown. Judging from the entries in Mrs. Brown's diary, the Camden family spent about as much time in the Brown home as in their own.

3 Milledgeville *Federal Union*, November 10, 1857, January 12, 26, 1858.
4 Augusta *Daily Constitutionalist*, January 23, 1858.

Brown next moved on Federal employees known to be hostile to him. "As Governor of Georgia I have the appointment of all the principal officers of the Western & Atlantic Rail Road and am responsible for its management," he wrote Postmaster General Aaron V. Brown. "I have upon it at present an excellent set of officers. I find that Mr. Hargrove, one of the traveling Post Masters on the Road, is not acceptable to the Superintendent. I am very desirous to have harmony among all the officers of the Road. I have therefore to request that Genl. Ira R. Foster of Cartersville, Cass County, Ga., be appointed post master in place of Mr. Hargrove." To Foster, the governor confided "Unless there is interference on the part of some Congressman I have no doubt you will receive a commission in a few days."[5]

Postmaster General Brown's reply was not satisfactory. The previous administration had complained about Hargrove, he said, but investigation had revealed him to be a man of good character. No immediate action would be taken. Governor Brown was irritated. The fact that two different administrations had complained against Hargrove, he retorted, should be proof of his undesirability as an officer. "I make no particular charge against the character of Mr. Hargrove. I only state that his demeanor toward the officers of the Road is not satisfactory to them." If the request for Hargrove's removal was denied, "those responsible for the management of the Road must submit to your decision till the termination of the present contract, when we must look to our own protection against so unpleasant a dilemma in future."[6] The postmaster general made no reply.

"The Regency by the assistance they could command in Washington have succeeded in controlling this matter," Brown reported to Foster.[7] "Regency" was the title the governor had given the disgruntled group centered at Rome. It was natural to suspect that Spullock, acting through Secretary Howell Cobb, Lumpkin, and possibly with the assistance of Congressman Augustus R. Wright, had exerted influence in Washington, but there is no evidence to support the charge.[8] It was

5 Brown to Aaron V. Brown, March 24, 1858, Brown to Foster, March 25, 1858, in Hargrett Collection.
6 Brown to Aaron V. Brown, April 5, 1858, *ibid.*
7 April 29, 1858, *ibid.*
8 In the midst of this controversy Governor Brown wrote a relative, the Reverend Joseph Brown of Giles County, Tennessee, A. V. Brown's home county,

true that Wright, sometime Methodist and then Baptist minister, and sometime Whig and then Democrat,[9] was eager for reelection. He had succeeded to the House seat vacated by Lumpkin, apparently with Lumpkin's blessing; yet he was a lifelong friend of Brown. John W. H. Underwood of Rome, Speaker of the Georgia House, was another friend of Lumpkin who had turned sour on Brown. He had his eye on the congressional seat held by Wright. Brown remarked to a friend "I am glad Col. J.W.H.U. has concluded not to demolish my administration till the next meeting of the General Assembly. Much of his ire will evaporate in thin air before that time and much more will then explode in gas."[10]

After weeks with no word from Postmaster General Brown, the governor became impatient. Early in August, 1858, he removed not only Hargrove but also Hibberts from their United States postal positions on the Western and Atlantic Railroad, and appointed Foster and A. G. Greer. "The sole charge" against the dismissed, Brown explained to Postmaster General Brown, was that they were "not friends of my administration." He had heard rumors, the governor said, that efforts were being made to persuade the postmaster general to order Hargrove and Hibberts restored to their positions. He could not believe that the department would do this. "I should very much regret any occurrence which might disturb the kind relations existing between this government and your department or which might compel me from a sense of duty or self respect to refuse to pass any agent appointed by you over the Road." This he would feel compelled to do even though it canceled the contract "between the Road and your department."[11] The governor sent a copy of this letter to President James Buchanan.

It is probable that Senator Robert Toombs was notified in advance of Governor Brown's intentions. One week after writing the postmaster general, Brown also wrote Toombs, thanking him for "protesting against the reappointment of the route agents lately removed." He reiterated the reasons for his actions and his determination not to permit

---

inquiring whether they were related to the postmaster general. The reply was "no." April 22, 1858, in Hargrett Collection.

9 Fielder, *Brown*, 65.

10 Brown to George D. Phillips, May 25, 1858, in Hargrett Collection.

11 Brown to A. V. Brown, August 19, 1858, in Telamon Cuyler Collection, University of Georgia.

"my enemies to keep spies in my camp." He hoped Secretary of the Treasury Cobb would not feel it his duty to interfere in this matter. He also hoped Toombs would speak to Congressman Stephens.[12]

As news spread that "heads were falling" along the state railroad, Governor Brown was deluged by letters from applicants and their friends, proclaiming their loyalty to his administration and the Democratic party. Brown was pleased to reward friends, but it soon became necessary to choose from among several friends; there were not enough vacancies. By mid-March, 1858, he reported thirty applicants for each vacancy. Applications of minor importance were usually referred to Superintendent Lewis. Those of major importance the governor answered personally.[13]

Soon his replies, although often written to personal friends, became rather formal in style and content: "I am very sorry that it is not now in my power to give you an office. There is no vacant office on the Road and there are over 500 applicants each desirous to fill the first vacancy which may occur. This is, of course, quite embarrassing to me, as many of them are my warm political and personal friends." The governor soon learned the political maxim that warm friends often grow cold when their quest for office is unsuccessful. This sometimes caused him to give vent to his true feelings: "I cannot give office to all who desire it, and I will be a tool in nobody's hands while I am the executive of Georgia. I will act independently according to the honest dictates of my own judgment."[14]

The governor further increased his unpopularity by discontinuing two daily trains and directing Superintendent Lewis to reduce the number of employees on the railroad. Such retrenchment became necessary, Brown announced, as a result of the decline in business and the low price of grain. "The commercial pressure has prevented the merchants from purchasing and shipping near as many goods as are usually shipped. . . . And for the want of money travel over the Road has been less than common."[15]

12 Brown to Toombs, August 25, 1858, in Hargrett Collection.
13 Brown to S. J. Smith, March 13, 1858, Brown to Z. P. Landrum, March 10, 1858, *ibid*.
14 Brown to J. A. Tolleson, August 24, 1858, Brown to John A. Tucker, March 10, 1858, *ibid*.
15 Brown to Z. P. Landrum, March 10, 1858, Brown to Richard H. Clark, April 7, 1858, *ibid*.

To those who complained about the change in the mail service the governor replied that discontinuance of the two trains would save the state twenty thousand dollars annually, and persons along the route would still get their mail twice daily. Less fortunate citizens in some other parts of the state, who also owned an interest in the state road, got theirs only once or twice each week. However, he would run as many extra trains and deliver the mail as often as residents desired "if the P. O. Department will pay the state for the extra service."[16]

Most dismissed employees and disappointed office seekers were residents of the area served by the Western and Atlantic Railroad. Congregating at Cassville, Rome, and Atlanta, they were outspoken in their denunciation of the Brown administration. When J. A. R. Hanks, sometime Baptist minister, was chosen from among a dozen applicants to succeed J. C. Longstreet, deceased, as solicitor general of the Cherokee Circuit, the Cassville *Standard* declared that "offices in the gift of the Governor have been secured to those of his particular faith, to the relatives and particular friends of himself and the Superintendent." Indeed they had made the Western and Atlantic the "Cherokee Baptist Railroad."[17]

The *Federal Union* challenged the *Standard* to prove its charge. As for the governor's Statehouse staff, the *Union* could say there was not a Baptist among them. The editor would suppose, however, that all appointments were made from among friends of the administration. "Now it cannot be expected, that the Governor or Superintendent would make appointments from among their enemies."[18] There is no evidence of political favoritism to persons of the Baptist faith.

James M. Spullock, dismissed superintendent of the state road, lived at Rome and made use of his close friend John H. Lumpkin, the most powerful political leader of the area. Brown and Lumpkin had patched up their differences during the recent political campaign, but after the removal of Spullock and many other friends of Lumpkin, communications between the two ceased. The point had now been reached where in many cases the friends of one were the enemies of the other

---

16 Brown to S. J. Smith, June 24, 1858, *ibid.*; Brown to A. V. Brown, May 29, 1858, Brown Collection, State Archives.
17 Quoted in Milledgeville *Federal Union*, August 3, 1858.
18 August 3, 1858.

and vice versa. Yet there were several men of prominence who tried to be friends to both Lumpkin and the governor.

Lumpkin's chief grievance was against Lewis rather than Brown. He confided to Cobb that he really could not complain about the governor's replacing Spullock and a few others with men in whom he had more confidence. His principal grievance was that Brown appointed Lewis, a man "I knew & he knew was my personal enemy" and then permitted the superintendent to make "war upon me and my personal friends."[19]

But Lumpkin made no open attack upon the Brown administration. He had large property interests along the state road, especially on the Chattanooga end, which could be adversely affected by the management. He no longer had political ambitions, and his few extant private letters reveal only two important interests. He wished to protect and promote his financial holdings and promote his friend Howell Cobb for the presidency. In those two endeavors he not only had no cause for a clash with the governor but could use his friendship and assistance.

Brown also recognized a need to mend and extend his political fences. Outside north Georgia, his policy regarding the state road had created little opposition. The politicians in other sections made fewer requests; therefore, there were fewer disappointments. After Thomas W. Thomas of Elberton came over to Brown's support during the recent campaign he gave no further difficulty. Shortly after taking office Brown employed Thomas to represent the state in an important suit involving the Alabama boundary. Privately the governor suggested, "It is a position where I think you may make some character as well as a good fee. When I say character, I mean you may add to that already made." Thomas had no close friends he wished to place in lucrative state positions. At times the governor even thought it advisable to write him, asking for recommendations.[20] And in January, 1859, the governor found it a pleasure to appoint Thomas himself judge of the northern Judicial Circuit vice James Thomas, resigned.[21]

The clash with Senate president John E. Ward of Savannah over the bank question did not prove too serious; the governor took no

19 Lumpkin to Cobb, October 25, 1858, in Cobb Papers.
20 Brown to Thomas, November 23, 1857, May 18, 1958, in Hargrett Collection.
21 Milledgeville *Federal Union*, January 11, 1859.

action against the banks in 1858. Before Ward resigned his legislative position and accepted an appointment as minister to China, he and the governor became completely reconciled. "The Gov. & I are now upon the most friendly terms," Ward wrote Howell Cobb. "Upon receiving a message from him I called at his office & received a most cordial greeting & an invitation to take my family to the Executive mansion & spend the session with him. I was of course glad to bury the hatchet with his consent."[22]

Frequent letters from Hiram Warner and William H. Stiles, two other political rivals, indicated they were not unhappy, although the governor was not always able to take care of their friends.[23] James Gardner alone of the more prominent aspirants for the nomination in the late Democratic convention remained aloof and sometimes hostile. He was still proprietor of the Augusta *Constitutionalist* but had turned over the editorship to James T. Nisbet as early as February, 1857. Although the *Constitutionalist* had given Brown strong support in his campaign for governor and had refused to publish harsh attacks upon him for his bank veto, Nisbet gradually grew lukewarm and then mildly hostile. By midsummer 1858, he was critical of the governor for reducing services on the state road in the interest of economy. Anti-Brown items from the Cassville *Standard* were copied with apparent relish. By June 24, Nisbet was publishing critical "communications." Soon the *Constitutionalist* began a series of long articles signed "Impartial," reviewing the bank controversy and the language used by Brown in his veto message.

When the editor of the Newnan *Blade* charged that the hostile attitude of the *Constitutionalist* was a result of Gardner's political disappointment, Nisbet replied that Gardner knew "no more about the articles, written or selected, which appear in this paper than does the editor of the *Blade*.[24] Finally, when the Dalton *Times* noted that "It is a significant fact that the gentleman to whom the Constitutionalist belongs is an aspirant for gubernatorial honors," Gardner himself spoke out. He denied any political aspirations or any attempt to influence anyone with regard to the next nomination for governor. He would throw

22 Ward to Cobb, November 8, 1858, in Cobb Papers.
23 Stiles to Brown, September 23, 1858, in Hargrett Collection; Warner to Brown, June 13, 1858, in Brockman Collection.
24 November 28, 1858.

no obstacle in the path of Governor Brown or anyone else. What course the editor of the *Constitutionalist* took was his business.[25]

Former governor Johnson, in retirement on his farm, remained extremely popular within the Democratic ranks. He recommended to Brown a number of friends. Some were appointed; others were not. The former governor, thinking the list of failures was too long, suggested to the governor that he felt like an unwelcome intruder. Brown hastened to reassure him, adding that although they had differed on some questions, he held Johnson in high esteem and would like to see him placed in some important position of honor and service.[26]

Brown also continued good relations with Senator Robert Toombs. During the recent campaign the two had developed considerable mutual admiration. Governor Brown also kept in close touch with a number of Georgia congressmen, especially Lucius Gartrell of Atlanta, Augustus R. Wright of Rome, and James Jackson of Athens. But the governor's most pleasant relations were with the Stephens brothers, Alexander and Linton. They seldom offered advice unless requested; they asked few favors. Probably no appointment during his governorship would give him as much real pleasure as that of Linton Stephens, "a man of clear head and close discrimination," to the state supreme court, succeeding Charles J. McDonald, who had resigned.[27]

Relations with Howell Cobb were cordial on the surface, but beneath there was distrust. Cobb and Lumpkin still resented the fact that Brown had secured the nomination that Lumpkin so desired, bringing to the fore a new north Georgia political leader and dooming forever Lumpkin's political aspirations. At the time, Lumpkin had assured Brown that he did not hold him responsible for what happened in the Democratic convention. Yet a few months later he gave ear to one Jefferson Fields of Gilmer County, a disappointed office seeker, who stated that Brown knew in advance that his friends planned to seek his nomination. Brown, Fields reported, did not discourage them. He only advised caution, fearing that if the plan failed it might ruin his future political prospects.[28]

25 January 11, 1859.
26 Brown to Johnson, June 10, 1858, in Hargrett Collection.
27 Brown to Hiram Warner, May 21, 1859; Brown to Linton Stephens, May 9, 1859, in Brockman Collection.
28 Lumpkin to Cobb, October 25, 1858, in Cobb Papers.

With the appointment of Dr. Lewis as superintendent of the Western and Atlantic and the subsequent dismissal of a number of Cobb-Lumpkin friends, the political atmosphere became clouded. Governor Brown, for political reasons if for no other, wished to see this cloud dispersed. Working through mutual friends Ira Foster and E. R. Harden, both employees on the state road, he attempted to reach an understanding. Lumpkin gave Secretary Cobb a full report.

According to Lumpkin's version, Brown and Lewis authorized Harden to say they were extremely anxious for Lumpkin to return to Congress and assured him E. W. Chastain, attorney for the Western and Atlantic, would not offer as an opponent. But Lumpkin replied that he had no desire to return to Congress. To Harden's assurance that the administration desired friendship, Lumpkin explained that when the governor stopped Lewis from "making war upon me and my friends" there would no longer be cause of difference or dispute between them. He gave this assurance, Lumpkin told Cobb, "to remove any obstacle from a cordial understanding between you and Gov. Brown if your interest should require it." He could not, however, speak to anyone at Rome on this subject. Some friends, especially Spullock, if they knew he was even considering reconciliation with the governor, would attempt to defeat it. But he added that even Spullock could be managed and controlled "if our interest requires us to unite with Governor Brown." Why not get Spullock a federal appointment? This could then be used to control him, and his great influence and management could be used "if compelled to act with Gov. Brown," whom he hated "with a most revengeful spirit."[29]

Lumpkin also had a conversation with Foster. Again there was assurance of the governor's desire for cordial relations. Foster put up a strong argument. Both Lumpkin and the governor were strong supporters of the Buchanan administration and opposed to Stephen A. Douglas in his break with Buchanan. Both were old-line Democrats, one of the State Rights wing, the other the Union. If they would but unite they could control the destiny of Georgia for many years. Lumpkin repeated his complaint against Lewis and urged that the superintendent cease acting to injure his interests and dismissing employees because they were his friends. Foster reported to Brown.

29 Lumpkin to Cobb, October 14, 1858, *ibid.*

A few days later Lumpkin and Foster again conferred. Foster reported Brown as speaking with strong friendship for the Buchanan administration and for Secretary Cobb as the principal member. The governor would speak to Lewis and persuade him to refrain from mistreating Lumpkin and his friends. Foster reported that when Brown expressed a desire to meet with Lumpkin, Foster advised the governor to take the initiative.

Lumpkin told Cobb he had no doubt of the governor's sincerity, yet he could not rid his thoughts of what he considered the principal grievance. Those removed from office by Brown were very hostile and "if we effect any union *with him it must be upon terms that will embrace our friends. I will not abandon the men who have stood firmly with me and for me.*" Brown and Lewis had acted with the hope of destroying him and his friends, Lumpkin asserted bitterly, and building up a combination friendly to the governor.[30] This was Lumpkin's account.

Although still bitter, Lumpkin was definitely interested in a reconciliation with the governor. Upon Cobb's suggestion he contacted Congressman James Jackson of Athens and apparently requested that he talk with Brown. Jackson reported that the governor expressed a most sincere desire for cordial relations and suggested that Lumpkin go to Milledgeville immediately for a confidential interview.

Lumpkin wrote Cobb that he was undecided what to do. Some of his friends were still hostile and not prepared for a reconciliation. Spullock, in particular, would bitterly oppose any negotiating with Brown. "He hates Brown, and nothing will restrain him from striking a blow when ever he can do so with any hope of success." Upon second thought, Lumpkin added that Spullock's only restraint would be regard for the possible effect his actions might have upon Cobb's future. Consequently, it was imperative that Spullock be given an appointment through which he could be controlled.[31]

Lumpkin did not go to Milledgeville for a conference with Governor Brown; neither did he write him immediately. But Howell Cobb did write. Lumpkin knew that should he confer with the governor, the news could not be kept from his Rome friends. Cobb, however, had no such fears, and he was extremely eager for a reconciliation. His letter

30 *Ibid.*, October 25, 1858.
31 *Ibid.*, November 14, 1858.

has not been preserved but its contents were reflected in Brown's reply. Cobb expressed pleasure that good relations between John E. Ward and the governor had been restored and hope that the same might be true of relations with Lumpkin. Brown expressed his eagerness and added that after conferring with Congressman Jackson and others he was convinced that Lumpkin was favorable to a restoration of their former friendly relations. He hoped that Lumpkin would visit Milledgeville soon.[32]

Unwilling to wait longer for a visit from Lumpkin, Brown took the initiative. He had sincerely believed that the removals he had made were necessary, he wrote. If Lumpkin had felt himself injured he was very sorry. No injury or lack of respect was intended. "The chief object of this letter is to assure you of my feelings of regard and friendship for you. I desire your success in every laudable enterprise, and trust our future relations may be cordial as our past have been kind."[33]

Lumpkin replied in a like vein, and Brown then shifted the discussion to the policies of the Buchanan administration.[34] Pleasant relations had at least been restored on the surface. "I shall offer no opposition to Gov. Brown's renomination," Lumpkin wrote Cobb, "and if he treats my friends as his friends he can make me cordially his friend—I am informed and believe that such is his intention for the future—and so I will be most cordial toward him." And with the hope of silencing Spullock, Lumpkin urged Cobb to secure for the former railroad superintendent an appointment as federal marshal for the state of Georgia.[35] This Cobb did.

Having reconciled their differences, Brown and Lumpkin began a steady correspondence on political matters. Soon the governor was appointing Lumpkin's nominees, urging him to make still more suggestions, and requesting that he pass upon the qualifications of applicants suggested by others.[36]

The one thread between Brown and the friends of Cobb and Lumpkin that was never broken or even seriously weakened was their mutual support of the Buchanan administration, especially on the subject of

---

32 Brown to Cobb, November 15, 1858, *ibid.*
33 Brown to Lumpkin, December 28, 1858, in Hargrett Collection.
34 Brown to Lumpkin, January 5, 1859, *ibid.*
35 Lumpkin to Cobb, December 28, 1858, in Cobb Papers.
36 Brown to Lumpkin, February 15, 21, April 14, 1859, in Hargrett Collection.

Kansas. This was the only national issue in which Georgians showed much interest. Brown was pleased by the plan to admit Kansas into the Union under the proslavery LeCompton constitution even though it had not been approved by the voters of the territory. His enthusiasm changed to grave concern, however, when news from Washington indicated that the LeCompton plan would not be accepted. "If Kansas is rejected," he wrote Alexander Stephens, "one of the contingencies of the Georgia platform has clearly happened, and the statute makes it my imperative duty to call the convention which must determine the *status* of Georgia with reference to the Union. . . . If Kansas is rejected I think self respect will compel the Southern members of Congress and especially the members from Georgia to vacate their seats and return to their constituents to assist them in drawing around themselves new safeguards for the protection of their rights in the future. When the Union ceases to protect our equal rights, it ceases to have any charm for me."[37]

When Stephens suggested that instead of rejecting the LeCompton plan outright Congress might smother it in committee, Brown was not so certain what his own course should be. He believed that such action would be a form of rejection and that because of slavery. And one of the contingencies listed in the Georgia platform under which a convention should be called was the failure of Congress to admit a state because of slavery. Yet he had some doubt that Georgians could be so convinced. He also had some fear that calling a convention might create great confusion in Georgia, although such a meeting would not necessarily endorse separate state action. It might be wise to adopt an ordinance to become effective when other southern states concurred.[38]

Governor Brown was also corresponding with Senator Toombs and at least two Georgia congressmen, giving his impressions and requesting theirs. He was much relieved when news came that a conference committee had endorsed what became known as the English bill, returning the LeCompton constitution to Kansas for a full vote. "I suppose the people will most probably accept the proposition of Congress, and the difficulty will be at an end," he wrote Toombs. And to Stephens, Toombs, and Cobb he expressed Georgia's appreciation for

37 February 9, 1858, in Stephens Papers, Emory.
38 Brown to Stephens, March 26, 1858, *ibid.*

the part they had played in solving this vexing problem. In his letter to Cobb he went a bit farther. "You occupy a proud position before the country; and should the Democracy in future determine to call you to a higher position I shall take pleasure in co-operating with my party friends in bringing about such a consummation."[39]

Kansas rejected the proposition set forth in the English bill and thus closed the door to immediate admission into the Union either with or without slavery. But even before results of the voting were known, Governor Brown was able to report, "The Kansas excitement is fast dying out."[40]

The most serious political repercussion of the struggle to admit Kansas was the break between Stephen A. Douglas and the Buchanan administration. Again Brown remained loyal to Buchanan even though his good friend Alexander Stephens became a Douglas man. "I am just from Milledgeville," wrote Thomas R. R. Cobb to his brother Howell, "& though you know I deal not at all in politics I saw enough to satisfy me that the Douglas movement in Georgia *is a failure*. Thomas—who went down as a feeler for Stephens *in my opinion*—left in disgust. Gov. Brown rejected their overtures—He wishes to ride with you & Jno Lumpkin & I think will do so yet."[41] This report pleased Howell Cobb and made it more imperative that he cultivate improved relations with the governor.

Administration of the Western and Atlantic Railroad brought to Governor Brown more grief than all other administrative problems combined, yet he loved it. Railroads fascinated him. Mixing business with pleasure, he often spent days riding up and down the line. He realized the potential of railroads in general both in economic development and as a field for investment. He consistently invested his own surplus funds in railroad lines within Georgia and neighboring states— Southwestern; Atlanta and West Point; Savannah, Albany and Gulf; Alabama and Florida; East Tennessee and Virginia; Nashville and Chattanooga; and Memphis and Charleston.

In operating the Western and Atlantic the governor insisted upon

39 Brown to Toombs, May 8, 1858; Brown to Cobb, May 7, 1858, in Hargrett Collection; Brown to Stephens, May 7, 1858, in Stephens Papers, Emory.
40 Brown to Lucius J. Gartrell, May 18, 1858, in Hargrett Collection.
41 November 13, 1858, in Cobb Papers. The legislature was in session at that time.

loyalty, efficiency, and economy. He made enemies but the road made money. He had employees salvage $20,000 of scrap iron scattered along the route. When one of his top officials was twice reported intoxicated, the governor exclaimed "This will be obliged to stop or I shall have to act. I am his friend and should deeply regret such a necessity, but if he were my own brother I would not tolerate dissipation and neglect of official duty and still retain him."[42]

Miles of track were repaired, a new passenger depot built in Chattanooga, dilapidated equipment replaced, and debts paid as they fell due, yet by March, 1858, the road was paying into the state treasury $20,000 per month. And in spite of the slump in business this amount continued to increase. When Superintendent Lewis made his report for the year ending September 30, 1858, he showed that receipts had exceeded operating expenses by more than $450,000. Construction and equipment had cost about $195,000. The sum of $175,000 had been paid into the state treasury.[43]

Although Governor Brown lamented that "we have more difficulty and wrangling in the Cherokee country than in all the rest of the state,"[44] he was proud of his achievements. But some of his enemies were not impressed. Ignoring all phases of the railroad report except the $175,000 paid into the Treasury, the Augusta *Constitutionalist* noted that a year earlier both Superintendent Spullock and Governor Johnson had stated that with proper management the Western and Atlantic should pay into the treasury $350,000 annually. Yet it had actually paid only $175,000. Therefore, the state had lost $175,000. The editor thought Brown had honestly and sincerely tried, but the governor himself knew he had signally failed. Those who praised his management were passing over facts hoping to receive a little crumb of patronage. All their shouts of praise, however, could not conceal the fact that there had been a great blunder in Brown's administration.[45]

Since meetings of the General Assembly had been changed from biennial to annual that body was scheduled to meet early in November, 1858. There was considerable uncertainty as to its probable relationship with the administration. There would be several new faces; a

42 Brown to James Milner, December 4, 1858, in Hargrett Collection.
43 Milledgeville *Federal Union*, December 28, 1858.
44 Brown to H. J. Sprayberry, September 25, 1858, in Hargrett Collection.
45 December 8, 1858.

number of new counties had been created from parts of old ones, and some old members had lost their seats as a result. The furor over patronage was limited almost entirely to the Cherokee area where the governor had a host of loyal friends.

The hostile bank forces were not very active. "The banks in this state have found themselves unable to keep up the war upon me," Governor Brown confided to Congressman Augustus R. Wright. "Finding that the weight of public opinion was overwhelmingly against them, they have resumed specie payment and have now engaged in a war with the S. C. bankers. . . . I am with the Ga. banks in that fight. In a word, I am against suspended banks wherever they may exist. I believe that whenever a bank suspends it should go into immediate liquidation. If this were known to be the penalty, few would suspend."[46]

But no truce was in sight in the bank war. Under the Banking Act of 1832 as amended in 1843 and 1850, the governor was required to call upon the banks, through public notice, for semiannual reports as to officers, stockholders, and financial condition. The notes of those failing to comply within thirty days were to be no longer accepted by the state treasurer in payment of obligations to the state. Previous governors had neglected to enforce this requirement. The act of 1857 had added still another requirement. Banks were forbidden to charge more than 7 percent interest or to purchase notes or debts at discounts of more than 7 percent. In their semiannual reports they were to make affidavit that they had not violated this restriction.

On June 1, 1858, Brown issued a call for all banks to make their semiannual returns. After thirty days had elapsed twenty banks had still not complied. On July 20, the governor issued a proclamation, declaring that since these banks had "utterly disregarded the will of the legislature, and set themselves above the law," their notes would no longer be accepted by the state treasurer. The noncomplying banks disliked this publicity but the penalty was not severe. The governor was "influenced by a spirit of vindictive persecution," declared the Augusta *Daily Constitutionalist*. He should delay action and refer the whole subject to the legislature at its next session.[47]

46 Brown to Wright, May 24, 1858, in Hargrett Collection.
47 Milledgeville *Federal Union*, July 27, 1858; Augusta *Constitutionalist*, July 28, 1958.

Chapter V

Little Dogs Must Bark

THE GENERAL ASSEMBLY, which had been elected the previous year, convened for its second session on November 3, 1858. Few persons other than members were present. How different from former years, recorded one observer, when eager crowds of aspirants flocked to the capital "anxious to serve their country by filling some position of honor or profit."[1] John E. Ward was again chosen president of the Senate and John W. H. Underwood Speaker of the House. These choices were certainly not due to executive influence.

The governor's message was read on the opening day of the session. He began with a review of the bank question, stressing his efforts to enforce the law. Some banks, he charged, were still in defiance of constitutional authority, having refused to file returns in accordance with the statute. He had applied the only penalty provided; their notes were no longer accepted by the state treasurer. This penalty was too mild. For the purpose of compelling obedience to the law he wished to recommend a penalty of 2 percent per month on the whole amount of the capital stock of noncomplying banks, payable in gold or silver. "There can be no just reason why wealthy corporations should be permitted at their pleasure to set the law at defiance, while individuals are compelled to suffer rigorous penalties for its violation. The mandate of the law should be obeyed as promptly and implicitly by the most influential and wealthy as by the poorest and most needy. This is Repub-

[1] Augusta *Daily Constitutionalist*, November 5, 1858.

lican equality, and our people should be content with nothing else."

The banks, although protesting, had resumed specie payment by May 1, making it evident that there had never been need for suspension. Through their uncontrolled issuance of "*promises to pay in the place of money itself*," banks had made huge, although often concealed, profits. As a safeguard for the future, the governor suggested that no new banks be created, none be rechartered, nor any increase in capital stock be authorized. Perhaps in the existing system, finances would be placed upon a firm specie basis, which he considered the currency of the Constitution. This was what was intended when the states were forbidden to make anything but gold or silver legal tender in the payment of debts. The governor further suggested that banks be forbidden to issue notes in small denominations. This would cause gold or silver to be used exclusively in small transactions. And he earnestly recommended the establishment of a state subtreasury system similar to that of the federal government. Let payments into the Treasury be in specie and then the state pay its obligations in specie.

Governor Brown next called attention to Superintendent Lewis' report on the operations of the Western and Atlantic Railroad, and paid tribute to the superintendent as "a most vigilant, active, and valuable public servant." Great praise was also heaped upon the agents and employees of the road. Although the economic depression had reduced income, the road had been able to meet its obligations, and make needed repairs and improvements, including the construction of a three-hundred-by-one-hundred-foot brick passenger depot in Chattanooga. The Nashville and Chattanooga Railroad had furnished half the money for this structure, and it was expected that the East Tennessee and Georgia and the Memphis and Charleston would soon be taken in as partners. In spite of all these expenses, the road was paying a considerable sum into the state Treasury each month.

So great was his confidence in the future of the state road, the governor exclaimed, were he "satisfied that it were the desire of the legislature and the people," he individually would be pleased to lease it for a period of ten years. He would agree to lay down ten miles of new track each year and keep the road and equipment in excellent condition and pay into the Treasury $25,000 per month. Furthermore, he would give bond to guarantee that the road would be returned to the state in good condition. So convinced was he of the importance of railroad development, he further recommended that the state lend its credit for construction of all roads which appeared to be necessary to prosperity.

The governor further recommended that the income from the Western and Atlantic during the coming years be pledged to the payment of the state debt and the development of public education. He submitted a detailed plan under which as much as $240,000 annually would be available for common schools. "Let the teachers be paid by the State," he explained, "and let every free white child in the state have an equal right to attend and receive instruction in the public schools. Let it be a common school, not a poor school system."

He also suggested that higher education bonds be issued, using the state road as security. Interest could be paid from the income of the road, and if and when the line should be sold, ample funds would be available to pay off the bonds. The bonds should be divided: $200,000 going to the University of Georgia, $50,000 to the Georgia Military Institute at Marietta, and $50,000 each to three denominational colleges. Each of the five institutions would be required to "bind itself" to educate annually one student for each two hundred dollars received. For all of this no additional taxes would be needed, the governor explained. If properly managed the Western and Atlantic Railroad could pay the public debt, educate the children, and become "a blessing to the whole people of Georgia."[2]

Small town newspaper editors in particular were very complimentary of Brown's message to the legislature. The Griffin *Empire State* related that as Brown delivered his address one "could almost have heard a pin drop upon the carpeted floor . . . so intense was the interest manifested." The great majority pronounced it the "soundest and ablest" document of many years, "while the *jaundiced* . . . were left to sneer at its style, without being able to state wherein it was defective."[3]

The Cassville *Standard*, which at times appeared to give some comfort to the disgruntled, was highly pleased that the governor from Cherokee had "sustained himself so handsomely. . . . Those who have regarded the people of this portion of the State as a set of hoosiers and blockheads,—fit only to help elect Governors, will soon be convinced

2 *Ibid.*; Milledgeville *Federal Union*, November 9, 1858.
3 November 11, 1858.

. . . that Cherokee Georgia can *furnish* Governors as well." Men were needed in public office who knew their duty and were "not afraid to do it, regardless of consequences. . . . Three cheers for Hon. Joseph E. Brown, the first Governor from Cherokee Georgia."[4]

Before the members of the General Assembly had digested the contents of the governor's message, he returned to that body a number of private or local bills vetoed by him after the close of the previous session. Most of these bills had to do with the granting or amending of corporate charters.[5] Continuing his hostility toward special legislation, before the close of the session he would veto no fewer than fifteen bills "for the relief of persons who have been divorced, and who, as the guilty party are not permitted under the statute to marry again." The legislature balked at passage of a general law to this effect, but granted relief to most individuals who requested it. In applying the veto, Governor Brown took the position that "these exceptions are wrong if the rule is right."[6]

Hoping to smooth some of the ruffled feelings resulting from his message and vetoes, the Browns entertained lavishly on Thanksgiving eve. A local baker made 150 pounds of cake, and more cakes were baked at home. There were cookies "without measure"; tables set in the huge dining room were loaded with "fruit, candy, nuts, beef tongue, oysters etc," which had been ordered from Savannah. Eggs were brought from Tennessee. The party continued until 2 A.M. "I can give you no guess how many persons were here," Mrs. Brown wrote her mother; "more than had ever been here before was said by many who had been in the habit of attending on such occasions."[7] Sarcastically "Reporter" remarked in the *Constitutionalist*, "Tomorrow is Thanksgiving day. We now give thanks to Gov. Brown for its appointment."[8]

The governor's praise of the management of the railroad and his prediction of a great financial future was received with enthusiasm, but it did not end dissension. "There is a great deal of rubbish to be cleared away," exclaimed the *Constitutionalist*, "before the people can examine into the merits of the many questions. . . . The 'outs' seem to be

4 *Ibid.*
5 Augusta Daily *Constitutionalist*, November 7, 1858.
6 Milledgeville *Federal Union*, December 28, 1858.
7 Mrs. Brown to Ma and Sister, November 29, 1858, in Hargrett Collection.
8 November 27, 1858.

in hot pursuit of the 'ins', and the 'ins' are throwing hot shots back at the 'outs.'" The road had never been better managed, the editor explained, than under the guidance of James M. Spullock. He then launched a comparison of Lewis and Spullock in which Lewis came out second best.[9]

Brown's indirect offer to lease the railroad himself was considered a mere expression of confidence. However, two months earlier, in a confidential letter to a Cherokee friend, he had made an almost identical suggestion of what he would be willing to promise in return for such a lease.[10] A bill to lease the road to a specific private company was introduced in the Senate, but the proposition was not nearly so attractive to the state as Brown's. The company proposed to pay the state $350,000 annually but did not propose to give security for repairs and proper care. No lease was granted.[11]

As the end of legislative session drew near, no action had been taken on the governor's recommendations relative to further regulation of banks, although a bill had been introduced in the House by George Hillyers of Walton and in the Senate by John A. Tucker of Stewart. But the governor demanded action, reported an unfriendly correspondent in the Savannah *Republican*. "His accidency, the little autocrat who presides over the Executive department," let it be known that unless action was taken on the bank proposal before adjournment he would immediately call the legislature into special session. "In fact our little Caesar puffed himself into a fury," and since a number of bank friends had already gone home the bill was pushed through at 2:30 A.M. Sunday.[12] The act provided a penalty of 2 percent per month on the entire capital stock of those banks that failed to file returns as required by law. The governor was to publish the names of those banks failing to comply.

As the legislators made their way home the Savannah *Republican* commended them for their negative performance. They had failed to grant the state aid to railroads and education requested by the governor.

9 November 24, 1858.
10 Brown to G. W. Garmony, September 24, 1858, in Hargrett Collection.
11 Atlanta *Daily Intelligencer*, November 13, 1858; Milledgeville *Federal Union*, November 16, 23, 1858.
12 December 14, 1858.

The proposed subtreasury had not been approved. They had even refused to grant Dr. Lewis an increase in salary. Millions of dollars had thus been saved. The bank bill was the only administration measure enacted.[13]

On January 7, 1859, Governor Brown sent to the principal newspapers a list of ten banks that had refused or failed to comply.[14] To George Hillyers, the sponsor of the act in the House, he confided that he had no doubt but that all banks would comply before the July 1 deadline. . . . They find that they have not yet the ability to govern the state. . . . Their feelings towards me have, I suppose, undergone little change." They would be pleased to defeat him in the coming election. "I do not know how well they may succeed."[15]

In a similar vein he wrote his friend Ira Foster: "They understand how much two per cent a month makes in a year. Some of them making a virtue of necessity are even fairly praising me. The fact is they are whipped before the people and whipped in the legislature and they are going to give up the fight with the best grace they can and become law obedient. They do not love me, but as their feelings are mostly in *their vaults* they will probably be glad to keep quiet lest some greater chastisement might happen to them."[16]

Before he had been in office six months, Brown had begun to give thought to the possibility of reelection and to suspect that his enemies were plotting to prevent it. He had tasted power and he liked it, and even his family had not found Milledgeville an undesirable place to live, although they would spend their summers in Cherokee. Life in Milledgeville was by no means a complete break with country life. He had the finest mustard bed in the city and plenty of lettuce, the governor wrote his mother. He also described his onions, beets, corn, and beans. The yard was covered with white clover for his cow and her heifer calf.[17]

Two months later Mrs. Brown was complaining of being unable to get any quilting done; she was sewing some and had found wonderful

13 December 18, 1858.
14 See several letters in Hargrett Collection.
15 Brown to Hillyers, January 8, 1859, *ibid.*
16 January 11, 1859, *ibid.*
17 Brown to Mother, April 5, 1858, in Spalding Collection.

bargains in gingham at twenty cents per yard. She had turkeys and chickens, a few of them large enough to eat.[18]

Comfortably situated in the Governor's Mansion, Brown definitely wanted a second term. As early as mid-March, 1858, he assured Congressman Wright that he was fully aware of the efforts being made in Rome and elsewhere to accomplish his defeat. He would do all that duty and honor would permit to avoid a clash with the influences to which Wright had called attention. "But if it is forced upon me I shall not hesitate to carry the war into Africa."[19] When Congressman Lucius J. Gartrell of Atlanta complained about the lukewarm support both he and Brown were receiving from the Atlanta *Intelligencer* Brown replied that the editor was a bank man and a pet of John E. Ward. "He is not my friend at heart." It was only through his friend J. H. Steele and a little patronage that the *Intelligencer* was held in line at all.[20]

Steele, late of the Griffin *Empire State*, had been appointed one of Brown's secretaries, but he soon resigned, apparently to take a position with the *Intelligencer*. Soon he would present to Brown a plan for establishing a new newspaper in Atlanta. Brown was enthusiastic. "I should be pleased to see a press established that would take bold, independent ground, and I would feel at liberty to direct the patronage of the Road mostly to such an establishment." If properly managed such a paper "could soon be made *the press* of the place and upper Georgia."[21] The plan did not materialize but Steele remained an intimate friend. To a number of other friendly editors the governor promised "all the patronage I can properly do from this office." He urged them to follow the lead of the Milledgeville *Federal Union* in publishing the financial reports of the Western and Atlantic and in meeting the charges hurled by the *Constitutionalist*.[22]

When the Columbus *Times* suggested, and the *Federal Union* concurred, that in view of the fact that opposition within the party to Brown's reelection was so minor there was really no need for a Democratic nominating convention, Brown privately agreed but he hastened

18 Elizabeth Brown to Nancy Brown, May 28, 1858, in Brockman Collection.
19 Brown to A. R. Wright, March 11, 1858, in Hargrett Collection.
20 Brown to Gartrell, April 17, 1858, *ibid.*
21 Brown to Steele, May 4, 1858, *ibid.*
22 Brown to A. A. Gaulding, June 12, 1859, *ibid.*

to make known the fact that this was not his suggestion.[23] The no-convention idea did not gain much strength; even most of Brown's friends agreed with the editor of the Athens *Southern Banner* that a convention was the only way to maintain party organization. Although the *Banner* did not wish to go on record as opposed to Governor Brown's reelection, it believed that when conventions were abandoned, confusion, disaster, and defeat would result. It might work well enough to run Governor Brown without a convention but the precedent would be dangerous.[24]

On second thought, even Brown decided that a convention might be desirable, if county delegations could be instructed to vote for him. This meant the groundwork must be done in the counties. The principal patronage opposition was centered in Cass (Cassville), Floyd (Rome), and Fulton (Atlanta) counties, and there was some bank opposition in cities like Augusta and Savannah. The Rome "Regency" had been weakened by the reconciliation of Lumpkin, but Spullock and Underwood were as hostile as ever. The appointment of Spullock as federal marshal for Georgia took Brown by surprise, and he was quick to sense the danger. "The office, as you are aware, will be one of great political power in the state in the next legislature and in 1860," he wrote Senator Toombs.[25] One of the duties of the marshal would be to appoint census takers for 1860.

Brown's fears were justified. Rumor soon reached him that Marshal Spullock was traveling over north Georgia promising to appoint certain local leaders as census takers provided their counties sent to the Democratic convention delegates opposed to the Brown renomination. Brown immediately contacted Lumpkin. "I am of opinion my informant is not mistaken," he wrote. "I shall rely on you & Gov. Cobb to control this matter if you have it in your power."[26] Lumpkin contacted Spullock and urged Cobb to do likewise. Spullock denied everything. Writing to Cobb, he declared "In reference to Gov. Brown while I do not like him on your account I am willing to pursue such course as will

23 Brown to Gaulding, January 11, 1859, *ibid.*
24 January 13, 1859.
25 Brown to Toombs, January 11, 1859; Brown to Alfred Iverson, January 14, 1859, in Hargrett Collection.
26 February 9, 1859, *ibid.*

best promote your interests. . . . I have not made the first appointment yet neither have I said a word against Brown." He thought if Brown and his friends were working for Cobb's promotion the administration newspapers would reveal it. "As their zeal grows for your interest mine will grow for Brown."[27]

No one seemed quite convinced that Spullock was telling the complete truth. Lumpkin assured Brown that the marshal would be controlled; he was willing to be personally held responsible that nothing would be done by Spullock to prejudice the governor's renomination. Further, he would be the first to "ask his removal" should the marshal refuse to be governed by Cobb and himself "in this particular."[28] Brown was satisfied.

Spullock had been silenced but other dissidents kept up the fight, striking hard at the Brown-Lumpkin coalition. The Atlanta *Confederacy* became their organ. E. V. Johnson, dismissed depot agent at Kingston, reported that Lumpkin offered to have him restored to office if he would support Brown for reelection. He spurned the offer! It was also charged that in return for Lumpkin's support Brown had promised to build a depot near the Lumpkin plantation in Tennessee "for his convenience in marketing produce and receiving supplies." "It seems that a parcel of vindictive discontents are determined to make mischief by propagating and publishing a falsehood every week," Brown wrote to Lumpkin.[29] This was true and there was still more to come.

House Speaker Underwood, most active of the Rome discontents since Spullock had been silenced, reported that Brown had told Robert A. Crawford of the Griffin *Empire State* that he preferred Alexander H. Stephens to Howell Cobb for the presidential nomination in 1860. He gave A. G. Greer, one of the mail agents on the Western and Atlantic, as his source of information. Both Brown and Crawford vigorously denied that there was ever any such conversation between them, and Crawford drafted a strong letter to Underwood. After reading the letter, Brown advised against sending it. "Underwood is hostile, unfair and unscrupulous," he explained, "and will take all the advantage

---

27 Brown to Cobb, February 12, 1859; Brown to Lumpkin, February 15, 21, 1859, in Hargrett Collection; Spullock to Cobb, February 22, 1859, in Cobb Papers.
28 Lumpkin to Cobb, February 21, 1859, in Cobb Papers.
29 Brown to Lumpkin, April 28, May 4, 1859, in Hargrett Collection.

he can, and will not in my opinion fail to misrepresent if he thinks it will help his cause."[30] This report of Brown's preference for Stephens was readily recognized for what it was—an attempt to drive a wedge between Cobb and Brown.

Brown had too many other things on his mind at this time to be giving much thought to the 1860 presidential nomination, but he was privately protesting Congressman Stephens' decision to retire to private life. Such a decision he considered a public calamity. "The ship of state has her difficulties ahead," he wrote Stephens. "We shall then need at the helm a mariner's skill sustained by acknowledged ability, enlarged experience and tried integrity." He believed he was expressing the feelings of sixty thousand Georgia voters when he said "I would most cheerfully support you for any position within the gift of the American people."[31] Was the governor referring to a presidential nomination? He had recently told Howell Cobb the same thing.

There is no doubt but that Brown's admiration for Stephens was great. When Linton Stephens presented him with a portrait of his brother, Alexander, Brown was overwhelmed. He wished for another just like it, he wrote Linton, so that he might use it to adorn the wall of the executive office.[32]

The rumor of the governor's support of Stephens for the presidential nomination could scarcely be reconciled with still another that was afloat. It was reported in the hostile press that Cobb, Lumpkin, and Brown had formed an "offensive & defensive" alliance. Brown was to be reelected as governor, Lumpkin was to return to his old seat in Congress now held by Augustus Wright, and the delegation to the 1860 Democratic convention was to be stacked with Cobb men. This report was so logical that many must have believed it, yet like most of the other rumors it had little foundation in fact. There is no evidence of any agreement among Lumpkin, Cobb, and Brown. There were wishes but no promises. Brown did hope for Cobb-Lumpkin support in the coming campaign and Cobb definitely wished the support of Brown in 1860. However, Lumpkin did not wish to return to Congress. Brown

30 Brown to J. H. Steele, April 13, 1859; Brown to Lumpkin, April 13, 1859; Brown to Crawford, April 20, 1859, *ibid*.
31 Brown to Stephens, February 14, 1859, in Alexander Stephens Papers, Duke University.
32 June 21, 1859, in Hargrett Collection.

stated privately that he informed Lumpkin he could not support him against Wright, yet at the same time he was urging Lumpkin to let the people decide whether or not he should return to Congress.[33]

Bargain or no bargain, Governor Brown felt confident of support of the more important leaders of his party. "I do not think Judge Lumpkin or Mr. Cobb or their friends will continue any war upon me," he wrote his intimate friend Judge L. W. Crook of the Cherokee Circuit. "I shall certainly make none on them or any other prominent men of the party. The influence of Messrs. Toombs & Stephens and Warner is, I have no doubt, friendly to me; so are the Colquitts, Judges Jackson, Thomas W. Thomas (once said to be otherwise), Tom Cobb, Judge Joseph H. Lumpkin and others."[34]

There were others whose friendship might be questioned who agreed that the governor had the political situation well in hand. "Gov. Brown is proving himself to be a pretty good diplomatist by his management of the various factions of his party," declared the Rome Courier.[35] "The Cobb and Lumpkin clique are said to be reconciled; the Gardner clan silenced; and now, we suppose Toombs, Stephens & Co. are appeased by the appointment of Linton Stephens to the supreme bench. Who will say that this is not right smart, to hand out the 'loaves and fishes' to the men he expects to work for him—and to log-roll for those only who have large forces to help him when he needs. We suppose there are a hundred men in Georgia better qualified for a seat on the supreme bench than Linton Stephens, but none of them have got 'little Alec' for a brother."

Observing the dissension within the Democratic party yet realizing the hopelessness of their own cause, some of the opposition press lashed out at the governor with reinforced invective. The Savannah Republican declared that many in the governor's own party regarded him as "an inflated upstart" and some of his acts as "prompted by the meanest prejudice or the grossest ignorance." Everyone knew that he became governor by accident—"the spawn of a party quarrel"—which pushed back into the shades of retirement those men whom the people wished to rule over them. It was also generally agreed that a single term in

33 Brown to J. H. Steele, Brown to A. R. Wright, February 23, 1859, ibid.
34 January 8, 1859.
35 May 25, 1859.

office was sufficient reward for such an accident. Therefore, it would be but becoming modesty for the governor to step aside so those who honored him might themselves be honored. "We would advise him . . . that a dignified retreat is better than waiting to be elbowed off the track." There was certainly enough opposition within his own party "to throw him clear overboard."[36]

"Here's opposition . . . with a vengeance," gleefully replied the confident editor of the *Federal Union*. If the governor had sold out "body and soul" to the banking and railroad corporations he would have endeared himself to the "*Republican* school of politicians." However, he considered the people the masters of moneyed tyrants and saw to it that these tyrants did not defy the law. Thus did he make himself "odious in their sight." Hence, "'The little dogs and all, Tray, Blanch and Sweetheart' bark at him." If the editor of the *Republican* could find a man "who wishes to test his fleetness with honest Joe Brown in the next Gubernatorial race, let him trot him out."[37]

Governor Brown carried on almost daily correspondence with personal and political friends urging that the county conventions not only select Brown delegates to the state convention but also pass resolutions endorsing his administration and instructing the delegates. The *Georgia Telegraph* relayed this message to the public when it urged counties to instruct their delegates "*who* to vote for." Thus would the wishes of the people be known prior to the convention. Mischief makers would be discouraged and few but the "true and faithful would attend."[38]

The governor was also concerned about the platform to be adopted. He considered a general endorsement of the Buchanan administration imperative. There was danger of a walkout of Buchanan friends unless this was done, thus producing division and confusion. Therefore, he urged that the state convention "reaffirm the principles of the Cincinnati platform," approve generally the Buchanan administration; and endorse his own administration. Further, he would have no objection to a Cuba resolution. He did not wish any new issues "to be lugged in." Nothing should be done that would place Georgia "in an awkward position after the action of the Charleston convention. . . . It is best not

36 Savannah *Republican*, March 8, 1859.
37 March 15, 1859.
38 Quoted in Milledgeville *Federal Union*, February 22, 1859.

to particularize too much in a platform," he suggested to Lumpkin.[39] Brown hoped that the mountain counties, his home section, would move early in selecting delegates to the Democratic convention and then make public their proceedings.[40] However, the early action he feared, but did not exactly expect, came from Fulton County. There a convention was called for 10:00 A.M. March 19. The anti-Brown forces arrived early and completed the selection of officials before the appointed time. Dr. E. N. Calhoun was made chairman, and Thomas J. W. Hill secretary. On the suggestion of B. M. Smith a committee of five was appointed "to report business and suitable delegates" to the coming state convention. T. C. Howard was made chairman of this committee. At this point Dr. John G. Westmoreland called upon all "Brown men" to walk out. This they did and held a meeting of their own. Those remaining proceeded with the business of adopting resolutions and selecting delegates.

The committee appointed to draw up appropriate resolutions reported: "We see nothing in the present juncture, literally nothing, which calls for our adhesion to a man, or a set of men, as a measure of salvation, or as a proper submission to a controlling public opinion. We think in the approaching gubernatorial convention, we should assemble in the same spirit which animated the party in the last convention. Private attachments were indulged on that occasion, without any thought of giving just offence to any, and they were freely surrendered when the general party weal seemed to demand it." Therefore it was resolved "That the Democrats of Fulton county send their representatives to the next Gubernatorial convention without further instructions in regard to measures more than this: 'go for nothing more or better than the old creed and the man who will best maintain it.'"[41]

When Governor Brown saw the names of the prominent participants in the hostile Fulton meeting he recognized several as among the "disappointed." Dr. Calhoun had wanted to be railroad physician, an office which was dispensed with "by having the masters of slaves pay

39 Brown to J. H. Steele, May 19, 1859, in McLeod Collection; Brown to Lumpkin, April 28, 1859, in Hargrett Collection.
40 Brown to S. J. Smith, February 26, 1859, in Hargrett Collection.
41 Atlanta *Daily Intelligencer*, March 20, 1859; Milledgeville *Federal Union*, March 29, 1859.

the d[octo]r's bills for their own negroes." Calhoun was then an unsuccessful applicant for the position of auditor. Thomas J. W. Hill wanted
to be secretary of the Executive Department; J. W. Duncan, one of the
delegates chosen, was offended because the railroad management refused to pay him "two prices for printing." A number of Atlanta merchants were angry because the road refused to pay their high prices
for oil. Another was a discharged depot agent; still another was a de-
faulter during a previous administration.[42]

The "seceders" adopted resolutions approving Governor Brown's
administration and selected Brown delegates. They also approved a
resolution calling for a meeting of "the whole Democratic party of
Fulton" April 5 to ratify or reject the delegates chosen. Apparently the
anti-Brown forces boycotted this April convention for the three delegates chosen by the "seceders" were unanimously approved.[43] Brown
professed to believe that the action of the first Fulton convention actually strengthened his cause. "It has waked up my friends in counties
where they were careless." He explained to a Cherokee friend, "You
are in the midst of the discontents. When you get below Atlanta there is
none of it."[44]

Brown was correct; there was no organized opposition below Atlanta, not even in the cities of Savannah and Augusta. But north of
Atlanta the discontents continued active. A meeting in Cass County
voted down a resolution denouncing Brown, but endorsed James Gardner for governor and selected anti-Brown delegates.[45] And Polk County
selected a split delegation. As the governor noted with pleasure the
favorable reports from other counties over the state, he gleefully remarked to friends that only one and one-half counties opposed him.
Many who were not enthusiastic supporters of the governor apparently
agreed with the editor of the Sumpter *Republican*: "We have no issue
to make with him, and it were almost factious to oppose him. Nor would
it be *politic*. Governor Brown's stern official integrity has endeared him
to the people, and his successful management of the State Road has

42 Brown to L. W. Crook, March 22, 1859; Brown to S. J. Smith, March 23,
    1859, in Hargrett Collection.
43 Atlanta *Daily Intelligencer*, May 6, 1859.
44 Brown to L. W. Crook, April 6, 1859, in Hargrett Collection.
45 Atlanta *Daily Intelligencer*, May 6, 1859.

made him thousands of friends. As long as he pays in $35,000 per month from that source, it were vain to oppose his election."[46]

The opposition press, although convinced that it was almost vain to oppose the governor, still refused to be charitable. Why should Brown be reelected, sneered the Savannah *Republican*. If Dr. Lewis had done such a marvelous job of managing the state road, why not elect him instead of Brown, for Brown had no standing with party leaders. The Democratic legislature had rejected his entire program except that relating to banks. His state aid plan would have "plundered the treasury, destroyed the credit, and corrupted the people." His "ridiculous Four Million Educational project" was about as well suited to conditions in Georgia as the Oconee River was to steamship navigation. Even the bank act was a farce.[47]

By late spring, of more concern to the governor than the smooth developing political picture was the condition of his own health. Mr. Brown was "scarcely able to be up," wrote Mrs. Brown to her mother. He needed "exercise and pure air, can not bear such constant confinement, he is wearing out very fast."[48] On April 5, the *Federal Union* noted that the governor was spending a few days at Indian Springs. For some time his health had been very bad and he was looking very thin. But three weeks later[49] the "iron-nerved, Jackson-willed patriot" was somewhat improved. In late May he journeyed to Brunswick and Savannah where he was "kindly treated to sail and fishing excursions." Upon his return he even agreed, in spite of "my temperance notions," to partake of some Georgia wine presented by Linton Stephens.[50]

The Democratic convention assembled in Milledgeville on June 15, 1859. Delegates were present from 117 counties. If the anti-Brown delegates from Cass and Polk counties were present, they remained silent. Brown was renominated unanimously. Also unanimously approved were resolutions endorsing the Cincinnati platform of 1856 and the administration of Governor Brown. The "honesty, fidelity, and ability which Joseph E. Brown has manifested," it was declared, en-

---

46 Quoted in Columbus *Times*, May 8, 1859.
47 March 25, 1859.
48 February 28, 1859, in Spalding Collection.
49 April 26, 1859.
50 Milledgeville *Federal Union*, June 7, 1859; Brown to Linton Stephens, June 4, 1859, in Brockman Collection.

titled him "to the confidence of the whole people" and reelection as governor. A third resolution expressing continued confidence in the Buchanan administration met with some opposition, but was approved by a vote of 371 to 34.[51]

A committee was dispatched to notify Governor Brown and bring him to the convention hall. The acceptance speech was short and contained nothing new. After a few words of appreciation and praise for the great state of Georgia, the governor reaffirmed his desire to place an education within the reach of every white child. "I am willing to labor to that point," he declared. "I am willing to devote the whole energies of my life to the accomplishment of that end." There would be no need for increased taxation. "We may even reduce the taxes while we are doing it and pay the public debt in the bargain." Then shifting to a discussion of the excellent condition of the railroad and its undoubted ability to pay in the future, he declared: "All I desire in the way of the education of the children of my State can be attained from the income of the Road if it be well managed."

He enthusiastically endorsed the party platform and in closing announced that he would not be able to carry on an extensive campaign. His official duties required too much of his time. He would simply appeal to the people to examine his administration. "I am willing to be judged by my *acts*." However, even if he had the time for campaigning the condition of his health would not permit it.[52]

"The Bankites, and the Know-Nothings, and the disappointed office seekers, all dwindled into insignificance before the Herculean strength of Joe Brown," remarked the *Federal Union*.[53] The Augusta *Constitutionalist* reported that there was "much noise and confusion, and some amusement" at the convention but admitted it was a very harmonious one. It immediately placed Brown's name at the head of its editorial column.[54]

Brown was highly pleased with the outcome of the convention. "In my opinion the democracy have at no time entered a canvass with

51 Milledgeville *Federal Union*, June 21, 1859; Atlanta *Daily Intelligencer*, June 18, 1859.
52 Atlanta *Daily Intelligencer*, June 23, 1859; Milledgeville *Federal Union*, June 28, 1859.
53 June 28, 1859.
54 June 18, 1859.

greater unanimity," he declared. He was proud of the unanimous endorsement given him by a convention "composed of such respectable material." Yet he was a bit concerned about the possible reaction to his decision not to carry on an active campaign. He immediately dispatched letters to Cobb, Toombs, and Stephens explaining his decision. "The condition of my health and my official duties forbid it," he explained. "And indeed I greatly doubt the propriety of it in case of an incumbent in office. . . . If my health were perfect there are so many collateral issues that might be sprung in the canvass, upon which an expression of opinion would be desired and upon which the public mind is divided, that I doubt whether any gains could be expected by the party from such course."[55]

For a time it looked as though the Democratic nominee would not have an opponent. But Brown was confident of his popularity, and wished to prove it by an overwhelming victory. The American party had nothing to offer; its name no longer appealed to voters. And neither Ben Hill, its vigorous candidate in 1857, nor any of his prominent supporters desired to carry the Know-Nothing banner into battle with the popular governor. There was no longer a place on the political scene for an American party based on its old principles, explained the Savannah *Republican*; it could win no future contests. To try again would be but to "stand alone, dreaming of the past." The battle must be "with the realities of the present."[56] Some American editors suggested that if no nomination was made, the Democratic vote in the counties would be light and American chances for victory on the local level improved. But others, including Democratic editors, could not bear the thought of a victory by default. Certain of victory, they gleefully taunted the weak opposition for refusing to fight.[57]

The executive committee of the American party formally announced the demise of that party in early June, 1859,[58] but from its ashes quickly arose an Opposition party which issued a call for all Democrats who wished to assert their independence, old Whigs, and

55 Brown to Stephens, June 21, 1859, in Stephens Papers, Emory; Brown to Toombs, June 21, 1859; Brown to Cobb, June 21, 1859, in Brockman Collection.
56 April 2, 1859.
57 Milledgeville *Federal Union*, July 5, 1859.
58 Savannah *Republican*, June 6, 1859.

Americans to assemble. At this meeting, at Macon on July 20, the delegates denounced and resolved but made no nomination; acceptable candidates were scarce. The Buchanan administration and all who supported it were denounced for failure to demand congressional protection of slavery in the territories. The convention then adjourned to meet again in Atlanta on August 10.

Probably few dissident Democrats attended the Macon meeting; it was too far removed from the centers of dissatisfaction. The Atlanta meeting would be different. The estimated one thousand who attended were a conglomeration of those who were politically unhappy. The *Federal Union* referred to the coming assembly as a "menagerie of opossums, coons, and wild cats" plus "many other animals." Later the same editor labeled the Opposition as "odds and ends of all parties that have existed in Georgia for the past six years." And then recalling the witches scene in Shakespeare's *Macbeth*, added: "Eye of newt, and toe of frog / Wool of bat, and tongue of dog"[59]

"Odds and ends" seldom furnish formidable gubernatorial timber. The opposition Macon *Citizen* offered a list of thirty-nine possible candidates any of which it could support. The editor proposed balloting until all were eliminated but the strongest. The one chosen should then make the race regardless of his wishes. "If the candidate thus nominated positively refuses . . . let his party friends *ignore* him for all time to come—in other words, let him be anathema to all political preferment in the future."[60] When the editor of the Savannah *News* read this suggestion, he exclaimed, "Look out gentlemen of the opposition, for there is no telling who is to be the victim."[61]

Finding no man of prominence willing to make the race for governor, the Atlanta convention nominated Warren Akin of Cass County, a part-time attorney for the railroad until Brown fired him. In accepting the nomination, Akin, like Brown, explained that poor health would prevent his carrying on an active canvass.[62]

In spite of ill health Akin did campaign in the principal cities,[63] but all he could do was denounce the Brown administration in general.

59 August 2, September 27, 1859.
60 Quoted in Savannah *Daily News*, July 28, 1859.
61 July 28, 1859.
62 Milledgeville *Federal Union*, August 23, 1859.
63 Augusta *Daily Constitutionalist*, September 4, 1859.

At Savannah on August 31 he flew into "Honest Joseph," declaring him a demagogue. While assuring the upcountry of his hostility to banking practices, the governor had been advising bankers how to evade the law.[64] Akin and his supporters also claimed that disgusted Democrats were coming over to the Opposition. When the Atlanta *American* published a long list of these deserters the Augusta *Constitutionalist* replied that some of those listed were not Democrats; others were supporting Brown; and still others had not deserted for they had never declared for Brown. Among the *American* list of deserters was the name of Patrick Brewster of Cherokee, Brown's brother-in-law. He was no deserter, declared the *Constitutionalist*, for he was a Know-Nothing and had not been on friendly terms with Brown for many years.[65] There was little chance to consolidate opposing forces. Those dissatisfied over the use of the patronage were mostly opposed to banks, and the bank forces had little interest in who did or did not have jobs on the Western and Atlantic. All Brown's friends needed to do was point to the achievements of his administration. The Opposition had nothing better to offer.

Brown's victory was impressive—more than 21,000 majority. He carried Floyd, Cass, and Fulton counties, the home territory of the discontents, and even Baldwin County, in which Milledgeville is located, which had not been carried by a Democrat in eighteen years.[66] To celebrate his second inauguration he placed an order with a Cherokee friend for "20 good old fat turkeys," including "as many old gobblers as possible." From Savannah came large quantities of rice, soda crackers, and beef tongue,[67] and from Tennessee forty dozen eggs, twenty dozen of which were broken in transit. This further increased the governor's wrath toward the express company, for two weeks earlier his Newfoundland puppy, Leo, enroute from Atlanta to Milledgeville was permitted to escape in Macon. Not even the offer of a five dollar reward resulted in his capture. The express company, however, not only paid

64 Savannah *Daily News*, September 1, 1859.
65 Augusta *Daily Constitutionalist*, September 10, 1859.
66 Milledgeville *Federal Union*, October 25, 1859; Brown to L. D. Collins, October 4, 1859, in Brockman Collection.
67 Brown to N. J. Camden, October 24, November 7, 1859; Brown to A. Haywood, November 16, 1859, in Brockman Collection.

for the broken eggs but also replaced Leo with "docile and good natured" Rover.[68]

The governor's levee was a great success, reported the *Federal Union*. The huge crowd included persons of "both sexes, of all classes, all sizes, and conditions, from the little ragged urchin who begs a penny by the wayside, to the man who sported his jewels of fabulous price." No invitation was required.[69]

Brown's overwhelming victory proved several points, exclaimed the Marietta *Advocate*.[70] It spelled death to those "heterogeneous elements whose battle cry was simply *opposition*, and death to the powers that be." It proved that mere personal abuse and vituperation could not succeed. It also proved the absurdity of attacking a person because of the dinners he gave, "the cut of his coat, his pronunciation, his grammar, and the most sacred arcana of his domestic existence." His detractors must have forgotten that simplicity was "pleasing to the eyes of the people." The "poor dupes with depleted pockets and disconsolate faces" who financed the Akin campaign would long remember the Opposition campaign of 1859. They had learned that people would not always be the "victims of humbuggery and intrigues of designing and unprincipled politicians and wire-pullers." And Atlanta, that citadel of Opposition, had learned the expensive way—her "free barbecues" were enjoyed by her *foes*, the friends of Governor Brown.

---

68 Brown to E. E. Brown, October 18, 1859; Brown to Adams Express Company, October 18, 1859; Brown to E. Hulbert, January 2, 1860, Brown to E. B. Walker, November 1, 29, 1859, *ibid*.
69 November 29, 1859.
70 October 14, 1859.

Chapter VI

Stephens, Not Cobb

BROWN WAS inaugurated for a second term on November 4, 1859. He congratulated the legislature and the citizens of Georgia on the "flattering evidences of prosperity" that had replaced economic gloom. A sound currency had promoted the rapid development of industrial and commercial interests, and the state road was paying into the Treasury about $400,000 annually. The remainder of the address was devoted to singing the praises of the Democratic party and his own administration.[1] "He has a philosophy and a breeding of his own, which, we apprehend nobody envies and none of his successors will be ambitious to imitate," growled the Savannah *Republican.*[2]

On the same day as the inauguration the governor's annual message was read to the General Assembly. It began on a critical note. The legislators in their haste to adjourn the previous session had sent to him bills not properly engrossed and signed. These he was returning without his signature. There were also evidences of hasty and inconsiderate legislation. "One of the great evils of the age is that we legislate too much," the governor charged. The failure of a bill with merit was often less serious than the passage of one without merit. Legislators were prone to neglect their duties during the earlier days of the session and then rush through many unworthy measures during the closing hours.

1 Milledgeville *Federal Union*, November 8, 1858; Savannah *Daily Republican*, November 7, 1859.
2 November 7, 1859.

He would not hesitate to veto such bills where he was convinced they had not been properly considered.

There was also too much local and class legislation, the governor explained. Some such bills were useless; others were unjust and mischievous in that they benefited a few at the expense of many. And each legislative day spent in passing such measures cost the taxpayers $2,500. There ought to be general laws to which exceptions would be few.

In exercising his power of veto, Governor Brown explained, he did not consider himself as showing disrespect for the General Assembly. Each house often failed or refused to pass or even to consider bills passed by the other. "If the Governor, therefore, out of respect for the two houses, signs a Bill which his judgment does not approve, he denies to the people the exercise of that Executive revision, which, under the Constitution, they have a right to demand as a protection against hasty or unwise legislation."

He urged that no more new counties be created until a real necessity existed and that both houses of the General Assembly be reduced in size. At present the only difference between the two houses was their names. The Senate should be reduced to 33 members and the House to 152. This reduction would result in great savings and improved efficiency.

During his term of office, the governor noted, he had seldom used the pardoning power. "I have no sympathy with that sickly sentimentality, which always, forgetful of the injuries inflicted upon the innocent by the guilty criminal, would in the name of mercy, turn loose upon the community every felon in whose favor a sympathetic appeal can be made." He had also refused to respite defendants in murder cases where investigation showed their conviction to be in accordance with justice and law.

The governor next proudly returned to his favorite subject—the state railroad. Twenty-five miles of new track had been laid during the past year, the rolling stock kept in good condition, debts paid when due, and $420,000 paid into the Treasury. Feeling that the road must be run by honest and competent men, he had not hesitated to exercise "moral firmness and nerve, without regard to personal consideration" in dismissing or employing personnel.

There was also a new topic to which the governor wished to draw attention. The military organization of the state was weak and neglected. Yet no one knew how soon it might be called upon for defense against "assaults of foreign ambition or fanatics within our own country." He subscribed to the advice of George Washington to prepare for war in times of peace. He recommended that the organization of volunteer corps be encouraged and that every effort be made to arm them. At present the only source of arms was the annual allotment from the federal government which was wholly inadequate.

To strengthen the military establishment the governor recommended that all existing laws relating to military service be suspended, leaving the volunteer corps as the only fighting force. A commutation tax should be assessed against all men above twenty-one years of age who were not members of these corps. The money collected should be used to purchase adequate arms. This accomplished, the remaining funds should be applied to the erection of a foundry for the production of arms and ammunition.

The governor again recommended state aid to necessary improvements through the endorsement of bonds and an increase in the appropriation for public education from the $100,000 voted the previous session to not less than $150,000.

In closing, Governor Brown apparently wished to let the banks know he was still thinking of them. He recommended that a 10 to 25 percent penalty be assessed against any bank that failed to redeem its notes in specie. Further, he would hold the officials of such banks guilty of a misdemeanor, punishable by five to ten years in prison.[3]

A correspondent of the Augusta *Constitutionalist* considered Brown's recommendation of prison sentences for guilty bank officials "eminently just," but he would further propose that should the state at any time fail to meet its obligations with specie the governor and the legislature "every man of them, should be hung without the benefit of clergy."[4]

Governor Brown's lecture to the legislature on the evils of special legislation had little effect. A total of 464 bills were passed; 54 of them

3 Milledgeville *Federal Union*, November 8, 1859; Savannah *Daily Republican*, November 4, 1859.
4 November 9, 1859.

were vetoed, 4 of which were passed over the veto. "I suppose therefore that I probably prevented 50 bad laws," Brown related to his brother-in-law.[5]

One of the bills vetoed would have pardoned William A. Choice, a convicted murderer. On December 30, 1858, Choice, a member of a prominent family, became involved in a heated controversy with Constable Calvin Webb over the collection of a ten-dollar debt. Choice, under the influence of liquor, became very abusive, and only the intervention of friends prevented violence. On the following day when the two chanced to meet near the Trout House in Atlanta, Choice shot and killed Webb without saying a word. Midst intense feeling and a threat of mob action the court sentenced Choice to be hanged. The defense attorneys were Ben Hill and Choice's brother-in-law, Daniel Printup.

In the fall of 1859 both Hill and Printup were elected to the state Senate, and early in the session a bill was introduced to pardon Choice on the ground of insanity. His insanity, it was claimed, resulted from a head injury he received as a youth, aggravated by the consumption of liquor. Ben Hill gave full play to his powers as an orator, and others joined him in support of the theory that one under the influence was not in control of himself and therefore could not commit a crime. The majority of each house of the legislature apparently agreed; Choice was voted a pardon.

In view of the governor's previous performances in such cases, intense pressure was applied by the Choice family and friends. Brown had known the mother in earlier years when she ran a hotel in Dahlonega. It was said that he had sold her vegetables from his father's farm. Nevertheless he refused to "permit my reason to be overcome by my sympathy," and he vetoed the bill. A cruel act of the defendant, he explained, had changed a happy family to a widow and dependent children with little means of support. "The laws must be vindicated and crime must be punished, or society cannot be protected." Only in those cases where mistakes had been made or circumstances had produced injustice, he reasoned, should the power of veto be exercised. Verdicts of juries and judgments of courts should not be indiscriminately annulled and "felons convicted of atrocious crimes" be again "turned loose upon the community." To exercise the pardoning power might

5 Brown to William S. Grisham, December 31, 1859, in Brockman Collection.

be Godlike, yet he also recalled God's command that "'ye shall take no satisfaction for the life of a murderer which is guilty of death: but he shall be surely put to death. So shall ye not pollute the land whereon ye are, for blood defileth the land, and the land cannot be cleansed of the blood that is shed therein, but by the blood of him that shed it.'" These were stern truths, he declared, and "the curse of God will rest upon that State or nation which disregards them, and his blessings will attend those who obey them."[6]

Attempts to override the governor's veto failed, but during the next session the legislature would pass another bill pardoning Choice and committing him to the insane asylum. Again the governor vetoed, but he was overriden.

Many persons bitterly denounced the governor for his hard-hearted position. Others vehemently defended him, pointing out that he was not only right but that the legislature had no original pardoning power; consequently, the bill was unconstitutional. And the governor must have been pleased with the reaction of the Savannah *Republican,* his most caustic critic. Brown's head would be "covered with maledictions," declared the editor, and his course would be denounced as "unfeeling, heartless and positively cruel." Therefore, "In anticipation of such a condition of affairs, we desire to bring to the support of Governor Brown whatever of influence the approval of this journal may possess. . . . In our best judgment he has discharged his duty, and the credit is augmented by the fearful responsibility that obstructed his path. He has encountered it fearlessly; and our opposition to him in almost all things else, shall not deter us from cordial expression of our approval and admiration."[7]

Before the close of the legislative session Democratic members were involved in controversy over the selection of delegates to the Charleston Convention of 1860. Friends of Cobb, well represented in the General Assembly, preferred action during the session. The majority of the Democratic Executive Committee appeared to have preferred some date after the close of the session, and they were joined by several important

6 Fielder, *Brown,* 117–18; Benjamin H. Hill, Jr., *Senator Benjamin H. Hill: His Life, Speeches and Writings* (Atlanta, 1893), 36; Atlanta *Daily Intelligencer,* January 1, 3, 4, 6, 1859; Milledgeville *Federal Union,* December 6, 1859.
7 December 3, 5, 1859.

newspapers. This aroused the suspicion of Cobb's friends. After observing the position taken by some key editors, Lumpkin wrote Cobb: "The Constitutionalist & the Federal Union both concur in recommending that the state convention be held after the legislature is adjourned—Gardner, Stephens and Toombs are represented by the first paper and the latter is the organ of Gov. Brown, and I am of the opinion that it foreshadows a combination of these worthies for your overthrow." He thought it might even be that Stephens had suggested to Brown that the governor's recent overwhelming victory entitled him to the presidential nomination at Charleston. "I do not doubt but that Gov. Brown has egotism and vanity enough to be influenced by such a suggestion." If this be true and the governor had the backing of Stephens and Toombs, he could cause Cobb much trouble. "He has forfeited my confidence and respect."

Lumpkin had a suggestion he thought might solve the problem. Underwood had expressed the opinion that Brown had his eye on Alfred Iverson's Senate seat. Then why could not Cobb's friends offer the governor support in this aspiration in return for support for Cobb at Charleston? Comfortably located in the United States Senate, Brown would no doubt be willing to wait a few years before trying for the presidency. Lumpkin had also heard rumors that Stephens had expressed a preference for Brown for president. Should Brown thus be temporarily sidetracked, then "Stephens & Toombs would have no other card to play."[8] The Brown-for-senator movement gathered no momentum; the governor was not interested at this time. Underwood and Lumpkin had engaged in wishful thinking. The Brown-Lumpkin honeymoon was definitely at an end; mutual distrust had burst through the thin veneer of reconciliation.

What Brown was thinking at this time was not revealed. He would have been pleased to head a Stephens-for-president movement but "little Alec" would give no cooperation. Brown had told Cobb that he *could* support him but he had never said he *would*. He and Cobb had professed true friendship, but it never existed. Brown correctly suspected that Cobb forces wished to use him, yet he welcomed their support. He would be the leader; he could not be a follower.

Writing to Stephens on June 4, 1859, Governor Brown expresed

8 November 18, 1859, in Cobb Papers.

a fear that "we shall have two delegations at Charleston."[9] He apparently meant pro-Buchanan administration and pro-Stephen A. Douglas. He could also have been thinking of a pro-Cobb delegation and an uninstructed one. To Cobb he wrote on November 21 that it was still in doubt when a convention should be held to select delegates to the Charleston convention. However, before closing he added: "I have just been informed" that a meeting was scheduled that evening to settle the question.[10]

A caucus of Democratic legislators did take place that evening. Ignoring the party executive committee, a meeting to select delegates to the Charleston convention was set for December 8. Those counties unwilling to permit their legislators to serve as delegates at this meeting were requested to select others. It was not explained, however, how this could be done in so short a time. On the following day, November 22, the state executive committee issued a call for a state convention to meet the second Monday in March, 1860. Only William K. DeGraffenried of the Committee dissented and joined in the plan of the legislators.[11]

The meeting called by the legislators met as scheduled on December 8. Some counties had selected delegates, others had designated their legislators as delegates, and still others had done neither. Fifty-seven counties were not represented. Some persons who attended refused to participate; others protested the proposed action and demanded postponement until March. It was no secret that this December meeting was sponsored by the friends of Howell Cobb.

A slate of twenty—four at large and two from each district—was chosen as delegates to the Charleston convention. These delegates were not specifically instructed to support Cobb, but the meeting endorsed Cobb as a man suitable for the office of president.[12] Another resolution promised support of the nominee of the Charleston convention only if he pledged defense of the rights of the South in the territories.

Fifty-two Democratic legislators published a protest against this unauthorized attempt to bind the Democrats of the state, and news-

9 Phillips, *Correspondence*, 444.
10 Brockman Collection.
11 The other four members were S. W. Burney, D. C. Campbell, Thomas P. Safford, and E. J. McGehee.
12 Milledgeville *Federal Union*, December 13, 1859; Savannah *Morning News*, December 10, 1859.

papers all over the state sprang to the attack. "We regard the movement as an unjustified assumption of power on the part of those who participated," declared the Savannah *Morning News*.[13]

There is no evidence that Brown was present at the December 8 meeting; yet he later stated privately, "I did not hesitate to say that in my opinion the convention should be adjourned over to the time fixed by the Executive Committee."[14] It is not clear whether the governor was displeased with the assumption of power by the legislators or the endorsement of Cobb or both, but he was definitely unhappy. As the clamor from newspapers and public meetings made it clear that the recent action would not be accepted, he turned to friends Toombs and Stephens for suggestions. He was concerned over the possibility of two Georgia delegations at the Charleston convention. Yet should the delegation selected at the December meeting be accepted, he thought the great majority of the party would be disregarded. However, he had one pleasant thought about the action of the legislators: "I think the particular interest which was intended to be advanced by this hasty move may have suffered by it."[15]

Stephens wished to refrain from active participation in the controversy, and Brown agreed "not to complicate" him. However, Stephens privately suggested a possible solution. If those responsible for the December meeting would agree to participate in the March convention then the latter might settle the controversy by confirming the delegates already chosen. Brown agreed with "almost every suggestion" Stephens offered. If the influences responsible for the December meeting would unite in the March convention he would agree to Stephens' suggestion. But he added that if they failed to unite he doubted "the propriety of reappointing all of them. . . . It would be a greater concession than they could reasonably ask."[16]

Brown made no public statement in favor of either the December meeting or the proposed March convention. Privately he claimed to "take no active part in the contest," yet he explained that the executive committee had merely performed its duty. He urged his friends, even

13 December 10, 1859.
14 Brown to Stephens, December 29, 1859, in Brockman Collection.
15 Brown to Toombs, December 29, 1859; Brown to Stephens, December 29, 1859, in Brockman Collection.
16 Brown to Stephens, January 5, 1860, Phillips, *Correspondence*, 453.

those who had been present in the December meeting, to be present in March and labor for harmony.[17] Some of Cobb's friends, however, did not attribute to the governor such lofty motives. James M. Spullock, still bitter from alleged mistreatment, reported that it was Brown and Linton Stephens who influenced the executive committee to call the March meeting. Through Baptist influence, Brown had controlled committeemen S. W. Burney and Thomas P. Saffold "against their will."[18] This accusation might have resulted from the observation that Linton Stephens was a guest in the Governor's Mansion during a portion of the legislative session.[19]

Cobb's friends were in a quandary. They were fearful that the March convention might not approve the action of the December meeting, yet they hesitated to oppose a convention of delegates specifically chosen. The Athens *Southern Banner*, a strong Cobb publication, disapproved of the convention as unnecessary since the December meeting had been in keeping with party custom and was therefore perfectly legal. A second convention would merely divide the party. "We hope therefore that those of our Democratic friends who have thought proper to dissent to the action of the December convention, will not suffer prejudice and bias to control and direct their deliberations." If the convention was made up of true representatives of the party then whatever was done should be accepted. "We repeat to all the Democracy—be present in the March convention."[20]

As supporters of Cobb, but a bit milder in their approach, the editors of the Atlanta *Daily Intelligencer* hoped that the same delegates chosen in December would be approved by the March convention and the same resolutions readopted. This would unite the party. Let the legality or illegality of the December meeting be ignored.[21]

There was much confusion and bad feeling throughout the counties as they selected delegates to the March convention. Some counties reappointed those who had served in December; others repudiated the December meeting. Some passed resolutions endorsing Cobb; others

17 Brown to C. E. Broyles, January 29, 1860, in Brockman Collection.
18 Spullock to Cobb, March 18, 1860, in Cobb Papers.
19 Brown to Linton Stephens, October 25, 1859, in Brockman Collection.
20 February 2, 1860.
21 February 21, 1860.

refused or failed to do so. The convention met at Milledgeville on March 14. Of the 132 counties, 90 were represented. Cobb's friends were able to select Alexander R. Lawton as presiding officer, but there success ended. A proposal to approve the December resolutions, including the endorsement of Cobb, was defeated. The delegates-at-large and all of the district delegates except two[22] chosen in December were confirmed, but the number of delegates to be sent to the Charleston convention was doubled.[23] If the friends of Brown worked for harmony, they accomplished little; much bitterness was in evidence.

Spullock and Daniel S. Printup rushed back to Rome to report to John H. Lumpkin why they had failed. Spullock also reported to Cobb. They had all the counties of the fifth district lined up for the Cobb resolution until Governor Brown succeeded in getting the delegates from three counties into the executive office and turned them against Cobb. Spullock claimed that he sent word to Brown that if he would line up his friends for Cobb he would be willing to forget all the differences between them. But by this time the governor was "so complicated with the opposition he could not act otherwise than he did & preserve his honor." Some counties were reconverted, Spullock explained, but Brown controlled Cherokee until the last; it voted against the Cobb resolution. Cobb lost, Spullock concluded, because "you had to contend with the Stephens, Brown, Warner, Iverson, McDonald, Cohen & diverse other lesser lights."[24] To this list Lumpkin added the names of Toombs and Judge James Thomas, father-in-law of Linton Stephens. Lumpkin charged Thomas with being the leader of the Cobb opposition in the convention.[25] This was truly an imposing list of opponents.

James A. Sledge of the Athens *Southern Banner* took a somewhat different view. He thought that Solomon Cohen of Savannah had organized the anti-Cobb forces before the session began action, and the friends of Alexander Stephens did both him and Cobb an injustice by continuing to discuss Stephens as a possible presidential candidate even after he had declined to have his name submitted. There was rumor that Stephen A. Douglas had agreed to support Stephens at

22 Arthur Hood and J. W. Evans.
23 Milledgeville *Federal Union*, March 20, 1860.
24 Spullock to Cobb, March 18, 1860, in Cobb Papers.
25 Lumpkin to Cobb, March 17, 1860, *ibid.*

Charleston if he himself could not get the nomination. This kept the Stephens hope alive. For the Georgia convention to endorse Cobb would endanger the success of such a plan.

Like most Cobb supporters, the *Banner* also placed much blame on Governor Brown. Cherokee County had voted against Cobb and the endorsement of the Dred Scott decision, the editor explained. "It was pretty generally understood" that this was the result of "the influence of the Governor." "If this turns out to be true we know *one* man who has been a warm friend and supporter of his, whose vote he will never get again."[26] A fact the editor did not note was that Solomon Cohen of Savannah was a close personal friend of Governor Brown.

Although as bitter as other members of the Cobb clan, Mother Cobb offered her "Beloved Howell" a bit of consolation: "Georgia will suffer disgrace, from a few mean & designing men, such as Stephens & Brown who both aspire to the honor themselves but I cannot believe a just & a good God will let them succeed in their sinful course."[27]

Outwardly, Howell Cobb assumed a philosophical and perhaps "patriotic" view of the situation. In a public letter to Isaiah T. Irwin, chairman of the December meeting which had endorsed him for president, Cobb expressed appreciation for "this manifestation of regard and confidence" tendered him by a "free will offering from the Democracy." He thought his friends in that meeting had acted in a legitimate manner and in keeping with the wishes of a majority of the Democracy. Yet he recognized bitter opposition in the "most unjust and illiberal attack" made upon that group. Therefore, when friends asked him for advice he had suggested that they go to the March convention and work for harmony, for "I neither desired nor would I accept the vote of the state at Charleston, against the will and voice of a majority of the Democracy of my own State." Further, he could not even consent to his name being presented at Charleston if the opposition at home was "of such a character either in numbers or feelings" as to endanger the harmony so much needed in the alarming crisis facing the nation. After reviewing the proceedings of both conventions, although still appreciative of "the warm and earnest support of a decided majority of the Democracy,"

26 March 22, 1860.
27 Mrs. S. R. Cobb to Howell Cobb, March 26, 1860, in Cobb Papers.

Cobb felt "I must withdraw my name unconditionally from the canvass."[28]

To the opposition, Cobb's letter was merely the announcement of withdrawal from a race in which he had already been defeated. His friends, on the other hand, thought his announcement the height of patriotism. "It is just what we expected from him," exclaimed the Athens *Southern Banner*, "and in unison and harmony with his life long devotion to the interests of his party."[29]

Brown claimed privately to have "preserved as much neutrality between the friends of the two conventions as I conveniently could," yet he did not hesitate to advocate nullifying the Cobb strength by the selection of additional delegates. He further claimed to have kept silent on the Cobb resolution, even though Cherokee County did vote against it. He was quick to point out that other counties in whose delegations he had close friends voted for the resolution. He regretted that Cobb's friends blamed him and Stephens for the results. "I owe Mr. Cobb no ill will, but I do not belong to him or his friends." As for Stephens, Brown would be "much gratified" to see him nominated at Charleston. "I think he would be a strong man in the race and that he would make an able and just chief magistrate."[30]

John B. Lamar, a strong Cobb supporter, advanced the idea that Cherokee's action was a result not so much of the governor's influence as that of his brother James, who wished to go as a delegate to Charleston, but was snubbed by Cobb's Floyd County (Rome) friends. James Brown then influenced the Cherokee delegation to oppose Cobb. Lamar also believed the whole action was encouraged by "the passive opposition of Stephens, brooding in silent malevolence."[31]

That a number of high ranking state employees who had received their appointments from the governor supported the Cobb resolution and were not punished was evidence that Brown was not determined to block Cobb. Yet it was also evident that had Brown actively supported the resolution it would have encountered little difficulty. Clearly, he

28 Cobb to Irwin, March 20, 1860, Athens *Southern Banner*, March 29, 1860; Savannah *Morning News*, March 31, 1860.
29 March 29, 1860.
30 Brown to Hiram Warner, March 27, 1860, in Brockman Collection.
31 Lamar to Cobb, April 5, 1860, in Cobb Papers.

wished Alexander H. Stephens, not Howell Cobb, nominated for president.

The National Democratic Convention met in Charleston on April 23, 1860. It was agreed that a platform should be approved prior to the nomination of a candidate for the presidency. The resolutions committee became hopelessly divided and presented both majority and minority reports. The majority group, consisting mostly of delegates from slave states, demanded congressional protection of slavery in the territories. The minority proposed readoption of the Cincinnati platform of 1856 with its policy of noninterference by Congress. When the convention adopted the minority platform, the delegates from the Gulf States walked out. A majority of the Georgia delegation later joined them. Unable to give any candidate the required two-thirds vote for nomination, the Charleston convention adjourned to meet in Baltimore on June 18. The "seceders" called a convention for Richmond on June 11.[32]

The Democrats of Georgia were stunned by what happened at Charleston. The walkout was no great surprise, for such action had been previously suggested. The great surprise was that those who remained in the convention made no serious effort to persuade the seceders to return. Never before had northern Democrats shown such independence. The hour of decision for southern Democrats had arrived and there was much disagreement over what it should be. Should the seceders be sent to the Baltimore convention; should a new delegation be chosen; or should no delegation be sent? If a delegation was sent to Baltimore, should the same group be sent to Richmond?

Brown privately attributed the breakup at Charleston to the longstanding quarrel between Stephen A. Douglas and the Buchanan administration as represented by Cobb. Douglas, with a feeling of strength, had "pushed his doctrines to an extreme," and Cobb had attempted counteraction "by advocating the protective doctrine forcing the issue upon the country prematurely," thus taking a position which two years earlier "he would have been the first to condemn." As for himself, Brown asserted, he was unwilling to see the Democratic party dissolved to gratify the ambitions of any man. But with some amusement he called attention to the fact that Cobb the Unionist had now

32 Nichols, *Disruption of American Democracy*, 296 ff.

become Cobb the Southern Rights leader. In 1850 the Cobb Unionists had denounced as traitors those who objected to surrendering southern rights in the western domain. Yet, now, when there was no present necessity for Congress to legislate on the subject of slavery, they appeared ready to dissolve the party and even the Union. Should the Union actually become endangered, Brown speculated, would they again do a "summer set" and claim credit for saving it?

Governor Brown further explained that he could not condemn the seceders, for he thought their action might eventually produce desired results, provided they could be prevented from moving too fast. He believed the majority report rejected at Charleston did no more than justice to the South, yet he questioned the expediency of insisting upon its adoption. Since the doctrine of congressional protection of slavery in the territories violated the doctrine of noninterference, many feared its adoption would open the door to other legislation. Furthermore, it could be of no practical benefits as long as free states controlled Congress and could determine what legislation should pass.

Brown proposed that the seceders be returned to the convention when it should meet in Baltimore, first going by Richmond and adjourning that meeting until after the Baltimore session. He had no doubt that the Baltimore convention would agree on a platform and a candidate the South could support. Should the convention fail to make this concession, there would be great trouble, and the results would be very uncertain. Brown did not speculate on acceptable candidates. He only stated "I have no fear of the nomination of Douglas and no one supposes Cobb can get it." He proposed that the Georgia Democratic Executive Committee call a convention to consider what action might be taken to protect southern rights and preserve party unity and integrity.[33]

In response to public demand the executive committee did call a convention for June 4, 1860. Meanwhile, a group of citizens called upon the more prominent Democratic leaders of the state to make known their views. No fewer than eight responded through public letters, but there was no unanimity. Secretary of the Treasury Howell Cobb vigorously defended the seceders and their demand for congressional pro-

33 Brown to James A. Nisbet, May 8, 1860; Brown to R. H. Clark, May 28, 1860; Brown to John W. Anderson, May 26, 1860; Brown to D. A. Wright, May 26, 1860, all in Brockman Collection.

tection of slavery in the territories. He wished these seceders reappointed to both the Richmond and Baltimore meetings, but to have no part in the nomination of Stephen A. Douglas. Senator Robert Toombs also wished the seceders sent to Baltimore and Richmond. At Baltimore he hoped they might assist in restoring party harmony. Should they fail, then appropriate action could be taken at Richmond. However, the tone and wording of his letter indicated his unwillingness to make extensive concessions in the interest of harmony.

Hiram Warner and Eugenius A. Nisbet condemned the seceders and charged that by their action they had cooperated with extremists who wished to disrupt both the party and the Union. The South had requested a guarantee of nonintervention and it had been granted. Why now violate the agreement by demanding the acceptance of the principle of interference?

Alexander H. Stephens and Herschel V. Johnson did not specifically denounce the seceders but they insisted upon respect for the compact which established the principle of nonintervention. They could see no wisdom in demanding the adoption of the principle of congressional protection when it would be valueless, of doubtful legality, and possibly dangerous.

Governor Brown's letter made public what he had been saying in private correspondence. Without calling names, he blamed the existing discord within the Democratic party upon rivalry between aspirants. He would not reflect upon the motives of either those who seceded or those who remained in the Charleston Convention. He believed in the principle of congressional protection of slavery in the territories, but at this time he considered it an abstraction that should not be insisted upon. The Supreme Court had spoken in the Dred Scott Decision. If this principle was added to the Cincinnati Platform of 1856 that should settle the question. Action at Richmond should be postponed until all reasonable efforts at Baltimore had failed.[34]

All political observers must have noticed the change in positions of Howell Cobb and Herschel V. Johnson over the past decade. Cobb the Unionist in 1850 was now Cobb the defender of southern rights. Johnson the defender of southern rights in 1850 was now urging unity. But the most astute political observer could not have seen in Brown's

34 Milledgeville *Federal Union*, May 22, 29, 1860.

moderate statement indication that before the close of the year he would be a rabid secessionist.

The state convention that met on June 4 reflected the same variations in opinions as those already expressed by the party leaders. James Gardner and Herschel V. Johnson spoke in opposition to insistence upon congressional protection of slavery in the territories. Gardner thought the Cincinnati platform of 1856 and the Dred Scott Decision guaranteed sufficient protection. Johnson added that such a demand was unnecessary, unless needed; there was no territory in which to apply it. But even if protection were needed, there was no probability of getting it in view of the growing Republican strength in Congress. Henry R. Jackson of Savannah, "a forcible, chaste, and eloquent speaker," defended his action at Charleston where he "had been actuated by pure devotion to the rights of the South." Howell Cobb concluded the speaking. He complimented Lewis Cass for his origination of the doctrine of popular sovereignty; and explained why he himself was a Union man in 1850. He thought he was right then, but he wished the people to judge him by what he "is now," not what he "was then." He was unwilling to compromise on the demand for protection in the territories. He saw no inconsistency between "nonintervention" and "Congressional protection."

When a vote was taken on whether to endorse the majority or minority reports made at Charleston, the majority (protection) report was approved 298 to 41. The same delegation was reappointed and accredited to both the Richmond and Baltimore conventions. Those favoring the minority report then met in separate convention, approved that report, and selected a delegation to the Baltimore convention. Johnson, Warner, and Gardner were among those chosen.[35] These plus Eugenius Nisbet and Alexander Stephens, who was too ill to attend the convention, would form the nucleus of Douglas support in Georgia in the months ahead.

At Baltimore there was no harmony. The regular Georgia delegation was finally offered seats but declined and joined another bolt. Hopelessly split, the two groups of Democrats nominated two different candidates—Stephen A. Douglas and John C. Breckinridge. Meanwhile

35 Atlanta *Daily Intelligencer*, June 7, 8, 1860; Milledgeville *Federal Union*, June 12, 1860.

a newly formed Constitutional Union party had nominated John Bell and the Republicans had chosen Abraham Lincoln.

Governor Brown recognized the disruption of the Democratic party for what it was—death to all hopes of victory. "I agree with you that we should do all within our power to defeat Lincoln," he wrote Linton Stephens. The big question was how could it be accomplished. In Brown's opinion the only place was in the House of Representatives. It was generally conceded that Lincoln coud not carry a single southern state; consequently, no southern combination in support of another candidate could assist in throwing the election into the House. As for himself, Brown explained, he would not support any combination that would require him to vote for Bell, "whose record is so very objectionable." The only combination that could be effective would be one formed in the free states. This he did not expect. "I am strongly impressed with the belief . . . that Lincoln will carry the Democratic free states under the plurality rule of voting and will be elected by the popular vote."

There was a trace of bitterness in Brown's reflection on the disruption of the Democratic party. He still believed in the correctness of the principle of congressional protection, yet he could not accept its failure of recognition as a sufficient cause for division. Since no legislation was requested, the question might well have been permitted to rest for the present. He could not agree with Douglas' interpretation of the Cincinnati platform; therefore, he could not vote for him. The South generally would support Breckinridge, he concluded, so "as a Southern man, I think it best to vote for him, while I condemn the action of the wire workers who produced the split more for the gratification of selfish motives and vindictive feelings than from patriotic emotions."[36]

Immediately after the June 4 convention, the Brown family moved to Rowland Springs, Cass County, for the summer, occupying a house generously furnished by John S. Rowland, who was being threatened with indictment for failure to make proper tax returns.[37] Mrs. Brown and the children had spent the previous two summers at Canton. Brown was still concerned about his poor health and thought the "mountain air and mineral water" would do him good, yet he relaxed very little at

36 July 27, 1860, in Hargrett Collection.
37 Brown to Rowland, May 26, 1860, in Brockman Collection.

Rowland Springs. He was never one to delegate much authority to others; therefore, he kept in close touch with Milledgeville. When not engaged in state business he was thinking about his private investments. Prior to 1860 his interest had been in railroad bonds. Now he was also investing in stocks. By the close of the year he owned numerous shares in the Nashville and Chattanooga, Macon and Western, and South Western railroads. His tax returns for 1860 valued his property at $44,790. Thirteen slaves—five at Milledgeville and eight at Cherokee—were valued at $9,000. Stocks and bonds accounted for $25,000; the remaining $10,790 in real estate. He had apparently disposed of some of his land.[38]

Returning to Milledgeville in late summer, Governor Brown became an interested observer but not an active participant in national politics. Although he thought the disruption of the Democratic party unwise and unnecessary he endorsed the Breckinridge-Lane ticket, joining Howell Cobb, Robert Toombs, and the bolters. Once in camp he moved toward an extreme Southern Rights position, parting political company with such friends as Alexander Stephens, Herschel V. Johnson, Hiram Warner, and Eugenius A. Nisbet. These moderates endorsed Stephen A. Douglas, and Johnson accepted the position of vice-presidential candidate on the ticket. The Opposition party endorsed the Bell-Everett Constitutional Union ticket, but many of its members drifted to other candidates. Ben Hill and Warren Akin led the Bell forces. The campaign was characterized by invective and vituperations; no one was safe from attack. There was a marked trend toward disunion.

In mid-October Thomas R. R. Cobb was in Milledgeville serving on a committee to codify the laws of Georgia, a position to which Governor Brown had appointed him two years earlier. News of Republican victory in the state election in Pennsylvania had just arrived. It is not known whether or not Cobb had consulted the governor but he spoke Brown's language when he wrote his wife: "I can see no earthly hope of defeating them in November and their success then, whether we

38 Brown to James A. Whiteside, May 4, 12, 1860; Brown to John W. Anderson, March 20, 23, 1860; Brown to S. R. McCamy, July 6, 1860; Brown to H. C. Moore, March 20, 1860, all in Brockman Collection; Brown to James A. Whiteside, August 11, 1860; Tax returns for 1860, in Hargrett Collection.

will it or not, is *inevitable disunion* .... *Separation is desirable,* peaceable if we can, forcibly if we must."[39]

Governor Brown was already at work on a special message in which he would recommend to the legislature retaliation against those states which by their "personal liberty laws" had nullified the fugitive slave act. And when the governor of South Carolina inquired what cooperation might be expected from Georgia in case Lincoln won and South Carolina should call a convention, Brown replied that Georgia also would likely call a convention. He thought a convention of all the southern states would be desirable in order to "take common action for the protection of the rights of all." He believed the Georgia legislature would pass retaliatory measures against the offending states even though Lincoln should be defeated. Should South Carolina remain in the Union he urged that state to adopt similar retaliatory measures. However, in direct answer to the South Carolina governor's question, he must state that, as things then stood, "Should the question be submitted to the people of Georgia whether they would go out of the Union on Lincoln's election without regard to the action of other states my opinion is they would determine to wait for an *overt act.*"[40] Soon Governor Brown would be working to prevent just such a delay.

A week before the presidential election Governor Brown, much depressed in spirit, dispatched a private letter to his trusted friend Dr. John W. Lewis. His son Julius was seriously ill with fever and election prospects forecast a Lincoln victory. He had about completed writing his proposed special message to the legislature which he suspected would be the first utterance of its type from any southern governor. "I pray God to direct my mind to such conclusions as may be for the good of our whole people." He agreed with those who were saying that the Union could not be perpetuated unless there was a radical change in northern sentiment; he did not expect such a change. Should the South submit to the election of Lincoln it might never again be able to make "a respectable show of resistance," for "Already the people of the North taunt us with inability and cowardice."[41]

The election results in Georgia were much as was expected; few

---

39 October 11, 1860, in Thomas R. R. Cobb Papers.
40 Brown to William H. Gist, October 31, 1860, in Brockman Collection.
41 October 31, 1860, *ibid.*

expected their candidate to receive a majority of the votes cast. Breckinridge received 51,893; Bell 42,855; and Douglas 11,580. Disunionists voted for Breckinridge, but not all who voted for him were disunionists. Bell and Douglas received the moderate vote, and their total exceeded the vote for Breckinridge. There was no Lincoln ticket. Since no one received the required majority, it would be left to the legislature to select Georgia's presidential electors.

Chapter VII

Delay Is Full of Danger

THE GEORGIA GENERAL ASSEMBLY convened on election day, November 7, 1860. The governor's annual message on the state of the state covered the usual topics of a general nature. He called special attention to the need for more money for the University of Georgia and the public schools, and urged further development of the Military Institute at Marietta. He commended the operators of the Western and Atlantic Railroad for their contribution to business and shippers for their use of the road. Mark Cooper's Etowah Manufacturing and Mining Company was given special attention. This company, operating two furnaces for pig iron, a rolling mill, and a nail factory supporting two thousand people, had paid many thousands of dollars in freight. However, it was now in some financial distress. In order to preserve and further develop this great industry, the governor recommended state aid. He also recommended the establishment of a foundry. Contracting with northern concerns for military supplies had not proved satisfactory, and even the small amount being received might soon be cut off.

Lastly, the governor wished to see Georgians have greater respect for the Holy Sabbath. It had long been the practice of the railroads of the state to run passenger trains on Sunday. This practice had been excused by the claim that the mails must be delivered. This excuse he considered insufficient. Yet, going along with the practice, he had permitted Sunday trains on the state road. However, he still believed the practice to be in violation of the Sabbath. Therefore, he recommended that each superintendent who in the future permitted such a violation be subject to fine or imprisonment. "'Remember the Sabbath day to keep it holy,' is addressed alike to the Legislator and to the private citizens."[1]

On the same day that Governor Brown's regular message was read to the General Assembly he also sent in his special message on state-federal relations and the right of secession. He covered the same points which had been covered so often by the late John C. Calhoun. The Union was a compact in which both the state and the federal government had spheres of power. The powers of the federal government were delegated and therefore strictly limited. Its duty was to protect, not to meddle. The control and regulation of property was left to the states.

Unfortunately, the constitutional obligations agreed to and respected by the Founding Fathers were no longer respected by some of their descendants. In earlier days many northern traders had grown wealthy selling slaves to the South. This southern money they had invested in business and industry. Now their descendants, while enjoying the income from business financed by southern money, wished to destroy the prosperity of the South by interfering with the institution of slavery. It would be no more a crime, the governor declared, for southerners to encourage the destruction of northern industry than for northerners to encourage the destruction of southern property in slaves.

Under the Constitution, the governor explained, states were obligated to return fugitives from justice and fugitives from labor. Fugitives from justice were to be surrendered to the executive of the state from whence they fled; fugitives from labor to those to whom the labor was due. Using Massachusetts as an example, it was pointed out how certain free states had ignored the Constitution. With their personal liberty laws they had nullified the federal fugitive slave laws, making it impossible for owners to capture and return fugitive slaves. Not only had Massachusetts refused to protect slaveowners against mob action, it had even placed legal penalties on persons who assisted owners. When in 1832 South Carolina had attempted to nullify a law which she

<hr />

[1] *House Journal*, 1860, pp. 7 ff; Milledgeville *Federal Union*, November 13, 1860; Atlanta *Daily Intelligencer*, November 13, 1860.

considered unconstitutional and ruinous she was threatened with federal force. Yet Massachusetts and other free states had nullified the fugitive slave laws and had been in no way threatened. If nullification of a law in South Carolina was treason, so was a similar action in Massachusetts.

The governor urged:

> Let us meet unjust aggression and unconstitutional State legislation with retaliation. To this end I recommend the enactment of a law authorizing the Governor of this state, in case any citizen of this State shall in future be deprived of his slave or other property, under the operation of the aggressive legislation of Massachusetts . . . or like legislation of any other State, or by the neglect of any such State to fulfill her constitutional obligations to Georgia, or her citizens, by delivering up to the owner, on demand, his slave which may have escaped into such State, to call out such military force as he may deem necessary for the purpose, and to seize such amount of the money or property of any citizen of such offending and faithless State, which may be found within the limits of this State, as may be amply sufficient fully to indemnify such citizens of this State as may have been robbed of his property by the failure of such faithless State to discharge its constitutional obligations.

If within thirty days the Georgian's property was not paid for or returned, the seized property should be sold and proceeds used as indemnity. The governor further recommended laws that would drive from Georgia markets the products from such offending states. To those who would say such laws would not be constitutional he would reply that since Massachusetts had violated her constitutional obligations to Georgia, Georgia recognized no obligations to Massachusetts. The above could be accomplished by levying excessive taxes on such goods. Although Governor Brown had used Massachusetts as an example, before closing he also included Vermont, Michigan, Maine, Rhode Island, Connecticut, New York, and Wisconsin. These, he said, were the states whose laws appeared to violate Georgia's rights.

In closing, Brown predicted that by the time of the reading of this message, the "Black Republican" party would probably have won control of the federal government. Therefore, Georgia must prepare to defend her rights. He recommended the calling of a state convention to decide the state's future course and the immediate appropriation of $1 million for military preparation. "To every demand for further concession, or compromise of our rights, we should reply 'The argument is exhausted,' and we now 'stand by our arms.'"[2]

Before taking action on the proposal to call a convention, the General Assembly invited a number of distinguished men to express their views before that body. The speeches of Toombs and Stephens were the highlights, for they expressed the views of the two large groups into which a majority of the people had divided. Robert Toombs, belligerent and impatient, demanded immediate secession. He was unwilling even to wait for the meeting of a convention. Let the legislature do it *now*. After March 4, he declared, the federal government would be in the hands of the enemy. "Will you let him have it? [The audience cried "No, No, Never."] Then strike while it is yet today. Withdraw your sons from the army, the navy and every department of the federal service. Keep your taxes in your own coffer—but arm with them and throw the bloody spear into this den of incendiaries and assassins, and let God defend the right. . . . Nothing but ruin will follow delay . . . . Then strike, strike while it is yet time."[3]

Stephens held different views. "My object," he explained, "is not to stir up strife, but to allay it; not to appeal to your passions, but to your reason. Good government can never be built up or sustained by the impulse of passion. I wish to address myself to your good sense, to your judgment, and if, after hearing, you disagree, let us agree to disagree, and part as we met, friends."

Who was to blame for the present condition? he asked. He thought the South partly to blame because it had split the Democratic party and made possible the election of a minority president. Had the South remained loyal to the principle of nonintervention and not split the party, the Democrats would have won as great a victory as the ones by Pierce and Buchanan. "Therefore let us not be hasty and rash in our actions, especially if the results be attributable at all to ourselves. Before looking to extreme measures, let us see, as Georgians, that everything which can be done to preserve our rights, our interests, and our honor, as well as the peace of the country, in the Union, be first done."

The only question demanding an immediate answer, Stephens

2 *House Journal*, 1860, pp. 33 ff; Milledgeville *Federal Union*, November 13, 1860.
3 Ulrich B. Phillips, *The Life of Robert Toombs* (New York, 1913), 200–201.

concluded, was what could and should be done by the legislature. His answer was that the legislature should call a convention. It did not have the power to vote Georgia out of the Union. "Sovereignty is not in the legislature. We, the people, are sovereign . . . . I shall bow to the will of the people. . . . I am, as you clearly perceive, for maintaining the Union as it is, if possible. I would exhaust every means thus to maintain it with an equality in it."[4] Many who heard Stephens must have been convinced he was right, yet the tide of disunion was beating heavily against them. A convention was called to meet January 16, 1861. Delegates were to be elected on January 2. Perhaps Stephens' speech did not greatly influence the coming election, but this was his finest hour.

The results of the recent presidential election in Georgia and words of caution and moderation from men like Stephens, Ben Hill, and Herschel V. Johnson caused concern in the ranks of the disunionists. On December 5 the Breckinridge electors recently chosen by the legislature appealed to Governor Brown to make public his views on the present situation. Brown gladly obliged. No doubt his reply was planned as an answer to Stephens.

He began by listing three questions for discussion. (1) Was Lincoln's election sufficient cause for secession? (2) If Lincoln's election and administration were submitted to by the South, what would be the effect upon the institution of slavery? (3) What effect would the abolition of slavery have upon the nonslaveholders and poor white laborers of the South?

If viewed in the mere light of the victory of a successful candidate, he did not think Lincoln's election sufficient cause for secession. But the election could not be viewed in that light, for Lincoln was the "representative of a fanatical abolitionist sentiment," the instrument of a triumphant party, "the principles of which are deadly hostile to the institution of slavery, and openly at war with the fundamental doctrines of the Constitution." It was not the victory of Lincoln the man that endangered the South and its institutions; it was the triumph of Lincoln the representative of a victorious sectional party avowedly hostile to the South. It was this victory that justified withdrawal from a union where equality, rights, and honor could no longer be protected.

4 Published in full in Richard M. Johnson and William M. Browne, *Life of Alexander H. Stephens* (Philadelphia, 1878), 564 ff.

It was the governor's candid opinion that the inauguration and administration of Lincoln would result in "the total abolition of slavery, and the utter ruin of the South in less than twenty-five years." To submit would convince the North that "we will never resist." By skillful use of patronage, the Lincoln party would so divide the South and destroy its moral power that a Republican ticket would be presented in 1864. If such a ticket received only five to ten thousand votes in each slave state, that would be as much power as was shown by the abolitionists in the free states a few years since. This bloc of abolitionists would hold the balance of power between the other two parties and gain control of the state governments.

Slavery would first be abolished in the District of Columbia and then in the federal forts, arsenals, and dockyards throughout the South. Next would come the abolition of interstate slave trade. Then after the acquiescing South had been sufficiently humiliated, slavery within the states would be completely abolished. "If we fail to resist now, we will never again have the strength to resist."

If slavery was abolished, the Governor argued, only misery and ruin would follow. If slaveholders were paid for their property at say $500 per head it would amount to a staggering $2,250,000,000 debt. Who would pay it? The North would not likely agree to pay its portion; so the South would be taxed for the full amount. That would average about $150 million for each of the fifteen slave states. If Georgia paid only the average and it was spread over a period of ten years, the tax burden would be multiplied thirty fold. Even if the North did assist in payment, Georgia would be assessed at least $75 million, thus increasing the tax burden fifteen fold over a period of ten years. Further still, it would be a great injustice to require slaveholders to pay taxes to compensate themselves for their loss of property. Consequently, it might be that the major burden of increased taxes would fall upon the nonslaveholders and the poor laborers.

Should the millions of slaves be freed what would become of them? inquired the Governor. The northern states had willingly harbored fugitive slaves but they would not welcome free Negroes. The idea of sending them to Africa was not practical. "With the means at our command," one might as well propose to send them to the moon. Even if an attempt were made to send them to Africa, another $1,125,000,000 would be needed for the acquisition of land and support until they could care for themselves. The North would not be interested in paying any portion of the bill, for it merely wished to free the slaves without compensation to owners and leave them where they were.

Even if slaveholders lost their slaves they would still be the landowners and the poorer whites the tenants. But what of the 4,500,000 former slaves? Those of them who worked must also become tenants. But many would not work, preferring instead to spend their time stealing, robbing, and plundering. Probably one-fourth of them would soon be in prison or poorhouses, supported at taxpayers' expense. Those who did choose to work would be in competition with white laborers, and employers would enjoy paying lower wages. "It is sickening to contemplate the miseries of our poor white people under these circumstances." Many nonslaveholders owned their own land, and those who worked for wages had the highest standard of living in the world. "They are a superior race, and they feel and know it." Abolish slavery and the black men would be their legal and social but not natural equal. God had provided natural differences which no law of man could change. Soon blacks and whites "must labor in the fields together as equals. Their children must go to the same poor schools together, if they are educated at all. They must go to church as equals, enter the courts of justice as equals, sue and be sued as equals, sit on juries together as equals, stand side by side in our military corps as equals, enter each other's houses in social intercourse, as equals; and very soon their children must marry together as equals. May our kind heavenly Father avert the evil, and deliver the poor from such a fate."

Continuing his efforts to alarm upcountry people, the governor prophesied that once free, the black man would move away from the hot cotton fields to the cooler mountain regions where they would live by "plundering and stealing, robbing and killing" throughout those lovely valleys. This he could "never consent to see," for this was his home and the home of hundreds of other "brave, honest, patriotic and pure hearted." These people loved the Union but they loved liberty and justice even more; they would never submit to abolitionist rule or continue in a Union dominated by an enemy who was determined to use "all its power for our destruction":

"Wealth is timid," the governor explained, "and wealthy men may cry for peace, and submit for fear they may lose their money; but the poor, honest laborers of Georgia, can never consent to see slavery abolished, and submit to all the taxation, vassalage, low wages and downright degradation, which must follow. They will never take the negro's place; God forbid."

The governor then called upon all Georgians to forget party differences and unite against the already united Black Republicans. They could not continue to live in a Union that did not give them sufficient guarantees of their rights, and the Republican party had no idea of granting such guarantees. Instead Republicans expected the South to continue to compromise and submit for the sake of peace.

Then what was the remedy? If the cotton states would secede from the Union their action might result in the meeting of a convention of all the states in which guarantees could be agreed upon. Should the North refuse to be a party to such guarantees then Brown believed the border states would join with the cotton states in forming a southern confederacy "in which, under the old Constitution of our fathers, our people could live in security and peace."

In closing, Governor Brown took issue with the rather widespread argument that the Lower South should take no drastic action without assurance of cooperation from the border states. "If we wait for this," he explained, "we shall *submit*, for some of those States will not consent to go," and the North would agree to no guarantees. "They will say that we have again blustered and submitted; as we always do."[5]

There could be no doubt as to the direction in which this broadside was aimed. Upcountry Georgia, where farms were small and slaves were few, had no tears to shed over the probability of the mighty planters losing a portion of their property. Yet they were no more abolitionists than the planters; they wanted no black neighbors, legal and social equals, or competition. Having grown up in the mountains, Brown was familiar with these fears and prejudices.

Two weeks after Brown issued his appeal for drastic action the news that South Carolina had seceded from the Union brought Georgia disunionists much comfort and hope. For thirty years a hotbed of discontent where nullification and secession were often threatened, South

5 This public letter, dated December 7, 1860, was printed in all the leading Georgia newspapers and also distributed as a broadside.

Carolina's action in this most serious of all crisis would have great influence in other cotton states. Privately, Governor Brown had been much concerned, and his concern was increased by a rumor that while South Carolina would probably vote secession it would not become effective until March 3, 1861, the day before Lincoln would take office. This news caused him to dash off three private letters in one day.

To Howell Cobb, who he had heard would be present at the meeting of the South Carolina convention, he declared: "In my opinion our success in Georgia depends upon the prompt action of South Carolina. If she goes out promptly her action will cause a thrill to pass through the great popular heart of Georgia and we shall certainly succeed in the election and follow her but if she passes an ordinance to take effect at some future day we are beat and all is lost." This note, he added, was not for publication, but Cobb might show it to members of the South Carolina convention.[6]

Mrs. Brown's brother, William S. Grisham, had written that he himself had been elected a delegate to the South Carolina convention. Brown replied, urging immediate action. If South Carolina failed to act at once "we may be beat in Georgia." This would leave South Carolina pledged to go out in February or March, "and she might have to back down in disgrace." On the other hand, immediate secession would strike such a thrill through the heart of Georgia that she would follow immediately. "Delay is full of danger. Act promptly and you will find in Georgia a faithful ally. Falter. . . and we may not act and you are disgraced. We hope to see you here within a few days from the Independent Republic of South Carolina."[7]

Still not satisfied, Governor Brown wrote directly to the governor of South Carolina. "While I have no right, nor wish to interfere in the internal affairs of South Carolina," he explained, "I feel a deep interest in this question. . . . if South Carolina dallies or delays . . . the so called cooperationists will carry Georgia. All depends upon your action. Go out immediately and we shall certainly follow. Your delay defeats us and all is lost. If you are attacked you will find in the people of Georgia a faithful ally. I shall permit no reenforcements of troops in the Forts of the United States in Georgia till the question is settled." The South

6 December 15, 1860, in Cobb Papers.
7 December 15, 1860, in Brockman Collection.

Carolina governor was free to show this letter to members of the convention.[8] It is not known what influence Brown's letter had upon the South Carolina convention, but it is certain that South Carolina's immediate secession greatly influenced the selection of delegates to the Georgia convention.

On December 27 a group of secessionists in Atlanta was still celebrating South Carolina's withdrawal from the Union. Francis S. Bartow of Savannah was speaking. In the midst of the speech a message arrived stating that Fort Moultrie in Charleston harbor had been evacuated and the federal garrison moved into much stronger Fort Sumter. South Carolina had called up two regiments of troops. The Atlanta audience broke into wild cheers. Bartow, folding his arms across his chest, remarked: "Yes, while you *talk of co-operation*, you hear the thunders of the cannon, and the clash of sabers reach you from South Carolina. Is this gallant, noble state of South Carolina, that had the boldness to take the lead in this matter, to be left to the cold calculating of the co-operationists of Georgia?"[9] The crowd thundered, "Never! Never!" (Bartow would lose his life in the first real battle of the Civil War.)

Little did the cheering crowd know of the seriousness of the problem that now faced South Carolina. Governor Francis Pickens rushed a letter to Governor Brown. Standing alone as it now was, what course should South Carolina take while Federal fortifications within her border were being strengthened? Brown replied immediately. He could understand the irritation the people of South Carolina felt at being menaced by a Federal force within their border. Yet, from a political viewpoint, he feared the beginning of actual war during the Buchanan administration would be unwise. An attack by South Carolina would cause the northern Democrats to rally to Buchanan's support and join the front ranks. Then when Lincoln came in he and his Republicans would take up where Buchanan left off.

On the other hand, Brown reasoned, if it was left to Lincoln to commence hostilities, the Democrats "for the purpose of thwarting his views and policy" would refuse their support and divide the country. Further, if Lincoln should begin hostilities soon after taking office, he would be at his weakest, having already offended many party leaders

8 Brown to Governor of South Carolina, December 15, 1860, *ibid*.
9 Atlanta *Daily Intelligencer*, December 29, 1860.

in dispensing the patronage. Time would be required to rebuild his strength. "Of course I do not wish to be understood as attempting to influence your decision," Governor Brown concluded, "should you be of opinion that the interest and honor of S. Carolina requires a different course."[10] South Carolina did not attack Sumter immediately.

The campaign for the selection of delegates to what became the "secession" convention in Georgia was very spirited with the tide running heavily in favor of immediate disunion. Scores of mass meetings were held and resolutions adopted. Most favored immediate action but a few strongly opposed it.[11] Almost daily some well-known Georgians made prominent announcements endorsing immediate secession. From Washington, Howell Cobb declared that the Union established by the Founding Fathers based upon equality and justice would soon be replaced by one based upon sectional hatred. Consequently, the only hope for the preservation of southern honor and safety was immediate secession.

"I entertain no doubt either of your right or duty to secede from the Union. Arouse, then, all your manhood for the great work before you, and be prepared on that day to announce and maintain your independence out of the Union, for you will never again have equality and justice within it."[12] Cobb resigned his position in President Buchanan's cabinet, immediately returned to Georgia, and began active participation in the campaign.

Also from Washington, Senator Toombs telegraphed the Savannah *Morning News*, "I tell you upon the faith of a true man that all further looking to the North for security for your constitutional rights ought to be instantly abandoned. It is fraught with nothing but ruin to yourselves and your posterity. Secession by the fourth of March next should be thundered from the ballot-box by the unanimous vote of Georgia on the second day of January next. Such a voice will be your best guarantee for liberty, security, tranquility, and glory."[13] On the day before the

10 Brown to Governor Francis Pickens, January 2, 1861, "Governors Letter Book, 1847–1861," pp. 767–68, Georgia State Archives.
11 For excerpts from many of these resolutions see Avery, *History of Georgia*, 135–37.
12 Ulrich B. Phillips, *Georgia and State Rights* (Washington, 1902), 197; Cobb to People of Georgia, December 6, 1860, Milledgeville *Federal Union*, December 18, 1860.
13 Published on December 24, 1860, and quickly copied by other newspapers.

election Toombs telegraphed the Augusta *True Democrat* announcing the resignation of the remaining southern members of the president's cabinet. "Mr. Holt of Kentucky, our bitter foe, has been made Secretary of War. Fort Pulaski is in danger. The abolitionists are defiant!"[14]

Even venerable former governor Wilson Lumpkin was induced to break his long silence on public issues and endorse immediate secession. Writing from Athens on December 14, 1860, he explained "I am forced to the conclusion that we of the South cannot save the Federal Union. We are a minority. The hireling States could save the Union, but they will not. . . . Under all the existing circumstances, I believe the best hope of prosperity left to all the slave holding states, is to secede from our present Federal Union at once, without delay, and as soon as may be, form a new and Independent Confederacy, allowing none but those recognizing the right of holding negro slaves within their limits a place in the new Confederacy."[15]

The election did not result in the overwhelming victory expected by those favoring immediate secession. Apparently the more cautious remained silent and voted against secession. Those candidates who later voted in favor of immediate secession received 50,243; those against 37,123. There was evidence of a voting pattern throughout the state, yet there were many exceptions. The upcountry, piney woods, and old cotton areas registered heavy opposition. The coastal plains, new cotton areas, and cities cast heavy votes in favor. Apparently the more prominent leaders exercised considerable influence in their home sections. Brown's appeal to north Georgia small farmers and mountain folk definitely frightened many into support of secession.[16]

While disunionists were whipping up secession sentiment throughout the state, Governor Brown and the legislature were moving in the same direction. On most points they were in general agreement, but they again disagreed violently on the bank issues. The election of Lincoln and talk of secession and possible war seriously deranged business activities and struck alarm in banking circles. Again bankers and their lobbyists descended upon Milledgeville urging legislative relief. Again the General Assembly reacted favorably and passed an act

14 Quoted in Phillips, *Toombs*, 215.
15 Milledgeville *Federal Union*, January 1, 1861.
16 For chart of votes see Phillips, *State Rights*, 209.

relieving the banks from all penalties imposed by previous legislation for refusal or failure to redeem their notes in specie. This relief was to continue until December 1, 1861.

For the same reasons as expressed in his 1857 bank veto, Governor Brown also vetoed this relief bill. He could not subscribe to the contention that suspension of specie payment was more for the benefit of the people than the banks. "The constant efforts made by bank men to practice upon popular credulity, by the declaration of this strange absurdity, are not a little remarkable," he averred. If this were true, why was it that when a suspension measure was up for consideration the lobbies were crowded with bank presidents, directors, and stockholders "constantly besieging" the legislators with "clamorous appeals for favorable action while their banks kept up the excitement by refusing to extend to the people the smallest accommodations." Why was it also that these same gentlemen never bothered to protect the people's interest by spending money to secure the passage of bills other than suspension measures? Further, if suspension was for the benefit of the people, why did not farmers and laborers demand payment in suspended notes rather than specie? The truth was that the masses of the people saw no need for suspension and did not desire the passage of this bill.[17]

The legislature not only passed the bill over the governor's veto but also objected to the language used in the message. Professing to see in the message an insinuation of legislative bribery, some members pushed through a resolution requesting an explanation from the governor. Apparently ignoring the House, Brown explained to the Senate that he intended no such a charge. His language was "general, and intended to be directed against what is usually known as lobby influence, when gentlemen leave their homes and spend money for traveling expenses, tavern bills etc for the purpose of hanging around the General Assembly to try to influence the minds of members so as to procure the passage of a particular bill. . . . I doubt not upon a calm review of the language used that each Senator will say that he sees in it no imputation upon himself." Brown sent no reply to the House.

The House, incensed at being ignored, passed unanimously another resolution declaring that in his intercourse with that body the

17 Milledgeville *Federal Union*, December 4, 1860.

governor had failed to maintain the "dignity of deportment, which becomes the chief Magistrate of Georgia." Further, he had evaded the charges he could not sustain, attempted to deceive, and used language "disrespectful to this House."

By this time the governor was becoming irritated. He denied having violated any privilege of the House, adding, "As the House, in debate upon said resolution, compromitted its dignity by permitting one or more of its members to make a personal attack upon the Executive . . . and to descend to low, personal abuse, unbecoming to character of a legislator, no rules of privilege known to parliamentary usage, entitled the House to a reply. . . . After the disclaimer made in my message to the Senate . . . should any member of the House feel conscious of guilt, and persist in applying to himself a charge of bribery or dishonesty, I have no wish to become his public prosecutor."[18]

Brown's distrust of banks was a part of his growing concern over corporate power in general. "A radical reform in our legislature is imperatively necessary, but I fear it will be very difficult to bring it about," he had confided to an editor friend a few months earlier. "Corporate power rules the state, and is constantly on the increase. Unless the masses of the people can be aroused upon this subject, and induced to take the power into their own hands by hurling corporate *tools* from place and power there is no remedy."[19]

On the subject of military preparation, the governor and General Assembly, both looking toward secession, found much in common. The office of adjutant general was created, $1 million appropriated for military purposes, and the governor authorized to raise ten thousand troops. Governor Brown immediately appointed Major Henry C. Wayne of the United States Army to the office of adjutant general, and began signing his own dispatches as "Commander-in-Chief."[20]

For the past two years Governor Brown had been encouraging the formation of volunteer corps and making every effort to arm them. Corps were created faster than they could be armed and the governor was sometimes embarrassed to tell his friends he could not give im-

18 *House Journal*, 1860, pp. 197, 198.
19 Brown to James H. Bethune, March 25, 1860, in Brockman Collection.
20 Allen D. Candler (ed.), *The Confederate Records of the State of Georgia*, 6 vols. (Atlanta, 1909–11), II, 8, hereinafter cited as *C. R. Ga.*

mediate aid.[21] The 1859 legislature did not pass the commutation tax suggested, but it did appropriate $75,000 for the purchase of arms. With these funds in hand the governor sent Cass County iron manufacturer Mark A. Cooper north to contract for arms. He was also to contact the secretary of war and request an advance on the quota of arms due Georgia for the next year.[22] The governor also entered into contract with D. C. Hodgkins & Son of Macon for 250 rifles, 700 revolvers, and 700 sabers, payment for which he promised from future appropriations. And with the new appropriation of $1 million he was able to report to the House on November 17, 1860, that he had ordered 2,000 Sharp's rifles. Brown also wrote Secretary of War John B. Floyd requesting samples of equipment other than arms used by soldiers with a view to having the same manufactured in Georgia. The quartermaster general endorsed on this request that such items could be furnished without inconvenience and noted the cost. But William Maynadier, captain of ordnance, added a second endorsement that Georgia's quota had been exhausted and such items could not be sold. However, he suggested a source where they might be purchased. On November 30, Governor Brown appointed Paul J. Semmes agent for the state to handle all military purchases and pay for the same in 6 percent bonds.[23]

Confident that the coming convention would vote secession, Governor Brown turned his attention toward Fort Pulaski which stood guard on the mouth of the Savannah River. The fort was not garrisoned,

---

21 Brown to Lucius Gartrell, December 20, 1859; Brown to A. M. Wallace, December 20, 1859; Brown to B. F. McDonald, December 29, 1859; Brown to M. A. Cooper, December 29, 1859, all in Brockman Collection.

22 Brown to John W. Anderson, April 1, 1860; Brown to M. A. Cooper, March 29, July 24, 1860, in Hargrett Collection.

23 *C. R. Ga.*, II, 3–5, III, 3; Brown to D. C. Hodgkins and Son, June 28, July 6, 27, September 8, 1860, in Hargrett Collection. In reply to an inquiry from Governor A. B. Moore of Alabama, Brown wrote: "We have, in all, some twelve to fifteen thousand stands of *small arms*, of various kinds, but mostly of approved patterns and makes, consisting of Minnie *Muskets*, *Rifles* (U.S.), *Colts* and *Adams pistols* and common U.S. Muskets. We have fifty or sixty cannon, including some now under contract, and we expect soon to receive. We have now sixteen hundred Sharps Patent Rifled Carbines; and have just closed a contract for three hundred Maynard Rifles and seven hundred Maynard Carbines. All the Minnie Rifles we have heretofore purchased have been new, but we recently bought 5,000 old U.S. Muskets (smoothe bore) which had been altered from Flint & Steel lock percussions. We got them at $2.50 each; and they are said to be good guns of the kind." Brown to Moore, December 18, 1860, "Governors Letterbook," Georgia State Archives.

contained few guns, and was in poor repair, yet its location gave it great importance. If strongly garrisoned, it would control Georgia's principal access to the sea. The federal government had not surrendered the forts in "independent" South Carolina and there was rumor that all southern forts were soon to be reinforced. Then came the news that John Floyd had resigned as secretary of war and had been succeeded by Joseph Holt, who was believed to be unfriendly to the South and favorable to aggressive action.

Governor Brown followed these developments closely. He did not wait to be reminded by Toombs that Fort Pulaski was in danger. To prevent possible regarrisoning by federal forces, he decided to send in state troops. On January 1, 1861, he went in person to Savannah and on the following day ordered Colonel Alexander R. Lawton, commanding the First Regiment of Volunteers, to occupy the fort, garrison it, and place it in good repair. According to the governor's own account, before making his decision he discussed the matter with military men, including Colonel William J. Hardee, who was still in the United States service. Most of those consulted advised against immediate seizure. The governor finally replied, "I take the responsibility," and ordered action.

Proud of his decision, Governor Brown immediately wired the governors of Alabama and Florida urging them to take similar action against forts within their states. Both replied that they would. He also telegraphed the governors of Mississippi and Louisiana, and after returning to Milledgeville, he urged the governor of North Carolina to seize the forts in his harbors.[24]

Excitement ran high in Savannah. There was much competition among military companies as to which would participate in the bloodless conquest of Fort Pulaski. Ladies sent in refreshments, including a huge cake decorated with the word *Secession*. On the governor's return trip to the capital he was greeted by cheering crowds at each railroad station.[25] "Governor Brown in this act has been guided by motives of peace, and a desire to save bloodshed in case hostilities actually begin," commented the *Federal Union*. "For his promptness and energy in this crisis, Gov. Brown deserves the gratitude of every citizen of

24 For documents relating to the seizure, see *C. R. Ga.*, II, 9–19.
25 Avery, *History of Georgia*, 145–47.

Georgia."[26] No doubt this view was shared by a majority of the people of Georgia. No one seemed concerned that, since Georgia was still in the Union, the governor's action might come within the constitutional definition of treason.

Upon his return to Milledgeville on January 5, Governor Brown found waiting for him John Gill Shorter, an agent from Alabama sent by Governor Albert B. Moore to consult on the probable course that should be taken by the cotton states. Three days later he dispatched John W. A. Sanford with a private and confidential letter to Governor Moore. Brown suggested the "expediency of taking immediate possession of the fortifications and works at Pensacola." He was aware that this would be a bold move but he thought it "better to look danger full in the face, than by inaction to give our enemies the advantage." Pensacola was in a key position controlling much of the commerce of the Gulf; therefore, in view of the attitude at Washington it should not be allowed to remain in federal possession. Since Florida alone might not possess a force adequate for this undertaking, Brown further suggested joint operation by Georgia and Alabama on a quota basis. He had sent Thomas Butler King to confer with the governor of Florida. No southern fort should be left in United States possession, he urged.

Sanford also carried with him a memorandum, prepared by Adjutant General H. C. Wayne, giving military details about the Pensacola fortifications. "Shrewd management, stratagem in all matters connected with the enterprise from its inception to its execution will be necessary," the adjutant advised. However, since such an important naval station was usually kept "well supplied with necessary materials," it would be a rich prize besides its strategic value.[27] By the time Sanford arrived in Montgomery, Alabama was busy with its secession convention. Brown's plan was not implemented.

On the eve of the meeting of the convention Governor Brown was determined and confident. "Georgia will not hesitate to follow the noble example of her Southern Sisters around her," he assured the governor of Alabama. "They may exterminate us if they have the power, but conquer us they never can." On the same day he also wrote the

26 January 8, 1851.
27 Shorter to Brown, January 3, 1861; Brown to Shorter, January 5, 1861, *C. R. Ga.*, III, 3, 13; Brown to Moore, January 8, 1861, in Hargrett Collection.

governor of Kentucky, who had suggested to him a plan for "adjusting the difficulties growing out of the slavery question." He liked the plan, Brown replied, but he had no hope that the free states would agree to "give these guarantees while the Southern States remain in the Union." What propositions those free states might agree to after they had "reaped the harvest of bitter fruits" that would result from "their wicked labor" after the cotton states had seceded could "only be ascertained by the developments of the future." At any rate, since three states had seceded and would soon be followed by four others, "I therefore consider it now too late for your proposition to arrest the secession movement."[28]

Prior to the assembling of the Georgia convention in Milledgeville on January 16, 1861, Alabama, Florida, and Mississippi had joined South Carolina in secession. This "secession" convention was not only the most important assemblage in the history of the state, its membership was the most distinguished. Few leaders of any political group were absent. Governor Brown, Howell Cobb, and Charles J. Jenkins were not delegates, but they were invited to honored seats on the floor. Never before had the state of Georgia occupied so important a position. If it voted secession, the movement would undoubtedly continue to spread; should it vote either against or for "cooperation" with the border states, secession would suffer a serious setback. Within the past month Governor Brown had been the most conspicuous leader in the secession movement. One can only speculate as to what might have been the result had he remained loyal to his earlier position as a cooperationist.

There was no doubt that the convention would vote secession, but the cooperationists were not ready to abandon the fight. Eugenius A. Nisbet, moderate turned secessionist, introduced resolutions declaring in favor of immediate secession and providing for the appointment of a committee to draft such an ordinance. Herschel V. Johnson countered with lengthy resolutions reviewing developments and declaring Georgia's intention not to remain in the Union unless her rights were secured, but calling for a convention of slave states to meet in Atlanta on February 16. However, after considerable speaking, highlighted by Nisbet, Thomas R. R. Cobb and Robert Tombs for immediate secession, and Ben Hill, Alexander Stephens, and Johnson for postponement and

28 January 12, 1861, "Governors Letterbook," Georgia State Archives.

cooperation, Nisbet's resolutions were adopted, and Georgia voted herself out of the Union 208 to 89.[29] Most of the eighty-nine who voted against the resolutions later signed the ordinance.

One Georgian who lived through those critical days later summed up the situation: "Had the milder policy prevailed, and Georgia been in the role of peacemaker, there is no telling how the end would have been. The conservative course was the wise one. It was too grave an issue and too awful a result to have been decided hastily, and not to have exhausted every possible means of friendly adjustment in the Union. But a higher power was ruling the occasion. The great and mysterious ends of Providence were in process of fulfillment. The frenzy of revolution was in the people: the counsels of prudence were subordinated to the honorable resentment of a chivalric section, and the work of the emancipation of four million slaves progressed to its bloody and final consummation."[30] Governor Brown had exerted all his influence to prevent the success of the "conservative course."

The convention approved Brown's seizure of Fort Pulaski, authorized the raising of two regiments of troops for probable use by a southern confederacy, selected delegates to a southern convention to meet in Montgomery on February 4, 1861, and adjourned to meet in Savannah at a later date to devise changes in the constitution as had been made necessary by secession.[31]

29 Percy S. Flippin, *Herschel V. Johnson of Georgia: State Rights Unionist* (Richmond, 1931), 179 ff; Johnston and Browne, *Stephens*, 380.
30 Avery, *History of Georgia*, 153.
31 Ralph A. Wooster, "The Georgia Secession Convention," *Georgia Historical Quarterly*, XL, 22; T. Conn Bryan, "The Secession of Georgia," *Georgia Historical Quarterly*, XXXI, 89 ff. The journal of the convention is printed in *C. R. Ga.*, I, 212 ff.

Chapter VIII

Would That I Could Accompany You

GOVERNOR BROWN shared the enthusiasm expressed by the wave of cheers and salutes that spread over Georgia following the announcement of secession; he too believed the state to be on the eve of greatness and was pleased to be in position to direct its new course. Among the shouts was also a demand that the United States flag no longer be permitted to wave over any portion of Georgia territory. This too met the governor's approval, for his attention was already directed toward the federal arsenal at Augusta.

Within three days following the passage of the Ordinance of Secession he was in Augusta. On January 23, speaking through Aide-de-Camp Henry R. Jackson, he demanded that Captain Arnold Elzey withdraw his United States force and turn over to the state of Georgia all property under his command. According to the law of nations, Elzey was advised, an attempt to maintain troops on foreign soil was an act of hostility. Therefore, "anxious to cultivate the most amicable relations with the United States Government," the governor requested immediate withdrawal. An answer would be expected by 9 A.M. the following day.

Elzey wired the secretary of war for instructions. Secretary Holt replied that although Brown's summons was "harsh and peremptory," no desperate defense should be made. If the choice was surrender or starvation, "stipulate for honorable terms, and a free passage by water with your company to New York."

Meanwhile some eight hundred state militia and minutemen had been ordered to Augusta. "Such a turn out of citizen soldiers was never witnessed in this city before," reported the Augusta *Constitutionalist*. "The ranks of the companies were full, and scores of citizens were doing all in their power to borrow uniforms and guns."

But there was to be no violence. Shortly before the deadline Captain Elzey requested an interview. There was considerable show of pomp, however, as the governor and seven officers of various ranks rode towards the arsenal for the conference. Terms were quickly agreed upon. United States troops withdrew and surrendered United States property to the state of Georgia. The property consisted of "two twelve-pound howitzers, two cannon, twenty-two thousand muskets and rifles," and a considerable quantity of ammunition.[1] Six months later, Captain Elzey would be one of the heroes at the Battle of Manassas as a Confederate colonel.

While Governor Brown was yet in Augusta, a still more spirited controversy was brewing, although the amount of property involved was not so great. In order to meet its contract with the state of Georgia, D. C. Hodgkins & Sons of Macon had purchased two hundred muskets in New York. As these guns were being loaded on the *Monticello* for shipment to Savannah on January 22, 1861, they were seized by New York police and deposited in the state arsenal. The Macon firm appealed to Governor Brown for assistance. On February 2, Brown wired Governor E. D. Morgan of New York: As Governor of Georgia I hereby demand that the guns be immediately delivered to G. B. Lamar of New York, who is hereby appointed my agent to receive them. I trust no similar outrage may be perpetrated in future." The tone of this dispatch indicates that Brown was not in a pleasant frame of mind.

Two days passed without reply from the New York governor. Brown wired the operator at Albany, New York, inquiring whether or not his telegram had been delivered and was advised it had. Realizing that his demand had been ignored, Brown immediately dispatched to Aide-de-Camp Jackson at Savannah an order for reprisal. "I am determined to protect the persons and property of the citizens of this state against all such lawless violence, at all hazards," he explained. "In doing

---

1 Augusta *Daily Constitutionalist*, January 25, 1861. The correspondence is printed in Avery, *History of Georgia*, 161–62.

so, I will, if necessary, meet force with force." Jackson was instructed to call upon Colonel Lawton for such force as was needed to seize "every ship now in the harbor of Savannah belonging to citizens of New York." Jackson had Lawton seize the *Kirby, Adjuster, Golden Lead, Julia,* and the *Golden Murray.*

In the meantime, Brown had received from Governor Morgan a request for verification of the authenticity of the demand. This did nothing toward improving Brown's disposition, but he replied in a long letter of explanation. He saw no need for lengthy correspondence, he declared. The situation required "action, not lengthy diplomacy. . . . The outrage was a public one. Citizens of this state have been robbed of their property . . . . I have demanded its re-delivery to its owners." The vessels seized would be held until his demand was met. If any of the vessels or cargoes belonged to New York citizens who had respect for justice, truth, and equal rights, he regretted any inconvenience that might be caused them. "I trust your Excellency may have no difficulty in arriving at the conclusion that this communication is 'official' and 'veritable.'"

Before this letter reached New York, Gazaway B. Lamar wired: "The arms have been put at the command of their owners here; please release all vessels." Brown instructed Jackson to release the vessels immediately. However, when Lamar called upon the New York superintendent of police for delivery of the arms the superintendent had changed his mind. The arms would not be released. Furthermore, he proposed to seize any other items that were considered "contraband." He did not say contraband of what. There was no war.

Lamar wired Brown of the change, and the much irritated governor ordered Jackson to make other seizures double the value of those vessels recently released. These vessels were to be held until the guns were actually shipped and beyond the reach of New York authorities.

Privately, he explained to Jackson "I feel greatly provoked at this bad faith and deception. . . . If you can get a steamer or two which are registered as New York vessels I shall be much gratified." When seizures had been accomplished, Jackson was to publish the names and the instructions under which the seizures were made. "I regret to disturb the commerce of our people," the governor explained, "but our honor as a state imperatively demands the proposed action and I cannot stop to count the cost. . . . When I have decided a question my rule is to act promptly."

Jackson seized the *Julia A. Hallack*, the *Martha J. Ward*, and the *Adjuster*. But upon learning that the *Adjuster* was loaded with cotton belonging to British and Russian subjects, Brown ordered it released. He further instructed that unless the property of which Georgians had been robbed was released in the meantime, the other seized vessels were to be sold at auction on March 25, 1861. The money received would be used to compensate for the property lost.

The vessels were advertised but not sold; both the guns and the vessels were released prior to March 25, and Governor Brown was much pleased; he thought he had taught the "abolition robbers to respect our rights." He proudly reported to his brother-in-law, "I presume you have noticed by the newspapers that no federal flag now waves over the soil of Georgia." He trusted also that he had taught New York authorities a lesson in distinguishing between "mine and thine."[2]

The governor's ego received an additional boost when a barrel arrived containing a plaster bust of himself. Some months earlier he had agreed to permit H. Dexter, a traveling sculptor from the North, to do a marble likeness. The plaster cast was a sample. Some of his friends were not too impressed with the "likeness," Brown wrote Dexter, but he supposed the marble would be more perfect. "If I take it I wish it finished in the best style of the art and pronounced by competent judges as perfect a performance as any in your collection."

The sculptor had suggested that the legislature purchase the bust for the state. Brown liked the idea and would consider it "a very high compliment, such as has never been paid to one of my predecessors," yet he could not himself suggest such an action. The legislature would convene again in November, he explained. "Should you as the sculptor think proper to lay the matter before them I can have no objection."

Dexter suggested that this bust would be among the last of the governors of the disintegrating United States. This gave Brown an opportunity to sound off. "The Government will never be reconstructed. Should the Federal Government at Washington be guilty of the mad-

2 *C. R. Ga.*, II, 26–29; Milledgeville *Southern Federal Union*, February 26, 1861; Brown to H. R. Jackson, February 15, 21, March 2, 1861; Brown to William S. Grisham, February 14, 1861, in Brockman Collection.

ness of attempting to coerce the cotton states back into the Union we may have a long and bloody war which will greatly injure both sections but the object never will be accomplished. The spirit of our people is fully aroused and is indomitable. You may exterminate us if you have the power but conquer us while we live you never will. We are generally out of debt and have vast resources. If need be we are prepared to sacrifice all in the struggle if forced upon us. Your people are mistaken about the true state of things here. We are united and vast numbers of our slaves are anxious to help us fight you if you come."[3]

The attempted "rape of arms" became front page news throughout the nation, and Governor Brown was praised and damned without restraint. G. B. Lamar, although he carried out Brown's instructions, did not approve of the governor's action. "The interruption of vessels by Gov. Brown causes more damage to Georgia than to N. York," he wrote Howell Cobb. "He ought to seize debts or some other property if he retaliates at all—which I think inexpedient at this time."[4] But another Lamar thought differently. "Joe Brown . . . is my kind of a man," wrote C. A. R. Lamar, "takes responsibilities & don't care a damn for consequences. . . . Hurrah then for Joe Brown."[5]

"Three cheers for Joseph E. Brown, the man for the times," exclaimed the Augusta *Evening Dispatch*.[6] The governor "feels impelled by the highest sense of duty, to protect the rights of our citizens against all such free booters and marauders as the New York police, by the use of every legal means at his command. From this duty he will not shrink," reasoned the *Southern Federal Union*.[7]

While Governor Brown was feuding with New York authorities, representatives from the seceding states met in Montgomery and formed a southern confederacy. There was still a widespread belief that secession could be accomplished peaceably, but judging from Brown's aggressive military efforts he did not subscribe to that belief.

---

3 Brown to H. Dexter, February 22, 1861, in Brockman Collection. Brown kept the plaster model. When Sherman's troops approached the capital in 1864, someone hid the bust under a woodpile. After Brown's death in 1894, it was sent to Italy, and a marble copy was made by William Waldo, Jr., in 1896. The photograph and note in Spalding Collection.
4 February 22, 1861, Phillips, *Correspondence*, 545–46.
5 C. A. R. Lamar to John B. Lamar, February 7, 1861, in Cobb Papers.
6 February 22, 1861.
7 February 26, 1861.

The recent legislature had appropriated $ one million for military purposes and authorized the governor to accept the services of ten thousand volunteers, and the convention had provided for the raising of two regiments for possible service to a southern confederacy. Without waiting for the formation of a confederacy, Governor Brown purchased sixteen hundred rifles from the Sharp Rifle Manufacturing Company of Hartford, Connecticut, paying for them with fifty state bonds of five-hundred-dollar denominations. He entered into contract with a Pittsburgh iron company for a number of cannon but was never able to get delivery. He then turned to the Tredegar Iron Works of Richmond for the manufacture of arms, a contract that would be later taken over by the Confederate government.[8]

Governor Brown also began immediately to appoint officers for the two regiments. William J. Hardee and William H. T. Walker, both Georgians who had resigned from the United States Army, were made colonels; Charles J. Williams (Muscogee) and E. W. Chastain (Fannin) lieutenant colonels; Lafayette W. McLaws (U.S.A.), Edward Harden (Whitfield), William M. Gardner (U.S.A.), and Alfred Cumming (U.S.A.) majors. "Our fine friend" John Jones was made quartermaster general and S. J. Smith (Towns), an original Brown-for-governor man, was made assistant quartermaster. Those appointed were either recent members of the United States Army or personal friends of the governor. Harden and Chastain had held important positions with the Western and Atlantic Railroad. In appointing these two men, the governor not only wished to reward friends but was also seeking to influence opinion in the mountain regions. To Chastain he privately suggested, "I trust you might be able to enlist a very considerable number in the mountains."[9]

Reports of widespread opposition in the upcountry regions were of much concern to the governor. He was clearly disappointed at his own influence in that area. "There is more difficulty in the upper part of the state . . . than was at first anticipated," he confided to Secretary of State Robert Toombs. "The results in Va. & Tenn. and the slave action of North Carolina have given confidence to those who are still for the

8 *C. R. Ga.*, II, 29; Avery, *History of Georgia*, 186.
9 Brown to Harden, February 2, 1861; Brown to Williams, February 4, 1861; Brown to Smith, February 4, 1861; Brown to Chastain, February 4, 1861, all in Brockman Collection.

Union, and there are influences at work to try to cause a division of the state. It is said there is an association of very considerable strength, having private meetings and taking secret obligations to stand by the Union in case of war. . . . There is more difficulty than I at first supposed."[10]

Brown's fears were well founded. "General" Harrison W. Riley of Lumpkin County declared he would lead a force in defense of the United States Mint at Dahlonega and a United States flag was raised in Jasper, Pickens County, in defiance of the Ordinance of Secession. Many friends urged Brown to take drastic action, but he wisely chose another course. "General" Riley, illiterate and eccentric, enjoyed considerable local popularity, but was evidently quite susceptible to flattery. Brown, working through friends rather than directly, let it be known that from his long friendship with Riley he could not believe the "General" would do anything rash or dishonorable. At the same time he notified the superintendent of the Dahlonega mint that he was taking possession in the name of the independent state of Georgia. There was no opposition.

The flag incident in Jasper was ignored by the governor. Instead of taking direction action against the opposition, he sought to increase his number of friends. It was reported that military companies from the upcountry were given special consideration in the distribution of arms and equipment. The news of favored treatment could be relayed by soldiers to friends back home.[11]

The appointment of officers was an easier task than filling company ranks with men. The governor withheld public announcement of his intention until officers were appointed; he did not want to be deluged with applications. Officers were then sent into the field to recruit men.

On March 1, 1861, the Confederate secretary of war, Leroy Pope Walker, sent to the Confederate governors an announcement that the president "assumes control of all military operations in your State having reference to or connected with questions between your State and powers foreign to it." The governors were requested to furnish an inventory of all arms and munitions acquired from the United States and also any other arms and munitions the state might wish to "turn

10 Brown to Toombs, February 28, 1861, *ibid.*
11 Avery, *History of Georgia*, 186–89.

over and make chargeable to this Government." Enclosed was a copy of the act of Congress authorizing the president to raise a provisional army.[12]

On March 9 Secretary Walker sent to the governors his first call for provisional forces for the Confederate states. Georgia was requested to furnish 1,000 men for Fort Pulaski and another 1,000 for Pensacola. Troops were to be furnished without public announcement if possible "to keep our movements concealed from the Government of the United States." As soon as troops arrived at their destination, they would be mustered into Confederate service.[13] This was the beginning of a situation that Brown thoroughly disliked but would be unable to prevent: when Georgia troops were mustered into Confederate service the governor lost all control over them.

To Secretary Walker's call Brown replied by wire: "I will furnish you two regiments of 1,000 each as soon as they can possibly be organized."[14] On the same day he explained by letter the condition of his regiments. He had appointed a full complement of officers for the two regiments but a total of only 450 men had been recruited. He wished to know whether the secretary would accept the regiments with their officers, but leave behind for recruiting those officers whose companies were not yet filled. "I cannot, in justice to the privates who have enlisted, tender the regiments unless they are received with the officers which I have appointed, as the recruits have nearly all been obtained by the officers appointed from civil life, with the understanding that they are to go under them." If the secretary would accept the regiments on these terms, "they are now at your service and subject to your order."[15]

Citing provisions of the law, Walker replied that complete regiments could be received, but he could not receive officers without men. He suggested that these officers be used to recruit "a volunteer force for twelve months amply sufficient to make up the defficiency." He regretted that it was not within his power to accept anything less than an organized company.[16] Brown tried again, offering to furnish "250 recruits

12 *C. R. Ga.*, III, 17.
13 *Ibid.*, 20.
14 *Ibid.*, 22.
15 *Ibid.*, 23.
16 *Ibid.*, 24.

and 750 volunteers" for both Pulaski and Pensacola. He did not, however, have sufficient equipment for volunteers. Walker replied: "I can only repeat what I have already said in previous letters."[17]

Whether or not it was at the request of Secretary Walker is unknown, but Secretary Toombs journeyed to Savannah for a conference with Governor Brown. Before hearing from Toombs, Walker wired Brown for a definite answer as to furnishing the organized troops requested. Toombs reported Brown's "temper and objects good." The governor would furnish troops for Pensacola, but there might be some delay for accoutrements. Walker agreed to a short delay and again warned that these volunteer units, as in the case of the regiments, must be completely organized before being mustered into Confederate service. As for the regiments in question, Walker would not give an inch; neither would Brown. Toombs wired Walker: "Can do nothing on your basis to arrange military affairs with Governor B."[18]

When Brown sent out his request for volunteer companies it was reported that 250 tendered their services. Only ten companies could be selected. Selection was made in order of priority of tender; the only exception being that of Captain Harris' company from Dahlonega. The governor wanted North Georgia units in the group.[19] Macon was designated as the place of rendezvous. Secretary Walker, assuming rendezvous would be at Columbus, arranged for transportation from that point. Brown insisted on Macon. Walker wired, "Very well." Transportation would be furnished from Macon for three hundred men daily. The troops would be mustered into Confederate service at Pensacola. Brown insisted they be mustered in at Macon, explaining that if troops left the limits of Georgia without first becoming a part of the Confederate force they would not be under any law whatsoever. Officers of Georgia forces objected to leaving the state under that condition. Walker refused. Such an arrangement would be to make an exceptional case of the Georgia troops; troops from other states were to be mustered in at Pensacola. This time Brown gave in. "After much difficulty I have succeeded in getting consent of the troops to go to Pensacola to be mustered into the service," he informed Walker. A

17 *Ibid.*, 27, 30.
18 *Ibid.*, 31, 32, 34.
19 Avery, *History of Georgia*, 188.

regiment consisting of ten companies and a battalion of four companies were being tendered for a period not to exceed twelve months.[20] By this time most of the units were in Macon. From the pettiness evidenced by both sides it would appear that Walker was not particularly eager to increase the Confederate forces; neither was Brown eager to help him.

Commander in Chief Brown went to Macon to welcome the troops. Mrs. Howell Cobb, visiting in Macon, made a typical Cobb report. Governor Brown and his adjutant general were "here in full blast," she wrote her husband, the former "casting bread upon the waters which no doubt he expects will return to him next October." He had also extended his electioneering by permitting even privates to vote in the selection of regimental officers. There was much grumbling that such a course was illegal. There was much politicking and maneuvering among candidates for the offices. Mrs. Cobb also understood there had been "considerable private cursing down here at the expense of Brown and his Adjutant." Brown was quartered at the Lanier House and on one of his doors was the sign "Gov. Brown's parlor." During the previous evening he was serenaded with music and musket fire. Mrs. Cobb agreed with her son who sent word "I'm so glad Papa is out of politics, that I may talk as I please."[21]

Election of regimental officers was held on April 3. James M. Ramsey, a lieutenant, was elected colonel of the Independent Regiment of Georgia Volunteers, James O. Clarke was elected lieutenant colonel and George H. Thompson major. As commander in chief, Brown reviewed and addressed the troops on April 4. He sang the greatness of Georgia, past and present, and of her two great living statesmen—Vice-President Alexander H. Stephens and Secretary of State Robert Toombs. He expressed great confidence in the justice of the cause that led to secession and the formation of the Confederacy. "Would that I could accompany you," he exclaimed, "and share with you your toils, and participate with you in your glory! My whole soul is in this movement and my heart swells with emotions which I cannot utter, when I am obliged to bid you adieu and return to my field of labors elsewhere.[22]

As the Volunteer Regiment moved off to Pensacola, the two regiments of regulars, their ranks still far from filled, remained inactive.

20 C. R. Ga., III, 35–38.
21 April 3, 1861, in Cobb Papers.
22 Macon Daily Telegraph, April 3, 4, 5, 1861.

Would-be soldiers preferred to enlist in volunteer companies, so recruiting of regulars became more difficult and then came to a complete halt as a result of further pettiness on the part of Secretary Walker. Upon learning that Governor Brown was still recruiting men with the hope of transferring the regiments to the Confederate service, Walker called his attention to the act of Congress authorizing the raising of provisional forces. The act provided for the acceptance of "forces now in service of said State." As Walker interpreted it, the provision did not apply to forces recruited after the date of its passage. The purpose of the act, Walker further explained, was "to relieve the separate States . . . of the troops already levied by them." This being the case, he suggested to Governor Brown that "it might be well to consider the propriety of further enlistments."[23]

With the complete failure of the Confederate commission which had been sent to Washington to work out details for peaceful separation, the situation became grim. To many who had previously been hopeful, war now seemed inevitable. Up until this time Governor Brown, although busily preparing for war and enjoying his work, had professed to believe there would be no war. On April 1, 1861, he had confided to Thomas W. Thomas the belief that Lincoln would not dare make war for fear of "driving out the border states." However, he himself feared that if there was peaceful separation and the border states remained in the Union a strong reconstruction party would appear in Georgia. "A reunion with the old government, and especially with New England would in my opinion terminate in our disgrace and ruin. Reconstruction of the whole Union as it existed last November would in my opinion be a greater evil than war."[24]

The Fort Sumter affair put an end to such speculation, and when the border states began to secede, Governor Brown was filled with joy. To the president of the Virginia convention he wired: "A descendant of Virginia ancestry, as the representative of Georgia, I send greetings, and one hundred hearty cheers to the Old Dominion. May God who defends the right enable her to protect the Cradle of Liberty, and the Grave of Washington from abolition desecration."[25]

Even before the Fort Sumter affair, Confederate authorities at

23 *C. R. Ga.*, III, 36.
24 Brockman Collection.
25 *Ibid.*

Montgomery had apparently concluded that there would be war. Immediately following the failure of the mission to Washington, a call went to Confederate governors for additional troops. Georgia was requested to furnish three thousand volunteers, "to be drilled, equipped, and held in instant readiness."

Brown sent out a general order to the volunteer companies throughout the state inquiring which were ready and willing to be included in the requisition. To Secretary of War Walker he replied that the requisition would be met. However, before making final preparation, he wished a definite understanding. Still smarting from having to give in in the case of the Pensacola regiment, he wished it understood that no precedent had been established. The new troops must be mustered into Confederate service before leaving the state. "I have every wish to accommodate, and Georgia will at all times be ready to do her part, but she will insist on having her rights and wishes respected when she is claiming the recognition of a principle of justice to her troops, as well as of obvious propriety."[26]

On April 13, 1861, Secretary Walker made a definite call on Governor Brown for one thousand men to be sent to Fort Pulaski. If he still refused to furnish portions of the regular regiments that had completed organization according to Confederate requirements, then volunteer companies were requested. Brown was further reminded that he had not met the original requisition for troops, dated March 9.[27] "The troops will be furnished immediately," Brown wired Walker on April 13, and two days later he had ten companies of volunteers enroute to Savannah. Upon arrival, it was expected that these companies would be organized into a regiment, permitted to elect their regimental officers, mustered into Confederate service, and placed under command of General Alexander R. Lawton.[28] Fort Pulaski and other United States properties seized by Georgia had recently been transferred to control of the Confederate government, and Lawton had been made a Confederate brigadier general and placed in command at Fort Pulaski.

On April 15, Secretary Walker wired: "The news today indicates general war."[29] This was a logical conclusion; Fort Sumter had passed

26 C. R. Ga., III, 40, 46.
27 Ibid.
28 Ibid., 48, 49.
29 Ibid., 50.

into Confederate possession on April 13, and President Lincoln had called for 75,000 troops to put down "combinations too powerful to be suppressed by the ordinary course of judicial proceedings." On April 16, Walker called upon the governors for additional troops. Georgia was asked for another 5,000. "I will have the 8,000 troops in readiness very soon," Brown replied. "I have a division of volunteers nearly organized under act of the Legislature. Will you accept them by division and brigades? This would greatly facilitate."[30]

With Brown's announcement of organization of state forces by division and brigades another clash with Confederate authorities was inevitable. The governor was familiar with that portion of Section 4 of the act of Congress which stated that forces tendered by states "may be received, with their officers, by companies, battalions, or regiments."[31] Yet he continued to raise troops under the 10,000-man authorization by the recent legislature, cause them to be organized by brigades, and appoint general officers. He originally intended to create two divisions and appointed Henry R. Jackson and William H. T. Walker major generals and Paul J. Semmes (Muscogee) and William Phillips (Cobb) brigadiers. But progress of recruiting in competition with other types of recruiting was slow; consequently, only one division was organized, Wiliam H. T. Walker commanding.[32]

Secretary Walker hesitated and pondered the question relative to receiving brigades or divisions, acting as though he might be contemplating circumventing the law. Even W. H. T. Walker, signing himself "Major-General First Division Georgia Volunteers," had wired the secretary for an answer. Brown telegraphed again on April 27, urging the secretary to "please say definitely." Two days later Walker replied: "The organization of brigades and divisions belong to the President."[33] Brown had also inquired about the appointment of surgeons and assistant surgeons, and had been told, "I appoint them." But he was not satisfied with this decision, having received a copy of "what purported to be an extract from a letter from you," stating that surgeons were

30 *Ibid.*, 53.
31 *Ibid.*, 18, 19.
32 Brown to William Phillips, April 1, 1861, Brockman Collection; Avery, *History of Georgia*, 186.
33 *The War of Rebellion: A Compilation of the Official Records of the Union and Confederate Armies*, 130 vols. (Washington, D.C., 1880–1901), Ser. IV, Vol. I, 238, hereinafter cited as *O. R.*; *C. R. Ga.*, III, 55, 64.

appointed by the governors. Therefore, although he had "no feeling of jealousy on account of your exercising the right," he wished to see a copy of the law. Secretary Walker supplied a copy of the law which definitely conferred the power upon the president.[34] This settled the issue, but did not soothe the governor's feelings or relieve his embarrassment, for he had already appointed four surgeons, including his brother, Aaron T. Brown, for the two regiments of regulars. At the secretary's request, he recommended five others.[35]

Amidst all the frustration, however, there did appear one measure of relief. Acting upon Brown's suggestion, Secretary Walker agreed to accept the long inactive two regiments of regulars "consolidated into one regiment of twelve companies." Officers were called in from their recruiting stations and began preparations for active service.[36]

Rumors that the federal navy would soon blockade Confederate ports and attempt to recapture all fortifications which had been seized produced a feeling of uneasiness from Norfolk to Galveston. Governor John Letcher of Virginia, fearing for Norfolk, called for help. Secretary Walker called upon Georgia for "two or three companies" to be sent to Norfolk *immediately*. Three days later *four* companies were on the way.[37]

Before these companies left the state, Secretary Walker called for two regiments of infantry "to rendezvous without delay in Richmond, Va." One week later came a call for another regiment to join General Braxton Bragg at Pensacola.[38] The requisitions were promptly met but Governor Brown was much concerned. Georgia regiments were leaving to fight on distant fields while Savannah, Brunswick and the entire Georgia coast was almost defenseless.

Shortly after the fall of Fort Sumter, Adjutant General Wayne, then in Savannah, had received "reliable information from Washington" that an attack upon Fort Pulaski was a part of Lincoln's plan to retake all southern forts. Brown relayed this information to Secretary Walker

34 C. R. Ga., III, 62, 66–67.
35 Brown to A. T. Brown, March 20, 1861; Brown to S. W. Thompson, March 20, 1861; Brown to A. Young, March 20, 1861, in Brockman Collection; Brown to Walker, April 27, 1861, in Hargrett Collection.
36 C. R. Ga., III, 55; Brown to H. C. Wayne, April 22, 1861, in Hargrett Collection.
37 C. R. Ga., III, 32; III, 55, 57.
38 Ibid., III, 57, 58, 65.

with a request that five thousand Confederate troops be sent to defend the Georgia coast. "I will respond promptly to all requisitions made on me for volunteers for that purpose." A week later, Brown reported that little progress was being made in improving fortifications. The few scientific officers on duty were doing the best they could, but more specialists were needed for locating batteries and mounting guns. There was little to hinder the largest enemy ships from entering at Brunswick, and "the whole navy of the United States could safely anchor there." The people felt insecure and were appealing for protection. Walker was not impressed. Brown was wrong about the United States fleet, he wrote General Lawton. "It lies off Pensacola and is not thinking of Savannah or Pulaski." He extended Lawton's command to include the entire coast of Georgia and ordered more scientific assistance for installing guns, but he did not order a concentration of troops.[39]

Brown was further concerned that with the Confederate government failing to provide adequate defense and departing regiments depleting the supply of guns, Georgia might be left without the means to defend herself. When the traffic manager of the Western and Atlantic informed him of Secretary of War Walker's orders to ship guns and ammunition on the road to Montgomery instead of Savannah, Brown replied: "Send them to Savannah. They are mine not his. The Confederate State Government has not sent a gun or shot or shell to Savannah. They cannot order off those I send there."[40] He then dispatched Quartermaster General Ira R. Foster as a special agent to check on all arms and munitions in Savannah and to remove to Milledgeville such as might be ordered.[41]

Another appeal was sent to Secretary Walker. The entire coast of Georgia was in a state of alarm. The governor was flooded with petitions for help. Citizens were sending away their valuable property and preparing to leave their homes. "Almost all business is suspended and the excitement and alarm are very great." There was great fear of the loss of slave property to the enemy. He had met all requisitions promptly, the governor declared, and would continue to do so; therefore, he did not feel that he was asking too much when he demanded protection of Georgia citizens who were "constantly exposed to the depredations of

39 *Ibid.*, 53, 54, 60, 63, 74.
40 Order quoted in Brown to Wayne, April 22, 1861, in Hargrett Collection.
41 *C. R. Ga.*, II, 37.

the enemy." Assuming a stiffer tone, the governor concluded that he still recognized the president's control over military operations, but "I demand the exercise of that authority in behalf of the defenseless and unprotected citizens of this State. . . . A prompt requisition of troops for this purpose is earnestly solicited, with the assurance that they will be supplied with the least possible delay."[42]

Copies of this letter were sent to Howell Cobb and Vice-President Stephens with accompanying notes urging their cooperation in applying pressure on the Confederate War Department for an increase and proper distribution of troops on the Georgia coast.[43] If Stephens and Cobb applied pressure, it was not sufficient. Confederate control was extended but authorities correctly assumed that Georgia was in no immediate danger. Troops were needed in other fields. And if Governor Brown expected even an expression of goodwill from Howell Cobb, he was deceived. "I can say to you rather confidentially," Cobb gleefully informed his wife, "that there is a fair prospect of a quarrel between President Davis and our *worthy* Joe Brown. The latter is trying to ride the high horse about certain acts of congress, which take out of his hands all control of the Ga. troops—I shall sustain Davis and our Congress & if they show the right spirit we will thoroughly put down the miserable demagogue who now disgraces the Executive chair of Ga."[44]

Since Savannah had long been a hotbed of anti-Brown sentiment, it was to be expected that his enemies would blame him for their defenseless situation. He was also accused of taking guns from troops near Savannah to give them to other more favored units elsewhere. When Foster began shipping off guns to Milledgeville the protest was so great that he asked the governor for further orders. "You will be expected to carry my instructions in effect," Brown replied. The Confederate government should "do something towards arming its troops." Yet it had been sending away to Virginia the best arms in Georgia. If those in Savannah were turned over to the Confederate authorities, they too would soon be carried out of the state. Should the necessity arise, these state arms should be available for state troops.[45]

---

42 *Ibid.*, III, 67–69.
43 Cobb Papers under date of May 4, 1861; Phillips, *Correspondence*, 565.
44 May 18, 1861, in Cobb Papers.
45 Brown to Foster, May 14, 1861, in Hargrett Collection.

Charles C. Jones, Jr., mayor of Savannah, protested to Governor Brown, requesting the reasons for the transfer of arms from his city, and intimated that the people of Savannah might not permit the execution of the governor's order. Brown explained that arms were needed to outfit two regiments for Confederate service, and it was necessary to sort and classify these arms. Also there was trouble with the Negroes in some sections, and arms must be sent to those exposed areas. As to the defense of Savannah, he explained, "I do not command the defences of Savannah." However, he had supplied all the heavy guns there. In case of invasion, all available state arms and men would be thrown into the fight.

The intimation that citizens might use physical force to prevent the execution of his orders clearly irritated the governor. "I very much regret that such an intimation should have come from the constituted authority of our usually law-abiding commercial metropolis. I should deeply deplore the necessity which might impel me to send any force to any point in the state which might be necessary to suppress *mobocracy*."[46]

There was some truth to the charge that Brown was most enthusiastic where military units were commanded by his friends. But there is no evidence that he took guns from one to give to another. Like others in charge of recruiting, he failed to encourage the enlistment of the maximum number of men while the fighting spirit was at its height. At times he even discouraged or ignored proposals to raise regiments. When Ambrose R. Wright of Augusta proposed to raise and equip a regiment or battalion without expense to the state, Brown refused to consent. Out of "justice & fairness to other sections," he explained, no large force should be raised in one section of the state. This would deny "equal participation in the service." He would be pleased, however, for Wright to raise a company which might be joined with companies from other sections to form a regiment over which he hoped Wright might be elected to command.[47] When Daniel S. Printup of Rome, a leader of anti-Brown forces, submitted a proposition, it was ignored. Printup appealed to Howell Cobb to influence President Davis to accept his regiment. "Governor Brown has failed to notice our applications

46 Brown to Jones, May 18, 1861, *ibid.*
47 Brown to Wright, April 24, 1861, *ibid.*

and has treated us with silence—if the Government at Montgomery fails to give us a chance we will be compelled to be silent spectators."[48]

Of course Governor Brown's recruiting activities were limited by law. The legislature had authorized the raising of ten thousand men and the secession convention two additional regiments. As these were inducted into Confederate service, however, he could fill their places with other recruits. Perhaps the governor was also influenced by a belief that the maximum number of troops would not be needed. As late as May 4, 1861, he confided to Ira R. Foster, who was supervising removal of State arms from the arsenal at Savannah: "My opinion is that we shall take both Fort Pickens and Washington City before a great while, and that all the slave states will soon be united in the same government, and that our independence will be recognized by the great powers of Europe and that we will finally be successful in the struggle, that the South will sustain republican government with civil & religious liberty and that the Northern states will be unable to do so and will in a few years run into monarchy."[49]

Governor Brown had labored diligently and successfully in meeting every Confederate requisition for troops and had sent them forth fully armed. It is understandable, then, why he was upset when he learned that Congress had authorized the tender of troops directly to the president independent of state authority. This meant that any body of troops wishing to leave Georgia for Confederate service could completely ignore the wishes of the governor. There was no evidence of Confederate intent to reflect upon the loyalty of any governor. The purpose of the law was to expedite the concentration of an adequate Confederate fighting force. But Brown denounced it as "a very dangerous infringement of States rights. . . . We went into this revolution to sustain the *rights of states*," and he regretted that Congress had chosen to infringe upon them. The action was supposed to have been taken in the interest of necessity, but he could see no necessity. He recalled that necessity was the plea used by Napoleon III in seizing complete control in France. "This is the plea of tyrants in every age."[50]

He immediately issued an order that any unit armed by the state

48 Printup to Cobb, May 12, 1861, in Cobb Papers.
49 Hargrett Collection.
50 *C. R. Ga.*, III, 81; Brown to J. H. Howard, May 20, 1861; Brown to Jared I.
    Whitaker, May 20, 1861, in Hargrett Collection.

which resorted to direct tender must leave its arms behind when leaving the state. He had equipped and sent to the field six regiments and two battalions and had two other regiments ready to move, and he would continue to meet requisitions by Confederate authorities, "but I say now once for all that I will neither arm nor equip any company which disregards the authority and the rights of the state and tenders its services and is accepted by the President without the consent of the state authorities."

Brown felt that he knew better than anyone else which troops could be spared; he did not relish the possibility of being forced to send other troops to protect the families and homes of those who had left all "to go glory hunting in Virginia. I do not think desertion of home when it is exposed to attack the highest evidence of genuine patriotism." If the president preferred to accept troops direct rather than through state authority, then he had no right to complain if they came without arms.[51]

One of the units soon to be accused of deserting its post to seek glory in Virginia was the Oglethorpe Light Infantry, Captain Francis S. Bartow commanding. This unit was the pride of Savannah. Organized in the mid-1850s, it had participated in the seizure of Fort Pulaski and was eager for real action. Governor Brown, seeing a need for its services for the defense of Savannah, had refused to assign it to any regiment going into Confederate service. Captain Bartow was a member of Congress and chairman of the House Committee on Military Affairs. It was assumed that he had exerted considerable influence in the passage of the Direct Tender Act. Telegraphing his unit to see if its members wished to go into Confederate service, and receiving an enthusiastic *yes*, he went in person to President Davis and made the tender. Amidst much fanfare, the Oglethorpe Light Infantry left for Virginia on May 21, 1861, taking with it the arms issued by the state of Georgia. Brown vigorously denounced Bartow, charging insubordination, disrespect for authority, and disregard for the defense of Georgia. Bartow replied that he intended no disrespect but found it necessary to disregard the governor's wishes. "I go to illustrate, if I can, my native State; at all events, to be true to her interests and her characters."[52]

51 Brown to J. H. Howard, May 20, 1861, in Hargrett Collection.
52 Augusta *Chronicle and Sentinel*, June 4, 1861.

These would soon become famous words in Georgia; Bartow would be a casualty of the Battle of Manassas.

Other units soon followed into Confederate service. Some took their arms; most did not. Governor Brown took no action to prevent their going, but is some cases, where units were determined to take their arms, he ordered the use of counterforce if necessary.[53] President Davis sent an urgent request that he rescind his Georgia arms order, but instead he urged Davis not to accept under direct tender any units carrying with them Georgia arms. "I am doing all I can to put every gun at my command into the service, and am sending in the State regiments fully equipped. This I will continue to do with all possible promptness. I deprecate anything like conflict between state and Confederate authority, and I feel sure you will not encourage any company to disobey my orders. I impose no restraint, only that they leave the State's arms. . . . I am anxious to have the spirit of subordination to State authority checked. If compelled I shall be obliged to use the means necessary to check it. . . . This insubordination will not last a moment after it is known it does not receive your countenance."[54]

President Davis replied through his adjutant general that he would sustain Brown's position, yet in the same message he called attention to the large number of Georgia units arriving in Richmond without arms. (The seat of Confederate government had now been moved from Montgomery to Richmond.) A few days earlier, General Robert E. Lee had also wired Governor Brown that many Georgia companies had arrived at Richmond without arms. He had nothing for them but old flint-lock muskets. He thought the governor might wish his men better equipped before meeting an enemy "whose arms are so much superior." The organization of a large cavalry force seemed necessary; a supply of pistols and carbines "would greatly further the common cause."[55] Brown had 800 Sharp's carbines available. He made a *loan* of 500 to the Confederacy and retained 300. But no sooner had the loan been agreed to than there came a request from Thomas R. R. Cobb for arms for a legion consisting of "300 horse 600 foot & 100 artillery."[56]

53 C. R. Ga., II, 43–44; III, 94.
54 Ibid., III, 88, 92; Brown to Davis, June 8, 1861, in Hargrett Collection.
55 C. R. Ga., III, 88, 94.
56 Brown to Cobb, June 11, 1861, in Hargrett Collection; T. R. R. Cobb to Howell Cobb, June 15, 1861, in Cobb Papers.

Although Governor Brown had insisted that things be done his way, always protecting what he considered to be state rights, his accomplishments had been considerable. By late spring, 1861, however, the program was facing some financial difficulty. To sell to the banks the bonds authorized by the legislature, the governor found it necessary to increase the interest rate from 6 to 7 percent, which he hoped the legislature would approve. To prevent assistance to the enemy and a weakening of Georgia's financial condition, he issued a proclamation "commanding and informing" all citizens "under any pretext whatsoever" to abstain from paying any debt owed to the United States, any free-soil state, or any citizen thereof for the duration of hostilities. Instead, the amount of such indebtedness when due should be deposited with the state treasury or to its credit in any bank. As security for these loans, the state would issue 7 percent certificates payable at the close of hostilities. Thus would citizens be enabled "to perform a patriotic duty and to assist the State" while denying assistance to "oppressive and wicked conduct" of the antislavery states.[57]

57 *C. R. Ga.*, II, 33, 37.

Chapter IX

If You Refuse, You Will Regret It

ON MAY 17, 1861, Governor Brown issued a public letter, "To the People of Georgia," calling attention to the great Union buildup of men and material for the purpose of crushing the South.

They threaten to invade our territory with large armies; to sweep over it with fire and sword; to incite our slaves to insurrection and murder; to violate the sanctity of our homes, and to inflict the most cruel and outrageous wrongs upon our wives and daughters. They appeal to the very basest passions of the human heart for the purpose of exciting their soldiers, and preparing them for the execution of their diabolical plans for rapine and plunder. They promise to appropriate our lands and divide our substance among their base mercenaries, as a reward for our extermination and butchery. In some of their cities, "beauty and booty" are made the rallying cry to induce the lowest rabble to enlist against us.

To meet this threat the Confederate government had called for many troops, the governor continued, and Georgia had responded nobly. It was reported that in the North great contributions of private goods were being solicited to support the planned invasion of the South. The South must also make such donations in the interest of defense. Soldiers must be supplied and their families cared for. Taxes in Georgia (in proportion to property values) were the lowest in any southern state. The value of Georgia property was estimated at $800 millions. Ten millions of this amount could be contributed to the support of the war as a "free will offering" and the state feel none the poorer.

Rather than resort to heavy taxation or debt to be paid by posterity, "let us show the world that we are fully enlisted in the noble cause of freedom, and that we have the ability and will by private subscription, to clothe and feed our glorious and gallant troops on the field and their families at home."

The governor made a special appeal for clothing to be made by patriotic ladies from any good homemade cloth. Such contributions were to be deposited with the county clerks who would keep a list of donors. County officials were urged to call public meetings to put the urgent need clearly before the people. All materials collected were to be shipped to the quartermaster general at Milledgeville. It was hoped that express companies and railroads would make no charge for handling the goods. Books containing lists of donors were to become permanent state records, and a "beautiful golden cup" was promised to the lady "making the most valuable contribution of clothing" prior to August 1.

From the gentlemen of the state, the governor hoped to raise $1 million dollars immediately for equipping troops. The state comptroller would furnish from the taxbooks a statement of what would be a just proportion of each county. A beautiful Confederate flag would be presented to the county that made "the largest donation in proportion to the value of its taxable property." A gold medal would go to the gentleman making the largest donation.

The governor further urged that since the enemy was attempting to block the coast and was reported unwilling to let anything but cotton through the blockade, that not one bale of cotton be shipped out. Instead, capitalists were urged to make extensive preparations to manufacture raw materials into needed items.[1]

As had been his practice in previous years, Governor Brown took his family to Canton for the summer. He set up a temporary office in Atlanta but spent much of his time with the troops concentrated at Camp McDonald, a few miles north of Marietta. He felt that camp life might improve his health. Troop concentration in northern Virginia continued and so did the stubbornness of Brown and Davis. Brown urged the appointment of his friend Henry R. Jackson as a brigadier general, complaining that even though Georgia had furnished many regiments,

1 This letter was published in all leading Georgia newspapers.

no Georgian had been appointed a general officer. If the president would send a commission for Jackson, three more armed and equipped regiments would be ready to move almost immediately.[2] Brown had apparently not learned of W. H. T. Walker's appointment as brigadier general on May 25. Jackson was commissioned a Confederate brigadier on June 4, 1861, and William J. Hardee received a similar commission on June 17.

Independent troops continued to leave Georgia without the governor's approval, some carrying their arms with them. When the Floyd Sharpshooters of Rome secretly smuggled their arms out of the state before they themselves departed, Brown demanded that President Davis order these guns seized and returned to Georgia.[3] The governor himself was sending thousands of guns out of the state, but he would tolerate no "palpable violation" of his order that none be taken out without his permission.

Brown had at Camp McDonald some 2,500 well-trained and equipped state troops, organized into two regiments and three battalions, and commanded by Brigadier General William Phillips. On June 18 he tendered to President Davis this brigade with its full complement of officers plus a "mountain regiment" which would be ready within a week. All would be well equipped and "go for the war." Ten days later he renewed this offer.[4] Davis made no reply. Yet on June 30 Secretary of War Walker notified Brown of the president's intention "to form and organize a reserved corps of 30,000 men." Georgia was requested to furnish 3,000 men organized by companies and assembled at two accessible camps for instruction. There the president would take them over and assign competent officers for drill and discipline. As needed, these troops would be organized into battalions or regiments and the president would appoint the field and staff officers. On the following day Walker requisitioned two more regiments of Georgia men, armed, equipped, and enlisted for the duration of the war. With this requisition came a flattering recognition of Brown's "patriotic response" in the past. The President had confidence that he would not "hesitate or falter now." Three days later there came a call from the

2 Brown to L. P. Walker, June 3, 1861; Brown to H. R. Jackson, June 3, 1861, in Hargrett Collection.
3 C. R. Ga., III, 98.
4 Ibid., 101.

president himself. Would Brown furnish a volunteer regiment of ten companies, half to be mounted and equipped with breech-loading carbines?[5]

Brown protested the president's plan to appoint field officers in the proposed camps of instruction, claiming that right for the state, but he agreed to recruit the companies. To satisfy the request for two regiments immediately, he again offered General Phillips' brigade at Camp McDonald. "Shall I order General Phillips' brigade to Bristol?" he inquired.[6]

A few days earlier Brown had reported to Vice-President Stephens that he had furnished the equivalent of twelve regiments for the Confederate service, all equipped by the state. Three other regiments, which he understood were commanded by Bartow and Lafayette Mc-Laws, had left the state as independent companies.[7] Brown's industry and patriotism were beyond question, yet the chief point of difference between him and the president had not been resolved. Davis would not accept a brigade with its brigadier, and Brown had no idea of sacrificing his Cobb County friend William Phillips.

He considered the recent requisition for two regiments to be in excess of Georgia's quota, Brown informed Richmond, but he did not wish to argue over quotas. As long as troops were needed, he would do all within his power to furnish them, provided the interest and honor of the state were respected. He would furnish Phillips' brigade as a unit but he would not agree to acceptance of the two regiments separately and then rejection of the battalions. If the only problem was that of accepting a brigade with its brigadier general, then the problem could be solved by accepting it in parts and then giving General Phillips a Confederate appointment.[8] To Vice-President Stephens, Brown confided that Phillips was extremely popular with the troops; they would be very unhappy if sent to the field without him. On this same date Davis wired: "Send the regiments to Bristol."[9] These were apparently the regiments of the Phillips brigade; no mention was

5 *Ibid.*, 104, 105, 107.
6 *Ibid.*, 108.
7 Brown to Stephens, June 25, 1861, in Stephens Papers, Emory.
8 *C. R. Ga.*, III, 110.
9 Brown to Stephens, July 8, 1861, in Stephens Papers, Emory; *C. R. Ga.*, III, 112.

made of Phillips. Two days later, in a confidential note to a friend Brown stated that Davis was willing to accept the two regiments only. "This would disband the brigade and cut Phillips' head off and give all his enemies the advantage of him."[10] Identity of Phillips' enemies was not revealed, but any person who became a friend of the governor automatically acquired a collection of bitter enemies.

On July 11 Secretary Walker replied to the several offers made by Governor Brown relative to the Phillips brigade. The president would not yield. Brown might furnish troops as companies or regiments with their state appointed officers; there could be no brigades. This was the law as passed by the Confederate Congress.[11] On the following day Walker wired Brown: "The crisis of our fate may depend upon your actions. The two regiments you have organized are indispensable to success. For the sake of our cause and the country I beseech you to send them, without standing upon the point of brigade organization. The president has no power to accept a brigade. If you refuse you will regret it. It is not necessary that I should say more." Brown would not budge. "You can accept it as a whole by commissioning the general now in command," he wired Davis. And to Walker he wrote: "If the threat of consequences to me for disobedience to your behests, which the language of your dispatch implies, is intended, rest assured it fails to intimidate." Walker denied any intended threat. His sole object was to appeal to "your well-known patriotism." The danger still existed and "in the best spirit toward you, both officially and personally, I renew the appeal."[12]

Brown was unyielding. To his confidant Alexander Stephens he wrote: "I shall continue to hold the Brigade subject to the order of the President as a Brigade and shall inform the public that I make the tender of this fine body of troops fully armed and equipped. . . . If they are not accepted and the public service suffers for want of their assistance the fault will not be mine, nor will the responsibility rest upon me."[13]

Several Georgia regiments participated in the Battle of Manassas,

10 July 10, 1861, Hargrett Collection. The last paragraph of this letter is illegible.
11 C. R. Ga., III, 112.
12 Ibid., 114, 116, 118.
13 July 20, 1861, in Stephens Papers, Emory.

July 21, 1861; several others were in Virginia; and still others were on the way, but Phillips' brigade was still at Camp McDonald. Great joy spread over the South with the news of a great southern victory. Governor Brown shared the elation and gave "thanks to our Heavenly Father," but he recognized there were great problems ahead; one small victory did not win a war. A determined North would soon call into action its great potential strength.

On August 1 Brown wired President Davis: "In view of the emergency I am obliged to yield the brigade organization, as I am determined to send the troops to the field." The rifle battalion and cavalry would be formed into a legion, commanded by General Phillips as a *colonel*. The regiments and legion would be ready to move by Saturday. "Where shall they go?" Davis replied: "Thanks . . . . Let the troops now offered proceed to Lynchburg, where they will receive further orders."[14] Brown had been influenced by an urgent request from Toombs to forward troops as rapidly as possible. "I felt that full justice had not been done the state in this matter," he explained to Toombs, "but the emergencies were such that I felt it my duty to yield the point."[15]

Brown next directed Davis' attention to the two camps of instruction and the 3,000 reserves called for six weeks earlier. He would move 800 men into Camp McDonald. Two regiments had already been assembled at Camp Stephens near Griffin, and Colonel E. W. Chastain was eager to move his mountain regiment into McDonald. The governor was very eager to take care of this mountain regiment, but this would be more men than requested. There was no objection to the addition of Chastain's regiment, replied Secretary Walker. The quartermasters and commissaries nominated by the governor had been appointed.[16]

Conscious of the fact that winters in northern Virginia could be rather severe, especially for thinly clad soldiers from the deep South, the War Department sent to the governors an appeal for warm clothing. Brown promised to use the entire resources of the state to acquire by donation or manufacture sufficient clothing for all Georgia men in Confederate service. On September 4 he published an appeal to the

14 *C. R. Ga.*, III, 120.
15 August 20, 1861, in Hargrett Collection.
16 *C. R. Ga.*, III, 123, 124.

people. He wished to acquire at public expense shoes and clothing for 30,000 men. All who could furnish such items would report to the superior court clerks the quantity, quality, and price. For the many Georgia soldiers sick in hospitals he solicited sheets, blankets, and coverlets. Ladies were urged to furnish such items from their own supply, all items were to be boxed, tagged, and shipped to the quartermaster general at Atlanta. "We believe God is with us and presides in our councils. Let us try to live near to Him and employ his continued favor. We have at the helm of State, the distinguished Statesman and invincible warrior, Jefferson Davis. By his side we have Georgia's own great Statesman. They are worthy of our confidence. . . . Their success is our success, their defeat would be our defeat."[17]

Many who read this praise of Jefferson Davis no doubt saw in it a bit of politics, perhaps an effort to offset a rumor of unpleasant relations between the president and the governor. It was again time to elect a governor, and although there was no constitutional prohibition, no governor had been elected to a third term for the past half-century. Perhaps no one had wished to be. Neither is there evidence that had times been normal Joseph E. Brown would have desired to break the precedent.

Speculation, both secret and open, often begins months before nomination and elections. Early in March, 1861, a letter published over the signature of Thomas C. Trice of Pike County brought to public attention the question: what should be done with Joe Brown? "I do not believe there is another man in Georgia, who is in every way as well calculated for Governor as Joseph E. Brown. I do not mean that Joe Brown has more sense than everybody else. I mean just what I say— that no man in Georgia will make such an executive as Joe Brown, and therefore I think that he should be re-elected. We need just a plain, sensible, practicable man as Joe Brown is to attend to the executive business of the State, while we try to make bread at home. It is no time now for fool parties among farmers, nor for swell-head Governors. We need strict economy at home, and prudent, plain investigating men to manage our State affairs."[18]

As early as March 14, 1861, Brown's friend George Hillyers of

17 Athens *Southern Banner*, September 11, 1861.
18 Milledgeville *Southern Federal Union*, March 12, 1861.

Monroe privately inquired as to his plans. In reply, Brown explained that "my ambition for the honor of the office I occupy has been fully satisfied and I look to retirement with much interest. It is true an election to a third term if made by general consent of the people without regard to past political differences, would be a very high compliment, such as I do not know that I could consistently with duty decline. I cannot expect however that politicians will permit such a compliment to be paid me." He would not under any circumstance enter a contest for a third time. For the present, he chose to let the matter rest. Two days later, as a follow up to a conversation the two had recently had, he expressed the same views to Alexander H. Stephens. A month later he told Alfred Iverson in strict confidence, "I am disposed to follow the time honored custom." He had been told there would be great unanimity in his favor. This he would consider a great compliment, but would "do nothing toward producing this state of things."[19]

Enemies as well as friends were speculating. The name of John W. H. Underwood of Rome was suggested. Writing to Howell Cobb, Underwood took himself out of the picture but speculated as to who would be the man. He thought Alexander Stephens was pushing his brother Linton. Should that fail, Stephens would turn to Martin J. Crawford or Ben Hill. As for himself, he preferred James Jackson of Athens. Underwood thought Brown's friends were no doubt pushing him for president, senator or governor. As for Brown himself, he was apparently watching developments and was delighted with "the prospects of a collision between Stephens, Hill and Toombs on the one side and you and your friends on the other, expecting to benefit by it himself. He has a certain strength and I think we had best let him alone, not advance him."[20] Underwood did not suspect that Stephens was privately urging Brown to accept a third term.[21]

On August 10, 1861, Jared I. Whitaker, Atlanta attorney, newspaper editor and grandson of Jared Irwin, the last governor to serve three terms, submitted two questions to Governor Brown for public answer. Did he favor holding a convention for the nomination of a candidate for governor? Would he accept a nomination for reelection?

19 Brown to Hillyers, March 26, March 28, April ?, 1861, in Brockman Collection.
20 April 11, 1861, Phillips, *Correspondence*, 580.
21 Brown to Stephens, September 28, 1861, in Stephens Papers, Emory.

Brown replied at considerable length. Under the present conditions he saw no need for a convention. No party caucus was needed since "party differences have passed away." He hoped that "vituperation and bitterness" would soon follow these differences to the grave. "Let us avoid everything that will revive party divisions and strife and vie with each other only to determine who shall do the most in proportion to his abilities for the advancement of our glorious, common cause."

As for accepting another term, the governor explained that he had stated privately to friends that "neither my personal interest nor inclination prompted me to give my consent." He had no desire to upset the two-term precedent. If he was to make a reputation, it had already been done; it would probably not be improved by another term. But his friends had pointed to his success thus far and stressed that his experience was needed in the present crisis. Further, since he as a secessionist had greatly influenced Georgia's withdrawal from the Union, he had no right even to consult his own wishes when his services were needed. Consequently, considering it the duty of every citizen to serve his state in the capacity most useful, "I cannot refuse to serve if the masses of the people without regard to old party lines, were by their united suffrages at the ballot to demand my services for another term."[22]

Earlier in the year Brown no doubt wished and intended to retire at the close of his term. He was still concerned about the condition of his health, and he was sensitive to the sting of opposition from many whom he thought should have given him support. But now, in the midst of the fight, he wished to continue. He believed it his duty and was convinced that no one else could do the job quite so well as he. Furthermore, he liked it. To Vice-President Stephens, the governor confided that the press and probably the politicians seemed "pretty generally opposed to my re-election." However, if he was reading the signs of the times correctly, "the masses of the people are still with me."[23]

The governor's expression of willingness to submit to the will of the people by no means silenced his old enemies. They now had precedent on their side and a convention must be held. By no other means

22 Milledgeville *Southern Federal Union*, August 10, 1861; Atlanta *Intelligencer*, August 14, 1861.
23 August 22, 1861, in Stephens Papers, Emory.

could opposition strength be lined up in support of a single candidate. A convention, without party designation, was called to meet in Milledgeville on September 11. The *Southern Federal Union* correctly observed: "The convention instead of being a representative body, bids fair to be a mass meeting of nearly all the enemies of Governor Brown."[24] This Brown organ had added *Southern* to its title following secession, and on July 9 had placed the governor's name at the head of its editorial column with the inscription: "He is the right man in the right place."

The argument had not changed much over the past two years, observed "A Laboring Man," writing in the Atlanta *Intelligencer*. Persons were still upset about the governor's favoritism, especially toward Baptists, when making appointments. The writer did not profess to know how many appointees were *friends* or *Baptists*, but he thought had Brown filled offices with *enemies* he would have deserved to be "'cut for the simples' and then taken out and hung." What a pity that the "Cherokee ox driver" had "ignored the claims of these patriotic and sacrificing gentlemen" who were denouncing him. "In the passage through this passion-rock and turbulent world, every man in his sphere, *must* reward his friends; if he does not and ignores their claims to his favor and bounty he will soon find himself in the unpleasant predicament of having none but enemies to punish!"[25]

Since the convention was certain to be anti-Brown in its composition, it was boycotted by the governor's supporters. According to reports, only 40 out of 133 counties actually sent representatives. Persons from eighteen others just "appeared" and were seated. Some of these came from counties that had actually decided *not* to send delegates. According to an unfriendly editor, the convention had a "very strong odor of Know-Nothingism" and "seemed to savor much more of revenge than patriotism." Although the hall was crowded with disappointed officeseekers, there were also a number of respectable men present, but they represented very few constituents.[26]

The editor of the Atlanta *Southern Confederacy* made an even more thorough analysis. He thought the convention did not represent

24 August 27, 1861.
25 Atlanta *Daily Intelligencer*, August 23, 29, 1861.
26 Milledgeville *Southern Federal Union*, September 17, 1861.

even a respectable minority of the people. He figured not more than fifty counties were represented by delegates chosen by public meetings and the average size of meetings was about twenty-five. Fifty times twenty-five or 1,250 was the number of constituents actually represented. And as to the plea for harmony, "the harmony which they advocate means that everybody else must think as they think, and act as they act or else everybody else is wrong and there is no harmony."[27]

The convention nominated Eugenius A. Nisbet, a prominent Macon lawyer, a moderate turned secessionist, who had introduced the Ordinance of Secession in the Georgia convention. In politics he had been a Whig, then a Know-Nothing, then a Democrat, supporting Stephen A. Douglas for president in 1860. The most ardent Brown supporter could express toward him nothing but the "most profound respect and esteem," although many wondered why he accepted the nomination. The *Southern Federal Union* suggested: "We believe most sincerely if left to his own unbiased judgment, Judge Nisbet would prefer that the helm of the ship of state, in these perilous times, should be left in the hands of him who has shown himself so skillful in piloting us among the rocks and quicksands of civil war." If his name was used "to divide and distract the people of Georgia," it would not be because he willed it but "in deference to opinions other than his own."[28]

Considering his unanimous nomination as an honor conferred upon him by a nonpartisan convention, Nisbet made public a letter of acceptance. Had such a nomination come from a group seeking to revive old party rivalries, he would have declined, he declared. Secession and the problems which followed had "obliterated lines of popular division" and he would not be a party to any effort "to arouse prejudices and animosities laid to rest by war." Whoever served as governor for the next two years would need to do little on the domestic front other than to preserve order and husband carefully the state's resources. His "most pressing duty and his most solemn trust," would be "to wield all power of the State on a bold and determined prosecution of the war."

Nisbet praised Jefferson Davis as a man with the cautious wisdom of Washington and great military genius and administrative talents. The state must prepare to resist a war "waged with unparalleled bit-

27 September 24, 1861.
28 September 17, 1861.

terness, relentless cruelty, and shameless disregard of the usuages of civilization and the obligations of Christianity." As to the office of governor, he thought "no man with a just sense of his accountability to God and the country, can desire the position of that office, but no true patriot can decline, if called to it by the people."[29] Governor Brown could just as well have written this letter.

About the time Nisbet's letter reached the daily newspapers Brown did analyze and pay his respects to the convention. He accepted the validity of the claim that recent practice had prevented a third term for governors, but he would also add that neither had it been the custom to have "revolutions." Neither, also, had the state been invaded and its soil drenched with blood, nor its governor been called upon to recruit, equip, and train thirty thousand soldiers.

He thought the convention must have approved of his administration, for in the resolutions adopted it was not condemned; neither was an issue made of a single act. He understood that in *private* balloting Judge Nisbet received the vote of only five districts. The other five were divided, but were later persuaded to make it unanimous. Therefore, a convention which was not representative had nominated a candidate who was not the real choice of a majority of the convention. Yet it was being argued that any candidate who might oppose Judge Nisbet would be "a disorganizer . . . seeking to engender party strifes by dividing the people." The people of Georgia had not sanctioned a convention, Brown concluded. In their refusal they had sanctioned the action of his friends in submitting his own name independently. "I now leave with them the determination of the question at the ballot-box, not doubting that they will pronounce a verdict as will best promote the general welfare."[30]

Brown made no active campaign and was opposed by all the major newpapers except the Milledgeville *Southern Federal Union* and the Atlanta *Daily Intelligencer*, although some did publish articles by writers favorable to the governor's reelection. This "no third term idea" was "*bosh and humbug*, gotten up for a purpose," declared "Chattahooche" in the *Intelligencer*. Although opposed by the politicians and much of the press, the governor was "*eminently one of the people.*" The

29 Milledgeville *Southern Federal Union*, September 24, 1861.
30 Atlanta *Daily Intelligencer*, September 19, 1861.

honest, solid farmers and working men were unwilling to "throw overboard this skillful pilot, though we were to vote for him the *Thirteenth time*." The people offered no objection to Judge Nisbet, "but we must be allowed to vote at least once more for 'honest Joe Brown.'"[31]

The points on which Brown's friends made their appeal for the governor's reelection were summed up by "Amicus" in the Savannah *Daily News*. The governor had been "careful and frugal with the peoples' money" and "liberal and generous in his own private benefactions." He had changed the Western and Atlantic Railroad from "an item of constant expense to the public" to a "magnificient and certain source of revenue." Through the exercise of great wisdom, finances had been adjusted, bank currency curbed to a safe limit, and taxes reduced. He had been "the true and manly exponent of State Sovereignty and State Rights," had exceeded all other governors in his effort to recruit and equip troops, and had "inaugurated wise and vigorous measures of defense of our exposed seacoast." Finally, Governor Brown had cast off the shackles of party and defied the action of the insignificant state caucus. Surely the people would reward him for his "incorruptible integrity and consummate ability."[32]

During the heat of the campaign Brown confided to Stephens: "Had I known the opposition to my re-election would be so bitter as it has been in some quarters I should not have consented to the use of my name, but I had gone too far to retract with honor before these developments were made." However, in spite of it all, he had confidence he would be elected.[33]

In his last issue before the election, the editor of the *Southern Federal Union* noted that "a very large portion of the politicians, the wire workers, and the press are opposed to Gov. Brown" but the people were with him. If the *Union* and the *Intelligencer* were the only newspapers supporting him the election returns would show they had "a very respectable crowd of readers." Governor Brown had made enemies by defending the rights of the people. It would soon be seen "whether the people will faithfully stand by him."[34] They did!

The election returns showed Brown 46,493 votes and Nisbet 32,802.

31 September 20, 1861.
32 September 25, 1861.
33 September 28, 1861, in Stephens Papers, Emory.
34 October 1, 1861.

The opposition centers remained strong. Brown lost Floyd and Cass counties and all counties in which there were cities, except Muscogee.[35] There was considerable shifting of votes in many counties. The results of the election disgusted many who had hoped against hope that Brown might be defeated. He had "no sort of an inclination" to support Brown during the recent campaign, growled an Atlanta editor to Alexander Stephens. "I am disgusted with him. My judgment is that he is a very dirty low-down man. I guess I know him much better than you do. He made a good Governor, I freely admit, and I hope will do so again. I shall throw nothing in his way; but he is *mighty* mean and low-flung with it."[36] No doubt Howell Cobb reached the heights of bitterness. Writing to his wife from Richmond he declared: "We hear by telegraph tonight that Joe Brown is elected—as a man—a Christian—a gentleman—and a Georgian I feel humiliated into the dust. For my life I can never feel the same respect for any man that voted for him, that I have heretofore felt. Our State is disgraced and if you will consent I will arrange to bring my family out of the state and if the war should last for two years I will not return there whilst the miserable wretch disgraces the executive chair. I cannot trust myself to write on the subject and I am glad that I do not have to meet with any person who by his vote and influence has contributed to this most humiliating event."[37]

Mrs. Cobb was equally bitter. She was troubled most by the fact that so many of Cobb's former supporters, including the relatives of the late John H. Lumpkin of Rome,[38] had voted for Brown. "The whole Lumpkin family from Great A to Izzard I understand voted the Brown ticket. Pope Barrow was the only relation of Jno H. L. that respected his memory and Joe Brown's villany toward him."[39] The "Great A" referred to was former governor Wilson Lumpkin, uncle of the late John H., then in retirement in Athens.

That which brought misery to the Cobbs brought joy to Governor Brown. The news of his support by Governor Lumpkin was "very gratifying," he wrote a minister friend. "I regard him one of the most

35 Milledgeville *Southern Federal Union*, November 12, 1861.
36 J. Henley Smith to A. H. Stephens, October 16, 1861, in Alexander Stephens Papers, Library of Congress.
37 October 4, 1861, in Cobb Papers.
38 Lumpkin had died on July 10, 1860.
39 Mary Ann Cobb to Howell Cobb, October 6, 1861, in Cobb Papers.

venerable and pure statesmen of his age. In the true sense of the word a gentleman of the old school, an ardent patriot and a zealous Christian, he is an honor to the age in which he lives, and I feel that I may well be proud of the support of such a man."[40]

Brown had not been deserted by all of the prominent active political leaders either. "The election of Gov. Brown is quite agreeable to me," wrote Thomas W. Thomas to Vice-President Stephens. "It is a triumph of the people over the newspapers and I think teaches a dangerous and evil engine a salutary lesson and administers to it a timely rebuke." Thomas thought the "animating spirit" back of Nisbet's nomination was "the old and defunct spirit of Know-Nothingism" which, in the absence of many true men, was endeavoring "to grasp the reins of power."[41]

Many unkind things were said and done during the campaign, but the unkindest cut of all came from the behavior of Brown's old friend Dr. John W. Lewis. In the midst of the campaign Dr. Lewis resigned as superintendent of the Western and Atlantic Railroad. Brown requested that the resignation be kept secret until the close of the campaign, but Dr. Lewis permitted a copy of his letter to reach the press. Approximately a year earlier the two had had a mild misunderstanding. Dr. Lewis was dissatisfied with the governor's interference with his management of the road, especially in the matter of appointments. Brown politely but firmly reminded the doctor of their original agreement that while he himself would not appoint a person against the wishes of the superintendent, he did reserve the power to appoint. He also apologized for any offense that might have resulted from carelessness or preoccupation with other matters.

According to Brown, Lewis acquiesced in his explanation and during the following months he himself had remained away from the road as much as possible, leaving the superintendent in undisturbed control. Dr. Lewis' resignation in the midst of the campaign came as a complete surprise, and its release to the press in such a critical time was more than Governor Brown could understand. "I did not deserve this at your hands," he informed Lewis, "and I confess I felt it keenly. . . . I do not attribute improper motives, but only say the coincidence was an unfortunate one for me."

In closing his letter Governor Brown made a rather pathetic plea that their temporary alienation not be made permanent. Family, church, and former friendly relations demanded otherwise. "You were my early friend and helped me up in life. When I had secured position and power, I invited you to the highest position within my gift. There may have been times when, laboring under the weight of cares and responsibilities, I have treated you with too little respect. There have been similar times when I felt that you treated me with coldness and indifference." But now, in parting, could not it all be forgotten and friendship restored?[42] John S. Rowland was appointed to succeed Lewis as superintendent of the Western and Atlantic.

While the Savannah press was denouncing Governor Brown, he was taking major steps to defend that city against a possible attack. He had not been much concerned about defense during the summer months, for he subscribed to the theory that Yankees would not come South to fight during hot weather. With the approach of winter, he feared attack most any day. Since some thirty thousand armed men had gone to fight on other fields Georgia had few troops and fewer arms for local defense.

As early as July 26, 1861, the governor, realizing what would soon be his plight, issued an appeal to the citizens of Georgia to loan to the state their rifles and double-barreled shot guns. He estimated that there were in private hands 40,000 of the former and 25,000 of the latter. At the close of the war these guns would be returned to their owners or compensation made for their loss.[43]

Early in September the governor made a tour of inspection of the coastal area of Georgia and found the defense woefully weak. There were only about three thousand Confederate troops present to defend 110 miles of coast. Before leaving Savannah he issued a proclamation explaining the emergency and his plans for meeting it. The Confederate Constitution, it was noted, forbade a state to keep troops in time of

---

42 Brown to Lewis, October 8, 1861; Brown to G. D. Phillips, October 29, 1861, in Hargrett Collection.
43 C. R. Ga., II, 47.

peace or engage in war unless "actually invaded, or in such imminent danger as will admit of no delay." In view of this limitation all forts and arsenals had been turned over to the Confederacy and that government had assumed the task of defense. Up until this date the danger of invasion had not been so imminent as to admit of no delay; consequently, the state had not attempted to interfere with Confederate authority.

But now the situation showed signs of rapid change. The tone of the northern press and enemy activities on the coast of North Carolina indicated a probable attempt to invade the coast of Georgia at no very distant day. Therefore the keeping of state troops was within both the spirit and letter of the constitution. Further, a force of up to ten thousand men had been authorized by the legislature during the 1860 session. Troops previously organized under this law had been transferred into the Confederacy. It was therefore ordered that all persons liable for militia duty, except those groups specifically exempt, report for organization and training. Volunteer companies would be formed and received into the state troops for coastal defense.[44]

Brown feared that recruiting, arming, and training of state troops would require more time than the Yankees were willing to grant; so he made frantic appeals to Richmond for help. The four regiments being instructed at Camps McDonald and Stephens were a part of the Confederate army, but they had not yet been armed. Brown appealed directly to Davis to order these regiments to Savannah and arm them with the guns which had just arrived there. Replying through Secretary of War Judah P. Benjamin, who had succeeded Leroy Pope Walker, Davis stated that the arms on the *Bermuda*, which had run the blockade, were private property. Should the government be able to acquire them they would be divided.[45] He *did not* order the four regiments to Savannah. It is doubtful that Secretary Benjamin had previously known of the existence of these four regiments, for on September 29, referring to correspondence of June 30 relative to reserve forces, he requested Brown to send complete information, including location and mailing addresses.[46]

44 Dated September 9, 1861, *ibid.*, 52.
45 *Ibid.*, III, 127, 128.
46 *Ibid.*, 131.

Brown next attempted to secure the return of some Georgia troops to their home state. Colonel Marcellus Stovall, whose incomplete battalion was stationed at Lynchburg, had appeared at Brown's headquarters. The governor, no doubt in response to Stovall's request, urged Benjamin to order this incomplete battalion back to Georgia where its ranks could be filled. Benjamin refused but ordered one thousand rifles to A. R. Lawton, Confederate general commanding at Savannah, to be distributed among such state troops as were tendered. "Grave reasons of policy forbid sending back any troops from Virginia," he explained. Brown expressed thanks for the guns but continued to demand men, also.[47]

Soon came the news that the four regiments (Twentieth, Twenty-first, Twenty-second, and Twenty-third Georgia) at Camp McDonald and Camp Stephens had been ordered to Virginia. Brown filed an immediate protest, although he had no control over these troops; he felt that the secretary of war might have at least extended to him the courtesy of an advance notice. Georgia already had twenty thousand men in Virginia, he informed Benjamin. Those remaining in Georgia were needed for state defense. But even if this were not true, it would be unwise and unfair to shift these poorly clad troops to Virginia to suffer in the extreme cold of winter. "In the name of the State and as an act of justice to the troops, I feel it my imperative duty to enter my solemn protest against the removal."[48]

Benjamin was unyielding. The troops could be armed in Virginia, but not in Georgia. They could be comfortably clad and were needed there. Confronted by superior forces and expecting an attack daily, he must do all within his power to reinforce Confederate forces. Should Georgia be attacked, defense forces would be sent. "I would do anything honorable in my power to prevent it, but fear it is not possible," the governor notified the regiments at Camps McDonald and Stephens.[49]

While engaged in a losing argument with the Confederate government, the determined governor was building up his state troops. He planned three brigades organized into a division. To command

47 *Ibid.*, 128, 129, 130.
48 *Ibid.*, 138.
49 *Ibid.*, 139; Brown to Colonels Smith and Worthem, October 28, 29, 1861; Brown to Colonels Jones and Hutchinson, October 28, 29, 1861, in Hargrett Collection.

two of these brigades he appointed his friends George P. Harris and Francis W. Capers from the Marietta Institute. Later he would persuade Henry P. Jackson and William H. T. Walker to resign their Confederate commissions, the latter to command the third brigade and the former to be major general of the division. So great was the response to the governor's call for volunteers that a second proclamation was necessary to put an end to enlistments. Commanders were instructed not to accept either companies or individuals who were not armed.[50]

The lack of arms continued to be a big problem. A check on the contents of the arsenal at Milledgeville revealed only thirteen hundred guns of all types. These were transferred to the generals at Savannah with instructions that they were to be issued to "*State troops solely.*"[51]

The landing of a small federal force on the coast of South Carolina early in November greatly increased Governor Brown's concern. He hastened to reopen enlistments, agreeing to accept the first thirty companies tendered. All must come armed with country rifles, doublebarreled shotguns or military guns "*fit for immediate use.*" Declaring that the city of Savannah was menaced by the enemy, the governor again appealed to the Confederate government. He urged the return to Georgia of William Phillips' Legion, the regiments commanded by W. T. Wofford and W. W. Boyd and Stovall's battalion. These had all been armed by Georgia and were now needed in her defense, Brown explained. "There are reasons of public policy which would make it suicidal to comply with your request," Benjamin replied. Ten other governors were making similar requests. Confederate forces must not be scattered into fragments "at the request of each Governor who may be alarmed for the safety of his people."[52]

Despairing of securing reinforcements, Governor Brown shifted his request to guns. "I now ask, not for men, but for guns," he informed Secretary Benjamin. A kind providence had guided through the blockade another vessel carrying arms. This cargo consisted of four rifled cannon and about 10,000 Enfield rifles belonging to the Confederate government. In exchange for 5,000 state guns carried away to Virginia,

50 *C. R. Ga.*, II, 69.
51 Brown to G. P. Harrison, October 4, 5, 1861; Report of T. M. Bradford, September 30, 1861, in Hargrett Collection.
52 *C. R. Ga.*, III, 142, 144.

might he not have 5,000 from this cargo? Brown inquired. He also wanted two of the four rifled cannon. Benjamin agreed in part. He would divide the arms equally between General Albert Sidney Johnston in Kentucky and General Robert E. Lee, commanding the southeastern coast. Brown was satisfied.[53]

This promise was acceptable to Brown but it did little to resolve the differences between him and Confederate authorities. He accused the Davis administration of attempting to gain control in military matters with a view to moving all Georgia troops to other fronts, leaving the Georgia coast exposed. It was Brown's idea to defend Georgia first, shifting to other fronts only those regiments not needed in home defense. And even those regiments shifted to other fields should be considered as Georgia troops on loan to the Confederacy.

53 Ibid., 143, 144, 145.

Chapter X

Regiments but No Brigades

CLAD IN A homespun suit, Governor Brown was inaugurated for a third term on November 8, 1861. About half of his short address was devoted to a severe denunciation of "the restless fanaticism, canting hypocrisy and insatiable avarice" which prompted the northern people to attempt the subjugation of the South. It was their "lust for power and love of plunder" that led to a sectional political victory and the seizure of the government. This left to the South a choice between "the position of subjugated provinces, yielding obedience to unrestrained power" or becoming an independent state, free from "encroachments of tyranny or the mandates of any superior." Convinced of the justice of its cause and appealing to God for guidance, the South chose the latter course.

The remainder of the address sketched the difficulties under which the South was waging its war of defense and made a plea for united support. He entertained no doubt of success. The separation of the sections would be final and perpetual. "Let us then lay aside all past differences upon minor questions . . . and, as a band of patriots, bury in one common grave every personal aspiration and every feeling of ambition, pride or jealousy" that would hinder the defense of "our beloved old State" or "the triumph of our glorious arms."[1]

The inaugural completed, the governor retired, and his annual message was read to an unfriendly General Assembly. His friends had returned him to the governor's office, but the friends of Eugenius A.

1 *C. R. Ga.*, II, 125–30; *House Journal*, 46 ff.

Nisbet had won control of the Assembly. Believing there was a similarity between British oppression of the American colonies and the oppression suffered by the South, the governor called attention to the
colonial struggle for independence. The colonies, after their remon-
strances against oppression and petitions for redress of grievances had
gone unheeded, chose the only alternative to tyranny and "threw off
the yoke and boldly defied the powers of the British Crown." Although
few in number and weak in material strength, they invoked the blessings of heaven and with stout hearts, strong arms, and belief in the inherent justice of their cause, they succeeded.

Independence, however, did not solve all of their problems, for there
were some among them who wished to substitute for the British government a strong American government dominated by an aristocratic
few. This idea, however, was rejected by the Constitutional Convention and the advocates of state sovereignty succeeded in establishing a
central government of delegated powers, reserving to the states all
powers not so delegated.

But even the adoption of the Constitution did not assure respect for
state sovereignty, the governor continued; there was still a group of
public men, headed chiefly by northern statesmen, who sought to accomplish indirectly what they had failed to do directly. Through interpretation of the new Constitution, they claimed to find power to
enact tariff and other laws for their own benefit without regard to
injury of others. "By the instrumentality of these laws, the government
of the United States has poured the wealth of the productive South into
the lap of the bleak and sterile North, and the people of the ice clad
hills of New England have grown rich and haughty upon the tribute
which they have levied on the production of the sunny South." The
people of the North, having profited by strong central government, supported it in enlarging its powers by diminishing the powers of the
states.

Meanwhile, the suffering South sought to stem the tide, ever insisting upon states' rights, only to be overwhelmed by the growing
strength of the North. Again and again the South protested against
oppressive measures and warned of probable consequences, only to be
answered by renewed acts of injustice. Finally, as a last resort, each
of eleven southern states "asserted its original rights by resuming all

the attributes of its original sovereignty," and then joined in the formation of a Confederacy based upon these rights.

And what had happened to the federal Union? It had become a "consolidated military despotism" with an executive who claimed and exercised unlimited powers over the life, liberty, and property of the people and was determined to force the seceding states back under control of his despotism. His soldiers had violated every rule of modern warfare, disregarded the rights of private property, and inflicted "the most grievous wrongs upon unoffending women and children." Yet, though greatly outnumbered, the South, with Divine guidance, had "repeatedly dispersed and driven them back with consternation and great slaughter." Still the war continued. But a gracious Providence had provided the means for ultimate southern victory; therefore, every patriot in every section should adopt as his motto "*Victory over the invader, or death to the last man sooner than acknowledge that we are vanquished.*" This portion of the governor's message was directed more toward the general public than the legislators. Although replete with inaccuracies, falsehoods, and exaggerations, it was needed to boost the war spirit which had been dampened by casualty lists and news of suffering.

The governor next heaped praise upon the government established under the Confederate Constitution. It had shown great ability, and in general the acts of Congress were "characterized by prudence, wisdom, and foresight." Yet he felt compelled to note two acts which could scarcely be reconciled with the letter and spirit of the Constitution. He objected to the act authorizing the president to accept volunteers from any state, organize them into companies and regiments, and appoint all officers above company level. He also protested the act that gave the president authority to accept organized groups without consulting the governors.

Brown classified volunteers as militia, not regulars, and contended that the president had no constitutional power to appoint officers of militia units. He also claimed that direct acceptance by the president resulted in inconvenience and disorder. Frequently, when the governor called upon a unit to report to meet a requisition, he found the unit had left the state, without leaving behind records of its organization.

The power of the president to raise troops without the services of the states was an imperial power, Brown contended. If placed in the hands of "an able, fearless, popular leader," supported by a subservient Congress, which also had the power to tax, his *will* could become the supreme law of the land. Perhaps there should be no fear that President Davis, guided by lofty patriotism and purity of purpose, would abuse his power. Yet this was not sufficient reason to place absolute power within his hands. "While I might not fear him as a dictator, I would not consent that he be made a dictator." His successor might have the ambition of a Napoleon.

Brown next traced in detail his successful effort to meet all requisitions while at the same time giving proper attention to local defense. He had concluded, however, that Confederate preparations for the defense of Georgia were not adequate. The state must assume responsibility for its own defense. Consequently, he asked for an appropriation of $3,500,000. "The only question proper for discussion now is how many men and how much money are necessary to protect the state and repel invasion."

There was also the question of how to raise the funds required. The Confederate war tax plus increased levies on the local level had created a burden, yet more money must be raised. Brown thought the public debt should be increased as little as possible, for it constituted a burden upon posterity. There was no choice left but to increase taxes. "The revolution has happened in our day; its burdens belong to the present generation and we have no right, by a very large increase in our public debt, to transmit the greater portion of them to generations yet unborn."

During the past year, the governor reported, he had encountered some difficulty in selling state bonds. With the interest rate on Confederate bonds at 8 percent, few individuals or banks would prefer state bonds at 6 percent. To offset this difference he had taken the liberty to promise 7 percent, and he now requested the legislature to legalize his action.

In view of the possibility that during the coming year the state might not be able to market all bonds authorized, the governor recommended the issuance of Treasury notes to meet the deficit. These notes should be acceptable in payment of all debts due to state or the state road.

The effectiveness of the blockade, the governor explained, had also contributed greatly to the financial plight. With planters unable to sell their cotton they would soon be unable to pay their debts and taxes without the sacrifice of property at ruinous prices. To meet this emergency, the governor recommanded that the state advance the planters Treasury notes in amounts equal to two-thirds the market value of their cotton. The cotton would be stored in approved warehouses and properly insured. The state would thus have control of the cotton until sold and the loan repaid.

As a measure of further relief, the governor reluctantly approved an extension of the suspension of specie payment by the banks and the law staying legal collection of debts. He noted that in normal times he had vetoed such legislation. But times were no longer normal, and he recognized the inability of banks to secure sufficient specie at any price or of persons to pay their debts without financial ruin. "I can imagine no greater cruelty than to permit the creditor, in absence of the soldier, to take from his family the small pittance left for their support."

The governor would also protect the people against unpatriotic speculation. There were "unprincipled public plunderers" who, gaining possession of commodities indispensable to health and comfort, would rob the government and wrong the soldier by charging exorbitant prices. It was the duty of government to protect the helpless against "the wicked avarice of these Shylocks." He recommended laws sufficient to give this protection. The State itself should also be protected against such impositions. He requested a grant of power to the governor to seize and appropriate any supplies or provisions needed for subsistence or comfort of the troops, paying for them at prices fixed by competent valuing agents. The price thus fixed by the state would then become the market price. The passage of such legislation would "not only be compatible with the dictates of humanity and the plainest principles of natural justice," but would also be within constitutional power to seize private property for public use.

Still another financial matter for concern was the Confederate war tax, based upon the value of property. Confederate assessors were to appraise property throughout the states, and Confederate collectors were to collect taxes. However, if any state wished to collect the tax itself and pay its assessment into the Confederate Treasury prior to a specific date, it would deduct 10 percent from the total amount. Payment could be made in either specie or Confederate Treasury notes. Governor Brown, disliking the presence of Confederate officials within the state, could do nothing about the assessors, but he recommended that no work be left for Confederate collectors. State agents should do the collecting, thus retaining for the state the 10 percent bonus.[2]

The governor's message was a straightforward, businesslike document, touching upon all the more important problems of the state. He stated facts as he saw them and requested nothing unreasonable. Yet in spite of the serious state of affairs, a bitter minority group preferred savage attacks upon the governor to sober consideration of state problems; an equally determined governor answered in kind. The state House of Representatives, which had chosen Warren Akin as its Speaker, opened fire on November 11 by passing a resolution requesting the governor to submit to that body copies of all correspondence with Confederate authorities relative to local defense. The governor declined, stating that "in the present critical state of affairs" he deemed it unwise to make public such correspondence. However, after consulting with a committee from the House, he did agree to submit select letters, which he requested be considered in secret session.[3]

In submitting this correspondence, he again stressed the lack of finances. The longer the legislature delayed in making appropriations, the higher the price for necessary supplies for the winter. The foot of the invader was now on Georgia soil, he explained, and there was not adequate defense against his further progress. Perhaps the Confederate authorities were doing all they could in view of obligations at many points, yet "whatever differences of opinion may exist upon this point, I respectfully suggest that it is not now the time to stop to balance accounts with the Confederacy, or to count the cost of defense."

Local and private bills might be important to particular interests, but they should give way to emergency measures.[4] Legislators do not like to be urged to abandon or even to postpone passage of their favorite local bills. Governor Brown further irritated legislators by his veto of two salary bills. Supposedly, in the interest of economy, a bill was passed

2 C. R. Ga., II, 77 ff; Georgia House Journal, 1861, pp. 10 ff.
3 C. R. Ga., II, 134, 146; House Journal, 1861, pp. 68–69.
4 C. R. Ga., II, 146.

lowering the governor's salary from $4,000 to $3,000 and the supreme court justices from $3,500 to $2,000. In another bill, forgetting the need for economy, the legislators raised their own daily compensation to $5.00. Brown vetoed both bills, but the increase for legislators was immediately passed over his veto. Although the reduction in salary could not apply to him during his present term, he disapproved the measure because it did not apply to all Statehouse employees and to circuit judges.[5]

Four weeks passed without the passage of a military appropriation bill. Governor Brown was borrowing money on the strength of a promise to pay when such an appropriation was made.[6] Winter was near and prices were increasing daily. In the legislature there was strong sentiment in favor of shifting the burden to the Confederate government. Before the House was a proposal to transfer the state troops to the Confederate forces, if President Davis would accept them. Such a transfer would not only shift the burden to the Confederacy but would take the troops from the control of the governor. The governor sent in a special message vigorously opposing the proposed transfer. As the correspondence placed before the House revealed, he explained, he had done all within his power to procure adequate Confederate defense of Georgia. The fact that he failed was not to criticize Confederate authorities, for they had many points to defend. However, it was not until after he realized failure that he resorted to raising a strong state force. The law authorized him to raise a force of ten thousand men, and the constitution gave to the states ample authority to defend themselves in such an emergency. "The Constitution gave me the right, and the Statute made it my duty to act." The condition of the state troops was now such as would make them "terrible to the invader." Had he not acted and the weak Confederate force proved insufficient to stop an invasion, he would have been justly condemned by the legislature and the people.

The enemy was now ready to strike, Brown explained. Was it possible that in the face of such an emergency the representatives of the people would spend their time discussing who was responsible or

5 Georgia *House Journal*, 1861, pp. 202–204.
6 Brown to G. B. Lamar, November 29, 1861, *C. R. Ga.*, II, 149.

should bear the burden of defense? Was it possible that "our action can be influenced by party considerations, or by personal hatred or personal favoritism," or whether or not they are "to advance the political fortunes of one man, or to injure those of another"?

To consider the situation from a financial viewpoint, the governor thought would be a grave mistake. Would it be too costly to spend $5 million to defend $700 million worth of state property? Would the proposed transfer result in great savings for the state? True, the Confederacy would assume the expense, and Georgia be required to pay only her apportioned share. But should there be no transfer, the Confederacy would at the close of the war reimburse the state for its expenses. Therefore, there would be no saving by transfer.

There were two other important points that must be considered, Brown continued. Could these state troops be transferred to Confederate service without their consent? Even with their consent, would the president have the power to accept them? These troops had been recruited as a state force for local defense. Their contract was therefore with the state, not the Confederacy. The state had no right to transfer to the Confederacy their contract for service. "They are not cattle, to be bought and sold in the market."

These troops had been organized into brigades and a division, and a number of their officers had, at the governors' request, resigned their commission in the Confederate army to serve their home state. Under the law the president had no power to accept brigades or divisions; consequently, the existing organization must be broken up and the major general and brigadiers left without commands. Further, the number of men in many companies and, therefore, the regiment they constituted was below the minimum required by Confederate law. Some regiments must then be dissolved and colonels, lieutenants colonels, and majors left without commands. What would happen to those units not accepted by the president? Had there not been a lack of arms, Brown explained, he would not have accepted companies below full strength. But there was an emergency and he felt compelled to accept all who could bring with them a country weapon.

The governor was certain that the troops would not agree to transfer unless their organization with its officers was preserved. This could

be done through a change in Confederate law, but there was no indication of such a change. To resort to any form of disorganization of
this fine body of soldiers, the governor thought would be "not only unwise but suicidal, and must result in the most disastrous consequences
to the State."

It was Brown's opinion that, should transfer be attempted without
the consent of the troops, they would refuse to go. To support this
opinion, he sent to the House a set of resolutions adopted by the regiment commanded by Colonel E. W. Chastain, which he had been requested to forward. These resolutions proclaimed loyalty to both the
state and the Confederacy, but boldly stated that if an attempt was
made to force a transfer "we will at once abandon the field and return
to our homes." There was no power on earth to force them into Confederate service without their consent. "We are not the property of the
General Assembly of Georgia to be sold and transferred from one
owner to another like a promissory note, and we do hereby enter our
solemn protest against any such sale." There is no evidence that the
governor was in any way connected with the adoption of these resolutions, but he was a frequent visitor to Camp Harrison where this regiment was located, and Colonel Chastain was a close personal friend of
long standing.

In concluding his special message the governor used very pointed
if not threatening language. "If this fatal policy should be determined
upon by the General Assembly, I will be responsible for none of the
consequences growing out of it; and, in the name of the people of
Georgia, I now, in advance, enter my solemn protest against it." Should
the Georgia troops be disbanded as a result of any legislative action, he
would consider it his duty "to proclaim to her people, that, while the
enemy is thundering at her gates, her representatives have left me
powerless for her defence, by withholding the necessary means, and
even taking from me those already at my command. If I have used
strong language, I mean no disrespect. When all that is dear to a people
is at stake, the occasion requires the utmost frankness and candor."[7]

Indeed, the governor had used strong language. It went to the
quick and produced an immediate reaction, when referred to an un-

---

7 *C. R. Ga.*, II, 149 ff, 168; *House Journal*, 1861, pp. 358–64.

friendly House committee. The committee reported resolutions declaring that the constitutional power of the governor to send to the legislature information and recommendations did not authorize him to send arguments for or against a measure under consideration any more than to appear in person and participate in discussions. Therefore, the message just received was "an unwarrantable interference with deliberations of the House and receives our unqualified condemnation." Further, it was charged that the governor's threats were unbecoming to his official position and "an infringement on the rights of free discussion and an invasion of the privileges of the House." His statement relative to legislative action amounting to disbandment was declared untrue and unwarranted. And his insinuations that the House was influenced by "party considerations or by personal hatred and favoritism" was declared "an aspersion which we indignantly repel."[8]

In support of its resolutions, the House committee report denounced the governor's message as "an argument thrust in unbidden and unasked, against a bill he wished to defeat." It was an assumption of power "which cannot and ought not to be tolerated." Had the point been reached where legislators could not engage in open discussion without being accused of "party considerations and personal hatred" if their views were not in harmony with those of the governor? "Who constituted him the judge of the motives which govern others in performance of their duties."? And was not the governor's threat of troop refusal to be transferred an invitation to insubordination? Was not the governor using a "threat of a disobedient soldiery" to influence legislative action?[9]

The House did not submit the committee's report and resolutions to vote, but did order them printed in the *Journal*. The governor was not sent a copy or notified of the action taken. Therefore, he was not given an opportunity to reply while the House was still in session. He did file a stinging protest after adjournment. The House, he explained, had an "unusual number of speaking members" with political aspirations, all of whom demanded to be heard on even the most trivial question. Consequently, the time was "consumed in lengthy discussions

8 *C. R. Ga.*, II, 166, 167.
9 *C. R. Ga.*, II, 160–66; *House Journal*, 1861, pp. 365 ff.

to the great hindrance of business, at a cost of thousands of dollars to the people, when the enemy was upon our territory, and the necessary appropriations had not been made to support our troops." But since the House had finally passed desired legislation, he thought the talking members must have finally listened to his own argument.[10]

A troop transfer bill passed the House but ran into difficulty in the Senate, which was more friendly to the governor. A conference committee revised the bill, removing the more objectionable features. As finally passed, the state troops were to be offered to the Confederacy only if they consented. If they were not accepted, $5 million was appropriated for their support. To raise this money the governor was authorized either to sell thirty-year 8 percent bonds or issue Treasury notes.[11] He would choose the latter.

Although the legislative session was stormy, the governor eventually got most of what he requested. He was authorized to sell twenty-year 8 percent bonds in amounts sufficient to pay the Confederate war tax levy. He sold $2 million to banks and $441,000 to individuals in time to meet the April 1, 1862, deadline and save 10 percent. He encountered no difficulty in selling the bonds. In fact, he was forced to call a halt to sales to banks in order to reserve some for individual purchase.[12] The legislature also appropriated $100,000 for relief of sufferers from the great fire in Charleston, South Carolina, $200,000 for hospitals, and $50,000 to promote the manufacture of salt, all of which were recommended by the governor.

Since this was the first session of the General Assembly after the formation of the Confederacy, it was necessary to elect two Confederate senators, one for a short term and the other for a full term. The fight for these seats became bitter; there were many aspirants. On the first ballot to fill the long term, Ben Hill received a majority over the combined vote for Robert Toombs, Herschel V. Johnson, Alfred Iverson, James Jackson, and William Law. These same candidates plus four others were then voted on for the short term. On the first ballot Iverson led with 85, followed by Toombs 49, Jackson 35, and Johnson 22. On the third ballot Iverson fell to 73 while Toombs moved up to 82. Iverson

10 *House Journal*, 1861, appendix, 441 ff.
11 Acts of General Assembly of Georgia, 1861, p. 141; Brown to Stephens, January 1, 1862, in Hargrett Collection.
12 Brown to G. B. Lamar, February 2, 1862, in Hargrett Collection.

withdrew after the fifth ballot, and Toombs was elected over Jackson 129 to 67.[13]

Governor Brown immediately notified Toombs, who had resigned as secretary of state and accepted a commission in the Confederate army. Toombs did not reply immediately, and rumor spread that he was much irritated by the opposition he had encountered in the legislature and would not accept. Finally, he notified the governor that "the manner in which the legislature thought proper to confer this trust upon me, relieves me from any obligation to sacrifice either my personal wishes or my conviction of public duty in order to accept it."[14]

Governor Brown, expecting such a reply, had made a conditional offer of the seat to Judge Joseph H. Lumpkin of the state supreme court. When the judge declined, he turned to Dr. John Lewis. How these two old friends had patched up their recent differences is not known, but the governor explained that "In view of your acknowledged position as a man of strong practical common sense, financial ability, and purity of purpose, taken in connection with your age and experience and your moral character, I am of opinion that it is my duty to the state and to the cause . . . to tender you the position and respectfully to solicit its acceptance by you."[15]

Much to Governor Brown's satisfaction, the General Assembly closed its session in a spirit of patriotism, as reflected in the approval of a resolution declaring separation from the United States "final and irrevocable." Under no circumstances would Georgia "entertain any proposition from any quarter which may have for its object a restoration or reconstruction of the late Union on any terms or conditions whatsoever. . . . Georgia pledges herself to her sister States of the Confederacy that she will stand by them throughout the struggle— she will contribute all means which her resources will supply . . . and will not consent to lay down arms until peace is established on the basis of the forgoing [sic] resolutions." Although the General Assembly did not request it, Governor Brown was so pleased that he sent copies of this resolution to other Confederate governors, "under the

13 Georgia Senate Journal, 1861, pp. 104–108.
14 Milledgeville Southern Federal Union, March 4, 1862; Atlanta Southern Confederacy, March 6, 1862.
15 Brown to Joseph H. Lumpkin, January 28, 1862; Brown to John W. Lewis, February 26, 1862, in Hargrett Collection; C. R. Ga., II, 207.

conviction that you will be pleased to learn the action of Georgia on the important subject to which it relates."[16]

The legislature did not grant the governor's request for authority to seize any provisions needed for the subsistance or comfort of the troops. However, during the legislative session he sent his assistant commissary general to Macon, Columbus, and Atlanta with orders to seize all salt about to be sent out of the state or being held for sale at more than five dollars per bushel. When questioned by the Speaker of the House as to his intentions, he replied that he hoped to secure adequate supplies for the army and prevent salt from either being shipped out of the state or held for unreasonable prices. There was no interference with the right of citizens to purchase salt for their own use.[17]

In accordance with legislative provisions, Governor Brown wired Confederate Secretary of War Benjamin on December 13, 1861, that he had several thousand six-months troops "organized into a division, brigades, regiments, battalions, and companies." Some companies had fewer than sixty men. "Will you accept them for local service as organized, if tendered?" Benjamin replied, "I will accept for local defense each armed regiment, battalion and company of six months men that you may transfer." He made no mention of brigades or divisions.[18] This reply was expected. Brown immediately ordered commanding officers to ascertain the wishes of their troops as to transfer. With "great unanimity," they refused.[19]

As Governor Brown had predicted, federal forces did take advantage of the cool weather to begin operations along the coast of Georgia and South Carolina. Several offshore islands were occupied, and there was evidence of concentration for attacks upon Brunswick and Savannah. By early February, 1862, General Lee was prepared to abandon Brunswick and center defense at Savannah. Also, in spite of the winter cold and heavy rains, federal forces moved down the Mississippi and up the Tennessee and Cumberland rivers. On February 2, 1862, the Confederate War Department sent to the governors a call for more troops. Georgia was asked for twelve regiments. They would be

16 *C. R. Ga.*, III, 147.
17 *Ibid.*, II, 145; Brown to Warren Akin, December 3, 1861, in Hargrett Collection.
18 *C. R. Ga.*, III, 146, 147.
19 Brown to Stephens, January 1, 1862, in Hargrett Collection.

armed and supplied by the Confederacy, and each soldier would receive a fifty-dollar bounty for enlisting.[20]

Brown did not receive his copy of the requisition until February 10. He immediately wired assurance that it would be met and apportioned to each county its quota. On the following day, he issued a proclamation to the "People of Georgia." As had become his practice in the issuance of public messages, he began with a lengthy denunciation of northern "abolitionists and protectionists" who had compelled southern states to secede, form a confederacy, and take up arms in their own defense. Northern troops had disregarded "all rules of civilized warfare," stealing and laying waste property and territory with "fiendish malignity," and shooting down in cold blood "unarmed and unoffending women and children." With "sacrilegious infidelity," they had "desecrated the altars of God" and "defiled and polluted our churches and places of public worship." The Lincoln government had suspended the writ of habeas corpus, and seized and imprisoned persons who expressed sympathy for the South. The federal Congress had ordered confiscation of southern property which would be used to pay the huge public debt. Ultimately, southern lands were to be colonized by Negroes working under northern masters. In order to accomplish this, Negroes were to be armed and incited to "destroy our wives and our children. . . . Soon the blow is to be stricken with terrible fury on many a bloody field."

To meet this crisis, Brown explained, President Davis had called for the immediate enlistment of troops for three years or the duration of the war. Georgia was asked for twelve additional regiments by March 15. These troops would be armed and supplied by the Confederacy and each soldier would be awarded a bounty of fifty dollars. They would be received at Camps McDonald and Stephens and a new Camp Davis, to be established on the Central Railroad about thirty miles from Savannah.

This proclamation was a call for volunteers, and the governor expressed confidence that the response would be immediate and sufficient. Should a draft become necessary, the law left it to the governor to decide the method to be used. No bounty would be paid to those drafted. "The bounty and the elective franchise belong, under the law, *only* to the brave volunteers." All men liable for military duty were ordered to assemble, together with such incomplete companies as existed in their county, on the regular camp ground on March 4. There officers would call for volunteers to complete their ranks. If the number of volunteers was not sufficient, the officers would resort to draft. Justices of the peace would be present to compile lists of those liable but not present.

The South had no strength on the seas, Governor Brown declared, but on land each enemy thrust must be driven back *"by the use of cold steel in close quarters."* In this type of conflict the enemy's courage would fail him, while southern troops, exhibiting their superiority and "most remarkable heroism," would drive him "from our genial territory back to his frozen home. . . . I warn you of the danger which surrounds you, my countrymen," concluded the governor, "and as your Commander-in-Chief I exhort you to lay aside . . . every other employment, and I now summon you immediately to arms. Strike before it is too late, for your liberties, your families, your homes, and your altars!"[21]

On February 18, Adjutant General Wayne issued a list of the categories exempted by the governor from possible draft: clergymen; Statehouse officials, including clerks and secretaries; judges; customhouse officials and clerks; postal workers; ferrymen and all marines employed by the government; express company superintendents and agents; officers and five workers in each iron mill or shop producing war materials; officers, guards, and select groups of assistants in state institutions; officers and cadets in the Marietta Military Institute; and superintendents and four employees in each cotton and woolen factory.[22] By a subsequent order the governor also exempted the faculties and students in the colleges.[23]

Two groups were conspicuously omitted from this list—plantation overseers and members of the General Assembly. This was not an oversight. Prior to the publication of the list, Senator Ben Hill had written the governor suggesting exemption of overseers. Brown replied that he had given much thought to this point, but had been unable to decide where to draw the line. How many slaves should an overseer be required to have under his supervision—a hundred? Ninety? Fifty? Twenty? All would demand exemption. And what about the small

21 *C. R. Ga.*, II, 187 ff, 208; *Official Records*, Ser. IV, Vol. I, 917 ff. This proclamation was also published in all leading Georgia newspapers.
22 Dated February 18, Athens *Southern Banner*, February 26, 1862.
23 *C. R. Ga.*, II, 207.

slaveholder who did his own supervising? "It is under these circumstances I have deemed it impolitic to prescribe any rule on the subject."[24] Brown had never been enthusiastic about extending special privileges to the planter class.

The list of exemptions included Statehouse officials and judges but made no mention of members of the General Assembly. Was the governor considering drafting some of those young hotheads who had given him so much trouble in the House? Many people no doubt wondered. To an inquiry from F. W. Adams, a member from Clarke County, Brown replied that there was no law exempting members of the General Assembly from military duty. During the recent session the members knew there was possibility of a draft, yet they passed no law exempting themselves. Some members had already volunteered. The governor did not presume many would be drafted, but he hoped that if they were, they would serve the state as soldiers as ably and faithfully as they had as legislators.[25]

Governor Brown encountered considerable difficulty in raising his twelve regiments. By 1862 eagerness to enlist was not so in evidence as a year earlier. Brown confided to Vice-President Stephens that it was "becoming difficult to get volunteers. So much has been said about the sufferings of our troops in Va. . . . that the spirit of volunteering is checked."[26] As a contemporary Georgia historian expressed it, "The hot fever of the early days of the war had very much quieted down. The effervescence had dissolved. . . . A year of actual service had dissipated the poetry of soldiering."[27]

Soon came the news that the thin Confederate line extending from eastern Kentucky to the Mississippi River had given way. The Confederates had been defeated at Mill Springs, leaving East Tennessee open to invasion. Forts Henry and Donelson had fallen, and General Albert Sidney Johnston was evacuating Nashville and Middle Tennessee. General Leonidas Polk had abandoned Columbus, Kentucky, and was falling back into western Tennessee. Federal pressure along the southeastern coast had not diminished. Brunswick and Savannah were threatened. And the people of Augusta were becoming appre-

24 Brown to Hill, January 24, 1862, in Hargrett Collection.
25 Brown to Adams, March 1, 1862, ibid.
26 January 1, 1862, ibid.
27 Avery, History of Georgia, 230.

hensive lest, if victorious at Savannah, Union forces might ascend the river to seize or destroy the eighty-two thousand bales of cotton stored there, the powder mills, and the factories.[28]

Governor Brown's reaction to the news of disaster on the Tennessee-Kentucky front was a call to prayer. By proclamation, he designated March 7 as a day of "Fasting, Humiliation and Prayer." In the beginning of this unequal struggle, he explained, the southern people had placed their trust in "the God of Israel," and their troops were blessed with victories. But soon, with hearts filled with vanity, they neglected to give God full credit for their success. They assumed the attitude that "'our hand is high; and the Lord hath not done all this,'" and confident of their own strength, were ready to say, "'Is not this the Babylon that I have built.'" In response to this haughtiness God had turned his back upon them, giving victory to their enemies, permitting their troops to be slaughtered and their land to be filled with mourning rather than rejoicing. The only hope for the South was to return to the Lord.[29]

Governor Brown trusted God but he had no intention of simple dependence upon Him. He was serious when he suggested that Georgia troops meet the enemy with cold steel at close range. On February 20, 1862, he appealed to the mechanics of Georgia to put aside all unnecessary work and make ten thousand pikes. Had there been five thousand men at Fort Donelson armed with pikes, he speculated, the results might have been different. The long-range gun might fail to fire or miss its mark, thus wasting ammunition, but the "short range pike and terrible knife . . . wielded by a stalwart patriot's arm, never fails to fire, and never wastes a single load." To those who were to use these pikes he suggested that when the enemy began retreat "let the pursuit be rapid, and if the enemy throw down their guns and are likely to outrun us . . . throw down the pike and keep close at their heels, till each man has hewed down at least one of his adversaries."[30]

The governor's specification for a pike was a six-foot staff with an eighteen-inch knife. Patterns were to be furnished by the Ordnance Office. Numerous mechanics, including those in the state road shops, began making pikes. The governor was very particular as to the metal and wood used. The first batch submitted was rejected; the handles

28 *C. R. Ga.*, III, 158–61.
29 *Ibid.*, II, 196.
30 *Ibid.*, II, 199.

were of red oak and the blades of iron rather than steel. "The handles must be of tough young ash or good hickory, all finished in neat style," he instructed, "and the blades and cross blades all ground to proper, smooth polish and made perfectly sharp, making the job a neat one . . . or not one of them will be received and paid for."[31]

As the situation in Kentucky and Tennessee grew steadily more serious, Governor Brown turned his attention to the problem of provisions. No doubt in accordance with previous arrangements, Linton Stephens requested that the governor make public his views "upon the necessity of greatly increasing our next provision crop, and lessening or dropping our cotton crop." Modestly stating that he did not suppose much importance would be attached to his views, Brown launched an extensive discussion of the subject.

Until recent months the Confederacy had within its possession the major portion of Kentucky and the entire state of Tennessee, "the great grain producing portion of the Confederacy." But much was now changed. Although the "magnificent valley of the Duck River" was still in Confederate hands, it was being threatened. No longer could the Confederacy depend upon provisions from the Tennessee area. The cotton and tobacco states must supply themselves and the Confederate forces with provisions. The "God of Nature," however, had so blessed them that they were quite able to assume this responsibility. If properly used, there was sufficient land and labor available to supply all people with needed provisions. The growing of cotton, on the other hand, was a burden, since it could not be marketed. "If we plant the usual cotton crop, my honest convictions are, we are in great danger of being conquered, not for the want of arms, or men to use them . . . but for want of provisions." This danger would be completely removed if cotton lands were planted in provision crops. But even if lands were not needed for provisions, continued production of large cotton crops would be unwise. The great surplus would only lead to lower prices when the market opened at the close of the war. And even during the war this great surplus would be further temptation to the enemy to make greater efforts at conquest in order to seize this rich prize.

Although the Union was winning on many battlefields, Governor Brown suggested that it might be sealing its own doom. The cost was

31 Brown to V. A. Gaskill, February 14, 1862, in Hargrett Collection.

too great. If complete victory did not come in 1862, the tax burden at the North would become so great that the people would demand an end to the effort to subjugate the South. If northern victory did come, southern property would be used to pay that enormous debt. The choice between producing provisions or cotton might well be the choice between independence or the confiscation of southern property to pay northern debts. Those who persisted in growing cotton and those distillers who "for money" insisted upon converting grain into liquor should beware "lest impartial history should hold them as justly obnoxious" and guilty of disloyalty to the South.[32]

Governor Brown had no power to force the substitution of the growing of grain for the production of cotton, but he could move against those distillers who were converting grain into liquor. On February 28 he issued a proclamation announcing that he had been reliably informed that "the distillation of corn into ardent spirits has grown to be an evil of most alarming magnitude." In one county alone, he had learned, no fewer than seventy stills were "constantly boiling, consuming more grain than was required to feed the entire population of the county. If not suppressed, that grain which was absolutely necessary to feed the armed forces would be made into strong drink, which the word of God declared to be "raging," which "dethrones the reason of our generals" and "degrades and demoralizes our troops," leading them to slaughter, with their flags trailing in the dust.

Therefore, effective March 15, 1862, he commanded every distiller in the state to desist "from the manufacture of another gallon of ardent spirits" until the next meeting of the legislature. The stills of all violators would be seized. This action was taken because the material used was private property needed for public use. Further, it was ordered that no liquor be hauled over the state road, and other railroads were urged to adopt this restriction. He was conscious of the probability that his actions would conflict with the interests of some influential people. Therefore, he appealed to all patriots, good citizens, and Christians not only to sustain him but to assist him in this discharge of duty.

There could be no other choice, the governor asserted, when faced with the probability of soldiers fighting "our battles on short allow-

32 Linton Stephens to Brown, February 22, 1862; Brown to Stephens, February 25, 1862, Milledgeville *Southern Federal Union*, Extra, March 4, 1862.

ance" while their families back home cried for bread and the poor wept bitterly from hunger, all in order that a few people might gratify their "unholy avarice and accumulate ill gotten gain." Besides, the metal used in making stills was needed for manufacturing cannon. Field pieces were 90 percent copper and 10 percent tin.[33] To be used with the copper he hoped to acquire from the destruction of stills, the governor ordered Captain V. A. Gaskill to seize all of the "block tin" found in Atlanta and hold it for public use.[34]

Probably no proclamation issued by the governor during the war gave him more pleasure than the one against the making of liquor. He hated liquor and had often been driven to the brink of despair by some of his friends' use of it. Again and again he had threatened to dismiss high-ranking officials on the state road for intoxication, and at least two of them, E. W. Chastain and E. R. Harden, had carried their habit with them into the army.

The governor was very serious about the enforcement of his order against distillers. He was "agreeably disappointed" at the reception of his order, he confided to Vice-President Stephens. Not even distillers had condemned it although a few had chosen to disregard it. These would have their stills seized. "I shall make a few very fine brass field pieces out of them."[35] When the seizure of a still near Ringgold was reported, the governor ordered it shipped to Noble Brothers & Company at Rome to be made into cannon. If any attempt was made to prevent seizure, militia officers were to meet force with force.[36]

Thomas W. Thomas was appointed to the governor's staff and placed in charge of enforcement of the order. Thomas had been on duty with the troops in Virginia, but had become dissatisfied and eager to return to Georgia. He wanted to be a brigadier in the state troops but Brown had no brigade for him to command. In his new position he was to visit the mountain counties enforcing the order "at any cost necessary." All stills seized were to be hauled to the railroad. A few distillers in Elberton, Lumpkin, and Murry counties, some said to be officers in the militia, were reported threatening to defy the military.

33 *C. R. Ga.*, II, 202; Milledgeville *Southern Federal Union*, March 4, 1862.
34 *C. R. Ga.*, II, 202.
35 March 28, 1862, in Hargrett Collection.
36 Brown to Stephens, March 28, 1862; Brown to W. A. Clemmons, June 25, 1862, *ibid.*

They must not only be arrested but court-martialed, the governor ordered. "I am determined to execute the order at every hazard and any cost."[37]

The prohibition of further distilling of liquor was destined to affect the supply thought necessary in hospitals. L. B. Northrop, Confederate commissary general, appealed to Governor Brown for a suspension of the restriction in order to permit the manufacture of specific quantities of liquor for "medicinal purposes." Brown readily agreed, but suggested the manufacture of as little as would "answer your purpose till the new crop is gathered."[38]

A few weeks later one Captain S. G. Cabel called at the governor's office and presented a contract with Confederate authorities for manufacture of one thousand barrels of whiskey. Brown approved, endorsing on the contract that Cabel was not to be hindered by Georgia officers in the carrying out of the contract. Cabel then stated that since the quantity was large and the time for production was short, he would need the assistance of other distillers. At this point the governor balked. He would permit no subletting for fear the matter would get completely out of control. Cabel continued to insist and the governor continued to refuse, adding a warning that should subletting be attempted, all stills would be seized and his approval of Cabel's contract revoked. The contractor went away unhappy but with plans in his mind. Making numerous copies of his contract with Governor Brown's endorsement and approval, Cabel began making contracts with numerous distillers to produce liquor for him at $1.50 per gallon. His contract with the Confederate Commissary Department was for $2.50. Should his contract be filled completely, he stood to make $120,000.

One can only imagine the extent of the governor's rage when he heard this news. He rushed off to General Northrop a biting letter. "I never anticipated that you would attempt to put all the stills in the State to running and give out contracts for hundreds of thousands of gallons," he exclaimed. Distillers all over the state were operating, some claiming to have direct contracts, others sublet arrangements. Northrop would consider the original permission granted him canceled. If the amount of liquor needed by the Confederacy should be apportioned

37 Brown to Thomas, January 1, 1862, April 22, 1862, *ibid.*
38 Brown to Northrop, August 20, 1862, *ibid.*

among the states, Georgia would furnish her quota, no more. For this production there must be specific agreements as to location and quantity. All other distilleries would be confiscated.[39]

Two days later Governor Brown issued a circular letter to all Georgia militia officers, explaining to them the situation. All contracts with Cabel were declared null and void. The earlier proclamation prohibiting distilling was to be strictly enforced against anyone who, after the publication of this order, should distill "a single gallon of whiskey in this State." The only exception was to be in a case where an individual produced an individual contract with the Confederate Government for the production of a specific quantity of liquor.[40]

The only commodity in sufficiently short supply to make it an item for speculation was salt. During the recent session of the legislature Governor Brown had sent Captain E. M. Field, assistant commissary general, to the principal cities to check on the salt supply. He was to seize for public use any that was being held for speculation or was in danger of being shipped out of the state. In Atlanta, Field seized one thousand sacks of salt in the possession of A. K. Seago, a prominent grocer and dealer in produce, making just compensation which was received and receipted by Seago. The salt was placed in possession of William Watkins, military storekeeper.

About two months later, Seago brought suit to recover the salt as his property. Unable to secure the $32,000 bond set by the court, Watkins was about to be placed in jail. Governor Brown, never one to tolerate interference with his authority, notified the sheriff of Fulton County that he would not permit the military operations within the state to be hindered by any civil process from any court. The sheriff would therefore release Watkins immediately and "abstain absolutely from all further interference with the military stores of this State, or the keepers thereof." Should the sheriff refuse, such military force as necessary would be used.[41]

A copy of this order was forwarded to General W. P. Howard, commanding, First Brigade, Georgia militia, with instructions to check on the sheriff's actions. The governor was now still more aroused; he

39 October 11, 862, *ibid.*
40 *C. R. Ga.*, II, 232.
41 *Ibid.*, 182.

had heard that certain "evil disposed persons" had advised the sheriff to disregard the governor's order. General Howard was instructed to use whatever means necessary to guarantee Watkins' freedom. If he had not yet been jailed, prevent it. If he was already in jail, request the keys and release him. If use of the keys was denied, use such force as was necessary to open the jail and release Watkins. Should the sheriff offer resistance, place him under military arrest.[42] Presumably, the sheriff offered no resistance.

As the supply of salt continued to dwindle, Governor Brown appointed Senator John W. Lewis as state agent to East Tennessee and Virginia to contract for the acquisition and transportation of salt. Lewis leased a portion of the saltworks at Saltville, Virginia, and began producing salt which the state of Georgia proposed to sell to the people at cost. "I confide the matter to your sound discretion," instructed the governor. "Have as much salt made as you possibly can." There was no state appropriation to defray the expense, so Brown transferred funds from the Treasury of the state road.[43]

The coming of spring, 1862, brought no improvement in the Confederate military situation. Grant continued his movement up the Tennessee and General Don Carlos Buell, at Nashville, was in position either to strike Chattanooga or join Grant. General P. G. T. Beauregard, second in command to A. S. Johnston, was concentrating Confederate forces at Corinth, Mississippi. And General Edmund Kirby Smith at Knoxville, threatened from both the north and south, was attempting to keep the East Tennessee railroads open. Federal troops occupied several points along the southeastern coast, and attack upon Fort Pulaski and Savannah appeared imminent.

Governor Brown had little difficulty in recruiting the twelve regiments requested by the Confederate War Department. Fear generated by news of federal victories apparently stimulated enlistment. But without training and arms these troops could be of no immediate assistance. By March 22 Governor Brown was able to inform President Davis that he tendered not twelve regiments but thirteen regiments and three battalions.[44] Yet appeals for Confederate reinforcements for the Savannah

42 *Ibid.*, 185.
43 Brown to Lewis, May 12, 30, 1862, in Hargrett Collection; *C. R. Ga.*, II, 219–23.
44 *C. R. Ga.*, III, 167.

area were in vain. Hard pressed on many fronts, the Confederacy had no surplus troops.

To make the situation even more serious the six-month period of enlistment of thousands of state troops was about to expire. Hoping to preserve their organization in position along side the Confederate troops as long as possible, Governor Brown made no public mention of this approaching crisis until the time arrived. On March 25 he informed Secretary Benjamin that eight thousand men would be needed to replace the state troops. Even with that number, replacement would be difficult, for the state troops had constructed the defenses and understood the situation. He had hope, however, that after a short leave most of the state troops might reenlist. Did the Confederate authorities wish the use of state troops to continue or was the Confederacy ready to assume total responsibility for defense, the governor inquired. "Keep the troops in service if possible a few weeks longer," replied George W. Randolph, who had succeeded Benjamin as secretary of war. In a follow-up letter the secretary informed Brown that soon there would probably be a sufficient number of troops, for there was before Congress a bill that would put into military service all men between the ages of eighteen and thirty-five who were not exempt.[45]

Before receiving this letter Governor Brown left Milledgeville to visit the state troops in Savannah. Fort Pulaski, isolated and under siege since late February, was tottering on the brink of surrender, yet numbers of state troops, their time expired, had left for home. However, news had arrived that Congress was considering a general conscription bill. On April 5, Governor Brown made a strong appeal for reenlistment. He heaped great praise upon the state troops for their patriotism and hard work on the Savannah defenses. For six months the enemy had lain offshore but dared not attack. However, this enemy, whose watchwords were *subjugation and confiscation,* was only biding his time. He knew of the expiration of terms of enlistment and the common longing of soldiers to return to their homes and families. Once the soldiers were gone this enemy would strike, and soon there might no longer be homes to defend. True, other soldiers could be recruited and trained but there was not time to wait. One trained soldier was worth more than two raw recruits. This being the situation the commander in chief urged

45 *Ibid.,* 170, 175, 177.

reenlistment for two and one-half years. Those who did would be placed beyond reach of Confederate conscription, leaving them to defend their home state. Those who did not reenlist would be subject to the Confederate draft. One week would be allotted for soldiers to make their decisions. Those who chose to reenlist would be given a thirty-day leave.[46]

Shortly after the governor returned to Milledgeville the wires carried news of the Battle of Shiloh, April 6–7. General Albert Sidney Johnston had been killed, and Confederate troops, victorious on the first day but suffering heavily on the second, were retracing their steps from Corinth, followed by a heavily reenforced federal army. Beauregard had succeeded Johnston.

President Davis wired the southern governors that Beauregard must have reinforcements. Would each send all available armed men? Brown replied that he would send his two best armed state regiments. He could also supply one thousand pikes and side knives. Davis accepted both with many thanks. But later in the same day, April 10, Brown received a wire from General J. C. Pemberton, now in command of the southeastern coast. Two Confederate regiments from the Savannah area had been ordered to Tennessee. He had no knowledge of any plan to replace them with other Confederate troops. Then before the close of the day the governor learned that Fort Pulaski was under bombardment. He canceled his offer to send troops to Beauregard. Davis agreed but urged that the pikes and knives be sent. If the route by Chattanooga was blocked, they could be sent via Mobile.[47]

Fort Pulaski surrendered on April 11. On the following day Governor Brown issued a proclamation calling for volunteers to fill the vacancies in the state troops left by those soldiers who chose to remain at home. Fort Pulaski had fallen, and Savannah and the surrounding area were at the mercy of a formidable enemy, he declared. The secretary of war had been requested to take over full responsibility for defense but had announced his inability to do so and "appealed to the state to continue to provide as far as possible for her own defense." Therefore, the state would accept the first thirty companies that tendered their services.

46 Athens *Southern Banner*, April 16, 1862.
47 *C. R. Ga.*, III, 181–83.

Companies were to consist of seventy-eight men and officers. They would be organized into regiments in groups of ten. A fifty-dollar bonus would be given each soldier when his company was mustered into service. With Georgia's "very existence as a State" threatened, "who will remain longer at home?"[48]

On April 15, 1862, Secretary of War Randolph sent out notices that Congress had passed an act "placing in the military service of the Confederate States for three years or the war all persons between eighteen and thirty-five years of age who are not legally exempt from military service."[49] This act would be commonly referred to as a draft, but, technically, it did not draft individuals into the service. Instead, by a single action, the armed forces were extended to include all white males between eighteen and thirty-five. Those exempt would not be required to serve. The problem, of course, would be to round up those not already under arms and compel them to perform their military service.

The draft, or conscription, act solved some problems but created others. Owing to the expiration of twelve-month enlistments, a considerable portion of the Confederate forces was threatened with disintegration. For several weeks there had been a running argument between Governor Brown and the War Department over the Georgia volunteers whose terms were about to expire. Brown insisted that since these men had been armed by Georgia, those who did not reenlist should bring their arms back to Georgia with them. Brown further insisted that where companies and regiments were reduced by departure to the extent that combination and reorganization was made necessary, the officers should again be commissioned by the governor. The conscription act and accompanying legislation settled these arguments in favor of the Confederacy. Those men within the age limits already in the service would be held for an additional two years; those not within the age limits would be held an additional ninety days; where reorganization was necessary, officers would be commissioned by the president; and no arms were to be returned to the states.[50] This displeased Governor Brown very much; it was only the beginning of a long period of unhappiness, bitterness, and almost open rebellion.

48 *Ibid.*, II, 213.
49 *Ibid.*, III, 184.
50 *Ibid.*, 183, 184.

The governor had erred when he assured state troops they would be beyond the scope of Confederate conscription; he was now embarrassed by his mistake. He had received the telegram announcing the passage of the conscription act, he notified Secretary Randolph, and he presumed the War Department's interpretation was that it disbanded state troops. He had been busily engaged in enlisting three-year men for state service, but he now proposed "to cease my operations and turn over the troops who yet remain in service, with the responsibility, to you immediately, in such manner as may be most agreeable to the President, as it is necessary to the safety of Savannah that the number of State troops be immediately increased if they are to be kept in State service." An immediate reply was requested.

Randolph replied immediately. He wished the state troops kept together until they could be enrolled in Confederate service. In this he would like to make use of state enrolling officers. "All between eighteen and thirty-five are to be in the Confederate service; the remainder may be organized by States."[51]

Governor Brown was already in Savannah, so without delay he called upon Confederate General Lawton and tendered over five thousand men, the entire force of state troops. Lawton assumed command, and Major General Henry R. Jackson, who had commanded the division of state troops, retired. The troops were allowed to keep their state arms with the understanding that should they ever be sent out of the state their arms would be left behind. The governor then withdrew his recent proclamation calling for volunteer companies to fill up the state forces.[52]

The transfer of the state troops to the Confederacy created problems of organization and command. They had been organized into a division of three brigades. The Confederate law still did not provide for acceptance of any unit larger than a regiment or battalion; consequently, the brigades must be broken into their component parts, leaving three brigadiers and a major general with state commission but no commands. With logic and reason, Governor Brown appealed to the War Department to commission Major General H. C. Jackson

51 *Ibid.*, 186.
52 *Ibid.*, II, 215; III, 187.

and Brigadier Generals G. P. Harrison, W. H. T. Walker, and F. W. Capers and reassign them to their old commands when reorganized as a part of the Confederate forces. No immediate action was taken, for General Lawton sent most of his new force home on leave.[53]

53 *Ibid.*, III, 208.

Chapter XI

Bold and Dangerous
Usurpation

NO PREVIOUS action of the Confederate government had upset Governor Brown quite so much as did the passage of the conscription act. Since President Davis had recommended and approved the measure, Brown considered him the chief culprit. It mattered not that a majority of Congress, including members of the Georgia delegation, had assented. As was his custom, he formed his own opinion without seeking advice and then began battling. He enjoyed being commander in chief of the state troops and even raising the regiments requested by the War Department. He took justifiable pride in his obvious success. Certainly no governor could have approached his duties with greater zeal.

Now he found himself suddenly pushed from the mainstream. He must surrender the state troops he had organized, and he was left without means of organizing others. The Confederacy was taking the prime portion of his manpower. Henceforth, he would not be needed to raise additional regiments for Confederate service; this would be done directly by Confederate officers. He had never tired of bragging about the number of regiments he had outfitted and sent to the front or his success in getting guns in through the blockade, even though he flew into a rage when several batches were "accidentally" seized by Confederate authorities and distributed elsewhere.

The governor opened fire on April 22, 1862, in a long letter to President Davis. Realizing his inability to retain state troops "without probably collision and conflict with Confederate authorities in the face of the enemy," he had tendered the state troops to Confederate General Lawton. In accepting them Lawton had promised to interfere as little as possible with their organization. Brown hoped the War Department would respect that promise, for should units be broken up and portions be assigned to other organizations, it would produce a very discouraging effect. He could see no need for this change in the method of recruiting. Georgia had always responded gladly and promptly to every requisition for troops and now had 60,000 men in the service. Another 20,000 could have been furnished if called for as the state's quota. "The plea of necessity, so far at least as this State is concerned, cannot be set up in defense of the conscription act."

Without waiting to see a list of those groups legally exempt from conscription, the governor envisioned complete destruction of the General Assembly. When that body convened enrolling officials might swoop down and attempt to carry away "to remote parts of the Confederacy" all legislators between eighteen and thirty-five years of age. This he would never permit, even if it required the use of all remaining state military force to defend that coordinate branch of government. (The governor had apparently forgotten that a few weeks earlier he had offered members of the General Assembly no protection against a state draft.)

Brown also expressed fear of attempts to conscript members of the supreme court; secretaries, clerks, and heads of departments of government; county tax officers; and even members of the commander in chief's staff. And what about officers and officials of the state military organization, the employees on the state road, the staff and students of the military institute, the state university and other colleges? Then there were the overseers of slaves who if conscripted would leave thousands of slaves without supervision and endanger the safety of women and children. (Again the governor had forgotten that he had refused to grant overseers exemption from a possible state draft.) If mechanics and those working in various factories were taken, there would be complete collapse of production. The governor did not promise to protect all these groups, but he declared that no conscription of persons essential to the operation of state government or the state road would be permitted.

Getting down to more concrete legal and constitutional points, Governor Brown charged that the conscription act gave the president power to enroll the entire state militia within the age limits and took from the states the constitutional right to appoint officers and train the militia. Under this power the president might conscript a major general of militia, reduce him to the rank of a private in the Confederate army, and place him "under the command of a third lieutenant appointed by the president, and . . . treat him as a deserter if he refuses to serve." He did not wish to imply that President Davis would resort to such action; he merely wished to illustrate the extent of power conferred upon the Confederate president. Further, this extensive control over state military power would make it possible for the president to limit or destroy state governments.

The conscription act also authorized the president, with the governor's consent, to employ state officers as enrolling officials. He had no intention of throwing obstacles in the way of enrollment, Governor Brown explained, but he was unable to see why state officials should assist in the enforcement of a law which "virtually strips the State of her constitutional military power, and, if fully executed, destroys the legislative department of her government, making even the sessions of her General Assembly dependent upon the will of the Confederate Executive. I therefore respectfully decline all connection with the proposed enrollment and propose to reserve the question of the constitutionality of the act and its binding force upon the people of this State for their consideration at a time when it may less seriously embarrass the Confederacy in the prosecution of the war."[1]

President Davis made a brief reply disclaiming any desire to interfere with the organization of troops in regiments, battalions, or companies. He enclosed a copy of the revised military law, however, which made it clear that he still could not accept divisions or brigades. As to the constitutional power to conscript, the president explained, it was derived from the power to raise armies, not from the power to call out the militia. The president also enclosed a list of the categories of persons exempt from conscription. Had Governor Brown waited to examine this list before writing his many pages of protest, he would

1 *C. R. Ga.*, III, 192 ff; *Official Records*, Ser. IV, Vol. I, 1082 ff.

have noted that the public officials whom he swore to defend against conscription were exempted by law.[2]

It would appear that the president's explanation, documented by copies of the acts of Congress upon which it was based, should have silenced the Georgia governor. But, never one to abandon a controversy as long as there was the slightest point on which to argue, Brown now took off in another direction. He did not question the contents of the laws but the power to pass such laws. Although completely without training in constitutional law and with limited knowledge in any intellectual field, the governor, in true Jacksonian fashion, would supply his own interpretation of the Confederate Constitution. Had there been a Confederate Supreme Court, Joseph E. Brown might not have openly disobeyed its decision on constitutional matters, but he certainly would have imitated Andrew Jackson in reserving to himself the right to interpret the constitution as he saw it.

Noting President Davis' statement that the power to conscript was derived from the power to raise armies rather than the power to call out the militia, Brown suggested close examination of Article I, Section 8 of the Confederate Constitution. That article and section contained three paragraphs relating to the armed forces. Congress was given power to raise armies, to call the state militia into service to repulse invasion or to suppress insurrection, and to provide for organizing and disciplining the militia, leaving to the states the power to appoint militia officers and train the militia in accordance with the discipline prescribed by Congress. Since these provisions related to the same subject and were incorporated in the same section of the Constitution, Brown insisted they "must be taken as a whole and construed together."

If all power were centered in the power to raise armies, giving the president power to commission all officers, then the other two provisions would be useless. Was it intended that state control over military matters was to be so completely nullified? Granted that Congress had the power to raise armies, the question was "How shall it be done?" If the state militia was called into service to repulse invasion, as was the present case, and the states commissioned the officers, then that would be the constitutional method. However, should the officers be appointed

2 *C. R. Ga.*, III, 200.

by the president, disregarding the reserved rights of the states, the action would be in violation of the Constitution.[3]

In reply to Brown's letter of May 8, President Davis explained that all the constitutional questions raised by the governor had been carefully considered by him before he recommended to Congress the passage of the conscription act. They had again been fully explored in the debate in Congress. And Brown's letter had been submitted to the cabinet and the attorney general asked for a written opinion. The majority of both houses of Congress and the entire cabinet had pronounced the act constitutional. Even so, because of his great respect for the governor and for the benefit of some other eminent citizens who shared similar views, he wished to give the subject a full discussion.

States formed confederacies in order to present their united strength against foreign powers, the president began. Although each state might be competent to manage its own domestic affairs, it did not possess sufficient strength to protect itself from outside foes. If the Confederacy was to possess sufficient strength to defend its member states, then the states must delegate some of their powers. After enumerating the powers delegated to the Confederate government, the states also agreed that Congress might pass any law "necessary and proper for carrying into execution the foregoing powers." Among the powers delegated was the power to "provide for the common defense," "declare war," "raise and support armies," "raise and maintain a navy," and raise money for all forms of common defense. In addition to granting these war powers the states also accepted limitations upon themselves. They agreed not "to engage in war, unless actually invaded, or in such imminent danger as will not admit delay."

The Constitution placed no restrictions on the power to raise armies, but there were only two methods by which armies could be raised— through voluntary enlistments or conscription. In the absence of restrictions, the president insisted that either of these methods could be used in any manner desired. Enlistments could be by individuals or units of any size or type of organization. Therefore, when Congress proposed a law to assist in exercising its power to raise an army, the only question to which an answer was necessary was: is the proposed law necessary and proper?

3 *Ibid.*, 212.

The president noted that in previous correspondence Governor Brown had questioned the necessity for the conscription act, contending that the states had always furnished more men than could be armed. The president disagreed. He considered the act not only necessary but "absolutely indispensable." Owing to the expiration of the terms of twelve-month troops, the armies were on the verge of disintegration. The immediate need was not to bring more raw recruits into camp but to keep in the field those who were trained.

Although this one fact established beyond doubt the necessity for the conscription act, the president explained, he wished to discuss the matter on a still broader base. When a certain law was proposed it was the duty of Congress, before passing it, to decide whether or not it was necessary. The test should be whether it was intended to accomplish what was needed. Certainly no one could doubt that the conscription act was intended "to raise armies." This being true, it was constitutional unless it came into conflict with some other provision of the Constitution.

Brown had contended that there was such a conflict, citing the provisions relative to the militia. The chief point in question rested upon the definition of the term *militia*. According to Davis, the militia was, in the words of the attorney general, a "*body* of soldiers in a State enrolled for discipline." It was an organized body, and the term could not be applied to separate individuals. Further, this body was not *troops*, for militia existed in time of peace, and no state could keep troops in time of peace. Therefore, there was no connection between the armies of the Confederacy and the militia of the states.

Congress had *exclusive* power over the armies, President Davis continued. As to the militia, the power was neither delegated exclusively to the Confederate Congress nor reserved to the states alone. Congress had power to provide for organizing portions of the arms-bearing population into a militia. The states had the power to appoint officers and train the militia in accordance with the discipline prescribed by Congress. Either could call the militia into active service to enforce laws, suppress rebellion, or repulse invasion. Therefore, the president could not see how Congress' *exclusive* power over the armies could in any way be diminished by the *divided* power over the militia. When called into active service by the Confederacy the militia did not become a part of "armies raised," but remained militia and returned home at the end of the emergency. Of course both the armies and militia must be recruited from the same arms-bearing population of the states. The call made through the conscription act was for men, not for militia. To deny to Congress the power to accept as volunteers or to draft members of a state militia would be denying to Congress the power to raise an army at all.[4]

From a practical viewpoint, President Davis definitely had the better of the argument. Since each had had his say, he no doubt expected the argument to end at this point. Also, he wished to make his views public, hoping to convince those "eminent citizens" who had views similar to those expressed by Governor Brown. Consequently, he released the correspondence for publication. Brown was furious; he had only begun to fight. Privately he accused Davis of wishing to give the public a one-sided view of the subject under discussion.

Davis' letter was delayed since the governor was at Canton rather than Milledgeville, but it was expected. In preparation for a reply Brown had studied Madison's *Journal*, the *Federalist Papers*, the Virginia and Kentucky resolutions, and Calhoun's *Disquisition on Government*. Having done his research, he intended to make use of the results. He pronounced Davis' letter the best argument possible in favor of the conscription law; yet he found it insufficient.

He could not ignore the disastrous consequences which he feared would result from the "bold and dangerous usurpation by Congress of the reserved rights of the States, and a rapid rise towards military despotism," he replied. He repeated at length the old states' rights argument that the federal Union and later the Confederacy were leagues formed by sovereign states. These unions were intended "to be rather the servant of several masters, than the master of several servants." He noted that Davis had ignored his previous citations from the Founding Fathers and assumed that the president chose not to consider as valid their interpretations of the Constitution. But, in spite of the president's attitude toward the interpretations given by the founders, Brown quoted at length from Madison and from the Virginia and Kentucky resolutions, and added more recent observations by John C. Calhoun, that "great and good man," in support of states' rights.

Davis' interpretation of the Constitution, Brown contended, would

4 *Ibid.*, III, 233 ff; *Official Records*, Ser. IV, Vol. I, 1133 ff.

place the "very existence of the State Governments subject to the will of Congress." If Congress had the power to conscript one man, it had the power to conscript all men, regardless of age or position, and make them privates in armies officered by persons appointed by the president. Of course, Brown had no fear that the Confederacy would attempt to conscript high-ranking state officials, for Congress had also passed an act exempting such officials. But Brown wished to argue. The fact that he himself might be wrong never occurred to him. To recognize the act exempting state officials would mean conceding that Congress possessed the power to conscript such officials. In short, he insisted that state officials were exempted "by *right*," not "by the *grace and special favor of Congress*." If this were not true, "of what value are *State rights* and *State sovereignty*?" Since the men conscripted would be the same men who might be called out as a part of the militia, Brown contended, the principal reason for conscription was that officers would be appointed by the president rather than by the states.[5] He might have added that this was his principal reason for *opposing* conscription.

In a postscript to his letter, Brown's language bordered upon disrespect if not contempt. He accused Davis of deliberately publishing *part* of an "unfinished correspondence," without waiting for his reply, for the purpose of "forestalling public opinion." President Davis explained that it had never been any part of his intention "to enter into a protracted discussion." He chose publication to get his views before people other than Brown. He had no knowledge of omitting any portion and had considered the correspondence at an end. However, since Brown had chosen to continue he wished "to disclaim in the most pointed manner" that he had ever said Congress was the "final judge of the constitutionality of a contested power." What he had said was that Congress was the judge of laws passed to execute a power. Governor Brown's long arguments had not changed his conviction that in passing the conscription act Congress had done no more than exercise its power to raise armies. Therefore, he could not share the governor's "alarm and concern" about destruction of states' rights.[6]

Brown was still not ready to terminate the correspondence. He certainly could not have hoped to change the opinions of either Presi-

---

5 *C. R. Ga.*, 251 ff; *Official Records*, Ser. IV, Vol. I, 1156 ff.
6 *C. R. Ga.*, 284; *Official Records*, Ser. IV, Vol. II, 2–3.

dent Davis or Congress. However, the probability of getting his letters in print along side those of Davis was appealing. As usual, he was positive that he was right, regardless of who disagreed with him. He now disagreed with Davis' disagreement: "You did assert that Congress is the judge," he declared, and "You did not qualify the assertion by saying 'the judge' in the first instance, nor did you annex any other qualification or exception in favor of the rights of a State or any other party." This he thought was the interpretation of "every fair-minded man" who had read the president's letter.

Brown could not close without returning to the real point of controversy. He again demanded that all Georgia troops be permitted to choose their own "company, field, and general officers," who would be commissioned by the governor. This right was "now denied them under the conscription act."[7] Brown refused to understand that when men reenlisted or were drafted following the expiration of their original term they were no longer state troops. Although Davis had recommended the conscription act, it was an act of Congress and as binding as any other law. Regardless of whether or not the act was wise, it was the president's duty to enforce it. In Brown's mind, however, the president was responsible for this alleged disregard of states' rights.

Davis made a mistake in allowing himself to be drawn into this controversy. No one ever won an argument with Brown, for he never stopped arguing. Although he never publicly announced it, good disciple of Calhoun that he was, he no doubt believed in the doctrine of "nullification" or "interposition." He refused to see the weakening influences of such a doctrine in times when total war effort was required.

While arguing with President Davis, Governor Brown continued other arguments, protests, and suggestions. He divided his time among Savannah, Milledgeville, Atlanta, and Canton. In Savannah he was concerned with both the defense of the city and the transfer of his state troops to Confederate service. He continued to urge that Major General Jackson and Brigadier Generals Walker, Harrison, and Capers be given Confederate commissions and restored to their commands with the state troops. This was a reasonable request, and, by failing to grant it, Davis gave evidence of as much obstinacy as Brown. About 5,000 men were being transferred, and another 3,000 who had gone home were expected

7 *C. R. Ga.*, 286–91; *Official Records*, Ser. IV, Vol. II, 10–13.

to rejoin their companies. This was ample for a division composed of three regiments. Brown was also justified in his insistence that the qualifications of these officers compared favorably with those of others in the Confederate service. No doubt encouraged by their commander in chief's views, the troops protested, almost to the extent of mutiny, but the division and brigade organization was not restored.[8] None of the commissions requested were granted. Perhaps the fact that Jackson and Walker had previously resigned from the Confederate army had some influence in their cases. The two were not reappointed Confederate brigadiers until 1863; Harrison and Capers never received Confederate commissions.

Following the capture of Fort Pulaski the Federals made no immediate threat to Savannah. Meanwhile, however, danger had appeared on the northern border. After the Confederates fell back from Corinth, Union General Don Carlos Buell was free to move eastward. Soon Chattanooga was threatened. General Kirby Smith at Knoxville, also threatened from Cumberland Gap, was moving first one way and then the other trying to protect the middle against both ends. Chattanooga was a valuable railroad center from which lines led through eastern Tennessee, northwest to Nashville, west to Memphis, and south to Atlanta. Through East Tennessee came Georgia's salt supply from Saltville, Virginia, and from points in Tennessee came coal for operating Georgia's industries.

Both concerned and angry, Brown rushed a note to Secretary of War Randolph: "The State has placed all her means of defense in the hands of the President," he began. "The enemy are near Chattanooga. If it is taken, the railroad bridges on both sides of it burned, we are cut off from the coal mines, and all our iron mills are stopped." It appeared that the Confederates would soon be forced out of Tennessee and would become dependent upon the cotton states for food. "It cannot last long." Rust had ruined the wheat crop, and the young men were being carried away by conscription officers. "If this policy is to be continued, hunger will at no distant day produce its natural result."

Could not an army of 50,000 men march from Chattanooga or Nashville and Louisville and seize the rich provisions of Kentucky, the governor inquired. If so, the results would be much more valuable than

8 *C. R. Ga.*, III, 188, 189, 206.

all the operations against gunboats along the coast. The defensive policy of fortifying the coast and falling back in the center would "end in starvation and overthrow. . . . Let me beg you to send heavy reenforcements to Chattanooga without delay." Since the president had all of Georgia's men and guns, the people had a right to expect him to protect them.[9] Brown's letter was referred to the president, and the reply was no doubt what was expected. "Such a campaign as you support has long been desired," he explained. The failure to carry out the proposal was due to a lack of power, not desire.[10]

Soon Governor Brown was receiving frantic requests from General Kirby Smith in East Tennessee for regiments or guns or both. There were already seven regiments and two battalions of Georgia troops under Kirby Smith's command, but illness had reduced regimental ranks to an average of four hundred. Some had no arms. Brown could send neither men nor arms, but he sent to the War Department an urgent suggestion. Could not Colonel William Phillips' Legion, stationed in South Carolina, be rushed to Chattanooga? This legion had been armed by Georgia and was composed for the most part of up country men.[11] Phillips' Legion was not sent, but Buell did not attack Chattanooga. Soon General Braxton Bragg's army from Mississippi circled around Buell and began moving into Chattanooga.

While President Davis and Governor Brown argued, Major John Dunwody was placed in charge of the enrollment of conscripts in Georgia. Brown was reassured by the War Department that no state officers would be enrolled. Upon arrival in Milledgeville, Dunwody called upon Brown for permission to use state officers to enroll recruits. He found the governor "pleasant and conciliatory, although firm and determined." He promised not to interfere with conscription, Dunwody reported, but "He absolutely refuses to give any State aid in the enrollment." While the governor did not suggest any extension of the exemption list, other than including 125 men who had been designated as guards at the bridges on the state road, he stressed that no militia officer was to be enrolled. Should this order be violated, the enrolling

9 *Ibid.*, 203.
10 *Ibid.*, 205–206.
11 *Ibid.*, 233, 246, 250, 283; Brown to Randolph, June 17, 1862, in Hargrett Collection.

officer would be arrested.[12] The governor considered militia officers absolutely essential to the exercise of local police power.

How much was fact and how much rumor was uncertain, but news soon spread that several militia officers had been conscripted. To Captain G. W. Hunnicut, who was alleged to have been conscripted, the governor sent orders to arrest any enrolling officer who tried to arrest him. Protests to Richmond brought reassurance that Dunwody had no authority to enroll militia officers, unless they had been appointed after the passage of the conscription act. Either Dunwody did not obey orders or those who spread rumors continued active. Finally, in desperation, Secretary Randolph suggested: "I think we might as well drive out our common enemy before we make war on each other." Brown retorted that he agreed, and he hoped the Confederate government would not force the state to choose between having its constitutional government "disbanded and destroyed or to defend the existence and integrity of its government by force."[13] He did not explain how a state with no troops could successfully defend itself against the Confederacy by the use of force. Neither did he explain what Georgia would do, if, by force, it severed its relations with the Confederacy.

Brown was proud of his controversy with Davis and apparently believed himself the winner. Although he had protested against Davis' publication of only a portion of their correspondence, he was pleased to have the complete argument before the public. His greatest disappointment was that so few Georgians of prominence saw fit to speak out as he had done. Many who agreed with his views felt that such views should not be insisted upon in time of emergency. Although Alexander Stephens did not always speak out, he was the one man to whom Brown felt he could turn for comfort and support. "I entered into this revolution to contribute my humble might to sustain the rights of the states and prevent the consolidation of the Government," he explained to Stephens, "and I am still a rebel till this object is accomplished, no matter who may be in power." Knowing of the coolness in the relations between Stephens and President Davis, the Governor added: "I was somewhat astonished at the course taken by the President in the publication. It was not fair

12 *C. R. Ga.*, III, 228, 229.
13 *Ibid.*, 224, 248, 249.

to publish part of the correspondence in the manner in which this was done. Can it be that the object was to obtain a verdict of the people without permitting the whole case to go to the jury? If so it was more like the trick of the politician than the act of the statesman."[14]

In writing to Herschel V. Johnson, Brown still professed to believe it was the intention of the Confederate government to destroy state government. If the conscription act should be carried out, he envisioned the forced enrollment of more than half of each branch of the General Assembly and thus the destruction of that branch of the state government. There might also be a threat to the judiciary. "This I cannot and will not submit to, until submission is yielded to superior overpowering force. While I may for the sake of our cause submit to a temporary disregard of the rights of the State . . . I cannot submit to the *destruction* of the State government." He would not actually hinder enrollment, but he did not feel "inclined to act as the instrument of the President in making the enrollment."[15] In explaining his actions to an out-of-state friend, Brown declared that if states' rights were "disregarded without complaint in war they will not be respected in peace when the force of precedent can be quoted to sustain usurpation."[16]

When General Bragg, having moved his army into Chattanooga preparatory to his Kentucky campaign, threatened Atlanta with martial law, Governor Brown viewed the act "with painful apprehensiveness." Yet strangely enough, he made no great issue of the matter. To Vice-President Stephens he complained: "It seems military men are assuming the whole powers of government to themselves and setting at defiance constitutions, laws, state rights, state sovereignty, and every other principle of civil liberty, and our people engrossed in the struggle with the enemy are disposed to submit to these bold usurpations tending to military despotism without murmur, much less resistance." He had decided to take no notice of the Atlanta affair until he received additional instructions from the state legislature. He doubted, however, that the present legislators properly reflected the sentiment of the people. Yet if the governor should go beyond that point where he would be sustained by the legislature, he would only "expose himself to censure without

14 Brown to Stephens, July 2, 1862, in Stephens Papers, Emory.
15 Brown to Johnson, April 21, 1862, in Hargrett Collection.
16 Brown to John S. Stell, July 28, 1862, *ibid.*

the moral power to do service to the great principles involved." In closing, the governor summarized his apprehensions in a single sentence; "I fear we have much more to apprehend from military despotism than from subjugation by the enemy."[17]

Although pleased with the position he had taken, Brown was displeased with the situation in which he now found himself. When friends privately suggested the possibility of his being elected to the Confederate Senate, he liked the idea. Dr. Lewis' appointment would expire with the next session of the legislature. In reply to C. B. Wellborn he explained "I am free to say that I have but little relish for the Executive office since the Conscription Act has taken it out of my power to be of service to our glorious cause in our time of trial. Were our relations to the military such as they were at the time of my last election I would exchange the office I now hold for no other in the gift of the people or their representatives. As matters now stand I might if I had my choice prefer another position." He could not agree with Wellborn, however, that there was a possibility that the legislature might choose him as senator. This, he felt, the legislators would not do "however much I might desire the place."[18]

Six weeks later the governor was even more receptive but no less cautious. He would feel it his duty to resign as governor to serve Georgia in the Senate "if I were satisfied it was the wish of her people." If the position "were tendered by the General Assembly I would not refuse to accept it." He had great respect for the president of the Senate, John Billups, who would succeed him as governor. However, although desirous of the appointment, he would not place himself "in the position of an aspirant for it." Neither would he permit the use of his name if Dr. Lewis wished to retain the seat.[19]

Although unhappy at the decrease in his importance, Governor Brown did not become inactive. The invasion of Kentucky by the armies of Bragg and Kirby Smith removed the immediate threat to Georgia's supply of salt and coal. Securing an adequate supply of salt was a matter in which the governor had the keenest interest. The lease at the Virginia salt works, secured through the efforts of Dr. Lewis,

17 Brown to Stephens, September 1, 1862, in Stephens Papers, Emory.
18 July 27, 1862, in Hargrett Collection.
19 Brown to J. R. Wright, September 12, 1862, *ibid.*

was supposed to produce 599 bushels of salt per day. The first three carloads arrived in Atlanta late in August, 1862. The governor had already secured from the principal railroads an agreement to haul state imported salt without charge.[20]

His plan was to use Cartersville, Atlanta, Athens, Augusta, Griffin, Macon, Albany, Columbus, and Savannah as centers for distribution. Commissary General Jared I. Whitaker was placed in general charge. To the widow of each deceased soldier was to go one-half bushel (25 pounds) of salt without charge. Justices of the inferior courts of the several counties were to supply the lists and supervise the distribution. Next, each widow or wife of a soldier might purchase one-half bushel at one dollar. Should an additional half bushel be desired by a widow or wife she would have preference to purchase at $2.25, the same price paid by others. Finally, as long as the supply should last, heads of families might purchase one bushel at $4.50.[21]

The movement of Confederate troops into Kentucky left the mountain regions of East Tennessee and Georgia a more attractive haven for deserters. Late in July, 1862, Secretary of War Randolph notified Governor Brown that a number of Georgia regiments had been greatly reduced in strength by prolonged furloughs or desertion. Brown expressed surprise at the extent of this problem but took action immediately. On July 31 he issued a proclamation calling attention to the fact that many soldiers were absent from their regiments without leave. Sheriffs, constables, and jailors were urged to be "vigilant in detecting and arresting all deserters." Those arrested were to be confined to jail and the secretary of war notified.[22]

On September 27, 1862, Congress amended the conscription act, raising the age limit from thirty-five to forty-five, but authorizing the president to suspend conscription in areas where it was found to be impracticable. In cases of suspension the president might accept troops under the law prevailing prior to the passage of the conscription act of April 16, 1862. These provisions gave Governor Brown renewed hope for victory, so he renewed the fight.

After the passage of the original "unconstitutional" Conscription

20 Brown to Lewis, August 28, 1862; Brown to John P. King, July 28, 1862, *ibid.*
21 Brown to Jared I. Whitaker, July 31, 1862, *C. R. Ga.*, II, 225.
22 *Ibid.*, III, 292; Atlanta *Daily Intelligencer*, August 2, 1862.

Act, Brown reminded President Davis, he had permitted the militia to be drained of those within the age bracket, rather than have his "fidelity to our cause" brought into question. However, the militia organizations had not been disbanded, for those above thirty-five had remained. Consequently, the state had continued protection of life and property. If the new amendment should be enforced, however, the state would be almost helpless against possible servile insurrection that might result in "indiscriminate massacre." He further predicted that if, as the law provided, the men in this new age group should be denied acceptance as volunteer units under officers elected by themselves and compelled to enter as individual conscripts, "your orders will only be obeyed by many of them when backed by an armed force which they have no power to resist." This injustice and possible difficulty could only be avoided by the president's exercise of his authority to suspend the conscription act and call up these men by companies and regiments.

Enforcement of the conscription act as amended, the governor contended, would not only do injustice to Georgia citizens but would utterly destroy the state's military organization, encroach upon reserved rights, and strike down her sovereignty "at a single blow," tearing from her "the right arm of strength, by which she alone can maintain her existence, and protect those most dear to her and most dependent upon her." Should the president persist in conscription rather than making requisition for the troops needed, the governor concluded, he himself could no longer avoid his responsibility to the people of Georgia. Consequently, "I cannot permit the enrollment of conscripts, under the late act of Congress . . . until the General Assembly of this State have convened and taken action in the premises."[23]

When the General Assembly convened on November 6, 1862, Governor Brown was able to make a rather optimistic report on state affairs. The state debt, including the issue of Treasury notes, was only $8,417,750. The value of property owned by the state exceeded that amount. Of the $5 million appropriated by the last legislature only $2,081,004 had been spent. About $2 million of this amount had gone for equipping and supporting State troops numbering about eight thousand.

Treasury notes to the amount of $2,320,000 had been issued. The

23 C. R. Ga., III, 294; Official Records, Ser. IV, Vol. II, 128.

only opposition raised to the issuance of Treasury notes, rather than the sale of bonds, was that they went into circulation and thus caused further depreciation of the currency. This was true, the governor explained, but the market demanded an increase in circulating medium. Had the state not supplied this need, it would have been necessary for the banks to do so. Through the issuance of noninterest-bearing Treasury notes the state also saved the interest that would have been paid on bonds. Had he been authorized to do so, the governor explained, he could have saved the state an additional $170,870 in interest by issuing Treasury notes instead of bonds in paying the Confederate war tax. Georgia actually paid $2,494,112.41 war tax.

Shifting to the war effort, the governor enumerated what had been done to strengthen the state and to meet its obligations to the Confederacy. He paid high tribute to the state troops recently transferred to Confederate service, especially to those officers who in spite of their great industry in organizing their commands had lost their positions as a result of the transfer.

There had been little success in the acquisition of small arms. Even a large portion of the 4,300 Enfield rifles brought through the blockade had been seized by Confederate authorities. Remonstrance had brought forth respectful replies and apologies but no return of arms. Some progress had been made, however, in the establishment of an armory within the state penitentiary. A few rifles were now being produced.

As of vital importance to the war effort, the governor explained, he had ordered a temporary prohibition on the distilling of grain. Although there had been some evasions of orders and some militia officers had no doubt failed to do their duty, "in the main" the evil had been checked and much bread saved for the people. He recommended the passage of a law prohibiting the distillation of grain into alcohol or ardent spirits, except for mechanical and medicinal uses. He believed both an "enlightened public opinion" and the "exigencies of the times" demanded such legislation. He further recommended that contracts for manufacture for Confederate use be strictly regulated as to location and quantity.

Since wartime inflation had brought much financial distress among persons of fixed income, the governor recommended some relief for public employees. He estimated that it would require a 500 percent increase in salary to restore them to their prewar financial condition, but he recommended an increase of only 50 percent. In this increase he would include members of the General Assembly. The governor himself could not be included since the constitution prohibited an increase in salary during his term of office.

There should also be a further increase in soldier's pay. The recent increase from eleven dollars to sixteen was inadequate. Some wealthier counties were assisting the families of soldiers, but poorer ones found such assistance impossible without a great tax increase. Therefore, the governor recommended that the state assume the obligation. All soldiers should be exempt from the poll tax and from property tax where property was valued at $1,000 or less. A bounty of $100 should be paid to each soldier signed for the duration of the war. The same amount should be paid to widows of soldiers and other widows who had a son in service. The entire net income from operation of the Western and Atlantic Railroad should be pledged to meet this obligation, and freight rates should be increased 25 percent. For additional funds, all persons found engaged in speculation should be taxed 33⅓ percent on the net income from their speculation. The governor should be authorized to borrow funds sufficient to meet all demands until income could be derived from the state road and taxation.

"We need not attempt to close our eyes to the stern reality," Governor Brown stressed. "The success of our cause depends upon the gallantry and endurance of our troops. They cannot fight unless they and their families can be supplied with at least the necessities of life. The wealth of the country must come to their relief, and contribute whatever the exigencies may require. The question for each property holder to consider is, whether he will give up part for the protection of the balance, or withhold the necessary contribution and lose the whole."

Continuing his discussion of the plight of the soldiers and their families, the governor stressed that some Georgia troops in the Confederate service were "almost destitute of clothes and shoes." During the hard winter ahead they were destined to suffer severely unless the state provided relief. He would recommend that the governor be authorized, if necessary, "to seize all factories and tanneries in this State and appropriate their whole products to this use, till a good pair of shoes and a good suit of clothes are furnished to every Georgia soldier in service who needs the assistance." If the Confederate government failed to pay for these items then the state should.

Shut in by the blockade, the South must look to all of its own needs for provisions. It possessed the means; all that was needed was a shift from cotton to grain. Cotton production should be limited to local needs. Indeed, "the lives of our people and the cause of the Confederacy," the governor asserted, depended upon this shift. To accomplish the shift there must be legal restrictions, for the high price of cotton was too strong a temptation to plant. Since there was little chance to export cotton, why produce more than needed? Storing it for possible future shipment offered a great temptation for seizure by the enemy. Neither should there be plans to store cotton in order to meet the needs of foreign nations after the war. "They have left us at a most critical period to take care of ourselves." Production of cotton could best be regulated through use of the taxing power, the governor suggested. Therefore, he recommended a tax of one hundred dollars per four-hundred-pound bale on all cotton produced in excess of needs. This would make excessive production unprofitable.

The only immediate threat to Georgia territory, the governor concluded, was the constant enemy pressure at Savannah. The Confederate commander there had signified his determination to defend the city to the last, and requested assistance in removing women, children, and other noncombatants from the city. As for himself, the governor declared, he would say "Let us hold the city as long as a house or a brick wall is left standing, behind which troops can fight." He thought the state should prepare to assume a part if not all of the loss and to make temporary arrangements to care for refugees. For the latter, he recommended an appropriation of $250,000.

To provide men for this and other local defense, including the possible horrors of insurrection, the governor recommended that all men between sixteen and sixty be made liable for militia service in their districts. Firearms should be provided for these militiamen to the extent possible. Beyond that point, resort must be made to pikes and knives. If slaves knew that whites had the means for protecting themselves, they would be less likely to attempt insurrection. To meet all necessary expenses of defense within the state the governor recommended an appropriation of $3 million.[24]

Many men of wealth in Georgia were not happy with Governor Brown's recommendation for taxation and restrictions. Among them was the irascible Robert Toombs, who was generally friendly toward Brown. "Our friend Brown has done some very foolish things which I greatly regret on his account and our own," Toombs wrote Linton Stephens. "His whisky proclamation was unconstitutional and as foolish as anything that Davis or Lincoln have ever done. His recommendations about taxing cotton show a want of knowledge of the first principles of political economy which is absolutely humiliating to his friends. He is running a fool's race with Davis and [his] tools, Bragg and Hindman,[25] robbing the sick and oppressing the poor. Lincoln could afford to pay them five hundred million dollars if they can succeed in burning all the cotton we have on hand and preventing the growing of more."[26]

On the same day that Brown's regular message was read to the General Assembly he also sent in a special message on the war and Confederate relations. Although as determined as ever, he did not feel comfortable since his position in opposition to the constitutionality of the conscription act was contrary to the views of the majority of Congress, the president, and the entire Confederate cabinet. While discounting the importance of the views of these men, he chose to elevate to great importance the decision of his political and personal friend, Judge Thomas W. Thomas, who had recently declared the conscription act unconstitutional. Thomas, a small-town circuit judge of some ability, had temporarily deserted the bench to do some soldiering in Virginia. However, he soon became unhappy with the situation there and appealed to Governor Brown for something better. The best the governor could do was give him a staff appointment and send him to break up distilleries in northeast Georgia. He apparently did some judging on the side, but he was not even a close approach to a constitutional lawyer.

The governor began his special message with an inaccurate and

24 *Senate Journal*, 1862, pp. 6 ff; *C. R. Ga.*, II, 241 ff.
25 Major General Thomas C. Hindman had declared martial law for the entire state of Arkansas.
26 December 1, 1862, Phillips, *Correspondence*, 607.

absurd comparison of the composition and motives of the federal and Confederate fighting forces. The armies of the South, he asserted, were composed of "her noblest and best sons, whose valor upon the battle field has been unsurpassed, and whose blood in abundant profusion has been poured out, a rich sacrifice upon the altar of liberty." With the armies of the North it was quite different. To a great degree, they were composed of "imported foreigners and paupers, and the worst classes of Northern society," serving as mercenaries. In many instances their destruction had been "rather a relief than a misfortune to society." These northerners were fighting a war for power and plunder. The noble sons of the South, on the other hand, were defending "the liberty and independence of themselves and their posterity." The North could stop the war at its pleasure, for the South asked nothing more than to be let alone. If not let alone, however, they would never stop fighting until subjugated; they could not be subjugated short of extermination.

Although the correspondence between himself and the president relating to the conscription act had been published in both the newspaper and pamphlet form and an official copy prepared for the General Assembly, Governor Brown entered into an extensive defense of his action. He was clearly sensitive to the charge that he was untrue to the Confederate cause even to the extent of obstructing the course to success. Rather than obstructionist, he wished to appear as the champion of the rights of the state and the citizen against the threat of military despotism.

Apparently the real purpose of this special message was to impress upon the General Assembly the necessity of its taking a definite stand. Brown had never had a friendly legislature, and the present one had been especially unfriendly during its first session. He had some fear of moving out too far in advance of legislative support in his battle with Richmond. It was to impress the General Assembly with its own importance, rather than to protect anyone from conscription, that had prompted him to forbid enforcement of the amended conscription act in Georgia prior to the meeting of the General Assembly. He explained that he felt he would have "justly forfeited the confidence reposed in him by the people" had he permitted such an encroachment upon state rights as virtually to disband state government "without first submitting the question of *surrender* to the representatives of the people. You have the power to adopt measures and give proper directions to this question." The General Assembly should "stand by the rights and the honor of the State, and provide for the protection of the property, liberty and lives of her people."

Since Judge Thomas of Elberton had declared the conscription act unconstitutional, the governor further explained, Congress had passed an act authorizing the president to suspend the writ of habeas corpus. This, he averred, was designed to give the president the power to free himself from decisions of unfriendly judges, placing the liberty of every citizen at his mercy. He could order imprisonment for any reason, and no judge could interfere even though the imprisonment might be illegal. In the face of such a threat, the governor thought it the duty of the General Assembly of the state to decide "whether the constitutional rights of her citizens shall be respected and her sovereignty maintained, or whether the citizens shall be told that he has no rights and his State no sovereignty."

Of further concern to the governor was General Braxton Bragg's declaration of martial law in Atlanta from his headquarters in Chattanooga.[27] Although the order was rescinded by the War Department, the governor declared it a "high-handed usurpation" which if acquiesced in could lead to subversions of the rights of the state and citizens. The states had delegated to Congress the power to suspend the writ of habeas corpus in time of insurrection or invasion, but Brown denied that any agency had the right to declare martial law, setting aside the civil process of a city or region.

In closing, Governor Brown urged the General Assembly to declare in some manner its opinion relative to the extent of Confederate powers in the matters discussed. He further requested that the Assembly "declare the extent to which the executive of this State will be sustained by the representatives of the people in protecting their rights" and the "sovereignty of the State against usurpation."[28]

27 *Official Records*, Ser. I, Vol. LVI, Pt. 2, p. 754.
28 *C. R. Ga.*, II, 283 ff.

Chapter XII

The Question Is One
of Bread

THE NOVEMBER–DECEMBER, 1862, session of the General Assembly
was to be another stormy one. Some of the governor's enemies refused
to support him although they agreed with his position on conscription.
Some of his friends hesitated to desert him even though they thought
him in the wrong. Although the governor made no mention of it in his
special message, another conscription case had been heard in the court
of Judge Iverson Harris, and the act was declared *constitutional*. This
case was later appealed to the Georgia Supreme Court where Harris'
opinion was confirmed.

Governor Brown's concern now became heavily influenced by irritation. On November 13 he sent to the General Assembly another
special message. It had been reported from Camden County that three
federal companies of Negroes had landed at St. Mary's, and "after insulting the few ladies remaining there and helping themselves to everything they could lay their hands on, returned to their gunboats without
the slightest molestation." There were also other reports of Federals
leaving their gunboats and seizing all livestock within their reach. In
an effort to protect their property, farmers were compelled to move
farther inland. Henry H. Floyd, colonel of militia in that district, requested from the governor authority to call out the militia of a number
of counties. Brown submitted the request to the legislature along with
his special message. Under ordinary circumstances, he explained, he
would use his constitutional power to call out the militia to protect

citizens against outrages, robbery, and insults by Negroes. But under the conscription act, which had recently been declared constitutional by the state supreme court, all militia, except officers, within the age limits were subject to the command of the president; consequently, the president might countermand any order the governor might issue and march off to other fields all militia called up to protect the people of Georgia. Thus the Confederate government had the power to destroy a state.

But Brown vehemently denied that any creature had the power to destroy its creator. The Confederate government could not have the power to deny states the means to protect their citizens against "invasion of the enemy and the unbridled savage cruelty of their slaves in actual insurrection." Yet the president, Congress, and the Georgia Supreme Court said it did. Brown was particularly bitter toward the supreme court for a decision "rendered under heavy outside pressure, and if not *ex parte,* under most peculiar circumstances."

In this embarrassing situation, the governor wished to appeal to the General Assembly for advice and direction. If he no longer had the power to command a force sufficient to protect the citizens then they should be told that, although they paid taxes for services, they would be left without protection from Negro invaders, insults, and plunderers. On the other hand, if the General Assembly should hold that the governor *did* possess the power to command sufficient militia to give protection, "I shall not hesitate to call them forth and hold them in service as long as the coast is invaded and our people are subject to the insult, robbery, and merciless cruelty of the enemy."[1]

The governor often referred to enemy "cruelty," yet cited no instances. Apparently in his thinking, every Yankee who participated in the invasion of the South was a potential fiend. His views were always greatly influenced by provincialism. As far as the records reveal, except for his trip to Connecticut for a brief period of study at the Yale Law School, he had never traveled farther from Georgia than eastern Tennessee and western South Carolina.

The Senate immediately granted the governor's request, approving his proposal to call out the militia in spite of the conscription act. But when the resolution reached the House it met with spirited opposition and produced much confusion. Thomas M. Norwood of Chatham de-

[1] *C. R. Ga.,* II, 317.

clared that he "opposed investing the Governor with special authority to throw himself in conflict with the Confederate authorities." But Linton Stephens thought, "We have the right to take issue with the decision of the Judiciary." Norwood took issue with Stephens. He stood by Davis in his interpretation of the power to raise armies. John Thomas of Whitfield said he had "never had the opportunity of rubbing his head against a college wall," but he thought the issue was leading toward "the organization of a new party, based in opposition to the decision of the court." Yet the great complaint against the "Yankees" had been that "they would not obey the decision of the courts." He would "never sanction hostility to the policy of Mr. Davis." J. S. Hook of Washington declared his dissent from the decision of the court, but he wished no conflict with the Confederate government. C. G. Cabaniss of Monroe denounced the governor for his attitude toward the court. The House tabled the Senate resolution.[2]

During the heat of discussion Confederate senator Ben Hill appeared on the scene and addressed the legislators on December 11. Since early in the fall, he had been in Georgia as an unofficial emissary of President Davis, attempting to neutralize the effects of Governor Brown's opposition. Before the legislature, he became the true champion of the administration. He vigorously defended the president's efforts to secure fighting men by any or all means. He then reviewed Brown's efforts to thwart Confederate authority in time of crisis, noting that the first official in the Confederate states to threaten to resort to conscription was Governor Brown. However, the only similarity between Brown's plan for a state draft and the conscription act was that both gave the individual an opportunity to volunteer before being drafted. Brown had no legislative authority for his action, Hill charged. President Davis would never have thought of such a step without prior congressional approval. True, Brown raised his quota of men, but it was by a method not sanctioned by law and with "little of the volunteer spirit." They certainly were not raised by a volunteer method.

Following the disastrous winter of 1861–1862, Senator Hill further explained, the Confederate government was forced to make grave decisions involving manpower. Many argued then and later that the gov-

2 *Confederate Union*, November 25, 1862; *House Journal*, 1862, p. 197.

ernment had no power of compulsion. To this he would reply that if there was no power of compulsion, the government was a failure. "We had defended—nobly defended by voluntary enlistment, until that system had exhausted its strength. We must *command* to fight or fail."

The senator then tore to pieces as thoroughly as President Davis had done, but not in the same calm manner, Brown's arguments against the constitutionality of conscription. He agreed that "Eternal vigilance is the price of liberty," but he denied that "eternal vigilance means perpetual snarling, snapping, fault finding, and complaining. I deny that vigilance means resistance to the government, disaffection to the laws, contumely to authority, or the disorganizing freedom of individual opinion to set itself up against legal enactments and judicial decisions."[3] Senator Hill knew the opinionated governor too well even to hope to influence him. What he planned and apparently achieved was to scotch the movement in the legislature to endorse Brown's actions.

On the closing day of the session, the General Assembly still had not taken a definite stand in opposition to the conscription act, so Governor Brown sent in another special message dealing with the appointment of company and regimental officers. Georgia troops in Confederate service were flooding him with pleas for relief from their situation, he explained. As militia in active service of the Confederacy, they were entitled to fill all vacancies by election and to have those selected commissioned by their governor. This right was denied by the conscription act, which gave to the president the right to fill vacancies by promotion or otherwise and to commission those chosen.

In this appeal the governor used a new approach. He pointed to the fact that several members of each house of the General Assembly held commissions in Georgia regiments in Confederate service. If they were classed as Confederate officers, then they could not constitutionally hold their seats, for the state constitution forbade all officials, except justices of the peace, justices of the inferior courts, and *officers of the militia*, from holding seats in the legislature. Therefore, such legislators were either militia officers or else they were not members of the General Assembly. If militia officers, they and their fellow officers were subject to election by their units and commissioning by the governor. The gov-

3 Hill, *Hill*, 252 ff.

ernor therefore urged the legislators to take steps to "vindicate the dignity and sovereignty of the State" and the rights of citizens now under arms.[4] There was no hope of immediate action; the governor wished to get his message before the public and hoped for action in the special session planned for the spring of 1863. He immediately sent copies to friendly newspaper editors, urging publication and favorable comment.[5]

During recess in the debate on conscription, the Assembly took up the matter of selecting a Confederate senator. One test applied to the candidates was how did they stand on conscription and the recent decision of the state supreme court. The name of neither Brown nor Dr. Lewis was placed in nomination. Their friends wisely chose otherwise. Only Herschel V. Johnson and James Jackson were nominated, but on the first ballot 55 votes were scattered among twelve other possible candidates. With 84 votes cast for Johnson and 59 for Jackson, no one received the required majority. Before another ballot was taken it was rumored that Johnson, who was known to be opposed to conscription, had however pledged his support to the law and the Davis administration. He received 111 votes and the election on the second ballot.[6]

Governor Brown, ignoring the rumor, was pleased with the selection; he expected the new senator to join him in battle against the administration. Before Johnson left to take his seat, the governor loaded him with documents—copies of communications with Richmond, his messages to the General Assembly, and all state legislative items touching on relations with the Confederacy. He further assured the new senator that "It will at all times afford me pleasure to furnish you from this office any information within my power."[7]

On matters other than conscription, Governor Brown got from the legislature most of what he requested. There was no general 50 percent increase in the salaries of state employees, but the governor was authorized to grant reasonable and just increases, not to exceed 50 percent, to workers on the state road. A sum of $500,000 was provided to supply the people with salt. The governor could use the money in production and transportation or in subsidies to persons engaged in manufacture

4 *C. R. Ga.*, II, 335 ff.
5 Brown to J. R. Parrott, December 19, 1862, in Hargrett Collection.
6 *Senate Journal*, 1862, pp. 111–13; Avery, *History of Georgia*, 250–51.
7 Brown to Johnson, January 2, 1863, in Hargrett Collection.

and distribution, provided there was no speculation. As much as $50,000 of the amount might be used to send trains to Saltville, Virginia.[8]

Large appropriations were made for the relief of soldiers and their families. If necessary, the governor was authorized to seize the output of factories and tanneries to the extent required to outfit soldiers. The sum of $1,500,000 was made available for purchase of soldiers' clothes; $2,500,000 for relief of indigent widows of soldiers and soldiers' families; and $300,000 for evacuation and care of indigent whites from invaded areas.[9]

No tax was levied on surplus cotton, but rather stringent limits were set on production. For each worker between fifteen and fifty-five years of age there was to be an allotment of three acres. For those under fifteen or over fifty-five the allotment would be half that amount. A fine of $500 was levied for each acre planted in excess of allotments. One-half of the fine collected would go to the informer and the other "for the benefit of indigent soldiers' families in said county."[10]

Still more stringent than the regulation on cotton production was the prohibition on the distillation of spirits. Henceforth, no alcohol was to be distilled from "corn, wheat, rye, or other grains except for medicinal, hospital, chemical or mechanical purposes." Violations were to be classed as misdemeanors, punishable by fines of $2,500 to $5,000 and twelve months in prison. Each day of operation was to constitute a separate offense. All fines collected would be divided, one-half to the informer and the other to the relief of wives, widows, and families of soldiers. The governor might grant licenses for the production of liquor not to exceed one million gallons for Confederate use, but the stills must be located at least twenty miles from a railroad or navigable stream. Preference was to be given to isolated areas in which grain was more abundant. The products were to be sold for not more than $1.50 per gallon for liquor and $2.50 for alcohol. In a kind of repudiation of the governor's previous seizure of stills, the act further provided that such stills were to be returned to their owners where possible and interest paid upon the value from the time of seizure. Where return was not possible, stills were to be paid for at their value at the time of

8 *Acts of the General Assembly*, 1862, pp. 6–7, 63.
9 For general appropriation act see *ibid.*, 10–16.
10 *Ibid.*, 5.

seizure plus interest from that date.[11] Most of the stills seized would not be returned; they had been melted down for use in the manufacture of guns.

Although the governor had not specifically recommended it, the relief to banks voted in the previous two sessions of the General Assembly was extended to December, 1863, provided banks would accept state and Confederate treasury notes at par with their own. Banks were also required to issue small bills, ranging from five to seventy-five cents, to the extent of 5 percent of their capital stock. They might also issue one-, two-, and three-dollar bills in amounts not to exceed 10 percent of their capital.[12]

Following the governor's suggestion, the Assembly authorized the increase of the state military force to two regiments for local defense and appropriated $1 million for military purposes. Brown had hoped that he might be authorized to form regiments into a brigade, thus enabling him to take care of his friend Major General Henry R. Jackson, who had been denied appointment by the Confederate War Department. He abandoned the plan for fear of "endangering the whole movement."[13] Privately, he expressed the opinion that "The legislature of Georgia has repudiated the constitutionality of the Conscription Act in the strongest practical manner: to the extent of forbidding its execution in the State when it conflicts with her decision to raise troops subject to it for State service."[14] To another friend he confided: "The action of the legislature in authorizing the organization of this force out of the men subject to conscription is a practical repudiation of the doctrine, of probable greater value than any set of resolutions that may be passed in the nature of a protest. This says, while we will not resist the execution of the law, we will hold our men when the State needs them, not withstanding the Conscription Act."[15]

The governor was reading into the legislative resolution more than was there. It did not forbid the execution of the conscription act; it did not even mention it. It did, however, make conscription almost impossible, for since the state and the Confederacy would be competing for

---

11 *Ibid.*, 25.
12 *Ibid.*, 18.
13 Brown to Jackson, December 23, 1862, in Hargrett Collection.
14 Brown to J. R. Parrott, December 19, 1962, *ibid.*
15 Brown to Herschel V. Johnson, January 2, 1863, *ibid.*

those within conscription age, those about to be conscripted would no doubt rush to join the state forces. Whether those who voted for the resolution knew it or not, it was Brown's intention to prevent conscription in Georgia to the greatest extent and for the longest period possible.

There was no doubt that more troops were needed in Georgia. The same was true in most other states. There was some danger of attack on Savannah, but many other portions of the Confederacy had already been hard hit. The problem was where could the limited forces of the Confederacy be used to the greatest advantage. Brown's answer to this question was always one word—Georgia. Late in November, 1862, while the General Assembly was in session, William M. Browne, aide-de-camp to the president, arrived in Milledgeville with an urgent request, a copy of which had also been sent to other governors. In this request, Davis pointed out that the year 1862 had not been a good one, and there was serious trouble ahead. In addition to the enormous increase in the United States land and naval forces there was a serious threat from bands of Negro slaves which might be incited by invading forces. To repulse these attacks, there must be "the most energetic action" on the part of all. "Appreciating the great value of cordial cooperation of the different State governments, and with unfaltering reliance on their patriotism and devotion to our cause, I earnestly appeal to them for all the aid it may be in their power to extend."

The president urgently requested assistance in five special areas—the enrollment of conscripts, the return of absentees, collection of supplies, recruitment of slave labor for work on fortifications, and in the breaking up the shameful practices of mercenaries.[16] Davis instructed his aide to stress upon the Georgia governor the necessity for filling up the much thinned ranks of Georgia regiments then in service by sending forward conscripts. He was also to express to the governor hope that the recent decision of the Georgia Supreme Court could be "regarded as conclusive of the constitutional question" concerning conscription. The president was looking forward with much pleasure to the governor's cooperation.[17]

16 *C. R. Ga.*, III, 305; *O. R.*, Ser. IV, Vol. II, 211.
17 Davis to Browne, November 28, 1862, Dunbar Rowland (ed.), *Jefferson Davis Constitutionalist: His Letters, Papers, and Speeches*, 10 vols. (Jackson, 1923), V, 378–79.

There is no evidence that Governor Brown informed the legislators of Davis' appeal, although they must have known of the presence of the president's aide in Milledgeville. Since Browne made an oral report to the president, the legislators would learn nothing of his conference with the governor. It is certain, however, that the mere mention of the recent decision of the supreme court did not add to the harmony of the conference; Davis was completely mistaken in thinking that Governor Brown would accept a court decision as the final word when it went contrary to his beliefs. Although it is not known what the two men said to each other, Browne did form an opinion of the governor and the more prominent men supporting him. "I am afraid I can do nothing with Joe B." he wrote a friend. "He is a slippery gentleman too much for me to hold. I trust that the State of Georgia will rid us of him this fall."[18] To Howell Cobb he explained "Bad designing men at Crawfordville [Alexander Stephens], in Hancock Co. [Linton Stephens] and elsewhere are doing all they can to bring Joe Brown into open rebellion."[19]

Governor Brown was quite willing to cooperate in all the president's requests, except the first. In fact he had asked the General Assembly for legislation to accomplish these ends. But he had no desire to assist in conscripting men to fill up the thinned ranks of Georgia regiments already in Confederate service. It was to thwart such an attempt that he urged the Assembly for authority to enroll more state troops. They would be under his command and their officers would be commissioned by him. Brown knew little about military matters, but he knew a great deal about politics. He disregarded the fact that most officers who had been elected through politics would perform as politicians, that many a good politician made a poor colonel. He appointed political friends to military positions with little regard for fitness. His most recent offer was to make Herbert Fielder of Cedartown colonel of one of the proposed regiments. Fielder, an old friend and future biographer, had been disappointed in politics and was out of a job. Neither did the governor hesitate to come to the rescue of friends who by "mistake" found themselves in undesirable positions in the Confederate service. He had recently appealed to General Kirby Smith for the release of

18 Browne to John ——, February 5, 1863, in Cobb Papers.
19 January 21, 1863, *ibid.*

L. N. Trammel, an original "Brown for Governor" man. He wished to make Trammel assistant quartermaster general.[20]

It was with great satisfaction that Governor Brown notified President Davis on December 29, 1862, of the Assembly's approval for the enrollment of two regiments of state troops to defend against invasion and to perform police duty.[21] According to the legislative resolution, he explained, the only men not to be considered for state service were those *already* enrolled in the Confederate service. Davis no doubt immediately recognized the conflict intended, but he did not choose to make an issue of it. Perhaps he was weary of arguing with Brown. Or maybe he recognized the fact that Brown could raise troops in Georgia with more ease than the Confederate enrolling officers. The president did not reply to the governor's letter, but he did express "great satisfaction" with Georgia's new law limiting cotton production.[22]

Governor Brown had little difficulty in raising his two regiments. He reported that he could have raised five. Eligible men had a choice between enlisting in the state force or forfeiting the governor's protection against Confederate conscription. Brown made it clear that these troops were to be used for local defense, including defense against depredation and terrorism from deserters concentrating in the mountains. "I intend that Georgia shall not be the resting place of deserters," he assured Senator Johnson. "I will hunt them if necessary with the state troops till they are driven from her soil. All who have volunteered and gone into service, or however tendered to the Confederacy by the State, must do their whole duty, and if they fail they will receive no sympathy among our people."[23] It might not have been intentional, but the governor mentioned only those deserters who had volunteered for Confederate service. No mention was made of deserters who had been drafted.

On January 17, 1863, Governor Brown issued a proclamation demanding that all deserters and others absent without leave return to their commands immediately.[24] Soon a detachment of Georgia troops,

20 Brown to Fielder, December 23, 1862; Brown to Kirby Smith, December 29, 1862, in Hargrett Collection.
21 *C. R. Ga.*, III, 317; *O. R.*, Ser. IV, Vol. II, 263.
22 *C. R. Ga.*, III, 324.
23 January 19, 1863, in Hargrett Collection.
24 *C. R. Ga.*, II, 359.

consisting of both cavalry and infantry, was scouring the mountains. Those in command reported success in capturing fifty leaders and two hundred members of the organization, and flushing out probably two thousand deserters to rejoin their commands.[25] The relief would be only temporary; the mountain area was too vast and rugged and too many natives were unfriendly to the Confederacy.

The companies to form the two new regiments were ordered to rendezvous on February 16, 1863, the first at Camp McDonald north of Marietta and the second at Fort Valley south of Macon. Brigadier General Hugh W. Mercer, commanding at Savannah, expecting attack and despairing of Confederate reinforcements, was calling upon Governor Brown for all the assistance possible. Once the two regiments were organized they were to be held in readiness to move to Savannah immediately.

By the close of the winter of 1862–1863, the economic plight in the South had become very serious. Many, including Governor Brown, were openly predicting that if the Confederacy suffered eventual defeat, it would be more from the lack of food and supplies than from a shortage of manpower. Following the failure of his brilliantly conceived Kentucky campaign, General Braxton Bragg had taken position at Murfreesboro, Tennessee. The federal army under General William S. Rosecrans faced him from Nashville, some thirty miles away. The two forces engaged in indecisive battle along Stones River as the year 1862 ended. Bragg then fell back to Tullahoma and Shelbyville where he remained inactive for months. His only supply line was the Nashville and Chattanooga Railroad to Chattanooga and the Western and Atlantic to Atlanta. The state-owned Western and Atlantic was also bringing into Georgia salt and coal from Virginia and Tennessee. Congestion was inevitable.

Growing impatient with what he considered civilian inefficiency, General Bragg ordered military seizure of the Western and Atlantic. He later professed ignorance of the fact that this line was Georgia state property. Nothing could have irritated Governor Brown more than military seizure of his beloved Western and Atlantic. He immediately wired President Davis: "I am informed that General Bragg has issued an order for seizure of the State railroad. I have done all in my

25 Avery, *History of Georgia*, 257.

power to accommodate him with transportation. The road is as absolutely the property of the State as is the State House. If he may seize the
one, he may the other. I must beg you to instruct him in his duties and
save me the unpleasant necessity of repelling his unwarrantable aggres-
sion by force from the hour the seizure is made. All operations on the
road will stop till the question is settled." Davis expressed a hope that
Brown's information might have been incorrect, but he gave assurance
that if such an order had been given it would be countermanded.[26] To
Bragg at Tullahoma, Davis expressed relief that although force was
threatened it had not been used to seize the railroad. Every effort must
be made to avoid conflict with state governments. In the future the
general would call upon Governor Brown directly when assistance was
needed.[27]

There was no clash of forces. Brown considered Davis' reply quite
satisfactory. In the meantime, however, he had instructed John S.
Rowland, superintendent of the state road, that should military seizure
be attempted, he was to stop all trains, call off from their jobs all employees, and lock up all depots until matters were satisfactorily settled.
The governor did not think Bragg would be so foolish as to attempt
seizure but if he did, the result would be failure. "While I remain in
office, he will never seize and hold the Road. If he undertakes it the
result will be his mortification."[28]

Seizure of the state road for military use might well have further
complicated the importation of salt from Virginia. Operations at Saltville had failed to meet expectations. A short supply of wood had at
times caused a shutdown in operation, but the most serious problem
was transportation. In order to reach Atlanta, salt had to pass over four
different railroad lines. The most serious problem was getting the salt
from Saltville to Bristol over the Virginia and Tennessee Railroad, for
Virginia and the Confederacy had priority on the use of cars. From
Bristol to Knoxville, traffic was often stopped by the work of East
Tennessee "bridge burners." In late March, 1863, no fewer than sixty
carloads of salt lay ready for shipment at Saltville. A more satisfactory,
but much more expensive, way to get out the salt would have been to

26 March 25, 1863, C. R. Ga., III, 329, 330.
27 Ibid., 331; Rowland, Davis, V, 453.
28 O. R., Ser. I, Vol. LII, 434, 435, 438.

send trains from the state road. But the president of the Virginia and Tennessee would not permit Georgia trains to operate on his tracks. He offered, however, to operate a Georgia engine and cars if they were sent to Bristol, paying ten dollars per day for use of the engine and two cents per mile for cars. This offer was being considered by Governor Brown. Further, the cost of production had greatly increased, and M. S. Temple, who was producing salt for the state under contract, was urging that an increase in the price be stipulated in the contract. Both Virginia and the Confederacy were paying more. All the governor of Georgia could do was promise to lay the matter before the General Assembly.[29]

Still more serious was the developing shortage of food and clothing. To encourage the production of more homespun cloth the state government was subsidizing the construction and operation of a factory at Milledgeville for the manufacture of cards for combing wool and cotton fiber. But wire and leather were in short supply, and the great demand for cards put the problem of fair distribution to individuals almost beyond solution. Governor Brown expressed the belief that "If the women of Georgia, who from the commencement of our struggle for independence, have acted so noble a part, were supplied with cotton cards they would not only clothe their families, but would, by untiring industry, contribute largely to the supply necessary for our gallant troops in service."[30]

Governor Brown appointed T. T. Windsor to arrange for the sale of cotton cards, and in the interest of fairness a rather complicated method of distribution was provided. Purchasers could do nothing to replace the wire used in producing their cards, but they could supply leather or animal skins. At the suggestion of the governor, Windsor publicly announced that cards would be exchanged for sheep, goat, dog, or deer skins, "whether tanned or not." A schedule of values was included in the announcement.[31]

More alarming than the probable shortage of clothing was the inevitable lack of an adequate supply of food. The year 1862 had not been a good one for the production of provisions, and too much cotton had

29 *C. R. Ga.*, II, 426–33; Brown to William M. Wadley, April 6, 1863, in Hargrett Collection.
30 *C. R. Ga.*, II, 360.
31 *Ibid.*, 363.

been grown. Further, Confederate officials were taking large quantities of provisions for military use. Governor Brown sent to President Davis a special protest against activities in the Cherokee region. A severe drought during the past season, he explained, had greatly reduced the production of grain. Corn was selling at three dollars per bushel and soldiers' families were suffering. Seizures by Confederate authorities were leaving little for relief. "If this continues the rebellion in that section will grow, and soldiers in service will desert to go to the relief of their suffering families." Plenty of corn could be had by the Confederacy in southwestern Georgia, Brown added, and the railroads were ready to haul it.[32] As his own personal contribution to the hungry, the governor journeyed to his plantation in Cherokee County and supervised the distribution of his surplus corn among the wives and widows of soldiers.[33] His desire to assist the unfortunate is beyond question, yet he could not have been unmindful of the fact that a gubernatorial election was only a few months away.

A further economic problem was that, as the planting season approached, a number of Georgia planters signified their intentions to ignore the regulations on the production of cotton. To his friend, Congressman Augustus R. Wright, Brown wrote: "If you have not yet disposed of the Exemption Bill, I suggest that you insert a provision that no manager of negroes shall be exempt who plants exceeding one-half acre of cotton or tobacco to the hand. The great question with us is one of bread. Lincoln's bayonets will never conquer us—starvation may."[34]

Brown issued a call for a special session of the General Assembly to convene on March 25, 1863. He had intended making the call for an April date but had moved it up hoping to get further legislation to "restrain the avaricious" in the planting of cotton and more stringent laws on the distillation of grain. At the governor's special request, President Davis granted furloughs to all Georgia legislators then in Confederate service.[35]

32 *Ibid.*, III, 328.
33 Brown to Justices of Cherokee County, February 17, 1863; Brown to William P. Hammond, February 18, 1963, in Hargrett Collection; Atlanta *Intelligencer*, February 22, 1863.
34 March 10, 1863, in Hargrett Collection.
35 *C. R. Ga.*, II, 366; III, 324, 330, 331.

The governor's message to the special session of the legislature came right to the point. First, he urged further controls on growing cotton. If three acres of cotton per workhand, as permitted by existing law, were planted "the result will be our subjugation by hunger, and the utter ruin of the Confederacy. . . . Attempt to conceal it as we may, the fact is undeniable, that the great question in this revolution is now a question of *bread*."

Equally as important as stimulating production of foodstuffs was the immediate protection of what was available. The law against distillation was being both evaded and violated. Distillers had in many cases shifted from the use of grain to potatoes, dried fruits, and molasses which were not protected by the law. Others, professing to use these items, were manufacturing behind closed doors and using much grain. Still others were openly defying the law, and people were afraid to report them. The governor recommended that the law be amended so as to prohibit distillation of potatoes, dried fruits, or molasses. Any distiller operating in secrecy should be held "*prima facie* guilty of a violation of the law." Any distiller operating without a license was to be considered guilty of using grain, burden of proof to the contrary resting with him.

The remainder of the governor's message was devoted to discussion of a proposal to have the states endorse the Confederate debt. Four states had already approved it in principle. Brown disagreed. The capitalists who owned the Confederate debt, he insisted, looked to the success of the Confederacy for security of their investment. Should responsibility for payment be shifted to the states "interest in the permanent success of the Confederacy ceases." Further, if the endorsed debt became extremely large the money lenders might decide that the chances of payment by the states might be better in the old Union than by continuing the new Confederacy. Such a reunion, the governor exclaimed, would be unthinkable. "Sooner than reunite with those now seeking to enslave us, and under the name of Union with them, become, with our posterity, hewers of wood and drawers of water for them, let us submit with more than Roman firmness, to the devastation of our fields, and if need be, the extermination of our race." The governor then engaged in extensive praise of the Confederacy. "The future happiness of our posterity is firmly linked with the Confederacy. . . . We should not only sustain the Confederacy at all hazards, but we should also sustain the administration." There would always be differences among men. "But while we contend earnestly for what we consider sound principles, we should do no act which can seriously embarrass the administration in the prosecution of the war."[36] Many listeners must have wondered if this was really the governor speaking. But on the eve of an election Brown certainly did not wish to appear antagonistic to the Confederacy.

Within a week after the governor's message was read to the Assembly he addressed a note to President Davis, warning him against believing a rumor that the government of Georgia and a few friends were attempting to organize an antiadministration party. "This I assure you is not true." Although he had disagreed with the president as to the constitutionality of the conscription act and on a few other points, he, in the main, had the greatest respect for the president's "high administrative ability" and "lofty patriotism." While in the old Union, he had been a disciple of the same doctrine as advocated by the senator from Mississippi and had ardently admired the senator's course.

In the new Confederacy, "upon the success of your administration depends the success of our cause and the freedom and independence of our people." While he would always freely express his opinion "when in my judgment the maintenance of sound principles requires it," he would ever be careful not seriously to embarrass the president "in the prosecution of the war with vigor, promptness, and energy." He could never have a part in organizing an antiadministration party which would be an evil without hope for good. In making such statements, Brown assured the president, he was seeking "no position within your gift"; neither did he expect ever to do so. "I trust, however, I am incapable of factious oppositions to the head of an able and vigorous administration, on account of the difference of opinion on a few points. Whether as a public officer or a private citizen, I shall do all in my power to sustain you and the Government in this struggle."[37]

In a special message to the assembly, Governor Brown renewed his previous request that the legislators take a definite stand in favor of increased pay for soldiers. This he thought was due the soldiers and

36 *Ibid.*, II, 395 ff.
37 April 4, 1863, "Governors Letterbook," 451.

he also thought it the best way to reach the wealthy who had hired substitutes while they remained at home to speculate. The wealthy must pay if the poor were to survive.[38] The legislature responded favorably, requesting Georgia congressmen and senators to support an increase in soldiers' pay to twenty dollars per month. Necessary funds should be raised from taxes on "the income of speculators and extortioners, and upon the wealth of those who are not in the army."[39] Governor Brown immediately forwarded a copy to President Davis.

The General Assembly refused to pass further legislation regulating the planting of cotton, but it did amend the distilleries act. Henceforth, it was forbidden that whisky, alcohol, or other spiritous or malt liquors be manufactured from "corn, wheat, rye, barley, millet, rice or other grains, nor from the articles of sugar, molasses, syrup, sugar cane, honey, sweet potatoes, pumpkins, peas, Irish potatoes, or dried fruit, in any form or condition of said articles, or from any mixture thereof, except for medicinal, hospital or mechanical purposes." Violators would be subject to fine of $500 to $5,000 and up to twelve months in prison for each day of operation.[40]

This special session of the legislature, in response to several recommendations by the governor, also made a move to curb speculation and profiteering. A tax was levied on profits from the manufacture or sale of goods and provisions. Profits of 20 percent were to be taxed at fifty cents on each $100. Profits of from 20 to 30 percent at $1.50 per $100. The rate continued upward indefinitely at an increase of fifty cents on each 10 percent bracket. Proceeds from this tax were to be divided among the counties for the relief of the families of indigent soldiers.[41]

There was, no doubt, much speculation in Milledgeville during the special session of the assembly relative to the coming gubernatorial campaign. No one had yet announced his candidacy. Of course the big question was would Governor Brown seek a fourth term. For the past two months the governor himself had been pondering this question. His first known mention of the subject was in a letter to Alexander H. Stephens, dated January 30, 1863, which began with the statement "I do not intend to be a candidate for election to another term." This point

38 *C. R. Ga.*, II, 433 ff.
39 *Ibid.*, III, 332.
40 *Acts of the General Assembly*, 1863, pp. 141–42.
41 *Ibid.*, 176–78.

disposed of, he added that he desired to see someone elected who would "contend for and sustain to the extent of his ability the rights and sovereignty of the state." After careful survey of the field of possibilities, he had placed Linton Stephens at the head of his list. He had not, however, mentioned to Linton or anyone else his decision to retire; he had thought it better for the time being to keep his "enemies and opposers" guessing. He now thought it time, however, "that a few of us who are friends and agree upon the great issues which are likely to come before the country should confer in advance about this matter." Would Stephens sound out his brother Linton? "I will exert myself to the extent of my power for Linton if he will run." Any newspaper discussion for the present he thought unwise.[42]

Linton Stephens considered the matter for some time. Meanwhile Alexander Stephens attempted to persuade Brown to change his mind. Brown replied that, while he had not said publicly that he would not under any circumstances be a candidate, "my convictions on that subject are so well settled that I do not think there is any state of facts likely to arise which can induce me to change my purpose." Should Linton decline, he thought Robert Toombs the best man. "I have the highest confidence in his patriotism, ability, statesmanship, and soundness on the vital question of state sovereignty."[43]

By mid-February Brown was receiving letters of inquiry from several sources. Clearly some were from persons who were considering making the race themselves should Brown not offer. Brown developed a stock reply. He would not be a candidate and would support no one whose stand on states' rights and sovereignty was in question. He thought no kind of announcement should be made until after the special session of the legislature. "When we all meet," he suggested to George A. Gordon, a member of the state Senate, "we must confer freely together and place in the field as our standard bearer the man of the proper principles and capacity who has the most general popularity and can most certainly carry the State."[44] To his old friend Congressman Augustus R. Wright he made similar statements. "My preference is to retire, and I feel that I have a right to consult my own feelings in

42 Stephens Papers, Emory.
43 Brown to Stephens, February 16, 1863, in Stephens Papers, Emory.
44 February 19, 1863, in Hargrett Collection.

the matter as affairs now stand." There would no doubt be "quite a scramble" for the office, and he did not propose to be "an indifferent spectator." He would support no man "who favors consolidation of all power in the hands of a central despotism."[45]

By mid-March, Linton Stephens had decided not to make the race and Brown had turned to Toombs. He wished Alexander Stephens to write Toombs to visit Milledgeville during the session of the General Assembly. He thought Toombs's refusal to limit his cotton production would be "the hardest thing he has to carry." It was also said that Congressman Augustus H. Kenan was trying to ruin Toombs by reporting that Toombs had sworn to come to Georgia and expose the Davis administration. This, Brown feared, might influence "the timid who fear the effect of opposition to the President upon any grounds."[46]

Almost two decades later Isaac W. Avery told of a meeting at the Executive Mansion, attended by the legislators James L. Seward of Thomas County and George A. Gordon of Chatham, Quartermaster General Ira R. Foster, Adjutant General Henry C. Wayne, and Comptroller Peterson Thweatt, at which Governor Brown announced his decision not to run and requested that those present look for a suitable candidate. The group protested, contending that no other man of similar views could be elected. They then insisted that if the governor "wished to take care of and sustain his friends," he would "withdraw his determination and let his friends run him again." The governor surrendered.[47]

In the extant correspondence of Brown there is no mention of such a meeting, but he had recently been in close touch with all of these men with the possible exception of Seward. Be that as it may, by April 1, the governor was weakening. He wrote Henry P. Farrow, "Were I satisfied that it is the general wish of the people of Georgia, with but little division of sentiment, that I remain in this office and discharge the laborious and responsible duties required of the incumbent, I should not hesitate, however contrary to my individual interests or inclination." His decided preference, however, was to retire.[48] On this same day he wrote a military friend that it was still his desire to retire "if we can

45 March 10, 1863, ibid.
46 Brown to Alexander Stephens, March 16, 1863, ibid.
47 Avery, History of Georgia, 260.
48 April 1, 1863, in Hargrett Collection.

find a man suited to the place"; however, "I may consent to the use of my name." He was much concerned over the attitude of the soldiers. He stressed to his friend, no doubt for relay to the troops, that he had "labored hard to promote their interest and comfort and to sustain their rights."[49]

Personal letters continued to arrive, and the governor continued to write personal replies. If he had made up his mind to run again he was not frank with his friends. There is little doubt that he really did desire retirement. "I say that nothing but a sense of imperative duty could induce me to accept for another term," he wrote M. C. Fulton. "There is no more honor in the place for me. There is no money in it, as the salary [$4,000] does not support my family; and there is indeed nothing but hard work, heavy responsibility and abuse to be expected by the incumbent."[50] To another friend he confided: "I prefer to retire if they [his friends] can harmonize on some other suitable man."[51]

Brown correctly suspected that his endorsement alone would not be sufficient to elect the man of his choice. Many who would vote for Brown would do so because he was the incumbent and was familiar with all the problems. Many who disliked him personally admired his ability, efficiency, and energy. Some thought his services indispensable in the existing crisis. Brown himself agreed with this; he thought no other person could handle the existing situation quite so well as he. He might have been correct.

To resist pleas from friends was easier than to ignore pressure from those who at times had been less than friendly. This was in evidence when on May 16, 1863, four prominent Augusta men[52] presented the governor with a request. In view of the present situation, they explained, the coming election had "an interest peculiar to itself." "We have not now shades of political bias and prejudice to gratify, but we are all united in one common struggle, with a malignant and vindictive enemy." Lives, liberty, property, honor—all were at stake. They now felt "bound by a common unity absorbing all other interests" and were opposed to the expression of individual preference for men being indulged in by the press. Therefore, "accepting the ability and fidelity

49 Brown to J. R. Parrott, April 21, 1863, *ibid.*
50 April 22, 1863, *ibid.*
51 Brown to Joseph B. Pate, April 21, 1863, *ibid.*
52 George Schley, B. H. Warren, James Gardner, and Robert H. May.

shown in the discharge of your duties as Governor, as earnest of your future career in that office," they requested permission to suggest him for reelection. In making this request, they concluded, they would call attention to the fact that they had often disagreed with the governor; yet "as honest men and sincere lovers of our country," they believed they could "best promote her cause by merging all past differences in your election again to the Governorship of Georgia, and in hoping that there will be no opposition thereto."

Brown replied at length, reciting his past efforts as praise of his own conduct in office, and putting the best front on his known controversy with President Davis. Although expressing reluctance in giving up his desire to retire, he declared "I am obliged to admit the right of the people to determine otherwise, and to acknowledge my obligation to respect and abide their decision when made without regard to past political differences of opinion."[53]

Now that the governor had decided to make the race for a fourth term, he began speculating as to who would be his opponent. He learned from several sources that his old friend Lucius Gartrell, now a colonel in the Confederate service, was considering running as an administration candidate. It was also rumored that Gartrell would depend largely upon the soldiers' vote. This worried Brown, for there was no way of knowing to what extent the government could or would influence the army. He opened an extensive correspondence with friends both in and outside the service, ever stressing that "As I may now be considered a candidate I of course do not wish to be defeated."[54] At every opportunity he sent greetings to soldiers in Lee's and Bragg's armies; pledged every assistance possible; and gave a sympathetic hearing to their complaints. A special effort was made to get before the soldiers the fact that he had long been urging an increase in their pay and was doing all within his power to care for their families.

What pleased the governor most was news of support from sources previously hostile to him. Both prominent Augusta papers—the *Constitutionalist* and the *Chronicle and Sentinel*—became active in his behalf.[55] Equally encouraging was news that many prominent families

53 Correspondence published in Augusta *Daily Constitutionalist*, May 24, 1863.
54 See numerous letters in Hargrett Collection, May–June, 1863.
55 Brown to James Gardner, June 10, 1863; Brown to G. W. Evans, May 22, 1863, in Hargrett Collection.

who previously opposed him were now urging his reelection. But the Cobb family was one that would not forget the past. "Joe Brown is out again," wrote a friend to Howell Cobb, "—nominated by the Banks! O Tempore tc Joe Brown & Jeff Davis—a regular Kilkenny Cats' fight. Decent folks ought to stand aside & let 'em fight. Gartrell I think is Davis' Tom to pitch into the ring. He seems to be making profuse offers of patronage. I think if such men as you, Toombs and the Jacksons, Hill etc—representing different parties were to ask a man to be candidate—Judge Bull for instance—old Joe Brown could be beat."[56]

Mrs. Howell Cobb herself could always be depended upon to express the most intense hatred of the governor. During the summer, when Brown visited Athens to enter his daughter in school, some of the Cobb children saw him standing in front of the Baptist Church. They reported to Mrs. Cobb in great excitement. She in turn reported to her husband: "I presume Joseph 1st is 'making a progress thru' his kingdom to [?] the people that he is governor 'by the Grace of God'— I would like just out of curiosity to see this Republican Louis Napoleon —It is unfortunate that every family in which our boys take a fancy to cast their lot should take to Joe Brown as naturally as ducks to water— and babies to their mothers milk.[57]

Rumor persisted, but Gartrell made no announcement. The name of Ben Hill was also suggested. This did not worry Brown, for although he did not "give Ben credit for very superior judgment" he thought him too smart to resign his seat in the Senate to take a chance on being elected governor.[58] Several other names were mentioned, but none generated much enthusiasm. Indeed, politics was at a low ebb in Georgia during the summer of 1863. All party organization had disintegrated. From the fighting fronts the major news was bad, and gloom was quite evident. Lee's second invasion of the North was stopped at Gettysburg; John Pemberton surrendered Vicksburg; and Bragg was being flanked out of Tennessee by Rosecrans, losing all that had been gained in his Kentucky campaign. Another force was assembling in Kentucky for movement into East Tennessee. The only good news was

56 John Whitens [?] to Cobb, June 3, 1863, in Cobb Papers. A. O. Bull was judge of the Coweta Circuit.
57 Cobb Papers. The first page of this letter is missing, so exact date cannot be determined.
58 Brown to Alexander Stephens, May 29, 1863, in Stephens Papers, Emory.

of Nathan Beford Forrest's capture of Streight's Raiders just short of Rome, Georgia. But there were many other potential raiders in the area from which Streight had come.

Shortly after Streight's capture, Governor Brown issued a call for "old men and young men to rally around the banner of our glorious old State. . . . The thunders are rolling towards our borders and the storm threatens to burst with fury upon our heads." He urged that one or two military companies be organized in each county, which units would be officially recognized and its officers commissioned by the state. This would give members the "rights of soldiers in service." It would not, however, protect from conscription those liable for Confederate service. He hoped, however, that many of conscript age would enroll until called into other service. The purpose for organization was local defense. Units would be called into active service in case of emergency only. All should arm themselves with whatever weapons they could command. The only weapons the governor could offer were pikes and knives.[59]

The governor was particularly eager to have some use made of his pikes and knives; there had been ridicule and many uncomplimentary remarks about "Joe Brown's Pikes." During a recent session of the General Assembly, he had been called upon for a complete report on the manufacture and use of these weapons. He responded with enthusiasm, citing the use of pikes by the Duke of Wellington in the fight against Napoleon when 79,000 pikes were placed in the hands of the Spaniards. The use of pikes had also been advocated by General Zebulon M. Pike in the War of 1812, who cited their superiority over bayonets in meeting a cavalry charge. If pikes had been useful in the hands of past military men, why would they not be effective in the hands of Georgia soldiers? The governor admitted, however, that he had planned to use the pikes only when guns were not available. He had purchased 7,099 pikes and 4,908 knives. At the request of Confederate authorities, he had issued 1,281 knives and 1,229 pikes. As of December 8, 1862, there still remained in the state arsenals 3,628 knives and 5,870 pikes.[60]

Before Governor Brown could get the organization of county defense units well underway, the War Department proposed a similar

59 *C. R. Ga.*, II, 447.
60 *Ibid.*, 344 ff.

plan. Unable to spare troops from the main theaters of operation, yet realizing the exposed conditions of other areas, President Davis urged the formation of local defense units. Georgia was requested to furnish eight thousand men. After a bit of sparring between the governor and Richmond authorities, the two plans were combined. Enlistment was to be on a voluntary basis, for neither the state nor Confederate law provided for drafting men over forty-five. Once organized, these troops were to be mustered into Confederate service, with the stipulation that when not active they would receive no compensation. They would become active only when called out in cases of emergency. Once the emergency had passed they would return to their civilian occupation. Under no condition were they to be called to serve outside their state without their consent. And as far as possible, service would be limited to their immediate area. Men of over forty-five and those otherwise exempt from conscription would be eligible to volunteer, and the Confederacy agreed that during the period allotted for enlistment, no Confederate enrolling agents would be active within the state. "If you will undertake to direct such organization," concluded the secretary of war, "and can thus obtain the whole number required in Georgia for the purpose explained, I will thankfully accept your aid, and from this time leave the matter in your hands for execution."[61] This was the type of instructions Governor Brown liked.

On June 22 he issued an additional proclamation to the people further explaining the great need for local defense and outlining the plan for meeting it. It was probably the strongest appeal he had ever made. The abolitionist government, he charged, had failed to conquer on the field of battle where rules of war were observed; so they now proposed to "violate all the rules of war . . . disregard the rights of private property, arm our slaves against us, and send robber bands among us to plunder, steal and destroy" with no respect for the aged or women and children. To meet these "plundering bands of marauders" the president had called for enrollment of eight thousand troops for a six-month period. If the number was not raised by August 1, a state draft would be necessary.

Once organized these volunteer local defense units would be mustered into the service of the Confederacy and become subject to the

61 *Ibid.*, III, 339 ff, 346, 347, 348, 349, 354.

command of the president. In the interest of both speed in enrollment and distribution of units, each county would be allotted a quota. On July 1, 1863, citizens of the several counties would be expected to put aside all other activities, assemble at their courthouse, form required volunteer companies, and report their organization to the state adjutant general. All officers, civil or militia, from the highest to the lowest, would be expected to be there. If necessary they were to travel throughout the country in the interest of enrollment. They should also realize that the best way to recruit volunteers was to have their own names on the list. "The crisis in our affairs is now approaching," the governor concluded. "*Georgia expects every man to do his duty. Fly to arms and trust in God to defend the right.*"[62]

The governor was usually sincere, but never before had his sincerity been so reinforced by fear of impending destruction. In addition to defense against organized enemy raids, he also hoped to use those volunteer units to control deserters in the mountain counties. To a friend from the mountain counties, apparently a militia officer, he suggested that enrollment be for defense in the "*mountain counties of the North Eastern part of the State.*" He would accept these units with this stipulation, thus limiting their service to the region where deserters were most numerous.[63]

The twin Confederate disasters of early July, 1863—the Battle of Gettysburg and the fall of Vicksburg—plus Bragg's retreat toward Chattanooga and North Georgia, greatly increased Confederate desperation. The fall of Vicksburg left the federal armies of Grant and Sherman available for other fields. Confederate secretary of war Seddon urged that the arms-bearing population of Georgia be brought to the defense of the northern portion of the state.[64] The great enrollment rallies of July 1 had not filled the quota required in some Georgia counties. On July 17, 1863, Governor Brown again appealed to the patriotism of Georgians, citing the two recent disasters. The time had come, he exclaimed, for "every Georgian able to bear arms" to attach himself to a military unit "with an unalterable determination to die free rather than live the slave of despotic power." Should there be a Georgian so

62 *Ibid.*, II, 456 ff.
63 Brown to James J. Finley, June 22, 1863, in Hargrett Collection.
64 *C. R. Ga.*, III, 368.

void of patriotism or "the noble impulses of our nature," or possessing "so little courage or manliness" as to fail to rally to the defense of home and family against insult and cruel destruction, then "let fellow citizens mark and remember him." Should anyone hide behind the pretext of exemption or be willing to "sacrifice his liberation for his avarice," then "let him be exposed with indignant scorn to public contempt."

Further, he called upon the secretary of war James A. Sedden to issue and enforce orders, pressing into service all useless subalterns, agents, officials, stragglers, and uniformed men who were wasting time in hotels and on trains. Without waiting for Confederate action, he ordered a state draft for August 4 in all counties which had failed to meet the quotas. Further, all militia and civil officers who failed to volunteer before that date would lose their protection against Confederate conscription.

Since Governor Brown's draft order would apply to all residents, not just citizens, it involved him in controversy with the British Consulate in Savannah. The acting consul, A. Fullarton, agreed that resident foreigners were obligated to assist in local defense, but he denied the state's power to place them in service against the United States. This would eventually be the result of this draft since these units were to be mustered into the service of the Confederacy; consequently, the consul petitioned the governor so to modify his order as not to apply to British subjects.

As was his custom, Governor Brown replied at great length. The purpose for which the consul admitted that British subjects might be used, he explained, was the exact purpose for which these units were being raised. There was no intention of using them against the regular armies of the United States. Instead, they were to be used for defense against possible cavalry raids and servile insurrection. Although the British government had refused to recognize or carry on diplomatic relations with the Confederate states, British subjects expected protection. Many of these subjects in Georgia owned land and slaves. Surely they could not object to service in protection of their own families and property. If British subjects wished to leave Georgia, they were at liberty to do so. If they chose to remain, they would be expected to assist in defense. There would be no modification of the draft order.

In view of this refusal to modify the draft, Fullarton advised British subjects to submit to compulsion for local defense, but in the event they were called upon to meet United States troops they were to "throw down their arms and refuse." To do otherwise would be to violate Her Majesty's proclamation of neutrality and subject themselves to severe penalty. Fullarton assumed the position that the existing conflict was a civil war, not an international conflict.

To this Brown replied that if the consul considered Georgia still a part of the United States, then he should make his complaints to Washington, not to Milledgeville or Richmond. Further, if British subjects "should be guilty of conduct so unnatural and unmanly as to throw down their arms and refuse to defend their domiciles, they will promptly be dealt with as citizens of this State would be should they be guilty of such dishonorable delinquency." There was no law to prevent aliens from leaving the state, but those who chose to remain would be expected to obey the law. "Trusting that my position is fully understood by you," the Governor concluded, "it may not be necessary to protract this discussion."[65]

The draft proved necessary in a very few counties. In the end, 15,000 reported to satisfy an 8,000 quota. Yet the governor's problems multiplied. General Bragg continued to fall back upon Chattanooga and North Georgia. In hope of filling the thinned ranks of regiments from Tennessee, North Alabama, and Georgia, he appointed General Gideon Pillow to use force to round up deserters and draft dodgers. Early in August, Pillow appeared at Marietta, Governor Brown's temporary headquarters, with a plan to send sufficient force into the mountains for recruiting. In addition to deserters and draft dodgers there were now in Georgia many men who were among the troops surrendered by Pemberton at Vicksburg. Brown liked Pillow's plan, for he knew strangers would not be inclined to grant favors to those who wished to escape service. He so notified Richmond but added that it would be very difficult to force Pemberton's troops back into service if they were again to be commanded by him. To a man, all who had been consulted had expressed no confidence in Pemberton.[66]

War weariness and "a sort of feeling of despondence" was in evidence in the Atlanta area, Brown wrote Alexander Stephens. It ap-

65 *Ibid.*, 372, 383, 391, 403.
66 *Ibid.*, 389.

peared to be stimulated by "constant croaking" of speculators who were ready to "curry favor with Lincoln," if need be, in order to save their property should Confederate arms fail. These dispensers of gloom "put the worst face on every mishap to our arms." While not yet guilty of positive disloyalty, they were doing all within their power to discourage the people. The fear was that this might prove the beginning of a reconstruction party. Brown urged Stephens to come to Atlanta and speak to the people. "There is no doubt you now have the ears of the people of the Confederacy and their confidence to an extent that no other man in the Confederacy has."[67] Stephens did not make the speech requested.

Ten days later the governor was still gloomy. He thought things in general were being badly managed. Major J. F. Cummings, Confederate commissary at Atlanta, had advised him of the great shortage of meat. Unless a method could be devised to get more cattle from South Georgia and Florida the meat situation was hopeless. The commissary was attempting to supply the armies of Bragg, Lee, and Joseph E. Johnston through Atlanta and had only about one million pounds of meat on hand.[68] Brown wired President Davis requesting that he be sure to read Cummings' report to the commissary general. Immediate action was imperative. It was impossible to get cow drivers in Florida to round up wild animals, and residents were refusing to sell their animals at the low prices offered, he explained. Could not Brigadier General Howell Cobb's command now stationed in North Florida be used to drive cattle and the people be paid fair prices for their animals?[69] Fortunately, Cobb did not immediately learn of Brown's proposal; he would have greatly resented such a suggestion, especially from the governor.

Davis replied that the commanding general was already acting in accordance with Brown's views. He did not say who would drive cattle, but he sent his aide-de-camp, James Chesnut, to confer with Brown "as to the practicability of sending re-enforcements" to General Bragg. Not only was Rosecrans pressing Bragg, but General Simon B. Buckner was being pressed at Knoxville and the East Tennessee railroads were in danger of complete destruction.[70] Davis also wrote Vice-

67 Brown to Stephens, August 12, 1863, in Stephens Papers, Emory.
68 Brown to Stephens, August 23, 1863, *ibid.*
69 *C. R. Ga.*, III, 402.
70 *Ibid.*; Rowland, *Davis*, VI, 19.

President Stephens, now at Crawfordville, stressing that "the gate of Northern Georgia" was being threatened. The Georgia militia and local defense forces "could render the most effective service" if rushed to "the defense of their own country. . . . If you concur as to the propriety of sending them up to co-operate with Bragg or Buckner you will oblige me by conferring with Governor Brown upon the subjects."[71] It is not known whether or not the vice-president conferred with the governor. The president knew of the close relationship between Brown and Stephens, and he also knew that his own suggestion would probably irritate the governor.

Without waiting for assistance from Stephens, Seddon wired Brown: "We are advised that a formidable force of the enemy is advancing on East Tennessee. Cannot the local troops organized by you be thrown to aid?" Brown replied in a spirit of cooperation rather than irritation. These men could not be forced to go outside the state, he explained, but no doubt many would agree if they were supplied with arms. If five thousand arms could be rushed to Atlanta he would furnish transportation and supplies for those who would agree to go. "I think we can get the men. . . . Who shall command them. Shall I assign them a commanding general for the time, or do you claim that as a right."[72] Brown did not say so, but he was holding his friend Henry Jackson in readiness to take command.

Seddon did not give Brown a direct answer. If these troops were militia, then Brown had the power to appoint, he advised, but if they were Confederate troops the power to appoint belonged to the president. However, arms would be sent to Atlanta.[73] There was no doubt that the president intended to appoint general officers, for he immediately assigned Brigadier General Howell Cobb to command. Cobb was already in Atlanta on other military business. Brown passed the disappointing news on to the Home Guard. The president had denied "my right to command you," he explained. But regardless of "my opinion of my rights," he wished no conflict with Confederate authorities while the enemy threatened "our homes." Therefore, he was turning over the

71 Rowland, *Davis*, VI, 20.
72 *C. R. Ga.*, III, 409.
73 *Ibid.*, 410; Horace Montgomery, *Howell Cobb's Confederate Career* (Tulscaloosa, 1959), 97–98.

command to General Cobb, "an eminent Georgian well known to all." He pledged to General Cobb every assistance possible.[74]

General Cobb was no happier with the turn of events than was the Governor. He had just been assigned to command the state troops raised by Brown, he informed his wife. "If the President had done his very best to place me in the most unpleasant position possible he could not have succeeded better—than by these orders—I am placed under Genl Bragg—for whom I have no respect—and have to cooperate with Joe Brown about whom—you know my opinions too well to repeat them. My duty requires me to submit without murmur or complaint— and I shall do it."[75]

Governor Brown must have heard more about the possibility of the formation of a reconstruction party in Georgia than he reported in writing. On September 5, 1863, he issued another proclamation to the "arms-bearing People of Georgia," in which he warned against false hope of escaping tyranny and oppression by abandoning the cause for which so much blood had been shed and seeking reconstruction of the old Union. Such "dastardly conduct" would be rebuked from the bloody graves of those who had fallen. No mercy could be expected from "wicked and heartless invaders." All of the property in the South would be required to pay the immense Yankee war debt. "Reconstruction is nothing but submission; and submission plunges us into the deepest degradation and the most abject poverty and misery." To everyone who even thought of such a thing he would say, in the words of the great Carolina statesman, "'It is the peace which the kite gives to the dove, the wolf to the lamb, Russia to Poland, and death to its victims.'" If there was determination there would be no defeat, the governor insisted. There were 40,000 men in Georgia capable of bearing arms. If but half that number would rally to the defense of their state the enemy would be driven from East Tennessee. Those who hesitated should recall the fate of Nashville and New Orleans. This should call forth determination that the same should never happen in Georgia.[76]

By mid-September Governor Brown was able to report the Home

74 *C. R. Ga.*, II, 476.
75 September 9, 1863, in Cobb Papers.
76 *C. R. Ga.*, II, 470.

Guard "responding nobly." No doubt 7,000 to 8,000 would soon be ready for service. He suggested that the entire force be organized into a division and Henry R. Jackson appointed major general, commanding. Cobb endorsed this recommendation.[77] Davis would soon appoint a major general, but it would not be Jackson. The Georgia Home Guard was not yet ready for action when Bragg's Army of Tennessee fought the bloody battle of Chickamauga. Neither was it subsequently pushed forward to participate in what should have been a knock out blow to the disorganized enemy shut up in Chattanooga. While Bragg did nothing, allowing the enemy to be heavily reinforced, Brown, celebrating the "brilliant victory" at Chickamauga and considering the pressure relieved, was urging Davis to send the guard home to harvest corn and plant new crops.[78]

At the time the Guard was mustered into Confederate service, Governor Brown had given assurance of his fullest cooperation, and had publicly expressed a desire to avoid any conflict with Confederate authorities. But Brown's formula for preventing conflict was to persuade the opposition to accept his views. Although he had never won an argument on the subject, he still insisted that it was the right of Georgia units in Confederate service to elect officers to fill vacancies. These officers would then be commissioned by the governor. This claim had been consistently denied by Richmond authorities, yet it had support of many troops, and they always called upon the governor for assistance. The claim was also denied by General Cobb; so a clash was inevitable. On September 29, Cobb called upon Adjutant General Cooper for a decision. Brown was insisting upon filling all vacancies, including field officers, under "State laws." "Whilst I am utterly opposed to all elections in the army," Cobb explained, "and regard them as the fruitful sources of trouble, I would recommend, if consistent with the president's views of the law, that the concession should be made and the vacancies be filled under the laws of the state. It is an evil, I know, but perhaps a lesser one than a conflict with the State authorities on this point." He wished instructions.[79] Secretary Seddon made the reply. When troops were accepted by companies and then

77 *Ibid.*, III, 416.
78 *Ibid.*, 417.
79 *Ibid.*, 420.

organized into regiments the president appointed the field officers. This was the law and there could be no departing from it.[80]

Soon the president visited Atlanta on his way to Bragg's head-quarters. He, Cobb, and Brown conferred on matters of major importance, and Cobb thought an understanding had been reached. Apparently Brown did not. On October 15 Brown wrote Cobb that he had not seen fit to engage in fruitless argument with the president; so had passed the matter off with a "simple dissent." However, he considered "the decision so flagrant a violation of the constitutional rights of the troops that I shall issue commissions to fill all such vacancies when election returns are sent to me." He would also place the matter before the General Assembly.[81]

Much disturbed, Cobb warned that such a course would bring state and Confederate authorities "into direct conflict" and would greatly endanger, if not completely destroy, the effectiveness of the Guard. He earnestly requested that the governor issue no commissions unless forwarded through the major general's headquarters. To do otherwise would "destroy all military rule and discipline and demoralize the troops under my command."[82] In requesting further instruction from the president, Cobb added that until otherwise ordered he would forward to Richmond all vacancies that might occur. Seddon replied "the course of the Department is clear."[83] The president would appoint the officers in question, but Joe Brown had not been convinced.

During the summer of apprehension and gloom resulting from Confederate disaster, Georgians had given a minimum of attention to the gubernatorial campaign. Until late summer it appeared as though Governor Brown would not have an opponent. No convention was held; no political parties offered candidates. Finally, in mid-August, the Atlanta *Gazette* declared for Joshua Hill and the Milledgeville *Southern Recorder* nominated Timothy Furlow.[84] Hill was a heavy load for any group to carry in a Georgia campaign. Apparently his nomination even proved too much for the *Gazette*; it ceased publication before the close

80 *Ibid.*, 421.
81 *Ibid.*, 423–24.
82 *Ibid.*, 424–25.
83 *Ibid.*, 422, 425.
84 Milledgeville *Southern Recorder*, November 17, 1863; Avery, *History of Georgia*, 261.

of the campaign. A former United States congressman from Morgan County, Hill had refused to walk out of the House with his colleagues when Georgia seceded. Instead, he submitted to the Speaker a formal resignation. Strongly opposed to secession, he had remained a conservative and often had been accused of giving comfort to North Georgia Unionists. The reconstructionist sentiment in evidence in the Atlanta area was no doubt responsible for his nomination. Furlow occupied the other extreme. A wealthy planter and state legislator from Sumter County, he was a strong secessionist and supporter of the Davis administration.

There was little campaigning, and Brown won an impressive victory, receiving 36,679 votes to 17,939 for Hill and 10,016 for Furlow. This gave the governor a substantial majority over the combined opposition. The army vote went heavily for Brown. Seventy-three regiments cast 15,223 ballots. Brown received 10,012; Hill 3,334; Furlow 1,887.

Chapter XIII

A Wicked Act

JOSEPH E. BROWN was inaugurated governor for a fourth term on November 7, 1863. Two days earlier he had sent to the General Assembly his annual message. The governor was in a somber mood and the tone of his message reflected the seriousness of the situation confronting the state and the Confederacy. A powerful federal army, though temporarily halted, lay at Chattanooga, gaining strength daily and preparing for an invasion of Georgia. General U. S. Grant had assumed command and the forces of Generals Sherman and Hooker were on their way to join him.

It was the governor's hope to arouse the fighting spirit of those who had never actively supported the cause or had grown weak in their support, by picturing what was about to be lost. The bloody war, "waged with more than savage cruelty, by a revengeful and unjust" enemy was approaching their homes, he exclaimed. Thousands of Georgians had already died, and many other thousands were risking their lives daily in protection of all that was dear to them. An enemy to whom no rights had been denied was determined to deprive the South of all of its rights. All the South had requested was the right to be let alone, but the answer was a war of "abolition, subjugation and confiscation."

The governor had heard it said that this was "the rich man's quarrel and the poor man's fight," for the abolition of slavery would not injure the nonslaveholder. "A greater error has never been conceived," he

explained. It was true that many of the rich had not met their responsibilities and thus "merited the condemnation of all true patriots," yet
many others had given their lives. But the question for consideration
was who would suffer most from the abolition of slavery. His answer
was, "the poor." The Lincoln government, the governor charged, had
avowed as its purpose not only the abolition of slavery but the elevation
of the blacks to equality with the whites. Although the wealthy would
lose their investment in slaves, they would still have enough wealth
to move their families to more pleasant places to live. With the poor
it would be different. Without the means to move, they would be
forced to remain and "submit to negro equality." And this equality
would be complete—at the polls, in the jury box, on the witness stand,
in the schools, and in competition for jobs. "Tell me not that the poor
man has no interest in the contest, when the social elevation, or degradation of himself and his children, depends upon its results." How could
the poor man be disinterested when it was a question of whether he
should be superior or "only the equal of a negro."

But abolition was not the only aim of the enemy. Mighty armies
were to be used to force complete subjugation. No states would be left
and the only political rights would be those the conquerors were willing
to grant to the vanquished. All property was to be confiscated to pay
the Union war debt, and insolent armies would be used to compel
complete submission, and "to rivet our chains more closely from generation to generation." But even if some property should be left to conquered owners, they would be taxed to the full amount of income,
leaving bare subsistence as pay for labor. It mattered not which method
was used, for people of the conquered South would be mere "subjugated
serfs—mere paupers and slaves to abolition power."

To those reconstructionists who professed to believe that the end
of war would restore things to their prewar status, the governor would
say they were laboring under false hope. The dead could not be returned to life, devastated areas could not be quickly restored, and
neither could there be compensation for "our injured females." The
only terms yet offered by the Washington government were "abolition,
subjugation, and confiscation." This would apply to all, regardless of
whether or not they favored the rebellion. This could not be very con-
soling to those friendly to the Union rather than the Confederacy.

The governor next turned to the subject of manpower. The hiring of substitutes by those who were conscripted was declared "productive of the most unfortunate results." If conscription was the right way to raise an army, then it should fall equally upon the poor and the rich. To permit the hiring of substitutes freed the wealthy from compulsory service but gave no such relief to the poor. "If every wealthy man would do his duty, and share his part of the danger of the war, but few complaints would be heard from the poor." But many who had hired substitutes for two or three thousand dollars had remained behind and made that much in a single month from speculation, and too often the unfortunate victim of this speculation and extortion was the family of the poor soldier serving for eleven dollars per month.

The system of hiring substitutes had also produced many deserters and stragglers. Some substitutes deserted and rehired again and again, each time exempting from the service an able bodied young man. If this war was to be won, Brown argued, then these and other exempt young men must be put into service. Some argued that the purchase of exemption constituted a contract that could not be annulled. With this the governor disagreed. All property of all kinds might be taken for public use, if the owner was justly compensated. A contract was property; consequently, it could be taken for public use and the owner compensated. Relieved of his substitute contract, the draftee would be eligible for service; so would the substitute, for he had already been compensated. Looking toward the implementation of such a plan, Governor Brown recommended that the General Assembly adopt resolutions urging the Confederate Congress to repeal the substitute clause and cancel all substitution contracts, with just compensation.

The governor also urged that funds be appropriated for relief of those counties subjected to enemy raids. He showed great concern over the provision supply in general, and again repeated in substance the very questionable statement he had made several times before—"This is the only point upon which we have anything to fear for the success of our cause." With ample provisions, he thought, the Confederate armies could fight for an indefinite period. He again urged legal restriction on cotton to one-fourth acre per workhand. Other acres should be planted to provisions. The grain crop in the upcountry counties had been an almost complete failure, and there was also a growing refugee problem. Many persons in invaded areas had fled their homes. "The bread question is *the* question in this contest."

The Confederate practice that irritated the governor most at this time was the impressment of provisions from almost destitute families in North Georgia. There were reports of the last milch cow, the last bushel of grain, the last hog, even the last work animal being taken by impressment agents. It was charged that many so-called agents were imposters, seizing and plundering for speculative purposes, and giving certificates that would never be honored by the Confederate government. The governor had protested again and again against "this system of moral robbery and plundering," but had failed to secure proper relief. Therefore, he recommended the passage of an act making it a felony punishable by ten years in prison for anyone claiming to be a Confederate agent who seized property in violation of the impressment act or refused to respect citizens' rights under that act. Any imposter who seized property should be given "thirty-nine lashes on the bare back" and then sent to prison for ten years. It should also be a felony for any commissary or quartermaster to send an impressing agent into a county without first making public his name and mission.

Governor Brown could not finish his message without taking a few shots at Richmond, but they were milder than usual. The Home Guard was now being kept in active service, he charged, when there was no emergency. This was in violation of the contract under which it enlisted. Such an act of bad faith would increase the difficulty of again enlisting men after their six-month term had expired. The Richmond government was also continuing to violate the rights of Georgia units in service to elect officers to fill vacancies. The governor urged the legislature to pass resolutions declaring these rights of the troops and demanding that Congress respect them.[1]

Throughout the session Governor Brown sent to the General Assembly several special messages, making specific recommendations. He urged a law giving the governor power to destroy every distillery found operating contrary to law, and either to use the metal for military purposes or sell it to the Confederacy. In the latter case, the income should be used for relief of families of indigent soldiers.[2] Two weeks

1 *C. R. Ga.*, II, 481 ff.
2 *Ibid.*, 540–41.

later, after receiving a complaint from the chief Confederate commissary for Georgia that he had been unable to arrange for manufacture of sufficient whiskey, Brown suggested another change in the existing law. Persons under contract to distill for the Confederate government should be permitted to use any corn furnished by the government. Further, such contractors in using barley, rye, or shorts should be exempt from the twenty-mile limit.[3]

As a further step in the conservation of provisions, Governor Brown urged the General Assembly to go on record in opposition to the Confederate "tax in kind." This tax required producers to surrender to the government a given percentage of their produce. Brown estimated that at least one-third of that surrendered spoiled or was wasted from want of efficient handling, storage, and transportation. It would be much more profitable to require payment of taxes in currency and then let the government purchase or impress its needs at market prices.[4]

The 1863 General Assembly was more responsive to the governor's requests than usual, but it stopped short of going all the way. In accordance with his recommendations, resolutions were passed urging that the appointments of all impressment agents who were liable to conscription be revoked, and that local citizens not liable to military service be appointed in their stead. Also passed was a resolution exempting from conscription all state civil and military officers.[5] Richmond authorities submitted the resolutions relating to impressment agents to Major J. F. Locke, chief commissary for Georgia, who declared the proposal "open to grave objections at all times, and particularly so at the present crisis." The officers suggested for removal had been chosen because of their qualifications, and had given "large bonds" guaranteeing faithful performance of their duties. He thought there was no other class of officers "against whom fewer objections can be urged." There had been a few complaints against these officers, but had it not been for "their extraordinary energy and unflagging devotion," Bragg's army would have suffered greatly for want of supplies. If there were imposters, the commissariat was not responsible, for names of all officers and agents *were* published throughout the state. "As the law now

3 *Ibid.*, 552–54.
4 *Ibid.*, 541–46.
5 *Acts of the General Assembly*, 1863, p. 104.

stands," Major Locke concluded, "it is altogether in favor of producers and altogether against impressing officers. The former can obtain redress if wronged, while the latter find scant favor, either at the tribunals of law or at those of public opinion."[6] It is clear that Brown and Locke had not been reading the same reports and complaints. Secretary Seddon refused to take further action.

Brown was pleased to pass on to Richmond resolutions passed by the assembly "almost unanimously" urging Georgia's representatives to work for a change in law that would guarantee to Georgia troops their "constitutional right" to elect their own officers. President Davis referred these resolutions and Brown's accompanying note to Secretary Seddon. The secretary noted that the resolutions were directed to Congress, not the Executive. However, he called the president's attention to recent correspondence with Brown on this subject and the governor's threat to take the matter before the legislature. The secretary concluded: "The Department did not consider it to be a part of its duty to vindicate to Governor Brown the legislation by which it was controlled, or to continue the correspondence further. It may be proper to add that the Department does not consider the claim to be well founded."[7]

Although rebuffed on two counts the governor was certain to win on the third. Before adjourning on December 14, the General Assembly passed resolutions declaring that the separation of the Confederate states from the federal Union should be "final and irrevocable"; the war should be prosecuted with "utmost vigor and energy" until independence was "unconditionally acknowledged"; Georgia would "contribute all the means which her resources will supply"; Georgia would not "tire of the war until her purpose is accomplished"; and would "not consent to lay down arms until peace is established on the basis of the foregoing resolutions." The governor was requested to send copies of these resolutions to the Confederate president and Congress and to the governor of each state.[8]

This session of the General Assembly also reelected Herschel V. Johnson to the Confederate Senate. Robert Toombs actively canvassed for the selection, apparently hoping to get in position to strike some

6 *C. R. Ga.*, III, 438–42.
7 *Ibid.*, 446–48.
8 *Acts of the General Assembly*, 1863, pp. 104–105; *C. R. Ga.*, III, 443–45.

hard blows at the Confederate administration. Prior to the election he made a strong antiadministration speech before the legislature. He was secretly supported by Governor Brown, but to no avail. Johnson was chosen on the third ballot.[9] Brown confided to Alexander Stephens, "While I had no reason to wish ill success to Johnson I regretted the defeat of Toombs. I think we need him in Congress."[10]

Before the assembly adjourned General Bragg's Army of Tennessee had suffered humiliating defeat in the Battle of Missionary Ridge and had fallen back to Dalton astride the Western and Atlantic Railroad. Governor Brown expressed grave concern but failed to grasp the real seriousness of the situation. The worst he predicted was temporary loss of upper Georgia and probable widespread suffering among the people in that area. To meet this possibility he began moving household things from his Canton home to a safer place in middle Georgia, where he apparently intended to send his family. He had recently purchased plantations in Lee and Dooly counties. The Dooly plantation, known as the Hamilton place, was located on Green Creek. He employed John G. Smith as overseer and sent down his slaves from Cherokee. Smith was to receive six hundred dollars per year for his services, but the contract was dependent upon his getting a detail from Confederate service to perform this work. Brown also directed members of the Grisham family to go down and take up residence in the big house and work such portion of the land as they pleased. The Lee County plantation, known as the Edward Jones place, was rented to H. Carlisle for one-third of the crop for the year 1864.[11]

While making these preparations Governor Brown continued to maintain that there was no emergency and to urge that the Home Guard be relieved from active duty. However, he did pinpoint one important cause of military disaster. "I wish we had a more able man at the head of our forces in that Department," he confided to Vice-President Stephens.[12] Soon he would join most Georgians in rejoicing that General Joseph E. Johnston had succeeded General Bragg.

9 William Y. Thompson, *Robert Toombs of Georgia* (Baton Rouge, 1966), 209.
10 November 27, 1863, in Stephens Papers, Emory.
11 Brown to Dear Brother, February 14, 1864, in Hargrett Collection; also contracts dated January 26, February 3, 20, 1864, *ibid*.
12 Phillips, *Correspondence*, 630–31.

General Johnston, efficient organizer that he was, lost no time before complaining to Governor Brown that the Army of Tennessee was not being adequately served by the Western and Atlantic Railroad. "Unless there is a change for the better, disaster will result," Johnston urged. A. R. Lawton, now Confederate quartermaster-general, and President Davis also urged Brown to action in improving the efficiency of the state road.[13] This struck the governor in a tender spot, for he had ever taken great pride in the road. He resented any suggestion of poor management and placed the blame on the loss of engines and cars to Confederate service elsewhere. He estimated the loss at over 200 cars and eight engines. To all who pressured him, he replied that if the government would only return two good engines and fifty cars, the Western and Atlantic could do its job. The rolling stock was not recovered immediately, but efficiency was in some way improved. On January 25, 1864, General Johnston could report with "great satisfaction" that "daily receipts of provisions and forage from Atlanta are now fully equal to the consumption." He had relieved the road of some of its burden by having beeves butchered in Atlanta rather than hauled or driven to the place of consumption.[14]

President Davis had some doubts about Brown's claim to have lost eight engines and over 200 cars. He cited reports made by state road officials to the governor for 1862 and 1863 to show that *no* engines had been lost and not more than 180 cars. He reminded the governor that it was improbable that the railroad management would have overlooked the loss of so large an item as an engine, and this also for a two-year period. Davis then proceeded to show how the rolling stock listed in the reports could be found quite adequate in supplying Johnston's army. "I am confirmed in my opinion that this road, as of today stands, can meet every reasonable demand upon it," the president concluded. However, should this prove not to be true, "every exertion will be made by the Government to furnish what is needed."[15] Just which of the two officials had the truth on his side is uncertain. But Brown and Stephens agreed between themselves that the Confederate government wished to take control of the road. To this Brown would never agree. "I know

13 *C. R. Ga.*, III, 450, 451, 454.
14 *Ibid.*, 453, 456, 457, 458.
15 *Ibid.*, 480–84.

as well as the Confederate authorities do how to manage the road."[16]

No doubt the insinuation that the state-owned Western and Atlantic was being poorly managed greatly irritated the governor. He appears to have vented his wrath on Major J. F. Cummings, commissary of subsistence at Atlanta. Since all early contracts for manufacture of whisky for the Confederate government had proved a failure, largely from inability to acquire grain, Major Cummings, with approval from Richmond, had made some new contracts during the winter of 1863–1864. Under the new contracts a portion of the grain received in payment of the tax in kind would be allotted to the distillers, who agreed to sell to the Confederate government their entire output. On January 18, 1864, Cummings addressed Brown a note giving some details of the type of contracts let. He also spoke of a recent conference with General Johnston during which it was agreed that since meat was in short supply a ration of liquor might be used as a supplement. The purpose of this note to Brown was to inquire of the governor whether or not the Confederate contracts conformed to Georgia law.

Brown let his temper get the better of him: "In reply to your letter I state that the laws of Georgia will not tolerate any such consumption of grain by distillation as you propose. . . . I shall order the prompt prosecution of every man who runs a still without license from the State, and I shall grant no license to stills in Upper Georgia." Only small stills would be licensed, and they must be in southern or southwestern Georgia and located at least twenty miles from a railroad or navigable stream.[17] Major Cummings explained that only grain belonging to the government would be used by stills near railroads. Would the governor please advise whether or not he would "attempt to prevent the distillation of grain belonging to the Confederate State Government . . . whenever and wherever they may deem proper." The army needed whisky and he was unable to supply the need.

Brown replied at length and in language little short of offensive. No matter what position one might hold, it was as much a violation of Georgia's penal laws to distill grain without a license as "to commit the crime of theft or swindling." While he was governor he would attempt to execute both the criminal and civil laws of the state. No

16 Brown to Stephens, January 28, 1864, in Stephens Papers, Emory.
17 C. R. Ga., III, 472, 473–74.

exception would be made for Confederate officials. "The ownership of the corn has nothing whatsoever to do with the question. You seem to think that because the corn is tithe corn the Government agents may distill it in violation of the criminal laws of the State without guilt." If ownership of grain were the only question, the government could purchase or impress as much as it wished for distillation. "No such pretensions will be acquiesced in a moment by the State."[18]

The tone of Governor Brown's communications with the War Department during this period was no less objectionable than his attitude toward the commissary. On January 13, 1864, Secretary of War Seddon inquired as to the possibility of enrolling the residue of the 15,000 men who had offered their services as State Guard. Only 8,000 had been accepted and even their term of service would soon expire. General Cobb had suggested that either they be held in service or the remaining 7,000 be enrolled to replace them. What course would Governor Brown suggest under the circumstances? inquired Secretary Seddon.[19]

As might have been expected, Brown was not interested in what Howell Cobb might suggest. These six-month men could not be relied upon for further extension of service, he advised Seddon. Their terms would soon expire, and they would return to their homes. Furthermore, since the government had not kept faith with them, they would not be inclined to reenlist. "While they were thus kept in camp eating out our limited supply of provisions, and were deprived of the privilege of sowing their wheat and preparing for another crop, they saw no enemy, there was no raid, no sudden emergency, and no use for their services. They felt and knew that this was a violation of both the letter and spirit of the contract. In their behalf I protested against it, but to no effect."

Brown suggested that if the war effort was to be successful then Confederate authorities must recognize that there must be a producing class as well as a fighting class. Georgia could not continue to meet demands of conscripting agents, furnish an additional force for either home or out of state duty, and produce adequate provisions. Unless there was a change of policy "the struggle for the future must necessarily be short." Should production be inadequate, all the enemy need do

18 Ibid., 473, 474–75.
19 Ibid., 452.

was to wait "till we consume our provisions, and they must conquer us."

He had no desire to dictate, the governor explained, or "to annoy you by voluntary advice," yet as a state executive he felt it his duty to give his opinion. There should be little if any further drafting of the producing class. Instead, those already on the muster rolls, "especially the almost countless number of young, able-bodied officers" who were wasting time in hotels and on trains, should be returned to active duty. Most every little railroad town had become a military post while "officers in brass buttons and gold lace" idled away time, keeping with them enough soldiers for a command, far removed from danger. Further, the quartermaster and commissary departments were using throngs of able-bodied young men in duties that could be performed by others. Send these men to the fighting front and the army would be increased by 50 percent. Call up the absentees and leave the producing class to produce. This was the only course to victory.[20]

Other duties, especially those relating to matters before Congress, delayed Seddon's reply for more than three weeks. When he did reply he explained that he did not wish to make "any reference to the acrimonious language you have thought proper to address to the Department." He reviewed the department's intentions and actions during the previous year in calling for the organization of the population not subject to the draft. This State Guard was for local defense, but the governor had been informed they would be raised as Confederate troops and paid by the Confederacy, when on active duty. Otherwise the governor had been given a free hand in raising these troops. Yet Brown had insisted that they were state militia. The War Department was thankful for the efforts made and wished to consider the failure to realize "its entire expectation or hopes . . . rather a matter of regret than for censure or complaint." The conditions on the Georgia border had remained so critical that a judicious administration would not justify disbanding the State Guard.

Although ever conscious of the great need for production, Congress had found it necessary to expand the draft, Seddon continued. The enemy's increase in manpower must be met as far as possible. "A cordial acquiescence and support of that legislation is called for by every

20 *Ibid.*, 458–63.

motive of patriotism, every sentiment of loyalty, and every consideration of public honor and private interest."[21] No one was convinced. The State Guard returned to civilian duties, and General Howell Cobb was left without a command.

No doubt Secretary Seddon had been seriously concerned with matters before Congress. Effective February 15, 1864, Congress for the third time granted permission to the president to suspend the writ of habeas corpus for a limited period. Two days later the conscription age was lowered to seventeen and raised to fifty. Industrial exemptions were abolished, but exemption was continued for public officials and necessary railroad workers. This left to the governors plenty of leeway. On this same date Congress took steps to reduce the volume of greatly depreciated currency. As of fixed dates, all noninterest-bearing Confederate Treasury notes were to be exchanged for 4 percent bonds or for new currency at the rate of three for two. Notes not so exchanged would eventually become valueless.

Governor Brown vigorously opposed each of these acts, and seeking support in his opposition, began considering a special session of the General Assembly. Meanwhile, Secretary of War Seddon sent Lucius Gartrell back to Georgia to encourage the enlistment of troops from men between seventeen and eighteen and forty-five and fifty. It was hoped that many would volunteer rather than be drafted. Gartrell reported that the young men were signing up, but the older ones chose to wait for the president's order. Gartrell appealed to Governor Brown for cooperation, but received none. The governor chose to make no statement until after the legislature should meet. During the last session the legislature had instructed him to enroll men from the forty-five to fifty group for state defense. It was uncertain whether that body would "recognize the right of the Confederate government now to take them out of the hands of the State." Even if conscription were constitutional, the governor concluded, that did not mean that Congress was authorized to take over the internal police regulation of the states, thus depriving them of "the power to execute their own laws or to suppress internal insurrections."[22] Despite the governor's attitude, Gar-

21 *Ibid.*, 484–88.
22 *Ibid.*, 489.

trell was able to report on March 5 that he hoped soon to be able to forward muster rolls for two regiments.

In preparation for a probable special session of the General Assembly, the governor again requested furloughs for those members serving in the Confederate army. This time, however, Secretary Seddon, upon the recommendation of General Lee, refused leaves, but suggested that officers could resign if they wished.[23] Before Seddon's note reached Brown he had held a strategy session with the Stephens brothers.

Since the previous December, these three bitter opponents of Confederate authority had been in especially close touch. Linton Stephens had become ill during the session of the General Assembly. Brown moved him to the Executive Mansion and wrote his brother Alexander to come at once.[24] What the three discussed or planned will ever remain a matter for speculation, but no doubt the ties of friendship were drawn even closer. Linton was able to return home at the close of the session. On January 2, 1864, Alexander Stephens wrote Brown that he had given much thought to the matter discussed, and owing to the "temper and feeling at Richmond," he was not very hopeful. "Still every one should do his duty in his own sphere as he from the best lights before him understands it, provided he so performs it as not to do injury by giving rise to injudicious conflicts, divisions and dissentions in public counsel from which divisions, strifes and factions may spring up amongst the people. Such a result can be but disastrous."[25]

Brown apparently received this letter just before leaving for Canton where he would assist Mrs. Brown in removing "bedding and household things to middle Ga before the opening of the Spring Campaign." From Canton he wrote to Stephens paying high compliment to Linton: "I admire his talents his honesty and stern integrity, and highly appreciate his friendship." Upon his own return to Milledgeville, the governor added, he would be pleased to receive Stephens' views on "the question alluded to in your letter." All letters should henceforth be marked "private" so they would not be opened by a secretary.[26]

Again, on January 13, 1864, the governor wrote Stephens that if the

23 *Ibid.*, 488.
24 December 8, 1863, in Stephens Papers, Emory.
25 Stephens Papers, Emory.
26 January 4, 1864, *ibid.*

Richmond government did not take some action he would call the legislature into special session. However, he did not want this known in Richmond. "No one but you and Linton know my purpose."[27] A month later the governor suggested that he and the Stephens brothers get together at Linton's Sparta home where they could "compare notes." He was eager to have the benefit of their suggestions. A week later he wrote again. He had heard that Congress had for the third time authorized suspension of the writ of habeas corpus which he thought every state "should denounce and condemn" as a "wicked act." Their proposed meeting was now even more necessary.[28]

The three met in Sparta on February 25, 1864. This must have been a very harmonious meeting, for they were in perfect agreement. There is no doubt as to what they discussed, and viewed in the light of their subsequent actions, there is little doubt as to what plans they adopted. With the assistance of Alexander Stephens, Brown would present to the legislature and the public a vigorous attack upon Congress and the president; Linton Stephens, a member of the House, would introduce resolutions embodying both denunciations and recommendations; and Alexander would address the legislature in support of both. And in order to supervise it all, he would be Brown's guest in the Governor's Mansion.

Brown returned to Milledgeville and began revising his proposed message. On March 4 he wrote Stephens that he had rewritten the section on habeas corpus. "It is the great question of the day and I do hope our legislators will have nerve and patriotism to put Ga right."[29] Meanwhile Linton Stephens wrote Mrs. Robert Toombs that if the legislature would "back the Governor in his effort to inaugurate State action for the preservation of rights and the obtainment of peace, I hope that the present year will close on us in peace and independence." He did not explain, however, how tactics designed to obstruct Confederate efforts to win the war could lead to success. But he added that "Peace can never be obtained by sword alone, and if it ever comes from negotiation the states or people will have to assume the initiative." Only those who opposed peace "because they find their profit in war," Linton Ste-

27 Stephens Papers, College of Sacred Heart.
28 February 13, 20, 1864, in Stephens Papers, Emory.
29 Stephens Papers, Emory.

phens concluded, considered it "degrading to our dignity" to offer terms to the enemy.[30] These words could just as well been spoken by Governor Brown.

The governor's message was read to the General Assembly on March 10, 1864, the opening day of the special session. It was of tremendous length.[31] Some contemporaries thought it the masterpiece of his public career; others no doubt were more impressed by its length than its contents. In his opening sentence Brown complimented the legislators for the patriotic zeal exhibited by them in the previous session and expressed thanks for the "personal kindness and official courtesy" shown him. In view of their faithful discharge of public duties, even at a sacrifice of personal preference and private interests, he had no doubt "that I can rely upon your counsels as a tower of strength in time of darkness and gloom."

On the civilian front, he explained, much difficulty had been encountered in the transportation of corn from middle and southwestern Georgia to indigent soldiers' families in other parts of the state. The governor recommended that some official be designated, "under the order of the Governor," to take control of the railroads of the state with instructions to haul supplies to the needy in preference to all other items, except troops and military provisions. Compensation could be made from relief funds already appropriated. In order to supply the destitute who lived far from railroads, he had purchased teams and wagons to be operated by the Quartermaster Department.

Although the governor felt a delicacy in doing so, he thought it his duty to report that too much cotton was being planted. A law should be passed making it "highly penal" for anyone to grow cotton in excess of one-quarter acre per hand. There were also many persons continuing to distill liquor from grain. The prospects for profits were so great that they evaded the law in every conceivable manner. Drastic measures alone could end these violations, for some public officials feared to incur the ill will of people of wealth and influence who violated the law daily. To correct this situation, the governor asked for authority to seize all illegal stills and convert the materials to war use. There should be just compensation for the loss of such property. Any civil or military

30 March 3, 1864, in Robert Toombs Papers, University of Georgia.
31 Sixty-nine pages as printed in *C. R. Ga.*

official who failed to exercise vigilance in destroying illegal distillation should be dismissed from office. Many producers were refusing to sell their surplus provisions for market prices while the needy were suffering from the lack of food. The governor requested authority to impress such provisions, making just compensation to the owner.

It was reported that numbers of persons in those Georgia counties near East Tennessee had moved their families within the enemy lines. Others had left their families behind and joined the enemy. The governor recommended that property belonging to such persons be confiscated and that any families left behind be transported to the Union lines. Such deserters should also be "*disfranchized* and *decitizenized*," should they ever attempt to return to Georgia.

Most of the remainder of the governor's message was devoted to a denunciation of the Confederate government, especially the acts passed during the previous month. "Probably the history of the past furnishes few more striking instances of unsound policy combined with bad faith" than the recent currency act, declared Brown. Earlier in the war, Treasury notes had been issued and accepted by the people under a promise to redeem two years after the conclusion of peace. It was further stipulated that these notes were fundable in Confederate bonds and were acceptable in payment of all public dues except export duties. But recently Congress had decreed that these notes must be exchanged for 4 percent bonds or new currency at a depreciated rate. Should this not be done the old notes would eventually become worthless. Was this not repudiation of honest debts? This measure was discussed in secret session so that the people back home would have no way to check on their representatives. "The *secret sessions* of Congress are becoming a blighting curse to the country," Brown charged.

The state of Georgia had been accepting Confederate Treasury notes in all of its transactions. Under the new law these notes would depreciate by one-third by April 1 as they were exchanged for new notes. It would seem advisable, then, that the state accept no more old notes, but instead wait for the new issue. Yet the state must have currency before April 1. Therefore, the governor recommended the issue of state Treasury notes redeemable on December 25 next in new issue Confederate notes. Further, all old-issue Confederate notes held by the state as of April 1 should be funded in Confederate bonds.

A second piece of recent Confederate legislation that greatly irritated Governor Brown was the extension of the conscription age so as to include all men between seventeen and fifty. Although the state supreme court had declared conscription constitutional, Brown explained, it had not conceded the right of the Confederate government to "enroll the whole population of the State," leaving to the state no command over its citizens or power to execute its laws. To raise armies was one thing, but it was entirely different to put the whole population under military law, compelling every man to secure a military detail before cultivating his farm or working at other tasks at home.

Accusing Confederate authorities of not making proper calculations as to manpower, the governor offered a plan of his own. He calculated that a fighting force of 200,000 men could be kept in the field and supplied for twenty years. "No power nor State can ever be conquered so long as it can maintain that number of good troops." There was always such a thing as "whipping the fight without fighting it," by avoiding pitched battles and allowing the enemy to become exhausted from heat, cold, or want of provisions. The governor cited Napoleon's Russian campaign as an example, but he made no comparison between Russian winters and those in Georgia. The true solution to the manpower problem, the governor suggested, was not to add more productive workers to the muster rolls, but to call to the fighting front those thousands of soldiers now wasting their time supposedly performing tasks that could be handled by civilians.

He realized that many of his ideas conflicted with those of Confederate authorities, Brown explained. He also recognized the fact that much of the press and many individuals denounced as "*agitators or partisans*" all who dared oppose Confederate encroachment. But. he would ask, when did Georgia ever embarrass the Confederate effort? It neither had nor would ever fail to do its full duty, yet at the same time "she will never cease to require that all her constitutional rights be respected and the liberties of her people preserved." If this be conflict then "conflict will never end till the object is attained."

Governor Brown next focused his wrath upon what he considered to be the unconstitutional attempt to suspend the privilege of the writ of habeas corpus. On February 17, 1864, Congress had for the third time granted to the president authority to suspend the writ for a limited period. Under the suspension the president, the secretary of war or the general commanding the Trans-Mississippi Department could arrest and detain persons thought guilty of any one of numerous disloyal activities. The suspension also denied the courts power to intervene. In passing this measure, Congress acted under its constitutional power to suspend the writ when necessary to repulse invasion or put down rebellion. Brown's first point of attack was upon the point of necessity. He denied that there existed civil situations which could not be handled by the courts. To thus tie the hands of the courts was "a fell blow at the liberties of the people."

He then recited the constitutional guarantees of the rights of the people relating to indictment, arrest, trial and conviction. All of these rights were denied by suspension of the writ of habeas corpus, he explained, even though these rights were specifically guaranteed and the right to suspend the writ was only implied. Further, the powers of the Executive were enumerated, and the power to issue warrants, make arrest, and detail those arrested were not among them. Neither could Congress give to the president such powers, for Congress itself did not possess them. "The power to *issue warrants* and try persons under criminal accusation are *judicial* powers, which belong under the Constitution, exclusively to the judiciary and not to the Executive," the governor declared. The president's power in such cases was strictly limited to the armed forces and those within their lines. The exercise of such powers beyond those limits was not only illegal but strictly forbidden by the Confederate Constitution.

Although the people had elected representatives to high position to guard and protect their rights, these representatives had taken a bold stride "toward military despotism and absolute authority." Therefore, Brown urged that "every patriotic citizen . . . sound the alarm" and that the state legislature "say in thundering tones to those who assume to govern us by absolute power, that there is a point beyond which freemen will not permit encroachments to go." The legislature should express its "unqualified condemnation" of this "most monstrous" habeas corpus act. Senators and congressmen should be called upon to work for its repeal or resign the trust with which the people had honored them. "What will we have gained when we have achieved our independence of the Northern States, if in our efforts to do so, we have permitted our form of Government to be subverted, and have lost *Constitutional liberty* at home?"

The remainder of the governor's message was devoted to a long, biased, often erroneous, even absurd, discussion of American history from the colonial period to the war. He dwelt at length upon the principles set forth in the Declaration of Independence, the recognition of state sovereignty, the aims of the Founding Fathers, and the departure from these principles which brought on secession and war. He wished to explain to the world in general and to generations to come the real causes of this cruel conflict. The whole people of the North were not to blame except that they permitted themselves to be dominated by the abolitionist minority.

He saw in Lincoln one of the great tyrants of all time, who not only sent armies to crush freedom in the South but kept enough force at home to crush liberty there also. Every semblance of freedom guaranteed by the United States Constitution to people of the North had been destroyed in an all out effort to subjugate the South, the governor declared. Lincoln's invading troops had committed every crime known to mankind. Originally claiming that laws protecting the slaveholder were a "'covenant with death and a league with Hell,'" they turned to the Bible for a "higher law." When they found that God favored slavery in both the Old and New Testaments, they then repudiated the Bible and "declared for an *anti-Slavery Bible and an anti-Slavery God.*" By an unconstitutional proclamation, Lincoln had declared the slaves free. They had long been encouraged to revolt against their masters. When it was found that slaves did not wish to be free, they were seized and dragged off to labor or fight. Many black women and children were taken from their happy homes to die from hunger or disease in crowded camps. "But federal bayonets can never reverse the law of God, which must be done before the negro can be made the equal of the white man of the South." Abolition, if achieved, would return the blacks to barbarism and "ultimate extermination from the soil, where most of them were born and were comfortable and contented under the guardian care of the white race before this wicked crusade commenced."

The closing portion of Brown's message was under the heading "How Peace Should be Sought." He did not know *when* the war would end, he asserted, but he knew *how* it would end. The South had no desire to conquer the North, and the North had not sufficient force to govern the South without its consent. Hundreds of thousands of lives might yet be lost, but the war still would not be "terminated by force of arms." "Negotiations *will* finally terminate it. The pen of the statesman, more potent than the sword of the warrior, must do what the latter failed to do."

But how could there be negotiations when Lincoln, since the beginning of the struggle, had refused even to receive representatives from the South? The governor's answer was that the South must ever keep before the northern people its willingness to negotiate on the basis of the right of self-government and state sovereignty. Immediately following each important victory of southern arms the proposition to negotiate should be made to the northern government. If declined, it should be repeated again and again, thus constantly holding that government in the wrong "before their own people and the judgment of mankind." What Governor Brown could not know was that there would be no more important Confederate victories on the battlefield.

When a proposition for negotiation should finally be accepted, the governor suggested the withdrawal of armed forces from all states, leaving it to the vote of the people to determine their own destiny. "This is all that we have been struggling for from the beginning." Should the border slave states decide to abolish slavery and remain with the Union that should be their privilege. They should also be entitled to the privilege of retaining slavery and joining the Confederacy. In the governor's mind, there was no "doubt that the cool-headed, thinking men on both sides of the line . . . will finally settle down upon this as the true solution to the great problem."

To the "timid among us" who would ask how Lincoln's great armies could be repelled should he continue to reject negotiation, Governor Brown would reply "The answer is plain. Let every man do his duty; and let us as a people place our trust in God, and we shall certainly repel his assaults and achieve our independence, and if true to ourselves and to posterity, we shall maintain our Constitutional liberty also. The achievement of our Independence is a great object; but no greater than the preservation of Constitutional liberty."[32] The governor's trust in God might have been strong but his knowledge of military might was weak.

32 *House Journal*, 1864, Extra Session, 5 ff; *C. R. Ga.*, II, 587 ff.

Joseph E. Brown as a young man

Joseph E. Brown, governor of Georgia

The home of eight Georgia governors, 1838–1868

The Georgia Statehouse where the Ordinance of Secession was passed

Joseph E. Brown about 1870

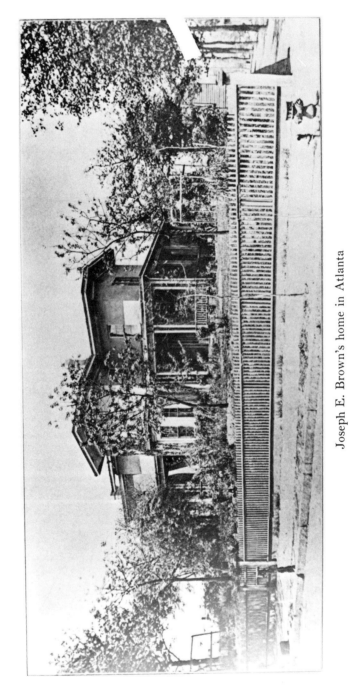

Joseph E. Brown's home in Atlanta

The "Buzz Saw Politician" circulated at the time of race for the Senate against Alexander R. Lawton

The Brown family, *circa* 1890

Chapter XIV

Let the States Decide

GOVERNOR BROWN'S message to the General Assembly contributed nothing to the possible success of the Confederacy. He openly opposed every major piece of legislation passed during the recent session of Congress, and by doing so he encouraged those who were inclined toward violating these laws. Peace by negotiation had no possibilities as long as Lincoln was in power and his armies victorious. And those victories would assure him success at the polls in the election of 1864.

Brown's charge of conspiracy on the part of Confederate Congress and the president to deprive the states and their people of their rights was false and he knew it. He also knew that Congress could at any time take from the president any additional power granted him. Further, he knew that congressmen must either represent the will of their constituents or be voted out of office. The governor himself was ever power hungry, and he resented any Confederate encroachment upon his realm. He insisted upon his own right to interpret the Constitution and act accordingly, but would not concede that right to the president and Congress. While denouncing them for disregarding the Constitution, he did not hesitate to seize salt, smash stills, and resort to state draft, none of which was authorized by the Georgia Constitution. What he did, he claimed to be in the interest of the people; what Confederate authorities did, he denounced as destructive of the interests of the people. He thought himself always right; those who disagreed were not only wrong but suspect. He interfered with and threatened to arrest

Confederate officials in performance of what they considered their duties, yet he would tolerate no obstruction of his own actions. And he hoped to be so convincing in his arguments that a majority of the people of Georgia would consider him their champion and protector.

Immediately following the reading of the governor's message, Linton Stephens introduced two sets of resolutions. Suspension of the writ of habeas corpus was denounced as an unconstitutional exercise of a power implied, but not expressly granted. It was an attempt to sustain military authority over the issuance of warrants and to "give validity to unconstitutional seizures of the persons of people." Therefore, it was "a dangerous assault upon the constitutional power of the courts, and upon the liberty of the people, and beyond the power of any possible necessity to justify it." Members of Congress were urged to work for repeal of this suspension, but in the meantime the question of its validity should be submitted to the courts.

The second set of resolutions was a plea for peace. Although the enemy was assessed with the responsibility for bringing on this "huge crime" against humanity, all who would escape "the guilt of its continuance" were urged "to use their earnest efforts to put an end to this unnatural, unchristian and savage work of carnage and havoc." The Confederate government, "immediately after signal successes of our arms, and on other occasions, when none can impute its action to alarm, instead of a sincere desire for peace," should make to the enemy "an official offer of peace, on the basis of the great principle declared by our common fathers in 1776." With such offers should be a "distinct expression of a willingness . . . to follow that principle to its true logical consequences, by agreeing that any border state, whose preference for our association may be doubted . . . shall settle the question by herself, by a convention to be elected for that purpose, after the withdrawal of all military forces, of both sides, from her limits."[1] Those who read must have noted the similarity between these resolutions and the governor's message. One of Alexander Stephens' contemporary biographers stated that Linton drew up these resolutions "without any concert with his brother." This of course was not true. It might be nearer correct to say that, in effect, Alexander Stephens wrote both the resolutions and

1 Quoted in Henry Cleveland, *Alexander H. Stephens* (Atlanta, 1866), 184–89; *O. R.*, Ser. IV., Vol. III, 234–37.

that portion of Brown's mesage that made the same suggestions for peace.

L. Q. C. Lamar, a visitor from Mississippi, Congressman Augustus H. Kenan, and General Howell Cobb were also in Milledgeville, hoping to offset the influence of Brown and the Stephens brothers. Cobb spoke in the hall of the House of Representatives on the evening of March 11. He was there, he explained, in response to a request of "a portion of the members," to discuss the conditions of the country, "its hopes, its fears, its prospects, and the responsibilities of its citizens both at home and in the field." There was no longer need to discuss the causes of the terrible war, but he did wish to note that it was an unusual war. It was not to settle boundary disputes or to determine the ownership of territory, but to protect life, liberty, property and "everything you hold dear on earth." It was, therefore, the duty of everyone to consider each word, thought, and act in the light of its effect upon the outcome. As to the grave responsibilities of the legislators, he wished to speak plainly and he hoped impressively.

He thought prospects had never been brighter. If there was gloom at home, it was not shared by the troops who had "with almost entire unanimity re-enlisted for the war." But the stern reality that a powerful enemy stood prepared on all sides to strike down everything, made it necessary to sacrifice or yield up temporarily many rights. There was no time to discuss mere technicalities. Public good and military necessity might require many acts that would not be sanctioned in time of peace. When soldiers and their families needed provisions they must be impressed, if not otherwise furnished. There must not be suffering because heartless persons refuse to sell.

Although Cobb did not mention the governor or his message, he followed rather closely Brown's argument, opposing him on practically every point. There must be confidence in the Confederate government he urged. The government's problems were the same as those of the states. If the flags of the states trailed in the dust, so would that of the Confederacy and vice versa. Those the people were being called upon to oppose and criticize were not strangers, but their own elected representatives. "Their cause is our cause, their prosperity our prosperity, their degradation our degradation." He thought no body of people had ever been called upon to exercise greater judgment, firmness, wisdom or patriotism than the past Congress. "If I were asked whether they exercised these virtues, I should answer in the honest sincerity of my heart, they did."

The people asked their representatives to check the great deprecia-tion in the currency, to protect the country against treasonable elements, and to enact adequate military measures. This Congress attempted to do in three important acts. While he himself did not entirely approve of what Congress voted, Cobb expained, he thought it acted with wisdom and merited the "thanks and gratitude of the country." He disagreed with those who declared that the constitutional right to suspend the writ of habeas corpus was by implication only; it was expressly granted. If not exercised in the manner prescribed by Congress, it could not be exercised at all. And what of passing measures in secret session? Were not both the federal and Confederate constitutions drawn up in secret sessions? What motive could have prompted the representatives of the people to give the president the power to suspend unless they believed "the public weal required it? . . . Have you no confidence in their wisdom their patriotism, their judgment?" Why should there be fear that the Confederate government would "attempt to crush the liberty of its citizens?" If the government was not worthy of trust, then all liberty was already hopelessly gone.

The recent Congress had also passed additional military bills which forced into the service those who had previously used substitutes. Was it not just that these "hale, healthy & able bodied men" should take position beside beardless boys and older men? As to the change in conscription ages, what did it matter whether one fought under state or Confederate flag. For three years, thousands of others had suffered and won victories under the Confederate flag. "Would you withdraw your admiration from this flag" and substitute another, even "that of our beloved old State?"

And what of the recent currency act? Was it an act of repudiation or of necessity? Was it repudiation to require exchange of currency for 4 percent bonds which could be exchanged for 8 percent bonds two years after a treaty of peace? If confidence in the government were de-stroyed, there would be no treaty of peace. "Do not, therefore, charge upon your government bad faith toward her people, or repudiation, when it has done all in her power to maintain her credit & to preserve her currency."[2]

Alexander Stephens did not address the General Assembly until March 16. Then for three long hours he poured forth denunciations of practically everything that had emanated from Richmond from the beginning of the war, repeating in different words almost everything said by Brown. In conclusion, he warned "against that most insidious enemy which approaches with her syren song, 'independence first, and liberty afterward.' It is a fatal delusion. Liberty is the animating spirit, the soul of our system of government; and like the soul of man, when once lost it is lost forever. . . . Without liberty, I would not turn upon my heel for independence. . . . I would not turn upon my heel to choose between masters. . . . As for myself, give me liberty as secured in the constitution with all its guarantees, amongst which is the sovereignty of Georgia, or give me death."[3]

Brown and Stephens, on the one hand, and Lamar, Kenan, and Cobb, on the other, brought to the legislators and the public full discussion on the matters in controversy. A number of Stephens' friends assured him that his speech was the greatest effort of his life. "It reads more like a speech in the House of Lords than a speech before a Georgia Legislature," wrote Richard M. Johnston.[4] Perhaps Stephens did rise to the heights of oratory, but he joined Brown in descending to the depths of disloyalty to the Confederate cause. They stopped short of an overt act of treason, but there could be no question of their intention to destroy the effectiveness of the Confederate government, that concentration of authority which alone could possibly lead to victory. It is inconceivable that two such intelligent men could believe that individual states could accomplish what centralized government could not or that disloyalty could contribute to success.

In view of Brown's effort to discredit the Davis administration in the eyes of the people, it was inevitable that he would be accused of aspiring to become president himself. And, as was to be expected, some friends proclaimed his qualifications for that office. In private

2 From notes taken by A. E. Marshall, in Hargrett Collection.
3 Printed in Cleveland, *Stephens*, 761 ff.
4 Johnston to Stephens, April 18, 1864, in Stephens Papers, Library of Congress.

correspondence he never mentioned the presidency, but he did later assert that he refused to permit the use of his name for any public office, and a friendly contemporary biographer claimed that he rejected the idea of a cabinet post, yet neither presented evidence of any offer. That Brown was an ambitious man, even his close friends would not have denied. To say that he aspired to the presidency is to place him in the same category with Stephens, Toombs, and Cobb. Perhaps he did.

Brown was by nature a schemer, and many times throughout his career his actions would defy explanation. He had great admiration for Alexander Stephens, but he was never dominated by him. There is no doubt that he intended to use Stephens' influence and prestige in discrediting Davis and possibly driving the president from office. His branding Davis as a tyrant could scarcely have been sincere. Brown did not dislike autocratic power; he merely disliked it in the hands of others. Had he himself been president, his dictatorial actions would have dwarfed those of Davis. Had he been president, would he have abandoned Confederate conscription, leaving the raising of troops to the whims of state governors? Would he have protected the right of citizens to undermine the Confederate cause by their words and action? No. Not Joseph E. Brown.

But what did Brown and the Stephens brothers hope to accomplish? In view of the war weariness, in both the North and the South, they apparently hoped that if the two stubborn antagonists, Lincoln and Davis, could be removed from power—one by defeat for reelection and the other by public pressure—the people, acting through state conventions, might force an end to the conflict. This was not merely an idle dream; it had some possibilities. But suppose the people in other states failed or refused to become sufficiently aroused. Did these "conspirators" advocate that Georgia take separate state action? They were accused of this, but they never advocated it. Had their hostility to the Davis administration become so intense that they preferred Confederate defeat rather than victory under Davis' leadership? The evidence points in that direction.

If defeat came—and Brown and Stephens certainly must have realized the strong probability—what then? Would Georgia have been left to resume her independent existence? No intelligent person advocated this. Then there was only one reasonable conclusion left. Georgia must eventually reunite with the Union. Should this come, Alexander Stephens, always a Union man at heart, would need to make few adjustments. With Brown it was different; no person in the Confederacy had more viciously denounced the Union and its people. Yet Brown possessed an uncanny ability to detect the probable winner and mount the bandwagon before it was too late. Could he have been adjusting his sails to meet the storm ahead? During reconstruction, when he courted favor with those in power, he would often refer with pride to his opposition to the Davis administration.

Even Senator Ben Hill had faint praise for a portion of Governor Brown's message, but he gave Stephens credit for having written it. He had read with "much pleasure and satisfaction" the latter part of the message dealing with "the cause of the war, how conducted, and who responsible," he wrote Stephens. "I know I must thank *you* for it. The whole country will owe you an everlasting debt for it. Gov. Brown can never pay you in kind for the great benefit you have bestowed upon him. You have given him a grandeur of conception, an enlargment of views, and a perspicuity of power and style to which he never could have reached. His only trouble can be the footprints are *too plain not to be recognized*."

Hill could also see Stephens' hand in the section of Brown's speech on the suspension of habeas corpus. He agreed in principle but thought that the public safety did demand its suspension. He had the highest regard for the president and did not believe the suspension would be abused. "I think his *heart* is right and that nothing could tempt him to be a dictator. He is *tenacious* of his *opinion* but does not seem to use *power* greedily." With the first portion of the message, "written by Gov. Brown," dealing with "finances, secret sessions, etc.," Hill "utterly and entirely" disagreed. "It is horrible that such a lame beginning and such a sublime ending should constitute the same message."[5]

Hill showed concern, but Herschel V. Johnson was alarmed. He reminded Stephens that as vice-president he was a part of the executive branch of the government. "How deeply to be lamented that holding that relation you should feel it to be your duty to avow your hostility to

5 March 14, 1864, in Stephens Papers, Emory.

and advise the Legislature to array the State against the Government!
. . . From Gen'l Toombs and Gov. Brown I expected rashness—I did
not expect it of you."[6] Stephens was quick to defend himself, Linton,
and Brown. He denied any antipathy to Davis. He was not even hostile
to the president, and had neither intention nor desire to organize an
opposition party. He knew as much as anyone about the recent resolutions introduced in the legislature; they were written by Linton after
"full consultation" with him. He informed Johnson that he was mistaken in thinking the movement in Georgia had as its aim the organization of an anti-Davis party. "I know all about that movement, if allusion
is made to Governor Brown's message. I advised it from stem to stern
and approve it." He did not provide the language of the message, but he
knew the policy and course intended.[7]

Two months later, Stephens was still defending himself and Brown.
They had no desire to degrade President Davis, he reassured Johnson,
but to him the president's actions had been "a source of deep pain and
mortification," and he thought Brown felt the same way. He had been
with Brown a great deal and felt that the governor's objects were much
higher "than the bare expression of this disapprobation of the President's conduct." Both he and Brown had seen Linton's resolutions
before they were introduced and had offered no objections.[8]

The frustration of the controversy apparently drove Stephens to
the brink of hysteria, but not Brown. As ever, he was cool and calculating. As would happen often throughout the remainder of his
career, he expected somehow to come out on top. He was proud of his
message to the legislature, and would make the fullest use of it for
propaganda purposes, completely ignoring the fact that to encourage
distrust of the government was to hinder the struggle for independence.
He sent copies of his message and Linton Stephens' resolutions to the
clerk of each county court within the Confederacy, and to stir discord
within the armed forces, he sent copies to the captains of each company
in each Georgia regiment. Although he did not get favorable attention
in as many Confederate newspapers as he had hoped, he was delighted

6 Johnson to Stephens, March 19, 1864, in Herschel V. Johnson Papers, Duke
  University.
7 Stephens to Johnson, April 8, 1864, O. R., Ser. IV, Vol. III, 278–81.
8 Stephens to Johnson, June 22, 1864, in Johnson Papers, Duke.

to hear that his message was being "published in *extenso*" in the northern press.[9]

Some military units reacted in a manner no doubt surprising to the governor. Brigadier General George T. Anderson's brigade adopted resolutions denouncing the calling of a special session of the Georgia legislature and the governor's message as "unwise and unpatriotic," sacrificing everything to promote "self-aggrandizement and personal ambition, . . . prostituting the dignity of high office to the accomplishment of unholy ends."[10] But, as usual, the governor had an answer. The officers who promoted the adoption of such resolutions were seeking presidential favor, he averred. Since they were members of the Confederate forces, possible promotion in rank would come from the president, not from the governor.

Brown was also highly pleased with Alexander Stephens' speech and desired the prestige that would come from having it circulated along with his own message. He arranged for Solomon and Leopold Waitzfelder, Milledgeville industrialists, to pay for fifteen hundred copies which would be printed by the *Confederate Union*. The Waitzfelders did not wish their names mentioned, Brown explained to Stephens, but "they are ardently with us and have plenty of money to pay for the copies and not feel it." He himself, Jonas Thweatt and Philip Russell would also pay for another fifteen hundred copies. Brown planned to send copies to each lieutenant in every Georgia regiment and the sheriff of each Confederate county.

The governor was also delighted with a report that Howell Cobb was "getting in the crazy state of fury." Cobb was reported to have denounced the governor as "a traitor, a Tory," who "ought to be hung and would be soon," and that he would travel a distance to witness the hanging. But Brown thought the general should not feel too mortified, for he had done the best he could to defeat favorable legislative action on the governor's proposals. Surely Cobb's master, the president, would reward him with an easy position far removed from danger. Cobb was also reported to have charged in Athens that Brown had either stolen public money or gotten rich in some other dishonest way or else he

9 Brown to Stephens, April 5, 1864, in Stephens Papers, Emory.
10 *C. R. Ga.*, III, 509–14.

could not have recently purchased two plantations in Southwest Georgia.[11] There were others who were also asking the question how a full-time governor with a large family and on a fixed salary of $4,000 could save so much money.

Throughout the period of debate in the legislature on the governor's proposals, lobbyists were reported extremely active. "Senex" in the Savannah *Republican* reported Brown very busy both in public and private. Cotton cards worth $40 to $60 were sold to legislators for $10. And each legislator was permitted to exchange $200 in depreciated Confederate Treasury notes for Georgia Treasury notes worth twice that amount. From these favors "Senex" estimated that the governor won thirty-four votes.[12]

Exhausted and ill humored, the Assembly voted to adjourn at noon on March 19 without having taken action on Linton Stephens' resolutions or either of the governor's three major requests. During the morning hours of that day, Brown sent in a message warning that he would call a special session two days later unless the Assembly took some action on whether the state should turn over all her active militia between seventeen and fifty years of age to the Confederate government; on the "suspension of the writ of *habeas corpus*"; and "the terms upon which peace should be sought."[13] Not wishing to be called again into session so soon, the legislators postponed adjournment for twelve hours, returned to their tasks, and ground out a number of resolutions.

Approved was that portion of the Linton Stephens resolutions for making peace overtures to the enemy, but added was a renewal of "our pledges of the resources of the power of this State to the prosecution of the war, defensively on our part, until peace is obtained upon just and honorable terms, and until the independence and nationality of the Confederate States is established upon a permanent and enduring basis." The assembly declined to express an opinion as to the wisdom of the act extending conscription to include all men between seventeen and fifty. It recommended, however, that the governor "interpose no obstacle to its enforcement." It was further recommended that the secretary of war be requested to exonerate from penalties those who had

11 Brown to Stephens, April 5, 12, 1864, in Stephens Papers, Emory.
12 March 26, 1864.
13 *House Journal*, 1864, Extra Session, 109–11; *C. R. Ga.*, II, 673.

failed to volunteer within the period specified. (The governor endorsed on this resolution: "Having given my views upon this question in my message to the General Assembly, and submitted it to their decision, I yield to this recommendation.") Finally, the legislators denounced the suspension of the writ of habeas corpus as unjustified and unconstitutional and urged its repeal, yet they also expressed "our undiminished confidence in the integrity and patriotism of Jefferson Davis, Chief Magistrate of the Confederate States."[14]

The governor got little of what he had requested, yet he considered the resolution on habeas corpus alone a great victory. His fear, however, was that the narrow margin of legislative approval might be wiped out in the next session. He suspected that General Cobb would act as "high priest" of the "consolidationists" (the supporters of the Richmond administration) in such an attempt. He offered Linton Stephens a circuit judgeship, but the two of them agreed that it was essential for Linton to remain in the House of Representatives; without his efforts the opposition might control the House. Toombs was also considered for the judgeship, but it was decided that his efforts on the bench would be nullified by the supreme court, which was dominated by consolidationists.[15]

Brown and Alexander Stephens received little support from the more important newspapers. "Troup," in the Macon *Telegraph*, used four columns in analyzing Stephens' speech and concluded: "We question neither the purity of his motives nor the sincerity of his convictions but we cannot refrain from saying that his speech was ill-timed, unfortunate, and illogical."[16] The press was never as kind to Brown as to Stephens, so he was concerned over the possible loss of some of the limited support he had received. When Henry Cleveland, editor of the Augusta *Constitutionalist*, notified him that majority stockholder James Gardner would no longer give him a free hand in publishing peace material and henceforth he would be obliged to change his course, remain silent, or lose his job, Brown rushed a letter to Stephens. Friends of the "rights line" must purchase control of that paper, he urged. He could raise part of the money himself and he wished Stephens to do

14 *House Journal*, 1864, Extra Session, 111–15; *Acts of the General Assembly*, 1864, Extra Session, 152–54, 155, 156–59.
15 Brown to Stephens, May 11, 1864, in Stephens Papers, Emory.
16 April 13, 1864.

likewise. "It would be a misfortune for the paper to be lost to the cause of liberty."[17] Gardner was not interested in selling.

Nathan Morse, another Augusta newspaper man, was also interested in assisting in the development of a peace movement. A Connecticut editor who was outspoken in his criticism of President Lincoln, Morse had fled to the South in 1861 and become a minority owner of the Augusta *Chronicle and Sentinel*. It does not appear that he and Cleveland were very friendly, although by mid–1864, they espoused the same cause. Both wanted control of a prominent newspaper. Brown was familiar with their desires and wished to use both if possible. On July 15, 1864, he wrote Cleveland: "I am trying to make arrangement for a good paper at Savannah. I prefer that you and Mr. Morse keep the matter in abeyance till I see what can be done as we may need you in Savannah. . . . I think we had as well say no more about the Constitutionalist."[18]

Cleveland forwarded this letter to Stephens on the same day and also made it known that he was interested in another paper which he did not identify. He noted, however, that it had the same circulation as the *Constitutionalist* and was the best bargain he had seen in two years. "I can make it the best paper in the State *and want it*."[19] No doubt he was referring to the *Chronicle*.

Before the close of the same day, however, Cleveland learned that Morse had purchased control of the *Chronicle* "on credit, at eighty thousand dollars." Morse "went to the Front," Cleveland reported to Stephens, "and I expect Gov. Brown endorsed his paper."[20] Brown probably did put up security for the money borrowed by Morse. For the remainder of the war the governor and the vice-president would call the plays executed by the *Chronicle and Sentinel*, and many columns of print would be devoted to denouncing the governor's assailants and extolling his virtues.[21]

On March 22, 1864, Governor Brown forwarded to Secretary of War Seddon a copy of the conscription resolution passed by the legis-

---

17 June 17, 1864, in Stephens Papers, Emory.
18 Brown to Dear Sir [Cleveland], July 15, 1864, in Stephens Papers, Library of Congress.
19 Cleveland to Dear Friend [Stephens], July 15, 1864, *ibid*.
20 *Ibid*.
21 As an illustration see issue of November 10, 1864.

lature, stating that he yielded to the recommendations of the assembly. He requested a thirty-day extension of time during which those seventeen to eighteen and forty-five to fifty might have the privilege of volunteering before being conscripted. These groups, he stated, had thought their enrollment under state law exempted them from Confederate conscription.[22] In other words, thinking themselves secure under the protecting wing of the governor, they had ignored the conscription act. The extension of time was granted by Seddon with an expression of gratitude for "the spirit of harmonious co-operation and patriotic zeal" evidenced by the action of the Georgia Assembly. Secretary Seddon was also pleased that Brown had relinquished his original objections in deference to the decision of the assembly. He hoped there would now prevail "a spirit of wise conciliation and forbearance which always avoid any conflict."[23]

Seddon was thoroughly deceived if he thought Governor Brown had experienced a change of heart. Blocked on one front, he merely shifted to another. Before receiving the secretary's letter he issued a public statement (in accordance with a resolution passed by the General Assembly) that *all* civil and military officers of the state were exempt from conscription. He then enumerated every elective and appointive office that had ever been provided for in the state, leaving the list incomplete for the addition of other appointive officials, and closing with a statement that if he had overlooked any office it would be added later. This he did. And when persons, regardless of age, were appointed or elected to such unimportant offices as notary public and constable, he issued them certificates of exemption. He even excused bankers as financial agents of the state since their banks had state money on deposit. He also continued to create new positions and declare the holders exempt. Further, he assured all state officers that they need not obey any orders from any Confederate officer. He did express regret, however, that some able-bodied young men were seeking offices that could easily be filled by older men.[24]

Major General Howell Cobb was appointed to command the Georgia Reserves now being forced into service.[25] Owing to the enmity be-

22 *C. R. Ga.*, III, 493–95.
23 *Ibid.*, 496.
24 *Ibid.*, II, 683–87, 689, 697, 701.
25 For Cobb's organizing activities see Montgomery, *Cobb*, 115 ff.

tween him and Governor Brown, Cobb was probably an unwise choice. The two immediately became involved in long and bitter controversy. On April 21, 1864, Cobb addressed a letter to Brown urging cooperation in bringing all able-bodied men into service. He called attention to the portion of the act of Congress which specified that only those state officers who were certified by the governor as necessary to state administration would be exempt from conscription. No such "sweeping exemption" as announced by Brown was ever contemplated. Cobb wished respectfully to inquire if all those declared exempt by Governor Brown were actually necessary to proper functioning of state government. Was it possible that there was need for 2,000 justices of the peace and 1,000 constables? Surely the few persons needed in these positions could be found among older men. And why 3,000 state militia officers when the active militia was being called into Confederate service? The few needed could be supplied from among men over fifty.

General Cobb further stressed that the law placed upon the governor the responsibility for determining what officers were necessary. The responsibility could not be shifted to the legislature. The only purpose of his letter, he explained, was to stress that the army needed able-bodied young men while thousands of them were being shielded in unimportant positions which could be filled by older men. It was farmers and mechanics who were needed at home, not justices of the peace, clerks, deputy sheriffs, or militia officers. The more unnecessary officers shielded in their unimportant positions, the more farmers and mechanics must be called into service.[26]

Brown replied at length restating much of the states' rights argument he had used so many times. The main point, he declared, was whether or not Congress had jurisdiction over state officials. He emphatically denied that it did. Therefore, it was the state legislature, not the governor as directed by Congress, who had power to say which officers should be exempt. The Georgia legislature had said all, and thus had bound both Congress and the governor. When he claimed the right of the state to exempt its officers he claimed it as a "reserved right," not as a "matter of grace or favor from Congress." The governor then again placed a halo over his own head and repeated his stock statement that he had never failed to do his duty. He had placed tens

26 C. R. Ga., III, 504–509.

of thousands of men in the field and labored incessantly to furnish provisions for them and their families back home. With 250,000 well-
equipped, well-fed men in the field, he continued, "we are in no danger
of subjugation." Twice that number, poorly equipped and half starved,
"must soon disband and we would be ruined." The governor would say
to the general that in his zeal to increase the number of troops he might
decrease production to the extent of ruining the cause he was attempting
to serve.[27]

It was now General Cobb's turn to reply and he did so at great
length. He had been informed that there were exactly 2,726 militia
officers within the state. Yet, according to Brown's own statements, if
the conscription act was executed it would deprive the state of her
whole active militia. "Well, the act is being executed," so now there was
"no active militia in the State." Then whom would the militia officers
command? "They should take military charge of themselves, for they
constitute in and of themselves their sole and entire command." He
could not allow to go unnoticed, Cobb further declared, the governor's
attempt to place upon the legislature "the odium and responsibility of
withholding these and other sinecure officials from the army." He himself knew enough of the opinion of legislators to convince him no such
sweeping exemptions were ever intended. Neither Congress, the Supreme Court, the legislature, nor anyone else, except the governor of
Georgia, had ever contended that "justices of the peace who never held
a court, constables who never served a warrant, and militia officers with
no men to command" were so important that without their services the
machinery of government must stop. Indeed, in several counties there
had been no justices of the peace or constables for several years prior
to the sudden rush by young men to fill these jobs in order to evade
military service. The fighting men in the field would scarcely consider
as befriending action the governor's attempt to shield young men from
being forced to come to their assistance.

Why was it, Cobb inquired, that persons could be spared from their
positions to serve in an active militia but not in the Reserve Corps? The
difference was that in the first case they would be under control and
command of the governor, in the second the president. "You seem to
think that its efficiency would be greatly increased by having the con-

27 *Ibid.*, 515–27.

trol yourself, but in this opinion I apprehend you will find few, if any, to agree with you." The legislature certainly preferred to see these men under Confederate authority, and its decision met general approval. "Your Excellency constitutes as far as I know the solitary exception."[28]

Governor Brown again replied in a long letter, saying nothing new on the subject, but at times becoming very bitter and sarcastic. If there was another pair in Georgia who had less respect for each other than the general and the governor the records do not reveal it. There was utterly no hope that anything constructive could emerge from the argument between the two. However, Brown did, in his latest letter, introduce another subject of interest. Cobb had suggested that the governor no doubt had knowledge of some "reprehensible speculation" during the war. This caused Brown to recall an earlier rumor, attributed to Cobb, that the governor had either stolen state money or engaged in other questionable transactions or else he could not have purchased two Southwest Georgia plantations. Brown now saw an opportunity to make a statement which he intended to reach the public.

Before the war, he explained, he possessed "handsome property" with a good yield. After the beginning of the war, his wife had inherited from her father's estate the equivalent of $20,000 in gold, which was invested before great depreciation began. In the depreciated currency with which he purchased his plantations this original $20,000 was worth more than the cost of both. Since this inheritance came through the rights of his wife, it could scarcely be classed as "reprehensible speculation." At the time he purchased his plantations, however, he did not wish to convert all of his securities; therefore, he borrowed $50,000 which he still owed. He hoped the general would accept this as a satisfactory explanation. But as to whatever opinion Cobb might have about the "merits of my official act [as] a public officer . . . I confess I feel a very cool indifference."[29]

28 *Ibid.*, 529–40.
29 *Ibid.*, 541–58. Governor Brown's tax returns for the year 1864 showed:
    Land: 1,316 acres in Lee County ($98,700, Confederate notes); 1,914 acres in Dooly County ($60,000).
    Slaves: 8 in Baldwin County ($16,000); 16 in Dooly County ($32,000). Other property in Baldwin County ($5,000); Dooly County ($5,000). Bonds, notes, etc., $50,000.
    No returns were made for Cherokee County since that area was under federal occupation. See Hargrett Collection.

In the midst of argument over Brown's having certified that *all* civil and military officials were necessary to proper functioning of the state government and therefore were exempt, he suddenly issued a proclamation for such officials within conscription age to report to Major General H. C. Wayne at Atlanta "to aid during the present emergency in driving back the enemy from the soil of this state. Neglect to obey these orders promptly will be visited by appropriate penalties." Only a select few whose duties were connected to the Statehouse, penitentiary, state road or the courts were to be exempt.[30]

This gave Cobb an opportunity for a rejoinder. Why was it that *all* state officers were necessary to state government when the Confederacy called for them, yet very few were necessary when the governor called them into service? "Do you not feel self-condemned," he asked the governor, "in having certified to a statement which is untrue, and which you knew to be untrue at the time you gave the certificate?" Further, Cobb inquired, while reiterating his "claim upon the gratitude of our soldiers" for providing for their needs and those of their families, why did the governor not give a little credit to the taxpayers of Georgia who furnished the money he used? "In your zeal to magnify your own conduct you should not forget what is due to others equally as deserving as yourself."[31] When Brown again replied in the same manner, style, and for the most part, contents, as previous letters, Cobb endorsed thereon: "This communication and the author are alike, unworthy of further notice."[32] Cobb forwarded copies of the entire correspondence to Adjutant General Samuel Cooper.

This exercise in mutual vilification served no good purpose. Both dealt in misrepresentations but developed some truths that produced discomfort. General Cobb's efforts to secure Governor Brown's assistance in building up the Reserve Corps was commendable; Brown's shielding of useless minor state officers from conscription was indefensible. And while General Cobb and the governor argued, General William T. Sherman's powerful force began moving southward along the Western and Atlantic Railroad toward Atlanta. General Joe Johnston's much smaller Army of Tennessee blocked the way. But, just as

30 May 18, 1864, *C. R. Ga.*, II, 703.
31 *Ibid.*, III, 562–66.
32 *Ibid.*, 569, 578

Bragg had been flanked out of Tennessee, so would Johnston be flanked southward through North Georgia. On May 28, 1864, Governor Brown issued an appeal to all able-bodied men of Georgia to report to General Henry C. Wayne at Atlanta for service "till the great battle is fought" and the invader driven back, bringing with them "a bed quilt or blanket" and "a good double-barreled shotgun." "He who remains at his home now will soon occupy it as a slave, or be driven from it. Rally to the rescue, and till the danger is past let the watchword of every patriot be, 'To arms, and to the front'; and the vandal hordes will soon be driven back."[33] No "great battle" was fought, for Sherman saw no need to fight when the Confederate forces could be flanked out of even their strongest positions. Serious threats to cut the lifeline to Atlanta compelled Johnston to fall back deeper and deeper into Georgia.

Brown appointed Major General Gustavus W. Smith[34] commander of his state troops, which, as of June 1, 1864, he estimated to number 3,000. To this force he added the two regular regiments that had been under arms for some time, and tendered the entire 5,000 to General Johnston. They were assigned to guard the bridges and fords along the Chattahoochee River.[35] As the situation became more serious, there is no doubt that Governor Brown did all within his power to bring to the front Georgia's complete manpower. Older men were urged to report on younger men who failed to respond. Militiamen who did not report were threatened with punishment as deserters. Officers, civil and military, were instructed to arrest and escort to Atlanta any evader. The fact that one might be exempt from Confederate service did not exempt him from state service.[36]

The governor also turned to Richmond, urging that reinforcements be sent to General Johnston. Writing from Atlanta, he told President Davis "I need not call your attention to the fact that this place is to the Confederacy almost as important as the heart is to the human body. We must hold it." To do this, Johnston's fighting force must be increased and Sherman's supply line broken. The Union army was being

33 *Ibid.*, 568.
34 Smith, a Kentuckian, was a West Point graduate and a veteran of the Mexican War. He was commissioned major general in the Confederate army in 1861 and saw service in the Peninsula campaign, but resigned early in 1863 as a result of disagreement over promotion.
35 *C. R. Ga.*, III, 574.
36 "To the People of Georgia," June 24, 1864, *ibid.*, II, 707.

supplied from Nashville along three hundred miles of railroad passing through some rough country and over many bridges. If the cavalry forces of Generals Forrest and Morgan could cut this line, destroying many bridges, it would be impossible for Sherman to subsist his army in a region so destitute of supplies as North Georgia. "I do not wish to volunteer advice, but so great is my anxiety for success of our arms and the defense of the State that I trust you will excuse what may seem to be an intrusion."[37]

Davis replied that he fully appreciated the importance of Atlanta, but he had no reinforcements available to send to Johnston. "The disparity of forces between the opposing armies in northern Georgia is less as reported than at any other point," he explained. He left open the possibility, but did not promise, that Forrest and Morgan might strike at Sherman's supply line. No change in disposition of forces seemed possible that would bring effective aid to General Johnston.[38]

Brown was much displeased by the position taken by Davis. He was convinced that 10,000 men under the command of Forrest thrown against Sherman's supply line south of Chattanooga would be a destructive blow. The people were pleased with Johnston's efforts, Brown argued, and expected Davis to assist by cutting off Sherman's supplies. They did not see how this could be done with Forrest operating in Mississippi and Morgan in Kentucky. "Your information as to the relative strength of the two armies in North Georgia cannot be from reliable sources," he told Davis. "If your mistake should result in loss of Atlanta, and the occupation of other strong points in this State by the enemy, the blow may be fatal to our cause and remote posterity may have reason to mourn over the error."

He was surprised that his estimates of the strength of the armies based upon official reports were unreliable, Davis replied immediately. "Until your better knowledge is communicated I shall have no means of correcting such errors, and your dicta cannot control the disposition of troops in different parts of the Confederate States. Most men in your position would not assume to decide on the value of the services to be rendered by troops in distant positions. When you give me your reliable statement of the comparative strength of the armies, I will be glad also

37 January 28, 1864, *ibid.*, III, 582.
38 June 29, 1864, *ibid.*, 583.

to know the source of your information as to what the whole country expects and posterity will judge."[39]

He regretted the president's "exhibition of temper" in denying the services of Forrest and Morgan in destroying Sherman and relieving the state, Brown responded. While he did not pretend to dictate, it did appear that with forty to fifty Georgia regiments defending Richmond there was no just cause for rebuke when her governor requested sufficient troops to defend Atlanta and the Gulf states. Should the president continue his policy of keeping forces divided and leaving three hundred miles of enemy supply line uninterrupted, he feared the results would be the same as "followed a like policy of dividing our forces at Murfreesborough and Chattanooga." Further if Atlanta should be sacrificed and other portions of Georgia overrun while the cavalry was away on distant raids, "you will have no difficulty in ascertaining, from correct sources of information, what was expected of you by the whole people, and what verdict posterity will record from your statements as to the relative strength of the two armies. I venture at the hazard of further rebuke, to predict that your official estimates of Sherman's numbers are as incorrect as your official calculations at Missionary Ridge were erroneous."[40] Here this chapter of the running controversy between president and governor appears to have ended. It is doubtful that anything the Confederacy could have offered would have stopped the stubborn onslaught of Sherman. Yet the plan offered by Brown, though not original with him, had merit. Forrest and Morgan could have seriously disrupted Sherman's supplies by destroying bridges faster than they could be repaired. And if they could have blown in the tunnel through the Cumberland Mountains between Sherwood and Cowan, Tennessee, the Nashville and Chattanooga Railroad would have been of no further use for the duration of the war.

General Johnston complimented the performance of Brown's state militia in the vicinity of Marietta and urged the governor to increase their number. Brown responded with a proclamation urging every man in the state able to bear arms to report for duty. He ordered all between sixteen and seventeen and between fifty and fifty-five to report. Men between seventeen and fifty who were exempt from Confederate ser-

39 July 5, 1864, *ibid.*, 588.
40 July 7, 1864, *ibid.*, 589.

vice were ordered to report for state duty. Also to report were all detailed men within this age range who were not actually in Confederate military service. He could not suppose, he declared, that the president, in this time of great emergency, would wish to protect from service those able-bodied men detailed for industrial or other types of work.[41]

Brown's "remarkable proclamation" again brought him into conflict with General Cobb and also Confederate colonel William M. Browne, who had been returned to Georgia and placed in charge of conscription. It was their contention that, from the date of the passage of the conscription laws, every man between seventeen and fifty, unless exempt, became *ipso facto* a party of the Confederate military service. Therefore, regardless of their present assignment, Brown had no control whatsoever over them. Cobb asked for instructions from Richmond and was advised to give in to the governor where he could do so judiciously, since the assignment of these men to militia duty would be temporary. But the instructions stated that if detailed men were to be called into service, the president preferred it be as a part of Cobb's reserves, not Brown's militia.[42]

Richmond authorities grew impatient with Johnston's continuous retreat, fighting small engagements, but never the great battle. On July 17, 1864, he was replaced by General John Bell Hood. Governor Brown sent assurance of "energetic co-operation," and Hood called upon him for more "men with muskets as fast as possible."[43] As the two armies faced each other in the Atlanta area, federal raiding forces struck at railroads and terrorized the countryside. One group visited Canton and burned Governor Brown's dwelling. Macon, Milledgeville, and Athens were threatened. Brown, with a portion of his militia, joined Cobb and the reserves at Macon. Also present was General Johnston who had been without assignment since being superseded by Hood. When the governor learned that Milledgeville was threatened he sent word for his family to flee the capital city.[44] This was a great

41 July 9, 1864, *ibid.*, II, 710–16.
42 *Ibid.*, III, 591, 592, 595, 596; Browne to Brown, July 20, 1864, in Hargrett Collection.
43 *C. R. Ga.*, III, 597, 598.
44 The governor also gave orders for the removal of public property. Should the enemy approach, he instructed the treasurer, John Jones, he was to remove "funds and valuables" by train if possible. If not, "take them in a

responsibility to place upon Mrs. Brown, for a large portion of the Brown clan was now housed at the Governor's Mansion. With the movement of Sherman deep into North Georgia, the governor had removed from the Cherokee area his aged parents, two sisters, and a sister-in-law. Fortunately, William McKinley, a Baldwin County planter living near Milledgeville, came to Mrs. Brown's assistance. McKinley was neither a political nor personal friend of the governor, but he was a man of compassion. Fearing that the governor's family might be abused by irresponsible soldiers, he hurriedly arranged for carriages and wagons to transport the group, incuding "all their Cherokee plunder," to his plantation home. Throughout the night of July 29 the moving continued, filling the halls with baggage and provisions.[45] The raiders did not strike Milledgeville; the Brown family was soon able to return to the Mansion.

General Hood had been expected to fight; he did, but lost. By early September, Atlanta belonged to Sherman, and central Georgia was wide open for invasion. During the fight for Atlanta, Brown had placed some ten thousand militia reserves under the temporary command of Generals Johnston and Hood. Many had seen some action and were reported to have fought well. However, the conditions under which these militia had been tendered was that the governor, their commander in chief, might withdraw or disband them at his pleasure. On September 10, 1864, Brown notified Hood that since his militia had been tendered for the defense of Atlanta, which had been terminated by the

---

wagon and start through the piney woods to such a place of safety as you may select until the raid is passed." Brown to Jones, July 24, 1864, in Brown Papers, Atlanta Historical Society.

45 Lucy Barrow Cobb, daughter-in-law of Howell Cobb, a visitor in the McKinley home, recorded a very unfavorable impression of the Brown family during this period of alarm: "They promise to afford us some amusement intermixed with pity," she wrote her husband. In describing the Brown children she referred to "blear-eyed Joe"; "poor little cripple," Franklin Pierce; Elijah, "a little hard of hearing;" Baby Sally with a "breaking out on her head which I believe to be scrofula"; and that vile negro nurse "with a consumptive cough." And there was "ole man Brown" whose withered "prying look" and "hanging jaws" frightened her; Nancy, the governor's sister of thirty-five, whose tall gaunt figure did not go well with the ringlets on her head and girlish ways; and the younger sister, who was "Josephs self in petticoats." Only the two Mrs. Browns—wife and mother—appeared to be normal. (Lucy Cobb to John A. Cobb, July 29, 30, 1864, in Cobb Papers). Lucy was born a Barrow but she was now a true Cobb!

fall of the city, he was withdrawing "said organization from your command."[46] On this same day Brown commended his troops for their "manly firmness and heroic valor" and sent them home on a thirty-day furlough to harvest crops and "put your houses in order." There was no longer an emergency, for it would require considerable time for the enemy to prepare for further invasion.[47] In other words, while the enemy was preparing to lay waste a large portion of the state, ten thousand Georgia troops would be at home performing their regular routine.

One day shortly after the fall of Atlanta, Joshua Hill and an associate called at the headquarters of General Sherman to request permission to go for the body of Hill's son who had been killed near Cassville. Sherman granted the request and then asked his visitors to remain for dinner. Conversation quickly turned to the condition of war-torn North Georgia and the probability that the same fate was in store for other sections of the state. According to Sherman, Hill readily agreed that further Confederate resistance in Georgia would be madness and also expressed the wish that Governor Brown would withdraw Georgia "from the rebellion in pursuance of what was known as the policy of 'separate State action.'"

Sherman was well informed on Hill's Unionist background, as well as of the words and actions of Brown and Stephens; therefore, he seized what he thought was an opportunity. He suggested that should Hill see the governor, he might say to him that "if he remained inert, I would be compelled to go ahead, devastating the State in its whole length and breadth; that there was no adequate force to stop us etc.; but if he would issue his proclamation withdrawing his State troops from the armies of the Confederacy, I would spare the State, and in our passage across it confine the troops to the main roads, and would, moreover, pay for all the corn and food we needed." Sherman also suggested that Hill invite Brown to visit Union headquarters in Atlanta. He would guarantee the governor adequate protection, and should Brown wish to make a speech, he would provide him with "as full and respectable an audience as any he had ever spoken to."[48] Sherman sent similar

46 *C. R. Ga.*, III, 608.
47 *Ibid.*, 609–12.
48 William T. Sherman, *Memoirs of William T. Sherman*, 2 vols. (New York, 1875), II, 137–38.

suggestions to Brown's friend Augustus R. Wright of Rome and to William King of Marietta, both of whom had been expressing themselves in the interest of peace.

Sherman was pleased with his plan to separate Georgia from the Confederacy, and in view of the peace talk that had reached him and Brown's well-known hostility to Richmond authorities, he had good reason to expect success. On September 15 he wired General Halleck: "Governor Brown has disbanded his militia, to gather the corn and sorghum of the State. I have reason to believe that he and Stephens want to visit me and have sent them a hearty invitation."[49] Halleck passed the word on to President Lincoln. Two days later the president replied: "I feel great interest in the subject of your dispatch mentioning corn and sorghum, and the contemplated visit to you."[50]

Sherman wired back immediately that Wright and King "are now going between Governor Brown and myself." He had explained to them that the rebellion "begun in error and perpetuated in pride" could be ended and Georgia "save herself from the devastation of war" now being prepared for her "only by withdrawing her quota out of the Confederate Army, and aiding me to expel Hood from the borders of the State." Sherman added that he was fully conscious of the "delicate nature of such assertions, but it would be a magnificent stroke of policy if we could, without surrendering principle or a foot of ground, arouse the latent enmity of Georgia against Davis." He would keep the president posted.[51] It should be noted that Sherman had now added to his original proposition the requirement that Georgia troops must assist him in driving Hood's army out of the state.

William King called on Brown and delivered Sherman's oral message, and the governor later gave to the press his version of the conference. His reply to Sherman was that since Sherman was "only a general commanding an army in the field, and I the Governor of a State, neither the Constitution of his country nor of my own, confers upon us any power to negotiate a treaty of peace. We probably hold but few sentiments in common, but if we should agree in every particular we would have power to bind no one by any compact we might

49 *Ibid.*, 138.
50 *Ibid.*, 139.
51 *Ibid.*, 138–39.

make. As our interview could therefore result in nothing practical I must decline the invitation."

According to Brown, he also stated that, while he was eager to do everything possible to relieve suffering in the occupied areas, he saw nothing that he could do. To Sherman's threat to overrun the remainder of the state, Brown's reply was that "no compulsion rests upon him to attempt this, unless it be the cruel orders of his Government." But should the attempt be made, the federal general would find greater difficulties than he had encountered between Dalton and Atlanta. "Georgia may possibly be overrun but can never be subjugated, and her people will never treat with a conqueror upon her soil."

Brown further stated that as a sovereign state Georgia had withdrawn from the old Union and joined a new one. "She is as sovereign today as she was the day she seceded from the old Union, and has the same power, by convention of her people, which she then had to resume all delegated power, and all the attributes of sovereignty, and then to declare war, negotiate treaties of peace, and do all other acts which a sovereign State may do." This power, however, rested with the people; it was not conferred upon the governor. But although Georgia possessed power to take separate action she was pledged to her sister states. She had entered the contest with full knowledge of her responsibilities; she would continue to respect those responsibilities.[52]

Robert Toombs, hearing of Sherman's efforts, rushed to Alexander Stephens a bit of advice: "Do not by any means go to see Sherman, whatever may be the form of his invitation. It will place you in a wrong, *very wrong* position. What is said to be Brown's answer . . . is the true position. If Sherman means anything he means to detach Georgia from the Confederacy. Better any fate than that. Davis is impregnable upon the peace issue. In every shape and form and at all times he has professed to seek peace, and in truth up to this time his actions conform to his professions. . . ."[53] Neither Stephens nor Brown agreed with the last portion of this statement.

William King visited Stephens after conferring with Governor Brown, and the vice-president released to the public his written reply. The termination of "this fratricidal war without further effusion of

52 Milledgeville *Confederate Union*, September 27, 1864.
53 Phillips, *Correspondence*, 652–53.

blood," he told King, was an objective "very dear to me." He would make any sacrifice "short of principle and honor to obtain it," yet he must add that neither he nor Sherman had the power to enter into negotiation. However, if Sherman thought there was any prospect of agreement and adjustment and would make the fact known in a "formal and authoritative manner," he "would most cheerfully and willingly. with the consent of our authorities," accede to the general's request and enter upon the "arduous task of restoring peace and harmony" with all the earnestness at his command. "This does not seem to me to be at all impossible, if truth and reason should be permitted to have sway."[54]

Brown and Stephens sent each other congratulations on their replies to Sherman. Brown had expected to be severely attacked, and was apparently disappointed that he had not been. He was pleased with Stephens' proposition to meet Sherman under certain circumstances. "It keeps the door open and I think this is wise." He also hoped that a copy of Stephens' letter would reach the northern press. Upon the suggestion of Governor Z. B. Vance of North Carolina, the southern governors were soon to meet in Augusta. Brown intended "to sound them a little upon their feelings in reference to a convention of the states."[55] Brown and Stephens had indeed left the door open, but in view of Lincoln's probable victory over McClellan in the presidential campaign, they could scarcely have expected that which might enter to be to their liking.

There appears to be no record of any report to Sherman by King, Wright, or Josh Hill. Sherman recorded that he had no doubt but that Brown "seriously entertained the proposition," but hardly "felt ready to act"; so the governor simply sent his troops home and called the legislature into special session to consider the "critical condition of

54 Augusta *Chronicle and Sentinel*, October 28, 1864; Johnston and Browne, *Stephens*, 472.
55 Phillips, *Correspondence*, 653; Vance to Brown, September 23, 1864; Brown to Vance, October 1, 1864, *O. R.*, Ser. IV, Vol. III, 684–85, 706–707.
    The southern governors met in Augusta on October 17, and adopted resolutions recommending the repeal of such state laws as prevented sending state troops outside the state; urging Confederate authorities to send all able-bodied men into active service; and suggesting the passage of stringent state laws for the arrest and return of deserters. They did not resolve on the subject of conscription, habeas corpus, or state conventions. Georgia *Senate Journal*, 1864, pp. 31–33.

affairs."[56] Sherman made no further report to President Lincoln. He might very well have been near the truth in his appraisal of Brown's position, but he was in error as to the special session of the legislature; the November session was a regular one.

It is not certain that either Hill or Wright conferred with either Brown or Stephens, but Brown heard from Hill in some manner. On September 30, the day King conferred with Stephens, Brown wrote the vice-president: "I learn that Hon. Joshua Hill agrees fully with us on the line of policy we have acted upon in Confederate politics." There was a vacancy in the state Senate from Hill's district, and he had "confidentially written Hill asking him to run. He is hesitating. I wish you would write him or see him and try to induce him to run. He can be elected and he would render a public service in my opinion."[57] Hill either did not make the race or was not elected.

There was definitely a widespread demand for peace in Georgia, but the movement was never organized. Destruction and suffering had eroded loyalty to the Confederacy, yet there was nowhere else to turn. Although many grumbled that the Confederacy had deserted Georgia, few advocated that Georgia desert the Confederacy. To desert the Confederacy meant to abandon all hope of eventual independence; no thinking person could envision Georgia as an independent power. Georgians were stunned by reality; the impossible had happened; their state had been overrun by a Union army. Brown and Stephens had cut the foundation from beneath loyalty to the Davis administration, yet had not supplied a more promising alternative. Although still in the future, the reelection of Lincoln, Sherman's march through Georgia, and Grant's determined movement upon Richmond, would relegate to the realm of wildest dreams the idea of peace through a convention of all the states.

Presumably with the hope of salvaging some of the loyalty to his administration and checking the spread of the Stephens-Brown influence, President Davis journeyed to Georgia late in September, 1864. On the evening of the twenty-third, he, Cobb, and Ben Hill addressed a gathering at Macon. Davis appealed to those absent from their com-

56 Sherman, *Memoirs*, II, 140.
57 Stephens Papers, Emory.

mands to return to duty. "Let us with one arm and one effort crush Sherman," he urged. He claimed to have given Georgia all of the assistance possible and scathingly rebuked that "miserable man" who accused the Confederate government of abandoning Georgia to her fate. The man who uttered that statement was a "scoundrel," the president exclaimed. He was not the man to "save our country."[58]

Davis' visit and speech recruited little support for a rapidly dying cause, but it gave the Brown-controlled press an excuse to speak out. "It is unnecessary to comment upon the bad taste and glaring impropriety of such an expression applied by the President of the Confederacy to a Governor of the sovereign State of Georgia," announced Morse of the *Chronicle and Sentinel*. "The people of this State will not be disposed to yield to President Davis, himself, the superiority over our noble and independent Executive in pure and lofty patriotism and unflinching and unswerving integrity."[59]

58 Macon *Daily Telegraph*, September 24, 1864.
59 Augusta *Chronicle and Sentinel*, September 28, 1864.

Chapter XV

I Therefore Decline

TWO DAYS after Governor Brown sent the Georgia militia on furlough following the fall of Atlanta, he received a communication from Secretary of War Seddon. From official reports to Richmond, the secretary explained, it had been learned that the governor had ten thousand organized militia. "I am instructed by the President to make requisition on you for that number, and such further force of militia to repel invasion as you may be able to organize for Confederate service."[1]

He and the people of Georgia regretted that the president was so late in discovering the danger of formidable invasion, Brown sarcastically replied. That invasion, which had begun in May, had overrun the "most fertile" section of Georgia, taken possession of Atlanta, and now threatened the railroad connection with Virginia. While this disaster was in the making, the governor charged, the president had thirty thousand available troops in Texas and Louisiana, and General Jubal Early with another twenty thousand was invading Maryland and Pennsylvania with no results other than to unite the North in support of Lincoln. Further, Morgan was raiding in Kentucky and Forrest was attempting to repulse raids in North Mississippi, an area no longer worth overrunning. Ignoring the tested rules of good generalship, the president had scattered his forces from Texas to Pennsylvania, while a severe blow was being struck at the heart of the Confederacy. The president and his advisers alone failed to realize what damage Forrest

[1] *C. R. Ga.*, III, 607.

and Morgan could have done to Sherman's supply line. Had all forces not necessary for the defense of Richmond been thrown against Sherman in Georgia, the war might have been brought to a speedy termination.

Further, the governor was astonished that the president failed to recognize that the troops he now sought to requisition had met their responsibilities with "distinguished valor" in the defense of Atlanta. For this the president extended no word of thanks, praise, or encouragement. "They were militia. Their Generals and other officers were not appointed by the President and their services are ignored by him." The object of this requisition then, the governor charged, was neither to get the militia into active service, for they were already there, nor to promote harmony, for relations between himself and Johnston and Hood had been perfect. While these troops were in Confederate service they were under complete control of the commanding general. Neither could the present requisition be for the purpose of increasing the number of men in service, for Confederate officers had constantly thrown every obstacle in his path while raising these troops. And it certainly could not be to force Georgia to furnish her quota; this she had done and more. Neither was this requisition being made upon other states. Therefore, there could be but one answer: the president's object was "to grasp into his own hands the entire control of the whole reserve militia of the State, which would enable him to disband its present organization, and place in power over it his own partisans and favorites," dismissing those distinguished officers appointed under state law. Although Brown did not mention it, he must have had in mind the fact that both G. W. Smith and Robert Toombs, the second in command of state forces, had resigned from the Confederate service because of disagreement with the administration.

Governor Brown further noted that the president's requisition was for "the whole militia of the State—all I have organized and all I can organize." The president, once he got control, could then order to some distant point outside the state the last man of Georgia's defensive force. To those who suggested that he should "trust the sound judgment and good faith of the President," he would say that he could not "forget the faith that was violated last fall," when the state guard was held in service long beyond the period of need. Indeed, there was nothing in the president's requisition that even promised this would not happen again. "I therefore decline to comply with or fill this extraordinary requisition." He himself would not hesitate again to call out these forces when necessity demanded it and even place them temporarily under command of the Confederate general. However, in such case he would "retain the power to withdraw them" when he thought proper. Furthermore, since the Army of Tennessee, even when reinforced by the militia, was not sufficient to drive back the invaders, "I demand as an act of simple justice that such re-enforcements be sent as are necessary." Unless this be done, "I then demand that he [the president] permit all the sons of Georgia to return to their homes, families, and altars." Upon their return they would either drive the enemy from their state or "nobly perish in one last grand and glorious effort."[2] As usual, Governor Brown seemed more concerned over possibilities than probabilities.

Secretary Seddon expressed "painful surprise" at the "tenor and spirit" in the governor's letter of refusal. "It requires forbearance in reply to maintain the respect I would pay your station, and observe the official propriety you have so transcended." The governor had reached conclusions not justified by facts. The president had requested organized militia. If organized, the units would have already chosen their own officers, who would accompany their commands. It had been reported that only a small portion of the militia had seen service and that at the pleasure of the governor. In the interest of unity and efficiency, it was reasoned that *all* should be under command of the general commanding, "subject not to your judgment or disposal, but to the control of the Constitutional Commander-in-Chief."

It was the duty of the Confederate government to provide for common defense, working through laws passed by Congress. The Constitution did not recognize the right of states to keep troops in time of war. But the Constitution did authorize the president to call state militia into active service and exercise complete control over it. The president had made such a call upon the governor, Seddon explained, and "You have met it with a distinct refusal." This was the first such incident in the history of the Confederacy, but there had been similar incidents during the war of 1812. During that war the governors of the

2 *Ibid.*, 612–22.

New England states had claimed for themselves the right to decide "whether the exigencies existed which authorized the president to make a requisition for militia to repel invasion, and denied his power to associate them with other troops under a Federal officer." Not only did those governors seriously obstruct the war effort but it was even suspected they were "in communication with the enemy, or at least proposed to give them encouragement and moral support." The secretary of war did not wish to make such an accusation against the governor of Georgia, he explained, but he would call attention to the fact that the two cases were analogous, and on the point of invasion the New England governors had the more plausible case.

In analyzing the reasons for Governor Brown's action, Secretary Seddon placed at the head of the list opposition to the Confederate government, especially the president. The military campaign in Georgia had not been conducted in accordance with Brown's conception and advice; therefore, the governor had resolved to retain control of troops rather than allow them to pass under command of the president. But the secretary would remind the governor that it was not the fault of the War Department that Georgia was "invaded by overwhelming numbers." If the governor understood the situation so well, why had he not organized his ten thousand militia and thrown them into the conflict early in May? Instead he had offered every obstacle against Confederate efforts to recruit.

As to the president's alleged design to disband the militia and reorganize it with Confederate officers, it could not be done without losing many men. Disband meant to discharge, therefore only those eligible for draft could be retained. "Your suspicions as to the motives and design of the President are simply chimerical." As to the governor's claim that state troops were needed not only for defense against invasion but also as "protection against the encroachment of centralized power," the secretary did not wish to comment. He could not believe the governor had duly considered the language used. He would prefer to class it as "inconsiderate utterances" rather than a real threat "to array your State in armed antagonism against the Confederacy." He did not wish to ascribe such a purpose to one occupying so high an official position. "I must, however, gravely regret that the spirit of Your Excellency's past action and public expressions, has caused grievous misconceptions in relation to the feelings and purposes of yourself, and perhaps of others of influence in your State, in the convictions of our enemies to their encouragement, and the mortification of many patriotic citizens of the Confederacy. Our enemies appear to have conceived you were even prepared to entertain overtures of separate accommodation, and that your State, so justly proud of its faith, valor and renown, could be seduced or betrayed to treachery and desertion." But rather than reminding the governor of "constitutional obligations and repelling unjust imputations," the secretary of war would prefer to be cooperating with him "in a spirit of unity and confidence, in the defense of your State and the overthrow of the invader."[3]

Secretary Seddon's analysis of Brown's motives was so near perfect that his letter could do no less than greatly arouse the governor's anger. More than a month passed, however, before Brown replied; he was busy preparing his message to the General Assembly. During this interval General Beauregard, commanding the southeastern coastal region, wired President Davis that he, General Cobb, and Governor Brown had satisfactorily arranged matters pertaining to exemptions and the state militia. Davis referred the telegram to Secretary Seddon. Apparently unable to believe that any kind of an arrangement could have been made with Brown that did not violate some Confederate law or principle, Davis requested Seddon to check whether or not the agreement referred to was "conformable to law and the necessities of the service." Seddon wired Cobb for information. Cobb gave assurance that Brown had done nothing more than place the militia under command of Beauregard with the same stipulations as when under Johnston and Hood. He himself, however, had agreed earlier that Confederate details not actually in the service were subject to militia duty. "You rightly suppose that Governor Brown is not only willing, but anxious to bring the Confederate authorities into disrepute with the people of Georgia. . . . whilst I have long since lost all respect for Governor Brown, and that feeling is on the daily increase, I am using every effort to have harmonious co-operation in the great work of the defense of the State and country."[4]

It was November 14, 1864, before Brown began writing his reply to Seddon. When completed it would fill twenty-five printed pages. But

3 *Ibid.*, 628–38.
4 *Ibid.*, 638, 639, 642.

for all its length it did not inject a single new idea into the discussion. It was a rehash of the points of conflict during the past two years, shifting to the Davis administration credit for all failures. His opposition to Confederate measures, he avowed, was not opposition to the government but to its errors and poor judgment. "Some men are able to distinguish between opposition to a government and unwillingness blindly to endorse all the errors of an administration, or to discriminate between loyalty to a cause and loyalty to a master. My loyalty is only due to my country; you can bestow yours where your *interests* or inclinations may prompt."

Brown denied that any sentence in his recent letter contained an "inconsiderate utterance." Neither was there anything in it that would justify an accusation that he would array the state of Georgia in "armed antagonism against the Confederacy." No state was more loyal to the Confederacy than Georgia, and as governor he stood ready to use her troops to defend all "just rights and Constitutional powers of the Confederacy. . . . But while I will employ all the force at my command to maintain all the constitutional rights of the Confederacy and my State, I shall not hesitate to use the same force to protect the same rights against external assaults and internal usurpations." There was a difference between loyalty to the Confederacy and loyalty to those who imagined themselves to be the Confederacy, yet recognized no individual state right which conflicted with their purpose or plans.[5]

As Governor Brown quarreled with Richmond authorities, he was already in serious confrontation with the General Assembly and public opinion. The assembly convened for its regular session on November 3. The governor's message was read on the same day. He opened with a stinging denunciation of Confederate authorities for not reinforcing General Johnston as the Army of Tennessee was compelled to fall back deeper into Georgia. He repeated the same arguments almost verbatim that he had previously written to Davis. If the president had only followed these suggestions, Sherman, with his supply line destroyed, would have been crushed and Georgia and Tennessee freed from his menace. But the "powers that be, determined upon a different line of policy. The world knows the results, and we must acquiesce. But the misfortunes following the misguided judgment of our rulers must not

5 *Ibid.*, 643–68.

have the effect of relaxing our zeal or chilling our love for the cause."

Many Georgians deplored Confederate "errors and mismanagement," Brown asserted, others "attempted to justify all its mistakes," but very few were disloyal to the extent of wishing to end the war without vindicating and establishing the "sovereignty of the several States. . . . Confederate independence with centralized power without State sovereignty and Constitutional and religious liberty, would be very little better than subjugation, as it matters little who our master is, if we are to have one." Military might could never end the bloody struggle, for the North had resources for many years and the South the power to resist and endure. Yet negotiations were unlikely as long as Lincoln and Davis headed the two respective governments, Brown contended. Either there must be a change of governments, or the people, "in their aggregate capacity as sovereign States," must exert sufficient influence to stop the war and force a settlement on the basis of "the principles of 1776."

The governor had his own proposal. He suggested a convention of delegates from all the states, north and south. Each state would enter the convention as "a separate, independent sovereign," and no action of the convention would be binding upon a state until its people approved. It would be left to each state to decide to which union it would belong. While Brown thought separate state action might be "necessary as a preliminary to a treaty of peace," he did not wish to advocate it. Yet he pointed out that the states of the Confederacy had seceded from the United States; they had the same right under the Confederacy. The fighting forces should not bear the entire responsibility. There should be statesmen working toward negotiations. Soldiers had just as much right to condemn statesmen for failure as statesmen did soldiers. "In a crisis like the present, statesmanship is even more important than Generalship. Generals can never stop a war, though it may last twenty years, till one has been able to conquer the other. Statesmen terminate wars by negotiation."[6]

There is no reason to believe Brown expected his plan to be implemented. The only hope of northern agreement to such a plan rested upon the possibility that Lincoln would not be reelected. There was much war weariness in the North, and although General Grant was

6 *House Journal*, 1864, pp. 5 ff.

grinding out eventual victory over General Lee, his terrific losses were sickening. Then came Sherman's brilliant invasion of Georgia. Perhaps the fall of Atlanta assured the reelection of Lincoln. At any rate, by the time Brown's message was presented to the General Assembly there was no doubt of a Lincoln victory. There was little chance that two men as determined as Davis and Lincoln would permit the treaty-making power to be exercised by a convention. And as far apart as the two presidents were on their war aims, it was unlikely that they would agree to negotiate. So it was war to the end, and that would not be long.

In spite of the gloomy prospects for negotiation, Linton Stephens again introduced resolutions calling for a suspension of hostilities and settlement of the controversy on the basis of sovereignty of each individual state. A convention of commissioners representing all states should "frame and propose a plan of peace," subject to approval by the Union and Confederate governments and by each state "whose sovereignty may be involved." It was further resolved that the Confederate government take the initiative and propose such a convention "on all suitable occasions and especially just after signal successes of our arms."[7]

Seeking assistance in blocking the passage of the resolutions, Senate president Ambrose R. Wright and others sent a copy to President Davis requesting his reaction. Davis replied on November 17. He had not contemplated the use of any "agency in treating for peace other than that established by the constitution." If the United States was willing to make peace, he thought it would treat directly. "If unwilling, it would refuse to consent to the convention of States." The author of these resolutions and his supporters, Davis observed, appeared "to commit the radical error of supposing that the obstacle to obtaining the peace which we all desire consists in the difficulty of finding proper agencies for negotiating"; therefore, what the resolutions did was to suggest that "*if* the enemy will treat, the best agency would be State delegates to a convention, whereas the whole and only obstacle is that the enemy will not treat at all or entertain any other proposition than that we submit to their yoke, acknowledge that we are criminals and appeal to their mercy for pardon."[8]

7 Augusta *Chronicle and Sentinel*, November 11, 1864.
8 Rowland, *Jefferson Davis*, VI, 402–406.

Most of the major press remained hostile to the Brown-Stephens proposals. In referring to the *Chronicle*'s conversion, the Augusta *Constitutionalist* declared "We utterly scorn and reject all ideas of a *convention* of the States."[9] And the Macon *Telegraph* regarded "the thing as impracticable." The plan would require that the states, north and south, "recall their delegated powers and assert their absolute sovereignty." Was there even a remote possibility of their doing so? "As for ourselves, we have neither time nor inclination to run tilts with windmills."[10]

Davis' letter and the adverse newspaper publicity had their effect; the House took no action on Linton Stephens' resolutions other than have two hundred copies printed, and the Senate passed resolutions expressing to the president the thanks of the people of Georgia for his "able, fearless and impartial conduct of our Government during the past year," and assuring him that "our confidence in his wisdom, purity and patriotism is unshaken and without abatement." The governor was requested to forward copies of these resolutions to the president and both houses of Congress.[11]

The session of the legislature was not only bitter, but also an uneasy one. Reports of Sherman's activities reached Milledgeville daily. Since taking Atlanta he had ordered the civilian population to remove themselves while he collected for military use all materials that were valuable. Munitions and other supplies continued to arrive from his Tennessee base. Raiding parties were sent out in all directions. Confederate General Joe Wheeler's cavalry kept watch but could do little more. On November 14, 1864, Wheeler reported rumors that Sherman was about to move toward either Savannah or Augusta. The next day he reported fires in Rome, Marietta, and Atlanta. The railroad north of Atlanta was being torn up; the bridge over the Chattahoochee River had been burned.

This answered the question of whether Sherman would follow Hood to Tennessee or move across Georgia to the coast. If the railroad north of Atlanta was being wrecked, then Sherman no longer had need for it. By the sixteenth, Sherman's army, reportedly reinforced to sixty

---

9 November 9, 1864.
10 *Ibid.*
11 *Senate Journal*, 1864, pp. 62–63.

thousand men, was moving toward Macon and Milledgeville. The state forces under Cobb and G. W. Smith fell back upon Macon. On the seventeenth, Governor Brown informed the legislature that Atlanta had been "burnt and laid waste." Other towns were experiencing similar fate. The Federals were moving toward Macon "and probably this city." But he was still hopeful that if the whole manhood of the state would rally and move toward the front, the enemy could be captured or destroyed. Therefore, he requested authority "to make a levy en masse," including every man able to bear arms. Once this authority was granted, he urged the passage of recommended appropriation and military bills, and that "the Governor and Legislature then adjourn to the front" to meet again at a place and time designated by the Governor.[12]

During lunch recess on November 23, news arrived in Milledgeville that Sherman was moving in that direction and his cavalry was probably not far away. Panic seized the capital city. Leaving "bills and other matters . . . lying on the desks," legislators hurriedly departed by "the best means of conveyance at their command." Many citizens joined them in flight. Those who had conveyances for sale or hire raised their prices to fabulous heights.[13] The Brown family remained in the city until the next afternoon. The governor had already ordered Quartermaster General Ira A. Foster to begin moving the more valuable records and other government property to places of safety. Some valuables were stored in the insane asylums. The bulk of property was to be sent to Macon by rail. Amid the consternation, the great problem was labor and conveyances to get the property to the station. Assuming that since the penitentiary was also a gun factory it would be burned by the enemy, Governor Brown set free all inmates (excepting a few hardened criminals) who would volunteer to aid in the removal of state property and then enlist in the Confederate service. The response was "almost unanimous," but most of them later deserted.[14]

Several years later General Foster was requested to give his account of the evacuation of the capital, with special reference to the persistent charge that Governor Brown "disregarded the State's property in order to take care of his own effects," including his "cow and cabbage." Foster

12 C. R. Ga., III, 671, 672; II, 790.
13 Avery, History of Georgia, 307.
14 Ibid., 309.

branded the story as *untrue* and proceeded to give the *true* account. In the first place, he recounted, the governor had no private interests in Milledgeville to protect, and his property consisted of a span of horses, a carriage, and a fine milch cow. The furnishings of the Governor's Mansion were the last items to be loaded. While loading, Foster recalled, he noticed in the garden a fine lot of collards. "Without the knowledge of Governor Brown or his wife," he instructed Aunt Celia, the cook, to cut them and bring them to the wagon for loading. Knowing how badly all the refugee families would need food, "I designed to have the last cabbage cut and put on the train if time would permit." Only a few cabbages had been cut when news arrived that federal troops were about to sever the rail connections with Macon. The governor gave the order to push off, and the few cabbages were thrown on top of other items. Meanwhile, Foster had noticed the milch cow and had her placed in a car.

The trip to Macon was made without incident, but very soon after the governor arrived, he received news that the Federals had cut the road over which the train had just passed. The train remained in Macon over night and then moved on to southwest Georgia. Governor Brown went as far as Montezuma and then returned to Macon. The Brown family left the cars at Montezuma and traveled thirty miles by dirt road to their Dooly County plantation.[15]

Sherman later recalled that most of the inhabitants of Milledgeville remained while the governor, state officials, and the legislators "ignominiously fled, in the utmost disorder and confusion." The Mansion had been hastily stripped of carpets, curtains, and furniture, and these and many other things, "even the cabbage and vegetables," carried away by "brave patriotic Governor Brown . . . leaving behind muskets, ammunition, and the public archives."[16] Sherman set up temporary headquarters in the Governor's Mansion, but he made no mention of the destruction of the "archives." Federal troops did considerable damage to public buildings, but they did not tarry long. Neither did they destroy the town while withdrawing. Sherman also bypassed Macon and headed for Savannah, which he reached on December 10, and ten

15 Foster wrote two very similar accounts. See *ibid.*, 310–11; Fielder, *Brown*, 313–17.
16 Sherman, *Memoirs*, II, 188.

days later Confederate troops moved out, leaving the city to the Federals.

As soon as Sherman's army had passed, refugees began moving back to their homes. Hundreds from Atlanta found they no longer had dwellings; the residents of Milledgeville had not fared so badly. Just when the Browns returned is uncertain, but they found the Mansion almost empty. What the Federals had not destroyed looters had carried away. On December 7 Brown issued an order calling attention to the fact that much property and many furnishings from the Mansion and Statehouse had been carried away by citizens. He ordered all such property returned immediately. All houses suspected of containing such property were to be searched, and if public property was found, the owner was to be committed to the common jail.[17] Some weeks later, in a letter to the governor's parents, Mrs. Brown stated that most everything in the Mansion had been carried away. Gone were blankets, tinware, water pails, washbowls, looking glasses, firedogs, and several bedsteads, yet several things had been saved. In one area, however, the Browns had done well. They carried away one milch cow and brought back three![18]

Owing to the bad condition of the Statehouse, the governor set up temporary quarters in Macon, where he continued his efforts to raise recruits for the state forces commanded by Cobb and Smith. Shortly before the General Assembly adjourned in haste, it had granted the governor's request that he be authorized to order a levy en masse. On November 19 he had issued such an order. All white males between sixteen and fifty-five who were not physically disabled were ordered to report to General G. W. Smith at Macon for a forty-day period of service. A subsequent order designated camps at Newnan, Athens, Macon, and Albany and instructed recruits to report to either. The only persons exempt were necessary employees of railroads, express, and telegraph companies and ministers of the Gospel. The law also exempted members of the legislature and the courts, but the governor invited them to report. Persons liable for service who failed to report would be arrested and treated as deserters. "The enemy has penetrated almost to the centre of your State," the governor concluded. If every

17 *C. R. Ga.*, II, 812.
18 March 13, 1865, in Hargrett Collection.

Georgian able to bear arms would rally to the defense, this enemy could never escape.[19]

Before this order could be implemented, Sherman was on his march to the sea. President of the state Senate, Ambrose "Ranse" Wright, at home in Augusta, reasoned that Sherman, by cutting across Georgia, had divided the state into two parts. Governor Brown, at Macon, would be unable to administer the Augusta area. The president of the Senate, first in line when the governor was incapacitated, therefore assumed power, canceled the governor's order, and issued his own order for all militia east of the Oconee River to report to him at Augusta. He immediately notified Governor Brown of his action and requested approval.

Wright should have known that a voluntary transfer of power was something the governor never considered. Brown immediately disapproved. If communications had been disrupted, how was it, the governor inquired, that his recent proclamation had reached Augusta two days after it was issued? "I cannot admit that the contingency contemplated in the Constitution had happened." Wright would send forward to General Smith all troops who had reported and discontinue the camp at Augusta.[20]

Brown inaugurated a vigorous system for rounding up those who hesitated to report. Small, well-equipped groups of men, usually six, were sent into the most difficult areas to make arrests. But as reporting progressed slowly, Sherman moved rapidly. By December 19, Brown was able to announce that except for the garrison at Dalton and the forces in the coastal area, Georgia was free from federal occupation. Therefore, he modified his recent order. All men in organization camps, who had not already been ordered to report to Major General Smith, were "furloughed until further order." Back home, these organized units would do police duty two days each week, giving protection against "depredations of thieves and marauders." They would also arrest stragglers and deserters and return them to their proper commands. Any unit failing to perform these required duties would be immediately eligible for field duty.[21]

19 *C. R. Ga.*, II, 799, 805.
20 *Ibid.*, III, 676, 677.
21 *Ibid.*, II, 814.

The governor believed that these units would be of more service to the people of the state as police units than as a fighting force. The greatest problem facing Georgians, other than repairing the damage done by Sherman's army, was to protect themselves against many forms of pillage and robbery. Roving bands of "bushwhackers," deserters, and draft dodgers had long been making life miserable for people of the North Georgia highlands. Of late, another type of thief had made its appearance. On November 24, the day his family fled Milledgeville, Governor Brown had issued a proclamation calling attention of the entire state to the activities of cavalry units in some areas. Some of the state cavalry, instead of striking terror among exposed enemy foraging parties, had divided into small groups "robbing and plundering the citizens indiscriminately." These "predatory bands of thieves and robbers" professed to be impressing property for military use, but had no authority whatsoever for their actions. Neither did the army receive any portion of what they impressed. The governor authorized all citizens to band themselves together for protection and to shoot on sight all such plunderers. Confederate General Richard Taylor, with temporary headquarters at Macon, had promised to execute all such persons brought in who were proved guilty.[22]

Even though the Confederate military situation continued to become more hopeless, field commanders continued to call for more troops. To General William J. Hardee, who after evacuating Savannah had moved into South Carolina, President Davis replied: "If your relations to Governor Brown enable you to influence him, that is a means to be employed."[23] Hardee's relations with Brown were good. With the governor's consent, General Smith led his militia across the state line to join Hardee.

Following Sherman's conquest, there settled over Georgia a feeling of hopeless gloom tempered with rage. Regardless of what suffering citizens wished to do by way of revenge, they realized it could not be done. Individuals, groups, and countywide mass meetings petitioned the governor and General Assembly to take whatever steps were necessary to end the bloody struggle.[24] The set of resolutions drawn up by

22 *Ibid.*, 802.
23 January 11, 1865, Rowland, *Jefferson Davis*, VI, 447.
24 See Hargrett Collection.

the citizens of Wilcox County expressed the situation and attitude very clearly. From the beginning they had given their best to the "bloody battlefields," but little had been accomplished. "We can't respond any more," except with old men. "Therefore we think the time has come when our authorities should go boldly to work to negotiate a peace before we are entirely ruined." Concerted action on the part of all the states would be desirable, but if this could not be arranged then "separate state action had better be resorted to." With starvation "certainly close at hand," citizens were "tyred of this most cruel, bloody war, having no hope that it will ever be settled until the people take it in hand themselves. Therefore we are disposed to speak out on the subject and make a strong effort to close the war and stop the murdering of the human family by such a wholesale way." The people had long hoped to hear the sound of peace from the great men in charge of government, but in vain. "We have lost the hope."

The people were willing to fight as long as there was a chance that fighting might bring peace. That chance no longer existed, so there must be efforts by negotiation "before the whole white male population is butchered." The governor and General Assembly were urged to begin such negotiations.[25]

Although Governor Brown urged a fight to the bitter end, he must have realized that that end was near. He was too intelligent not to have known that ultimate Confederate victory was impossible, yet he was undecided what should be done. In mid-January, 1865, he privately explained to Hiram Warner some of his thoughts on the situation. He still charged that the Confederate government had "usurped as absolute power as can exist in the hands of a government hard pressed by a powerful enemy." Unless there was a "change of policy soon we are ruined," but "Davis prides in not changing and Congress is entirely subservient." Yet, with all the mismanagement, he still thought "we have men and means to succeed." But to do so "we must abandon odious conscription and treat white men as free not as slaves." From the very day the conscription act was passed, Brown contended, the "ardor of the people has been chilled," and men had sought to evade service they had previously been "constantly striving to enter." Further, it would be necessary to abandon the policy of supporting the army by pillage

25 January 14, 1865, in Hargrett Collection.

and plunder. Citizens must be paid for their property in sound currency, not quartermaster receipts.

Brown was still unreasonable on the subject of conscription. He failed to see that no man was ever conscripted who wished to volunteer instead. And no Confederate conscription agents ever used methods as drastic as those used by the governor in enforcing state conscription. The point of conflict that enraged the governor most was that Confederate conscription denied men the privilege of volunteering for state service, not for Confederate service. If Confederate conscription chilled the ardor of free men, treating them as slaves, as Brown contended, why did not state conscription do likewise? And as for the impressment of supplies, no Confederate officer ever came nearer to taking what he needed when and where he needed it than did Governor Brown. True, some persons posing as Confederate officers robbed the people, but this occurred on the state level also.

Brown admitted to Warner that he had not made up his mind as to the best course remaining. Reconstruction or rejoining the Union on the basis of whatever terms were offered, he thought, would leave "neither honor nor property except such as we hold mortgaged to pay the war debt of the U.S. Government." Then what was left but to "fight it out." This would "save our honor." To sue for peace on Lincoln's terms would be degrading. If Georgia called a convention and proposed terms, she would be "made the scapegoat for the future." It would be said that, after leading her sister states into the difficulty, she had then deserted them and brought ruin to the Confederate cause.[26]

The proposal for separate state action had developed considerable support in Georgia, and it seems probable that the governor favored it as a last resort. Yet he had stopped short of advocating it, knowing that he would be denounced for deserting the cause. It was rumored, not only throughout the South but in the North as well, that Georgia was on the verge of seeking separate peace. Governor Z. B. Vance of North Carolina, a strong states' rights man himself, became much concerned. On January 18, 1865, he wrote Brown advising against separate state action. He thought no separate action would be taken in North Carolina unless Georgia led the way. It was largely Georgia's influence that led North Carolina into secession. Attempt at separate state action,

26 January 18, 1865, *ibid.*

Vance argued, would be but another revolution. And there would be minorities, probably backed by the army, who would inaugurate "a state of anarchy more horrible than anything we have yet endured."

News from Richmond, Vance continued, indicated that President Davis was "inclined to make earnest efforts for peace, on a basis as modest as I suppose you or I could willingly agree to. I am anxious therefore, to see this, the legitimate and proper channel, fairly tried and thoroughly exhausted before we take matters in our own hands and inaugurate revolutionary measures." Therefore, he appealed to Brown, "in all candor and honor, to ask if Georgia should not in this great matter show deference to the opinions and wishes of her Northern [border] sisters, who moved mainly out of sympathy for those who got first into trouble." The chief aim should be "to hold the demoralized and trembling fragments of society and law together and prevent them from dropping to pieces until the rapidly hastening end of our struggle shall be developed."[27] By the time Governor Vance's letter arrived in Milledgeville, Governor Brown had left for a week's vacation at his Dooly County plantation. An aide replied to Vance that Brown's views would be embraced in his forthcoming message to the General Assembly.[28] The Assembly had already been called to meet at the Macon city hall on February 15, 1865.[29]

Governor Brown's message to the legislature began with a denunciation of that "bold and skillful General" whose army had recently passed through Georgia. Much of the remaining portion of the message was devoted to a denunciation of the Confederate government for creating a situation that made such an invasion possible. The governor was always careful not to assume any responsibility for failure. Of the tens of thousands of Georgians in Confederate service, Brown charged that only about three hundred were in Georgia during Sherman's march. Only one brigade of other troops was sent to aid, and it arrived after the capital was in enemy possession. Thus had Georgia been left to her fate with only the Confederate reserves and the militia, composed of boys and old men, to defend her soil. Had Georgia Confederate troops alone, fifty regiments of which were in Virginia, been available to

27 *C. R. Ga.*, III, 702.
28 February 6, 1865, *ibid.*, 706.
29 *Ibid.*, II, 817.

meet Sherman, Brown declared, the federal army would never have crossed Georgia. But neither they nor any other competent force was present when Sherman cut loose from his supply base and headed for the sea. Had Sherman been forced to fight, his supply of ammunition would soon have been exhausted and his defeat inevitable. To accomplish this result would have been worth the evacuation of Richmond and the throwing of Lee's entire army into the fight in Georgia. There would never again be such an opportunity for Confederate victory, Brown lamented.

He thought it his duty to refer to this tragic blunder in view of the fact that Georgia had been so "systematically, if not wilfully, misrepresented" by Confederate officials, "without the magninimity or common honesty to publish the facts." One of the misrepresentations had been that he had kept 15,000 men out of Confederate service under the exemption act. Yet the whole number of state officers was only 1,450, including those above conscription age. He had publicly made this correction, but his explanation had been ignored. The governor further related in detail the recent attempt of the president to get control over the state militia, and justified his own action in refusing to permit it. He wished the General Assembly to tell him whether or not his decision was proper.

One of the casualties of Sherman's march was the state penitentiary which had been destroyed by fire. Governor Brown expressed doubt as to the advisability of rebuilding it. He doubted that it had served the purpose for which it was established. Instead of it being a place for reform it had been a "school for theft, lawlessness and villainy." Therefore, the governor recommended that the penitentiary be abolished and "other modes of punishment, such as hanging, whipping, branding, etc., be substituted." He further recommended that the penalty of death be fixed as punishment for "robbery, burglary, and horse stealing." And those convicted of "illegal traffic with slaves" should be whipped.

Even at that late hour, Governor Brown failed to face the fact that the institution of slavery was doomed. The Confederate administration, he explained, having abandoned the proper method of raising troops through the agency of the states and having failed with its policy of conscription, was now ready to fill the ranks with slaves. This, he declared, would be a great error. In the first place, they were needed for production of provisions. But even if this were not true, placing them under arms would be unwise. Brown always contended that slaves in general were contented and happy, unless subjected to outside influence. He now saw them "quietly serving at home, because they do not wish to go into the army." Their great fear was that they might be taken over by the enemy and forced to become soldiers. Therefore, if the Confederacy attempted to conscript them they would "leave us by the thousands." Certainly, if they remained with the Confederacy, they could not be expected "to perform deeds of heroic valor, when they are fighting to continue the enslavement of their wives and children." To compel them to fight would not bring down the blessings of heaven upon the cause. Providence did not design them as both slaves and a military people. And once they were made a military race, it could no longer be claimed that they were unfit to be free. He was aware of the suggestion that slaves might be given their freedom in return for their assistance in winning southern independence, but the governor could not conceive of giving up slavery along with "personal rights and State sovereignty, for independence." He was sure that freeing the slaves could be used to make a better bargain than could ever be won by their use on the battlefield. But he was completely convinced that once they had been "taught the use of arms, and spent years in the indolent indulgencies of camp life," the institution of slavery could no longer exist. And the governor vehemently denied that the Confederate government possessed the power to take slaves and set them free.

In the middle of his message the governor observed the obvious fact that "all is not well." This was the introduction to a renewal of his attack upon the Richmond government. He repeated every argument and denunciation used in former messages to prove inefficiency, dishonesty, attempts to destroy personal and state rights, and an all-out effort to establish despotism. According to Brown, all original war aims had been sacrificed to the ambition of tyrants, who through the use of patronage, civil and military, had made a mockery of democracy. Constitutional restrictions had been disregarded in the interest of centralization of power. The country was flooded with an almost worthless currency, debts were repudiated, provisions were seized without just compensation, people were mistreated by impressment agents, and unconstitutional taxes were levied. Yet with all the power illegally seized, the Confederacy was losing the war; the army was disintegrating; disloyalty was everywhere manifest; and deserters and other lawless elements terrorized the country, robbing and murdering honest citizens.

However, in spite of total mismanagement, there was still the "ability to succeed," the governor explained. In spite of the waste, there was still sufficient men and means to achieve independence and restore the constitutional liberties which had been so completely crushed. Success must begin with a reversal of policy. Conscription must be abolished, and all armies be raised and officered by the states. Thus could all Confederate enrolling officials be brought into active service and deserters returned. It was Brown's contention that most desertions were a result of tyranny of officers appointed from Richmond. There must be no more repudiation of debts through currency regulations, and no further impressment of supplies except when paid for in acceptable currency. There must no longer be representatives in Congress who had no constituencies and no more secret sessions of that body.

Discipline must be restored to the armies. This could be done by substituting state officers for those appointed through Confederate patronage. Since the president had failed to furnish efficient military administration, he should be removed as commander in chief by the appointment of another to that position, who would be entirely free from presidential control. This change would require a constitutional amendment, so the governor recommended that Georgia take the lead by calling a state convention to propose changes in the constitution. If as many as two other states joined with Georgia's demands, Congress would then be compelled to call a convention to consider these proposals. It was also proposed that the General Assembly appoint commissioners to visit the other states and urge them to join the movement. As the situation now stood, the governor asserted, Richmond authorities seemed to consider independence the only aim. But independence was not even the principal aim. Russia and Turkey were independent, yet they were despotisms. "Let us beware how we trifle with the rights, the liberties, and the happiness of millions."

Of course the governor knew that he was treading on dangerous ground, and he could not have had even a slight hope of success for his proposals. But clothing himself in self-righteousness, he hoped to carry the people of Georgia along with him. Boldly declaring his willingness ever to fight for civil and religious liberty, avowing his support of all rights of the people, and citing his own personal losses in the conflict, he concluded: "My destiny is linked with my country. If we succeed I am a free man. But if by the obstinacy, weakness or misguided judgment of our rulers, we fail, the same common ruin awaits me which awaits my countrymen."[30]

The relations between Governor Brown and the General Assembly during the 1865 special session were conciliatory. The only major defeat for the governor was the refusal to authorize a state convention. Resolutions were passed requesting that he forward to each brigade commander of Georgia troops a copy of the declaration in support of the war passed in 1863. And the Georgia congressional delegation was urged to support repeal of the conscription act. The delegation was also requested to support a measure authorizing the president to accept troops with elected officers. Brown stated that he had not changed his mind on the subject of a convention, but he did not wish to question the integrity or patriotism of the legislators. He considered the difference of opinion an honest one and was willing to leave to the people and future developments the decision as to who was correct.[31]

In a brief special message near the close of the session, Brown congratulated the General Assembly and the military and civilian population at large on the appointment of General Johnston to command the remnant of the Army of Tennessee, which he had once so efficiently and proudly led.[32] To the end Brown's attitude toward the military remained a puzzle. Only his energy and determination remained beyond question. On February 24, 1865, he again withdrew the state militia from Confederate command and sent the men home on furlough, explaining to General Beauregard that the interior of Georgia was in no immediate danger and most of the men were exempt from Confederate conscription.

At times Governor Brown appeared interested in filling up the thinning ranks of the Confederate armies; at other times he appeared determined to shield able-bodied Georgians from Confederate service. The inconsistency was more apparent than real. He agreed to release

30 *Ibid.*, 818–55.
31 *Ibid.*, 867; *Acts and Resolutions*, 1865, p. 84.
32 *House Journal*, 1865, pp. 14 ff.

to Confederate authorities only those he could not hold in state service. And since he considered service with the state so much more desirable than that with the Confederacy, he used possible Confederate conscription as a threat to compel obedience. But whichever way he moved, he assumed an air of self-righteous determination that impressed those he proposed to assist. Thus he created a popular image that even resembled his personal appearance. A young lady who met him on the train in mid-April, 1865, wrote in her diary: "He is a regular Barebones in appearance, thin, angular, with a sallow complexion and iron-gray hair. His face wears an expression of self assertion rather than obstinacy and I couldn't help thinking how well he would have fitted in with Cromwell's Ironsides. He had on a rusty short-tailed black alpaca coat that had a decidedly home-made set. He looked 'Joe Brown,' every inch of him, and if I had met him in Jericho, I would have said 'There goes Joe Brown.'"[33]

There could be no doubt but that Joe Brown was eager to promote what he considered the best interests of the people and state of Georgia. His honesty and integrity were beyond question. The degree to which he was loyal and patriotic depended upon one's definition of those terms. It was his contention that Confederate authorities had departed from the principles established by the Founding Fathers; patriotism or loyalty did not require one to support them in their disregard of the Constitution. At times Brown greatly assisted the Confederate cause; at other times he hindered its progress, and he could not have been ignorant of that fact. By publicly denouncing and openly refusing to obey Confederate laws, he encouraged disobedience in others. At least in his own actions, he sought to justify disobedience. He never expressed admiration for any important civil official of the Confederacy. To him they appeared as a part of a conspiracy to deprive people and states of their rights. Among the more prominent military commanders, he had praise for only Lee, Beauregard, and Johnston. Had Jefferson Davis not constantly interfered with them, Brown thought they might have succeeded. Before the end of the war he had built up an aversion to everything that emanated from Richmond. Georgia was his world; he had great difficulty seeing beyond her borders. That a Georgia victory

33 Eliza Frances Andrews, *The War-time Diary of a Georgia Girl, 1864–1865* (New York, 1908), 159.

was completely dependent upon a Confederate victory was apparently not a part of his thinking. He advocated a type of confederacy in which each state retained complete sovereignty. When he realized that Richmond authorities entertained no such idea of government, he lost interest in and even became hostile to the Confederacy per se. His attitude, expressed and implied, indicated that in the end he preferred defeat to victory for what he considered Richmond despotism. Near the end Brown would have supported separate state action if it offered hope of acceptable terms of peace, yet he stopped short of advocating it. Instead, he urged the people of all the states to rise up and free themselves from Confederate tyranny and seek peace through a convention. Yet, with Confederate power to resist completely broken, he could not have expected the enemy to grant terms of peace that did not include restoration of the Union.

The end came on April 9, 1865, when General Robert E. Lee surrendered to General U. S. Grant. General Joseph E. Johnston surrendered to General W. T. Sherman on the twenty-sixth. General James Wilson, moving in from Alabama, had already taken possession of Macon. When Brown learned that Sherman and Johnston had agreed to a truce preparatory to peace, he was at Augusta. From Abbeville, South Carolina, Mrs. Jefferson Davis wrote to the president, then in flight: "Be careful how you go to Augusta. I get rumors that Brown is going to seize all Government property, and the people are averse—and mean to resist with pistols—They are a set of wretches together, and I wish you were safe out of their land."[34] Davis no doubt shared his wife's wish, but Brown had no idea of seizing Confederate property.

34 April 28, 1865, Rowland, *Jefferson Davis*, VI, 566–67.

Chapter XVI

Private Citizen Again

THE DAY BEFORE Johnston's surrender, Governor Brown wrote Vice-President Stephens from Augusta: "I am now remaining here to learn the result of the conference going on under the armistice. When that is announced I will try to shape my course as best I can. I have made up my mind to remain in the state and do all I can to aid in the restoration of order and to mitigate suffering as long as I am allowed to do so. If I am arrested and carried off I have prepared my mind to meet my fate with coolness. As matters now stand I am very anxious to see and confer with you as to what is best to be done. Genl. Toombs is here and I am anxious that you come down."[1] In his coolness, Brown suspected the worst. He must have known, however, that it was no longer within his power to determine what was "best to be done."

On April 27, the day following Johnston's surrender, General Wilson, at Macon, dispatched a messenger with a note for Governor Brown: "I have the honor to request a personal interview with you in regard to the existing status of affairs in Georgia." The bearer of this message would "explain more fully the objects for which I solicit a meeting. Any point or time you may designate will be agreeable to me." On the twenty-eighth General Wilson wired the governor that he wished to reopen the railroad from Atlanta to Dalton and would like to confer with Brown or his representative on the matter. Brown was agreeable to both the interview requested and the reopening of the

1 April 25, 1865, in Stephens Papers, Emory.

railroad; a meeting would be held in Macon on May 5.[2] Meanwhile, on May 3, Wilson forwarded to Brown, addressing him as commander in chief of the Georgia militia, a request that he "take the necessary steps to surrender the troops under your command, with all the arms and military stores pertaining thereto." The terms offered were similar to those granted by Sherman and Grant. Officers would give individual paroles and sign a group parole for those under their command. The surrender of arms and stores would not include officers' side arms, horses, or baggage. Once paroled all were free to return to their homes, "not to be disturbed by military authorities of the United States, so long as they preserve their parole and obey the laws which were in force previous to January 1, 1861, where they reside."[3] On the same day that Wilson issued these terms for surrender and two days before the two met in Macon, Governor Brown issued a call for the General Assembly to convene in special session on May 22. In the interest of "the safety, security and welfare of the people" it was necessary for civil officials "to do all in their power to prevent anarchy, restore and preserve order, and save what they can of liberty and civilization."[4]

Brown left no account of his May 5 meeting with General Wilson, but years later Wilson recorded a very interesting story: Knowing that the governor "had defied Confederate authorities," Wilson expected that he "might consider himself an independent authority." Brown arrived in Macon on the afternoon of May 4 and took suite 28 in the Brown Hotel. Immediately, he sent "a natty major in a brand new Confederate uniform" to inform the general of his arrival and to say that he would be pleased to receive the general in his suite at 8 P.M. Wilson replied: "'General Wilson's quarters are at the Lanier House in Parlor A, where he expects to see His Excellency Governor Brown promptly at nine o'clock tomorrow morning . . . if His Excellency has the slightest doubt as to the significance of this message, General Wilson will send a sergeant of the guard and four men to escort His Excellency.'" The governor understood the message; he arrived at the appointed time.

Wilson described the meeting as "a pleasant and interesting one."

2 C. R. Ga., III, 714–16.
3 Brown Papers, Duke; C. R. Ga., III, 715–16.
4 C. R. Ga., II, 878.

Having heard amusing stories about the governor and his family from the "wiregrass country of Cherokee, Georgia," where they had enjoyed "few educational advantages and none of the cultivation of the graces," the general was surprised. He found Brown "smooth, suave, deferential, and polite, as well as more than usual intelligent. He carried himself with easy self-possession and appeared well dressed and prosperous, as might have been expected of one who had grown rich by blockade running, while the majority of his fellow-citizens had lost most everything they had from the ravages of war."

The general immediately informed the governor that he would not permit a meeting of the legislature, which had been called "against my warning." When Brown argued that such a session was necessary to establish social order and restore prosperity, Wilson agreed to permit an appeal to Washington. It was then demanded that all Georgia militia under arms, including its commander in chief, be surrendered and paroled. This demand, Wilson thought, caused the governor great concern, for it would "rob him of his power and influence." These points agreed to, the two engaged in general discussion.

Wilson quickly sensed the bad feeling between Brown and Howell Cobb, whom Brown considered "overbearing, bombastic, and inconsiderate." In discussing other prominent Georgians, Brown "talked freely of all and unkindly of none." Wilson got the impression that the governor thought himself "not only the most considerable man of the State, but its safest guide back to full and harmonious relations with the other states of the Union." He "dwelt complacently on his strenuous opposition to Davis" and his own activities in organizing state militia as an independent force, yet Wilson could see no indication that the governor had even thought of a parole that would "protect him as commander-in-chief from arrest and imprisonment." As Brown was preparing to leave, Wilson handed him a parole and suggested he read and sign it. Brown replied: "'Yes, yes, I thought of that some time ago, but it had escaped my mind.'"

As Brown read the parole, his countenance saddened. Dropping it on the table, he remarked: "But, General, I can't sign that document.'" Wilson, in surprise, assured him that it gave the same protection General Johnston received from General Sherman. But, Brown replied, "'It requires me to recant and abjure all the political acts and opinions of my life.'" Well, it was "in no way compulsory," Wilson suggested. With a "deep and audible sigh," the governor explained, "'If I sign that paper it will destroy all my political prospects forever'" Rising from his seat and facing Governor Brown "squarely," General Wilson replied: "'My God! Governor, is it possible that you imagine, in the face of the part you have taken against the United States for the last four years, you have any prospect in this country but to be hanged?'" Hesitating a moment, the governor said, "That view of the matter had not occurred to me.'" He signed, giving his parole, and departed "with his countenance somewhat sicklied o'er with a pale cast of thought."

Howell Cobb and others were waiting at the Brown Hotel to learn the results. On the following day Cobb himself conferred with Wilson, displaying much satisfaction with Brown's crestfallen position. According to Wilson, Cobb "showed quite plainly not only his contempt for the Governor as a 'poor white from Cherokee, Georgia,' but as a scheming politician whom he was glad to see foiled in his efforts to beguile me while striving to avoid responsibility for his own acts." Throughout the conversation with Cobb, Wilson noted that not even the adversities of war and defeat had "leveled the distinction between the rich and the poor, the slave-holder and the non-slaveholder, the military man and the politician, with their varying shades of interest and belief."[5]

Despite forty-seven years of fading memory, General Wilson's dramatic account has a ring of considerable accuracy; yet on several points it is in error as to fact and interpretation. Brown came from the yeoman farmer class, not the "poor whites"; Cherokee and the "wiregrass" country were not the same region; Brown was not a nonslaveholder; neither had he grown wealthy as a blockade runner; and to say that he had never thought of a parole for himself or the possibility of being hanged was to reflect upon his intelligence. Certainly, he had thought of everything that could possibly result from defeat, and he was conscious of his helplessness in the presence of military control. Neither was the question of parole first raised near the close of the

5 See Hargrett Collection under date May 8, 1865; James H. Wilson, *Under the Old Flag*, 2 vols. (New York, 1912), II, 250–56.

May 5 meeting; conditions of surrender and parole had been sent to the Governor on May 3. He issued his call for a special session of the legislature before, not after, receiving "warning" from General Wilson. No doubt the account of the conference with Cobb is essentially accurate; it fits Cobb's known attitude toward the governor. (There is in the Andrew Johnson Papers a long letter from Cobb to Wilson setting forth what he thought should be done about the situation in Georgia.) Although Wilson described his meeting with Brown as pleasant, the subsequent attitude of each toward the other indicates otherwise.

At 1:30 P.M., May 6, General Wilson wired General J. M. Schofield: "Without my knowledge or consent, Governor Brown has issued a call for a meeting of the Georgia Legislature for the 22d instant. I don't think it proper for either Governor Brown or his Legislature to exercise any control or influence in shaping opinion or policy in the re-establishment of Georgia with the Union. I shall therefore not allow the Legislature to meet, unless directed to do so by the Government at Washington. I see no necessity for conventions at best, and certainly not when controlled by prominent secessionists. Please forward this dispatch to proper authorities for orders in the case." True to his promise, General Wilson also forwarded Governor Brown's appeal. To President Johnson, Brown explained that the collapse of the currency and the great want of provisions made a session of the legislature imperative. This, however, General Wilson had forbidden. "Does he reflect the views of the Government, or will you order that no force be used to prevent the meeting of the Legislature?"[6]

The president was not impressed by the governor's tale of woe. Replying through Secretary of War Edwin M. Stanton and General Wilson, in a tone of bitterness rather than sympathy, he informed Brown that the plight of Georgia was a result of "rebellion, treason and insurrection against the laws of the United States, incited and carried on for the last four years by you and your confederate rebels and traitors." Whatever "loss and woe" had been suffered by the people was chargeable to those state governing officials who had usurped their power and by treasonable acts "provoked the war to extremity." Now

6 *C. R. Ga.*, III, 717, 718; Andrew Johnson Papers, Library of Congress, under date May 10, 1865.

that rebellion had been crushed, the restoration of peace could not be entrusted to those "rebels and traitors who destroyed the peace and trampled down the order" which the people of Georgia had enjoyed for more than half a century. The legislative body that had incited and waged war would not be permitted, "at the call of their accomplice," again to usurp powers that might "set on foot fresh acts of treason and rebellion." In calling that body together "without permission of the President," Governor Brown had been guilty of a "fresh crime that will be dealt with accordingly."[7]

At 7 P.M., May 7, 1865, one hour after he had telegraphed to Wilson the president's reply for relay to Brown, Secretary Stanton wired Wilson: "The President directs that you immediately arrest Joseph E. Brown, who pretends to act as Governor of Georgia, and send him in close custody under sufficient and secure guard to Major-General [Christopher C.] Augur, at Washington, and allow him to hold no communication, verbal or written, with any person but the officer having him in charge after the receipt of this order."[8] The precaution prescribed in this order seemed to indicate that the skinny little governor of Georgia was a very dangerous man.

For some unexplained reason, Stanton's order dated 7 P.M., May 7, did not reach Macon until 3:40 P.M., May 9. General Wilson immediately dispatched Captain G. H. Kneeland to Milledgeville to arrest Brown and "seize his papers." Meanwhile, Wilson reported to Stanton that on the previous day Brown had been paroled as commander in chief, "but his parole in no way acknowledges him as Governor."[9] The governor was at the Executive Mansion in Milledgeville on the evening of May 9 when Captain Kneeland and his escort arrived. He protested vigorously against arrest but made no attempt to escape. It was his contention that his parole ensured him against being molested in any way by military authorities as long as he obeyed the law. He had not violated either the law or the condition of his parole. This argument did not suffice; he was given only thirty minutes to prepare for departure and his parole was taken from him. But Kneeland did not

7 *C. R. Ga.*, III, 719, 724; Brown Papers, Duke.
8 *C. R. Ga.*, III, 721.
9 *Ibid.*, 722, 723.

seize the governor's papers. After the party had left, Mrs. Brown and son Julius, fearing the governor's papers might later be seized, destroyed those stored in the Governor's Mansion.[10]

Governor Brown left Macon for Atlanta on the 8 A.M. train, May 10, 1865, under guard of Lieutenant William Bayard and five men from the Fourth Cavalry. Since the railroad north of Atlanta was not in operation, General Edward Winslow, commanding in Atlanta, was ordered to furnish "a strong escort and the necessary horses" for Brown and his party to Dalton. The party was in Dalton by the thirteenth. The commander in Chattanooga wired General George Thomas in Nashville for further instructions. Should the prisoner "be forwarded here and on to Nashville, and in what manner?" Thomas sent instructions for forwarding Brown to Washington. President Davis, who had been captured in Georgia, was also expected in Chattanooga, but Brown was not to be held until Davis arrived.[11] Perhaps there would have been some interesting conversation had the president and governor been permitted to travel together to Washington.

At Washington, Governor Brown was placed in Carroll Prison. When the conditions under which Brown was arrested were placed before General Grant, he was not as enthusiastic about the affair as some other officials. If the call for a special session of the legislature was issued after parole was given, he thought Brown was probably liable for arrest; if before, the situation was different, he informed Stanton. Although he would not recommend that the governor be returned to Georgia, "I do not think a paroled officer is subject to arrest so long as he observes his parole without giving him notice first that he is absolved from further observance of it."[12]

Brown apparently had little difficulty in arranging an interview with President Johnson. In his request, he suggested that all matters pertaining both to his own case and the status of affairs in Georgia could be better discussed in a personal interview than in writing. Presi-

---

10 Brown to Andrew Johnson, May 20, 1865, in Hargrett Collection; Brown to Mrs. W. H. Felton, February 4, 1887, in Rebecca Latimer Felton Papers, University of Georgia.

11 Wilson to Stanton, May 10, 1865; Thomas to Commanding Officer, May 14, 1865, in McLeod Collection; Charles Cruft to W. D. Whipple, May 13, 1865; Whipple to Cruft, May 13, 1865; James Wilson to E. F. Winslow, *O. R.*, Ser. I, Vol. XLIX, Pt. 2, p. 766.

12 *C. R. Ga.*, III, 729.

dent Johnson agreed and the interview was set for 3:30, May 20. Josiah R. Parrott of Cartersville later told Alexander Stephens that he himself, as a friend of President Johnson, had arranged Brown's interview.[13] There is nothing in the Brown papers to substantiate this claim, although Brown and Parrott were friends. It is more likely that if any influence was used it came from David Patterson, the president's son-in-law. Before the war Patterson had been a federal judge; recently he had been elected United States senator from Tennessee. How or when Brown and Patterson became friends is unknown, but in view of subsequent correspondence it would appear that they had some common prewar railroad interests. The two were definitely in touch during Brown's prison term; on May 23, 1865, Brown wrote the president: "I am very desirous to see Senator Patterson today and will be much obliged, as I learn he spends part of his time with you, if you will so state to him."[14]

Regardless of who applied influence upon the president, it is doubtful that any was needed; the interview was granted the same day it was requested. There is no record of what was said during the interview, but there is basis for speculation. Their common plebeian backgrounds gave the president and the governor much in common. Both had risen to prominence by the exertion of much determination, although Johnson's path had been a bit rougher. The president was very hostile toward the southern aristocracy, which had denied him acceptance or even recognition. Surely Brown must have reminded him that he too had never been accepted by the aristocracy. The two were poles apart on the subject of secession, but Brown was ready to close the gap by admitting that he erred in 1861 and by showing a willingness to accept the results. Perhaps the two needed each other. At any rate they parted as friends.

Immediately following the conference, acting upon a suggestion by Secretary Stanton, Brown prepared for the president a detailed statement of the conditions under which he had issued his call for a special session of the General Assembly, stressing the fact that it was done prior to his parole. In closing, he declared: "Frankness requires that I

13 Myrta Lockett Avary (ed.), *Recollections of Alexander H. Stephens: His Diary Kept When a Prisoner at Fort Warren, Boston Harbor, 1865* (New York, 1910), 414.
14 Hargrett Collection.

state further that I was an original secessionist, and an ardent and I trust honest believer in the correctness of the doctrines of that school of statesmen. But when the decision was made against that right by the most powerful tribunal known among nations—the sword—I felt and still feel that it is the duty of the people of the South to yield and accept it as the law of their conduct in future, and do all they can in the new state of things to repair the losses sustained by the war." Three days later Brown wrote again, inquiring if the president was in need of any further information. In closing he stated "If I could be released on parole in the city, pending the investigation of my case, it would be a great relief, and would enable me with much greater facility to prepare any point in the case that may require my attention."[15]

On May 29 Johnson granted Brown's request for a city parole, under which he was permitted to pass to and from his quarters without interruption. He was to report to the president from time to time. On June 3 the president requested Secretary Stanton to grant Brown a brief interview. "I would suggest that he be permitted to return to Georgia upon his parole and that free transportation be furnished him. I discover in conversation that you have succeeded in making a decided impression upon him. I think that his return home can be turned to good account. He will at once go to work and do all that he can in restoring the State. I have no doubt that he will act in good faith. He can not under the circumstances act otherwise."[16]

The interview was granted immediately and was very satisfactory to Brown. On the same day he gave his "parole of honor" to return to Georgia, "be of good behavior" toward the government, "give no aid nor comfort to its enemies," to work faithfully toward restoration of federal authority within the state, and "to induce the inhabitants thereof to return to their allegiance and fidelity to the Federal Government." Stanton ordered that he be released from prison and furnished transportation to Milledgeville via New York and Savannah. With the president's approval, a happy former Confederate governor of Georgia wired his wife at Milledgeville: "Released on parole. Home, I hope, by New York and Savannah, by 20th instant."[17]

15 May 20, 23, 1865, *ibid.*
16 *Ibid.*
17 June 3, 1865, *ibid.*; *C. R. Ga.*, III, 729.

Brown's prison life had produced inconvenience only; he experienced no real hardships. The entire ordeal had covered less than a month. Meanwhile, back home, his pregnant wife had tried to hold things together but had suffered great concern over the possibility of his extended absence. Her only extant letter to him was dated May 26, 1865. It is doubtful that it reached him before his release. Mrs. Brown reported that son Julius had gone to the farm to check on the Negroes. The ones at the Mansion seemed content and would probably remain so "unless some outsider . . . would induce them to leave." She was concerned over what she and her family would do when forced to leave the Mansion. Their friend Leopold Waitzfelder urged them to come to his home, but she preferred a house of their own if possible. There was a serious money problem. Only United States greenbacks and silver were readily accepted. State notes would not pass at all, and bank notes had limited circulation. Before sending out her letter she added a postscript: Julius had returned from the farm. Crops were good and there were plenty of corn and other things to eat. The meat was keeping well. The Negroes were all there and doing well, but the "tories" were stealing and killing.[18]

What concessions, agreements, or promises, other than those reflected in his parole, were made between Brown and the president are not a matter of record. But when the former governor returned to Georgia he was a different man. The past was past; only the future mattered, and it belonged to those who were wise enough to seize its advantages. He was much impressed with President Johnson, and the two would soon be engaged in extensive correspondence. Although not permitted to take the oath of amnesty, no one could possibly have taken the terms of his parole more seriously than Brown. On his return trip from Washington he traveled by buggy from Savannah to Macon "to see and converse with" as many people as possible. Exposure to rain and sun made him ill of "billious fever" for several weeks.[19]

Meanwhile, on June 17, 1865, President Johnson appointed James Johnson, a Columbus lawyer, as provisional governor of Georgia. James Johnson was not one of the better known Georgians. In the early 1850s he had served a single term in Congress, representing the Union party.

18 McLeod Collection.
19 Brown to Andrew Johnson, July 15, 1865, in Hargrett Collection.

He had opposed secession in 1861, and refused to take any active part in the war. Upon arrival at Milledgeville to take office as governor, he would become a boarder in the Executive Mansion, which was still occupied by the Brown family. Several persons other than Johnson had been suggested as a possible appointee. Joshua Hill wanted the position badly. On May 10, 1865, he wrote the president suggesting that he be remembered "as one of the Representatives of Georgia at the time of secession—who condemned that movement—standing alone—amongst her public men—in the national councils."[20] Several others also wrote letters and, as did Hill, made trips to Washington. Brown was in Washington at that time, but there is no evidence that he was consulted.

Before leaving Washington, Brown had begun the preparation of a farewell address to the people of Georgia, which he issued on June 29, 1865. After expressing his sincere thanks for the honor and trust bestowed upon him during the past eight years and assuring the people he had done his honest best to merit their confidence, he resigned the office "into the hands of the people who have so long and so generously conferred it upon me." Unlike the Brown of previous years, he dwelt but briefly upon the past. "The contest has been long and bloody. Each party has learned to respect the manhood and the chivalry of the other. But the South has been overcome by the superior numbers and boundless resources of the North. We have no further power of successful resistance, and no other alternative but to accept the result."

In his brief travel through the North, Brown explained, he had talked to private citizens and officials in high places and had read their newspapers carefully. He found them in unanimous agreement that slavery must be immediately abolished. They had the power to accomplish this and they would exercise it in spite of any obstacles "we may attempt to throw in the way." Indeed, abolition was already considered an accomplished fact. He did not wish to advise others what to do, but he now considered his Negroes free and henceforth would pay them for their labor. Also, he had found in the North much less bitterness than he had expected. "If we act prudently, and do nothing to cause unnecessary agitation or to provoke angry and unprofitable discussions, I think there are strong reasons to hope that a sentiment of Justice and liber-

20 Andrew Johnson Papers, Library of Congress.

ality will prevail so soon as we have given up slavery, and the passions engendered by the unfortunate and wicked assassination of the late President have had time to subside." He had hope that the people of the North would realize that they alone were sitting as judges, for their adversaries had no opportunity to be heard. He hoped they would realize the necessity of restoring unity, harmony, and prosperity throughout the land. Although flushed with victory, they should "exercise magnanimity to their fallen foes, whose heroism they are obliged to respect."

Once slavery was abolished, Brown had confidence the president, a man of the people who had had experience from the lowest office to the highest, would "cast his immense power and influence into the scale of equal rights and popular government," leaving to the states "the undisturbed management of their own internal affairs." He therefore recommended that the people of Georgia give generous support to Johnson. He further recommended that all who expected to remain in Georgia take the prescribed oath and prepare themselves to vote. Those who could vote would soon be called upon to elect a convention to reshape the state constitution. To refuse to take the oath because it provided for the acceptance of abolition was of no value; slaves were already free. And certainly no one should object to taking an oath to support the government under which he expected to live. If one did not intend to support his government then he "should seek a home and protection elsewhere. . . . I will only add in conclusion that I shall carry with me into retirement a lively appreciation of the generous confidence which you have so long reposed in me, and my constant prayer to God will be for your prosperity and happiness."[21] This truly was a new Joseph E. Brown speaking.

He sent a copy of his address to President Johnson and presumably to some northern newspapers. When Alexander Stephens, incarcerated in Fort Warren, Boston Harbor, read the address in the New York *Herald*, he wrote in his diary on July 18: "I like its general tone, style and views as I do most that comes from him. I have differed with him on many important matters, and on none other so important as secession; yet I have regarded him as a man of unquestionable ability and patriotism. In his address, I see he has been released upon the ground

21 *C. R. Ga.*, II, 884–92.

of his being at the head of the State forces, and entitled to a parole on surrendering them, under the same conditions as generals in command. Rather a fictitious ground, I think; but I am glad of his release. There is much in luck. Some seem to have been born under propitious stars, and by nature to be lucky. He is of this class. I have often remarked it. In the greatest difficulties that threaten him, when one sees hardly any chance for his escape or for his surmounting them, some little lucky incident turns up in his behalf. With me, the contrary is true. Luck never was my forte."[22]

On July 13, 1865, Provisional Governor Johnson issued a call for a state convention. Delegates were to be elected on the first Wednesday in October; the convention would meet on the fourth Wednesday. Brown made an immediate report to President Johnson on conditions and prospects. He was pleased with the reception of his own address; the people were in need of leadership. He thought the convention would abolish slavery, although there would be some opposition; it was very difficult for slaveholders to accept the facts. He would do all within his power to influence the convention both to abolish slavery and endorse the proposed amendment to the federal Constitution on the same subject. Since Governor Johnson was boarding at the Mansion, the two would work in close harmony and do everything possible to carry out the president's policy. The most immediate concern was to get the people to take the oath and thus qualify themselves to vote. In the more remote counties very few had even had an opportunity to take the oath. Brown urged that officers be sent to these counties to administer the oath, for these were the counties that would certainly send delegates favorable to immediate abolition of slavery. "I should be very happy to have any suggestion you may think proper to make," Brown assured the president.[23]

Three days later Brown was again writing a "private" letter to the president. He had contacted the editors of the Atlanta *Intelligencer*, Macon *Telegraph*, and Milledgeville *Federal Union*,[24] and they promised to support the president's policy. He hoped to see other editors soon. No pains would be spared in his efforts to achieve success. "If I

22 July 18, 1865, Avary, *Recollections of Stephens*, 352–53.
23 July 15, 1865, in Hargrett Collection.
24 This newspaper had recently readopted its original title.

were relieved of my disability by the generous tender to which you made allusion in our conversation, which you did not then think policy, I am quite sure I could now turn it to good account for the cause. I shall however await your own time without complaint, believing you are my friend and knowing you will do what you think best."[25] (Apparently, while in Washington, Brown and the president had discussed the possibility of a pardon, but the president had thought the time not yet right. Brown belonged to one of the categories to which Johnson had denied the privilege of taking the oath.)

Provisional Governor Johnson was not aggressive enough to please Brown. He complained to the president that the governor "puts a very limited construction upon his powers: thinks about all he has to do is call a convention and to take care of the public property til it meets." Brown was also displeased with the progress being made toward the selection of favorable delegates. On July 21 he telegraphed the president again, urging that officers be sent into every county to administer the amnesty oath. The "backwoods counties," the most loyal, were the most neglected. The president replied that Governor Johnson "ought to proceed at once" to appoint sufficient officers. Any military or civil officer loyal to the administration could administer the oath.[26]

Immediately after wiring the president on July 21, Brown left for a visit to the Cherokee country. On July 25, at Canton, he was again writing the president, at length. Across the top of the letter he wrote "I must beg the President to read this letter long as it is!" Throughout the country north of Atlanta he had advised the people to take the oath and vote for "good men" who favored abolishing slavery and restoring Georgia to its place in the Union. He had assured them that the president was their friend, eager "to build them up," not "to crush them." Particularly effective was his assurance that, while the president demanded the abolition of slavery, he was willing to leave the matter of suffrage to the states. The people were kindly disposed and ready to take the oath but many had no opportunity. Throughout the hundred-mile distance from Marietta to the North Carolina line, he could not hear of anyone authorized to administer the oath. Such officers should be sent immediately with "plenty of printed blanks." If he him-

25 July 18, 1865, in Hargrett Collection.
26 July 15, 24, 1865, ibid.; July 21, 22, 1865, in Andrew Johnson Papers.

self were permitted to circulate freely among these upcountry people, Brown thought he could assure success. However, he was being hindered by the military authorities, although "I never interfere with their business nor prerogatives."

Ill feeling between Governor Brown and General Wilson had not disappeared when the governor returned to private life. Shortly after Brown had issued his recent address to the people, Wilson had wired General George Thomas at Nashville that unless the former governor's counseling of the people was done "by direction and permission of the President," he should be arrested and sent to a northern prison. Wilson apparently knew nothing of the contents of the parole issued Brown by Secretary Stanton. Thomas replied: "I am inclined to think that the President permitted J. E. Brown to resign as Governor, but you are right to forward his resignation and address to the people to General Steedman."[27] Thomas was correct.

When Brown left Milledgeville for Atlanta thence into the Cherokee country for more counseling of the people, Wilson sent an officer to follow him and demand a copy of his parole and all other papers from the War Department. If Brown did not have such papers with him, he was to be brought to Macon. The officer found Brown without the papers, but too ill to travel. No arrest was made, but Brown promised to return to Milledgeville via Macon. What use General Wilson intended making of the copy of his parole Brown did not know; yet he complained that such an order as that issued by Wilson was not only annoying but tended "to lessen my influence with the people."

In reporting this event to the president, Brown explained that he had not made public the contents of his second parole. Should it be published to the people that, in order to obtain his release, he had promised to use his influence "to induce them to return to their loyalty," his influence would be destroyed. The people would charge that what he was saying might or might not be his own honest convictions since he was under pledge to the government. Consequently, he urged the president to order General Wilson to make no public use of the parole. Fearing that Wilson might resort to some unfavorable publicity before his own letter arrived in Washington, Brown wired the president on

27 July 2, 1865, *C. R. Ga.*, III, 730; July 4, 1865, *O. R.*, Ser. I, Vol. XLIX, Pt. 2, p. 1064.

July 29: "Please direct Gen Wilson by telegraph immediately to with-hold public use or publication of my parole to Sec of War till you receive my letter mailed here today—All working well in the State—I go from here to Macon."[28]

On June 30, Brown was in Macon, where he had "just seen Genl. Wilson." He wired General James B. Steedman, who had been appointed to command the Department of Georgia, that he could come to Augusta, if necessary, and "explain to your satisfaction. The part of the document [Address to the people] referred to was read to and approved by the President before it was used."[29] Apparently not only his plan to resign, but also the contents of his address had been discussed with President Johnson before Brown left Washington.

Brown went to Augusta to confer with Steedman; what they discussed is not known. However, a few days later Steedman issued an order that Brown was to be permitted "to receive all messages or packages sent him by mail, and to use the telegraph without restraint."[30] On August 7, Brown wired the president: "I think it important that I have an interview with you about affairs here. If my health will permit, I should like to start to Washington in about ten days. Please send me passport to this place. No telegraph at Milledgeville."[31] The president granted the request, and Brown made the trip to Washington in company with Linton Stephens. The exact nature of his business is unknown. It is certain, however, that foremost in his mind at this time was the status of his application for a pardon and a desire to secure the release of Alexander Stephens from prison. On August 26, 1865, Stephens wrote in his prison diary: "A letter from Washington in the N. Y. World says Linton and Governor Brown are there endeavoring to have me released on parole."[32] Brown did not accompany Linton to Boston; his continuing illness and that of his wife made it imperative that he return to Georgia.[33]

Before leaving Washington, however, he put the finishing touch on his application for pardon. He is known to have had assistance from at

28 July 25, 1865, in Andrew Johnson Papers.
29 Hargrett Collection.
30 August 4, 1865, *ibid*.
31 Andrew Johnson Papers.
32 Avary, *Recollections of Stephens*, 487.
33 Brown to Stephens, November 9, 1865, in Stephens Papers, Emory.

least two other men of influence. On August 14 Provisional Governor
Johnson had stated to the president that Governor Brown "has cooperated with me and given the Government his influence and support.
His efforts have materially benefited the cause, and no doubt he will
everywhere continue to prosecute the good work. He deserves com-
mendation and amnesty." No doubt Tennessee senator David Patterson,
the president's son-in-law, also spoke a good word. On July 21 Brown
had asked the president, "Where is Senator Patterson?" The president
replied "Judge Patterson is somewhere in Tennessee; will be here
soon." A week later Patterson was in Nashville on his way to Washington. From Nashville he wrote Brown, "If I can be of any service to
you in procuring a pardon for you while at Washington, call upon me
and I will take pleasure in doing all in my power."[34] Brown probably
saw Patterson in Washington.

On September 6, 1865, President Johnson granted Brown "full
pardon and amnesty for all offences by him committed, arising from
participation, directly or indirectly in the said rebellion," upon condition that he (1) take the amnesty oath as prescribed May 29, 1865;
(2) never acquire property in slaves or make use of slave labor; (3)
pay all costs of any "pending proceedings against his person or property; and (4) not "claim any property or the proceeds of any property"
sold by court order "under the confiscation laws of the United States."[35]

Brown had taken the oath on the previous day. He immediately
accepted the other conditions and Secretary of State William H. Seward, on September 8, 1865, certified that the conditions had been met.[36]
Mission accomplished, Brown hurried back to Georgia to be even more
active in the selection of delegates to the coming convention. However,
he was soon faced with the possibility of a return trip to Washington.
On September 30, 1865, General John T. Croxton, now commanding at
Macon, relayed to him a summons from the judge advocate's office to
appear as witness in the Henry Wirtz case. Wirtz, the commander at
Andersonville Prison during the war, was being tried before a military
commission on charge of responsibility for the deaths of twelve thousand federal prisoners of war.

34 Hargrett Collection, July 31, 1865; C. R. Ga., III, 730, 731.
35 Original in Brown Papers, Atlanta Historical Society.
36 Hargrett Collection.

Brown was much disturbed. He knew nothing of the Wirtz case and wanted no part in any trial for "war crimes." Further, his wife was expecting a baby any day, and her health had been very poor during the period of waiting. He immediately dispatched a letter of explanation to General Croxton and enclosed a telegram to be sent to the president that also explained the situation and added: "I never saw Capt. Wirtz. Was never at Andersonville prison. Do not believe I know any fact important in the case. There are other important reasons with which you are acquainted why I regret to leave Georgia at present."[37] The operator at Macon refused to send Brown's telegram, so Croxton sent one of his own relaying the substance and so notified Brown. The president replied on October 4, instructing Brown not to report "until further notice."[38] Such a notice never came, but no testimony from Brown could have saved Wirtz from the death penalty.

Brown's relations with the federal military were generally good, except in the case of General Wilson. When General Croxton, who had succeeded Wilson, learned that he might be transferred, he reported it to Brown with the suggestion: "If you can conveniently do anything I would be obliged." Brown immediately wrote the president that Croxton's conduct had been such as "to merit and receive the good will and esteem" of the people of the Columbus District. He had ever "maintained the interest and dignity of the Government with ability and energy" and preserved order, yet he had acted with such courtesy and kindness as to make a most favorable impression upon the people. "His decisions have been just, while he has been firm and decided in his administration . . . in behalf of the people generally." The former governor petitioned that General Croxton be retained in his present position. "By granting this petition," he assured the president, "you will add another to the many obligations under which you have already placed me and the people of this State."[39] Brown's interest might have been stimulated by Croxton's prediction that, if he were relieved, General Wilson would return as his successor.

The convention chosen to revise the Georgia Constitution met in Milledgeville on October 25, 1865. Its personnel lacked the distinction

37 September 27, 30, 1865, in McLeod Collection.
38 October 1, 2, 1865, in Hargrett Collection; October 4, 1865, in Andrew Johnson Papers.
39 October 2, 4, 1865, in Hargrett Collection.

of that convention which had voted secession in 1861. Death had taken its toll, but few of the more distinguished living were present as delegates. Absent were Brown, Toombs, the Cobb brothers, the Stephens brothers, Ben Hill, Bartow, Nisbet, *et al.* Only twenty-two of the almost three hundred members had served in the 1861 convention. In general this was a convention of moderates, most of whom had voted for Bell or Douglas in 1860 and had opposed secession.[40] Fortunately, leadership of the new convention did pass into the hands of those best qualified. Herschel V. Johnson was chosen president and Charles J. Jenkins chairman of the committee on business.[41]

The convention's pattern of action was cut in advance; it had no real choices to make. Georgia must be restored to its former position within the Union. This was done by repealing the Ordinance of Secession. There were no dissenting votes. But there was not such unanimity of feeling on the question of the abolition of slavery, although no one could have had any doubt about its abolition. In his proclamation of July 13, 1865, Provisional Governor Johnson had declared, in accordance with his instructions from the president, that "slavery is extinct, and involuntary servitude no longer exists." Georgians realized this fact and were not happy about it. The convention voted to abolish slavery but specified that this action was "not intended to operate as a relinquishment, waiver or estoppel of such claims for compensation or loss sustained by reason of the emancipation of his slaves, as any citizen of Georgia may hereafter make upon the justice and magnanimity of that Government."[42] Thus was a spark of dim hope of compensated emancipation kept alive.

Joseph E. Brown, occupying a seat of honor on the floor of the convention, heartily approved the two steps thus taken; this was the action he had been publicly advocating for several months. His views on the next topic of great importance are not so clear. Acting upon instructions from Washington, Provisional Governor Johnson virtually demanded that the convention repudiate the Georgia war debt. As gov-

---

40 See C. Mildred Thompson, *Reconstruction in Georgia* (New York, 1915), 148–49.
41 The complete Journal of the convention is found in *C. R. Ga.*, IV, 133 ff.
42 *Ibid.*, 145–46, 171–72.

ernor, Brown had opposed extensive sale of state bonds to finance the war. Possibly he feared a demand for repudiation in case of defeat. He definitely opposed passing to the next generation a debt which it had no part in contracting. At any rate, wise financier that he was, he preferred investing his own money in lands, rather than state or Confederate bonds, while land could be purchased with inflated Confederate notes.

During the war Georgia's debt had increased by $18,135,775. To erase this obligation completely, would be an act of tremendous importance both to the state government and the people. There was much opposition in the convention. Some members owned state obligations, others were opposed in principle. Yet since this was a debt resulting from rebellion, if rebellion was to be disavowed, then so should its means of support. When the convention showed definite signs of refusing to repudiate, Governor Johnson turned to Washington for reinforcement. "We need some aid to reject the war debt," he wired the president. "Send me some word on the subject. What should the convention do." The president replied that there should be no hesitation about repudiation. It would be unjust to tax those who had opposed the rebellion for the purpose of paying for its support. Those who had invested their capital in rebellion "must meet their fate and take it as one of the inevitable results of the rebellion." Secretary Seward further increased the pressure when he wired that the president could not recognize the people "as having resumed the relations of loyalty to the Union" as long as they admitted war debts as legal obligations.[43] The convention had no choice but to repudiate.

November 15, 1865, was set as the date for election of state officers and members of Congress. Many loyal Brown supporters of long standing could not envision any other but him in the executive office. It was to be expected that they would strongly urge his election for a fifth term. He gave them no public encouragement, for he truly did not desire another term. Yet privately he did give some consideration to making another race for governor. When he learned that Charles J. Jenkins, who was being extensively urged as a candidate, would possibly be under the influence of men like A. H. Kenan of Baldwin County, he

43 *Ibid.*, 50, 74.

privately resolved to be a candidate himself if the rumor were found true. However, when in an interview he received the assurance desired, Brown publicly announced his support of Jenkins.[44]

As usual, Brown's first choice was Alexander Stephens, but Stephens was still in prison and Brown had received no statement from him. Before the former vice-president arrived in Georgia on parole, Brown had endorsed Jenkins. Even though Brown had not heard from his friend, some others had, and Stephens had unofficially agreed to be a candidate provided he was convinced it was the general will of the people. Relying upon this unofficial assurance, some newspapers had announced for Stephens. But when he returned to Georgia and learned that Brown and other prominent men had endorsed Jenkins, he quickly withdrew his name from consideration.[45]

Stephens was disappointed; he wanted to be governor. To his brother Linton he complained of Brown's apparent lack of friendship in this matter. After a "full and very satisfactory account" from Brown, Linton replied that brother Alexander had done the former governor an "injustice in your thoughts." No favorable message from Stephens had been received at Milledgeville "until after the arrangement had been made in favor of Mr. Jenkins and acceded to by Brown himself." Brown had held up action as long as he could, but was "beaten at last by his inability to give an assurance that the place would certainly be accepted by you or myself." Linton was convinced that "Brown's course was neither selfish nor unfriendly to you." He had further understood that Brown had made a public statement "that of all living men you were his first choice for any place you would have."[46] Stephens was pacified. Charles J. Jenkins was elected governor without serious opposition.

The election of a new governor brought to an end Brown's tenure in the Executive Mansion. In the earlier years of his administration he had kept in close touch with his home village of Canton and Cherokee County. His family returned there each summer, and he himself fre-

---

44 Brown to Stephens, November 9, 1865, in Stephens Papers, Emory; Brown to Jenkins, October 30, 1865, in Hargrett Collection.

45 J. R. Parrott to Stephens, November 3, 1865, in Stephens Papers, Emory; Stephens to Brown, November 11, 1865, in Hargrett Collection.

46 Linton Stephens to Alexander Stephens, November 20, 1865, in Stephens Papers, College of Sacred Heart.

quently spent many weeks there, believing that mountain air was more heathful than that of central Georgia. He often expressed great affection for the people of the Cherokee country, yet he surely must have felt rather keenly the fact that his greatest political opposition came from certain points in that general region. The war changed almost everything. Sherman's troops burned the Brown home at Canton. He did not wish to rebuild. The postwar Brown was not seeking seclusion or the quiet life. He wanted to be where the action was, and Canton was certainly not the place. Although then in ruin, its location marked Atlanta as a future center of commercial and industrial progress. Brown purchased the Sidney Root house on Washington Street and made it his home in December, 1865. This would be his home for the remainder of his life.[47]

The Georgia Convention of 1865 had met all presidential requirements for reconstruction. The amnesty oath had been required of voters in the election of delegates but was not made a requirement in state elections. However, there remained very few leaders who had not received presidential pardon, and even most of them were directly or indirectly seeking Brown's influence in securing the removal of their disabilities. Robert Toombs was in hiding and would later, from his Cuban place of refuge, loudly denounce Brown and Andrew, James, and Herschel Johnson, but back home his brother Gabriel was seeking Brown's assistance in Robert's behalf. It was Gabriel's, and no doubt Robert's, contention that since Robert Toombs was at home, not on active duty, at the time Governor Brown surrendered the state troops, no parole was required of him. Neither was there legal justification for his being chased from his home to escape arrest. Brown agreed that Toombs was at home at the time of surrender, for he had visited him there three days earlier. Neither did Toombs have any intention of returning to active duty. Brown further explained that he surrendered only those troops under arms; persons not under arms were not troops and consequently needed no parole. He hoped, however, that a parole would still be granted Toombs if it should be ruled that one was neces-

---

47 In 1877 Brown's former business partner, H. I. Kimball, would supervise for him an extensive remodeling of the house and grounds. (See Brown-Kimball correspondence, July 20 to August 20, 1877, in Hargrett Collection.) In the mid-1880s his son Julius would build a palatial home in the same block.

sary.[48] Gabriel Toombs was authorized to show this letter to General Steedman. Robert Toombs made no direct application but fled the country instead. Had he remained at home and bridled his tongue, he certainly would have fared no worse than Stephens and Brown.

The case of the former Confederate senator Ben Hill is something of a puzzle. When he was paroled from prison in July, 1865, he apparently made application for a pardon. Months passed with no action taken. On November 1, Hill reported to President Johnson the progress of the convention which he had, along with Brown, observed from a seat of honor on the floor. In a most ingratiating manner, he also reported on conditions in Georgia and heaped the highest praise upon the president for his enlightened and humane policy. Then, in closing, he stated "If you are satisfied the act will be in perfect accord with the public weal and not otherwise, I would be pleased to have favorable action on my application for pardon filed in July last." This letter, written and signed by Hill, is in the Brown family papers.[49] How did it get there? Neither of Hill's biographers make mention of it, and there is no reference to it in the Andrew Johnson Papers. It is hardly conceivable that, in view of the unfriendly relations between the two, Hill himself would have sent Brown an autographed copy. The only reasonable conclusion is that President Johnson forwarded it to Brown for suggestion. The pardon was not granted.

The new General Assembly convened on December 4, 1865. Charles J. Jenkins was not inaugurated as governor until December 14. Meanwhile, Provisional Governor Johnson had urged upon the legislature the necessity of ratification of the proposed Thirteenth Amendment to the United States Constitution. In so doing, he reminded the assembly that "Georgia has, in good faith, abolished slavery. She could not revive it if she would; and the ratification of this amendment will make the people of the United States homogenious—will remove from among us the cause of bitterness and sectional strife, which has wasted our property and deluged our land in blood."[50] Regardless of whether or not individual legislators approved, as a group they had no choice. The Thirteenth Amendment, abolishing slavery, was immediately rati-

48 Brown to Gabriel Toombs, October 7, 1865, in Hargrett Collection.
49 McLeod Collection.
50 *C. R. Ga.*, IV, 115.

fied.[51] Brown was keeping in touch with President Johnson by telegraph. On December 6, he reported the adoption of the amendment and added that the assembly "will pass laws amply protecting Freedmen in their rights to sue & to be sued & testify."[52]

Following the inauguration of Governor Jenkins, the General Assembly adjourned until January, 1866. During the interim a committee appointed by the late convention to suggest measures for regulating the rights of freedmen reported to Governor Jenkins.[53] No doubt the question of the rights of freedmen was the most difficult subject with which the legislators had to deal. Five members issued an appeal to former governor Brown for an expression of opinion "as to the legislation which is proper, under existing circumstances, relative to the freedmen of this State." Brown replied on February 14, 1866. Legislation wise in antebellum days might now be unwise and vice versa, he observed. Wise men would be influenced by the "circumstances by which they are surrounded." The war had resulted in a complete change in the relations between whites and blacks. "The fact is undeniable that those who were our slaves prior to the war, are now *free*, and so far as *legal* rights are concerned, are placed upon terms of equality with us. This is a fact which is mortifying to our people, but is none the less true on that account. The sooner it is realized to its fullest extent, the better for us. I do not say that negroes are the *equals* of the white race. God did not make them so, and man can never change the *status* which the Creator assigned them. They are not our equals intellectually or socially, and unless madness rules the hour, they will never be placed upon a basis of political equality with us."

Brown believed it was generally agreed that blacks were not competent to govern themselves; neither could they be competent to assist in governing the whites. This fact, however, did not affect legal equality. Even if Georgians wished to do so, the federal government would not permit the adoption of separate codes of law for blacks and whites. This did not mean that blacks must have equal rights with whites to serve on juries or cast the ballot in elections, but it did mean that blacks must have the right to sue and be sued and to give testimony

51 *Senate Journal*, 1865–66, pp. 9, 16, 17, 18; *House Journal*, 1865–66, pp. 16–17.
52 Andrew Johnson Papers.
53 Macon *Daily Telegraph*, January 9, 1866.

in all courts. Of course the *"credibility"* of all testimony must be determined by the jury under such rules of evidence as might apply. Blacks and whites must be subject to the same criminal code and the same penalties for their crimes. To every black the "rights of life, liberty, and property, including the full enjoyment of the proceeds of his labor, must be amply secured . . . by law, with all the guarantees necessary to their protection." There must be equal and impartial justice in all cases. When these legal rights were guaranteed and respected by the courts, Brown suggested, there would no longer be justification for the Freedmen's Bureau. Until this was done, however, "No one can reasonably expect such result."

Brown strongly advised against the enactment of a separate freedmen's code. The existing code should be amended so as "to embrace all persons of African descent, and extending to them all the civil rights in our courts enjoyed by white persons, except the right to sit in the jury box, together with the same rights of marriage as between persons of their own color, and the same rights of inheritance, with the same laws of guardianship, apprenticeship, etc., in all the legislation relative to them which is expedient or proper."[54] In general, the General Assembly followed the pattern sketched by Brown.[55] On paper, blacks became legal equals of whites, except for jury service and the franchise. How they would fare in court was another question. The Freedmen's Bureau did not suspend operation immediately.

In order to complete reorganization of the state government, it was necessary that the General Assembly select two United States senators. Of course Brown's name was proposed, but there is no evidence that he sought an appointment. His friend and future biographer, Herbert Fielder, investigated the situation and reported he did not believe the former governor could be elected even if he desired it. Stephens was reported to be a certain choice, and Fielder's informants predicted Lucius Gartrell as the other. Fielder did not wish Brown's name to be presented, for he did not want him defeated by Gartrell or Ben Hill. Furthermore, Fielder explained, the time was not right for true southern statesmen to take seats in Congress. "All we need is a set of men who can unqualifiedly submit to insult, degradation and gross injustice."

54 Atlanta *Daily Intelligencer*, February 18, 1866.
55 Thompson, *Reconstruction*, 158–59.

The situation might be different after Republicanism had run its course; therefore, Brown should wait.[56] Brown made no argument to the contrary, but he did pressure Stephens to permit the use of his name. Stephens at first balked, then hesitated, then gave in, on condition that his re-election would reflect the true will of the people.[57] He and Herschel V. Johnson were chosen over Joshua Hill, Gartrell, and James Johnson.

Brown wired President Johnson immediately: "While I regret much that has happened I trust the election of Stephens and Johnson will not be misunderstood. They will both support your policy zealously. I write you fully."[58] He wrote on the same day, explaining that he did not approve of the results of the election. He thought one of the defeated candidates should have been chosen. "I did not advocate this because I believed they were better men than those elected, or because I believed they would, if elected, labor more faithfully to sustain your policy and support your administration, but because I believed they would be more acceptable to the senate and the northern people. I still think this may be so."

But Brown felt certain that in making their selection the General Assembly was not prompted by disloyal motives. The members simply did not believe Joshua Hill or James Johnson truly represented the people of the state or were sympathetic with their problems. What the assembly did was to select Douglas men of 1860 who had opposed secession and supported the Confederacy "in a rather inactive way," yet were men of talent and "national character." Such men, it was believed, might be acceptable to the North. Brown further assured the president that neither senator elected sought the position, but both were "open, active zealous supporters of your administration."[59]

56 Fielder to Brown, December 21, 1865, in Hargrett Collection.
57 Stephens to Brown, November 15, 30, 1865, *ibid.*
58 January 31, 1866, in Andrew Johnson Papers.
59 Andrew Johnson Papers. This letter was made public by the Atlanta *Daily Constitution*, November 15, 1877.

Chapter XVII

Agree with Thine Adversary Quickly

NEITHER BROWN'S friends nor enemies would permit him to return to a peaceful private life. His friends constantly urged his return to active politics, and his enemies still hoped to uncover evidence of wrongdoing while in office. One who is reputed to have grown wealthy in wartime is usually suspected of profiteering and, if an officeholder, of making private use of public funds. Brown's enemies saw to it that he was suspected of both. He did manage his wartime financial assets with skill and efficiency. As of April 1, 1866, he owned 6,818 acres of land scattered over several counties. The larger tracts were in Dooly County (1,941 acres), Lee (1,316½), and Cherokee (1,210).[1] For the year 1865, the first in which he considered himself liable for federal income tax, he paid $230.23 tax on an income of $5,204. It is not known, however, whether this was for the full year or for that portion of the year subsequent to his parole.[2]

The 1865 convention authorized its president to appoint a committee of three to make "a thorough examination and investigation of the financial operations of the State" from January 1, 1861, to the present, and report its findings to the next legislature.[3] In accordance with requests from Provisional Governor Johnson, Brown had already sub-

---

1 See tax returns, in Hargrett Collection. Other tracts were in Floyd (80 acres), Paulding (40), Thomas (250), Terrell (202½), Decatur (750), and DeKalb (100).
2 See income tax returns, in Hargrett Collection.
3 *C. R. Ga.*, IV, 432.

mitted two detailed reports on state activities relative to the purchase, transportation, and sale of cotton during the war.[4] According to Brown's figures, the state had purchased and paid for 6,392 bales. Of this number, 1,556½ bales had been safely exported and only 58 lost at sea. The enemy had captured 305 bales, and 2,847 bales had been burned to prevent capture. Benefits from running the blockade had been considerably reduced by the unreliability of some consignees. Although the state's participation in the cotton business could not be classed as a great success, Brown took pride in being able to account for every bale purchased.

The investigating committee "invited every one who knew anything that would throw light upon the investigation, to come and tell it." Brown gave extensive testimony. In his opening statement he explained that, since the committee had seen fit to place him under oath, he would give full information as to all public financial operations. But "upon principle," he denied that the committee had a right to investigate his private affairs. However, he would not hesitate to explain any private matter upon which he had been assailed. His testimony on public matters reiterated much that was already known but revealed little that was not. Its greatest value would be in the publicity produced and the committee's ultimate decision. All cotton transactions were reviewed in detail, but many records were reported destroyed when Sherman's troops scattered "bushels" of documents "all over the House and grounds." As for his own cotton transactions, Brown explained, they were limited to the purchase of but a few bales as a part of his plantation business. In no case had he ever used one dollar of state money "for any private purpose or benefit to himself."[5]

Under oath, the former governor denied that he had ever been a private partner in the firm of E. Waitzfelder and Company or had ever owned any stock in the Milledgeville Manufacturing Company. His two Southwest Georgia plantations had been purchased with depreciated Confederate notes that had cost him "but a few thousand dollars in gold assets." A part of these assets had been acquired through his wife's inheritance from her father's estate of which he was ad-

---

4 August 12, October 30, 1865, *C. R. Ga.*, IV, 54–56, 62–72.
5 The wording is that of the author of the committee's report, not of Brown himself.

ministrator. Most of the remainder had been realized from trading
in bonds, especially railroad bonds. Most of his investments were now
in land and city property in Atlanta. Land had appeared to be the
safest investment. To those who charged that he had made a "large
fortune" during the war, he replied that he would take $10,000 less in
gold for his present possessions than his property was worth at the
beginning of the war.

Brown further explained that he had never been a heavy investor
in slaves. He owned "twenty odd" when they were set free. His salary
of $4,000 in depreciated currency was not even sufficient to care for his
family. But he had always observed the rule, Brown continued, of paying all obligations promptly. This had established his credit to the
point where instead of his seeking sources from which to borrow
needed money, people with money came to urge him to borrow from
them. His bank credit was almost unlimited, he boasted, and he had
often used this credit when he recognized "an opportunity to make a
good trade in stocks, bonds, and other things." Some investments had
proved very profitable. For instance, he purchased a small piece of
land near Canton for a "wood lot," paying $500 for it. It later proved
to be copper land, and he sold it for "over $20,000 on the gold basis,"
retaining some stock in the company.

Brown also wished to explain "the matter of the State Treasury
notes" received from the Treasury as reported by the treasurer, John
Jones. During the winter of 1861–1862, when the state had several
thousand troops at Savannah but no money to support them or pay other
expenses, the General Assembly authorized the governor to raise such
funds as needed by issuing either interest-bearing bonds or noninterest-
bearing Treasury notes. The banks, wishing to invest their money,
urged the issue of interest-bearing bonds. But, wishing to save money
for the state, the governor decided to issue Treasury notes. There was
some question as to whether or not sufficient paper could be brought
through the blockade for the printing of such notes. Pending the printing, the governor persuaded the banks to make temporary loans to the
state which would be repaid in bonds should he be unable to print
Treasury notes. James Jackson was sent to New Orleans to arrange for
the printing. He was able to get out of the city with some notes, plates,
and paper just before the city fell into federal hands. The banks ac-

cepted the notes. The governor had thus saved the state more than a million dollars in interest that would have been paid on bonds.

Brown further revealed that he had also urged "citizens and capitalists" to make similar temporary loans to the state to be repaid in Treasury notes when printed. His argument was that such notes would continue to increase in value and might eventually command a high premium. He himself had some surplus funds at the time and borrowed others, and friends entrusted him with still others. These funds, totaling $327,000 in "bank bills and Confederate notes," were loaned to the state for two or three months without one dollar of interest. The loan was repaid with Treasury notes when that was all the state had with which to pay. In making such a loan, Brown explained, he had in mind two reasons. In the first place, the state was in need of funds and as governor he was responsible for raising them. A second reason was his belief that state Treasury notes would eventually be worth a premium and were therefore a good investment. This proved to be true; he later sold some at "a considerable premium" and he still had some. Thus was he "more than compensated" for the loss of interest while his money was on loan to the state.

The committee's questioning next turned to events immediately preceding the federal occupation of Milledgeville. Brown reaffirmed the report that upon arrival of news that federal troops were approaching, the members of the General Assembly took off in many directions, making no effort to save papers and documents. The governor and most executive officials remained another twenty-four hours, and made an effort to save everything possible. Light furniture and silverware from the Executive Mansion were saved. Each department head was urged to save all papers from his office, but the task proved too great. "Bushels of papers were left." Brown enumerated some losses, but admitted that the list was incomplete. Apparently the most extensive loss was the papers of all description relating to cotton transaction. Although Brown did not so remark, this left many questions forever unanswered.

Regardless of newspaper reports to the contrary, Brown asserted, state-owned powder and ammunition at the arsenal were saved, but Confederate officers made no effort to save that which belonged to the Confederacy. He gave the highest praise to Quartermaster General Ira Foster. And as to the charges that favoritism had been shown to

E. Waitzfelder and Company, he would say that the quartermaster arranged with that company the "most advantageous contracts made with any Factory." Much clothing, cloth, and thread were furnished to the state at about one-half their market value. In public and private matters, he had "never dealt with more correct merchants."

Brown no doubt expected criticism of his public activities, yet he resented greatly any meddling with his private affairs. He thought he had a right to engage in trading while holding the office of governor, he informed the committee. He had made some money through trading before he was governor, while governor, and since resigning and expected to make still more. But all of his dealings had been honest and fair; therefore, he thought no one had a right to complain. He denied that the public had "a right to meddle in his private affairs." Should anyone feel that he had been wronged, the courts were open to his complaint; however, he believed no man had ever complained of injustice in private dealings with him.

The former governor declared that he "claimed no laudation for the good deeds" performed by him while in office, yet he proceeded to call attention to his accomplishments. He thought it only fair that his assailants, while exaggerating the errors they claimed he had committed, should at least occasionally "present the other side of the picture." He regretted that even the committee, in its search for every dollar due the state and every mistake made by a public official, had not been charged with placing the state "in the position of a party coming into equity." It had long been recognized, he explained, that "a party coming into a Court of Equity must come with clean hands; and that he who asked equity must do equity." This definitely was not the case in this investigation. In fact the investigation was a completely one-sided affair. While the committee sought to determine and recommend collection of claims due the state, it would take no action on state obligations to the very persons being investigated. A rule that did not work both ways was a bad one. He himself held claims against the state for "nearly three years salary" and for some trust funds invested in notes and bonds which had been repudiated. In the mildest terms, this was unfair.[6]

6 *Report of the Committee, Appointed Under Resolution of the Convention, on the Financial Operations of the State During the War* (Milledgeville, 1866), 16–26.

In submitting its report to the General Assembly, the investigating committee declared: "Our conclusion is, after the most rigid scrutiny into the public and private affairs of these officers, from Governor Brown down, that no one of these rumors has been sustained by the slightest proof. Instead of fortunes having been made by them, we have found them generally poorer than when they went into office."[7] This investigation and report no doubt pacified the general public, but the governor's enemies were not impressed.

During the second portion of the legislative session, Brown spent almost as much time in Milledgeville as if he had been a member of the assembly. On January 22, 1866, he was retained as counsel for four Augusta banks,[8] for a fee of $5,000. He was to represent these banks, "on all points looking to proper remedies," either legislative or judicial, "for protection of the rights and interests of the stockholders."[9] On the same date he gave Alfred Baker, representative of the banks, a receipt for $3,000 advance payment.[10] Alexander and Linton Stephens were also on the payroll of these same banks. The most bitter opponent of the banks over the past eight years had now become their leading lobbyist.

Linton Stephens joined Brown in Milledgeville, and Brown reported to Alexander Stephens on their progress. "The bank bill . . . has passed the Senate," he wrote on March 2. "Its fate in the House is very doubtful. Indeed it will be very hard to carry it. I do not however despair of its prospects. If we had a skilful leader in the House it could pass. The prejudices are high and hard to combat."[11] Stephens replied: "I do hope the Legislature will pass some such measure as the one which passed the Senate upon the subject of winding up the banks. . . . Some rule of evidence ought to be established by which honest, bona fide bill holders should be secured in the collection of the full amount of their demands and by which stockholders ought to be put upon the same equitable principles of settlement toward sharpers and speculators as all other citizens are placed under the ordinance of the State.

7 *Ibid.*, 35.
8 Bank of Augusta, Mechanics Bank of Augusta, City Bank of Augusta, and Union Bank of Augusta.
9 Brown to Alfred Baker, January 22, 1866, in McLeod Collection.
10 McLeod Collection.
11 Stephens Papers, Emory.

This is reasonable, right and just, it seems to me in my view of the subject."[12] On April 3, Brown was reimbursed by Baker for $2,600 "used for such legitimate purposes as per understanding with Mr. Baker as were thought by me necessary to aid in procuring just and proper legislation for the relief of the banks of this State and their stockholders."[13]

In recognition of the almost complete economic chaos that existed and the total inability of many persons to pay their debts, the General Assembly passed a stay law. It was vetoed by Governor Jenkins but passed over his veto. However, some relief advocates were still not satisfied. Jesse W. Jackson of Morgan County made a strong plea for the repudiation of all private debts. He received little support in the assembly, but after the close of the session he appealed to Brown to read his speech and give an opinion. After Governor Jenkins' veto of the stay law he was no longer classed as a friend of relief "*but a staunch friend of the banks*," Jackson explained. Brown's opinion was "not sought for *any public use*" but "to assist me to direct my course aright." Jackson was considering taking the matter to the people. He apparently did not know that Brown was an attorney for the banks.

Brown replied immediately. He was favorable to "every constitutional relief which the legislature can afford to our distressed and impoverished people," but he did not think Jackson's proposal was constitutional. The federal Constitution forbade a state to pass a law impairing a contract. Debts were contracts and could be legally collected through suit in court. To cancel a debt would be to cancel a contract. With the state it was different; it could not be sued except with its own consent. Therefore, it could repudiate its debts by refusing to permit suit. "While I sympathize with you in your desire to do all that can be done to relieve our unfortunate people," Brown advised, "I do not see how your plan can succeed. I have no personal interest in this question, as all who owed me paid me during the war in Confederate money."[14] Jackson did take his plan for repudiation of private debts to the people and soon had in circulation a false rumor that Brown

12 March 6, 1866, in Hargrett Collection. This bill providing relief for stockholders did not become law.
13 Hargrett Collection.
14 Jackson to Brown, April 5, 1866; Brown to Jackson, April 6, 1866, *ibid.*

had endorsed the plan and agreed to run for governor in the next election *"in favor of repudiation."*[15]

Brown was also engaged in another activity which was at least unusual, if not questionable, in nature. On December 28, 1865, J. Condit Smith, an agent of the United States Treasury Department, wrote him from Eufala, Alabama: "Your letter of the 19th was received a few days since. I am at present and shall be for the next ten days exceedingly busy, after which time I will have leisure, and will meet you at Atlanta if it will suit your convenience."[16] The letter mentioned has not been found, but on January 18, 1866, Brown and I. C. Plant, president of the First National Bank of Macon, signed an agreement with D. C. Anthony and J. Condit Smith, agents of the Treasury Department, whereby Brown and Plant were promised 25 percent of any amount realized by the Treasury from information furnished by them relative to railroad and cotton deals involving railroads, individuals, and the Confederacy. Specifically involved were the Albany and Gulf and the Brunswick and Florida railroads, which were reported to have sold their iron to the Confederacy for use on other roads. All Confederate property was subject to confiscation. Apparently Brown and Plant had already reported that the president of the Brunswick and Florida had invested the money received in five hundred bales of cotton. If this cotton was found and seized, Brown and Plant were to receive their 25 percent. The contract further stated that "The said Smith and Anthony as agents . . . are to act upon the information given by said Brown and Plant and to use all proper diligence for the identification and recovery of said iron as soon as possible. They are not to expose the names of said Brown and Plant as informers."[17]

Brown was now devoting much time to private business. He owned thousands of acres but he had no desire to become a planter. He purchased land mostly for speculative purposes. In November, 1865, he offered to sell his Dooly County plantation for $10,000 in greenbacks or 50,000 pounds of cotton, but finding no taker, he then rented each

---

15 W. M. Lewis to Brown, December 21, 1866, *ibid.*
16 Hargrett Collection.
17 Agreement dated January 18, 1866; Smith to Brown, January 16, 1866, in McLeod Collection; Plant to Brown, January 29, 1866, in Hargrett Collection.

plantation for a percentage of the crop or twenty bales of cotton. He refused to sell any of his Cherokee lands.[18]

There is no record of how many former slaves remained with the Brown family to work for wages. Some apparently did. In the few extant letters written by Mrs. Brown she mentioned names as if they were very familiar to the family. In writing to her husband while he was lobbying in Milledgeville, she stated that "Andy is living at Uncle William's; it is a good home for him, but I am sorry for such stingy folks to be waited on for nothing. Maria, Alice and Gus work for $120 per year; and now they have Andy they will get along better than of old. . . . The children send howdy to the negroes."[19] The last sentence would seem to indicate that some Mansion servants had remained in Milledgeville.

On January 12, 1866, Brown employed John and Neal Bateman and John's wife Ellen as hired servants. Under the written contract, Brown was to feed the servants and furnish a comfortable room and firewood. At the end of the year John and Neal were to receive $100 each. Ellen was to work for the support of herself and two children. The servants were to clothe themselves and always dress decently. They were to take good care of the livestock, tend the garden, cut and haul wood, wait tables, and "do any work they are put at." Ellen was to "cook, wash, milk," and do house work. All were required "to be respectful, obedient, and attentive and obey orders promptly. If they become disobedient, inattentive or disrespectful, or fail to do faithful labor, they forfeit their wages for the time they have stayed. When they do their duty faithfully they are to be well treated and well fed." Neither of the servants could write; each made his mark. The contract was witnessed by Brown's son Julius.[20] This contract does not appear to have been much of an improvement over the deal offered by "Uncle William." At any rate, it did not work out very well; both John and Neal left before the end of the year. However, Brown paid them for the time they had worked.[21]

18 Brown to D. M. Cox, November 25, 1865; E. F. Winslow to Brown, January 2, 1866; rental agreement with S. P. Salter, January 10, 1866, *ibid.*
19 February ?, 1866, *ibid.*
20 Hargrett Collection.
21 Note written on original contract

The legislative session and lobbying having ended, Brown returned to general law practice in Atlanta. On May 19, 1866, he formed a partnership with John D. Pope. The two agreed to share equally all expenses and income. It was further agreed that Brown "does not bind himself to give close attention to the office, as he wishes time to read and to give some attention to other matters." Although Pope would do most of the office work, he was not to be considered as "simply an office lawyer." Both would take cases to open court "having proper regard for the wishes of clients."[22] Brown was an immediate success as a practicing attorney. Within a few months, the services of no other lawyer within the state were in so great a demand. Nor was there one who charged higher fees.

By the summer of 1866 state and local courts had been organized and were hearing all types of cases, except those relating to freedmen's affairs, which were handled by the Freedmen's Bureau. Judge John Erskine reopened the federal district court in Savannah in May, 1866, with Henry S. Fitch as district attorney. Erskine was a very close friend of Brown. The details of Erskine's appointment are not clear, but in midsummer, 1865, he wrote Brown from New York, requesting verification of certain "facts," for there was some question as to whether or not he would be able to take the required oath. Brown had stopped briefly with Erskine in New York on his return from imprisonment. Erskine now very flatteringly assured Brown that all who met him there were much impressed, gave him "credit for candor," and pronounced him a "fair enemy." "Now all you have to do is neither to be apathetic to public matters nor too personally seclusive, and it will not be long till you are at the head of affairs, at least in Georgia, again."

After sending greetings to Generals Foster and Wayne and Judge Lockrane, and advice to "Support the President on all occasions," Erskine got down to the facts he wished verified. During the greater portion of the war he had practiced law in Georgia, but "never bore arms against the U.S." or "gave aid, countenance or encouragement to persons" engaged in hostilities against the United States. In order to avoid Confederate conscription he had requested and received a position on Brown's staff. Later Brown had offered to make him a military

22 Hargrett Collection.

aide, but he refused and accepted only an honorary position. He "never wore any insignia of office." But in June, 1864, he resigned this honorary position and passed "out of the Confederacy *via* Mississippi." This being his history, he contended "If I cannot take that oath, who that was *in Ga.* during the war can?"[23] Brown must have confirmed this story; the two remained close friends.

Judge Erskine's former home had been at Newnan. He returned to that locality and spent several months before moving to Atlanta, and he and Brown carried on an extensive correspondence. No doubt the friendship was mutual and genuine, but the fact that he was a friend of the judge did not hurt Brown's legal practice. No sooner had Erskine opened his court than William Law, an attorney of long practice, applied for permission to resume practice without taking the test oath. Brown appeared as Law's attorney. Here was a man, Brown explained, who had practiced law for half a century and maintained a private and professional character of the highest type. He had remained a Union man as long as there was a possibility of preventing the rupture. He never bore arms against the United States; held no Confederate office; was never convicted of crime or even indicted; and had received full pardon from the president "for every act which might, even by implication, be construed as a violation of the law."

Although Law now refused to take the oath, where were those who would venture to accuse him of treason, crimes or misdemeanors, Brown inquired. Unless some such accusation should be made and proved Congress possessed no power to prevent his practicing before the courts. Brown next entered into a long discussion of history, including biblical times, in reaching the conclusion that the statute requiring the test oath was unconstitutional. The Divine law and the laws of nations agree, he argued, that when war is at an end, and peace is proclaimed or amnesty and pardon granted to the vanquished as to the applicant in this case, "*all the past must be buried in oblivion.*" No one was to be called to account for acts during the war. "And he who forfeits the property of those who have made peace for acts done during hostilities, violates the law of nations; while he who sheds blood of those who have conformed to the terms of the capitulation after hostilities have ended 'sheds the blood of war in peace,' and violates not

23 July 31, 1865, *ibid.*

only the law of nations, but the law revealed by the living God."[24] The fact that Brown had his argument published in pamphlet form is evidence that he wished it to be read by those outside the South who were talking of possible confiscation of property.

Of course District Attorney Henry Fitch argued in favor of the legality of the test oath, but Judge Erskine had little difficulty in reaching a decision in which he concluded: "That the imposing of this oath (so far as the retrospective part of it is concerned) is virtually compulsory, and effectually punitive, cannot, in my judgment, be denied. It makes the party swear to a life long innocence, and to testify against himself, and herein it is an infraction of the fundamental law of the land." Although the judge was not "unmindful of the magnitude—nay awfulness—of the responsibility which devolves upon a Court in pronouncing against even a part of a solemn Act of Congress . . . it is ordered and adjudged by the Court, that the Act of Congress . . . so far as it was intended to apply to this case, is repugnant to the Constitution of the United States."[25] Someone also paid for having Judge Erskine's opinion printed in pamphlet form.

On June 1, 1866, Judge Erskine wrote attorney Brown that he had "pronounced judgment in Law's case," based upon the "facts before me." "I have named you in such way as I could with propriety in the 'opinion.' I thought it due to the Dist. Atty. to mention him handsomely today. I may now say of your argument that it is an honor to any lawyer in the United States. Go on! You must succeed. You need not be second to any lawyer in this State if you will half try."[26] Following the Law decision, Judge Erskine made a hurried trip to New York, but was soon back in Newnan, and he and Brown resumed their correspondence on state and national matters. A bit on the vain side, the Judge noted with pride the remarks about him in the Atlanta *Intelligencer*. Would Brown send him "half a dozen copies of *that* paper"? he suggested.[27] This extensive and extremely friendly correspondence between the two continued. In whatever decisions Judge Erskine would make on matters

---

24 *Argument of Ex-Governor Joseph E. Brown on the Unconstitutionality of the Test Oath as Applied to Attorneys-at-Law in the United States District Court* (Savannah, 1866).

25 *Opinion of Honorable John Erskine, United States District Judge, in Ex Parte William Law* (Savannah, 1866).

26 Hargrett Collection.

27 June 24, 1866, *ibid.*

of public importance during the next few years Brown no doubt exerted influence.

On December 18, 1865, Secretary of State William H. Seward proclaimed the Thirteenth Amendment an addition to the Constitution. Since Georgia had completed all requirements set by the president, the process of restoration to good standing within the Union appeared completed. This was far from reality, for the Radical element in Congress had no idea of permitting prewar leaders again to assume command in those states recently in rebellion. With the abolition of slavery, the three-fifths clause in the Constitution had been rendered inoperative. Henceforth, a black would be counted a whole man, not three-fifths of one, in determining population. This would increase southern representation in Congress. Should the blacks be counted in determining representation, yet not permitted to vote, southern white political strength would be increased considerably as a result of the abolition of slavery.

Regardless of whether welfare of the blacks or of the Republican party was foremost in the thinking of the Radical Congress, neither could be adequately guaranteed by the president's plan of reconstruction. Declaring reconstruction a legislative rather than an executive function, Congress took control. In January, 1866, a joint congressional committee on reconstruction began holding hearings. Just what was gained from these hearings still remains a question. Almost 150 witnesses were questioned on such related topics as treatment of Negroes, Unionists, and Yankees in the southern states. "What the inquisitors were after, and what they got, was just that much more of what they were convinced of already. . . . The committee was interested in only one side of the story, and most of the informants were summoned because of their special knowledge of that particular side."[28]

From committee hearings and long, drawn-out congressional maneuvering, there eventually evolved a proposed Fourteenth Amendment to the United States Constitution, which declared Negroes citizens and forbade a state from depriving "any person of life, liberty, or property, without due process of law" or "deny to any person within its jurisdiction the equal protection of the laws." A possible penalty was provided

28 Eric L. McKitrick, *Andrew Johnson and Reconstruction* (Chicago, 1960), 330.

for states who denied citizens the privilege of voting, but the suffrage was not specifically conferred upon the blacks. The right to hold office was denied to all persons who, prior to the war, had taken an oath to support the Constitution and later engaged in rebellion or aided those in rebellion. This disability could be removed by a two-thirds vote of Congress. And lastly, the public debt of the United States was declared valid, but neither the United States nor any state might pay any "obligation incurred in aid of insurrection or rebellion against the United States" nor compensate for any loss of slaves as a result of emancipation. This proposed amendment was approved by Congress and sent to the states for ratification before the congressional campaign of 1866 got well underway. A National Union Convention was held in Philadelphia in August, 1866, to devise means of checking Radical progress by rallying to the support of President Johnson. Georgia sent a delegation of eighteen distinguished men, including the Stephens brothers and Herschel V. Johnson. Brown was not a delegate, but he participated actively in the Fulton County convention called for the selection of delegates.

The National Union Convention was a failure, but President Johnson had already taken a firm position in opposition to the Fourteenth Amendment and signified his intention to take the issue to the people in the congressional campaign. In late August and early September, he made his "swing around the circle" on which he met with much protest and ridicule and "retorted with much indiscreet and foolhardy word-bandying." He did the Radical cause little harm; neither did he help his own.[29]

"The President has returned to Washn. from a tour that it were better had never been made," wrote Judge Erskine to Brown, "but experience teaches us, and by frequent inductions we soon or later come to a logical conclusion. Now what I wish you to do is to write him a carefully penned letter, stating to him how grateful the people of Georgia, as well as yourself, appreciate all he has done; let it be of an encouraging nature; let him understand that his views of the *status* of the states is the true constitutional one, & that the people of the *whole* Union must necessarily come to it." Erskine prophesied that within the next few months there would likely be a reconstruction of the presi-

29 *Ibid.*, 428 ff.

dent's cabinet. If Johnson could but know Brown as he was known to people in Georgia and the South, "he will be certain to invite *you* to a seat." This was "the opinion of many thinking men." Although Judge Erskine did not say Alexander Stephens was one of those "thinking men," he did speak of spending the past evening with the former vice-president. He was pleased to hear Stephens speak so highly of Brown's statesmanlike ideas of government.[30] Brown apparently did not write the suggested letter; he realized that the president's cause was a losing one.

The proposed Fourteenth Amendment was placed before the Georgia legislature for approval in November, 1866. Governor Jenkins urged that it not be ratified, a joint legislative committee recommended likewise, and few members wished to support it. It was rejected by the Senate unanimously, and only two favorable votes were cast in the House.[31] All other southern states, except Tennessee, took similar action, thus rejecting the first condition of restoration demanded by the Republican Congress, even though the overwhelming Republican victory in the recent congressional election placed that party in position to ignore the president if it chose. The fact that Johnson failed to exert positive influence on congressional plans made him of little further service to the South.

Brown was quick to realize this situation. By the close of the year 1866 he was wondering on which side of the bread was the butter. After a few weeks of meditation he decided to go to Washington to make a firsthand investigation of the political situation, taking with him Judge Dawson A. Walker and Chief Justice Joseph Henry Lumpkin. Brown also had other business in Washington. Through his friend Senator David Patterson of Tennessee, he had reported information to the Treasury Department "relative to a certain railroad at the South which has in its possession iron or cotton," which the federal government was entitled to seize as Confederate property. The secretary, desiring more definite details, suggested that Brown come to Washington. If the information resulted in seizure, the informant could expect "liberal compensation."[32] Since this was a private and secret matter, no record

30 Erskine to Brown, September 21, 1866, in Hargrett Collection.
31 *Senate Journal*, 1866, pp. 65–72; *House Journal*, 1866, pp. 68–69.
32 William E. Chandler, assistant secretary, to David Patterson, December 29, 1866; Patterson to Brown, January 11, 1867, in Hargrett Collection.

needed to be kept, so the secretary of the Treasury returned Brown's letter to Patterson. In relaying this message to Brown, Patterson also urged him to come. "When here we can talk freely about the condition of the country." Patterson no doubt had plenty to talk about, for the hostile Brownlow legislature of Tennessee had recently voted him out of the United States Senate because of his relationship with the president. Nothing more is known about the iron-cotton information.

Judge Walker accompanied Brown to Washington, but Judge Lumpkin declined because of illness. In declining, he stated that "bad as it is, if we could have peace by a general pardon and negro suffrage, I am inclined myself to accept it." He would appreciate a letter from Brown while the former governor was in Washington. However, four days later, his illness probably getting the worst of him, the judge lamented "I fear that vain is the help of man—and unless God in his mercy should deliver us by sending confusion of tongues among our persecutors as he did the builders of Babel—or rescue us by some other miracle we are a ruined people."[33]

In Washington, Brown visited in the home of James M. Wayne of Savannah, associate justice of the U.S. Supreme Court.[34] The two had been communicating directly and through their friend Judge Erskine since October 31, 1866. On that date Wayne had noted: "The Radical violence continues to manifest itself in their newspapers, but the President continues firm in his constitutional views." In the capital, Brown "conversed freely with persons high in authority in every department of the government and with men of distinction of every shade of political sentiment." Judge Erskine urged him to have a private interview with the president and to call upon members of the Supreme Court and sent a letter of introduction to Associate Justice David Davis. Erskine also reminded Brown that Supreme Court justices did not call upon anyone "first," except the president; so if Brown called and failed to make contact, he should call again.[35] His old friend of military occupation, General John T. Croxton, put Brown in touch with General James A. Garfield, congressman from Ohio, and arranged for General Henry Boynton to accompany him to see William D. Kelley, congressman

33 Lumpkin to Brown, January 25, 1867, *ibid.*; Lumpkin to Brown, January 29, 1867, in McLeod Collection.
34 Wayne was from Savannah.
35 Erskine to Brown, February 6, 9, 1867, in Hargrett Collection.

from Pennsylvania. Croxton also suggested "you need apprehend no unpleasant newspaper notoriety."[36] Brown never made public the names of those with whom he conferred, but he soon entered into correspondence with William D. Kelley.

After careful examination of the situation, Brown made a lengthy report to Justice Lumpkin, who had remained at home in Athens. Having conversed with "many prominent men on both sides," Brown expressed regret that he could not make a more favorable report. "It would be better for our people if every man who enjoys their confidence would represent the State of things faithfully as they exist, and not as we would have them. Our theories and our interests often have to yield to stubborn facts which we have no power to change. The statesman must look to the condition of the Country, and the circumstances by which he is surrounded and not simply to his own abstract ideas of wise government, in determining what is best for his Constituents." Conditions had changed, and "we must change our action in conformity to it."

With this introductory statement, Brown launched a detailed discussion of prewar and wartime activities and results which led to the existing situation. The South had demonstrated its gallantry and manhood, but "we were conquered." Georgia had submitted to the president's requirements for reconstruction, but that had not proved sufficient. A Radical Congress had asserted that the body with the power to make war also had the power to make peace, and had submitted the Fourteenth Amendment for adoption as a condition of reconstruction. But the southern states had rejected that requirement.

Results of the recent congressional election had shown the people of the North to be in support of the Republican party, and had guaranteed sufficient votes in Congress to override any presidential veto. Consequently, the president was powerless to command acceptance of his own ideas or to block action of the Republican majority. Acceptance of the Fourteenth Amendment by the South might have solved the major problem, but now Congress was determined to enforce its demands, adding universal suffrage to the list. The South must choose between acceptance or utter ruin, Brown explained, for military government was to be substituted for civil government, whites were to be

36 Croxton to Brown, February 10, 1867, *ibid.*

disfranchised, and blacks given the power to dominate. And the more radical element in Congress was also demanding confiscation of rebel property. In view of the helpless condition of the South and the determination of the Republican Congress, Brown saw no choice but to accept the terms and hope for the best. He would like Judge Lumpkin's private opinion. "If you think it best for our people that I make these views public, send me back this letter written in much haste and I will revise and publish it, whatever may be its effect upon me personally."

When Brown's letter arrived in Athens, Judge Lumpkin was seriously ill. His son James read the letter to his father and returned it to Brown with a note that the judge "says your sagacity and opportunities of judgment are so much better than his—even if capable of mental exertion—he begs you will give that direction to your views which you may think best for our people & the country. That for himself— whether his time be long or short—he sees nothing but gloomy future before him."[37]

Brown returned from Washington on February 18, 1867. A few days later twenty citizens issued a request that the former governor report on his sojourn in Washington. Addressing him as a "sentinel upon the watch tower," they wished to ask him "What of the Night?" "We sincerely and earnestly call upon you, as we believe, for the good of our State, and every interest of the great masses of our people, to present to us fully, freely, and frankly, your views upon the condition of the country; and what course in your judgment should be pursued by the people of Georgia in the present crisis."[38] No doubt Brown had prior knowledge of this request; his reply was ready.

Were he "a sentinel," Brown replied, he would report that "The night is dark, dreary, gloomy; no rainbow of hope spans the black impenetrable cloud that overshadows us. Scarcely a ray of light is seen upon its margin." But he was not a sentinel; he held no position of responsibility; he had sought no position since the war; neither did he "ever expect to hold any in future." But even if the people of Georgia wished him to hold public office again and he were willing, there was "a higher power than their will, which will deny my eligibility." This

37 Brown to Joseph Henry Lumpkin, February ?, 1867; James M. Lumpkin to Brown, February 21, 1867, in McLeod Collection.
38 Atlanta *Daily New Era*, February 26, 1867.

being the case, he could speak "with perfect frankness." He felt it his duty to state the facts even though aware that they were "unacceptable to the good people of Georgia, but they are none the less facts."

In Washington he had been received with kindness and courtesy and had conversed with prominent men of all political views. It was his purpose "to learn the true state of affairs, and I believe I succeeded." He learned that the "Radical party" had the support of the majority of northern people, and the congressmen of that party could be considered as "generally representative." On the other hand, the Democratic party not only did not have the support of the northern people, it was "not gaining ground." The president's policies were not sustained by the northern people, and the Radical Congress possessed the power to override his veto, thus further limiting his power. These facts, however, had not altered the president's determination to stand by the Constitution and defend the "just rights of the states." The president still maintained that no state could withdraw from the Union, and it was the president's right to reconstruct republican governments in the insurrectionary states. This the Radicals denied, contending that the power to re-establish state governments was vested in Congress. They further denied the validity of the reconstruction under the president's plan and insisted upon adoption of the Fourteenth Amendment. The recent rejection of this amendment by the southern states had irritated Congress and increased its determination. There was little doubt but that the amendment would be ratified by three-fourths of the northern states.

Brown further explained that the extreme Radicals were advocating still more drastic action. They would deny the suffrage to "*all persons who voluntarily* participated in the rebellion," leaving the franchise with the few loyal men and extending it to the freedmen. New state constitutions adopted by these two groups would no doubt disfranchise the white majority. It was also believed, Brown explained, that the ultimate design of the extreme Radicals was the confiscation of property of former Confederates to pay the United States war debt. This would be done as soon as "the popular mind of the North could be educated or excited to the proper point" and the Constitution adequately amended by three-fourths of the northern states.

In Brown's opinion, there was no longer a question of whether or not suffrage would be granted the freedmen. The only question was

whether or not it would be denied whites who were former Confederates. This would most certainly happen if the South continued "to throw
obstacles in the way of reconstruction upon the basis of the constitutional amendment and universal suffrage." The dire consequences predicted, Brown believed could still be averted if action was immediate.
"Our prompt adoption of the constitutional amendment and universal
suffrage would, in my opinion, settle the question. Nothing less ever
will."

Such favorable action on the part of the South, Brown reasoned,
might improve the relations between the president and Congress, for
Johnson had always contended that control of the suffrage "belongs to
the States." Therefore, the President could not be displeased with such
action, and Congress would maintain "its point of honor." In this fight
between the president and Congress the South had been caught between
"the upper and the nether millstones, being ground to atoms. The
longer it lasts, the worse we are ruined." To the all important question
as to what to do, Brown would advise "'Agree with thine adversary
quickly.' We are prostrate and powerless. We can offer no further resistance. The conquerors dictate their own terms, which are heightened
in severity by the delay of the conquered to accept them. Because we
have lost immensely, is it wise stubbornly to sacrifice the little that is
left to us?" It was already decreed that Confederate leaders, including
himself, Brown asserted, were to be deprived of all political rights, but
it would be unwise for the masses to lose control of their own destiny
through continued support of those so denied. "If peace, quiet and returning prosperity can be restored to our unhappy country by the sacrifice, we should make it without further hesitation or delay." All laws
should be faithfully executed; and the "most proscriptive loyalist" and
"degraded freedman" should be meted out the same justice as "our own
people." All who had chosen to spend their future in the United States
rather than migrate should now do all within their power, "while claiming its protection," faithfully to perform their duties as citizens.

A new era was dawning, Brown concluded. The South with all its
resources needed capital and labor. "Neither will come till our difficulties are settled, and our political status defined." Every man, be he
northerner or foreigner, who brought capital or physical strength into
the South brought improvement and should be received as a friend. In

their depressed condition, southerners should "refuse to bandy words" with those who would insult them. "Time will heal most of our wounds, and we who in war were enemies, will soon be in peace friends. The sooner this is the case, the better for the whole country."

In view of the existing conditions, Brown thought it the duty of the governor to call the General Assembly into special session. The assembly should ratify the Fourteenth Amendment and authorize a convention to alter the state constitution to provide for universal suffrage. Congress had already given assurance that this would settle the question of readmission to the Union. "We shall never get better terms. Let us comply with them, and be ready to be represented in the next Congress as soon as possible."[39]

The contemporary historian I. W. Avery stated that gentlemen with whom Brown conferred advised him not to "immolate himself" by publishing this letter, but Brown rejected the advice, stating: "'In the present excited state of the popular mind, the chances are that bold leaders will inflame their [the people's] passions and prejudices, and they will reject the terms proposed, and suffer the consequences.'" He knew that his action would make him the most unpopular man between the Potomac and the Rio Grande. Further, Avery related, when Brown was advised that since he was no longer a public official he was not obligated to speak out, he replied: "I am indebted to the people of Georgia for all I am as a public man, and I have made up my mind to *tell them the truth*, and warn them of danger, be the consequences what they may to me as an individual."[40] Avery did not identify the gentlemen consulted by Brown. There is nothing in his extant correspondence to indicate that he conferred with anyone other than Judge Lumpkin, but since Judge Walker traveled with him to and from Washington, it seems reasonable that the two talked freely. Shortly before leaving for Washington, Brown had entertained at dinner Bishop Lynch, Father O'Reilly, and Father O'Neal.[41] It is quite probable that he discussed with them the purpose of his proposed trip, but there is no evidence that he conferred with these churchmen after his return.

As Brown no doubt expected, his letter brought forth abuse the

39 *Ibid.*
40 Avery, *History of Georgia*, 364.
41 February 2, 1867, Franklin Pierce Brown Diary, 1867–68, in Hargrett Collection.

like of which no Georgian had ever known. There was no exaggeration in the contemporary statement that it produced "alteration in public favor, so sudden, so complete, so overwhelming and savage as to constitute the most extraordinary personal vicissitude of the extraordinary period. . . . It was a frightful struggle. . . . It battered and ostracised him."[42] From a position of popular champion of constitutional and personal rights, the former governor's image quickly changed to that of a "traitor," "scalawag," "Benedict Arnold," "Judas Iscariot." Even those newspaper editors who were inclined toward moderation revealed disappointment, distrust, and disgust. "Listen to the voice of the lamb, Joe Brown," sarcastically advised the Griffin *Star*. "With what Christian resignation he submits to disfranchisement! What tender regard he has for our wives and children! We can assure him the feeling is reciprocated. We sincerely hope his tender ones may never be without their full allowance of 'collards,' and that his brick and rock tower in Atlanta may continue to increase in altitude until its summit shall pierce the clouds."[43] The editor of the Augusta *Constitutionalist* said he merely wished "to pit Brown against Brown; the man of '61 versus the man of '67 . . . . If Brown was blind in '61, how can we bespeak the integrity of his optics in '67? If political somersaulting is a test of skill, the Hanlon Brothers may as well surrender at discretion."[44]

The Milledgeville *Federal Union*, probably the most consistent supporter of Brown throughout his political career, still thought him "one of our wisest, and purest patriots," whose advice "claims our profoundest respect and earnest consideration"; yet the editor was at loss to see "with the lights before us, how our situation will be improved by following his advice."[45] The Atlanta *Intelligencer* was a bit more tolerant. It thought the outburst of abuse poor reward for one who had contributed so much to his state and its people. The presses which were denouncing Brown's stand "should remember that there is no argument in abuse, no logic in scurrility; and that no weapons in political warfare are so *impotent* as they."[46] The editor of the recently established Atlanta *Daily New Era* stood almost alone when he asserted "We must face the

42 Avery, *History of Georgia*, 364.
43 Quoted in Augusta *Daily Constitutionalist*, March 2, 1867.
44 *Ibid.*, February 28, 1867.
45 March 5, 1867.
46 March 13, April 8, 1867.

music, and the quicker the better for all concerned. . . . This is a practical common sense question, not to be lightly treated by a starved,
distracted people—such as ourselves."[47] Howell Cobb, Jr., predicted
that "Should this Joe Brown ship come safely thru the storm Little
Aleck will emerge from the hold."[48]

47 April 24, 1867.
48 Howell Cobb, Jr., to Howell Cobb, March 3, 1867, in Cobb Papers.

Chapter XVIII

In Support of
Congressional Reconstruction

NOT ONE PROMINENT Georgian publicly joined Brown in his new position. He no doubt expected Alexander Stephens to give him some support, although he definitely did not consult the former vice-president before making his announcement. Stephens remained silent for two weeks. When he did write Brown on March 8, he pleaded ill health as the principal cause for delay, and quickly added that what he had to say was in strictest confidence. "I fully and thoroughly sympathize with your views and apprehension of the future," he explained. "And if I saw the least prospect of anything that we can do averting those great threatening ills now impending I should most certainly give action on such line my most hearty approval." But he had no such hope. "Restoration of the union under the Congress plan will inevitably I think end in political ruin North as well as South." Such a plan would ultimately end in the extinction of one of the two races. There was no possible way to avert such a catastrophe.

If confiscation of property came, it would be a result of total disregard of "all constitutional barriers" by the Congress and courts, Stephens explained. In this case, no "sacrifice would appease such fanaticism." Since there would be no power to prevent political doom "we might just as well stand still & take what comes—We may just as well bear the force and fury of the tornado in an open field as to take shelter under something that may ultimately make our ruin more complete." Stephens further stressed that these were his own private views;

he had no desire to impose them upon others. He did not wish to exert influence or place obstacles in the way of anyone who wished to follow the line suggested by Brown. As for himself, however, he would abide by the law, "leaving results & consequences to the mercy of God and the judgment of mankind. . . . As Caesar wrapped himself in his mantle and received the blow when he saw the blade of Brutus even so now would I do."[1]

With the passage of three more weeks Stephens had reached some more definite conclusions, but he still declined to make his views public. He thought the policy of Congress would be carried out, and he did not propose to offer any "impediment or obstacle to it by word or act." He believed, however, that the portion of the white population that did have the franchise could control affairs, provided it acted with wisdom and prudence, and he would not oppose extending the franchise to qualified freedmen.[2] When asked privately why he remained silent, Stephens replied that it was because he saw "no prospect of being able to do any good by anything I could say to the public." He thought nothing a southern man might do or say would have "any effect in arresting the tendency of affairs." He had remained quiet because he had no wish further to contribute to division among southern people, causing "old friends to grow angry with each other," when nothing could be accomplished. "If Gov. Brown and others see fit 'to take to life-boats' in our stranded condition, I have no quarrel to make with him or them, for pursuing that course; though I believe that he . . . will be swamped in the surf at last." As for Brown personally, Stephens stated, "I have a very high regard for him, and esteem him as a man of very great ability, as well as integrity. He is, in every respect, entitled to high rank among our public men and statesmen."

When the interviewer asked Stephens if he believed Brown had been taken to the "High Mountain" of temptation while in Washington, he replied that he did not. Instead of a "Mountain of Temptation" it was more likely that the former governor had been taken to the rim of the "Bottomless Pit" from which he could view the horrors "where his *fears* instead of his *hopes* were operated upon." It was fear of what might come, not promise of reward, that had prompted Brown. "His

1 McLeod Collection.
2 Stephens to E. M. Chapin, March 29, 1867, in Stephens Papers, Emory.

course has been taken more from apprehension awakened by threats of Attainder, of Confiscation, and the thousands of other ills."

When questioned about the charge that near the close of the war Brown was ready to make a separate peace, Stephens declared "No, sir, never!" He thought "no truer man to our Cause lived, while its standard was up, than Brown." Such charges were "utterly untrue." Brown and Davis were at times in "very decided disagreement," Stephens admitted, "but the difference was on what was the best and surest way to success." Brown often endeavored to secure a change of policy, but "never for a moment" did he cherish "the dastardly idea attributed to him. When the principle involved in the conflict failed to be maintained by arms," Stephens thought Brown "gave up, not only the cause, but the principle itself, as lost. His public acts, since, have been governed by this conviction."[3] This interview was not made public until 1870.

From outside Georgia, Brown received a number of messages of approval. On March 22, 1867, William G. "Parson" Brownlow, governor of reconstructed Tennessee, wrote: "I take this occasion to say to you that I have attentively perused your late published letter and pronounce it the most sensible and patriotic document I have seen from the South since the surrender of Lee before Richmond. You and those who act with you may be abused for a time, but you will finally be sustained. All who wished to avoid the horrors of *confiscation* had better act with you."[4]

Some of the northern press also heaped upon Brown great praise for the bold stand he had taken. "The value to 'a state lately in rebellion' of one able, sensible, moderate, and conscientious public man is beyond reckoning," declared the New York *Daily Tribune*. "Such a man ex-Gov. Brown of Georgia appears to be." The editor was particularly pleased that Brown had "found out" the Democrats and wanted nothing more to do with them. "There are many Browns in this world," the editor concluded, "but ex-Gov. Brown of Georgia is, for the present, the flower of the family." The editor believed that the thousands who thought as did Brown, "needing only a spokesman and a leader," would

---

3 Quoted in Alexander H. Stephens, *A Constitutional View of the Late War Between the States*, 2 vols. (Philadelphia, 1868, 1870), II, 654–58.
4 McLeod Collection.

gladly give their support to "a policy which means peace and prosperity. They want bread, and not revenge; peace, and not another desperate revolt; status in the Union, and not a eternal abiding out in the cold. Brown speaks their mind now; but give them a chance, and we shall hear them speaking it for themselves."[5]

This statement was correct except for Georgians not wanting revenge. They did want revenge for their physical and material suffering, but most of them no doubt realized they could not get it. What they needed was leaders who could convince them of the necessity of accepting what they could get. If at this point Brown had received the support of other prominent leaders the path might have been much less difficult.

Few Georgians at the time gave their former governor credit for his true motives in taking such an advanced position. They could see in him nothing but a selfish, dishonest, scheming traitor, who had been bought by his former enemies. In this they were completely in error. Brown had become a realist, who, regardless of how much he loved the past, recognized the fact that it must be accepted as past, Georgia was in the depths of ruin and despair. She needed help and there could be no advantage in remaining out of the Union. Turmoil and uncertainty would not attract capital for economic restoration and expansion. Neither was there a chance to be readmitted to the Union except through conformity to congressional demands. Delay would only increase, not lessen, those demands. Then why not accept what could be had and start rebuilding from that foundation. The only hope of avoiding Radical reconstruction was in the possibility that northern public opinion would not support it. The recent congressional election had proved otherwise.

All arguments to the contrary notwithstanding, Brown's course was the only sensible one, for there could be no reason in blighting the future by adhering to the dead past. If Joe Brown did not sincerely believe the position he was assuming was the best, if not the only, hope for restoring the devastated economy of Georgia and the South, then his action defies explanation. Knowing the voters of Georgia as he did, he could not have expected political reward. And to say that he was interested in saving his own property from possible confiscation was but

5 May 20, 1867.

to place him in the same category with all other property owners, even including Bob Toombs.

By favoring extending the franchise to the Negro, Brown was not expressing concern for the black man. Having belonged to the master class, he was not free from bias. He had no desire to see semiliterate freedmen governing their former masters, but he had confidence in the powers of intelligent leadership. As he saw it, there was no way to prevent extension of the franchise to the blacks, so why not boldly make the concession and then control them. He knew the extent of racial bias, even in the upcountry where Negroes were few. The number of whites disfranchised by the Fourteenth Amendment would be small when compared to the total white population, and even they might soon have their disabilities removed. With skillful leadership, Brown foresaw what actually did happen a few years later. The whites would regain complete dominance, and the blacks would be relegated to political insignificance.

While former Confederates in Georgia denounced their former governor, Congress put the finishing touches on a reconstruction bill (Sherman Bill) which was passed over the president's veto on March 2, 1867. All males, black and white, who were not disfranchised by the Fourteenth Amendment were to register and vote for delegates to state conventions. These conventions must write Negro suffrage into the state constitutions, and the new legislatures must ratify the Fourteenth Amendment. Once the revised constitutions had been ratified by the eligible voters, they were to be submitted to Congress; only after approval by Congress were representatives and senators from the reconstructed states to be seated.

Three weeks later Congress passed the Supplementary Reconstruction Act which provided arrangements for implementing the first act. The late Confederacy, except for Tennessee, was to be divided into five military districts. The generals in command were to supervise the selection of delegates to conventions and the submission of the approved constitutions to Congress. General John Pope was placed in charge of the district composed of Florida, Alabama, and Georgia, with headquarters at Atlanta. A complimentary public dinner was given for the general at the National Hotel on April 12. Following his expression of appreciation for the manner in which he had been re-

ceived in Atlanta, numerous toasts were read. One declared: "Reconstruction—Let it proceed under the Sherman bill without appealing to
the Supreme Court of the United States—the arbiter of civil rights,
and not political rights." Brown replied, pledging his support of reconstruction measures and urging others to do likewise. He did not
believe the court would hear a Georgia petition that these measures
be nullified.[6]

Brown and Pope became friends immediately, and the general was
soon a guest in the former governor's home. "Pa" gave a "big dinner"
at 4 o'clock for General Pope and other distinguished guests, wrote
Franklin Brown in his diary on May 9. It was rumored that Brown
would use his influence to persuade Pope to remove Governor Jenkins
from office. This was not true, Peterson Thweatt assured Alexander
Stephens, for Brown thought it would be "a *disaster* to this State for
Gov. Jenkins either to resign or be removed." Thweatt had recently
dined with Brown and had even gone with him to call on General Pope.
"He and Gen. Pope I find on *very good terms*."[7] Many other persons
also *dined* with Brown during the spring of 1867. Although severely
denounced by and isolated from many of his former supporters, he
was by no means deserted. Among the partakers of hospitality in the
Brown home were Generals William Phillips and William T. Wofford
and Judges Erskine, Warner, and Walker.[8]

Brown was always a determined man; severe criticism never caused
him to waver. Once he had taken his stand on reconstruction he intended to convince the people he was correct. Even before Pope took
command, he was engaged in both a private and public campaign in
support of the congressional plan for reconstruction. To George W.
Ashburn of Columbus he wrote "As I feel conscious that I have acted
in the manner which will be most productive of the public good under
all the circumstances, and that no selfish motive or self interest has
controlled me, I can bear with patience the unfair and ungenerous assaults which are made upon me. I neither expect nor desire public
position in the future." Considering his political career at an end, his
only desire was to see the return of "peace, prosperity and stable gov-

6 Atlantic *New Era*, April 14, 1867.
7 Thweatt to Stephens, April 27, 1867, in Stephens Papers, Library of Congress.
8 Franklin Brown Diary, March 13, April 5, May 20, June 1, 6, 1867.

ernment." Henceforth he wished to live and conduct his business as a private law-abiding citizen. He had hope that "upon mature reflection" the people would realize "the propriety of terminating the strife" by compliance with the terms set forth by Congress. "As we now have one common country, with a government fully established, and a Union indissoluble, it should be the object of all to sustain the flag, maintain its credit, and uphold its rightful jurisdiction against every obstruction."[9]

To a citizen of New Albany, Indiana, Brown wrote in a similar vein, but added something for people of the North to consider. He explained that he had "acted from a conscientious conviction of duty," wishing to see this "vexed question" speedily settled forever. As the conquered, the South could hope for nothing better than the Sherman bill, but he warned that the northern conquerors themselves could never attain great prosperity as long as the South lay prostrate and paralyzed. "Under existing circumstances the welfare of the whole country will be best promoted by the prompt acceptance of the terms on our part, in good faith, and a faithful adherence to the pledges contained in the act on your part. We must accept the act as a final settlement, and you must then admit us to representation, and we must all shake hands over past differences. . . . The Government of the United States is now my government; its flag is now my flag."[10]

Brown was equally as eager to stress northern responsibility for acceptance as southern necessity for acquiescences. "My sincere desire is to see the Union restored as speedily as possible," he told the editor of the *Pennsylvania Press,* "and with it amnesty for the past and fraternity and harmony for the future, each section bearing its just share of the burdens and receiving its fair proportion of the benefits of a common government." He had done all within his power to convince the people that once they "faithfully complied" with the terms set by Congress that body would redeem its promise of readmission and that "we shall re-enter with sufficient strength to be respected."[11]

Brown took his message to the public in speeches at Atlanta, March 4; Savannah, April 18; Augusta, April 27; and Milledgeville, June 6. At

9 March 16, 1867, in McLeod Collection.
10 Brown to D. Williams, March 21, 1867, in Hargrett Collection.
11 June 17, 1867, *ibid.*

Atlanta a citizens meeting adopted resolutions urging that restoration be no longer postponed. It had already been delayed "until the interests of the entire people of Georgia are bleeding at every pore." Reason should be substituted for passion and prejudice and Georgia should accept the congressional proposal "without the least hesitation." As the meeting was about to adjourn, Brown conveniently entered the hall. Although he denied any intention or desire to speak, he was soon on the floor. The time had arrived, he declared, when oil should be poured on the troubled waters. When the military should take over the government of Georgia, all punishment would be left to the general's discretion. The great trouble with most of the people, he exclaimed, was that they failed to face "the fact that we are *a conquered people*," totally without power to resist any terms that might be imposed by the conqueror.

To the accusation that he was being inconsistent Brown's reply was that "I admit it." Born in the Calhoun country, he had grown up on Calhoun principles of government. But the sword had decided against that doctrine, and "I bow to the decision of the august tribunal that dictates between States and nations in the last resort"; therefore, he was no longer a secessionist. True, that was inconsistency, but he thought the man who remained consistent regardless of circumstances acts very unwisely. To be disfranchised, as he himself was, was humiliating but not degrading. It was never degrading to accept what could not be avoided. If people could abrogate the Ordinance of Secession, abolish slavery, and repudiate the war debt as Georgians had already done, then surely they could "take the balance of the dose" without making the ugly faces some were making. "Let us put a little sugar-coating around it, and swallow the pill at once, and be done with it—waiving the 'dignity' for a time as we have so often been compelled to do." All who remained in this country rather than migrate chose the government as their government. They owed it their allegiance. "There is neither manliness, dignity, nor good faith in any other course." [12]

Before Brown made his next major speech, which would be to the people of Savannah on April 18, several important events had occurred.

12 Atlanta *Daily Intelligencer*, March 9, 1867.

General Pope assumed command of his district; Governor Jenkins petitioned the U.S. Supreme Court for an injunction restraining the secretary of war, General Grant, and General Pope from enforcing the Reconstruction Acts; Senator John Sherman introduced a bill to remove the disabilities of Brown and Governor Robert M. Patton of Alabama; and Brown learned of an effort being made in New York to bring a damage suit against him for the seizure of Fort Pulaski, the Augusta Arsenal, and the Dahlonega Mint.

The rumor of a possible damage suit naturally disturbed the former governor, although he saw no probability of its being successful. He immediately dispatched a letter to Secretary of State William H. Seward explaining the conditions under which this federal property was seized and the ultimate disposal of all materials acquired. If his actions constituted an offense against the United States, they had been "forgiven by the President's pardon to me and forgotten by the amnesty." Brown suspected that the threat was for the purpose of annoying him, yet he wished to be certain. He requested Seward to state whether or not this matter had "come to your knowledge" or been approved by the government. Seward's reply simply stated that he had submitted Brown's letter to the President.[13]

News that Senator Sherman had introduced a resolution to remove Brown's disabilities brought forth numerous charges of bargain between the two whereby Brown would push acceptance of the Sherman bill in the South, and Sherman would secure the removal of Brown's disfranchisement. Although without foundation, these charges were embarrassing to Brown's efforts toward reconstruction. On March 21, 1867, he expressed to Sherman his appreciation of the expression of confidence and personal kindness implied. Yet he wished to stress that it was completely unexpected. "If it is thought best for the public interest that I be relieved Congress will no doubt do it. If this is doubted by any considerable number of members, I beg you to withdraw the resolution so far as it applies to me." He had anticipated all kinds of bitter assaults and charges of "all sorts of bargain and sales," but he had the private satisfaction of knowing that he had not been influenced

13 Brown to Seward, April 13, 1867, in Hargrett Collection; Seward to Brown, May 7, 1867, in McLeod Collection.

by improper motives; therefore, he did not "suffer under the lash of my revilers."[14]

Brown spoke in Savannah on April 18. He had met General Pope, he stated, and thought Georgia very fortunate in having such a "liberal minded, enlightened and highly cultivated gentleman" in command. He saw no probability of good, however, from Governor Jenkins' legal action. The quickest action the Supreme Court could be expected to take on the governor's petition would be "next December." Then with the "usual demurrers, pleas and answers," no decision could be expected under two years, probably three or four. Meanwhile, should Georgia, relying upon a favorable decision by the Court, refuse to act, the congressional policy would be carried out "to our utter ruin." Even if the Court's decision should be favorable, what effect would it have upon Congress? The decision in the *Milligan* case had been ignored on the ground that it involved a *"political question"* over which the Court had no jurisdiction.[15] "I regard the whole movement of the appeal to the Supreme Court as ill-advised and unfortunate, tending to excite hopes that can never be realized, costing the State a large sum of money, and imperiling everything by probably inducing our people to reject the terms rendered by Congress." What good could result? What prosperity could be expected under such conditions? What Georgia needed was "peace, stability of Government, and capital for development."

Brown denied that he had the slightest knowledge of Senator Sherman's intention to introduce his relief resolution, yet he would not say that he was indifferent on the matter. Should Congress see fit to grant relief, "I shall properly appreciate their action." He also denied that he ever intended again to seek public office. "I therefore say, I do not want your votes. But I am no idle spectator."

To the blacks present Brown stressed that since they now had equal political rights they must also accept responsibilities. Rights

14 *Congressional Globe*, 40th Cong., 1st Sess., 118; Brown to John Sherman, March 21, 1867, in John Sherman Papers, Library of Congress.
15 The court eventually dismissed the Jenkins case on the same ground. Writing from Washington, Jenkins urged the people of Georgia not to acquiesce but to adopt "firm but temperate" refusal and "patient, manly endurance of military government" until "better counsels prevail at the Federal capital." *C. R. Ga.*, VI, 71–76.

were "neither bread nor meat"; they only protected one in his labor. The right to participate in government carried with it the duty to pay taxes for its support. Since the freedmen were now enfranchised, the South, when readmitted, would be entitled to twenty additional seats in Congress. This strength, once present, would be courted, not despised, by northern politicians. Reconstruction, once completed, would bring relief to "the down trodden South," and the threat of panic in the North. To the whole country it would eventually bring "unity, peace, prosperity and happiness. . . . My motto is *action, reconstruction, and relief.*"[16]

At Augusta on April 27, Brown was introduced by Mayor Foster Blodgett, who assured the people that whatever advice Brown might give them would be in accordance with what the former governor honestly and conscientiously believed best for the common country. Brown began by addressing himself to those who were denouncing him, especially the "small journalists and newspaper scribblers . . . who, unable to meet an opponent in the forum of reason, and maintain their cause by argumentation, use no weapons of assault but abuse and slander, and when vanquished, like the famous cuttle fish, cover their retreat by muddying the water with the filthy slime they emit behind them." He would not attempt to judge "how much and how little good such men have done the country." Instead, he wished to appeal to the reason of the sober, thinking, laboring men of the country, "who rejoice with it in its prosperity, and suffer with it in its adversity—the bone and sinew of the country."

In 1861, Brown related, the South claimed to be no longer in the Union. When the Union denied this claim "we went to war." Had the South "whipped them," the South would have remained out of the Union. Georgians claimed they seceded. To be consistent they should still claim to be out of the Union, yet, instead, they claim they are in the Union and entitled to all rights and privileges and "arraign the consistency of secessionists who are in favor of the plan of reconstruction laid down by Congress. . . . You took up arms against the United States, and swore to support another Government, and said the Union was dissolved; and yet when we failed, you resumed your allegiance to

16 Atlanta *Daily New Era*, April 24, 1867.

the United States. You said that it was *no rebellion*. Since that you have gone and laid your hands upon the Bible and taken the oath which said it was one. Are you consistent?"

Suppose it now be admitted, as things stood in 1861, that the South was out of the Union, then Georgians had no rights, and could be re-admitted only on such terms as might be offered. "Now take that horn of the dilemma—how do we stand?" Now a conquered people, the laws of nations gave no protection against such terms as the conqueror might wish to impose. Indefinite military rule could be applied. What right did Georgia have to petition the Supreme Court or demand any other privilege? "None."

Taking the other horn of the dilemma, that the northern view was correct, then the attempt at secession was void and "we were in rebel-lion, and each of us who took up arms was guilty of treason, and liable to be hanged." Furthermore, the crime of treason carried with it the additional penalty of confiscation of property. "We either did go out, and the Government had the right to deal with us as a conquered people; or else we did not secede, and we were rebels and liable to be dealt with as rebels." Regardless of which position was taken, the South still had no choice but to accept such terms as were offered.[17]

In a speech at Milledgeville on June 6 Brown made an appeal to "reason and common sense." Those with "common misfortunes and common dangers" should not spend their time quarreling among them-selves. Past differences and party strife should be buried in the interest of what was best to do now. As for himself, he belonged to "the re-construction of Georgia," to which he thought all other Georgians should belong. He stood for the Sherman bill which he interpreted to mean "prompt reconstruction in strict good faith." Not until after re-admission to the Union did he propose to become affiliated with any political party. He would then be inclined toward "whatever progres-sive national party shows the greatest inclination to stand by principles and deal justly by us." In making his selection of party he would not be governed by past prejudices, for in looking backward "I think I see that the South acted unwisely. In order to maintain consistency, we took the hull and gave the North the kernel." The South opposed the tariff and internal improvements, yet it had both. "We gave the North

17 Augusta *Daily Press*, April 29, 1867.

all the substantial or material benefits, and in return, they generally gave us the Presidency and a large share of the offices." The children of the South, who were put "upon their own energies" as a result of the abolition of slavery, "may live to see that the war with all its troubles, destruction and privation, was a national blessing in disguise."

Brown urged all blacks to register and vote for convention. There must be no war between the two races; it would lead both to the verge of ruin, but the blacks would suffer greatest. In numbers, training, and experience the whites would have the advantage. The whites were accustomed to managing for themselves; the blacks to dependence upon others. Such a condition could not be changed at once. "Mark this," Brown advised the freedmen, "and when any man, whether from the North or South, whether white or black, encourages you to quarrel with us, or to make war upon us, recollect he is neither your friend nor our friend, nor the friend of the country, but he is controlled by selfishness, and has some bad object to accomplish."[18]

Wishing the maximum publicity for the cause he was now promoting, Brown granted an interview to a reporter of the Cincinnati *Commercial* on May 7, 1867. The reporter, never having seen the former governor, expected to find "a man of not less than sixty, big whiskers, cross, sour and self-willed." He had formed this image, he wrote, largely from reading Brown's correspondence with President Davis. Instead, he found "a man of about forty-five, tall, straight, with the most amiable of human countenances, and a smile that many a charming woman might borrow and wear to her advantage." His graying hair was "rather long, but not profuse." A "high, broad, intellectual forehead . . . overarched a pair of dark blue eyes, capable of the genuine Calhoun stare of wildness or of the mildest benevolence of expression, at the owner's pleasure, and a smooth-shaved face, strongly marked with furrows of thought rather than of time."

The reporter thought Brown might well be mistaken for an "educated Southern Methodist preacher—one of the divines who earnestly and conscientiously believed and preached that slavery was ordained of God, and who, if he didn't think Abolitionists would all go to hell, certainly never expected to meet one in heaven." The reporter realized immediately that he was not in the presence of a "negative or milk-and-

18 Milledgeville *Federal Union*, June 11, 1867.

water person, who seeks to compromise every quarrel with a half-way proposition, and has a holy horror of extremes." No conservatism was reflected in the governor's countenance. He could have as easily been a Wendell Phillips in Boston as a John C. Calhoun in South Carolina. The reporter was also much impressed with Brown's conversational powers and charming unreserved manner. With simple candor Brown spoke of his days as a secessionist. He spoke not of repentance but treated the matter as a big game at which he lost. After it was over he was ready to "hand in his checks."

What Brown related in the interview covered familiar ground, but he was so impressive in the telling, the reporter concluded that under the leadership of men like Brown, the South could be reconstructed; therefore, disabilities set forth in the Fourteenth Amendment should be removed from such men as quickly as possible. "One Brown is worth to the South and the nation more than a million Hunnicutts or Honey-pots, or whatever that crazy Virginia devil's name may be.[19] He is worth more than a standing army, or a dozen acts of Congress; and he is as good a Union man today as there is in the United States. No mistake about that."[20]

Judging by his speaking engagements, Brown was very active during the spring and summer of 1867. Ben Hill alone of the more prominent Georgia leaders saw fit to attempt publicly to counteract Brown's arguments. Speaking in Atlanta on July 18, Hill declared there was never any difficulty in detecting a dying nation. There were many symptoms of pending death, but the leading one was "*disregard* of the fundamental law of that government. . . . I charge before Heaven and the American people this day, that every evil by which we have been afflicted is attributable directly to the violation of the Constitution. . . . I declare to you that there is no remedy for us, and no hope to escape the threatened evils, but in *adhering to the Constitution*." Hill explained that his remarks would not be directed at anyone "individually," for he would cooperate with even his bitterest enemy in preserving the Constitution. "But if I have an enemy, and have a vindictive spirit and desired him to become forever infamous, I could ask no more of him

19 For the extreme radical activities of James W. Hunnicutt see Hamilton J. Eckenrode, *The Political History of Virginia During the Reconstruction* (Baltimore, 1904), 67 ff.
20 Cincinnati *Commercial*, May 7, 1867.

than that he should support the hellish schemes of those who are now seeking to subvert the Constitution and destroy our liberty. He is digging a grave for himself which posterity will never water with a tear. Let him alone." As for himself, Hill exclaimed, he would respect his obligations under his amnesty oath but "I will not bind my soul to a new slavery, to hell, by violating it." He made no mention of his own effort to secure a pardon!

Hill charged that the military bills would produce war between the races. Persons who would accept disfranchisement of the most intelligent population because it was dictated by those not affected by it had no conscience. Those same persons who took the oath to support the Constitution knowing that they planned to violate it immediately were "not fit to be trusted by any animal, dog or man! Such a man would betray his pointer, and such a woman sell her poodle!" Hill also denounced those who would accept the military bills to save their own property. "It is like going out into the highway and surrendering your purse to the robber to keep him from taking it! . . . Confiscation is the law of enemies in war, and in peace it is the law of robbers." He could advise persons to register but not vote for a convention. "Never go half way with a traitor, nor compromise with treason or robbery. If they hold a convention, vote against ratification."[21]

Most of what Hill said was aimed directly at Brown. Probably no better presentation of the two opposite positions could have been made than the speeches of these antagonists of long standing. But with all of his wit and ranting, Hill offered no solution to the problems of reconstruction; neither did he make an attempt to repudiate Brown's explanation that either the South went out of the Union or it did not. If out, it could not expect to be readmitted unless it met requirements. If it did not go out, then all who participated in the late war were traitors subject to the noose.

Throughout the spring and summer of 1867 Brown was in communication with Congressman William D. Kelley of Pennsylvania. Only one Kelley letter has been found, but the general contents of others can be determined by Brown's replies. Uneasy lest Congress should add other requirements for reconstruction, he urged Kelley to use his influence to prevent what would be considered bad faith. Brown

21 Atlanta *Daily Intelligencer*, July 18, 1867.

had promised the people that acceptance of the terms already proposed would be a "*finality*." No action had been taken on Sherman's resolution to remove the disabilities of Brown and Governor Patton of Alabama, and Brown continued to hope there would not be for the present. When he heard that Patton had gone to Washington to urge passage of the resolution, he urged that his own name be withdrawn from consideration at that time. To remove his disabilities, Brown believed, would "tend to retard the reconstruction movement in the South"; therefore, it would be bad policy on the part of Congress.

Brown also insisted that Kelley use his influence to get some government printing for Dr. Samuel Bard, editor of the Atlanta *New Era*, the most spirited reconstruction paper in Georgia. The editor could also use some extra funds to expand the activities of his publication. Brown cordially commended Bard to Kelley and any northern friends who might be interested. "Dr. Bard fully comprehends the new era under which we live, and, laying aside obsolete ideas and the political dogmas which produced the war, his course will be onward & upward with the march of events."

As in most of his other correspondence, Brown stressed to Kelley how hard he himself was working for the cause. "Notwithstanding the known and I may say active opposition of some of our former leaders, such as Cobb and Ben Hill, and the silence of others, as Stephens and Johnson, we intend to carry the State for reconstruction upon the Sherman Bill and the Supplement. Thus far I have the public aid of no man of decided prominence, but it is not the first time I have had to carry the State over the opposition of the newspapers and politicians. Give us a fair opportunity and all will come out right."[22]

On July 11, Herschel V. Johnson ended the silence noted by Brown. In a letter to James G. Westmoreland and others he admitted a reluctance to put his views in writing. He had yielded under pressure from friends who felt that those who had honored him in previous years now had a right to know his views. He denounced the Sherman Bill and all who would willingly accept it. He denounced Congress for assuming that it was supreme, "the Executive a nullity and the judiciary 'a nose of wax,' and that the States, or the people thereof, are entitled to such rights only as Congress might permit."

22 Brown to Kelley, May 20, July 1, 9, 1867, in Hargrett Collection.

Johnson disagreed with those who advised nonparticipation in the election of a convention. Failure to participate might be classed as *consent*. All should register and vote against a convention. Should a convention be held, those who voted against it would not be obligated to ratify its work. But those who refused to vote placed themselves at the mercy of the Radicals. His advice was to vote but vote against the Radical proposals. To consent would make ruin inevitable; nothing worse than ruin could result from rejection. "Property and life are nothing without good government. We bequeath to our posterity a heritage of woe, if we surrender them to the mercies of despotism." He saw no chance that Congress would of its own will "ameliorate pending issues." The only hope was from possible pressure brought by the people of the North. "They can, if they will, save liberty; we cannot, without their co-operation. Our oppressors can put chains upon us, if they will, seeing us impotent and prostrate at their feet; let us *consent* to it never. . . . They can rob us of freedom, but let us never *agree* to be *slaves*. They may overthrow *constitutional liberty*; but let us never *embrace* their *despotism*."[23] Johnson made no mention of Brown.

It was noticeable that Brown never advocated going beyond what was required by Congress. He considered himself a realist, not a radical. This made him suspect by both sides. In mid-June, 1867, he received a letter from Henry M. Turner, Negro minister and political leader. Judging from Brown's reply, the Reverend Turner wished to know what the Negro might expect out of reconstruction. Brown explained that his own views had been clearly expressed in his recent Milledgeville speech. He stood for the Sherman bill, but could see no possible good from affiliating with any national party. A convention should be held, and that body should comply with the terms prescribed by Congress. The people should then ratify the work of the convention and elect to Congress good, sensible men who would represent both races. In all matters both races must seek harmony and understanding. The responsibility resting upon the members of the black race was very heavy. Persons on both sides would attempt to mislead and use blacks for selfish purposes. There should be no misstep, for missteps were difficult to correct. Brown explained that he wished to see the

23 Atlanta *Daily Intelligencer*, July 16, 1867.

black race prosper, but he never expected to ask for black votes; consequently, he could have no motive for misleading them.

Reverend Turner had inquired about the possibility of confiscation and redistribution of lands. If confiscation came, Brown replied, he himself would be just one among many sufferers. The black race, however, should not expect to profit, for all such property would be needed to pay the Union war debt and pensions to soldiers. The black man would still be forced to work for a living. White people of the North would first satisfy their own interests before looking to the interests of the southern blacks. "This is human nature as you very well know." Neither should the blacks expect pleasure or profit from exchanging landowners with whom they were raised for strangers who had little sympathy with their habits and needs.[24]

By midsummer Hill and Brown had become the spokesmen for the two sides to the controversy. Beginning on June 19, 1867, and continuing through August 1, Hill published in the Augusta *Chronicle and Sentinel* a series of letters under the heading "Notes on the Situation." It soon became evident that a considerable portion of the series would be devoted to an attack upon Brown. The latter then requested that he be permitted to reply to these "ill natured assaults."[25] The *Chronicle and Sentinel* was no longer edited by Brown's "peace movement" friend Nathan S. Morse. In March, 1866, he had sold the paper to Ambrose R. Wright and Henry P. Moore and left for the North. The new owners had not been friendly to Morse's peace policy; neither could they be classed as friends of Brown. In their first issue (March 24, 1866) they had announced: "We disclaim all responsibility for the sins of the past, and ask to be judged by our conduct in the future."[26]

Editor Henry Moore granted Brown's request for space, but he was not happy about it. To his readers he explained that "we oppose and condemn the policy and course which Gov. Brown has seen fit to pursue." His own views, he said, corresponded with those of Stephens, Jenkins, Hill, and Johnson. "In publishing Gov. Brown's 'review,' we abate neither jot nor tittle of these views. We simply extend to the

24 June 17, 1867.
25 Brown to Editor, July 22, 1867, in Hargrett Collection.
26 For the history of the *Chronicle and Sentinel* see Earl Bell and Kenneth Crabbe, *The Augusta Chronicle, Indomitable Voice of Dixie* (Athens, 1960).

Governor the use of our columns to destroy, if he can, the impregnable position within which Mr. Hill has fortified himself."[27] In reality this exchange between Hill and Brown was but another battle in the old war of words; the only ammunition available had already been used many times, for there was nothing new to say on the subject. Hill's "Notes" were a long profound discussion of the well-worn topic of state-federal relations, interspersed with vilification of Brown and the reconstructionists. He led off by denouncing those who "urged us into secession as the only peaceful method of securing our rights" and then later "led us to subjugation as the only method of escaping military despotism." He thought General Pope "must have felt an almost nauseating pity for the poor men who gathered around him in Atlanta, and forgetting the history of their fathers and the character of our institutions, welcomed in feasting and rejoicing, the inauguration of military despotism." If the policy advocated by these depraved reconstructionists should be put into operation, complete anarchy would follow. No pen could adequately picture the horror that would "spread over the land during this reign of disorder, discord, and decay." Commerce would be prostrate, industry paralyzed, and legal protection and restraint destroyed. Adults would be demoralized, children starved, while robbers and assassins prowled the land.

There was but one way to avert such horrible destruction, Hill explained: "Trust in no party, listen no longer to men who have deceived you; who have been false to every promise, faithless to every principle, and treacherous to every government. Return. Oh! my deluded and prostrate countrymen, return to the Constitution! It alone is safe. . . . Let us resolve to accept whatever is according to its provisions, and reject every thing that is contrary thereto, and then *fear nothing*." Without referring to Brown by name, Hill next took up the arguments set forth in the former governor's February letter and denounced them at every point. The people had been robbed by foes and "friends," Hill charged, and a few of those "friends" had shown great "talent to make money while their dupes showed a will to lose blood." These "friends" might well fear the confiscation of property. They might also wish to see destruction of the archives which contained the

27 Moore to Brown, July 21, 31, 1867, in Hargrett Collection; Augusta *Chronicle and Sentinel*, August 1, 1867.

records of their wrong doings. The Confederacy had not been conquered by military might but was "crushed by *ideas* . . . born in treachery and disappointment." Some who had been most active in destroying the Union later became most active in destroying the Confederacy they had helped to organize. "And these are now the favorites in the South with the Radicals of the North."[28]

Since Brown had made several major speeches after the publication of his February letter, he had nothing new to say on the subject of reconstruction, yet, as was his custom, he continued to talk; he could not permit an adversary to go unchallenged. In his "Review" of Hill's "Notes" he dwelt at length upon Hill's inconsistencies, lack of loyalty, bad judgment, and failure to make maximum contribution to the cause. He castigated the former Confederate Senator for failure to face reality and an attempt to lead the people along a false road of hope. He then stressed what he believed to be the only hope. Since Congress exercised the "power of the conqueror," its requirements must be met. This alone could lead to restoration and prosperity.[29]

Henry W. Grady was quoted as later saying of Hill's "Notes": "In my opinion they stand alone as the profoundest and most eloquent political essays ever penned by an American. They were accepted as the voice of the South, uttering her protest and her plea. . . . Even now they stir the blood and kindle the pulses of the most phlegmatic reader, but this is but a hint of the sensation they produced when they were printed."[30] It is noticeable that Grady, the champion of the "New South," stopped short of evaluating the contribution these "Notes" made toward solving the problems of Georgia in that critical period.

The registration of prospective voters began in April, 1867. Even many conservative individuals and newspapers urged those not disqualified to register. The results showed 95,214 whites and 93,457 Negroes. A supplemental registration a few months later increased the total to 102,411 whites and 98,507 blacks. The heaviest registration of blacks was in the cities, to which many had drifted after the war. In Atlanta alone of the larger cities did white registrants constitute a majority.[31]

28 These "Notes" are also found in Hill, *Hill*, 730 ff.
29 *Chronicle and Sentinel*, August 1–9, 1867.
30 Quoted in Hill, *Hill*, 51–52
31 Thompson, *Reconstruction*, 186–88.

An election was held October 29–November 2, 1867. Voting was on whether or not to hold a convention and for delegates to such a convention. Only 106,410 votes were cast and 102,283 of that number favored a convention. In the black counties very few whites voted—only seven in Baldwin, three in McIntosh, and one in Jefferson. There exists some disagreement among experts as to the classification of the delegates selected. Mildred Thompson classified the 167 elected as 12 conservative whites, 37 Negroes, 9 carpetbaggers, and the remainder scalawags.[32] In a more recent study Elizabeth Nathans makes a somewhat different analysis based upon voting records on measures that came before the convention. Of the 165 delegates who took their seats, she classes 46 as staunch Democrats. Another 20, "probably elected as Democrats," usually voted with the more radical Republicans. The remaining 99, which included the Negro members, were Republicans.[33] From any view, one fact is clear: Negroes and carpetbaggers were much in the minority.

The convention, although strongly Republican, would not prove extremely radical. It was scarcely as bad as pictured by the Milledgeville *Southern Recorder*: "A political bastard, sired by military power upon the dam, negro ignorance, crossed with white perjury and cowardly policy."[34] Among the Negro members were a few of ability, though, in some cases, shady character. Foremost among them was the Reverend Henry M. Turner of Macon, who had previously been in communication with Brown, Tunis G. Campbell of McIntosh County, and Aaron Alpeoria Bradley of Savannah who was said to have a prison record.[35] The editor of the Columbus *Daily Sun* declared "We don't like Turner, for we regard him as the worst man black or white in the State except for Joseph Brown."[36] The vicious attacks made upon Negro delegates in general and the comparison of Brown with them was indicative of the degree of racial bias and the low status of the former governor in the minds of many Georgia whites.

While further infuriating irreconcilable Democrats, Brown had

32 *Ibid.*, 189.
33 Elizabeth Studley Nathans, *Losing the Peace, Georgia Republicans and Reconstruction, 1865–1871* (Baton Rouge, 1968), 56–57.
34 February 18, 1868.
35 For sketches of these three, see E. Merton Coulter, *Negro Legislators in Georgia During the Reconstruction Period* (Athens, 1968).
36 July 20, 1867.

disappointed the leaders of the newly formed Republican party. With
his decision in favor of strong support of the congressional plan, they
had expected him to become a full-fledged Republican and assume the
lead in forming a political alliance between the newly enfranchised
blacks and the yeoman white farmers. Brown did neither. He favored
going no farther than Congress demanded, and instead of courting
votes he lectured the blacks on the responsibilities which their new
status required them to assume. He urged support of the congressional
plan, but he made it clear he was not affiliated with any political party.
He would play the field and await developments.

The convention assembled in Atlanta's city hall on December 9,
1867. It had been scheduled for Milledgeville, but was moved to Atlanta
when General Pope learned that adequate accommodations for Negro
members were not available in the capital city. This was a first step in
the removal of the capital to Atlanta. J. H. Nisbet wrote Brown from
Milledgeville, urging that the convention not be moved to Atlanta. It
would not benefit Atlanta and would injure Milledgeville. He feared
ultimate removal of the capital which would ruin property values in
Milledgeville. Atlanta could grow great without it.[37] Brown did not
intervene; he favored Atlanta as the future capital.

As the delegates assembled, an unfriendly correspondent of the
New York *Herald* reported: "Without exaggerating, I can say that a
more seedy looking body of men never assembled together in Georgia.
As the men warmed themselves by the stove, the scene was decidedly
rich. Unshaven, uncombed, unwashed, and in most cases very dirtily
dressed, stood and set the legislators of the State, deep in conversation
which was only interrupted by the continual squirting of tobacco juice
into small tin spittoons, of which there are over two hundred scattered
over the room."[38] Few members of the convention were well known
throughout the state; none, of course, had held prominent office before
the war. To bitter former Confederates it appeared that the bottom
rail of the fence had reached the top. Brown, though not a member, was
to exercise considerable influence. J. R. Parrott of Cartersville was
chosen president. This was the same gentleman who claimed credit
for arranging Brown's first meeting with President Johnson. Brown

37 September 27, 1867, in McLeod Collection.
38 Quoted in Augusta *Daily Constitutionalist*, December 20, 1867.

no doubt exerted some influence in the selection. He was reported to have told a correspondent of the New York *World* some time before the selection that Parrott would be chosen. The correspondent expressed an opinion that "Joe Brown is a demagogue and a deep one . . . He will manage to out-wit all the hungry office-seekers and come in winner."[39]

The general picture of the convention, as he saw it, caused the editor of the Rome *Weekly Courier* to come forth with a bit of hate-inspired humor:

> Parrott in the Chair, Monkey on the floor,
> Scattered round the hall, five and twenty more,
> Hundred odd white skunks, mean as they can be
> That the *tout ensemble* of this Menagerie.
> Way off in the corner is the keeper of the show,
> A-balancin' accounts. Name is Snaky Joe.[40]

After completing organization, the convention adjourned on December 24, but the members went home without Christmas money. No money had been appropriated to pay the expenses of the convention. General Pope ordered State Treasurer John Jones to pay out forty thousand dollars from such funds as were available. Jones refused because the governor had issued no warrant for such payment. There the matter stood when General George Meade succeeded General Pope on January 6, 1868. Meade ordered Governor Jenkins to issue the warrant. Jenkins refused, explaining that the convention had been called under federal law and could not be paid from state funds. On January 13 Meade removed Jenkins and Jones from office and appointed Brigadier General Thomas H. Ruger, governor, and Captain Charles F. Rockwell, treasurer. Jenkins immediately left for Washington carrying with him all the money in the Treasury. When Rockwell took over, he could find only ten cents but he soon secured funds elsewhere.[41]

Brown had already begun to apply the brakes to check the extremists. On December 23, 1867, he informed Brigadier General Wagner Swayne of the Freedmen's Bureau just how far he was willing to go. Swayne had made some kind of request. Brown expressed regret at

39 January 23, 1868.
40 February 28, 1868.
41 Avery, *History of Georgia*, 378–79; Thompson, *Reconstruction*, 179–180; Alan Conway, *The Reconstruction of Georgia* (Minneapolis, 1966), 156–57.

not being able to go along with the request, and then made a definite
statement of his position. He would sanction no test oaths or proscription of any group of whites in the new constitution. If there was to be
universal suffrage, "let us have it pure and simple." If all blacks over
twenty-one were to have the privilege of voting then so should all
whites of like age, regardless of past political opinions or participation
in the war. He supported the reconstruction policy set forth by Congress, but was "not prepared to go further than Congress has gone."
To do so, in his opinion would be both "wrong in principle" and a
"most wretched policy."[42]

By the time the convention reconvened early in January, 1868,
Brown had received from "a respectable number of members" an invitation to address that body. He spoke on January 9. The friends of
reconstruction, restoration and peace, he announced, "anxiously desire
that your action may be characterized by wisdom, moderation, and
justice," conforming to the requirements of Congress but "going no
further than Congress has gone." All "test oaths and all proscription"
should be avoided. The one simple requirement fixed by Congress was
that "you give the freedman, as well as the white man, the elective
franchise." And the only requirement set for the next legislature was
ratification of the Fourteenth Amendment. After the convention met
this single requirement, approved a few needed relief measures, and
changed the mode of election and tenure of some officeholders, "the
sooner you adjourn the better for all."

Brown would call attention to the fact that the opposition was
watching, waiting to take advantage of the first misstep made. Many of
those watching, were "unscrupulous demagogues" who "denounce all
who differ with them as *knaves*, fools, or *perjured* traitors." Although
these men would "spare no pain wilfully to mislead and deceive the
people," there was little to fear from them. But there were other men of
"judgment and sagacity" who did the thinking for the opposition and
had the confidence of the people who were ready to "turn to account all
your excesses and blunders." Therefore, wisdom demanded that the
convention not go one step beyond the requirements of Congress. To do
so would reflect upon Congress and misrepresent the people. Congress

42 Brown to Swayne, December 23, 1867, in Hargrett Collection.

had demanded the franchise for the Negro, but it had not demanded that he be permitted to hold office or sit on juries.

Brown then lectured the blacks at some length, urging them not to attempt to seize more than Congress was guaranteeing them. "You have nothing to gain by making issue with the white race. . . . Do not forget that he who attempts to leap from the bottom to the top of the ladder at one bound is certain to fall—clinch it step by step, and you may hope to stand."

As to disfranchisement, Brown pointed out that the Sherman bill prohibited certain whites, him included, from voting "in all elections to any office" under the provisional governments; therefore, so long as the state government was "provisional" they could not vote. There the prohibition stopped. No limit beyond that point was required by Congress. Personally, he would not support a provision that would disfranchise any white man, unless he be a lunatic or felon.

If Georgia Negroes came under the influence of northern men, Brown charged it would be because the opposition refused to treat them with "kindness and conciliation." He further charged that those who refused to participate in the recent election were seeking to give control to the Negroes. But in spite of this "we came very near electing a majority of conservative moderate men to the convention." He believed that if all elected members were present there actually would be such a majority. But a number of "weak-nerved" delegates had been deterred from taking their seats, so extensive was the claim of white subordination to Negro domination. Brown was now speaking more to the public than to the convention. "When you say that I contemplate the subordination of my own race to the black race, or any other race, or that I favor social equality of the races. I hurl the charge back, branded as an infamous falsehood, and defy you to sustain it from any act or utterance of mine." In connection with the recent election, he said he desired to offer "a word of justice to Gen. Pope." There was no truth in the charge that Pope gerrymandered the state in order to give control to the Negroes. For the purpose of apportionment of seats Pope had used the senatorial districts which had been set up by the constitutional convention of 1865. He challenged Pope's critics to come up with a better method of apportionment, keeping in mind the acts of Congress as guides. All persons accused of crime could have been tried by military commission, yet not one such trial had been held.

As though he were still governor, Brown made a number of specific recommendations to the convention and the next legislature. He suggested that judicial officials be appointed by the governor with approval of the Senate and their length of term be doubled. He wished the terms of governor and state senator increased to four years. Education should also be encouraged. The appropriation for the university should remain at $8,000, and $4,000 should be set aside for separate Negro education. "When I use the term separate institution for the blacks, I intend it to have significance," he exclaimed. "Social equality does not exist, and cannot exist between the two races. The God of nature did not intend it."

Brown further recommended relief for debtors and homestead exemption on at least "one thousand dollars' worth of land." He hoped the day was forever past "when the sheriff, for the debts of the husband, can turn the wife and children helpless beggars into the streets and highways." His enemies had charged that he himself was very rich and very selfish, Brown asserted. If this were true, why would he be interested in relief for the people? "If I were half as selfish as they charge, and half as rich as they represent, it would certainly be to my interest to do away with all relief laws, and to turn loose the sheriffs without mercy upon the people." This would result in much income from lawyers' fees and he could take twenty-five thousand dollars and buy up enough land at sheriffs' sales to be worth half a million dollars by the time his youngest child became of age. But he denied being very wealthy and he hoped he was not as selfish as charged. He thought losses of the war should be divided between creditor and debtor.[43]

The banks were singled out by Brown as being in special need of relief. Many banks that flourished before the war were now in sad plight. Much stock was owned by widows who were faced with loss of everything left them by their husbands. Where banks had issued three dollars in notes for each one in specie, the stockholder was faced

43 Perhaps Brown was correct in denying that he was *very* rich, yet his tax returns for 1867 showed him the owner of 7,425 acres of land scattered over twelve counties, a home worth $15,000, and the Brown Building in Atlanta valued at $25,000. For federal purposes he reported an income of $16,224 and paid $658.42 in taxes. Hargrett Collection.

with not only loss of his stock but an additional amount equal to three times the face value of the stock, for stockholders were "bound for the ultimate redemption of all bills of the bank, in proportion to stock owned by each." No other groups which lost property in the war had any such debt hanging over them. Northern brokers had purchased southern bank notes at depreciated values and were now suing for the full amount. As needed relief, Brown urged passage of an ordinance "declaring all bills of any of the banks of this State, issued during the war in aid of the rebellion, illegal and void, and that no recovery shall ever be had upon said bills, or any of them."[44] Judging from newspaper accounts, a number of Georgians (as well as northerners) were engaged in buying bank notes at a small percentage of their value, claiming they were doing the holder a great favor, even saving him from a threat of starvation, by paying *anything* for these *worthless* bills.[45]

Brown's speech made little impression among the major editors and politicians who had already denounced him as a traitor, but it was not totally without favorable comment. *The Madison News* thought it reflected "great credit upon its author" and indicated the "forsight and statesmanship he possesses." The editor urged all antireconstructionists to give it "careful and attentive perusal." He thought it would "do them good, in the way of blowing dust out of their eyes which Andy Jackson and Ben Hill had been throwing in by the handful." Only by the acceptance of such moderate counsel could more extreme measures be avoided. And extreme measures would make the whites "uneasy and restless" and the Negroes "ridiculous and uncomfortable and there would be no peace. Moderation is the word—universal amnesty and universal suffrage."[46]

From far away Detroit came an expression of thanks from General Pope for Brown's kind remarks about him. The two had developed a close personal friendship. Pope closed all of his letters with regards to Mrs. Brown and daughter, Miss Mary. In this letter the general offered a number of suggestions. He thought the convention should order state and county elections at the same time as the ratification of the constitution. General Meade should then require the same election

44 Atlanta *Daily New Era*, January 11, 1868.
45 See *ibid.*, January 24, 1868, ff.
46 January 25, 1868.

officials to report all results. "He will not refuse, I think I can assure you." Pope also reported that while in Washington he "headed off Butler's bill empowering the convention to fill offices of the Provisional Govt & I think there will be no further interference with the reconstruction acts." He trusted that Brown was satisfied with General Meade, whom he thought a man of ability. The acts of Congress would no doubt be enforced "without partiality or fear." He urged Brown to keep him posted, for he was deeply interested in Georgia, and considered the former governor his best source of information.[47]

In order to understand Brown's interest in relief for banks, which in previous years he had declared should pay every dollar for which they were obligated, it must be remembered that he and the Stephens brothers were paid lobbyists for four Augusta banks. In addition, in February, 1867, he had contracted with the stockholders of the Mechanics Bank to defend them "in any court in Georgia." The fee was $9,000. Apparently the first suit of any consequence against this bank was brought in the United States Circuit Court by Scott, Zerega and Company of New York, which held $60,000 in notes. Two months before Brown was employed by the Mechanics Bank, Scott, Zerega and Company had approached him to take their case. Perhaps the fee asked was too high. Subsequently, Brown was also requested to take a case involving $90,000 in notes. In the early days of the session of the convention the spokesman from the Mechanics Bank stockholders wrote him: "Your influence can accomplish a great deal in the convention, and if you go to work I think there is no doubt but you can get such relief as will exempt stockholders entirely."[48] Brown did go to work preparing his speech of January 9, 1868.

Although the constitutional convention of 1867–1868 was predominantly Republicans, it was so divided between Radicals and moderates as to make a number of compromises necessary. The most aggressive leadership came from the Augusta Radicals who included Rufus Bullock, Foster Blodgett, Benjamin Conley, and John E. Bryant, but

47 Pope to Brown, February 3, 1868, in McLeod Collection.
48 Alfred Baker to Brown, February 27, 29, July 26, September 2, 19, 20, November 10, December 17, 1867; Isaac Scott to Brown, December 21, 1867, in Hargrett Collection and Brown Papers, Atlanta Historical Society. Several times Baker reported that lawyers and upcountry people were eager to know what the banks were paying Brown. He refused to say and hoped Brown would do likewise.

Brown's moderating influence was constantly in evidence. No doubt his speech set the pattern of action that would be followed by the convention.[49] Extreme Radical Republicans, led by John E. Bryant of Augusta, coeditor of the *Loyal Georgian*, proposed disqualification of all former Rebels while guaranteeing to the freedmen both the suffrage and the right to hold office. Homer V. M. Miller, a Democrat, countered with a proposal that followed Brown's suggestion that only criminals and lunatics be denied the franchise. Here the Republicans divided, but the Miller proposal was overwhelmingly approved. Even the great majority of the Negroes voted in the affirmative. Bryant and Bullock were among those who voted in the negative. This settled the question of suffrage but not that of the right to hold office. A conservative proposal was made that would have disqualified all blacks by limiting officeholding to those who had been citizens for seven years. But moderates of both parties realized that, in view of the known attitude of Congress, this would be a hazardous step. The problem was solved by leaving the new constitution silent on the right to hold office.[50]

With the exception of the suffrage, the most discussed topic during the recent campaign had been debtor relief. The economic plight was such that even bankers joined in the demand. Indeed, "reconstruction and relief" became a campaign slogan. Brown had dwelt at length upon this subject in his speech to the convention. This was a subject of minor concern to the blacks; no one had extended credit to them. But the debtor-class whites were in need of relief. Most Republicans felt they had no choice; they must look to the yeoman class for votes, and this was the group most heavily in debt. This was also the group upon which Joe Brown had the greatest influence. Early in the session the convention approved an ordinance temporarily suspending the collection of all debts until permanent action could be taken.[51] It then appointed a Committee on Relief to study the question. This committee made both majority and minority reports. The majority, headed by Rufus Bullock, proposed that all debts contracted prior to June 1, 1865, be declared invalid and the state courts be forbidden to hear suits for their collection. The minority report, filed by Amos T. Aker-

49 The minutes of the convention are printed in *C. R. Ga.*, VI.
50 *C. R. Ga.*, VI, 583–84, 597–99.
51 *Ibid.*, 1932–33.

man and Thomas P. Saffold, suggested that creditors had also suffered and were as much entitled to relief as debtors. Besides, to invali-
date debts would be to impair contracts, which was forbidden by the
federal Constitution. After considerable discussion the Akerman proposal was tabled by a more than two-to-one majority, and the majority
proposal was approved. There were, however, a number of exceptions and limitations, including debts against corporations. Also approved was a homestead exemption of $2,000 and $1,000 in personal
property.[52]

While the proposed relief measure was being considered by the
convention there was considerable confusion in the public mind. The
temporary ordinance had incorporated the same provisions as the permanent proposal, but *without the exceptions*. Should the proposed new
constitution, *with the exceptions*, be approved by the voters it would
apparently supersede the temporary ordinance. But suppose the voters
rejected the new constitution. Would the temporary ordinance remain
in force? This also raised the question as to whether or not General
Meade would approve the convention's exercise of legislative power in
the passage of the earlier ordinance.

Linton Stephens wrote Brown in much concern, urging him to
influence General Meade to make a public statement, clarifying the
situation. Stephens had a number of clients who wished him to begin
suit for collection of debts, and he did not know how far to go in preparing his cases. He also suspected ulterior motives on the part of convention leaders. "The schemes considered in conjunction—the one as
successor to the other—," he charged, "reveal a manifest purpose. That
purpose is to use the unmitigated horrors of the ordinance as a *goad*
to drive the people into the mitigated horrors of the Constitution—to
make the people *accept* the miseries of Purgatory as the only refuge
from the greater miseries of Hell." It was about like a condemned
criminal being forced to go "*voluntarily*" to the gallows to escape being
shot by the guards.

Stephens insisted that he did not wish to say "one word" at present
relative to the constitutional provisions. "I confine my strictures to the
ordinance which is intended to serve the ignoble purpose of a torturing

52 *Ibid.*, 224–25, 306–308, 453–55, 715–22.

goad to the people. Does Gen. Meade recognize its validity?" Since the ordinance then in force applied to debts contracted after June 1, 1865, as well as before, much injustice was being done. As an illustration, many, on whose crops there were liens for supplies furnished, were ignoring such liens and selling their crops without making payments of their debts.

In closing his letter to Brown, Linton Stephens added a most impressive personal note: "We have widely differed in our views as to the best policy to be pursued by our people in regard to the Reconstruction Acts. That difference has been the source of real and deep regret to me; but it has never changed my feelings toward you personally in the least degree. I have often defended your motives while expressing my dissent for your policy. I believe that your course was taken with conscientious conviction that it was the best for our people. In saying this I can scarcely suppose I am saying but what you already believe; but I say it because I wish you to be assured that I do not in the least sympathize with the denunciations which have been so freely hurled at you by others."[53] Among the public men of Georgia, Linton Stephens was no doubt Brown's best friend.

The relief measures incorporated in the new constitution were scarcely a concession to Negroes and carpetbaggers, who were not burdened with debts. Further, Negro leadership was asleep on the job when it permitted the omission of a specific clause on officeholding. But engineer Brown was definitely at the throttle. As ever, he was conscious of the voting power of the common whites who had no love for the blacks. Although there was no sound reason to doubt his sincerity, it was quite evident that "Snaky Joe" did well by himself. From a long range view, it might be that he also did well by his state. This was later admitted by many who condemned him then.

Before the convention adjourned it approved a list of prewar men of prominence whose disabilities the members wished to see removed. This action was probably suggested by Brown. Early in March he received a note from his Pennsylvania friend, Congressman William D. Kelley, stating that the attitude of the House toward southern leaders had softened somewhat. He suggested that the convention prepare a

53 February 10, 1868, in Hargrett Collection.

list of men whose disabilities should be removed and that the name of Judge Dawson A. Walker be included.[54] Kelley and Walker had become acquainted when the judge accompanied Brown to Washington in February, 1867.

J. R. Parrott and Foster Blodgett were sent to Washington with a copy of the new constitution and the list recommended for relief from political disabilities. They found members of Congress reluctant to remove disabilities until it was seen how those recommended would perform in the coming ratification campaign.[55] However, a relief bill was introduced in the House and Brown's name was included. When John A. Logan of Illinois denounced Brown as a mere politician, Kelley sprang to his defense. When this news reached Brown he again became much concerned. He rushed a letter to Kelley thanking him for his kindness, but explaining again that he was not asking for relief. "I can live without it and without office." He had stood firmly by the Reconstruction Acts and done all within his power to make them a success. In doing so, he had "sacrificed social position to a great extent" and "driven off and made bitter enemies of a host of old friends personal and political. No year's work of my life has cost me more difficulty and embarrassment. . . . I have been denounced as a renegade and a deserter of the interests of my race on the one hand; and by a few, brainless, extreme Radicals here who desired me to attempt impossibilities, on the other, as untrue to reconstruction." He had tolerated this abuse, he explained, because of a sincere desire for a restoration of peace and prosperity. Instead of being the target for abuse he could have easily "floated with the current and retained an almost unbounded popularity in the State." He thought he had done his duty and was prepared "to endure the results," but it was discouraging to be denounced within the halls of Congress. Therefore, "I authorize you in your discretion to have my name stricken from the pending bill." He had not requested that his name be placed on the list, yet he would admit that removal of his disabilities would be agreeable. Still he had "no anxiety on the subject" and thought it of "very little consequence to the country."[56]

---

54 Kelley to Brown, March 8, 1868, in McLeod Collection.
55 Atlanta *Daily New Era*, April 18, 1868.
56 Brown to Kelley, March 18, 1868, in Hargrett Collection.

The new Georgia Constitution was not a radical document. Brown had exerted his full influence to prevent the convention from going to the extreme, and in so doing he had disappointed the Radicals, yet not endeared himself to the conservatives. His was the voice of moderation, accepting what Congress demanded, but unwilling to make unnecessary changes. He shrewdly calculated that this was the position the majority of white Georgians must eventually accept, and he intended to emerge as the leader. This is not to say that he played the demagogue. The principal changes in the constitution were not what he wished but what he thought Georgians must accept.

Chapter XIX

Full-fledged Republican

THE CONVENTION set April 20, 1868, as the date for voting on ratification of the constitution and the election of state officials. The Democrats had reorganized their party in convention at Macon in December, 1867. The meeting was not reminiscent of "old times"; absent were Toombs, the Stephens brothers, the Cobbs, and Brown. Ben Hill was selected to preside, and he struck the keynote when he exclaimed: "Let it be in your hearts, in your actions, in your determination, that this fair land in which we were born and reared, ought not, need not and *shall* not be brought under the domination of the negro and destroyed as the heritage of our children." It is interesting to note that among those present and participating in the denunciation of reconstruction measures and all who supported them were Brown's future biographers—Herbert Fielder and Isaac W. Avery—who later became his ardent admirers.[1] No Democratic nominations were made, for it was not yet known that there would be an election in 1868.

Since the Republicans were in control of the constitutional convention, they used that body as a nominating convention. Rufus B. Bullock was their choice for governor. According to a later statement by Brown, he himself was not an original Bullock man and gave him support only after it became evident that Judge Dawson Walker could not be nominated. There is no proof that Bullock bargained with Brown for

1 *Proceedings of the Conservative Convention Held in Macon, Georgia, 5 December 1857* (Macon, 1868); Avery, *History of Georgia*, 373–75.

support, but later he did support Brown for the Senate. Bullock was not an unknown, although he did not have a wide political reputation. New York born, he had arrived in Georgia in the 1850s and become connected with the Southern Express Company. He was a member of the Oglethorpe Infantry and was present at the surrender of the Augusta Arsenal. He did not, however, go into active Confederate service. Instead, he continued with the Southern Express Company and performed services in the field of transportation. Late in the war, he was appointed assistant quartermaster general with the rank of colonel. His political activities began after the war when he became associated with the "Augusta Ring." During the convention some of Bullock's friends had urged the removal of Governor Jenkins and his appointment as provisional governor.[2] At the time of his nomination he was president of the Macon and Augusta Railroad.

A friendly contemporary described Bullock as "a large, handsome, social specimen of a man, pleasant-mannered, and well liked."[3] But another contemporary, avowedly hostile, saw him as "a big, flabby, long-haired, beefy looking animal . . . of heavy lumbering action docile only to negroes, bites and kicks at whites."[4] Brown and Bullock had not been closely associated prior to the convention, but since December, 1867, Brown had been riding the Macon and Augusta Railroad without charge, thanks to the generosity of its president.[5]

In the campaign the Republicans would urge approval of the constitution and the election of Bullock as governor. The Democrats would be in somewhat of a quandary. Their true desire was to reject the constitution and elect a Democratic governor. Yet this would seem to be an exercise in futility; if the constitution should be rejected there would be no civil government over which a Democratic governor could preside. No one with any knowledge of Washington politics could have been so naïve as to expect Congress to readmit Georgia without the enfranchisement of the Negro. Although the Radicals in Congress had failed to remove the president by the impeachment process, they had lost none of their radicalism toward the unreconstructed states. Had

2 C. R. Ga., VI, 261–62, 264–68.
3 Avery, History of Georgia, 384.
4 E. Merton Coulter, William Montague Browne, Versatile Anglo-Irish American, 1823–1883 (Athens, 1967), 169.
5 See McLeod Collection under date December 11, 1867.

the Democrats acted wisely, they probably could have elected a governor along with approval of the constitution, which they could not prevent anyway. The only glimmer of hope left to those who opposed congressional reconstruction was a remote possibility that the people of the North, having grown more lenient toward their late enemies, would elect a more moderate Congress in 1868. This was a weak reed upon which to lean; the "bloody shirt" was waving in the North as well as in the South.

Politically astute, Joseph E. Brown had thought all of this through. He had long since adopted the businessman's view. To continue to pay taxes to and be dominated by a government in which you had no representation was unthinkable. Economic progress and prosperity must be preceded by restoration to the Union. Therefore, the new constitution must be ratified and acceptably administered. This was the Republican platform. The Democrats had nothing to offer but continual opposition. They apparently preferred continued military rule to rule by Negroes, carpetbaggers, and scalawags.

Brown neither wished nor feared Negro domination; he knew the low-income whites could be depended upon to prevent that. But he did want Georgia on the track toward economic progress. Writing *"in confidence"* to a congressman friend before it was known just who Bullock's opponent would be, Brown expressed serious doubt that Bullock could be elected. To a great extent, white voters were dropping him, for he and his friends had "been injudicious in forcing upon the people several candidates for Congress who are newcomers, or it is said carpetbaggers, over good men here who are actively for reconstruction." Brown himself had decided to take the stump for the Republican nominee; yet he considered it "an exceedingly doubtful contest."[6]

Brown did take the stump, speaking at Atlanta, Marietta, Rome, Kingston, Ringgold, and McDonough.[7] Shortly before the convention adjourned he spoke at a "Great Ratification Meeting" at Atlanta's city hall. He explained that his first choice for governor had been Judge Dawson A. Walker, but the judge preferred to remain on the bench. While he and some others worked for their candidates in various ways,

6 Brown to William D. Kelley, March 18, 1868, in Hargrett Collection.
7 Frank Brown Diary, March 20, 27, April 17, 1868.

the friends of Bullock "outplayed us a little, and I think we should all acquiesce with a good grace." Nominations were aways made by *caucuses*, a few men meeting behind closed curtains, and the defeated always complained. He knew the Republican candidate to be "a gentleman of ability, of unimpeachable character, of industry and energy, and of first-rate business habits, and strong common sense." These were the qualities required in a good governor.

The Democratic party had not yet nominated a candidate, but it no doubt would do so, Brown speculated. Although it had added *National* to its title, it was the same states' rights group to which he so long belonged. He himself still honored the memory of states' rights; yet, regardless of his former position, he was now obliged to admit that states have no right to secede; therefore, "primary allegiance is due to the United States Government." The doctrine of secession and primary allegiance to the state must be abandoned. The same was true of the old opposition to the tariff. With the national debt so heavy and taxes so high, the South should favor raising all funds possible by this indirect means. Once restored to the Union, Georgians themselves should engage in manufacturing to the greatest degree possible in order to reap some of the profits while bearing their portion of the burden. Neither could the South afford longer to oppose internal improvements at federal expense. In the past southerners had helped pay the bills of others and got only political offices in return. That was a "bad trade." In the future the national government would engage in extensive internal improvements. The South must take her part, Brown proposed, securing as much money as possible to rebuild "broken fortunes and restore Prosperity" to her "impoverished people."

Since the war destroyed old issues, future party division must be on new ones, even though old names might still be used. The convention that nominated Bullock adopted no principles other than those incorporated in the Constitution being submitted to the people. "All who favor reconstruction under the Sherman Bill, are cordially invited to act with us and support the platform and the nominee." As to the new constitution itself, Brown thought it might prove to be the best Georgia had ever had. Many who had denounced the convention as a group of "scalawags, negro worshippers, and carpetbaggers" were now ready to support the constitution provided they be allowed "*to have the offices* under it."

Brown asserted that not more than a half dozen members of the convention were living in the North at the close of the war. Yet all who were of northern birth were being denounced as carpetbaggers. "It is time we ceased this everlasting outcry against Northern men. We need capital and energy, and muscle and nerve, to aid in building up, and the development of our State." Northern people should be invited "to settle among us and bring their capital, and their energy to aid us." But what encouragement would they have as long as they were ostracized? "This appeal to prejudice is wrong in every view of it. It does infinite harm. It prevents harmony and retards prosperity. It is the weapon of demagogues, wielded only for mischief, and is never productive of any good." Brown predicted that within six months Rufus B. Bullock would be occupying the governor's office in the new capital of Atlanta. The city of Atlanta had promised to furnish necessary accommodations for a period of ten years. During that period "a splendid granite Capitol" could be "hewn out of Stone Mountain with convict labor, at very light cost."[8]

When Brown spoke in Marietta on March 18, the Democrats still had not made a final choice of a nominee for governor; so Brown would discuss all whom he thought possibilities. He praised Bullock as one who, having had a prominent part in framing the constitution, would stand "fairly and squarely upon it." As a strong relief man, he would execute the laws on that subject "in good faith and without equivocation or double dealing." And having had Union sympathies during the war, he could work "smoothly and harmoniously" with the federal government. This would be infinitely better than to elect someone known to be hostile toward the government.

In surveying the possible opposition candidates, Brown remarked that he had little to say about Judge Augustus Reese except that he was "known to be bitterly opposed" to the reconstruction plan. He thought Judge David Irwin was "riding the race with a foot on each horse. He is *sorter* for and somewhat against reconstruction." Irwin had been elected to the convention, but, undecided which side he was

8 Atlanta *Daily New Era*, March 11, 1868.

on, declined to serve, stating that judges should not "mingle in politics."
Brown charged that Irwin was opposed to the relief measures in the
constitution and challenged him to come out and make a definite
statement.

Then there was Governor Jenkins, Brown continued, recently
removed from office by General Meade because his conscience would
not permit him to "*pay out*" 1867 convention expenses from the Treasury when appropriated by the convention. However, when a member
of the 1865 convention, his conscience had permitted him to "*receive*"
money appropriated by the convention of that year. But Brown preferred to devote most of his time to Ben Hill, the "acknowledged dictator" of the so-called National Democratic party of Georgia. Here was
a man who had "spent nearly all of his political life in bitter denunciation and vilification" of the party he now proposed to lead. In a recent
speech in Atlanta, Hill, as ever, acting "Sir Oracle," had lamented the
depravity of the times, corruption among the people, and the fact that
members of his audience loved falsehood better than truth. Brown
charged that Hill thought himself alone to be "pure and undefiled, a
prophet whose vision is unerring." Further, Hill had lamented the fact
that the constitution would not give the General Assembly power to
pass social legislation. This would permit blacks to socialize with
whites, even to the extent of intermarriage. Brown would remind Hill
that since the legislature had no power to pass social legislation, neither
did it have power to repeal social restrictions already in force.[9]

The Democrats held no nominating convention in 1868, leaving to
their executive committee the task of selecting a candidate. The committee had difficulties. It first chose Judge Reese, but General Meade
declared him ineligible. Judge Erwin was then selected, but he too was
declared ineligible when it was revealed he had served as a presidential
elector prior to the war. The choice then went to General John B.
Gordon, Georgia's most celebrated military hero. He had not held office prior to the war.

The campaign was bitter. Midst charges and countercharges, there
were threats of violence. "Stop and reflect the people is determined not
to bear every thing," ran a semiliterate anonymous note addressed to

9 *Ibid.*, April 14, 1868.

Brown. "You will here of several assinations before the 20th of this month."[10] This note might have been merely for annoyance, but it was dated the day following real violence at Columbus. About 2 A.M., March 31, a group of disguised men entered a Negro boardinghouse and murdered George W. Ashburn, a member of the recent convention. Ashburn had the type of background and reputation that marked him as a probable victim of the newly organized Ku Klux Klan. During the war he had fled to the Union lines. After the war he became an outspoken radical reconstructionist. He was what might have been considered a typical scalawag. Upon returning from the recent convention, he was denied quarters in the white boardinghouses of Columbus, so he turned to one operated by a Negro woman. Later stories declared it to be a house of prostitution. Although the city government of Columbus offered a reward for the apprehension of Ashburn's murderers, General Meade removed the mayor and aldermen and appointed a military government. Within a week the new mayor arrested ten suspects, most of whom were from prominent Columbus families. Trial would not be set until after the election.

A few patterns of operation were in evidence during the campaign. The Republicans or reconstructionists concentrated on getting out the Negro vote and holding the upcountry whites in line while doing so. It was stressed that Bullock and his friends were responsible for the relief clause in the new constitution, and efforts were made to revive the hostility against the old slaveholding aristocracy, which for the most part was Democratic. "Be a man!" exclaimed one Republican handbill. "Let the slaveholding aristocracy no longer rule you. Vote for a constitution which educates your children free of charge; relieves the poor debtor from his rich creditor; allows a liberal homestead for your families; and more than all, places you on a level with those who used to boast that for every slave they were entitled to three-fifths of a vote in congressional representation. Ponder this well before you vote."[11]

Bullock relied heavily upon Brown and his influence among the debtor-class whites. The upcountry people wanted copies of Brown's speech in pamphlet form, Bullock wrote on March 25. He urged Brown

10 April 1, 1868, in McLeod Collection.
11 Spalding Collection.

to arrange with Dr. Bard, editor of the *New Era*, to print them "at my expense" and place them in wide circulation.[12] Brown followed the suggestion, and ten thousand copies were printed immediately. Five thousand additional copies of a revised edition were subsequently put in circulation.[13]

Bullock made numerous reports to Brown on the situation in various sections. What Brown was saying to Bullock is not known. Bullock felt certain the "*Union* men of the mountains will work hard & vote solid in the right direction," he assured Brown. Reports were generally good except in Morgan County, "and we shall beat out the Morgan County 'Clique' in their own bailiwick."[14] Two days later he passed on to Brown word of the fear expressed by a local leader that he could not carry his district for the Republicans unless he could distribute to certain key men promises of appointment to offices. Bullock gave assurance that he would confer freely and fully with Brown on the matter. The same local leader also reported fear on the part of "our real friends" that Bullock might appoint to office "only carpetbaggers & perhaps niggers." To quiet this fear, Bullock published and circulated numerous copies of the constitution, along with an address to the people. He also reported to Brown that he was replying to each applicant for office "in such a manner as to energize his action without binding my own. . . . All our men are wide awake to the great necessity of bringing out the black vote—& nothing is more sure to secure it than the fact that colored men are on the county ticket."[15] If Brown disagreed with these campaign tactics, there is no record of it.

The effect of the murder of Ashburn upon the ratification of the constitution and the election of a governor is uncertain. Bullock urged that the murderers be dealt with "severely and promptly," fearing that the event might intimidate party workers.[16] No doubt the murder caused General Meade to tighten military restrictions. Apparently Brown had reported to General Pope that Meade was agreeable enough but not too aggressive. Pope replied: "I never supposed he would take

12 McLeod Collection.
13 See Henry P. Farrow Collection, University of Georgia, for list of documents circulated by the Republicans. They numbered more than 100,000 pieces.
14 March 25, 1868, in McLeod Collection.
15 March 27, 1868, *ibid.*
16 Bullock to Brown, April 1, 1868, *ibid.*

much interest in the success of reconstruction, though I knew he would do his duty under the law. I trust you are strong enough to ratify your constitution without the aid or sympathy of any U.S. official though of course it would have been both pleasant & useful to have had both from the District commander." He himself had enjoyed the relief from "such harrassing & thankless duty." He had read Brown's speeches with much interest.[17]

Great concern on the part of reconstructionists was not really justified; their opponents could offer nothing more than a continuation of existing conditions—military rule and federal taxation, but no representation. The Democrats had a good candidate and a losing cause. Their only appeal was to bias and prejudice. They had no chance to win the black vote, so they appealed to the prejudices of the whites. Like the Republicans, they made use of numerous handbills. The constitution was attacked for its establishment of political, social, and educational equality of the races, which was certain to result in higher taxes and a depreciation in property values. It was not a Georgia-made document but one ordered from Washington and "framed by adventurers from New England, by convicts from penitentiaries, and by ignorant negroes from cornfields." And as for the promises of relief, they were but a trap to catch votes; the court would declare them contrary to the Federal Constitution. Then "White men of Georgia! Read and Reflect! Rescue Georgia! The issue involved in the election on the 20th of April is whether or not Georgia shall pass into the hands of negroes and Yankee political adventurers."[18]

The whites did become much more aroused than in the previous election, and there is no doubt that a great majority of them shared the hostility to Negroes and northern adventurers. But the economic plight of Georgia was frightful, and the only promise of relief was incorporated in the proposed constitution. Even Ben Hill soon realized that defeat of the constitution was not possible. In desperation, he implored the people of Georgia: "Even if you do ratify the hated Constitution, influenced by fraud and force, at least give us the noble Gordon, native to your hills to administer it."[19] The idea of the constitution and

17 Pope to Brown, March 29, 1868, *ibid.*
18 Quoted in Thompson, *Reconstruction*, 203–204.
19 Macon *Telegraph*, April 8, 1868.

Gordon was an impressive one; the manner in which Hill presented it was far from impressive. Yet the vote indicated that some voters accepted the suggestion. The constitution was approved by a 17,972-vote majority, and Bullock was elected over Gordon by a majority of only 7,171.[20]

No doubt there was much violence and intimidation during the campaign and election. Republican Amos T. Akerman was most unhappy. Although his party had elected a governor, the Democrats had cast three-fourths of the votes in his county. "The result is easily explained," he wrote Foster Blodgett. "The Democratic bullies have been active for several weeks terrifying Republican voters by threats of assassination and other injuries." Many Republican candidates flinched and withdrew. Lawlessness reigned on election day. Negroes were threatened with death unless they voted Democratic. Even the few soldiers present assisted the Democrats. "Liquor and other bribes were freely given." Akerman concluded that these "disgraceful doings ought to be set aside and a new election held under the protection of sufficient military force."[21] These "disgraceful doings" would not be set aside, but Akerman would soon be rewarded with a seat in President U. S. Grant's cabinet.

The part played by Brown in the drafting and ratification of the "hated" constitution did not increase his popularity among former Confederate whites. And, as if to destroy what little popularity he enjoyed, he accepted an offer of chief prosecutor of those accused of the Ashburn murder. This astonished even his close friends. His acquaintance with Ashburn had been brief and of a political nature, yet Ashburn had dined in the Brown home during the recent convention. Young Frank Brown wrote in his diary: "He is large and *very ugly* and a radical."[22] Brown's decision to head the prosecution could not have been designed to influence the election, for he was not employed until two months after the election.

On June 26, 1868, General Meade wired General John M. Schofield, secretary of war, that in the interest of justice and "my personal vindi-

20 Thompson, *Reconstruction*, 204–205.
21 April 23, 1868, Amos T. Akerman Papers, Georgia State Archives. New Hampshire born, Akerman had been living in Georgia for about a quarter century. At this time Elberton was his home.
22 January 22, 1868.

cation" the Ashburn murderers should be tried before a military commission. He had tentatively retained Joseph E. Brown as counsel. "I deem his services of the utmost importance not only for his legal ability but for the influence his position in the state will give the prosecution." The only difficulty was that Brown had set his fee at five thousand dollars. Before contracting to pay so large a sum, General Meade wished authorization from higher authority. "In view of the great importance of the case, of the value of Gov. Brown's services, of the fact that a large fee will have to be paid him for what he has done, I would strongly recommend my being authorized to pay the amount asked, as I am satisfied he would have received double, if not quadruple the amount from the other side who approached him after I had retained him, and said any amount of money could be raised." The evidence already collected by Brown was of the most positive nature; there could be little doubt about conviction. Schofield replied: "Your proposition relative to employment of counsel in the murder case is approved."[23]

Brown was to be assisted by two army officers. It is not known whether or not they were experienced trial lawyers. The accused were defended by an imposing array of seven experienced lawyers headed by Alexander Stephens, all of whom had once been Brown's friends. The defendants were imprisoned in Fort Pulaski and, it was reported, very inhumanly treated. The report might or might not have been true, but it greatly inflamed the public. The trial was never completed. The military commission convened in Atlanta, but was suspended by General Meade on July 22. Two days later he turned the case over to the civil authorities. The prisoners were released on bond, and the case was never called up by the civil courts.

One of Brown's contemporary biographers later stated that the Ashburn case "left a more lasting and bitter legacy of hard feeling than any event of reconstruction. It wounded Gov. Brown more deeply than any other incident of his life."[24] This might well have been true, yet he certainly could not have been ignorant of such a probability when he took the case. Eleven years later, when, as he explained, there was "no reason why the relations of counsel and client, or any

---

23 June 26, 27, 1868, in Hargrett Collection; *Major General Meade's Report on the Ashburn Murder* (Atlanta, 1868).
24 Avery, *History of Georgia*, 287–88.

public policy" should longer require his silence, Brown explained his reasons for taking the case. He stated that he had no knowledge of the case until he was approached by General Meade. Neither did he have anything whatsoever to do with the confinement of the prisoners. When Meade suggested that he take the case, he himself suggested that trial be delayed until the civil courts were again functioning. Meade's reply was that, since there was so much violence, some defendants must be tried by the military courts. Before he would seriously consider taking the case, Brown related, he demanded complete control of the prosecution and explained that his idea was to delay action until the legislature had acted upon reconstruction requirements. He also demanded that in case the death penalty should be decreed it would not be executed until reviewed by civil authorities. Under these conditions, Brown felt that he could be of service to the people and the nation, and it would prevent the case from falling into the hands of persons of "ultra and extreme views." Still, before making a final decision, he consulted his friend General William Phillips. No other person was consulted. After due reflection, Phillips advised: "You are the only man who can save the lives of these prisoners. If you take the case under your understanding with General Meade, you can accomplish that great object, and at the same time save the state from greater calamities, and I see no other possible chance to avert the danger. I therefore recommend you to accept the position."

By the time Brown made this public statement General Meade was dead, but Campbell Wallace, superintendent of the Western and Atlantic Railroad in 1868, stated that Meade had given him essentially the same account. And Alexander Stephens, who had been chief counsel for the defense, also confirmed the story as to Brown's desire for delay. Brown had even suggested that the prisoners be tried separately.[25] Unless one believes this account, Brown's decision to lead the prosecution of the alleged Ashburn murderers remains a mystery.

Brown was pleased with Republican victory on the state level, yet he was conscious of the fact that the fruits of victory depended upon an unanswered question. Would the governor and General Assembly-elect be permitted to assume authority as a provisional government

25 Atlanta *Daily Constitution*, June 3, 1868, September 24, 25, October 1, November 2, 1879; *Governor Brown and the Columbus Prisoners* (n.p., n.d.).

until the requirements of the Sherman Bill had been met? This was essential to political use of the patronage, and patronage was essential to success on both state and national levels. On May 6, 1868, Brown dispatched a letter to General Grant. This was a presidential year and it appeared certain that the Republican nomination would go to Grant. Brown called the General's attention to this probability, and assured him of victory in Georgia provided there was some cooperation from Washington. If Governor Bullock and the legislature were permitted to assume power, the wheels of government, including the patronage, could be turned in Grant's direction. If this was not permitted, then the state would be much under control of the "*so-called* democracy" and Republican defeat would be certain.

Brown used the Western and Atlantic Railroad as an illustration of the power of patronage in Georgia. At present the road was being operated by the military, but its manager had been appointed by Governor Jenkins and he controlled the personnel. This patronage was worth 1,000 to 1,500 votes which in the recent election had been cast for the Democratic candidate. If Governor-elect Bullock could get control of the road, those votes could be turned to the Republican presidential candidate. As he often did, Brown referred to his own record of no defeats at the hands of the people. He knew the secret of success, yet he would be powerless to deliver Georgia to the Republican presidential candidate unless the military or Congress should hasten the inauguration of the new state government. He was aware, however, that such an inauguration must be provisional until requirements had been met. "If any of our friends who have been elected are not eligible, let Congress relieve them [of their disabilities] at once. This is absolutely necessary as we are obliged to have earnest, fearless native white men to lead, or the Democracy will control a large part of the freedmen."[26]

By this time Brown had decided to go all the way. In May he went to Chicago as a delegate to the National Union Republican Convention and had a wonderful time. His reputation had gone before him. Here was an original secessionist who had broken with President Davis, and who after the war supported President Johnson's program, only later to abandon it and espouse the cause of Radical reconstruction. This branded him as a very unusual person. During a break in the activities

26 Hargrett Collection.

of the convention, a delegate from Louisiana arose to announce that there was in their midst a former governor of a rebellious state who had become reconstructed and "proved himself, in the fire, true as steel, a genuine convert, and in full fellowship with the Republican party." He then moved that Joseph E. Brown of Georgia be invited to address the convention. After loud and continued applause, Brown arose on the floor and responded: "I came here . . . a reconstructed rebel. I was an original secessionist." Here he was interrupted by loud calls to take the platform. "We want to see you." He yielded to the demand.

This gave Brown the opportunity he desired. He was "born in South Carolina in Mr. Calhoun's district," he began. "Charmed with the fascination of his manner and the splendor of his intellect, I early imbibed his State rights doctrine; and . . . religiously believed they were correct." He then praised the compromising efforts of Henry Clay and Daniel Webster and added that after they were gone "the storm again arose" and "there was no one who could pour oil upon the troubled waters and stop the deluge." The result was secession and he himself, as a states' rights man, had cordially supported it. However, when the president of the Confederacy deserted states' rights, he deserted the president. Then the South fell, and "I had sense enough to know I was whipped." Upon being released from prison he realized the time had come to make a "choice between this land and this government and some other land and some other government. I still loved my land the best." He therefore sought and received amnesty and protection and promised to make a good citizen. He urged acceptance of President Johnson's plan "because we had no other to negotiate with but him." Then when Congress, "which had the legitimate control of this question," proposed the Fourteenth Amendment, he urged its adoption. "But the tide of feeling was so overwhelming against it that no voice could stay it." The rejection he considered very unwise for he feared a worse demand would follow. He now saw the suffrage question as the only "living issue" in this amendment, and this "Congress left with the States to determine for themselves; if we voted the blacks we might count them in our representation; if we refused to vote them we could not count them. That was right." The requirement for repudiation of the Confederate debt was of no importance, Brown explained, for such action had already been taken by the state. And as for the provision that disbarred him and others this was only temporary; they themselves would soon pass from the scene and their places be taken by other and probably better men.

When he endorsed the Sherman bill, Brown further explained, he expected "hearty denunciation by my people," yet he did not consider himself a traitor to the "Lost Cause." He considered his course more honorable than that of those Rebels who received protection from the government yet remained "an enemy prepared to sting it when opportunity offers. . . . I staked all upon the arbitrament of the sword. When I fought you, I fought you openly and boldly. When I surrendered, I surrendered in good faith. When I took the amnesty oath, I took it intending religiously to observe it. . . . I abandoned the doctrine of secession, for I could not support the union of the States and encourage secession from the Union." Brown thought Georgia now on the way if Congress would pass pending legislation permitting the governor-elect and legislators, a majority of whom were Republicans, to take office. They would then adopt the Fourteenth Amendment and elect Republican senators, "and you should receive us back into Congress again. Give us what we have won, and we will succeed in this contest, and roll up a majority for Gen. Grant in November next."[27] Brown knew what Republican convention delegates wanted to hear, and he gave it to them. They considered him something of a curiosity and applauded madly. But back in Georgia he merely further inflamed the fury of former Confederates.

The new state government *was* permitted to organize prior to congressional acceptance of the constitution. The General Assembly ratified the Fourteenth Amendment on July 21, 1868, and Governor Bullock was formally inaugurated on the following day. He was escorted by Brown, followed by Judge Erskine and General Meade. According to an analysis made by reconstruction historian Mildred Thompson, the new state Senate was composed of seventeen Radical Republicans, ten Moderate Republicans, and seventeen Conservative Democrats. House membership was made up of seventy-five Radical Republicans, nine Moderate Republicans, and eighty-eight Conser-

27 *Speech of Ex-Governor Brown of Georgia, Delivered in the National Republican Convention at Chicago, May 20, 1868* (n.p., n.d.).

vative Democrats. This analysis has been challenged by more recent writers.[28] It appears probable that the Republicans had more strength in the House than Thompson calculated.

Although Georgia had again "reconstructed" herself, her new constitution was yet to be accepted by Congress. Members of both houses of Congress registered strong objections to the "relief measures." Brown rushed letters to Senators James Wilson and John Sherman and Congressman Schuyler Colfax, Republican vice-presidential nominee. If these relief measures were stricken out, he told Colfax, the result would be so disastrous as to defeat the Republican candidates in Georgia in the coming election. He pictured the dire circumstances of thousands of debt-ridden Georgians, some of whom were once prominent and wealthy. Should their lands be sold "under the sheriff's hammer" at this time, they would lose everything, and lands would be concentrated in the "hands of a few capitalists." That section of the constitution under attack did not cancel debts contracted prior to the close of the war, Brown explained. It only denied the state courts jurisdiction until the legislature should "think proper to restore it." Such a stay of execution would be necessary only until the return of prosperity. Then why should not such questions be left to the judiciary and legislature of the state. It did not affect northern creditors for they could sue in federal courts.

It was these relief measures, Brown further explained to Colfax, that had brought about ratification of the constitution and the election of a Republican governor and legislature. If they were now abrogated by Congress, Republican success in the fall would be impossible. "We have a desperate fight to make against the press, the politicians, and the property of the State which are in a great measure combined against us. Why should our friends in Washington load us with more weight than we can carry?" Leave the constitution as presented, and Georgia would be carried for Grant and Colfax. "Cripple us in the manner proposed & you give us over a prey to our enemies." Would Colfax please call this to the attention of Thaddeus Stevens?"[29] Brown's plea

---

28 Thompson, *Reconstruction*, 208; Nathans, *Losing the Peace*, 105–108; Charles G. Bloom, "The Georgia Election of April, 1868" (M.A. thesis, University of Chicago, 1963).

29 June 9, 1868, in Hargrett Collection. See also Brown to Reuben E. Fenton, governor of New York, June 11, 1868.

was not sufficient; the relief clauses were deleted by Congress, and Georgia had no choice but to accept the change. However, the deletion did not produce the disastrous results predicted by Brown; the General Assembly would write legislative provisions similar to those stricken from the constitution.

By midsummer, 1868, the presidential campaign in Georgia was as warm as the weather. On July 23, the day following Bullock's inauguration, the Democrats held their celebrated "Bush Arbor" meeting in Atlanta for the announced purpose of selecting nominees for presidential electors. More than a thousand delegates came from 108 counties, and the throng that came to see and listen made this meeting the largest gathering that had ever been held within the state. Cobb, Toombs, and Ben Hill furnished five hours of entertainment; Joe Brown was their principal target. "Let him go with the negroes, they are good enough for him," exclaimed Cobb. "White men of Georgia, cut loose from him; overboard with him. When I see a white man talking to Brown a feeling of revulsion comes over me; when I see him talking to a nigger I am sorry for the nigger." When Ben Hill spoke in apparent reference to Brown, some one in the audience cried out, "Joe Brown." Hill came to a dramatic stop, and then remarked: "I did not call that name. It should not be mentioned in decent company." Toombs also harangued the huge audience. After denouncing everything and everybody connected with reconstruction, he exclaimed "Your country says come, honor says come—duty says come—liberty says come—the country is in danger—let every freeman hasten to the rescue."[30]

Toombs continued his denunciation of the "Browns, Bullocks, and Blodgetts" in speeches at Augusta and Cedartown. Brown, he declared, "is false to nature. He went to Chicago. What more can I say to commend this wretch to your detestation; he has fatigued public indignation, it is no longer equal to his crime. Ignoble villain, buoyant solely from corruption, he only rises where he rots."[31]

On July 29, less than a week after the Bush Arbor meeting, the Georgia legislature completed reconstruction reorganization by electing United States senators. Bullock's Radicals supported Brown for the long term and Foster Blodgett for the short. The Conservatives

30 Atlanta *Daily Constitution*, July 24, 25, 1868.
31 *Ibid.*, August 25, 27, 1868.

(Democrats) offered Alexander H. Stephens and H. V. M. Miller. Although Brown received 102 votes to Stephens 96 on the first ballot, he had no chance of ultimate victory. The Conservatives would give him no support whatsoever, and there was little difference of opinion between them and a number of Moderate Republicans. The two groups combined in support of Joshua Hill, electing him by a vote of 110 to Brown's 94, and selected Miller over Blodgett for the short term.[32] When the defeat of Brown was announced the spectators broke into cheers. The Speaker ordered the chamber cleared and the excitement spread into the streets. Former governor Brown, once the idol of the masses, must have been the most depressed man in the state as he made his way home on that July evening. Young Frank Brown wrote in his diary that the Assembly had elected Hill and Miller and added "I am disgusted with that body."[33]

Brown made a serious mistake when he permitted his name to be placed in nomination for a Senate seat. His usual political shrewdness deserted him when he calculated that his strength combined with that of Governor Bullock would be sufficient. Perhaps he seriously believed that with his connections in Washington he could be of real service to Georgia, yet there is no evidence that he really wished to go to the Senate at that time. Defeat by Stephens would have been bearable, though not welcome, but to be defeated by Josh Hill was a bitter experience. Hill was a Republican, yet he had not come out strongly in favor of the Reconstruction Acts. On the surface, he and Brown professed friendship, and during the recent convention he had been a dinner guest in the Brown home. Still the former bitterness had not been erased.[34]

The rejoicing over Brown's defeat quickly spread throughout the state; it was music to the ears of those who had denounced him at Bush Arbor the previous week. "As to the senatorship," wrote Robert Toombs to Alexander Stephens, "I preferred Brown should be beaten by Joshua Hill to almost any other man. It is impossible for you [to] think worse of the scoundrel than I do, but it could only be done by a Radical, and there was political justice in making the earliest traitor

32 *Senate Journal*, 1868, pp. 91–92; *House Journal*, 1868, pp. 100–108.
33 Frank Brown Diary, July 29, 1868.
34 See Brown to Joshua Hill, June 20, 1868, in Hargrett Collection; Frank Brown Diary, January 15, 1868.

defeat the worst one and break down his party. I differ with you as to the policy of beating Brown." Toombs figured that Brown already had "the whole patronage of Bullock at his feet." If to this should be added the patronage of a senator it "would have cost us not far short of 10,000 votes." Brown's "knowledge, especially of all the rogues of the State, is prodigious, and I think it was about worth the State to beat him." As for Josh Hill, Toombs thought him "a poor devil," forlorn, powerless, unable "to help himself or hurt us." All he asked of the new senator was that he not "join us or speak to me."[35]

Bullock failed in his effort to make his friend Brown a senator, but on August 17, 1868, he appointed him chief justice of the state supreme court for a twelve-year term, dating from July 21, 1868.[36] Brown no doubt wished to be rewarded for his political service, but it is very doubtful that he wished to be chief justice. It would take him out of active politics, eliminate his lucrative legal practice, and limit the time he could devote to business interests. The salary of $2,500 was much less than he could collect in fees from one good lawsuit, and Joe Brown liked money. He could not have intended to remain on the bench for a lengthy period.

Some Georgia lawyers who had been denouncing him so severely for the past ten years must have felt a bit uneasy. Federal judge John Erskine wrote congratulating Brown on his appointment and added: "I want to be in court when B. H. Hill, Cobb, Toombs and some dozen others I could name make their first bow. Poor fools!" Judge Erskine also suggested: "You must push for the Cabinet. . . . The Chief Justiceship will be nearly as good a stepping stone to move from as the Senatorship." He had spoken to several persons in Washington while on a recent trip, including Senator Charles Sumner, "with whom I spent a whole morning at his house." He had mentioned to these persons Brown's administrative ability and suitableness for a cabinet appointment. "I also cleared up some trashy lies that were in the way." Erskine hoped Brown could find time to stump for Grant in several states. "By doing this *at once* you help yourself. . . . Besides it is due to those who at Chicago & by letter invited you to speak to respond to their calls. . . . Were I you, I should make my arrangements—bundle up and go on

35 Phillips, *Correspondence*, 703.
36 Hargrett Collection; "Executive Minutes," 1866–1870, p. 163.

this electioneering tour immediately."[37] Brown had earlier considered taking the stump for Grant in other states and made such a suggestion to the Republican National Committee. William E. Chandler, secretary, replied urging him to remain in Georgia until after the Ashburn murderers were convicted. If sufficient time remained, Brown might then spend three or four weeks speaking in the North. Chandler was unable to get northern speakers to go South during hot weather.[38]

On August 18, a few days after his appointment as chief justice, Brown took another swing at his critics, especially those who had reviled him so bitterly at the Bush Arbor meeting.[39] Speaking in Atlanta city hall, he explained to his audience that, since he had not yet taken the oath of office as chief justice, he did not "transcend the bounds of propriety" in raising his voice in warning against the dangers which threatened the "very existence of civil government." The issues before the country now were "peace or war," "life or death," "government or anarchy."

The "so-called Democracy" had vowed the intention to "tear down" the reconstructed governments in all southern states "by the sword." On the other hand, the Republican party had declared for peace, law and order, prosperity and retention of the reconstructed governments. This was the lineup; the choice was left to the people. "Shall we have peace and stability, or shall we again plunge the country into war, bloodshed and chaos, with all their attendant horrors, privations and miseries?" There was no need further to discuss the merits or demerits of congressional reconstruction. It was now an accomplished fact, not according to the wishes of Georgians, but according to the dictates of the conqueror, yet it was a fact, and Georgia had been readmitted into the Union. Peace and the return of prosperity were at hand. But now the "so-called Democracy" had declared its determination to "undo all that has been done—to trample the Acts of Congress into the dust, and to disperse the governments that have been established, by the use of the sword in defiance of the laws of the land."

This was Brown's interpretation of the Democratic platform and

37 Erskine to Brown, August 18, 1868, in McLeod Collection.
38 Chandler to Brown, July 6, 1868, *ibid.*
39 The speech was in response to an invitation from a Grant-Colfax committee composed of P. M. Sheibly, S. C. Johnson, and George S. Thomas, dated August 18, 1868, in McLeod Collection.

the letters of acceptance written by Horatio Seymour and Francis P. Blair, Jr., nominees for president and vice-president. What the platform actually said was "We regard the Reconstruction Acts of Congress, so-called, as usurpation, unconstitutional, revolutionary and void." Brown also quoted from a letter from vice-presidential candidate Blair to James O. Broadhead. There was no hope to break the Republican control of the Senate, Blair said; therefore, reconstruction could not be undone by congressional action. The only hope was to elect a president who would "declare these Acts null and void; compel the army to undo its usurpation at the South; disperse the carpetbag State governments." The president must "execute the will of the people by trampling into the dust the usurpations of Congress known as the Reconstruction Acts." And Democratic presidential candidate Seymour promised to strive to carry out the platform. These statements by Seymour and Blair, Brown thought, justified the classification of the Democratic party as determined upon destruction. Neither could there be hope for intervention by the supreme court, Brown asserted, for it would continue to consider the question a political one and claim lack of jurisdiction.

Brown next proceeded to analyze the Georgia Democratic leaders individually. That "poor political maniac" Ben Hill was a scourge to every popular cause he espoused, a guarantee of defeat. It was the Democrats' misfortune when they permitted him to join their ranks. He had learned their secrets and had "no better sense than to disclose them." If the Democrats could but control "his diarrhea of words," perhaps they could use him to some advantage. "But man can not impart judgment, common sense, and moral honesty to those upon whom nature failed to bestow them." One way to assure a Grant victory would be to permit "Ben to canvass the state thoroughly" for Seymour.

However, with Toombs, Cobb and "lesser lights who revolve around them," Brown thought it was different. They represented their party and what they said had significance. But Cobb, an original Union man, became the enemy of the United States the day Stephen A. Douglas "got the inside track on him for the Presidency." Henceforth, treason rankled in his heart and he "sought to ruin that he could not rule. . . . The personal abuse he has poured forth against me I pass with silent contempt. I will not bandy words with a blackguard. I will not exchange epithets with a man who at the end of the war swore to support the Union of the states, and now again plots revolution, bloodshed and carnage for its overthrow." As for Toombs, Brown thought him a "bold, open, frank enemy," yet was unable to see how he could complain about mistreatment. Toombs had fled the country rather than surrender. The president later permitted him to return without taking the amnesty oath, yet he was still on the warpath.

Brown explained that he was aware of the presence of some original Union men within the so-called Democratic ranks. He wished to ask them what they expected from the leadership of men like Hill, Cobb, and Toombs. To follow in the train of these men was to be "chained to the car of their ambition" and dragged "down the steeps of revolution and ruin." With their political fortunes already wrecked, these men were "ready for bold adventures. War may give them position. Peace leaves them in retirement with none to do them reverence." After four years of bloody war followed by three years of almost hopeless misery, Georgia had finally been able to put in motion the wheels of a new government, which was able to protect life and property and promote prosperity. Were the Democrats to be permitted to destroy and declare void all of these gains? They declared illegal every existing branch of state government and void every act performed by its officials. If this interpretation should prevail, "You are in the midst of anarchy, and the law of physical force is the supreme law of this state."

Brown further charged that, with the exception of Cobb, those who were seeking to lead the Democratic party were not Democrats. Three of them had been his opponents for governor; none adhered to old time-honored Democratic principles. He would especially warn the original Union men of North Georgia against the trickery of these false leaders. And as for the 90,000 colored Republicans who owed their freedom to the government of the United States and their franchise to the Republican party, he would say these rights could not be taken from them except by war. "When in the history of the past did you ever know 4,000,000 of people with the ballot in their hands surrender it without bloodshed? It cost revolution to give it to them, and nothing short of bloody revolution can take it from them. If you will allow them to exercise it without disturbance, they will do it peaceably. If there are outbreaks of disturbance, they, I predict, will grow out of the attempts of the white race to deprive the colored race of this right, or to interfere with its free exercise. I warn you, my friends, to be cautious on both sides, how you put your lives in jeopardy and your homes and families in peril. And I especially warn my own race of the extreme danger to them in case of collision. The colored people have but little except their lives to risk in the fight if it should unfortunately come. The white race have the same risk, and in addition to this they have their property to lose. Your houses, your villages, towns and cities are pledged to peace. Be careful then how you excite discord and bloodshed."[40] Brown's analysis of Democratic leadership was close to the mark, but the extent to which he believed his own prediction of violence and destruction is open to question. When hostile editors got hold of his prophecy of possible black revolt the hounds of war were let loose again.

Although Brown predicted bloodshed should an effort be made to take from the blacks their newly won privilege of voting, he made no mention of the Negro's right to hold office. This right was already under attack in the legislature and a Democratic member had cited Brown's Marietta speech of March 18 as evidence that Negroes had no such right. Early in September, 1868, the legislature "unseated" its Negro members and seated their white opponents in the recent elections.

The appointment of Brown to the supreme bench took him out of active politics, but it by no means silenced his enemies. In October, 1868, the attack upon him sank to the level of pure slime. One James H. Martin placed in the hands of the editor of the La Grange *Reporter* two letters purported to have been written by Brown to Martin's late wife. These letters revealed an illicit relationship between the two. Martin stated that he married his wife, a widow with children, in the spring of 1864, but that she spent most of her time with Brown. Further, Martin stated, on September 13, 1864, Mrs. Martin gave birth to a child by Brown. The first Martin knew of her pregnancy was when he got possession of these letters.[41] This was new grist for the mill of hate—just what some newspaper editors were looking for, although

40 Copy in *ibid.* For the Broadhead letter and its probable effect upon the campaign see William E. Smith, *The Francis P. Blair Family in Politics*, 2 vols. (New York, 1933), II, 405 ff.
41 Atlanta *Daily New Era*, October 25, 1868.

no man in Georgia had a better reputation for strict adherence to the moral code than Joseph E. Brown.

At first Judge Brown ignored the charge. But when the *Reporter* and some other hostile papers "defied him to come out over his own signature" and explain his conduct, Brown published a reply in the *New Era*. For the past two years, the judge explained, he had "borne in silence an amount of misrepresentation, vituperation and abuse, on account of my political position, that has seldom fallen to the lot of any public man or private citizen. . . . Relying confidently upon returning reason and a sense of justice, when passion had subsided and *results* are seen, I have held my peace. . . . But as an effort is now made to establish a charge injurious to my reputation, and destructive of the peace of my family . . . I feel justified in appearing before the public in my own vindication."

A friend of his, Brown related, had secured the original letters from the *Reporter*, brought them to Atlanta in his absence, and had them examined by a "large number of the most intelligent and respectable citizens," representing both parties and different religious faiths, who were thoroughly familiar with his handwriting. He produced statements from fourteen of these men pronouncing the letters "base forgeries."

Brown admitted having known Mrs. Martin and having seen her in public, often with her husband. During the war he had assisted her in getting through the Confederate lines in order to visit her son in a northern prison, and he later learned that she too was thrown into prison for a short period. At the very time she was said to have been living with him, she was beyond the federal lines. If she gave birth in September, 1865, she was in the north at the time of conception and "I could not have been its father." He suspected that even the charge that Mrs. Martin had a bastard child was also false.

Brown admitted having seen Mrs. Martin many times after the war and that she had consulted him on legal matters, particularly as to attempts on the part of her husband to get control of her property. He remembered her as "intelligent, fluent in conversation, and rather sprightly, but sometimes rather erratic or extravagant in her expressions." He thought her "an unhappy woman, and looked upon her more as an object of pity than lust. I never had any reasons to call in question her chastity."[42]

The Macon *Journal* and the Columbus *Times* were the only two newspapers yet persuaded to publish Brown's "reply," reported a friend on October 31. The Atlanta *Constitution* and the Augusta *Chronicle and Sentinel* had "added insult to injury."[43] No doubt many enemies were chuckling at the judge's effort to defend his moral reputation, even though they must have been conscious of his uncanny ability to extricate himself. Many times in Brown's stormy career, just as his enemies were ready to write his political obituary, he scratched out of the grave to which they had consigned him.

After Brown assumed the duties of chief justice he no longer served as close adviser to Governor Bullock. It is not certain who was responsible for this change in relationship. Perhaps it was desired by both. Brown wished to minimize his political activities, and Bullock was already developing ideas which he must have known would not have been approved by Brown. With the expulsion of the Negro members, the governor lost whatever chance he might have had of controlling the legislature, and the overwhelming victory of the Seymour-Blair ticket in Georgia confirmed the minority status of the Republican party in the state. It had definitely lost control of the black vote. The fact that not one vote had been cast for Grant in eleven Georgia counties was evidence that coercion in some form had played a prominent part in the election.

What President-elect Grant would do about patronage was uncertain. Andrew Johnson appointees feared the loss of their jobs; Georgia Republicans were eager to get those jobs. Moderates quickly spotted the potential dangers that lay ahead. Alexander Stephens expressed hope that Brown would use his influence with the new president in favor of "making no changes in the subordinate offices of the government *except for cause*." This he thought would be of vast importance in restoring harmony both between section and party factions. Where there were vacancies to be filled he hoped the president would not look exclusively to the ranks of his own party. Some "moderate, conservative men" should be appointed. Stephens then turned to his own private desires. He was through with active politics and public affairs,

42 *Ibid.*
43 Peterson Thweatt to Brown, October 31, 1868, in McLeod Collection.

he explained. He had not wished to be a senator and the only reason he yielded to pressure in 1866 was the hope that he could help bridge the "chasm which then separated the two sections in Federal legislation." As for the recent election of senators, his name was presented "not only without my authority but against my expressed injunction." His name was not even used in a complimentary manner but rather for "ulterior purposes."

Returning to the subject of the president, Stephens hoped he could avoid control by either of the extreme groups. "The future to me is still dark and gloomy. The extremes on both sides are already as rabid as they were in 1860." He considered Grant a "remarkable man—one of the most remarkable men I ever met with." He could not doubt that the president's "rare combination of extraordinary qualities" would be exercised in the interest of public good. All of this was written in the "same confidence" as ever, he reminded Brown. He further noted that he and Brown had often differed widely and did now, yet "your integrity —personal integrity—I have never questioned nor have I questioned your patriotism. . . . Ponder what I say. Consider it well before you adopt a line of policy differing from that herein indicated." He thought Brown's influence and counsel during the months ahead would be "fraught with good or evil. See to it that it be not evil. Look more to country than to party. Let this if possible be the policy of the administration."[44] Brown pondered Stephens' advice as he always did, but he would not have great influence with President Grant.

After analyzing the results of the recent election and reflecting on the many rumors in circulation, Brown expressed himself privately to Governor Bullock and Joshua Hill. To Bullock he expressed regret that their friend Blodgett had been defeated for mayor of Augusta. "This is the loss of the last stronghold of the Republican party in the State. The result of the late elections prove very clearly that the negro vote will not do to rely upon unless there is a white party in the locality of the election strong enough to give them the necessary moral support." As he himself had often privately predicted, Brown continued, as soon as Democrats accepted the fact that Negroes had the freedom and right to vote and ceased to make an issue on that point, they would receive a large portion of the black vote in every election. Indeed, they

44 Stephens to Brown, November 20, 24, 1868, *ibid*.

got such a vote in the last election, even though the "mass of the party denied their right to vote and proposed to take away their franchise."

To maintain the Republican party in the South, Brown explained, division of the white vote was absolutely necessary. Republicans must unite with a strong wing of the Democrats which might be managed into support of Grant's administration. If Republicans failed to do this, it would be "utterly hopeless" to contend with the Democrats. "They possess most of the intelligence and wealth of the State which will always control tenants and laborers." The Democrats were already divided into two wings held together by a common name only, Brown noted. Those who were leading those wings hated each other and would not act together for any length of time "unless by our blunders we enable the leaders of the crazy wing to apply the party lash so strongly, by appeals to prejudice, as to hold them together." The Republicans should make terms with the moderate Democrats and (as Stephens suggested) persuade the Grant administration to "treat them with such consideration as to gratify them." This plan would result in victory in the next election. "Let the Ben Hill and Toombs wing go. We have no terms to offer them and no wish to coalesce with them."

To promote this combination, the only hope for the Republican party, Congress should be urged to move cautiously with regard to the status of affairs in Georgia. "They should take no step backward." What had been done should not be undone by destroying the existing state government. The Fourteenth Amendment was now a part of the Constitution, and Congress had power to pass all laws necessary to its enforcement. "They should in my opinion stop there."

It was with the "utmost candor" and "kindest feelings" that he presented these views, Brown concluded. He hoped the governor would "reflect maturely and carefully before you condemn them as erroneous." Reorganization of the state government on the basis of the test oath would so embitter the white people as to make it impossible to divide the Democrats. Overwhelming Democratic victory in the next election would be the result. "I repeat, our only chance is 'divide and conquer.' We must conciliate the moderate wing, or this is not possible."[45] Governor Bullock had not requested this advice; neither would he heed it. He already had other plans.

45 Brown to Bullock, December 3, 1868, in Hargrett Collection.

Judge Brown also offered Joshua Hill some unsolicited advice. Hill had been elected senator over Brown, but since Congress was not in session when he arrived in Washington he had not yet been seated. The Democratic celebration over his defeat for the senate, Brown explained, had been even more mortifying because he believed Hill in sympathy with them. However, it was not his nature to bear malice, and since he thought Hill would stand firmly by the Grant administration there was "no just reason why we should quarrel or act as enemies." He thought Hill and Miller legally elected and should be seated by the Senate. After being twice reconstructed, it would be unwise again to remand Georgia to military rule. To again set aside the government and "begin *de novo*" would cause the people to "lose all patience and become desperate under the belief that we are never to have stability." If people considered this "set aside" as being for the purpose of putting Democrats out and Republicans in, it would give the Democrats an overwhelming majority two years hence, "which will become permanent."

Repeating much that he had told Governor Bullock, Brown again stressed that the Negro vote could not be depended upon unless the Democrats could be divided. There was nothing in the Reconstruction Acts that guaranteed the Negro the right to vote. And Brown thought the question of officeholding should be left to a decision of the courts through interpretation of the constitution and the laws of the state. Hill might show this letter to such senators as he saw fit, Brown concluded, but it was not for the general public.[46] Before Brown's letter to Hill reached Washington, Governor Bullock had arrived there, and it became known immediately that he would endeavor to convince federal authorities that Georgia still had not been reconstructed. "I regret to see the statement of Gov. Bullock's memorial to Congress," Brown wrote Stephens, "& cannot concur in his views."[47] Brown neither preferred nor believed in eventual success of Bullock's radical plan. He saw in it complete destruction of Republican hopes for the future. Only through a combination of the moderate wings of both parties could Georgia be spared continued turmoil and be placed on the road to true recovery.

46 Brown to Hill, December 7, 1868, in McLeod Collection.
47 December 8, 1868, Stephens Papers, in Library of Congress.

Chapter XX

Action, Action, Action

BY THE WINTER of 1868, reports of mistreatment of blacks were numerous. As General Pope had predicted to Brown, General Meade acted in a legal manner but was never very aggressive. After affairs were turned over to civil authorities conditions grew worse. That the black man was suffering from fear, intimidation, and violence was beyond question. There was also no doubt that many reports were exaggerated. The Ku Klux Klan was active and also got credit for acts with which it was not connected. Both Bullock Republicans and Negro leaders turned to Congress for relief. The former had lost political control, and the latter were losing their right to vote.

During December, 1868, a United States House of Representatives Committee on Reconstruction held hearings on the "Condition of Affairs in Georgia." Governor Bullock and several other Radicals, black and white, testified. They presented a horrifying picture of the situation. It was stressed that, through violence and threats of violence, blacks had been virtually deprived of the suffrage granted them. Negro members had been expelled from the legislature, while seats were held by more than fifty whites who were ineligible since they had not taken the oath required by the Reconstruction Acts. In short, Georgia had not been reconstructed; therefore, according to Bullock, the General Assembly should be called into session, the Negro members restored to their seats, and all whites who did not take the oath expelled.[1]

---

1 For these testimonies see *House Miscellaneous Documents*, 40th Cong., 3rd Sess., No. 52.

Meanwhile testimonies were also being collected by Georgia congressman Nelson Tift of Albany. More than a hundred persons replied to a list of questions sent out by him. With one exception, they gave generally moderate reports on race relations. They thought carpetbaggers rather loathsome people but welcomed honest northerners into their midst. Of course Congressman Tift chose those to whom he sent his questionnaire, but the list did include many highly respected men of local and state prominence.

Judge Brown replied at length. He thought "justice and candor" required him to report that much lawlessness and crime had gone unpunished and that blacks and Republican whites had been the chief sufferers. He thought judges had made an honest effort, but that this had not been true of juries in some localities. Some juries had feared "a few desperate characters"; others had been "under control of leaders who are bitter and vindictive, because of their political disfranchisement and were able to inflame passions and prejudices to a point which makes them unwilling to execute the laws impartially." For these deplorable conditions, Brown saw no hope of relief short of the improvement of public morals. He had observed that juries had been more under control of passion and prejudice during the military period than at any other period double that length throughout his own public life. Military commanders could permit jury trials, but were "powerless to reach the conscience of juries." Therefore, he considered it "simply absurd to talk of correcting this evil by military government." The best the federal government could do, Brown advised, was to pass such laws as would develop resources, stimulate industry, promote education, and tend to restore prosperity. This alone could nullify the influence of the "unpatriotic and unprincipled demagogues" and "restore order, promote loyalty, and secure the faithful and impartial execution of the laws" to an extent that could never be attained by "military government, test oaths, and political disabilities."[2]

Confused by much conflicting testimony, Congress took no immediate action on Bullock's request for another reconstruction of Georgia. However, the Senate did refuse to seat Joshua Hill. On January 15, 1869, Bullock boldly placed the matter before the legislature he hoped to wreck. All members elected to the legislature in 1868 should be

2 *Ibid.*, 141–46.

called together and the test oath applied, he explained. Those who could not take the oath should be denied seats. Those who could should retain their seats. This action alone would meet congressional requirements and thus avoid another reconstruction. He disapproved of the suggestion that the question of eligibility be left to the decision of the state supreme court.[3] When the legislature passed such a resolution and agreed to abide by the court's decision, Bullock vetoed it.[4] Such a decision might settle the question of Negro officeholding, but it would not apply any remedy for the holding of office by ineligible whites. Although two of the three supreme justices were his appointees, Governor Bullock was unwilling to risk a decision. Justice Hiram Warner was a Conservative, and Chief Justice Brown had previously publicly stated that the Georgia constitution did not confer upon the Negro the right to hold office.

In the meantime, Congress had approved and submitted to the states a proposed Fifteenth Amendment to the Constitution, which would deny to a state the power to deprive any person of the privilege of voting because of race, color, or previous condition of servitude. When Governor Bullock submitted this amendment to the legislature for ratification the House approved by a vote of 64 to 52, but the Senate rejected it 16 to 13. Many in each house dodged the issue by abstaining.[5] Some historians, contemporary and later, accused Bullock of secretly working against ratification, hoping to use the act of rejection in convincing Congress of the need for further reconstruction.[6] This might very well have been true, for it fit into his plan. Rejection definitely was not solely the work of the Conservatives, for many of them favored the amendment in order to force Negro suffrage upon the North. Regardless of who was responsible, rejection of the Fifteenth Amendment marked Georgia for further discipline.

Although the governor wished no decision by the state supreme court on the subject of officeholding, the court made one in June, 1869,

---

3 For more complete discussion see Conway, *Reconstruction*, 175 ff; Thompson, *Reconstruction*, 255 ff; Avery, *History of Georgia*, 419 ff; Nathans, *Losing the Peace*, 147 ff.
4 *Senate Journal*, 1869, pp. 5–9; Atlanta *Daily New Era*, February 17, March 2, 1869.
5 *House Journal*, 1869, pp. 665–66; *Senate Journal*, 1869, p. 806.
6 Avery, *History of Georgia*, 411; Thompson, *Reconstruction*, 261.

in the case of *White* v. *Clements*. The case had been appealed from the superior court of Savannah. William J. Clements and Richard W. White had been opponents in the race for a local office. White polled the majority vote, yet was denied office since he was one-eighth black. The supreme court was composed of Chief Justice Brown and Associate Justices Hiram Warner and H. K. McKay. Brown and McKay were Bullock appointees. Warner had been on the bench for many years.

In a two-to-one decision, the court declared White entitled to his office. Brown and McKay constituted the majority. "Whatever may or may not be the *privileges* and *immunities* guaranteed the colored race, by the Constitution of the United States and of this State," reasoned Brown, "it cannot be questioned that both Constitutions make them citizens. And I think it very clear that the Code of Georgia, upon which alone I base this opinion . . . confers upon *all* her citizens the right to hold office, unless they are prohibited by some provision found in the Code itself. I find no such prohibition in the Code affecting the rights of the respondent. I am, therefore, of the opinion that the judgement of the court below is erroneous." Justice McKay was of the same opinion, but Justice Warner dissented. He was of the opinion "that there is *no existing law of this* State" that conferred upon colored persons the right to hold office; therefore, White had no *legal* right to hold the office to which he had been elected.[7] Whether so intended or not, this decision would make it easier for Governor Bullock to have the expelled Negro members of the General Assembly reseated.

Chief Justice Brown could not stay out of politics. On May 10, 1869, he attempted to exercise some of the influence Stephens thought he had with the new president. "I am as decided and determined a supporter as you have in Georgia," he began a letter to Grant, "and my wish and aim is to build up a strong party to sustain your administration." The most powerful weapon available in Grant's support was a moderate and wise use of the patronage. By skillful use of the patronage the Democratic party, "made up of antagonistic elements, and banded together on the single issue of opposition to reconstruction," could easily be split and the moderate wing brought to the support of the Republican administration. The 45,000 Democratic victory in the recent election

7 *White* v. *Clements*, 39 *Georgia Reports*, 232 ff.

was conclusive evidence that the Republicans could never control Georgia "till the democrats are divided." Unfortunately, this fact was being ignored by the "faction of extreme ultra men in the republican party . . . determined to rule or ruin." These were men of little political experience, and "I fear but little love for any party longer than the spoils last." They seemed bent on driving from the party the most competent men because of their conservatism. These same ultra Republicans, through "misrepresentation, detraction, and abuse of better men and truer republicans than themselves," had controlled completely the patronage, yet a majority of those who had been appointed to office could not influence a dozen voters to support the administration.

He did not make these remarks in a spirit of fault finding, Brown assured the president, but rather to stress what he had learned from long years of political experience. He was no disappointed officeseeker; he was not an applicant for any office "within your gift"; neither did he have a friend to recommend. His sole object was to picture matters "plainly and without reserve," believing that the president preferred frankness to false flattery. "One after another, the heads of Conservative Republicans fall in Georgia, and their place is filled by extreme men, who have neither influence nor experience to add any thing to the party." Brown had just learned of the replacement of two Treasury officers in Atlanta and Savannah, both men of moderate views, but among the more "intelligent and influential" Republicans within the state. They could be worth more to the party than the whole faction that was seeking "to destroy reconstruction in the state and renew military government, anger, strife, and anarchy. . . . Let me beg you to stop this movement if it be on foot, and to give the moderate true influential portion of the republicans at least some little share in the offices."[8]

Shortly after writing this letter to the president, Brown visited Stephens at Crawfordville. As was often the case, Stephens was confined to his room by a recurrence of his old ailment. Very despondent, he had urged Brown to come talk with him. There was no recording of their conversations, but on the return trip Brown had an experience that affected him deeply. Of course he had heard all kinds of reports

8 May 10, 1869, in McLeod Collection.

of hatred, intimidation, and violence, and had himself been sometimes insulted, but this demonstration of how sons reflect the attitude and opinions of their fathers made a deep impression upon him. Several students from Mercer University were on the train, and upon learning from the news boy the identity of Judge Brown, they began calling out "Josey cabbage, collards," referring to his departure from Milledgeville upon the approach of Sherman's troops. When they got off at Union Point for dinner and also to take another train to Athens, the boys called out, "Come on, we will have cabbage for dinner." After dinner they stood on the platform between the trains and called out, "Here is old Joe Brown, come up boys and see him for only 25 cents." By this time the judge could take no more. He spoke to them, explaining that he was passing along the road quietly and peaceably "and had not bothered them. Would they go home and tell their fathers and teachers about their conduct and see if they approved?" Two boys answered, "Our fathers will approve it, they are Southern men, there is no negro in them." As Brown's train for Atlanta pulled away, the boys called, "Atkins is waiting for you." Brown thought he heard one say "Atkins' fate will soon be yours." (Joseph Atkins, a Radical member of the General Assembly and reputedly very obnoxious to whites because of his cohabitation with black women, had been murdered by a Ku Klux Klan band.)[9] In reporting to the president of Mercer his unpleasant contact with the students, Judge Brown asked for no disciplinary action, but he very clearly would have welcomed news that some had been taken. What action President H. H. Tucker took is not known.

The Fortieth Congress, during its third session, heard much testimony and did much discussing, yet it adjourned without taking action on the Georgia situation. The Forty-first Congress was in session when the Georgia legislature rejected the Fifteenth Amendment and it had already taken cognizance of the Georgia problem by refusing seats to her congressmen and senators.[10] Throughout the summer and fall of 1869, Congress discussed many proposals but approved none. The situation changed, however, with the reading of Grant's annual mes-

9 Brown to Reverend Dr. H. H. Tucker, May 24, 1869, in Hargrett Collection.
10 *Congressional Globe*, 41st Cong., 1st Sess., XLI, 16, 102.

sage to Congress on December 6, 1869. He suggested the action
Bullock and his friends had been insisting upon for the past year.[11]
Congress quickly passed a bill directing Provisional Governor Bullock
to do what he most desired. All members of the legislature elected in
1868 were to be called into session. All must take the test oath unless
they could prove that their disabilities under the Fourteenth Amendment had been removed by Congress. Federal troops were to furnish
such assistance as was needed in enforcing the act. It was reported
that Governor Bullock, in Washington at the time, was so elated that
he accompanied the bill to the White House and witnessed President
Grant signing it without reading it.[12]

When news of Bullock's success arrived in Georgia, editor I. W.
Avery of the *Constitution* requested a number of prominent men to
make public their views as to the legal scope of the new act and what
should be done. Thinking a case might come before the court, Chief
Justice Brown declined to answer the first question. The second gave
him an opportunity to remind the whites that had they acquiesced in
the reconstruction measures in 1867 reconstruction would now be complete and Georgia represented in Congress. Instead, popular orators had
aroused "feelings of resentment, and reason and judgment were de-
throned by prejudice and passion." And the fact remained that good
relations still must be reestablished with the federal government. This
could never be accomplished by nonaction. Henceforth, the watchword
should be "*action, action, action.*" There must be reorganization in
accordance with the acts of Congress. "We may offer resistance, or
refuse to act, for years to come, and live under military government, or
in a state of anarchy, and we will still be compelled, in the end to come
to the terms dictated by the conqueror. Then why longer delay?"[13]

With the support of General Alfred H. Terry, who had succeeded
General Meade as commander in Georgia, Governor Bullock called into
session on January 10, 1870, all persons who had been elected to the
legislature in 1868. Neither house, however, was to be permitted to
exercise its constitutional power to serve as sole judge of the qualifica-

11 James D. Richardson (ed.), *A Compilation of the Messages and Papers of
the Presidents*, 20 vols. (New York, 1897), IX, 3982.
12 U.S. *Statutes at Large*, 41st Cong., 2nd Sess., Chap. 3, p. 59; Avery, *History
of Georgia*, 423.
13 Atlanta *Daily Constitution*, January 5, 1870.

tion of its own members. Although the law gave them no specific power to do so, the governor and General Terry would supervise organization of each house. The Fourteenth Amendment had disqualified from holding office all persons who had held office prior to the war and had later given active aid or comfort to the Confederacy. It did not, however, define the term "office" nor "aid or comfort." The governor asked State Attorney General Henry P. Farrow, a good Bullock man, for an opinion. Farrow ruled that "office" meant any public position from notary public to governor, even including the state librarian. And "aid or comfort" might even include quiet acquiescence as well as active support.[14] This threw the field wide open for investigation of all who were not supporters of Bullock.

A group of moderate legislators, led by Republican John E. Bryant, who had abandoned his earlier extreme radicalism, called upon Chief Justice Brown for his interpretation of the disqualifying clause. Since cases involving such disqualifications could not come before a state court, Brown explained, he saw no reason why state judges should not give their opinions. According to the principles of the reconstruction amendments, as interpreted by subsequent legislation, all who had held state offices prior to the war which were a part of the administration of law or justice and later assisted the Confederacy were ineligible to vote or hold office. But, Brown explained, those public employees who had no executive or judicial duties could not possibly be included, for they merely performed tasks created by law. Those who held minor positions such as librarian, or road supervisor, or worked for municipal corporations could not be administrators.[15] Brown's opinion "knocks to atoms" the elaborate document of the attorney general, declared editor Avery of the *Constitution*. "It riddles his law to smithereens. It is absolutely unanswerable. And it is none the less forcible or potent because it comes from a Republican source."[16]

There were many rumors of corruption within the state government. Brown was now concerned over possible political pressure upon the court in defense of the Bullock administration. "If no terms are attempted to be put upon me I may remain on the Bench," he wrote

14 *House Journal*, 1870, Pt. 1, pp. 10–16; Atlanta *Daily Constitution*, January 8, 1870.
15 Atlanta *Daily Constitution*, January 19, 1870.
16 *Ibid.*, January 20, 1870.

Stephens, but he would not submit to pressure for political approval of "extravagance or public plunder. I trust the financial schemes are not so bad as many good people suppose." Clearly, Brown was no longer within the inner circle of the governor's friends. He had not seen Blodgett in a month, he informed Stephens. Neither had he "conversed with Gov. Bullock about any public matter since his return from Washington." Therefore, he did not consider himself well informed. "There are all sorts of rumors afloat here."[17]

For judging the qualifications of members of the legislature, General Terry appointed a military board of three. The result was that, through the use of martial law, twenty-one persons were denied seats in the Georgia legislature. However, sixteen of this number admitted their own ineligibility by applying for relief from disabilities.[18] "Oh! degenerate days! Oh! lost liberty!" screamed the editor of the Rome *Weekly Courier*. "When cornfield niggers and imported scalawags thus disgrace the halls of Georgia legislation, where Troup and Toombs and Stephens lent the power of their geneous [*sic*] to give prestige to the great commonwealth."[19]

Once the Negro members regained their seats and twenty-one conservative whites lost theirs, the Bullock Radicals were ready for reorganization of the legislature. There was no difficulty in electing Bullock's friend Benjamin Conley president of the Senate. In the House, however, there was a spirited fight for Speaker between the supporters of John E. Bryant and Robert L. McWhorter. Bryant, once a Bullock man but now in opposition, was the candidate of the more conservative members. McWhorter was chosen. There is evidence that Brown played a quiet part in this reorganization of the House. Robert Toombs, who had visited Atlanta at the opening of the session but left before organization was completed, wrote Alexander Stephens that Bullock was "perfectly reckless, fully supported by the military, stakes all upon success, and offers all the offices, places, money and the plunder of the people for help to aid him to obtain the dictatorship of the state." Toombs feared that some so-called Democrats would "bite at the bait," yet be believed there was still enough firmness within the party to "hold

17 January 5, 1870, in Stephens Papers, Library of Congress.
18 Thompson, *Reconstruction*, 263–64.
19 January 14, 1870.

the weak and timid and overawe and intimidate some of the villains on their own side. . . . Bryant is the candidate of the Democrats for speaker of the House, and I and Joe Brown are trying to elect him! Rather a strange conjunction, is it not? But you know my rule is to use the devil if I can do better to save the country."[20] Two weeks later Toombs had still more to say about the situation at the capital. While there, he had consulted with Brown, Bryant, and others. "Politics does make us acquainted with strange bedfellows," he explained. "Brown seems really in earnest in his endeavour to defeat Bullock and his schemes. I don't know whether or not he sees where his present course will land him, but I suppose he does."[21] Brown knew quite well the direction in which he was moving.

Peterson Thweatt reported to Stephens that Brown appeared "determined not only to cut loose from, but to fight Bullock & his schemes, whenever he has time from his duties in the Supreme Court. . . . I think he is anxious to quit the Bench & probably would have done so but for your advice & the advice of other friends." Governor Bullock and his friends were "lobbying for Bob McWhorter. He *pays well.*" In the limited association he himself had had with the governor, Thweatt had found him "kind & clever," yet he still considered him "an *unmitigated scoundrel, thief* & everything else that is *mean.*" To another friend Thweatt confided that Brown would help all he could to "head" Bullock.[22]

The Bullock-Terry dominated General Assembly quickly ratified the Fifteenth Amendment and also the Fourteenth. The latter action was in accordance with the claim that the previous legislature had been illegally constituted. Following this same line of reasoning, the legislature declared illegal the 1868 election of Hill and Miller as senators and proceeded to select in their stead Henry P. Farrow and Richard H. Whiteley. Since the short term to which Whiteley was elected would end in 1871, the legislature went still further and chose Foster Blodgett to succeed Whiteley for the term 1871–1877.[23] "Bullock's Boys" were

20 January 24, 1870, Phillips, *Correspondence*, 707.
21 Toombs to Stephens, February 8, 1870, *ibid.*, 708.
22 January 20, 1870, in Stephens Papers, Library of Congress; Thweatt to John Screven, February 7, 1870, in Arnold-Screven Family Papers, University of North Carolina.
23 *House Journal*, 1870, pp. 95–98.

in control and riding high, but they were digging their own political graves and also that of the Republican party in Georgia for a hundred years to come. No one versed in Georgia politics could have failed to detect the gathering storm. Judge Brown was already trimming his sails to meet the gale. Bullock and his clique had moved too far too fast, and looking back, they soon saw supporters both in Washington and Georgia falling behind and dwindling in numbers. There was evidence that Congress was growing tired of the Georgia question; the president had never had much of an appetite for the subject.

In Georgia, dissension and feuds were tearing the Republican party apart. Supporters of Bryant continued hostile to Bullock; the governor and the state treasurer, Nedom L. Angier, were charging each other with the misuse of state funds. There was also a trend toward moderation in both the Republican and Democratic parties. Owing to control of state patronage, the Radicals were very powerful, Bryant reported to White House secretary Horace Porter. They were also seeking to convince federal officeholders that "they control the patronage of President Grant. . . . They are bold and reckless and they squander the money of the people openly evidently expecting to escape punishment on account of their power[.] They *expect* Congress and the President to sustain them by extending the terms of the members of the General Assembly." The object of his own efforts now, Bryant explained, was to break the influence of the Bullock-Blodgett ring and reorganize the Republican party under the leadership of Amos T. Akerman.

Bryant also reported the division within the Democratic party and noted the little difference between the moderate wings of the two parties. "Personally the leaders of these two wings are on the most intimate terms and all look to ex-Gov. Brown as their leader." Brown, Bryant continued, was a strong supporter of the Grant administration, "but he is bitterly opposed to the policy of Gov. Bullock." Should Congress and the president permit Bullock and Blodgett to control federal patronage, Bryant predicted that within six months the moderates of the two parties would "unite under the leadership of Gov. Brown who I regard as the ablest leader in the South." Such a combination would not only gain control in Georgia but shape the policy of "the great mass of the white men of the South," and probably give support to a man like

Salmon P. Chase for the presidency in 1872. However, if the president and Congress did not sustain Bullock and Blodgett, the Republican party could be saved. Bryant hoped Porter would give this matter much thought and probably put it before President Grant.[24]

At heart, the majority of white Georgians were Democrats, and the Democrats held most of the elective local offices. In view of these facts, plus the hostility resulting from the Bullock-led "third reconstruction" of Georgia, the governor realized that a Republican victory in any statewide election in 1870 would be highly unlikely unless the military continued in control. Therefore, he spent much time in Washington during the late spring and early summer lobbying for a bill declaring the Georgia government provisional and postponing the election of a new General Assembly until November, 1871. Although this plan was championed by Benjamin Butler, successor to Thad Stevens as Radical leader in the House of Representatives, and thousands of dollars were rumored to have been spent in the "right places," the movement failed. In mid-July, 1870, Congress readmitted Georgia to the Union and stipulated that nothing in the act was to be so construed as to deny the election of a General Assembly in accordance with the Georgia constitution.[25]

If the election of a new General Assembly could not be postponed, Georgia Republicans reasoned that the next best thing to do would be to regulate the election in such ways as to give maximum advantage to their party. In late summer United States Attorney General Amos T. Akerman, Georgia's contribution to Grant's cabinet, appeared on the scene. Although no friend of Bullock, his interest in the welfare of the Republican party prompted him to supervise the drafting of a bill, which as passed, fixed the election dates as December 22–24, and provided that election officials were to be appointed by the governor and approved by the (Republican) assembly. No voter could be challenged at the polls. In the interest of success, if not of harmony, the supporters of both Bullock and Bryant assisted in the passage of this bill. Brown opposed the bill and authorized the editor of the *Con-*

---

24 May 21, 1870, in John E. Bryant Papers, Duke University.
25 U.S. *Statutes at Large*, 41st Cong., 2nd Sess., XVI, 363–64. For a detailed discussion of congressional maneuvering relative to Georgia bills and amendments see Nathans, *Losing the Peace*, 182 ff.

stitution to say that he considered some of its provisions "in palpable violation of the constitution" and that he therefore condemned and denounced it.[26]

When the Atlanta *New Era*, no longer edited by Samuel Bard and no longer friendly to Brown, made derogatory comments, Judge Brown took exceptions and made a public explanation of his connection with the Akerman bill and his objections to its provisions. He had not seen a copy of the bill until it had already passed the House. Upon reading it he was convinced that it violated the state constitution. He then urged that it be so amended as to secure a fair election and not violate the plain provisions of the constitution. His suggestion was not heeded, for the "party lash had been used freely," and Republican members feared censure should they fail to support the bill.

Brown's objections to the new law were specific. The law stated that voting should take place in the county seats and in any other precinct that existed or might be established in other incorporated towns. But the constitution did not give the General Assembly power to "make or change established precincts," Brown contended. The people alone, acting through their courts of ordinary, possessed that power. If the act should be carried out, there would be but one voting precinct in most counties, for they had but one incorporated town. This inconvenience to voters would greatly reduce the rural vote. The aged, ill, and poor who lived in remote sections would be subjected to virtual disfranchisement. To deny people the privilege of voting in their regular precincts was also wrong, and should be "condemned by all honest Republicans. . . . We may obtain power for the time by unconstitutional and unfair means; but we can never maintain a party in power long by such means"; there would come a day of reckoning and retribution.

Further, Brown explained, the constitution stated that no one should be permitted to vote, "if challenged," unless he took the oath. But the new law denied to both election managers and bystanders the right to challenge a voter. What then was the situation when a prospective voter, if challenged, coud not vote unless he took the oath, yet no one could challenge him or deny him the ballot? The constitution also re-

26 *Senate Journal*, 1870, p. 274; *House Journal*, 1870, p. 874; *Acts and Resolutions*, 1870, p. 62; Atlanta *Daily Constitution*, October 1, 1870.

quired that a voter must have resided six months within the state and thirty days within the county. Yet the new law required only residence within the county. Residence of even one day would meet this requirement. Also the constitution denied the ballot to any member of the armed forces even though stationed in Georgia. But soldiers could certainly meet the one-day residence requirement; therefore, under the new law they could not be denied the ballot. Still further, the constitution denied the ballot to all persons who had been directly connected with a duel. The new law would permit one to vote although he had killed his man only an hour earlier. In total, the constitution denied the ballot to seven distinct classes of persons; the new law denied it to none who appeared to be of voting age. In conclusion, Brown declared: "I think what I have said shows conclusively that the act in question is in conflict with the plainest principles and provisions of the Constitution, and is to the extent of such conflict utterly null and void, and should be so held and treated by every patriotic, law abiding citizen of this state."[27] Thus spoke the chief justice of the Georgia Supreme Court.

Whether by design or accident, the Akerman Act threw the Georgia election of 1870 wide open for the perpetration of every conceivable fraud. No doubt both parties made considerable use of the opportunity. But Radical leadership in Georgia had faltered, and, tainted with rumors of corruption, it failed to attract new voters. The one bit of real political excitement during the campaign was Ben Hill's announcement through the columns of the Augusta *Chronicle and Sentinel* on December 11. Although he considered the Fourteenth and Fifteenth amendments usurpations, they had been added to the constitution and were now law, Hill explained. It was criminal "to aid in committing usurpation," but it was also a crime to break the law. "Successful usurpation is the strongest expression of power; and law itself, in its last analysis, is only power." He saw no probability that public opinion at the North would ever force the eradication of these amendments; therefore, they would remain law. All good citizens must obey the law regardless of whether or not they favored it. In the midst of the political campaign he would urge the importance of electing honest men, men who could not be bought. An honest black man was

27 Brown to Editor *Daily New Era*, October 29, 1870, in Hargrett Collection.

better than a dishonest white; an honest Republican better than a dishonest Democrat.[28] Hill had not only "yielded adhesion" to Brown's views, exclaimed editor I. W. Avery of the Atlanta *Constitution*, but he had "absolutely leaped clear over the head of the Chief Justice, and landed some mile or two beyond the 'reconstruction' and 'accept the situation' platform. . . . Joe Brown and Ben Hill cheek by jowl, politically, is a merry piece of humor."[29] Except for timing, there was much similarity between the new position assumed by Hill and that taken by Brown three years earlier. But Brown had acted when there was no certainty that Georgia would acquiesce; Hill waited until reconstruction provisions had been legally adopted and were in operation in Georgia. Both urged acceptance of congressional requirements and obedience to law. Brown must have chuckled when he read Hill's announcement and thought of the lambasting that was in store for his bitterest critic.

Hill's announcement, coming at a time when a Democratic victory was certain and when he himself had nothing of a political nature at stake, was generally puzzling. Naturally there was much speculation. Many who had been much less extreme than he denounced him as a traitor. Some expressed surprise at Hill's action, wrote Alexander Stephens, but as for himself he considered it convincing proof of "his total unfitness to lead. In his present position he is but a follower."[30] Linton Stephens was a bit more to the point: "He is truly a traitor—a base traitor," he wrote Brown. "No other word can fitly describe him."[31]

The state election of December 22–24, 1870, resulted in crushing defeat for the Republicans. Half the seats in each house of the General Assembly were to be filled. Of the eighty-six House members elected, seventy-one were Democrats. The Democrats also won nineteen of the twenty-two Senate seats filled. Four of the seven congressmen elected were Democrats.[32] These newly elected congressmen would be seated. And as if further to stress the decline of radicalism in Georgia, the United States Senate seated Joshua Hill and H. V. M. Miller, rather than Henry P. Farrow and Richard Whiteley.

28 Also widely copied in other newspapers.
29 December 28, 1870.
30 Stephens to Brown, December 15, 1870, in Hargrett Collection.
31 Linton Stephens to Brown, February 22, 1870, *ibid.*
32 Thompson, *Reconstruction*, 270–71.

When Ben Hill made his announcement, the public quickly observed that the path he had chosen was quite similar to the one chosen by Brown three years earlier. Could it be that these political antagonists were about to meet on common ground and possibly organize a new moderate political party? Only time would tell and time did not delay for long. One of the "scandals" of which the Bullock administration was accused was the misuse and even disappearance of public funds. The most noticeable case was the management of the Western and Atlantic Railroad. This state road had always been a source of patronage for the party in power, but under the management of Governor Bullock and Superintendent Foster Blodgett, it had become "a public grab-bag into which one sufficiently favored politically might plunge a hand."[33] It no longer paid profits into the State Treasury, and by mid-1870, the smell of corruption was so evident that not even good Republicans could defend its management. Yet a bill was actually introduced in the legislature to appropriate $500,000 to be used by Blodgett in putting the road in repair. As Ben Hill suggested, however, this bill might have been intended to hasten the leasing of the road.[34]

There was a widespread public demand that the road be taken out of politics. This had not been Brown's idea, however; testifying before an investigating committee in 1868, he had declared it impossible to divorce the Western and Atlantic from politics as long as it was owned and operated by the state. The same would be true if placed in charge of an appointed commission. He thought the present system had one definite advantage—the governor could always be held responsible for the management of the road. Naturally the governor would prefer the assistance of those whom he could trust, but if things went wrong the governor himself must assume the blame. "It is my deliberate judgment, therefore, that the present system, which has met the approval of our wisest and best men," was the best that could be devised. If those in charge were found guilty of error or mismanagement and failed to meet the "just standard of popular expectation, displace them at the next election and try other men." The only other alternative Brown saw was to sell the road. This he did not believe to be the wish of the people;

33 *Ibid.*, 245.
34 *Testimony* [Joint Committee of General Assembly to Investigate the Western and Atlantic Railroad, 1872] (Bound without title page), 119.

yet he thought many capitalists would be eager to buy such valuable property.[35] By 1870 there had been much change since Brown recorded this opinion in November, 1868. His advice was now rising up to convict the governor he had helped to elect, and he himself had joined those capitalists who had their eyes on this valuable piece of state property.

In October, 1870, Dunlap Scott, a Democrat, introduced a bill to take the Western and Atlantic out of politics by leasing it to a private company. The bill was hastily drawn and introduced in order to get it on the calendar. Scott then called at Chief Justice Brown's office and requested him to put the bill in finished form. When Brown suggested that the requirement of an $8 million bond by the leasing company might be a bit high, Scott, according to Brown, replied that he wished it high so "Bullock could not lease the road to carpet-baggers and adventurers." Brown redrafted the bill, but, as passed, the lease act differed from this bill in several particulars.[36] Brown did not say what particulars.

Many Republicans joined Democrats, and the bill passed both houses of the legislature by large majorities. Governor Bullock approved it on October 24, 1870. The new act authorized the governor to lease the road to a private company for a period of twenty years for a monthly payment of not less than $25,000. The leasing company was required to give bond for $8 million. This of course made the pledging of railroad property necessary. A majority of the lessees must have been residents of Georgia for the past five years.[37] The fact that Republican legislators supported a measure taking from them their principal source of patronage caused considerable public speculation. Had some interested parties used money where it could work most effectively? Or did the Bullock clique, realizing that their days in power were numbered, wish to deprive the opposition of future patronage? Bullock immediately announced that he would receive bids from interested companies until December 25, 1870.

Ever interested in both money and railroads and having been very

---

35 *Senate Journal*, 1869, pp. 470–73.
36 *Testimony*, 128–29, 177.
37 *Acts and Resolutions*, 1870, pp. 423–27.

successful in the management of both, Judge Brown immediately became involved in the formation of a company to bid for the lease.[38] Prominently associated with him in this venture were his law partner Hannibal I. Kimball, a financial power of questionable ethics, John P. King, president of the Georgia Railroad, Edward W. Cole of the Nashville and Chattanooga Railroad, and Ezekiel Waitzfelder of New York, formerly of Milledgeville. At his own request, Alexander Stephens was also admitted to membership to the extent of $10,000. Stephens suggested to Brown that the lease might be worth considerably more than $25,000 per month, but Brown replied that he would not be a party to any lease above that amount, citing as reasons the condition of the road and the increasing competition from other roads. He thought, however, that with good luck and proper management there would be a "handsome margin for profit," and the leasing company would be doing the people of Georgia "a great kindness in taking the road out of politics." At the same time, he noted, the guaranteed income to the state would equal "all the State tax paid this year." It would be a pleasure to have Stephens a member of the company, Brown concluded, for Stephens could always be relied upon "to uphold honesty and fair dealing by the company with the State and all other parties. I will have nothing to do with it on any other basis."[39]

News of King's association with Brown and Kimball alarmed managers of the railroads serving Macon. They feared that a combination of the Georgia and the Western and Atlantic railroads might adversely affect their business. Their first idea was to purchase interest in the Brown company. Having no success, they then organized a company of their own in which Ben Hill became a leading figure. They also went outside and recruited as members Senator Simon Cameron of Pennsylvania, Walter T. Walters of the Baltimore and Ohio Railroad Thomas Scott of the Pennsylvania Railroad, and John S. Delano, son of the secretary of the interior. Hill later testified that these men were brought into the company for purely business reasons, and Brown

38 Since becoming chief justice, Brown's income had decreased considerably. For 1869 he reported only $9,981. This was only slightly more than 50 percent of his 1867 income. Hargrett Collection.
39 Stephens to Brown, December 10, 1870, *ibid.*; Brown to Stephens, December 16, 1870, in Stephens Papers, Library of Congress.

added that it was because of their large railroad interests which they were extending southward.[40]

A third group, which became known as the Seago-Blodgett-Dobbins Company, was formed in the Atlanta area. Its organization was never quite complete. Management of three railroads offered as security later claimed the offer was made without their consent. But this company submitted a bid of $36,500 monthly for the lease. There is no evidence that Governor Bullock ever seriously considered awarding the lease to Seago-Blodgett-Dobbins, although Brown stated privately, "The Gov's sympathies were with Blodgett's company."[41] Perhaps he should have said "with Blodgett," not the company.

What apparently concerned the governor most was that both the Brown and Hill companies were seeking the lease at $25,000. Hill later told of having two interviews with the governor in behalf of his own company. He found that the feeling between Brown and Bullock was not very friendly. "I had always supposed to the contrary, until that time," Hill added. The governor "spoke very disparagingly of Brown, and declared that he would never accept the bid of any company with Brown in it, until he had his resignation in his hand." In a second interview, Hill further related, he inquired of Bullock as to the truth of the rumor that no lease would likely be made to anyone. Bullock replied that he hoped a company could be formed that would represent "all parties in the State."[42] Hill did not make this revelation until after Governor Bullock had resigned and left the state.

The governor no doubt applied pressure in behalf of the merger of the Hill and Brown companies, but it was Brown who took the lead. As early as December 19, 1870, he was in private correspondence with A. J. White, president of the Macon and Western Railroad, a member of the Hill company. "Form no alliance with any northern man or company till I see you," Brown urged. "Say the same to the Central. I know facts that I consider vital to *Georgia interests*. Let me see you when you come before you do anything. Say the same to Genl. Holt [of the Southwestern]. Tell him to come with you. I know I can confide in

40 *Testimony*, 128–29, 177.
41 Brown to Linton Stephens, January 30, 1871, in Hargrett Collection.
42 *Testimony*, 127–29.

you. We must have a conference strictly private."[43] Brown sent a similar message to Alexander R. Lawton urging him to be in Atlanta the next Saturday "with power to represent the Central R. R." Lawton was also urged to form no positive alliance until the two could confer. The conference should be private. Brown also repeated the statement that he knew some facts "important to all of the *Georgia interests*."[44]

Members of both companies, including Columbus Delano, were assembling in Atlanta by the twenty-first. Simon Cameron had been there, but had now returned to Pennsylvania. William C. Morrill of the Macon group reported to Cameron: "We at last succeeded in making a compromise with our opponents . . . . The interests were so large and conflicting that we found the Governor would not let it [the lease] unless we did come to terms— Divisions of interest also had to be made to meet the requirements of the Governor. . . . For two nights we did not go to bed until abt daylight." On the evening of the twenty-fourth the two groups met in separate rooms in the Kimball House; negotiations were carried on by messenger. The most difficult matter to settle was who would control the management of a combined company; there was no inclination for the two companies to bid against each other for the lease. Brown no doubt stated a fact when he later revealed that he was unyielding in his opposition to giving the other company control. He valued very highly his own knowledge of railroading and would not agree to give power to any group that "would manage it loosely." About midnight the two companies agreed to a merger, and Brown became president of the Western and Atlantic Railroad Company. A bid was immediately sent to Governor Bullock. Brown, H. I. Kimball, and Senator Simon Cameron of Pennsylvania owned one and one-half shares each in the new company. Twenty others owned one or one-half share each. Each of the combining companies furnished eleven shareholders. Share "No. 23" was assigned to W. B. Dinsmore of New York, president of the Southern Express Company and friend of Governor Bullock. All shareholders were designated as directors. Morrill excitedly reported to Cameron that the new

43 Brown to White, December 19, 20, 1870, in Hargrett Collection.
44 Brown to Lawton, December 19, 1870, in Alexander R. Lawton Papers, University of North Carolina.

company was "certainly the strongest ever in the South & the security embraces every road from here to St. Louis & every road in Ga." He gave Delano much credit for the success.[45]

Brown immediately resigned as chief justice, specifically requesting that Governor Bullock accept his resignation "before you consider the respective proposals or decide between the different companies on the question of the lease of the road."[46] This was Brown's second resignation. No record of his first resignation, which occurred in August, has been found, but he was reappointed on October 22, 1870.[47] Neither is there a clear reason for his first resignation. One recent writer labels Brown's action as a trick to get rid of Associate Justice Warner and to get an increase in salary for himself.[48] The Savannah *Morning News* explained that the first resignation was "to secure an increase in salary" and the second "to get hold of the State Road. . . . 'J. B. is sly sir: devilish sly is Joey B.'"[49] This is confusing, for neither the acts of 1869 nor 1870 provided for a salary increase for judges. As for Warner, Bullock might have wished to be rid of him, but it is doubtful that Brown shared the desire. He and Warner had been close friends for many years, and although they disagreed on some legal points, there is no evidence of hostility. In reporting the second resignation the Augusta *Weekly Chronicle and Sentinel* observed: "As a matter of course the little game is understood between them. Bullock accepts the resignation and after the lease (stealing) of the State Road is accomplished will reappoint Joseph."[50] But if Hill quoted Bullock correctly, Brown had no choice other than to resign if he wished his company to secure the lease. Hill also testified that he himself refused to go into any company with Brown unless he resigned from the court.[51] There was

---

45 W. C. Morrill to Simon Cameron, December 29, 1870, in Simon Cameron Papers, Library of Congress. For official papers relating to the lease, see "Executive Minutes, 1870–74," pp. 1–6. Names of lessees are affixed. The combined total personal wealth of the lessees was givn as more than $4 million. Brown was listed at $100,000. This of course was too conservative.

46 Brown to Governor Bullock, December 24, 1870, Atlanta *Daily Constitution*, December 28, 1870. Bullock appointed A. O. Lockrane, Brown's former law partner, as his successor.

47 "Executive Minutes, 1870–74."

48 Darrell C. Roberts, *Joseph E. Brown and the Politics of Reconstruction* (Tuscaloosa, 1973), 69.

49 December 31, 1870.

50 January 4, 1871.

51 *Testimony*, 126.

no need for heavy pressure upon Brown to resign; he had frequently threatened to do just that, and a salary of $2,500 was scarcely attractive to a man of Brown's abilities.

Although Governor Bullock had no doubt made his decision prior to Brown's resignation from the supreme bench, the award was not announced until several days later. Brown learned of the governor's decision on December 27, and he, Hill, and Delano set to work drawing up the papers required by law; the governor immediately affixed his signature. Brown took possession of the Western and Atlantic Railroad at 5:30 P.M. the same day.[52] That evening Bullock gave a "celebration" dinner at the Kimball House, apparently in honor of the out-of-state lessees. "Truly we have here the lion and the lamb lying down together," observed a reporter to the Augusta *Weekly Chronicle*, "and yet there was no commotion in the heavens, as very many would have expected had such a queer gathering been brought together two years ago."[53]

There was much uncertainty as to just what happened in the case of the Seago-Blodgett-Dobbins Company. Bullock stated that the group did not offer sufficient security. Members of the company insisted that there was sufficient security, but Bullock acted before it could be organized. As would be brought out in later investigation, Blodgett was taken into the company because of his close relationship to Bullock and then when he failed to deliver there was a desire to discard him. Regardless of whether or not he officially withdrew from the company, Blodgett used his influence in behalf of the opposition. He later revealed in private correspondence that through an arrangement with Kimball and Brown, "with the knowledge and advice of Gov. Bullock," he was paid $60,000 for "services rendered the Western & Atlantic R. R. Co."[54] He gave no indication of the nature of his services.

No deal with which Bullock, Brown, and Kimball were connected could have escaped charges of fraud, and the addition of the name of Ben Hill merely added his newly acquired enemies to the list. It was quickly charged that "No. 23" among the lessees was Bullock, not Dinsmore. Then when the Seago-Blodgett-Dobbins group revealed that

52 *The Lease of the Western & Atlantic Railroad, with Correspondence and Other Papers in Relation Thereto* (Atlanta, 1871); *Testimony*, 170.
53 January 4, 1871.
54 Blodgett to H. I. Kimball, January 11, 1875, in Hargrett Collection.

they had actually bid $36,500 per month for the lease, the charge of favoritism was added to that of fraud. Expecting a sympathetic hearing, A. K. Seago told his story of injustice to Robert Toombs, and Toombs took it to Stephens.[55] Upon seeing the list of lessees, Toombs had already written Stephens, "It is a lot of the greatest rogues on the continent, your name alone excepted." He was surprised to see Stephens' name among them.[56]

Stephens, ill at Crawfordville, had been much pleased with Brown's efforts in his behalf in company affairs and had sent to him the power of attorney to be used in all company matters. His only concern, he explained, was that Brown would no longer be chief justice.[57] He had also authorized Brown to transfer one half of his share to Sebastian K. Johnson. He was thinking of transferring the other half to the Educational Fund of Georgia. Upon hearing the Seago story he determined to complete the transfer. "I could not think of continuing to be interested in any way with a lease of this property of the State made under the circumstances stated by Mr. Seago," he informed Brown. He cared not whether all of Seago's account was completely accurate; it was enough that a man of his standing had made such a charge.[58] Stephens immediately gave to the press a complete account of his connection with the lease and withdrawal from the company, and assured his readers that during his participation he had no idea of any wrong doing. Now convinced otherwise, he was transferring his interest to the state.[59] Brown replied in three columns of details relative to the leasing and Stephens' voluntary participation. The company was defended, but no effort was made to discredit Stephens.[60]

Linton Stephens reassured his brother that he had taken the right course. Linton knew not what fraud might be proved but would "confess the thing has a bad look to me, and I believe there was fraud in it." On a recent trip to Macon he had learned that Bullock really did reject a higher bid. It was also reported that in return for the lease Bul-

55 Seago to Stephens, January 9, 1871, in Stephens Papers, Library of Congress. Seago declared that every word he had written Toombs was true.
56 December 30, 1870, Phillips, *Correspondence*, 265.
57 Stephens to Brown, December 28, 1870, in Hargrett Collection.
58 Stephens to Brown, January 4, 7, 1871, *ibid.*
59 Augusta *Daily Constitutionalist*, January 8, 1971.
60 *Ibid.*, January 13, 1871.

lock was promised by Cameron and Delano that "Bullock Senators" should be seated in Congress. It was also generally believed that Bullock was a member of the company. He himself thought Bullock had been involved with Kimball in many shady deals. "I don't believe you have a conception of the depth and breadth of his corruption, and I don't believe that Bullock is much, if any, worse than Joe Brown." Linton was also suspicious because Republicans Cameron and Delano had been made a part of the company. Further, he believed Ben Hill's coming into the company "so freshly after his tergiversation" was a part of his reward. And Judge Erskine was also at the Bullock dinner. No doubt "the connection between the lease and the dinner was very close and intimate."[61]

There was a considerable outburst of public protest and suspicion when the lease was announced, yet there was also evidence of a feeling of relief. "While we disapprove of leasing," explained the Savannah *Morning News*, "yet the people need not have any fear that the twenty-five thousand dollars will be paid into the Treasury promptly. So far as we are concerned, we would be perfectly willing for Gov. Brown to take the road, and trust him to pay that or any other amount he might agree to pay into the Treasury, without bond."[62] There would be no doubt about Brown's promptness in making payments and he was usually careful to see that the public was informed of the same.[63]

Expecting the granting of the lease to be severely challenged and probably officially investigated, and apparently ignorant of Linton Stephens' hostility to the Western and Atlantic Company, Brown suggested that Linton accept "a retainer in favor of the lease." Stephens refused, stating his reason to be distrust of the validity of the lease and suspicion that Bullock had a personal interest in the shares held by both Kimball and Dinsmore. "I would not pay the slightest attention to any denial which either he or Kimball might make, in this or in any other matter where they might have an interest." He thought them "a pack of swindling adventurers." Brown replied that he had no compaint about Stephens' refusal of a retainer from the Western and Atlantic Company, but he did wish to state that Stephens was mistaken

---

61 Linton Stephens to Alexander Stephens, January 8, 1871, in Stephens Papers, College of Sacred Heart.
62 December 31, 1871.
63 See Atlanta *Daily Sun*, October 2, 1871.

about Bullock's being interested in the lease. "I think I know *positively* that he is not."[64] No proof was ever submitted that Brown was incorrect. However, the opposition required no proof; they were convinced that Bullock was financially involved.

In view of the numerous charges of fraud and scandal against Bullock and his associates, it was inevitable that the Western and Atlantic Railroad Company would be subjected to litigations and investigations. The Seago group, which Brown referred to as the Dobbins company, protesting against being denied the lease when they were higher bidder, employed Robert Toombs as counsel to threaten suit, but suggested that a compromise might be arranged. "In my opinion it would be best for us to compromise with the Dobbins Co. and stop difficulties," Brown wrote director A. J. White. "They ask $35,000 and half Stephens's interest." They could cause "ten years litigation" plus a heavy legal fee and expense "to lobbyists before the legislature." But "with them satisfied we could get along with little difficulty." The $35,000 would place a considerable burden upon the Western and Atlantic Company, still with careful management "I could soon work out of it all. . . . I have always found it best to compromise out of such difficulties. I have made it a rule as a lawyer to law for other people who desired it and compromise for myself." Brown suggested that White see the other Macon directors and let him know their views.[65]

In the same envelope with the above letter from Brown to White is an undated, unsigned statement, supposedly made by a number of railroad officials, copies in Brown's handwriting: "We state unequivocally that neither the Central R. Road & Bk. Co. nor the South Western R. Road Company, nor the Macon and Western Railroad Company authorized said company to use their names, as they were used as sureties for said Company composed of Seago, Blodgett & others and we state positively that said Companies would not then and would not at any time since have gone on the bond of said Seago, Blodgett & others." This would appear to be a statement which Brown planned to use in case of litigation with the Seago group.

64 Linton Stephens to Brown, January 26, 1871; Brown to Linton Stephens, January 30, 1871, in Hargrett Collection.
65 Brown to White, January 27, 1871, *ibid.*

In addition to silencing by compromise those who threatened legal action, President Brown urged the development of a friendly press. Apparently James Gardner, owner of the Augusta *Constitutionalist*, had wished to be a member of the original company but was not so favored. On March 27, 1871, Brown wrote director John P. King, president of the Georgia Railroad, that he had conferred freely with Gardner. The only way Gardner would now agree to become a member of the Western and Atlantic Company would be through a transfer of a portion of King's share "to relate back to the formation of the company." Brown thought Gardner would be pleased with a one-fourth share, and he stated that the company would compensate King for the loss of interest. "I think Col. G. would use his pen with vigour & energy in defence of the lease & the Co." King was urged to contact Gardner. "He has a warm friendship for you and wants to defend you against all assaults," Brown concluded.[66] King agreed, since it was thought that the lease was "in a rather ticklish condition" and "every *honest* means of protecting it" was considered justified. He also agreed that the services of a "respectable & influential" newspaper were expedient and wise.[67] When the transfer of one-fourth share was made it was to Gardner "in trust for the sole & separate use of his wife Martha G. S. Gardner."[68]

Bullock, Kimball, and Brown also made a $5,000 loan to Dr. Samuel Bard, late of the *New Era* and now editor of the *True Georgian*. To secure this loan a lien was taken on the entire printing establishment. Payment for all job work done for the Western and Atlantic Company was to be applied to the loan.[69] The company received little service from this new press; Bard failed to repay the loan, the *True Georgian* folded, and Brown, in whose name the loan was made, took over the printing office and equipment. He subsequently formed a partnership with Wilson Rice, printer, in a job printing business.[70]

Rumors relating to the Western and Atlantic lease multiplied. Robert Cowart circulated the report that Brown had paid legislator

66 Hargrett Collection.
67 King to Brown, n.d., *ibid.*
68 King to Brown, April 27, 1871, *ibid.*
69 Hargrett Collection under date of July 18, 1871.
70 See agreement in Hargrett Collection under date of January 18, 1872.

C. H. Hooks and others $4,000 to support the lease. Brown denied it; so did Hooks.[71] The *Augusta Chronicle and Sentinel* reported a rumor that a Brown-Bullock "ring" was being formed to control the next legislature. The editor had no confidence in the report that Brown "would not become an active participant in movements looking to the security of Bullock's position in the Gubernatorial chair." The truth was, continued the editor, the connection between Brown and Bullock had been so "close and intimate" during the past three years that "the safety of one involves the security of the other." Bullock would not be impeached nor would there be close investigation "into the conduct of Bullock, Brown & Co." if Brown could by "juggling and duplicity" prevent the appointment of "an honest or intelligent" investigating committee. State road money would no doubt "flow freely."[72]

The Atlanta *Sun*, in which Alexander Stephens was major stockholder, editorialized on the *Chronicle* charge, and warned legislators to beware and to remember the "Yazoo Ring." Legislators were also warned that the "hungry wolves" who had gnawed into the vitals of political action during the last session would no doubt "attempt to save themselves from exposure, disgrace and punishment they deserve, by manipulating the next legislature as they did the last."[73] Brown reacted quickly in a letter to the "Political Editor" of the *Sun*, denying any knowledge of such a ring but adding that he had heard of a ring *opposed* to the lease. He did not believe, however, that legislators, "knowing the popular sentiment," would "commit *political suicide*" by stopping the flow into the Treasury from the Western and Atlantic. He then launched a discussion of benefits that would accrue to the state.[74] Although Stephens held the title of "Political Editor," the letter fell into the hands of general editor J. Henley Smith. Perhaps Stephens was not in Atlanta at the time.

When several days passed and Brown's letter did not appear in the *Sun*, he inquired as to what had happened to his article on "combinations and rings." Smith forwarded the inquiry to Stephens, suggesting that the article might be published "with proper comments,"

71 Brown to Hooks, October 10, 1871; Hooks to Brown, October 17, 1871, in Hargrett Collection.
72 October 5, 1871.
73 October 5, 1871.
74 October 1, 1871, in Hargrett Collection.

but he thought Brown had "laid himself very wide open" on some points. Smith also inquired of Stephens what he thought of his own recent article. Toombs had informed Smith that it went a bit too far. Toombs was convinced that Bullock could not be impeached without the "aid of the R.R. ring"; therefore, "we must not drive Democrats who voted for and are interested in the R.R. charter over to the support of Bullock."[75] Stephens apparently did not think well of the publication of Brown's article; he returned it to the author.

The Democratic legislators chosen in December, 1870, did not take their seats and assume control of the General Assembly until November, 1871. Meanwhile, charges of fraud and corruption against the Bullock administration continued to mount. Added to mismanagement of the Western and Atlantic prior to lease were charges of fraudulent endorsement of railroad bonds. The Bryant wing of the Republican party desperately called upon Washington for help. Bullock and Blodgett were their principal targets. After election, Bryant wrote Columbus Delano, Bullock had turned his back on those who elected him and surrounded himself with corrupt men. Reorganization alone could save the Republican party in Georgia. No reliance could be placed upon the black vote "until the Ku Klux Klan and all other organizations of violent men are broken up." And recruiting whites was very difficult as long as Blodgett was head of the state central committee. Bryant thought Brown concurred in these views.[76]

What assistance Bryant hoped to secure from Washington is uncertain, but Georgia was soon to be rid of Bullock-Blodgett influence. Governor Bullock had no desire to face a hostile General Assembly and probable impeachment; so to the almost complete surprise of everyone, he resigned on October 23, 1871, leaving the governorship to his friend Benjamin Conley, president of the Senate. Before his resignation was made public, he had left the state. To many Georgians, the governor's flight was sufficient evidence of guilt.

The General Assembly convened on November 1, 1871. The moderate whites had finally regained control in Georgia. L. N. Trammell, Brown's long-time North Georgia friend, was chosen president of the

75 Brown to Editor of *Daily Sun*, October 17, 1871, in Stephens Papers, Library of Congress. Smith's note to Stephens is written on this letter.
76 May 18, 1871, in Bryant Papers.

Senate. James M. Smith was elected Speaker of the House. The Democratic Assembly had no intention of permitting Republican Conley to serve out the unexpired term of Governor Bullock; so, by special act, December 3 was set as the date for electing a new governor. A Democratic nominating convention met in Atlanta only three days before election day and chose James M. Smith, Speaker of the House, as their candidate. The dispirited Republicans, suffering from the charges of fraud and corruption hurled at the Bullock administration, held no convention and made no nomination. Although without competition, Smith polled only 39,705 votes. He was inaugurated as governor on January 12, 1872. Brown was among the distinguished men who escorted the new governor to the chair. A friend reported that Brown not only voted for Smith but also contributed one hundred dollars toward the expenses of the inaugural ball.[77]

Brown was clearly on the road that would return him to his political home. For several months Linton Stephens had been privately urging him to rejoin his old political friends. In February, 1871, Stephens had written: "I never blamed your motive but only your conclusions. I thought you despaired too soon. When you said there was no hope, I thought there *was* hope." He still had hope and felt certain that the next president would be a Democrat. This would bring an end to revolutionary reconstruction governments and restore the constitution and a republican form of government. At no time since the war had he thought that the minds of the people were more eager for the truth. He also thought that even God, having "exhausted his wrath upon us," would exert his power toward the "re-establishment of the Constitution and constitutional liberty."

"I appeal to you by the ties of our old friendship and by the memory of the many conflicts in which we have stood side by side for the cause of liberty," Stephens entreated. "Reconsider your position. Does not *consistency* require that you should say under the present changed aspects of affairs—you were mistaken in *point of fact*—you *now* see there *is* hope, and henceforth the whole weight of your intellect and character shall be cast in favor of the cause which has never *ceased* to be dearest to your heart?" Stephens was certain that Brown's old

77 Peterson Thweatt to Alexander Stephens, January 14, 1872, in Stephens Papers, Library of Congress; Avery, *History of Georgia*, 467–68.

friends would welcome him with great enthusiasm; and "you would have a glorious revenge on the traitor, Ben Hill." There was no doubt that "your power thrown into the right scale at this time would be tremendous" and greatly appreciated. "I entreat you not to decide this question hastily. Ponder it." This letter was being written by his wife, Stephens concluded, and only she and "my brother" would know of it.[78] If anyone could have a persuasive influence upon Brown it was Linton Stephens.

The Democratic General Assembly began immediately to investigate the conduct of the recent Republican regime—management of the Western and Atlantic under Bullock and Blodgett, lease of the Western and Atlantic, illegal endorsement of bonds, and the official conduct of Governor Bullock. As everyone must have expected, most of the sins of corruption were charged to absent former governor Bullock. Testimony was so voluminous and conflicting as to prove most anything one wished to believe. Evidence of fraud in connection with the issuance or endorsement of bonds was most damaging. However, this was a subject on which there was disagreement. Brown always believed that a bond legally issued became an obligation of the state, regardless of who received the money for its sale. Toombs and Ben Hill, on the other hand, maintained that evidence of fraud invalidated the state's obligation. This was the view of the legislature when it repudiated that portion of the bonded indebtedness which it considered had been fraudulently created by the Bullock regime.[79]

The investigating committees found little to praise but much to condemn in the conduct of Governor Bullock and his close associates. The only investigation in which Brown had a prominent part was as to the legality of the granting of the Western and Atlantic lease. This unfriendly committee even employed Toombs as its attorney, and he did much of the questioning of witnesses.[80] Brown and Hill testified at length, disagreeing at some points and at times departing from what others stated as facts; both were always careful to exonerate themselves from any wrongdoing. A. J. White testified that after much discussion the Western and Atlantic Company had authorized President Brown

78 Linton Stephens to Brown, February 22, 1876, in Hargrett Collection.
79 *Acts and Resolutions*, 1872, pp. 5–8.
80 Members of the committee were W. M. Reese, G. M. Netherland, C. B. Hudson, G. F. Pierce, Jr., and A. D. Nunnally.

to use $50,000 to satisfy certain parties who claimed to have performed services for the company. Brown denied this, but admitted that he had wished to compensate some friends who wanted to get into the company but failed. Hill had objected, Brown said, for he too had some disappointed friends. The money mentioned by White, Brown asserted, was used to improve the road—$40,000 for the purchase of two hundred boxcars and fifty coal cars from the Ohio Falls Car Company. When the committee asked Brown just who the persons were outside the company he wished to compensate, he named Generals George D. Phillips and John B. Gordon. But in their own testimonies both Phillips and Gordon denied that they had any interest whatsoever in the lease.

The most interesting and probably the most informative testimonies came from members of the Seago-Blodgett-Dobbins group. Miles G. Dobbins stated that he, Seago, and William McNaughton went to see Blodgett and he subscribed $50,000. They were interested in Blodgett because they thought he had "a good deal of influence with Governor Bullock." Seago substantiated this story. Blodgett testified that the group wanted him to see Bullock in behalf of the proposed company and assure the governor that "he could have whatever interest he or his friends desire." As inducement to Blodgett to use his influence, the Seago group permitted him to sign up for $50,000 although they knew he was insolvent. Further, they wanted him to put Bullock down for $200,000. He not only refused, but he did not even speak to the governor about the matter. Displeased with his failure to perform, Blodgett continued, the other members of the proposed company tried "to turn me out," and then insulted him by offering $10 for his share. Seago and Dobbins, however, disputed Blodgett's testimony, denying that they made any effort to get Bullock into the company.

Throughout the hearings no one testified that Bullock was a member of the Western and Atlantic Company or offered proof that he acted illegally in granting the lease. Neither was Blodgett accused of secretly assisting the Western and Atlantic Company. No mention was made of the $60,000 Blodgett later privately stated he received from Brown and Kimball with Bullock's approval. Further, no mention was made of the $35,000 "hush money" demanded of Brown by the Seago group after the lease had been made.

In making their report, the majority of the committee made it clear that they had little confidence in the testimonies of Hill and Brown. They thought there was sufficient evidence that "H. I. Kimball, one of the lessees, *manipulated* Governor Bullock in procuring the lease. . . . It is certainly established that Kimball had an absolute control over Governor Bullock, in all matters of legislation and official patronage, from which money was to be made for himself, his relations and friends." The committee further stated that no company that had failed to take into consideration Kimball's influence could have secured the lease. In view of the evidence it was concluded that the lease "was unfairly obtained."

A. D. Nunnally, a committee member, filed a minority report which concluded: "Taking all the testimony, I am unable to see any fraud that could possibly justify a court in setting aside the contract lease." He proposed that the legislature adopt resolutions declaring that the evidence did not support a charge of "fraud or unfairness" and that on the contrary the lease was considered "a most fair and advantageous one."[81] The legislature approved the substance of the minority report.

The majority report was about what Brown had expected. On July 12, 1872, he wrote G. D. Phillips that "Judge [Augustus] Reese and one or two other members of the Committee are controlled by Genl. Toombs, and will report unfavorably."[82] When Bullock, writing from New York, congratulated him on his successful defense of the lease, Brown replied: "The assaults upon it were as bitter as partisan hate and personal malignity could devise. But the transaction was, as you know, an honest, fair one, and it could therefore stand the severest test and defy all assaults."[83]

Expecting an unfavorable report from the committee and not quite certain of what the legislature might do, Brown felt the need for more vigorous newspaper support. He sounded out Stephens on the possibility of purchasing the Atlanta *Sun*. Stephens was not interested in selling, he explained, for he had hopes of greater success as a journalist than in any of his previous occupations. He expressed great disappointment, however, that so little patronage was coming his way. As for the Western and Atlantic lease, he had not changed his opinion. The lease

81 *Testimony* . . . . Bound in with the *Testimony* are also majority and minority reports.
82 Hargrett Collection.
83 November 15, 1872, *ibid.*

was "unfairly let" and the price was too low; however, he was willing for the courts to decide its fate. "Its validity is a question I do not intend to discuss myself in the columns of the *Sun*." He thought his time and energy could be devoted to other things of "more practical interest." After making his own position clear, Stephens then stated to Brown that the columns of the *Sun* were open and urged him to use them. Owing to its large circulation, Stephens insisted that nowhere else could a full and ample hearing before the people be had for so small a cost. All of this was being written in strictest confidence and he was not keeping a copy. Brown could do what he wished with the original.[84] It was clear that Stephens had no *free* space to offer.

While Brown was feeling out Stephens, he was also resorting to a bit of psychology. In a long public letter addressed to R. W. Phillips, he stated that were he convinced that the taxpayers of Georgia wished the Western and Atlantic "returned to the State Government, and again made a political machine, I would not, so far as I am concerned, hesitate to surrender the lease."[85] He was on safe ground; he knew very well the public did not wish the road returned to the type of management that paid no profits.

Although Brown often bought and sold Georgia bonds, he apparently had no connection with those which were repudiated.[86] He disapproved of the unbusinesslike, if not corrupt, manner in which Bullock and Blodgett had managed the Western and Atlantic Railroad, yet he must have derived much pleasure from the comparison with his own administration. The most violent critic of Governor Bullock and all who were in any way associated with him was Robert Toombs. Regardless of whether or not investigation revealed wrongdoing, Toombs was convinced that every action of Bullock, Brown, and Kimball was tainted with corruption. "If I can do nothing else I will teach as far as I can the next generation to hate the vile scoundrils [*sic*]," he told Alexander Stephens.[87] Within his category of scoundrels he also placed the majority of the Bullock "purged" legislature. So violent were his

84 Stephens to Brown, July 14, 1872, in McLeod Collection.
85 Atlanta *Daily Constitution*, July 11, 1872.
86 E. Waitzfelder & Co. to Brown, June 12, August 31, 1871, in Hargrett Collection.
87 Toombs to Stephens, February 14, 1870, in Stephens Papers, Library of Congress.

charges relating to legislative action in the Mitchell heirs case that he and Brown were brought to the brink of a duel.

In 1842, when the Western and Atlantic Railroad was in the early days of construction, Samuel Mitchell donated to the state five acres of land in Atlanta on which to construct a terminal and other necessary buildings. The area proved to be larger than needed, so a portion was traded to the Macon and Western Railroad, and in 1859 the city of Atlanta was authorized by legislative action to beautify and use the remainder for a park.

In 1867 the heirs of Samuel Mitchell employed the law firm of Brown and Pope to bring suit for the recovery of that portion of the land being used as a park, since the state road had never used it for the purpose for which it was donated. Before final action could be taken both Brown and Pope were appointed to judicial positions, and the case was turned over to A. O. Lockrane, Brown's new law partner. Subsequently Lockrane would be appointed to succeed Brown on the supreme bench. The retrocession proposal was opposed by Governor Bullock and defeated in the legislature. But later the legislature approved a compromise, retroceding the property to the heirs for $35,000, even though an Atlanta company offered $100,000. Brown and his friend Ezekiel Waitzfelder subsequently purchased a portion of the property. This was about all the public knew, but there were many rumors.

Two years and much controversy later, Robert Toombs opened attack upon the Mitchell retrocession. In the meantime Bullock and his financial associate, H. L. Kimball, had fled the state, and a Democratic legislature had investigated almost every act of the Bullock regime. On June 27, 1872, Toombs published an opening shot in the Griffin *News*, charging that the rejection by the legislature of a $100,000 bid to accept a $35,000 offer was a result of the political engineering of Lockrane, Kimball, and Brown. It was "the result of bribery, pure and simple."[88] Brown replied: "Now if Gen. Toombs intends by his language to say that I have been guilty of bribery in 'engineering' this bill through the Legislature, I pronounce his statement an infamous falsehood and its author an unscrupulous liar." Chief Justice Lockrane also replied: "Too long have the interests of Georgia been cursed by

[88] Quoted in Atlanta *Daily Sun*, July 16, 1872.

the bewildering folly of Toombs. May the God of justice interpose to save the state from further infliction of his pestilential influence."[89]

Brown expected drastic reaction to his denunciation of Toombs as an "unscrupulous liar." On the same day that he published his statement, he wrote James Gardner of Augusta: "I may receive a note from Genl. Toombs on the subject. If so I want your advice and assistance as a friend and shall put the matter in your hands. Will you do me the favor to serve me in the matter if I need a friend? If so, please telegraph me 'I can come.' If not, say 'I cannot come.' . . . I have borne in silence Genl. Toombs' assaults as long as I can and it is I think my duty to stop it." Gardner wired "I can come," and wrote, "I will cheerfully and promptly go to Atlanta if you notify me that I can serve you. My opinion is that you will not be invited even to a war of words. Our bellicose General does not relish a prolonged contest even of that character. I am very sure he will wilt before a firm front opposed to his gasconade. There is no fight in him. There never was. If he makes another move you will have the opportunity of demonstrating that fact to the world. It will be a public service, and this reflection will be your consolation under the disagreeable necessity."[90]

Brown was now in dead earnest. He inquired of Gardner what to do if Toombs sent no note by a friend but instead published an abusive article. Would it be wise simply to state that since he had denounced Toombs as an unscrupulous liar he would take no further notice until Toombs showed he had "personal courage to protect his honor as a gentleman"? If a hostile note came, he would wire Gardner, Brown concluded. In case of hostile publication, he would write. Gardner thought Brown's position precisely correct. If Toombs should demand "a retraxit, simply reply declining to retract," he advised.[91]

No formal personal note came, but a personal messenger did. On July 9, John C. Nicholls appeared at Brown's Atlanta office. He had been sent by Toombs to inquire whether Brown would give satisfaction according to the code. According to Brown, he replied: "Say to Gen. Toombs I hold myself ready to give him any satisfaction which may be due him, or to which he is entitled as a gentleman." But according

89 Atlanta *Daily Constitution*, July 3, 1872.
90 Brown to Gardner, July 3, 1872; Gardner to Brown, July 3, 5, 1872, in Hargrett Collection.
91 Brown to Gardner, July 7, 1872; Gardner to Brown, July 8, 1872, *ibid.*

to Nicholls' version, Brown replied that if Toombs sent a note, he would consult his friend and then reply.[92] As soon as Nicholls departed, Brown wired Gardner, and Gardner arrived in Atlanta on the next-morning train. The only criticism of Brown's action offered by Gardner was that he had not put in writing the conversation with Nicholls. Brown then set out to find Nicholls; the hotel reported that both he and Toombs had left for home. Gardner was assigned Toombs's vacant room. Brown then wrote down his version and forwarded it to Toombs by special express. In giving this information to the public, Brown charged that Toombs left town because he preferred to "respond in the *newspapers.* . . . I leave the public to judge who is the poltroon, and whether Gen. Toombs preferred *newspaper* artillery to heavier metal."[93]

Dueling was illegal in the state of Georgia and contrary to the rules of the Baptist church. Brown temporarily withdrew from the church; apparently he and Gardner intended to ignore the Georgia law. Toombs sent no challenge, but Brown made careful preparation for the acceptance of one. Henry W. Grady later recorded an interesting speculation of what might have happened had there been a duel:[94]

In the first place, Gen. Toombs made no preparation for the duel. He went along on his careless and kingly way, trusting, presumably, to luck and a quick shot. Gov. Brown, on the contrary, made the most careful and deliberate preparation. He made his will, put his estate in order, and then clipped all the trees in his orchard practicing with the pistol. Had the duel come off—which fortunately it did not—Gen. Toombs would have fired with his usual magnificence and his usual disregard of rule. I do not mean to imply that he would not have hit Gov. Brown; on the contrary, he might have perforated him in a dozen places at once. But one thing is sure—Gov. Brown would have clasped his long white fingers around the pistol butt, adjusted it to his gray eye and sent his bullet within the eighth of an inch of the place he had selected. I should not be surprised if he drew a diagram of Gen. Toombs, and marked off with square and compass the exact spot he wanted to hit.

Although Toombs sent no challenge, he continued to publish. On July 16, he inserted a long article in the Atlanta *Sun* in the form of a letter to the editor. "A brace of ex-Chief Justices, of this State, honored

92 Atlanta *Daily Constitution,* July 19, 1872.
93 *Ibid.,* July 18, 1872; Avery, *History of Georgia,* 479, 484.
94 Atlanta *Daily Constitution,* August 29, 1880.

me with their notice and vituperation in *The Constitution* of the 3d instant," he began. "There were a trio of these *chevaliers d'industrie* engaged in the transactions referred to. The third member of the firm (Mr. H. I. Kimball) is absent from the State, I suppose, 'from circumstances beyond his control.'" Toombs then entered upon a long discussion of the Mitchell heirs case, involving Brown at every point possible.[95] Brown had been advised by Gardner that he should give no further attention to Toombs other than through an address to the public. Accordingly, under date of August 5, 1872, he published in the Atlanta *Constitution* a long letter addressed to the editor,[96] giving his version of the Mitchell heirs case.[97] Both Toombs and Brown fell far short of giving the full story. Toombs did not know the facts; Brown preferred not to reveal all of them.

A duel had been averted, but Toombs was not through with Brown. Early in March, 1873, he filed suit in the superior court of Atlanta, Judge John L. Hopkins presiding, "exercising jurisdiction in Equity." The case was docketed *John H. Mitchell et al* vs. *Joseph E. Brown, A. O. Lockrane, H. I. Kimball et al.* Clearly Toombs hoped to bring to light much of what he had been fishing for for several years. Alleging fraud and deception on the part of the defendants and others, the Mitchell heirs, through attorney Toombs, requested the court to declare null and void all deeds of transfer made by them involving the property retroceded to them by the state. In informing his partner, E. Waitzfelder and Company, of the pending bill in equity, Brown declared, "This will give us some trouble and a bitter law suit as the whole thing is founded in Toombs' malice and he will work very hard. It will run us to some expense in the way of lawyers' fees etc but I am satisfied they can never recover."[98] Brown lined up an imposing group of defense attorneys, headed by Ben H. Hill.

In the bill, the Mitchell heirs admitted that they had signed the contracts and deeds relating to the property in question, but they charged that, being ignorant and unlearned in legal matters, they had

95 See also *ibid.*, July 16, 1872.
96 Journalist-historian I. W. Avery was editor.
97 See also *A Statement of Facts Connected with the Compromise Between the State and the Heirs of Samuel Mitchell, for the Park Property in Atlanta,* written by Joseph E. Brown (Atlanta, 1872).
98 March 13, 1873, in Hargrett Collection.

allowed themselves to be misguided and deceived by their agents and
lawyers. There was considerable conflict in testimonies and depositions
introduced during the hearing, but the essential facts are fairly clear.
This is the story that was now made public. At the inception of their
efforts to recover the Atlanta property, the Mitchell heirs designated
Robert J. Powell, husband of Eliza Mitchell, as their agent and attorney
in fact. Powell contracted with the firm of Brown and Pope to handle
the case for one-fourth of the property involved. No court action had
been taken when J. D. Pope was appointed superior court judge for
Atlanta and Brown chief justice of the supreme court. They placed the
case in the hands of A. O. Lockrane. Having little hope for success in
the courts, agent Powell and attorney Lockrane decided to ask the
legislature for a direct retrocession of the property to the Mitchell
heirs. Powell testified that Lockrane and an assistant were to receive
half of such property as might be recovered. The request was not
granted by the legislature since most of Governor Bullock's friends
voted in the negative. Powell thought the vote was pretty much along
party lines—Democrats for and Republicans against. The failure of
this effort canceled Lockrane's contract.

Several months of inactivity followed during which time H. I.
Kimball became connected with the case. There seemed to be no reason
to try the legislature again unless Governor Bullock could be persuaded
to support the measure, and Kimball appeared to be the only man who
could supply sufficient influence upon Bullock. Testimonies in the trial
disagreed as to who first contacted Kimball, but by this time Lockrane,
Kimball, and Brown had formed a law partnership. Powell claimed,
however, that many persons around the capital advised him to secure
the services of Kimball and that Brown had no knowledge of the plan.

On June 11, 1870, the Mitchell heirs, through their agent, R. J.
Powell, contracted with H. I. Kimball "to use his best efforts and give
his personal attention and services toward the consummation of a settlement for the recovery of said lands from the City of Atlanta and the
State of Georgia." He was not, however, to pay the state more than
$35,000 nor the city more than $25,000 in any compromise settlement.
For his services, Kimball was to receive one-half the retroceded property and was to pay all expenses connected with compromise.

Whether or not Brown and Lockrane had prior knowledge of this agreement is not evident, but they clearly did not intend to be bypassed and lose all compensation for services they had rendered. One June 17, Kimball signed a contract with Brown and Lockrane under which he would seek to "purchase all outstanding titles to the property so as to perfect the title in himself to the whole." Brown and Lockrane were to "aid by their services" in carrying out this plan. They were also to furnish one-third of the money required to make reasonable compensation to other lawyers who had served in some capacity—John D. Pope, L. E. Bleckley and D. E. Pittman. Kimball was to pay the other two-thirds. Should the title to the property be perfected, Kimball would own two-thirds and Brown and Lockrane one-third. Written on the initial page of this contract is: "Cancelled June 17, 1870 H. I. Kimball." This was the same date it was signed. Supposedly, the cancellation was by mutual consent.[99] There is no evidence that Powell knew of this contract.[100]

Kimball refused to honor his agreement with the Mitchell heirs to take the case for one-half the retroceded property. He wanted control of all of it and so informed Lockrane and Powell. He would pay the heirs $25,000 for their claim—$5,000 cash and $20,000 after retrocession, he paying all expenses connected with the case from the beginning. Powell and Lockrane carried the news to the Mitchell family at Barnesville. All of the heirs lived in Pike County. According to testimony, the heirs protested that the offer was not sufficient, that the property was worth hundreds of thousands. Lockrane assured them that it was worth no more than $75,000 to $100,000, from which all expenses would need

---

99 Kimball later paid Lockrane $7,500, Pitman $5,000, Beckley $2,000, and Pope $2,000. Kimball to J. C. Kimball, April 7, 1873, in Hargrett Collection. Kimball made a special agreement with Brown.

100 A copy of this contract fell into the hands of one E. D. Atwater of Atlanta. When Brown and Toombs were on the verge of a duel Atwater attempted to blackmail Brown into giving him a lucrative position with the Western and Atlantic. Brown gave him no position, although Atwater later claimed he was "positively promised" one. He greatly resented what he considered Brown's failure to pay off. In February, 1873, he again wrote Brown reviewing the situation and accusing him of acting in bad faith. "It may be politic," he threatened, "for you hereafter to keep in mind the fact that nobody is too insignificant either to serve or injure your interests. . . . Whenever this question is reopened (as it will be) the necessary *proof* will be brought forward to *Substantiate* charges originally made, & as *positively denied by you*; the original agreement with your signature attached will be forthcoming." Atwater to Brown, July 17, 1872, February 25, 1873, in Hargrett Collection. Atwater did not carry out his threat.

be subtracted. The amount of $35,000 was finally agreed upon, and on June 18, 1870, the Mitchell heirs deeded their claim to the Atlanta property to H. I. Kimball. Kimball then made a special arrangement with Brown. If and when the property should be placed on the market, Brown would purchase *"all cash down"* at least $50,000 worth of the property. This would give Kimball cash with which to pay the Mitchell heirs. Kimball on his part agreed to give Brown $20,000 "of the notes and mortgages realized from other purchases."[101] No copy of this agreement between Brown and Kimball has been found; so it is not certain whether it was made before or after the retrocession by the legislature.

On June 20, 1870, two days after he had been given a deed to the Mitchell claim, Kimball deeded it back to the heirs. He later explained in his deposition that at first he had thought his influence with the legislature would be greater if the title to the claim was in his own name, but he later decided otherwise. However, the deed to the heirs was not delivered until they gave to Lockrane "the power of attorney irrevocable," dated November 4, to sell the property and place all proceeds in the hands of Kimball. Through Lockrane, Kimball petitioned the governor for retrocession of the property, the heirs paying $35,000. Bullock sent it to the legislature, and it was approved by joint resolution October 25, 1870, although an Atlanta company offered $100,000 for the property. Four days later Bullock deeded the property to the Mitchell heirs. The property thus deeded lay on Decatur, Alabama, Pryor, and Loyd streets adjacent to property already owned by Kimball, on which he had constructed the Kimball House.

Agent Powell, who had passed into the employ of Kimball, claimed all credit for "engineering" the measure through the legislature. He later explained that he was forced to deal with all kinds of lobbyists who thought they had influence and "wanted a finger in the pie. . . . Some of them had a system of blackmail and had to be either fed or fought. Some were hired to work and some to keep still." Kimball paid all the bills. Not one witness connected Brown in any way with "engineering" the measure through the legislature. Kimball stated positively that Brown was not even consulted relative to the contracts made with the Mitchell heirs. However, Brown was not a member of the supreme

101 H. I. Kimball to J. C. Kimball, April 7, 1873, in Hargrett Collection.

court when the Mitchell request was presented to the legislature. He had resigned in August and was not reappointed until October 22.

The property was sold at auction on November 3, 1870, by real estate agent G. W. Adair. Brown, taking in his friends the Waitzfelders of E. Waitzfelder and Company as partners, purchased a portion for $52,000. He also, according to agreement, received notes and mortgages from other sales totaling $21,000. However, according to Kimball, before Brown would go through with his part of the deal, he demanded evidence that Kimball had carried out the provisions of all agreements, and that the Mitchell heirs were satisfied. Such evidence was furnished, Brown himself drawing up the statement of satisfaction signed by the Mitchell heirs.[102] The suit cost Brown and his associates several thousands of dollars in lawyers' fees, but Toombs failed to establish wrongdoing against any of the accused. As in the case of the duel that never happened, Brown's standing was probably enhanced rather than damaged.

---

102 *Senate Journal*, 495–502, 550. The voluminous papers relating to Mitchell heirs case are in the Hargrett Collection.

Chapter XXI

Democrat Again

THE FACT THAT Brown had come out in support of Horace Greeley for president early in 1872 had contributed to Robert Toombs's bitterness. In his publication in the Griffin *News* on June 27, Toombs declared that all "public plunderers" who called themselves Democrats "from Tammany Hall down to the smallest petty larceny thief on the State Road" had come out in support of Greeley.

On the national scene many Republicans had turned sour on the Grant administration and were demanding reform, including a softer policy toward the South. This group, generally referred to as "Liberals," nominated Horace Greeley, editor of the New York *Tribune*, for president and B. Gratz Brown of Missouri for vice-president. Although sparked by much enthusiasm, the Liberal Republicans realized that their only hope for success lay in possible endorsement by the Democrats. On June 20, 1872, Joe Brown wrote Carl Schurz, one of the foremost leaders of the Liberal movement, that the South had "taken hold of Mr. Greeley with remarkable unanimity. The few politicians who attempt to dictate will have to yield and follow or be left behind. Greeley if nominated [by the Democrats] at Baltimore will carry every Southern State except South Carolina. Any movement by the friends of reform to put out another candidate will cause greater confusion and secure the election of Grant. Such action will be condemned by the mass of the people and I protest against it. . . . I am not actively in politics and this is not intended for publication. Show it to our friends."[1]

1 McLeod Collection.

The Democratic convention at Baltimore did endorse Greeley. Some "straight out" Democrats, refusing to support him, held a meeting in Louisville and nominated Charles O'Connor. It was difficult for former Confederates to accept Greeley. Even though of late he had opposed Radical reconstruction, those whom he had so vigorously denounced during the war had difficulty in forgetting. However, most Georgia Democrats realized he was their only hope for defeating Grant; so in convention in Atlanta, on July 24, they endorsed Greeley and B. Gratz Brown. A few, like Toombs and the Stephens brothers, refused to cooperate. Toombs denounced Greeley supporters as "Know Nothing villians & thievish democrats who are united solely 'by the cohesive power of public plunder.'"[2]

Brown came out in public support of the Greeley-Brown ticket and the reelection of Smith as governor. When John L. Hull of Thomason, Georgia, inquired what Liberal Republicans should do in the campaign, Brown replied that since the Democrats had endorsed the Liberal Republican platform, which was essentially the same position he and other liberal Republicans had taken in 1867, "let us give Governor Smith and our State ticket such a majority in October as will gladden the hearts and strengthen the hands of the Liberal party in the Northern States. . . . and thereby swell the glorious triumph which awaits Greeley and Brown."[3]

Most Democratic editors throughout the state were complimentary of Brown's stand. They welcomed the generosity exhibited in his willingness to join hands with those who had so vigorously denounced him. He had demonstrated "eminently practical sense," remarked the Augusta *Constitutionalist*.[4] The Griffin *Semi-Weekly Star* declared: "This coup-de-main places Joe Brown fair and square in the bosom of the progressive Democracy. Henceforth he will be among them, and of them; and whether Grant or Greeley wins the race old Joe has fairly reinstated himself with the dominant party in Georgia."[5] The Columbus *Sun* noted that "Whenever ex-Governor Brown speaks, there will never be a lack of listeners. . . . With none of the furious, unchained

2 Toombs to Stephens, August 26, 1872, in Stephens Papers, Library of Congress.
3 Atlanta *Daily Constitution*, September 24, 1872.
4 September 26, 1872.
5 September 27, 1872.

whirlwind eloquence of Toombs, the sophistry, vanity and savage denunciation and invective of Hill, he is more natural and practical than the latter two combined. He never wastes ammunition, always following the advice of Oliver Cromwell to Trust in God, but be sure to keep your powder dry! . . . He is a true Quaker, and we have no doubt, if sent as a missionary by President Greeley to the Indians, he would pray the horns and hoofs off Buffalo Hump and restore peace to the frontier. In cunning he would prove a match for Little Fox, and in that 'soft low voice,' so eloquent in women he would silence Roaring Bear and Striped Lightning."[6] There was not to be a President Greeley. He carried Georgia 75,896 to 62,485 but lost decisively to Grant in the total national vote. O'Connor received only 3,999 votes in Georgia.[7]

Now a private citizen with no apparent political ambitions, Brown was definitely a Democrat again. As a man of business, he was well on the way to great success. In his tax returns for 1872, he valued his Fulton County property at $114,000. Of this amount, $70,000 was invested in Atlanta real estate and $25,000 in stocks and bonds. His 1,695 acres of Cherokee land were valued at $11,000. He now owned 1,520 acres in Gordon County worth $22,000. And he reported 1,708 acres scattered over eight counties but gave no estimate of value. He had disposed of his Lee County plantation in 1868 and that in Dooly the following year. The Gordon plantation was acquired in 1868.[8] This was not a complete financial picture, for it did not identify his railroad and other stocks nor his coal and iron interests in Bartow, Cherokee, and Dade counties. He owned stock in a sleeping car company and the Nashville and Chattanooga and the East Tennessee and Virginia railroads. And during the present year he had also invested $60,000 in shares in the Texas and Pacific Railroad.[9] He was not a charter member of this railroad but had no doubt become interested through association with Thomas A. Scott of the Pennsylvania Railroad who was also president of the Texas and Pacific. Scott was a director of the Western and Atlantic Company. As later related, Brown purchased the Texas and Pacific shares believing it a very good investment, owing to the liberal land grants made by Texas and the federal government.

6 Quoted in Atlanta *Daily Constitution*, October 22, 1872.
7 Avery, *History of Georgia*, 502.
8 See Hargrett Collection.
9 Brown to E. Waitzfelder and Company, November 2, 1872, *ibid.*

He also calculated that being largely free from snow during the winter, this line would "empty the wealth of the Pacific to a great extent into the lap of the South."[10]

Since the federal income tax was repealed in 1872 Brown made no report of income for that purpose, but his account book gives $17,036.[11] During the previous year he had reported $11,614.75,[12] broken down into $2,314.75 from rents, $800 from farming operations, $1,500 interest and dividends from railroad, bank, and insurance company investments and $7,000 from salary.[13]

Whether a controversial public figure or a private man of business, a hostile press would permit Brown no peace. Probably the most hostile of all was the Atlanta *Herald* edited by Alexander St. Clair Abrams. A paper that denounced Brown was assured of many readers, and the *Herald* was trying desperately to increase circulation. Abrams denounced the leasing of the Western and Atlantic, Brown, and all of his business activities. He accused Brown of granting railroad passes to friendly newsmen only and of responsibility for frequent accidents and delays due to mismanagement. Abrams subsequently claimed that he was eventually pressured out of control of the *Herald* by a threat of foreclosure of a mortgage of $5,000 by the Citizens Bank unless he ceased attacking Brown and the Western and Atlantic Company.

Robert A. Alston assumed control of the *Herald* with young Henry W. Grady as an associate, but the attack on Brown and his associates did not end. "If Governor Brown is to own coal mines and force manufacturers to buy coal or allow their shops to stand idle, and citizens to burn it or suffer," exclaimed the *Herald*, while at the time using "a public highway worth ten milions of dollars, of which he obtained the control without paying one cent, as an engine of oppression, then he becomes the most mighty potentate of modern times, and can force the people of an entire state to knuckle to his will or suffer for their temerity." Brown replied in a letter that filled four printed columns, justifying his activities and advertising his businesses. The *Herald* printed the letter but classed it as advertising, and business

10 Brown to Alexander Stephens, December 27, 1873, in Stephens Papers, Library of Congress.
11 Account Book No. 2, in Brown Papers, Atlanta Historical Society.
12 His Account Book shows $15,333.
13 Hargrett Collection.

manager Grady sent Brown a bill for $25. Brown screamed "black-mail" and Grady replied: "How natural it is for a man who knows that he would steal if he had the chance, to conclude that everybody does steal, who, he supposes, has the opportunity."[14]

Attacks on Brown did not bring financial security to the *Herald*. Hard pressed by his creditor, Alston turned to H. I. Kimball who had recently revisited Atlanta preparatory to facing his own creditors and resuming business life there. Alston presented a glowing picture of the great services he and the *Herald* could be to Kimball's future in-terests if some financial relief could be found. If he had $10,000 on which to operate the paper in his absence, he could travel over the state making contacts and securing subscriptions. He could sell the paper and retire to his plantation, but he did not wish to do so because of his interest in his young partner, Henry W. Grady. Kimball pleaded in-ability to furnish financial assistance, adding that while he did not ques-tion Alston's personal friendship he feared they could not agree on public matters. No doubt Kimball had conferred with Brown while in Atlanta and become familiar with the policies of the *Herald*. Alston reassured Kimball of his support, but no financial aid was forthcoming.[15]

Alston's attack upon Brown and his enterprises continued and even Kimball was brought under fire. It was charged that the Atlanta *Con-stitution* had been organized with bribes from Kimball and state road money. This was followed by a story of a railroad "pool" led by Brown to form a monopoly on cotton transportation. Then the Brown com-pany was accused of spending $70,000 to secure legislative approval of the Western and Atlantic lease. Still further, an attack was launched upon the convict lease system from which Brown and a few others were reported to be reaping considerable profits. Finally, Brown would take no more. In the words of Grady, he "sat down" on the *Herald* like Humpty Dumpty. The Citizens Bank, in which Brown was a major stockholder, sold the *Herald* at a sheriff's sale.[16]

Even though Brown no longer had any business connections with "exiles" Bullock and Kimball, after repaying them their portion of the loan to Bard following the take over of the *True Georgian*, he corre-

14 Atlanta *Herald*, May 14, 20, November 9, 1873.
15 Kimball to Alston, March 7, 1874; Alston to Kimball March 30, 1874, in Hargrett Collection.
16 Atlanta *Daily Constitution*, December 8, 1876.

sponded with them fairly regularly as to the situation in Georgia. If Bullock profited from the alleged frauds of his administration he spent his ill-gotten gains very rapidly. When Brown sent him $800 from the Bard transaction in November, 1872, he thanked Brown profusely, stating, "Unfortunatey I am *not* revelling in ill gotten (or other) gains in Paris, London, Egypt or other places named for me by the accommodating newspapers."[17]

Both Bullock and Kimball were in New York where financial circles were greatly concerned over Georgia's repudiation of "Bullock bonds." Naturally, Bullock was eager that the repudiation be rescinded. It is doubtful, however, that he himself owned any of these bonds. In view of Kimball's intense interest in the matter, it is reasonable to suspect that he either owned repudiated bonds or had been promised compensation for the use of his influence. In February, 1873, Thomas L. Snead of New York, agent for the bondholders, presented to the Georgia legislature a proposed compromise whereby Georgia would compensate the bondholders to the extent of their actual investment— approximately $1,500,000. During the prolonged debate, the Atlanta *Constitution* requested the opinions of a number of prominent men on the subject. Brown obliged in five columns of newsprint, pointing out the probable difficulties and evils associated with wholesale repudiation and closing by proposing compromise.[18] The legislature rejected the proposed compromise.

After learning of the action of the legislature, both Bullock and Kimball turned to Brown for advice on what might yet be done. Was there a possibility of a reversal of the legislative action? How could it be accomplished, and what would it cost? They knew that if any man was familiar with the situation in Georgia it was Brown; he had contacts with persons in all walks of life. Brown replied in what he considered utmost frankness. The prospects were not good. Georgians had been led to believe that their legislators had acted correctly in repudiating corruption and thus relieving the people from unjust taxation. Further, the claim that repudiation would ruin Georgia's credit had proved false; a new issue of Georgia bonds had recently sold at par. Before the legislature could be persuaded to reverse its action, public

17 November 21, 1872, in Hargrett Collection.
18 Atlanta *Daily Constitution*, February 13, 1873.

opinion must be changed. Although he thought the cause a just one, Brown declared, in order to accomplish the object, which was in opposition to public opinion, "it would be necessary to silence certain presses that are now urgently pandering to popular error and passion, and to interest several prominent influences, which in my opinion would cost $50,000 in cash and a much larger sum conditional."

If Georgia would permit bondholders access to her courts, Brown had no doubt she would be compelled to pay. He would grant that there might have been irregularities in a few cases; still he believed that the great mass of the repudiated bonds was issued by proper authorities and in accordance with the law. These bonds were also held by persons who had no legal notice of any "irregularity or invalidity" when purchased. Therefore, it was the obligation of the state to pay. He had observed, however, that as time passed, the people seemed even more satisfied with the decision and were less likely to change their opinion. Therefore, unless repudiation was reversed by the next General Assembly, Brown asserted, he himself would not give five cents on the dollar for those bonds. To Kimball, Brown stated frankly what he considered the only possibility. The bondholders must put in Kimball's hands, to be used at his discretion, funds sufficient to control the leading presses, conciliate those politicians who enjoyed popular confidence, and hire lobbyists. If this was not done, Brown concluded, "my advice is that you retire from the whole matter & let them take their own course, & it is easy to predict what will be the result."[19] The bondholders did not supply the funds.

The return to power of the native white Democrats in Georgia left the Negro just where Joe Brown thought he should be. Under the pressure of necessity, Brown had favored political and legal rights for Negroes. On paper, at least, they now had these rights. Brown had steadfastly opposed social equality. As the fall elections of 1874 approached, there was before Congress a proposal designed to guarantee to Negroes equal accommodations in education, public transportation, hotels, and places of amusement. Brown joined the majority of white Georgians in bitter opposition.

As usual, some of Brown's friends requested his opinion. He obliged

19 Bullock to Brown, March 30, 1874; Brown to Bullock, April 3, 1874; Brown to Kimball, April 21, May 16, 1874, all in Hargrett Collection.

under date of August 31. For background, he reviewed his position on reconstruction. Acquiescence in those measures in the face of the threat of force he still considered the only reasonable course. "I thought by acquiescence at once, and raising no issues with the colored people . . . we would retain their confidence, and keep them out of the hands of the carpet-baggers and designing men, who would come among them for the purpose of misleading them, and exciting their prejudices against the native white population, who are in fact their best friends." This position brought him and his associates "persecution and ostracism seldom endured by those who have in view nothing but the best interest of the State." Yet such acquiescence enabled Georgia to escape the fate of South Carolina and Louisiana. Georgia was now prospering under a constitution which enabled her "native original citizens" to return to the control of public affairs. In some other states the constitutions had vested the government in the hands of former slaves and carpetbaggers who, bankrupt in both purse and character, played upon passion and prejudice rather than common sense. There was no doubt, Brown explained, that the "property, intellect and intelligence of any State can govern it, when it unites in a determined effort to do so."

Brown considered South Carolina a good example of unwise action. There the great mass of whites declared hostility to the reconstruction acts and Negro suffrage, thus forcing the Negroes to look elsewhere for friends. The carpetbaggers stepped in "with flattering promises" and bound them by ties "too strong to be easily broken." But reconstruction was now past; the proposed civil rights bill was another matter. It was a Republican measure designed to make the Negro voter a stronger supporter of the Republican party. It was a "social equality" proposal, not a civil rights measure. He would say that social equality could never be accomplished; it would never be submitted to regardless of consequences. "God has created two races different, with different tastes, capacity and instinct for social enjoyment, and no human legislation can ever compel them to unite as social equals."

As president of the Atlanta school board since its organization, Brown felt that he could proudly say that "separate public education" was available to all who wished it. He would be pleased to continue to assist colored people "if they act in their proper social sphere." However, if this so-called civil rights bill became law, he would favor repealing all laws relative to public education and abolishing all public schools. This would not be in violation of the state constitution, for it did not require a system of public education.

Brown prophesied that should an attempt be made to force equality in public facilities and transportation there would be strife and bloodshed, race war and anarchy, and probably the extermination of the black race. Although he disapproved of mob action, he could see it as a probable result, and soon white juries would refuse to "convict white men for killing negroes who undertook to force themselves upon them as social equals." The only solution to the problems facing the country, Brown concluded, was an "overwhelming defeat of the Republican party" in the fall elections. "This would check the passage of this most iniquitous measure, and relieve the country of horrors subsequent upon its passage. . . . To this end I shall cheerfully contribute my humble mite."[20] The civil rights bill did become law but was declared unconstitutional by the Supreme Court.

Brown had struck a popular chord, just what Georgia whites wanted to hear. Newspapers large and small throughout the state sang his praises. "No white Southern born man now in Georgia, who has the slightest claim to self-respect, or the respect of any living creature, will for a moment remain with the civil rights infamy, after reading Gov. Brown's great letter," declared the editor of the Albany *News*. He vigorously denounced those "few dirty, lying, mischief-making press correspondents" who were busily engaged in denouncing Brown's "exposé" of Civil Rights. "Would it not be just as easy to give Gov. Brown credit for patriotism." If those "anonymous scribblers," who were "unfit to unlatch Gov. Brown's carriage driver's shoe buckle," would only reveal their names, "seventy-five thousand of the best men in Georgia would spit upon them."[21] The editor of the *News*, Carey W. Styles, was the *same man* who, as editor of the Atlanta *Constitution* during the stormy days of reconstruction, had so vigorously denounced Brown.

"Joe Brown is still in the ranks of white men," announced the Alapaha *Georgia Forester*. In the days of reconstruction his eyes were

20 This copy was taken from the Gainesville *Eagle*, September 11, 1874. The letter was widely printed.
21 September 10, 24, 1874.

"open to the situation," and he endured much persecution for the sake of his state. "We all see now what Joe Brown saw in 1865." The colored people could not wish for a better friend. He was now attempting to protect them against a measure that could result in the destruction of their race.[22]

Not all Democrats exactly welcomed Brown back into the party. Many still considered him a deserter and refused to forgive him for his support of Radical reconstruction. But apparently a majority thought otherwise. After receiving his contributions to the political and economic welfare of the state, the Atlanta *Constitution* declared, "We deprecate those flings at him." Would it not be "good sense and sound policy" to "accept the services of so able an ally and turn them to the best advantage against a common enemy!"[23]

The editor of the Atlanta *Daily News* placed himself among those who were "outraged" by Brown's proposal to "accept the situation" in 1867, yet he felt that "the ceaseless, unequalled denunciation of him for that step ought to satisfy the most vindictive and revengeful." It was Brown's influence that had brought Georgia through "the reconstruction mill" with a better constitution than any other southern state. This alone should have redeemed him, but when one added to this feat his services in restoring the Democratic party to power and "putting the thieves and plunderers to flight," surely he had "fully atoned for the past." Brown was no doubt honest in his views when he supported reconstruction and thought he was advocating what was best for the state. And now that he had returned to his old party, he had "brought with him very nearly all the brains, respectability and decency who went off with the reconstructionists in 1868. We would rather to-day see him in any important office than scores of blatant Democrats who are so zealous in the cause. We are not his champion, but we are ever ready to do any man justice."[24]

Few white Georgians were bold enough, or even desired, to take issue with Brown on the Negro question; yet among his former Republican friends there was considerable resistance to his suggestion that all vote Democratic. The Gainesville *Advertiser* praised him for

22 September 22, 1874.
23 October 14, 1874.
24 October 16, 1874.

his stand in 1867–1868 and on the present civil rights bill. "So far, so good. But Joseph closes [his letter] by advising all of us to join the Democracy!—Farewell, Joseph! wife, world and cotton patch. Joseph has at last returned to his old love. Farewell Gov. Brown, but before shaking hands with you for ever, we propose now to ask God to forgive us for voting for you in 1868 for U.S. Senator."[25]

Welcome or no welcome, Brown was again a full-fledged Democrat, and recognition of his political leadership was not limited to Georgia. During the presidential campaign of 1876, however, he was more an observer than a participant. For several years, in private correspondence, he had often spoken of his poor health. A throat ailment gave him much discomfort and at times his lungs were involved. Yet he kept driving. His energy was almost boundless, and he never wasted it on light or frivolous things. He had no hobbies; every day was a workday. Vacations were extremely rare; consequently, by the summer of 1876 he had reached a point of physical exhaustion that demanded relief. In August he, Mrs. Brown, and their son Elijah traveled to Colorado to try the effects of a higher altitude. Most of the time was spent in Pueblo and Denver. On October 3, Mrs. Brown reported her husband much improved. He was coughing very little but continued to have some trouble with his nose. His flannel drawers had caused a rash on his legs, but fortunately he had brought with him his doctor's prescription.[26]

The Browns were back in Atlanta by late October, having returned by way of Philadelphia. Political friends were eager to know what he observed during his travels; so he granted an interview to a correspondent of the Atlanta *Constitution*. The unidentified interviewer was much impressed by the former governor: "It is universally conceded in all this section that Gov. Brown has more judgment than any living man—when he has had opportunity of judging. He never decides hastily. He never talks carelessly. Even in the most casual conversation, he goes slowly, while his long fingers outstretched inquiringly, winnow the air carefully, as if they were hunting about for the right words."

Brown considered the presidential race between Rutherford B.

25 Undated clipping in Spalding Collection.
26 Mrs. Brown to Mary Brown Connally, October 3, 1876, in Spalding Collection.

Hayes and Samuel J. Tilden a close one, but he thought Tilden was gaining in favor. He believed this was probably a result of President Grant's sending troops into South Carolina. If after twelve years of reconstruction, troops could still be sent into a southern state during an election "our liberty is at the point of a bayonet." Brown thought the southern question would soon "crop out of politics." The recent Democratic victory in Indiana would definitely influence the national election, the Democrats winning over the "neutral or floating vote." He had detected in the North a desire for a change in administrations. The "bloody shirt" or "solid south" would have very little effect. These predictions, Brown explained, were based upon conversations with numerous "ordinary people"; he had not sought the opinions of political leaders.[27] His predictions might have proved sound had elections in Louisiana, Florida, and South Carolina been free of military pressure and fraud. When the voting was over, both parties claimed victory in these three states. Who would be the next president depended upon which electoral votes were counted. Tilden needed only one vote from these three states; Haynes needed all.

The situation in Louisiana was hopelessly confused, and the alleged use of federal troops at polling places in South Carolina presented a still different problem. In Florida both parties charged fraud, so the outcome would likely depend upon who canvassed the vote. The election was held on November 7. At 10 P.M., November 11, S. M. Inman of Atlanta telegraphed John H. Inman in New York: "Our leading citizens request you see Governor Tilden tonight if possible and have him request Governor Joe Brown to go to Florida and represent him in this election matter. It is thought he can be of much service." John H. Inman wired back at 1 A.M.: "Have seen parties in highest authority," and they urged that leading citizens prevail upon Brown to go. Later in the day Inman again telegraphed from New York: "Assure Gov. Brown that I have seen party mentioned in your telegram & that my other dispatch was sent with his hearty approval." In addition to Tilden, Inman had apparently seen Abram S. Hewitt, chairman of the Democratic National Executive Committee, for on November 12, Hewitt wired Brown: "We earnestly desire you go immediately to

27 Atlanta *Daily Constitution*, October 3, 1876.

Florida & see that there is a fair and honest count & return."[28] Brown left for Tallahassee, Florida, on the evening of November 12. There he would meet with several men of national prominence, some representing their party, others the candidates. When William E. Chandler, representative of the Republican National Committee, arrived he wired back to New York for money and help: "Florida is swarming with prominent Democrats. Send some Republican lawyers and eminent men."[29]

Also to Tallahassee went Henry W. Grady who would report regularly to the New York *Herald* and Atlanta *Constitution* on the situation in Florida and Brown's activities. He had joined the staff of the *Constitution* the previous month; this would be his first major assignment, and his association with Brown would result in a complete change in attitude from his days with the Atlanta *Herald*. He began his November 15 report: "Wellington did not need Blucher more sorely in the crisis of that memorable day at Waterloo, than did the democrats of this state and the nation need Joe Brown when that gentleman quietly walked into the Warwick hotel this morning. I was never so glad to see a man in my life! The democrats down here are not the men for the crisis."[30] With his "throat tied up in a red bandana," Brown was soon hard at work and was quoted as saying, "We will sustain the democratic majorities or we will make the throwing of them out so ridiculous and outrageous that the civilized world will not stand it."[31]

Brown immediately plunged into detailed study of Florida election laws. He always preferred examination of constitutional and statutory law to any other legal challenge. The Republican governor of Florida was claiming the power to appoint his own agents to canvass the popular vote as reported by the counties and thus decide who was chosen as presidential electors, although the Canvassing Board had been created by law. The Democrats went to court asking an injunction against the governor and a writ of mandamus to compel the Canvassing Board to perform its duty. The case was set for November 23. As Brown pre-

28 Copies of telegrams in Hargrett Collection.
29 William W. Davis, *The Civil War and Reconstruction in Florida* (Facsimile of 1913 edition; Gainesville, 1964), 714.
30 Atlanta *Daily Constitution*, November 18, 1876.
31 *Ibid.*, November 16, 1876.

pared his argument, young Grady, through days of close association with him, decided that the former governor was a most exceptionable man. Neither a threat of pneumonia nor the blare of a brass band from the hotel dining room seemed to interfere with Brown's rest or concentration. When Grady expressed concern, Brown replied: "I can will myself to sleep at any time I want to." And a servant confided to Grady that Brown could also will himself awake when he wanted to. Grady closed his dispatch: "Joe Brown is a very smart man."[32]

Brown's argument before the court was the high point in the Democratic case. As his first task, he intended to prove that presidential electors were state, not federal, officials and their selection, therefore, was governed by laws regulating election of state officials. Under Florida law, as revised in 1872, precinct officers were chosen by the county commissioners who in turn were appointees of the governor. Precinct officers made their reports to a committee composed of the county judge, clerk of the district court, and one justice of the peace, all of whom were appointed by the governor. This committee then had thirty-five days within which to file its returns with the secretary of state. All returns were then canvassed by a board composed of the secretary of state, comptroller, and attorney general. Thirty-five days were allotted for the canvass unless returns were complete within a shorter period. The governor issued the certificates of election.

Brown contended that since the Republican governor appointed and therefore controlled all officers who handled the vote from the precincts to the Canvassing Board, he had an advantage no Democrat could equal. Should he be permitted to usurp the power of this board also, his control would be complete. Brown discounted the argument that since the thirty-five days allotted the board extended beyond the date for casting the electoral vote, Florida's vote might be lost. There would be no such delay unless some of the governor's appointees caused it. Neither could the governor function more rapidly than the Canvassing Board, for neither could act in less than thirty-five days unless all returns were in. The Democrats were urging rapid action on the part of the Canvassing Board. If there was not rapid action, it would be because the Republicans did not wish it. To the contention that the governor's assumption of jurisdiction was based on the ground

32 *Ibid.*, November 22, 1876.

of necessity, Brown would reply that "this is the plea by which usurpation is always attempted to be justified."[33]

Without waiting for the judge's decision the Canvassing Board began its work. The board was composed of Secretary of State Samuel B. McLin and Comptroller C. A. Cowgill (Republican) and Attorney General William A. Cocke (Democrat). Grady thought Cocke honest and McLin and Cowgill "not irredeemably bad." Brown himself expressed hope; "We have the state fairly and I think we shall be able to hold it. If we do not, we shall show the American people very plainly that it does belong to us."[34] Brown's optimism must have been centered in the latter portion of his statement; with his knowledge of partisan politics, he could scarcely have believed the two Republican members of the board would award Florida to Tilden. The Board did hear testimonies, one side or the other contesting the returns from every county. But the Republicans had a two to one vote on the board, and on December 6, it declared the Republican electoral candidates successful. On the same day the electors met and cast their votes for Rutherford B. Hayes.[35]

Brown was pleased with his efforts in Florida. He felt that he had done his duty at his own expense, he wrote his old friend L. N. Trammell of Dalton. He did not suppose that "any effort or human foresight could have prevented the results." The minds of the radicals in control were already made up, and they were "ready to perpetrate any sort of outrage to accomplish the results." The Canvassing Board threw out those votes that did not serve their purpose. As for his own future, Brown explained, "I have no desire to hold any political position under either the State or Federal government." He thought the country was passing through a very critical period and that "every southern orator & statesman should at present act with great caution and circumspection. We must leave this matter in the hands of our northern democratic friends. If they stand firm & show no disposition to waver, we will inaugurate Tilden without difficulty."[36]

Regardless of whether or not Brown had political ambitions, his

33 *Ibid.*, November 29, 1876.
34 *Ibid.*, November 26, December 3, 1876.
35 Davis, *Civil War and Reconstruction in Florida*, 713 ff.
36 Atlanta *Daily Constitution*, December 8, 1876; December 12, 1876, in L. N. Trammell Papers, Emory University.

political standing was enhanced by his labors in Florida, even as his physical condition deteriorated. (Shortly after his return, he developed pneumonia.) The editor of the Rome *Evening News* proclaimed him "a perfect man, the noblest work of God." Even though he disavowed interest in public office, the people should return him to the governor's office without consulting him.[37] A writer in the *Constitution*, after enumerating the probable candidates in the coming senatorial election, declared them all good men but not one of them up to the "requirements of the times." Only Joe Brown had the "ability and firmness the times demanded."[38] Brown was too ill to become active in politics. When on December 13, national chairman Hewitt urged him "to return to Tallahassee & take command of our case," Brown replied: "Command belongs to Congressional committee. Would cheerfully go and aid but I am unable from attack of pneumonia contracted while in Florida."[39]

Since Congress had not yet "counted" the electoral vote, Democrats still had hope for a Tilden victory. On the evening of December 12, they held a big celebration in Atlanta. Houses were illuminated and street marchers carried placards declaring "The end of fraud and corruption"; "Let the thieves beware"; "No account is a radical count"; "Rads into your holes"; "Beaten at their own games"; "A man named Brown took them down." Brown, too ill to participate, sent his regrets and a long letter to be read.[40] And on December 30, in response to a request by thirteen prominent Georgians, he gave to the public his "views on the present political situation." He did not "entertain the shadow of a doubt that Tilden and Hendricks were legally and fairly elected president and vice president." Of course he denounced the "radical" effort to seize the votes of South Carolina, Florida, and Louisiana. He gave some credit to the rumor that the (Republican) United States Senate would attempt to have the electoral vote counted by the (Republican) vice-president. He also noted the rumor that the Radicals in Washington were determined to inaugurate Hayes even by military force if necessary. That of course woud be in complete disregard of the law and Constitution, he asserted, and would result in a

---

37 December 15, 1876.
38 December 23, 1876.
39 Hewitt to Brown, December 13, 1876; Brown to Hewitt, December 13, 1876, in Hargrett Collection.
40 Atlanta *Daily Constitution*, December 13, 1876.

revolution in our form of government, changing the republic to a military despotism. That would indeed be the end of all liberty. "History shows that power once usurped by military force is never surrendered but at the point of the bayonet."[41]

With the publication of this letter Brown's political stock again registered an increase. Senator Thomas M. Norwood should pray that the former governor Brown did not aim at the senatorial "hole in the ground," exclaimed the Augusta *Constitutionalist*. "He always comes out of the hole ahead of everybody, you know."[42] Brown was not aiming at the Senate at that moment. He supported Governor Smith for the Senate seat as long as there was hope and then shifted to Ben Hill. "By that course," remarked a reporter in the Athens *Georgian*, "the Ex-Governor has visibly softened old-time resentments and animosities, and has made a host of friends among the class known as 'coming politicians,' young and ambitious men who will figure in the political struggles of the future."[43] Among those young men was journalist Henry W. Grady. During their association in Florida he and Brown had become warm friends.

During January, 1877, the political situation in Washington remained somewhat at a standstill. The Republican Senate and Democratic House could not agree on who should count the electoral vote. Finally, on January 29, the president signed into law a congressional compromise creating an electoral commission composed of five members from each house and five from the Supreme Court. Politically, as organized, it would include seven Democrats and eight Republicans. The Commission began canvassing the electoral votes on February 1 and concluded its work on March 2, two days before the date for inauguration of a new president. By a strict party vote of eight to seven, all electoral votes in question were awarded to the Republican candidate, giving Rutherford B. Hayes a 185 to 184 victory.

Continued illness confined Brown to his home during most of the winter of 1876–1877. Numerous rumors had him suffering from different maladies. In answer to many requests, his church paper, the *Index and Baptist*, published on March 8 a bulletin on his health. After re-

41 *Ibid.*, December 31, 1876.
42 January 5, 1877.
43 January 18, 1877.

covering from pneumonia he had "suffered a severe attack of Bronchitis" early in February. His recovery had been slow but he was now going for short walks and long rides. "His lungs are perfectly sound; nothing is involved beyond the bronchial tubes; he has no consumption, and no fatal disease of any kind. Still he suffers quite severely from cough, which sometimes disturbs his rest. . . . On the whole, his condition may be said to be serious but not dangerous." He also suffered from "catarrh of long standing."[44]

On March 29, 1877, the New York *Sun* carried a detailed account by Charles Foster, a representative from Rutherford B. Hayes's home district, of his connection with the alleged agreement with certain southerners relative to what the new president would do after taking office. He related that, during the "final hours of the count under the Electoral bill," a number of southerners who had opposed a threatened filibuster to prevent the count were eager for some definite assurance as to what the president's policy would be. An informal meeting of a group of Hayes's friends and a number of these southerners was held for the purpose of arriving at "a better understanding in regard to the policy of the incoming Administration." Foster related that the southerners did not demand such assurance as the price of continued support of the electoral bill, but they did wish a definite statement that they could use to convince their constituents that they had acted in good faith. Hayes's friends pointed out that a definite promise by him at that time would be "improper and indelicate," but they as his friends felt certain "his policy would favor local self-government and home rule in the South." There was no written compact, Foster asserted; therefore, Hayes could not have given any approval in writing. However, Congressman John Young Brown of Kentucky and Senator John B. Gordon of Georgia did request a letter from Foster stating his opinion as to what Hayes would do. Foster gave such a letter signed by Stanley Matthews and himself.

Shortly after this issue of the *Sun* reached Georgia, the Atlanta *Daily Constitution* published a contribution headed, "The Evil Genius," and signed, "Citizen." It expressed the "general feeling of disapprobation" of the failure of Democrats in Congress to delay the electoral count

44 April 7, 1877.

until after March 4. Such a delay, "Citizen" believed, would have thrown upon the House of Representatives the responsibility for electing a president and Tilden would have been chosen. As president, he would already have delivered South Carolina and Louisiana from "bayonet rule." But instead, Hayes had been inaugurated because a group led by J. Y. Brown and J. B. Gordon had sold out to the friends of General Hayes for a "promise" that troops would be withdrawn. "Citizen" protested that "they sold too cheap," for the South got nothing but what already belonged to it and at the same time lost four years of Democratic administration. Gordon and J. Y. Brown had proved themselves "very unfortunate and unskillful traders." Of course the participants denied that there was a "bargain," but "Citizen" recalled that Henry Clay and John Quincy Adams had also denied a "bargain" in 1825. If here was no "bargain," then "there certainly was *a capital understanding.*"

"Truth" replied to "Citizen," defending Gordon and asserting that all southern senators, save one, voted as Gordon did. All realized there was no possible chance for a Tilden victory. Had Democrats failed to accept the decision of the electoral commission, they would have been charged with bad faith in failing to support what they had created. What Gordon did, "Truth" concluded, was map out "a course that secured the only alleviation of the outrage. He rendered certain the redemption of South Carolina and Louisiana." Furthermore, the senator alone of the Georgia delegation remained in Washington after the session of Congress and secured for Georgia $200,000 compensation for federal use of the Western and Atlantic Railroad in the period immediately following the war.[45]

"Citizen" was not convinced. "Truth" had not answered a single question, he charged. Why take credit away from J. Y. Brown and give it to Gordon? He supposed that it was because "We are so accustomed, under certain supposed arrangement with certain reporters, to see all the credit given to Gordon, for everything that is done in Washington." Why did they see so little of what Hill, Felton, Candler, and Stephens were doing in Washington? A "reasonable degree of newspaper puffing is tolerable" but there was "such a thing as carying it *ad nauseam.*" The reason for Gordon's remaining in Washington after the session

45 Atlanta *Daily Constitution*, April 8, 1877.

was to be present at the birth of a fine daughter whom he named "Carolina," supposedly because the press had placed him "upon the calendar as the patron saint of South Carolina."

Another activity of Gordon in Washington, which the press had failed to stress, "Citizen" reminded, was his part in the appointment of "his friend Bob Alston" as marshal. "And just let me remark that those who know Alston's standing cannot account for his positive control over Gordon." And as for the $200,000 payment for the use of the Western and Atlantic, even the *Constitution* had recently stated that "lobbyist" Alston had "engineered" the bill through Congress. Gordon had not even been mentioned. It had also been reported that Alston *et al* were to receive $50,000 of the $200,000 as their commission. Why reward Gordon if Alston was responsible? "Citizen" did not wish to attack Gordon, for the people owed him much honor, yet "in spite of his services, dash, and chivalrous manner," when he made mistakes he should expect criticism.[46]

"Citizen's" mention of Alston brought from that gentleman a protest and a demand that the *Constitution* reveal "Citizen's" identity. Joseph E. Brown authorized the editor to reveal that he had written the articles signed by "Citizen." This brought a letter from Alston to Brown. This was the same Robert Alston whose Atlanta *Herald* had been "sat down upon" by Brown and the Citizens Bank. Alston considered Brown's recent reference to him as "offensive and derogatory." Brown, apparently with some pleasure, pointed out that, although Alston apparently exercised much influence upon Gordon, his standing was inferior to that of Gordon in every respect, clearly degrading Alston as he praised Gordon. Yet Alston considered the reply satisfactory.[47] Gordon himself denounced as "basely false in every syllable and in every sense" the charges that he made either promise or bargain. Brown then added a final blow. He considered the evidence of Gordon's connection with the affair as "irresistible and conclusive, notwithstanding the denial. . . . I certainly never would assume the responsibility as he did of making a trade for my party, if I could not make a better one than was made by him and his associates."[48]

46 *Ibid.*, April 17, 1877.
47 *Ibid.*, April 22, 1877.
48 *Ibid.*, May 2, 1877.

Senator Gordon was both offended and puzzled. "No greater outrage ever was perpetrated upon any man than is the effort made just now . . . to make me responsible for the counting in of Hayes," he explained to a friend. "My only agency was this: when I saw the count was to be completed & that all was lost to our party I decided to do all in my power to save from wreck the suffering people of S. C. & La. I did this—nothing more. I stand or fall on my record."[49] Was Brown jealous of General Gordon's popularity? He never appreciated the fact that wars bring glory and acclaim to military men only. His attack upon the general was both unjust and unfortunate, and it did damage to his image as one who could recognize and face reality. But he had survived damage before and would do so again.

Prior to the Brown-Gordon controversy there was already much speculation as to the policies that might be adopted by the new president. When the Augusta *Chronicle and Sentinel* asked a number of public men for their opinion of the policies said to be intended by President Hayes and whether or not "Southern men should apply for or take office under him," Brown came forth with another long letter. He denounced "the counting in of Governor Hayes to the Presidential office as the greatest fraud ever perpetrated upon the American people." In view of the fact that this electoral majority was compiled in defiance of popular will, he could "as a Democrat, under no circumstances" accept an appointment from Hayes. Neither could he "with propriety" recommend any friend for appointment. True, Hayes had in his inaugural address, through the use of "general and indefinite" phrases, "indicated a more liberal policy toward the South." Some journals had announced his intention to distribute the patronage so as to divide the Democratic party. He had already appointed one southern Democrat to his cabinet. However, Brown warned all Democrats who accepted appointments from the new Republican president that they would be required to "conform to general policy" and conduct themselves so as to strengthen the Republican party. They should also realize that henceforth they would be classed as Republicans who had helped divide the Democratic party. They would be "without Democratic following."

As was his custom in most speeches and public letters, Brown reviewed the history of reconstruction, and added that the victor usually

49 Gordon to L. N. Trammell, April 14, 1877, in Trammell Papers.

dominated the defeated for several years after the close of a conflict. The defeated could do no better than recognize helplessness and hope for change. It appeared that by 1876 that time for change had arrived, for the Democrats did at the ballot box condemn "bad faith and usurpation" and elect a president. Northern Democrats should have "stood firmly" by this verdict, determined to inaugurate their candidate, and the "solid South should have moved up to their support." Yet that did not happen. Instead, Democratic leaders at Washington allowed themselves to be "outgeneraled by the superior management of their antagonists."

Rutherford B. Hayes was now de facto president, Brown concluded. All, through obedience to the law, should aid him in giving a fair administration. However, the South was not on the market; it could not be purchased by patronage. The administration should offer "no bribe of office," but should "do equal and exact justice to every state." The war issue should be buried and no longer alluded to, and no longer should the Republican party "flaunt the bloody shirt in our face." Let the administration concede the right of local self-government to all states. This done, public attention could then be turned to internal improvements, banks, tariffs and other important topics.[50]

Illness did not prevent Brown from continuing to give attention to his business interests. His secretary came to his home both mornings and afternoons to help with correspondence. For some time he had been concerned about what could be done for former governor Bullock. In his home state of New York, to whence he had fled from Georgia, Bullock had not prospered. In the fall of 1874 Brown had written Simon Cameron that Bullock was "very poor" and suggested that something should be done to secure for him "a position where he can make an honorable & liberal support" for his growing family. Brown thought the administration at Washington should do something for Bullock. He also assured Cameron that Bullock was "an excellent business man" with railroad and express company experience. His "enterprise, ability, promptness & industry" fitted him for a position with a railroad or in the post-office department. Further, "I think under all the circumstances that those who may have been benefited by his acts, while he was in the

50 March 27, 1877.

plentitude of his power, & his old friends with whom he then dealt liberally and justly ought now to exert themselves to be of service to him in his time of need." Brown further suggested that Cameron urge Thomas A. Scott, president of the Texas and Pacific, Secretary of the Interior Columbus Delano, and Walter T. Walters, of the Baltimore and Ohio, to use their influence with the post-office department.[51] Brown sent a copy of this letter to all persons mentioned. All were members of the Western and Atlantic Company. Scott, president of the Texas and Pacific with offices in Philadelphia, replied that he would recommend Bullock to Mr. Jewett of the Erie Railroad. Delano promised to confer with others, but warned that there were "very great difficulties" in the way of an appointment for Bullock.[52] Bullock received no appointment.

While Brown was attempting to assist Bullock, Foster Blodgett again appeared on the scene. He now resided in Newberry, South Carolina, but both he and his son, Edwin, were in legal difficulties in Atlanta. He wished Brown to get the cases "dropped from the docket." More important, he wanted to go to Washington as lobbyist for the Texas and Pacific Railroad, in which Brown was a stockholder. He had already notified "some thirty odd of my Congressional friends" that he would be in Washington next session to advocate a measure "beneficial to myself and my section." He felt confident of great influence with South Carolina and some Georgia representatives. He further suggested that Democratic victories in the recent congressional election would help; defeated Republicans would be easier to handle than if they had been reelected.

Blodgett, probably the most corrupt man in Georgia during the Bullock era, was his old self again. "You know my zeal and energy when I undertake anything," he reminded Brown. "You also know my experience and my success in managing men, and you know that I do my work in such a way that there are no afterclaps or investigating committees. My tracks are always covered and when I embark in a cause I do so to *win*." Blodgett did not mention a fixed sum for his proposed services, but he did suggest that his wardrobe had "become

51 October 24, 1874, in Hargrett Collection.
52 Scott to Brown, November 3, 1874; Delano to Brown, October 31, 1874, in Hargrett Collection.

somewhat delapidated [*sic*]," and he would "need an advancement to set me up all right." He further suggested appointment as an agent of the company with "a month or two's salary advanced."[53]

There had been some correspondence prior to this letter, for Blodgett mentioned having received a letter from Brown with copies of two letters from Scott. Who initiated the correspondence is not known. Scott was definitely not enthusiastic about the idea of using a man like Blodgett. He himself would go to Washington within the next few days, Scott wrote Brown on November 21, 1874, and would survey the situation to be "better able to say exactly what service Mr. B. will be to us, and will then advise you." However, Scott urged Brown and "other gentlemen as are influential with the Southern members" to come to Washington. "We intend to put in our bill at once."[54]

The Texas and Pacific Railroad, in which Scott and Brown were heavily interested, was in financial straits. Construction was progressing rapidly, and the president, Scott, was attempting to market more bonds in Europe when the panic of 1873 brought operations to a halt. The promoters then turned to Congress with a petition for more help, and Brown turned to his friend Alexander Stephens, now a member of Congress. What the Texas and Pacific was asking, he explained, was no more than had already been done for the Union and Central Pacific. The request was that the government endorse bonds at the rate of $35,000 per mile of track constructed. As security for these bonds, the Texas and Pacific would give a first mortgage on the entire line and its vast holdings of Texas lands. Brown urged Stephens to explain to other southern congressmen the importance of the Texas and Pacific project and the fairness of the request.[55]

A year passed without relief and the Texas and Pacific was again preparing to present to Congress a renewal of its request. If Blodgett's services were used, he had lost some of his skill "in managing men"; no bonds were voted by Congress. A year later, Scott was still petitioning Congress, and Brown was publicly proclaiming the great advantages that would result from the completion of a southern railroad to the Pacific. Could not the line be completed without further govern-

53 Blodgett to Brown, November 16, 1874, *ibid.*
54 Hargrett Collection.
55 Brown to Stephens, December 27, 1873, in Stephens Papers, Library of Congress.

ment aid? a reporter of the *Constitution* inquired. Brown said, "No." About 330 miles were now complete and another 180 had been graded. This would take the line to Fort Worth. From that point, if constructed, the road would open up the wilds of Texas and Arizona and reach the Pacific at San Diego. Its national utility would be great, and running along about the parallel with Savannah, the route would be 500–700 miles shorter than the northern route. And surely the government could lose nothing by endorsing bonds secured by the entire line and 15 million acres of land.[56]

Unable to get money from the Texas and Pacific, Foster Blodgett turned to his old "friends," the Western and Atlantic lessees. On January 11, 1875, he wrote H. I. Kimball, now back in Atlanta and in business again, reminding him of their earlier association. For "services rendered" to the Western and Atlantic Company he had been promised $65,000 in cash. "The arrangement," he recalled, "was made by yourself and Gov. Joseph E. Brown with the knowledge and advice of Governor Bullock." He had elected to take $10,000 in cash and the remainder in $500 monthly installments. He claimed to have the original of this agreement in his possession "in the handwriting of Gov. J. E. Brown." Shortly after the lessees took over, Blodgett further recalled, Kimball had requested that he accept the unpaid balance in cash, and "have an end of the matter." This he still preferred not to do. However, Brown soon paid over to his representative the remaining $50,000 for "interest." Against this deduction he protested vigorously, and he still maintained that the lessees owed him $15,000.

Blodgett now called upon Kimball to arrange for him a settlement "without litigation." This he much preferred, for "I fear if I was once on the witness stand, that matters not connected with this case might be drawn out, that possibly might be damaging, for instance about the Mitchell Property or the Tennessee Car Company. *You understand!!!!*" However, should he be forced to bring suit for the remainder of his money, he would "not employ Toombs or any of the Company's enemies." In conclusion, he appealed to Kimball to "confer a favor on *one who has done you much good and no harm.*"[57] Apparently there was no lawsuit; neither is there record of Brown and Kimball

56 Atlanta *Daily Constitution*, October 10, 1875.
57 Hargrett Collection.

denying Blodgett's story. Judging by Brown's previous position on such matters, it seems reasonable to assume that he, as president of the Western and Atlantic, paid the remaining $15,000.

Whether satisfied or not, Blodgett died shortly thereafter, but Bullock lived for another thirty years. In May, 1876, he agreed to return to Atlanta to meet his accusers, yet his trial would not be held until January, 1878. In the meantime he spent most of his time in Albion, New York, brooding over alleged mistreatment by his old friends. He was unable to understand why those he had befriended should enjoy affluence while he continued in want. In March, 1877, he traveled to Baltimore to place before Walter T. Walter for his signature a paper approving a proposition to appoint him "confidential attorney" for the Western and Atlantic Company at a salary of $4,000 per year. Walters, of the Baltimore and Ohio Railroad, was the largest shareholder in the Western and Atlantic Company. Bullock explained to Walters that there was no "covert meaning or intent" connected with his request. The question involved was simply whether the lessees, "receiving a fair equivalent for the risks incurred by themselves," would in "their *generosity* . . . grant compensation to me about equal to the return for *one* share in the Lease." He was certain that Brown "as one Lessee *would* be willing."[58] Walters would not commit himself without first receiving a "cue from Atlanta."

Both Walters and Bullock wrote Brown immediately following their conversation. Walters enclosed the paper presented by Bullock. He was suspicious as to just what Bullock was after and wanted Brown's opinion, adding, "I need not tell you that I hope we are in a position to reject the matter in toto."[59] Bullock explained to Brown that he had presented to Walters a paper, which he hoped to get signed by all lessees, approving his appointment as "confidential attorney." He was confident that Cameron, Scott, and the other northern lessees would sign cheerfully if Walters signed first; however, he had found Walters hesitant, desiring first a cue from Brown. "Now what I ask of you is that you will respond to Mr. W. by writing 'Joe E. Brown' on my paper." Should he receive the appointment, Bullock was sure he could

58 Bullock to Walters, March 28, 1877, *ibid.*
59 March 31, 1877, *ibid.*

be of service to "*yourself* personally" and also to the Texas and Pacific interest.[60]

The lessees were in a quandary. Not even Brown wished to have Bullock, who was still under indictment in Atlanta, connected with the Western and Atlantic Company. Yet all must have felt some obligation for his known favor in granting the lease. Just what a "confidential attorney" would have been is not clear. Certainly the identity of any attorney performing actual service for the company could not have been long concealed. And for Bullock to have been so rewarded by the Western and Atlantic would have intensified the hostility that had kept the company under almost constant legislative investigation.

Brown attempted to play both sides. He wrote Walters that he did not consider Bullock in position "to injure us." "I regard him honorable in such matters and do not think he will try to do harm." This left Walters in position to act independently. Brown could understand Bullock's feeling that since others were "making good income as the result of his favor and assistance, and as he is needy, he would like to share something in it." As to his own position, Brown felt it wise for him to express favor "in a modified form," and leave it to others to object. This would settle the matter and "might leave me with more control over the party [Bullock]."[61]

To Bullock, Brown sent only a short note, pleading illness as an excuse. He was "perfectly willing" that Bullock be employed, should the other lessees approve; however, he did not think approval should originate with him. It should begin with others and come to him only after they had acted.[62] Brown sent Walters a copy of his reply to Bullock, noting that he supposed others would object. He doubted whether others would sign unless Walters signed first. If Bullock should ask what reply Brown had given, Walters should say Brown was "willing if the other parties at interest would consent."[63]

Bullock took Brown's reply to him for just what it was—a definite reluctance to approve. "I greatly regret that you did not act upon my request and return the paper with your signature to Mr. Walters," he

60 March 29, 1877, *ibid.*
61 April 4, 1877, *ibid.*
62 April 14, 1877, *ibid.*
63 April 18, 1877, *ibid.*

retorted. Had he not needed employment and compensation he would never have given himself consent to make the request. "But when it *has* so occurred & I *do* ask for employment, can, will, ought the gentlemen of the lease Company to refuse me?" He wished to ask frankly would Brown "push this request to a favorable conclusion?" He had no doubt of success if Brown would give the matter his "active sympathy & support." However, without that kind of aid "the matter must fail." He had not brought the request to Brown first, Bullock continued, because he felt a delicacy in asking such a favor "from one whom I felt sure could not & ought not to refuse me"—one who might even feel gratified at promoting his interests. He reminded Brown that many times he had promoted his interests "unasked & done it effectually. . . . Will you now comply with my wish," which required no "discredit or expense to yourself or your associates? Don't put me off with pleasant phrases. Let it be a positive affirmative or a definite negative."[64]

Caught in a corner, Brown professed a lack of understanding of Bullock's letter and hinted at an interpretation that there was an attempt being made to hold a rod over him. But there was no ground for misunderstanding. An old friend, whom Brown no longer considered a public asset, was requesting a favor that he did not wish to grant. In his reply to Bullock he became a bit more definite. As for past favors, he wrote, he would admit that Bullock had granted several, but he also called attention to the fact that there was "another side to the account without which you would not have been in position to bestow favors." He thought there was no chance for Bullock's employment at the salary suggested. There were several directors of the company over whom he had no control. Owing to this fact and poor health, "I cannot undertake to say to you that I will press it to a favorable conclusion." However, "I will cheerfully second and aid the movement." He planned to leave for Hot Springs, Arkansas, the following day with hope of gaining "relief from my disease."[65]

Bullock replied at length, reviewing the entire matter, and concluding: "Mr. Walters will sign if you recommend it. In fact he will do only what you advise in the matter. With your approval & his signature,

64 April 20, 1877, *ibid.*
65 May 2, 1877, *ibid.*

I will try for the others. Without that I shall make no further effort."[66] This appears to have concluded the correspondence. Bullock was not employed as "confidential attorney." It is convincing to note that, in this strictly private correspondence, there is no mention of any compensation having been given or promised Governor Bullock for awarding the lease to the Western and Atlantic Railroad Company.

Brown remained in Hot Springs until almost mid-June. During his absence from the state, Georgians approved and selected delegates to a constitutional convention scheduled to meet on July 11, 1877. Brown was not nominated by the Atlanta convention for delegate to the convention. Many politicians were still afraid of him; they knew that when Joe Brown participated it was as a leader, never as a follower. A movement was begun among Brown's friends to place his name at the head of a list of independent candidates, and also a list opposing the holding of a convention. His son Julius requested that no such action be taken until his father could be contacted. Brown telegraphed the editor of the *Constitution* a note for publication: "I have just received copy of your paper of Tuesday, and see my name at the head of a ticket in opposition to the Convention. I can neither permit its use against the nominees who are good and true men, nor in opposition to the Convention. I think it best that the Convention be held." He further commented that he thought those who had been nominated for delegates would safeguard the interests of the people of Georgia.[67] He hoped the people of Atlanta would vote for a convention.

When a number of Brown's friends urged him to "keep quiet; neither accept or decline," he weakened and authorized Julius to publish that he was "no candidate" and add, "But I have no authority for saying he would refuse to serve if the people at the polls demand his services." Later in the same day, however, he telegraphed both Julius and the *Constitution* to cease publication relative to his candidacy.[68] It seems reasonable to assume that secretly he, like many others, saw no

66 May 25, 1877, *ibid.*
67 William Phillips to Mrs. Brown, May 22, 1877; E. L. Connally to Brown, May 30, 1877; Brown to Julius Brown, June 6, 1877; Brown to Editor of *Constitution* (telegram), June 8, 1877, all in Hargrett Collection.
68 C. D. Phillips and W. T. Winn to Brown (telegram), June 8, 1877; Brown to Julius Brown (2 telegrams), June 9, 1877; Brown to Editor of *Constitution* (telegram), June 9, 1877, all *ibid.*

need for any substantial changes in the Constitution of 1868. Yet the fact that it was written during the Bullock era was reason enough for most white Georgians to desire a new one. Defense of the Constitution of 1868 would be in a sense to defend radicalism; this Brown did not wish to do. To push his independent candidacy for delegate would be to risk defeat. Even small defeats can be damaging to one looking toward higher goals.

Either to carry out his part of the "bargain" or out of a sincere desire to bring Radical reconstruction to an end, President Hayes had already, during April, 1877, withdrawn the federal troops from South Carolina and Louisiana. Since the Democrats still held control in the House and the slight Republican majority in the Senate had not been increased, the president would need southern support for such measures as he might wish to push through Congress. In the interest of such support, President Hayes visited Atlanta in September and was honored with a banquet at the Markham House. This was not just a Republican affair. Judge James Jackson presided and at the head table sat Governor Alfred H. Colquitt and Chief Justice Hiram Warner. Chairman Jackson read toasts in the names of several states. For Georgia he proposed: "Georgia—the Empire State of the South: 'Her swords turned into plowshares'—her armories into factories." Brown was called upon for a response.

He traced the history of slavery, stressing that original Georgians neither had nor desired Negro slavery. It was introduced by New England shipowners seeking profits. Then when Georgians found slave labor profitable in the production of cotton, they concluded "it was right." Outside the South, many believed it wrong. Each side justified its opinions "by the Bible." Politicians seized upon slavery as an issue, yet when war came neither side expected its abolition. Following the Battle of Manassas, Congress passed a resolution declaring preservation of the Union, not the abolition of slavery, as the war aim. But war continued to the bitter end, slavery was abolished, and Georgia again stood as it was originally—a free state.

Brown conceded that during the war "We were equally honest"; then came the bitterness of reconstruction. During the past year, "our distinguished guest led one of the great political parties as its standard bearer. . . . I did all in my power to secure its defeat. I did not believe it right that he should be elected." Georgia cast the largest majority against him of any state in the Union. But now, as president, he was Georgia's guest and would receive her "warmest welcome." "Differ as we may about the struggle, I, as his opponent say that his general course in office has been that of an honest man—'the noblest work of God.'" As president, he had hauled down the "bloody shirt" and "buried it, I trust, forever in the grave dug by common patriotism." The South now was looking to the future, Brown concluded. Where money was once invested in slaves it was now invested in manufactories, and Georgia would soon be "a formidable rival of your northern states." Raw materials, labor, climate, and water power would make it to the interest of northern manufacturers to move their machinery to Georgia.[69]

Although Brown and other orators spoke of prosperity, few Georgians were prosperous during the 1870s. The economy had still not adjusted to the changes resulting from war and reconstruction. As on the national scene, applicants for public jobs were greatly in excess of the number of jobs. Those who were unsuccessful became disgruntled, and appointing officials became the objects of great abuse. Governor Alfred Colquitt managed the state's financial affairs with considerable efficiency, collecting hundreds of thousands from sources indebted to the state, still he was loudly denounced for the fees paid to those who assisted in the collection. He was also denounced for his endorsement of certain railroad bonds. Finally, at his request, his actions were investigated by a committee of the General Assembly. He was completely exonerated, yet his enemies were not silenced.[70]

This investigation, although revealing no evidence of wrongdoing, touched off numerous other investigations and trials, increasing personal bitterness that would be reflected in politics. Brown, out of office and almost out of legal practice, had no active part in these controversies. Through intelligent investments he was quietly making money while others growled over the crumbs. The panic of 1873 seemed to have stimulated rather than decreased his income which totaled more than $19,000 for each of the years 1874 and 1875. And his Atlanta property alone was assessed at $142,525 in 1876.[71]

69 Atlanta *Daily Constitution*, September 25, 1877.
70 Avery, *History of Georgia*, 537 ff.
71 Account Book No. 2, in Brown Papers, Atlanta Historical Society.

Brown now had extensive interests in coal and iron mines in north-west Georgia. By the early 1870s he and a small group of associates controlled thousands of acres of coal and iron lands in that area, most of which they incorporated as the Dade Coal Company in 1873,[72] with Brown as president. The following year his interests in Bartow and Walker counties were incorporated as the Rising Fawn Company and the Walker Coal and Iron Company. The same year, he and six others created the Marietta Paper Manufacturing Company.[73] The Dade Company apparently owned controlling interest in these companies, and Brown controlled the Dade Company. No doubt they had a monopoly on the coal, coke, and iron business in North Georgia.

In 1874 the Dade Company began using convict labor. Finding the keeping of the ever-increasing number of convicts a serious problem, the Georgia legislature authorized the governor to lease them to companies for a period of five years.[74] The Dade Company immediately secured the lease of one hundred convicts to be worked in general mining operations at a cost of $1,000 per year plus food and clothing. Two years later, under a revised law, the number was increased to three hundred and the period of lease to twenty years at $75,000, payable in twenty equal installments.[75] At this time the Dade Coal Company was composed of Brown (president), John T. Grant, W. C. Morrill, and Jacob W. Seaver. The last lived in Boston.

Rumors of Brown's wealth, though exaggerated, made him a marked man. So numerous were the requests for gifts and loans from individuals and the promoters of causes that he felt it necessary to prepare a printed letter of reply: "It is entirely out of my power to comply with the numerous requests of the character mentioned. I must be excused therefore for adopting this mode of expressing my regrets that I CANNOT GRANT YOUR REQUEST."[76]

---

72 *Acts and Resolutions*, 1873, p. 185.
73 *Ibid.*, 1874, pp. 273, 363.
74 For details of the convict lease system in Georgia, see Elizabeth Taylor, "Origins of the Convict Lease System in Georgia," *Georgia Historical Quarterly*, XXVI (March, 1942).
75 "Executive Minutes, 1874–77," pp. 1, 395, 641, 731–35.
76 See Hargrett Collection for printed copy.

Chapter XXII

New South Versus the Old

BROWN'S RAILROAD interests kept him before the public more than any of his other enterprises. The panic of 1873 followed by ruinous competition among railroads caused them to turn to cooperation and consolidation. The Southern Railway and Steamship Association was organized in 1875 "to prevent as far as possible ruinous competition" by regulation through pooling agreements and the distribution of business among member roads.[1] Brown was made president. Persons hostile to railroads saw this organization as an attempt to create monopoly and fix freight rates. Rumors of illegal state aid and of favoritism and unjust discrimination by the railroads resulted in further public protest. The Constitutional Convention of 1877, under the leadership of Robert Toombs, adopted provisions prohibiting further state aid to railroads and giving power to the legislature to regulate railroads so as to prevent unfair rates and unjust discrimination. Toombs would spend the remainder of his active life fighting railroads.[2] In 1879 the legislature created a railroad commission to implement its powers of regulation.

On November 5, 1879, a rumor reached Atlanta circles that E. W. Cole of the Nashville, Chattanooga and St. Louis Railroad had acquired the shares of northern members of the Western and Atlantic Company. His design was to strike a severe blow at the new Cincinnati Southern

---

1 Brown's testimony in *Report of the Joint Committee of the General Assembly of Georgia Appointed to Investigate the Lease of the Western and Atlantic Railroad, 1880–81* (Atlanta, 1881), 60.

2 Thompson, *Toombs*, 243 ff.

Railroad linking that city with Chattanooga by denying it use of the Western and Atlantic. A reporter of the Atlanta *Constitution* sought an interview with Brown to learn the truth about this reported transaction. Brown admitted that Cole had bought some shares but claimed that this would not materially affect the management of the Western and Atlantic. As long as he himself was in charge there would be no discrimination against any line. He wished to do business with both the Nashville, Chattanooga and St. Louis and the Cincinnati Southern. Furthermore, Cole, with whom he was on very friendly terms, did not expect any favors.[3] Cole later testified that he did buy seven and one-half shares from nonresidents of Georgia, but he denied that he ever voted these shares. His only vote was that of his own share as an original lessee.[4]

Rumor persisted and soon had Brown and Cole leasing the Central Railroad, thus through their combined lines making connection from St. Louis to Savannah.[5] There was truth in the rumor, but the proposed deal was never completed. Victor Newcomb of the powerful Louisville and Nashville Railroad, with interests centered in New York, stepped in and without the knowledge of Cole, acquired control of the Nashville, Chattanooga and St. Louis. Brown granted an interview on February 1, 1880, to say that Newcomb's control of the Nashville, Chattanooga and St. Louis would not give him control of the Western and Atlantic. He, Cole, and a few friends were still in control, and there would be no bottling up of the Cincinnati Southern at Chattanooga.[6] Even as Brown spoke reassuringly, he knew that Victor Newcomb was looking through Chattanooga and Atlanta toward Savannah.

This was the situation when John B. Gordon exploded a political bomb on May 15, 1880, by submitting to Governor Alfred H. Colquitt his resignation as United States senator. He gave as the principal reason for his action "a long cherished desire to retire from public life." For many years he had subordinated his desire to his sense of duty and a reluctance to leave the service of "a noble and generous people" who had honored and exalted him by their confidence. Now that the

3 Atlanta *Daily Constitution*, November 5, 1879.
4 *Report of Committee . . . to Investigate Lease of Western and Atlantic Railroad*, 77.
5 Atlanta *Daily Constitution*, January 7, 8, 1880.
6 *Ibid.*, February 1, 1880.

right of self-government had been restored in South Carolina and Louisiana and full representation in national affairs accorded the South, he felt free "to consult my inclinations and the imperative interests of my family, with the least deteriment to the public service."

According to published accounts, Governor Colquitt immediately telegraphed Senator Gordon urging that he reconsider, if not unconditionally, "at least until the meeting of the general assembly." Gordon expressed appreciation for "your flattering request," but although "anxious to oblige" felt "constrained to decline." Governor Colquitt accepted the resignation in a letter filled with compliments and good wishes.

In placing before the public Gordon's resignation, the editor of the *Constitution* declared that it "came to the executive office like a bolt out of the blue. Its coming had been heralded even by rumors, and all to whom the news first found its way were incredulous, and only became believers in its genuineness when there was no longer room for doubt." And Henry W. Grady, reporting from Washington, quoted Gordon as saying the first thing he wanted was a few weeks of rest and then added that the senator had received "several flattering offers," but would delay his decision for the time being.[7]

No doubt the news was a bolt that would produce expressions of surprise, disappointment, and anger, yet there had been rumors. According to the Athens *Watchman*, Grady had stated in Athens, on May 10, that Gordon would soon resign and be succeeded by Brown. However, perhaps as the fiery Mrs. Rebecca Latimer Felton later explained, Grady's "careless handling of facts" was so well known that the "statement carried no force."[8] Neither was the resignation a great surprise to Governor Colquitt, as would be later revealed by him, and there was even a "leak" in Atlanta as to Gordon's successor. A second "bolt" came on the following day with the announcement that Joseph E. Brown had been named Gordon's successor. The *Constitution* accompanied the announcement with the statement that "It is recognized as a proper appointment and as good as could have been made."[9] Many persons disagreed, and thus were unleashed the enemies of all three participants.

7 *Ibid.*, May 20, 21, 1880.
8 Mrs. William H. Felton, *My Memoirs of Georgia Politics* (Atlanta, 1911), 303.
9 May 21, 1880.

Cries of "bargain" and "trade" came from all parts of the state. Heretofore, Gordon had been an idol "classed with Lee and Jackson, Beauregard, and Johnston, and the noble Semmes," declared "Paul Pry" in the Savannah *Record*. But now, regardless of his excuse, Gordon had "committed a grave mistake, an irreparable wrong to Georgia," and "imperiled the Democratic cause." He had been "indiscreet and negligent of his duty to his State and to his constituents." It was his duty to "stipulate with the Governor" as to a successor before surrendering. Knowing the "previous history and damnable antecedents of this said Joe Brown," Gordon should have either remained in the senate or insisted upon naming his successor. However, if there was not a "shadow of suspicion" against Gordon "farther than fitful indiscretion and temporary weakness, nothing can excuse Governor Colquitt's reprehensible and insulting appointment. Joseph E. Brown, Esquire, commonly called Joe Brown for shortness and familiarity, and 'Pike' Brown through derision of his military equipment—could not obtain a constable's berth in any single county in Georgia unless by bribery." The said Brown could neither "be depended upon nor trusted by any party." He was for sale to the highest bidder "be he Grant, Sherman, Blaine, or the d—l." He was "venal, mercenary, mediocre, vindictive, ever veering his sails to suit the wind." Regardless of who else was down, "Joe Brown is sure to be uppermost." [10]

In Columbus, the home of the "Columbus prisoners," a mass meeting adopted resolutions protesting the appointment of one who had betrayed his state into the hands of the enemy "in her darkest hour." Gordon's action was regretted; Colquitt's was "deserving of censure so strong that we fail to find words adequate to express our indignation thereat." The people of Muscogee County wished to express their "disapprobation of the shameful and disgraceful manner" in which Brown was forced upon them. [11]

As the storm of protest and denunciation gathered momentum, a reporter from the Atlanta *Constitution* gathered statements from the participants. Governor Colquitt denounced the charge of "bargain" as "utterly, wantonly false" and declared that "no one but a liar or a thief would make such a statement." "Was there no sort of understanding?"

10 May 24, 1880.
11 Columbus *Times*, quoted in Atlanta *Daily Constitution*, May 21, 1880.

inquired the reporter. "None—not the hint of one—none directly or indirectly," exclaimed the governor. For several months he had known of Gordon's desire and of course had looked about for a possible successor; he did confer with Brown. At first the former governor flatly declined the possible offer, but when Colquitt continued to urge, he consented to think it over, all the while insisting that everything possible be done to keep Gordon in the Senate. "I was both surprised and gratified at his prompt acceptance" when the official offer was made, Colquitt added.

When questioned if he had represented Gordon "in any proposition tendered to Governor Brown," Colquitt replied "None whatever." He did not even know what Gordon's plans were. He respected every man's right to express an opinion as to the resignation and appointment, Colquitt explained, "but I have nothing but loathing and contempt for the man who hints of corruption or questionable methods" in arriving at his opinion. The governor further stated that in casting about for a successor to Gordon he had consulted friends and had eventually told some persons of his intentions to appoint Brown. This was the possible source of the "leak" in Atlanta that Brown would be appointed.

When the reporter left the governor's office, he called upon Brown and asked questions similar to those which had been put to Colquitt. Brown declared "The statement that there has been any trade or bargain or condition in this matter is an infamous falsehood." Then what was the true story? the reporter inquired. Brown substantiated Colquitt's story as to their conference, his reluctance, and his urging that every effort be made to keep Gordon in the Senate. This the governor promised to do, but he had also urged Brown to accept an appointment in case the effort failed. Brown, after consulting friends, decided to do so. (He did not say whether or not he so informed the governor. Colquitt had stated that he did not know at the time whether Brown would accept.) "There was no suggestion or hint of any bargain or understanding or condition, then or at any other time. I was simply urged to take the place, and finally agreed. There never had been the slightest hint of a condition."

When questioned whether he had previously conferred with Gordon on the matter, Brown replied that no word in any form had passed between them. "Nor has any friend passed one word between us in any way." Had there ever been a suggestion that Gordon replace him as president of the Western and Atlantic Railroad Company? the reporter queried. "Never at any time," Brown replied. "On the contrary, the only suggestions I have had are urgent requests from my stockholders that I should remain in charge of the road." It was his intention to do so.[12]

Senator Gordon told a similar story with a few additions. He denounced the charge of trade or bargain as "a base calumny and falsehood in all its length and breadth and depth. . . . Governor Brown had nothing to give me. The offer [of a railroad position] came to me from Mr. Newcomb and was the consequence and not the cause of my resignation. I had already sent my resignation to the governor, intending to accept another position." When Newcomb learned of his resignation, he then made the offer. His position with the Louisville and Nashville Railroad would be that of general counsel.[13]

Later Senator Gordon, speaking before an Atlanta audience, vigorously defended the governor in the appointment of Brown. He admitted that "as a matter of sentiment, most of us would have preferred some other Georgian," yet under "the circumstances surrounding our present momentous issues" involving future political contests, Brown was the best possible selection. In the South the time had come when, in the interest of the "integrity of our society, the security of our property, and the supremacy of our political principles," policies should be liberalized and the olive branch extended to those who had differed during the transition stage following the war.

Governor Colquitt, Gordon asserted, saw in Brown "a man of large property, deeply interested in the material progress of the country and in stable government—a life-long Democrat, who, although denounced by us for voting for Grant and reconstruction in 1868, was joined by us in voting for Greeley and reconstruction in 1872." Gordon thought Colquitt also saw in his appointment of Brown a great service to the Democratic party. The Democrats were in serious trouble in several areas. Two of their strongest districts had been lost in the last election, and in two others the fight had been close. In short, the party was

12 May 23, 1880.
13 May 27, 1880.

threatened with dissolution. Among the dissatisfied who were ready to break up the party were the "hardy yeomanry of the mountains," friends and "life-long followers" of Brown.[14]

At this point, Senator Gordon stated, he wished to repeat that everyone knew he was "not the champion of Gov. Brown." Yet he also wished to assert that "it is due our manhood that we either cease hostility to Gov. Brown, or cease to ask his time and talents and money for the benefit of our party." For the past decade Brown had been unfaltering in his support of the party. He had even supported Gordon himself against a life-long friend—Herschel V. Johnson. In conclusion, Gordon stated that he was but performing a simple act of justice when he testified to the "earnest, unswerving, potential aid" given him by Brown's friends of the mountain districts.[15]

These were the "facts" concerning the resignation of Senator Gordon and the appointment of Brown as his successor that the public and future historians were asked to accept. I. W. Avery, in his *History of Georgia* published the following year, declared that there was "no collusion, no condition—no trading"; that Gordon knew nothing of a plan to appoint Brown; that Brown was already a supporter of Colquitt, so there was no need for a political agreement; and that Brown had nothing to do with Gordon's appointment to a position with the Louisville and Nashville Railroad.[16] Avery was either very naïve or less than truthful. He was executive secretary to Governor Colquitt and a close friend of Brown. For some months Brown had been giving him considerable assistance in the preparation of his proposed history, and thanks to the generosity of Brown, he and his family had been riding the Western and Atlantic Railroad at reduced rates.[17]

Even Mrs. Felton, wife of Seventh District congressman William H. Felton, who learned to hate Brown for alleged meddling in district politics, later recorded in her *Memoirs* that she did not believe it was Brown's money that induced "money-loving General Gordon" to resign. Brown would buy other men's influence, but he never made a practice of selling his own. He was inclined to leave "money trading to

14 This reference was to the independent revolt in North Georgia led by the Reverend Doctor William H. Felton of Cartersville.
15 Atlanta *Daily Constitution*, June 8, 1880.
16 Avery, *History of Georgia*, 561.
17 Avery to Brown, May 17, 1880, in Hargrett Collection.

smaller men, and weaker natures." Mrs. Felton further noted that Brown kept well posted on what other politicians were doing and kept men about him who could ferret out "the invisible, if not the unknown." In this case, she thought Brown took what "weak Gov. Colquitt" offered him, and then refrained from exposing what he knew about Senator Gordon's politics and financial affairs. She conceded that Brown was a very able man and added that he was "a dictator in Georgia politics, even while he was being roundly abused by the majority of Georgia's Democratic politicans."[18] Mrs. Felton was nearer the truth than she knew; all of the participants had "refrained from exposing" what they knew.

No one seemed to have suspected that Henry W. Grady had a prominent part in making the resignation-appointment arrangement. Young Grady, envisioning a "New South," had become much interested in railroads and in Atlanta as a possible hub of the wheel of transportation. Of particular interest to him was the known business friendship between Brown and E. W. Cole, president of the Nashville, Chattanooga and St. Louis Railroad, and the possibility that arrangements by them might bring a flood of traffic through Atlanta. Early in 1880 he secured leave from his responsibilities with the Atlanta *Constitution* and journeyed to Nashville and other points to study railroad possibilities. In Nashville, he learned that the Louisville and Nashville Railroad, headed by Victor Newcomb, had acquired controlling interest in the Nashville, Chattanooga and St. Louis. He soon became not only a friend but a paid assistant to Newcomb and was with him in New York at the time of Gordon's resignation. His known friendship with Brown was certainly no hindrance to his becoming a close associate of one who had an eye on possible control of both the Western and Atlantic and the Central Railroad.

How early Grady and Brown began discussion of the possibility of Gordon's resignation is unknown, but by early May, with the assistance of W. H. Pittman, he had placed in Brown's hands an undated code to be used in their telegraphic dispatches. Telegraphic operators might talk! The code was in Grady's handwriting, on his personal letterhead, and enclosed in a Nashville, Chattanooga and St. Louis Railroad envelope. The code:

18 Felton, *Memoirs*, 527.

These words are to be used in reverse, that is Jones means Newcomb.

State road—neck

Jones—Newcomb

Smith—Brown

Agrees—shoots

Gordon—Williams

Senatorship—Wash

Presidency—wood

Attorney—more

Thousands—slow

Refuses—poor

Year—proud

Colquitt—Jim

Appointment—break

Resignation—play

Send in—pass

Where a word not included in the list is used, it stands for itself

H.W.G.

I will telegraph as soon as I know.[19]

The first telegram *in code* was sent by Grady from New York, on May 15, and received by Brown on the following day. As translated: "Gordon will send in resignation certain. Newcomb highly pleased with Brown's assurances & anxious to do all wanted. He would like you to make Ravill vice prest if agreeable to you with no increase in duties while you hold senatorship. He wants all roads be interested in pool Gordon's salary & will fix at twenty thousand if your road will pay three to five thousand. Please do this. It fixes everything precisely as wanted. Answer."[20]

Brown's reply has not been found. Grady again telegraphed in code on the 17th: "Everything is fixed. Gordon's resignation sent in to Colquitt & Newcomb agrees that Brown shall hold [road?] and senatorship but says in adjusting Gordon's salary four thousand should come from Brown's road. He begs that Brown come to New York on tomorrow's train as he wishes to have conference with him for better understanding. He is anxious. Can't Brown come. Newcomb says Brown must guarantee that Cole who is bitterly opposed to him shall not have charge of road while Brown is in Washington. Answer tonight."[21]

Brown replied in code: "Brown cannot come to New York. Important engagement in Nashville Thursday prevents. General manager

19 Original in Hargrett Collection.
20 Hargrett Collection.
21 *Ibid.*

under Brown's instruction will control in his absence. Vice President will have nothing to do with it. Brown cannot speak positively about four thousand. Directors under rules control that. He will urge three thousand. Thinks that would be certain. He wants to meet Newcomb soon. When could he come here or meet Brown at some other agreed point."[22]

A. Anderson, representing Newcomb, also wired Brown expressing fear that "a delay might cause miscarriage of your wishes as the time is short," and urging that Brown come to New York. He thought it would be the following week before they could return home.[23] Brown, now in Nashville, replied it would be out of the question for him to come to New York at that time, yet he desired to see Newcomb and had no doubt of a cordial understanding.[24] On the same day Grady was again on the wires. Newcomb was eager "to meet your wishes in every respect. I advise you to break engagement & leave tonight without fail. Come to St. James Hotel."[25]

By this point Brown had become irritated. "I have twice stated I cannot come to New York," he telegraphed A. Anderson. "After the assurances I have given if distrust is shown by delays I shall decline to go to Washington and confine myself to my duties here. In that case we will assume no part of the salary of anyone. I have acted frankly & in good faith with the most ready intentions and can say no more."[26]

Brown could now afford to be independent. During the day he received a telegram from Governor Colquitt sent to Nashville in care of E. W. Cole: "Gen Gordon has resigned his seat in the U.S. Senate. If you can accept appointment to vacancy please notify me & return immediately." Brown replied: "I accept the appointment. Will return Friday."[27] Here the extant telegraphic correspondence ended. When Brown received Colquitt's telegram he was at a dinner given by Alexander Porter in honor of General Joseph E. Johnston. On the following day he attended the unveiling of an equestrian statue of Andrew

22 May 17, 1880, *ibid.*
23 May 18, 1880, *ibid.*
24 *Ibid.*
25 *Ibid.*
26 May 19, 1880, *ibid.*
27 *Ibid.* See also "Executive Minutes, 1877–1882," I, 705.

Jackson on the Tennessee Capitol grounds, and returned to Atlanta on May 21.[28] He left for Washington on the twenty-fourth.

The correspondence between Atlanta and New York leaves several questions unanswered. Why was Grady so interested? The biographers of neither Grady nor Gordon mention his participation. Did he represent his friend Brown in negotiations with Gordon and Newcomb? Brown denied that "any friend passed one word" between him and Gordon. When Grady reported from Washington that Gordon had received "several flattering offers" but would make no decision at present, he knew very well that the general had already taken a position with the Louisville and Nashville Railroad. Was Gordon not in touch with Brown and Newcomb while they were negotiating his future? Why was Newcomb so interested in securing Gordon's services and Brown willing to pay a considerable portion of his salary? Why was Newcomb so eager for Brown to come to New York for a conference if the only thing involved was the appointment of Gordon to a position with the Louisville and Nashville system. The landing of Gordon would be no great catch; he was not among the foremost members of the Georgia bar. Further, did Brown really want to go to the Senate? And what was Governor Colquitt's role?

Even though there are gaps in the evidence, certain conclusions seem justified. Perhaps Gordon did need a more lucrative job. Newcomb hoped to make use of his name, for the general was among the more popular Confederate heroes. At first Newcomb definitely hoped to gain control over the Western and Atlantic Railroad by placing a friend in charge while Brown was in Washington; Brown vetoed that plan. This did not deter Newcomb, however, for he still had hopes of control and a favor to Brown might pay good dividends. The real reason for Newcomb's desire for a conference with Brown in New York was later revealed in the latter's testimony before an investigating committee. Shortly after Brown went to Washington as a senator he was requested to attend a Louisville and Nashville board meeting in New York. There he was informed that Newcomb and his friends had acquired majority shares in the Western and Atlantic. Again Brown applied the damper. Regardless of who owned the shares, he explained, only the original lessees could sit at board meetings and participate in

28 Atlanta *Daily Constitution*, May 21, 1880.

the management of the road.[29] Newcomb had begun to learn what many others already knew—Joe Brown usually came out on top.

It is doubtful that Brown really wanted to go to Washington as a senator, leaving behind all of his business interests, yet he thought the honor due him. This honor had previously been denied him by the legislature, not the people. There is no reason to question Governor Colquitt's sincerity; still it was also true that, facing a difficult fight for reelection, he needed all the political assistance possible. One wonders, however, if he seriously considered the fact that while acquiring the support of Brown's friends he could not escape the hostility of his enemies. Amid all the speculation, one fact stands out: Regardless of who else won, truth suffered a defeat.

Denials on the part of the "triumvirate"—Colquitt, Brown, and Gordon—did not silence the hostile outburst. An "ex-journalist," speaking through the Savannah *Recorder*, expressed dissatisfaction with Colquitt and Gordon, but declared he could tolerate them. "But Brown!— Joseph E. Brown! The third of this triumvirate!!!" How could he possibly find union of any kind with the other two when his name had become "a stench in the nostrils not only of the Democratic party, but of everything in the nature of a Southern element?" Like the Apostle Paul, Brown had been "'all things unto all men'"—Democrat, "mad on State Rights," scalawag, Radical, Independent, then Democrat again. What would this political acrobat be tomorrow?[30] A "regular bargain and sale" charged the Americus *Republican*. The Augusta *News* thought this was a blow that would sever Colquitt from many of his friends forever. The governor had shown too great a "desire for office and a mamouth pull on the wires."[31]

But all was not hostility; there was mild and even strong defense of the triumvirate. The Covington *Star* thought Brown's appointment satisfactory. He would do Georgia no dishonor, and probably no one could do more for the state in Washington than he. Yet "*as a party man*," he probably should not have been chosen; he had not exerted himself for the good of the party.[32] The Quitman *Reporter* thought

29 *Report of Committee . . . to Investigate Lease of Western and Atlantic Railroad*, 60.
30 May 30, 1880.
31 Quoted in Savannah *Record*, May 26, 1880.
32 May 26, 1880.

Gordon had "a perfect right . . . to resign," and Colquitt "a perfect right" to appoint "any good, competent, capable and reliable citizen." In appointing Brown he showed "great wisdom," for Brown had "no superior, if he has a peer in the State, in point of astute statesmanship." Why the "disgraceful hot-mouthed howling?"[33]

The editor of the Albany *News* considered the outburst of denunciation "an outpouring of venimous spleen," which had been "awaiting an opportunity." He gave no credit to the rumors of bribery; there were insufficient reasons for "unjust insinuations." Yet he could not understand why Gordon could not have remained in the Senate a few more days without serious contribution to his "financial embarrassment." No doubt the senator would give a public explanation. As to the appointment of Brown, the *News* thought Colquitt made "a very great mistake" if he intended to appoint "*a popular man.*" The governor had overestimated the former governor's popularity, for the past had not been forgiven and forgotten.[34]

The Monroe *Advertiser* refused to believe there was any bargain or trade. Gordon wished to resign, and Governor Colquitt wished to secure "the services of perhaps the most capable man in Georgia." If people would only "forget the animosities of the past" they would be "abundantly satisfied" with Senator Brown.[35] The Madison *Madisonian* declared Brown "the peer of any man in this State in intellect, and over and above all in judge-m-e-n-t."[36] His appointment should give satisfaction. There was not the "least foundation" for the charge of bargain or sale." When Gov. Colquitt, Senator Gordon and ex-Gov. Brown have been convicted of bargain and sale, then 'we'll all jump into the wagon and take a ride.'"[37]

He had no sympathy with the "hue and cry" against the governor; he was a victim of "unfortunate circumstances," explained the Fort Valley *Mirror*. The "organized democracy" should welcome an opportunity to secure the support of "Brown's adherents," many of whom had been acting outside the party as independents. The time had come to

33 May 27, 1880.
34 *Ibid.*
35 May 25, 1880.
36 This refers to Brown's pronunciation of the word which had long been a subject of amusement.
37 May 28, 1880.

"heal the breach between the white people of Georgia." There were "as many good men among the independents as there are among the organized democrats." The editor was not afraid to risk Brown in Washington. The former governor had strong and bitter opponents, yet he was very popular "outside of the politicians."[38]

The editor of the Thomasville *Times* probably expressed most accurately the attitude of the majority of Georgians: The governor had acted in good faith and appointed one of the best workers in the state, a man well versed in state and national affairs. "We did not approve, nor do we now, of Gov. Brown's course during the reconstruction period, but no man in Georgia has a fairer or more consistent record during the past few years. He has been true as steel."[39]

Brown took the oath as senator on May 26, 1880, escorted by Senator Ben Hill, his long time adversary, who himself had been elected to that body in 1877 with Brown's support. Only about three weeks of the session remained. Probably one reason for pressure on Gordon to resign so near the end of the session was that Brown might acquire status of incumbent and receive publicity before time for election by the General Assembly. (Certainly Newcomb and the Louisville and Nashville Railroad could have waited three weeks for the services of a second-rate legal adviser.) From his first day in the Senate, Brown intended to be seen and heard. As demonstrated when he entered the Georgia Senate in 1849, he felt none of the reluctance or deference for seniority generally associated with freshmen legislators. Even though short on experience, Joe Brown would never accept the classification of novice in any field of activity.

"Pork barrel" legislation had already become the name of the game in Congress, and Brown had long insisted that Georgia must get her share. He immediately thrust his own arm into the "barrel" and came out with $10,000 for improvement of the harbor at Brunswick, and "almost" pulled out an additional $35,000 for improvement of the Savannah River. He also sponsored a measure to authorize the Savannah, Florida and Western Railroad to bridge the St. Mary's River. But the fight that he enjoyed most and from which he hoped to get the greatest publicity was on a bill to grant soldiers' pensions. The Senate was

38 *Ibid.*
39 May 29, 1880.

ready for debate on a bill to grant pensions to certain veterans of the Mexican and other wars. Amendments were suggested, proposing to pension all Union veterans of the late war; pension only those veterans of the Mexican War who were on poverty; deny pensions to veterans of the Mexican War who later fought for the Confederacy. Brown thought veterans of the Mexican War, now old and probably in need, should be pensioned. He did not, however, favor distinction as to need. All should be pensioned, including those who later fought for the Confederacy. He did not feel that sufficient time had elapsed for granting general pensions to the Union veterans of the late war. At the proper time he would favor pensions for all, not just the needy.

When Roscoe Conklin of New York suggested "gently, delicately, mildly" that ex-Confederates on the floor held their seats by grace rather than right, this gave Brown his opportunity. He would discuss the war—its causes, prosecution, and results—giving full treatment to his own participation and reaction. Much of what he would say was not new to Georgians, but he was now speaking to a national audience, and he would add some new conclusions. The Constitution, he declared, had provided for two senators from each state. Regardless of how long a state was in rebellion, when it was ended, to deny that state its two senators was to destroy the Union one fought to preserve. If the Union had been preserved, then Georgia was a member, and no power on earth could rightfully deny its senators their seats. He admitted that Georgia had tried to leave the Union and that he was "a secessionist, earnest and active." As governor, he sent a hundred regiments of soldiers into the field, and others from Georgia were enlisted by Confederate conscription, "which, as all know, I did not approve. We fought you honestly. We were as earnest, as honest as bold, and as gallant as you were in the struggle. We believed we were right." And he still did.

There were two causes for the late war, Brown contended—"slavery and our differences on the right of secession." The South believed the right to own slaves was guaranteed by the Constitution of their fathers. When the North elected a president opposed to the extension of slavery, Brown continued, it left the South with one of two choices—give up slavery or exercise the right of secession. The South chose the latter, and the North resorted to arms to prevent it. The use of arms, "the highest of human tribunals," decided against both slavery and secession and removed them from the picture forever. "I would have given my life then to maintain our institution of slavery believing it for the best interests of both races, morally, politically, socially, and religiously, yet, if by turning my hand over today I could reinstate it I would not do so." He accepted the verdict and did not wish a new trial. The same was true of secession. "If we had succeeded we would have been heroes, but having failed we were rebels; consequently we must accept the term 'the war of the rebellion.'" The war settled the questions of slavery and secession, yet it did not alter the equality of the states within the Union. Although the doctrine of Jefferson and Calhoun was no longer applicable, still "we can stand upon the doctrines of Clay, Jackson, and Webster as to the rights of the States."

Brown could not refrain from tracing his own course during the reconstruction period. He thought President Johnson made a "great mistake" by not first submitting his plan to a special session of Congress before attempting to apply it. Yet Brown admitted that he had advised Georgians to accept the president's terms. When Congress repudiated the president's action and dictated its own terms, Brown, although he thought them severe, saw no way to avoid acceptance. Therefore, he advised quick agreement with the adversary, for he considered restoration of the Union the matter of first importance. The position he assumed, Brown related, put him through a "hard ordeal," but convinced that he acted wisely, he had never regretted it. He continued to stand upon the platform of acquiescence and the Democratic party finally joined him.

Brown next admitted that the late war might have been a mistake, yet he did not believe slavery could ever have been abolished in any other manner. During the war it was said that the South was not and could not get out of the Union; yet after the war it was forced to seek readmission to the Union from which it could not withdraw. The conqueror dictated the terms. Now the South was called upon to help pay pensions to disabled Union soldiers. "I think you should sympathize with the poor maimed soldier who on our side felt that he was fighting in as sacred a cause as yours, and believed he was right, who can draw no pension because he was on the weaker side." In closing the new senator made a strong appeal for understanding and cooperation between the sections. "Let us move grandly and gloriously in united effort to restore to every section of the Union substantial, growing, material prosperity; and we will then bring to the whole country peace, happiness, and fraternal relations. This seems to me to be a consummation devoutly to be wished by patriotic people of all parts of the Union."[40]

This speech and the calm manner in which he delivered it elicited many favorable comments from Brown's colleagues. When he returned to Georgia in mid-June he had a feeling of a job well done. He had delivered three speeches in three weeks. Alexander Stephens privately observed that the new senator's speeches had "added vim to the current events in the direction it seemed to me to be drifting—i.e. to the re-election of Gov. Colquitt & the electing of Brown to the Senate."[41] Brown's work for the summer and fall was already cut out for him. To be appointed by the governor to fill a vacancy was one thing; to be elected in his own right was entirely different. But he was determined upon election by the next General Assembly. His appointment to the Senate made him no additional friends; Colquitt and Gordon lost supporters. Yet the three now formed a triumvirate which none of their friends could afford to oppose. Colquitt would seek reelection as governor; Brown the election of enough legislators to keep him in the Senate; and Gordon to vindicate his own action.

After days of balloting and bitter controversy, the Democratic convention, meeting in Atlanta in early August, was unable to make a nomination for governor. The friends of Colquitt agreed to a two-thirds rule and then were unable to get the required number of votes. The opposition, divided among several candidates, eventually offered to compromise on almost any man other than Colquitt; the supporters of Colquitt stood fast. Finally Colquitt's friends, who constituted a majority of the convention, issued a statement endorsing him as a candidate. The minority endorsed former senator Thomas M. Norwood.[42] The coming campaign might well have been "the most intense and desperate political contest" Georgia had yet known. Colquitt and Gordon would take the stump; Brown, for the most part, remained behind and pulled wires.

40 *Cong. Record*, 46th Cong., 2nd Sess., Pt. 5, pp. 4479 ff; Fielder, *Brown*, Appendix, 593 ff.
41 Stephens to Mrs. A. H. Lawton, September 20, 1880, in Lawton Papers.
42 Kenneth Coleman, "The Administration of Alfred H. Colquitt as Governor of Georgia" (M.A. thesis, University of Georgia, 1940), 66 ff.

Norwood had little personal support, but he profited by the intense hostility to Colquitt and Brown. Colquitt already had enough enemies of his own, yet in acquiring Brown supporters he also added Brown's enemies. And those who supported Colquitt soon realized that, especially in North Georgia, they could not oppose Brown and expect his friends to vote for their candidate. The campaign would produce many interesting inconsistencies among prominent men. W. T. Wofford, long-time friend of Brown and frequent visitor in the Brown home, opposed Colquitt but remained loyal to Brown. Robert Toombs offered little opposition to Colquitt, even while denouncing Brown. And Alexander Stephens, Brown's consistent friend, could find nothing good to say about either Colquitt or Gordon. He wrote Mrs. W. H. Felton that he did not think Colquitt fit for the office the first time and he had not changed his opinion; however, he thought Norwood "no fitter than Colquitt." As for Gordon, "he is so utterly hollow-hearted, deceitful, unprincipled and dishonorable and unreliable . . . I should question his sincerity."[43] Stephens had little admiration for military heroes.

The person most prominently mentioned during the campaign as a possible opponent of Brown for the Senate seat was Alexander R. Lawton of Savannah. After an acceptable military career General Lawton had served as confederate quartermaster general. The first mistake of his campaign for the Senate was the announcement of open opposition to Colquitt. Patrick Walsh of the Augusta *Chronicle and Sentinel* was quick to catch this error. He warned Lawton that Colquitt would be reelected governor and that a majority of the legislators would be the governor's friends.[44] But James D. Stewart of Augusta doubted that many of Colquitt's friends "would be inclined to sustain Brown"; they thought Colquitt's present position was a result of bad advice from Brown.[45] A. R. Lamar, editor of the Macon *Telegraph* thought otherwise. "Colquitt and Gordon having been saved by the management and money of Brown will be compelled even if averse to do so, to stand up to the compact," he wrote Lawton. Even though

43 Felton Papers.
44 Walsh to Lawton, September 9, 1880, in Lawton Papers.
45 Stewart to Lawton, August 19, 1880, *ibid.*

Walsh and "a large portion of the intelligence of Georgia" might rebel against the election of Brown, they would be unable to prevent it. The principal Augusta, Savannah, and Macon newspapers might continue their fight but they would fail. It would be unwise to attack Brown's war record. Diplomacy would be the better course. As for himself, Lamar did not prefer to attack Brown. "I have already the animosity of Colquitt and Gordon. If I assail Brown I shall add it to his undying enmity and his untiring and devilish ingenuity for revenge."[46]

The Georgia voters gave Colquitt an overwhelming victory— 118,349 to 64,004 for Norwood.[47] It was also known immediately that Colquitt's friends would control the legislature. Even so, some of Brown's enemies refused to concede that a Colquitt victory necessarily meant a Brown victory. They thought many of Colquitt's friends "can not swallow Brown."[48] W. P. Price, president of the Gainesville and Dahlonega Railroad and member-elect of the General Assembly, was not certain of the eventual outcome, but he knew what had already happened. Colquitt's friends in North Georgia had learned that they could not win by fighting Brown. He himself was obligated to give Brown a complimentary vote, he wrote Lawton, but "I shall do nothing to induce others to vote for him."[49]

Lawton's wife, if not he himself, was undecided what he should do about permitting his name to go before the legislature. Mrs. Lawton wrote Alexander Stephens shortly before the election seeking advice. Stephens suggested that if Lawton found that Brown *did not* have a majority in the legislature he might "put in—not otherwise."[50] Lawton either made a very inaccurate count of Brown's supporters or decided to disregard Stephens' advice. The legislature convened on November 3, 1880. Lawton opened his campaign with Atlanta speeches by attorney J. C. C. Black of Augusta, Robert Toombs and himself. When he learned that Brown had arranged to speak in the De Gives Opera House on the evening of November 15, the day prior to the date set for electing a senator, he requested an opportunity to appear on the pro-

46 October 9, 1880, *ibid.*
47 Avery, *History of Georgia*, 601.
48 N. Y. Atkinson to Lawton, October 17, 1880, in Lawton Papers.
49 October 18, 1880, *ibid.*
50 Stephens to Mrs. Lawton, September 20, 1880, *ibid.*

gram in reply. Brown declined the request, citing the fact that he himself had not been invited even to attend Lawton's programs.[51]

On the evening of the fifteenth the opera house was "packed from pit to dome with ladies and gentlemen."[52] Among those near the dome was A. R. Lawton. Brown's speech was later reported to be the greatest of his long public career; it was probably so advertised in advance. "John Temple," a contributor to the Athens *Banner*, was present to sketch the scene. With "the stirring strains of music," the "prominent figures of the General Assembly filed in and took seats upon the stage, and then a pause, a hush, and a burst of passionate applause as a gray-bearded and attenuated man walked awkwardly in. The members of the assembly arose and bowed profoundly. The gray beard bowed ungracefully in return. Its wearer sunk into a sofa, and, while the band played a stirring lyric," the audience "had time to scan him well. Nothing in the man's appearance or manner suggested the idea of a more than ordinary occasion. Not a line of the calm, meek face betrayed emotion. . . . It was a singular face—not line or a curve that suggested birth or blood; not a touch of the aristocrat had been born of the twenty years of affluence that had rolled over him; a calm face, with a wonderful depth of quiet patience and tranquil determination in its outlines— the face of a man who would have smiled calmly at the stake, not from warrior pride or fortitude, but because the equable pulse of his discipline and philosophical temperament accepted the inevitable."

In the gallery there was another "with arms folded proudly and gracefully, showing just one aristocratic hand in whose blue veins the rich blood coursed calmly in the tranquil flow of his high-bred composure." His erect soldierly carriage and "flawless dignity of dress and manner . . . proclaimed the old blooded Southerner."[53] This man in the gallery was the rival of the man on the stage; both were seeking the same honor. When Brown rose to speak his "first sentence, awkward like himself, spoken in the vernacular of the masses" branded him as of the people—"a commoner indeed." Since the recent speeches of Lawton and Toombs had been devoted almost entirely to Brown's record and

51 Brown to Lawton, November 15, 1880, 2 P.M., *ibid.*
52 Fielder, *Brown*, 529.
53 Quoted in Avery, *History of Georgia*, 602–603.

political character, his would be mostly in reply. He expressed surprise that General Lawton had not announced a platform of principles to which he proposed to adhere should he be chosen senator. Instead the general had chosen to turn back to the past and drag "from their graves the carcasses of the dead issues which divided and embittered our people in years gone by." It was clear that the general hoped "to rise by his assaults upon my record rather than upon his own merits." Brown might have been surprised; he certainly was pleased, for it gave him an opportunity to review again his reconstruction record. This record was now more of an asset than a liability. Much of what he had proposed in 1867–1868 was what the Democratic party now advocated, so, he questioned, why tear "the scabs off the healing wounds" and again seek "to arouse the bitter prejudices and passions" of the past. The South was now living in a new era brought on by "a revolution in our labor system" which had "engrafted new provisions on the political system."

Brown denied that he had ever been a traitor to his party, for the principles upon which the so-called Democratic party stood in 1868 were not old party principles; neither were they the principles of the present. He refused to stand upon the platform of 1868 because "I knew it could result in no good, and must, if carried out to its legitimate results, end in revolution and blood." If he was a traitor, then the whole Democratic party was now in the same position, except for "a few Bourbons who can never accept the situation." In 1861 most Georgians were secessionists, yet some were Unionists. Should either group now denounce the other as traitors?

At this point Brown read to his audience a short letter: "My dear Major: . . . I think there can be no doubt in the minds of those who reflect that conventions must be held in the Southern States under the Sherman bill, that the people are placed in a position where no choice in the matter is left them, and it is the duty of all who may be entitled to vote to attend the polls and endeavor to elect the best available men to represent them and act for the interest of their States. . . . Wisdom dictates that the decision of the conventions should be cheerfully submitted to by the citizens of each State, who should unite in carrying out its decrees in good faith and kind feeling." Someone from the audience

called out, "That's Joe Brown talk." Brown replied, "No," but it was
very much like him. The letter was written by Robert E. Lee on April
3, 1867. Brown was reading from the original.

While he and Lee were advising acceptance and cooperation,
Brown further explained, his opponent, General Lawton, was advising
whites to resist by refusing to participate. That was the type of advice
South Carolina, Louisiana, and Florida acted upon thus giving full
control to negroes, scalawags, and carpetbaggers. The results were
well known to all. Had those states acted wisely in 1868, they would
not have been the scene of controversy in 1876. Brown suggested that
the people decide whether his active support of reconstruction or his
opponent's folding of the arms and doing nothing was the wiser course.

Lawton had brought up Brown's relations with President Davis
and accused him of hindering the prosecution of the war. To this Brown
gave the same reply he had given many times. He had met every
requisition upon the state for troops. On all occasions he had defended
"State sovereignty and slavery" which he considered to be the true
purpose of the conflict. He had opposed conscription as "unconstitutional and subversive of the very principles of State sovereignty which
lay at the foundation of our political fabric." His discussions with the
president were on "questions of constitutional law and principle" and
resulted in no practical embarrassment. He never offered any obstacles
to the execution of the conscription act except where officers showed
disrespect for law and states' rights.

Brown went into considerable detail in relating how he had cooperated with Confederate commanders in Georgia and how they had
complimented him for his aggressive loyalty. He quoted General J. E.
Johnston as saying that he did more for the cause than all other Confederate governors combined. Brown inquired if Lawton also wished
to include Stephens and Toombs as being untrue to the Confederacy.
"We acted in perfect harmony." To convict one was to convict all three.
And was it not well known that Toombs was now Lawton's strongest
supporter for election to the Senate. Further, if he was disloyal to the
cause, why did the soldiers give him such an overwhelming vote in the
election of 1863?

Brown next stressed what a loyal Democrat he had been since the
party decided to accept the situation. The Democratic experiment in

the election of 1868 he pronounced a complete failure. He made no apology for supporting Grant and "conciliation." And by 1872 the Democratic party "came squarely upon the reconstruction platform upon which I stood in 1868," and nominated Horace Greeley for president. Who made the greatest leap? "I in voting for Grant in 1868, or my opponent when he voted for Greeley in 1872?" His acceptance of reconstruction measures, Brown insisted, was a "matter of necessity only, and not as a matter of choice. I felt no attachment to them. I had no devotion for them." But he accepted them in good faith as the best terms that could be had from the conqueror. He then supported them in the same good faith.

If returned to the Senate, Brown promised to represent not only agricultural interests but also the interests of industry and commerce. Abundant raw material, cheap labor, and suitable climate gave to the South all the advantages needed. In Washington he had already talked with numerous persons who were interested in investing in the South. He would also work for federal assistance in improving harbors and rivers for transportation. He was conscious of continuing opposition to federal support of such projects, but since the South paid its share of taxes it should also receive its share of the distribution of funds. By working in behalf of these advancements, he figured he could serve the people better than by delivering a few polished speeches on "the sentimentality of the South and the bourbonism of the past."

Brown also promised to work for the advancement of public education. "Disguise it as you may," New England's support of common schools and colleges had given her people "great advantage in the contest for power and place in this government." Men educated in New England were leaders in their businesses and professions throughout "the broad plains of the mighty West." If the South was to compete, it too must educate the masses and give advantages to bright intellects wherever found. Brown liked the Prussian system of seeking out and developing those who showed great promise. Only by following the example of Prussia and New England would the South be able to "move forward to the front." But public education was expensive and those who had suffered greatest from the late war were in greatest need, yet least able to bear the burden. This being the case, it was the duty of the federal government to bear some of the burden of educating

the people. Brown favored setting aside for education the income from
the sale of public lands. These funds should be distributed among the
states annually in proportion to illiteracy and used for the education
of both races. The South with its large illiterate colored population
would of course receive more of the money than New England. Still he
believed "the enlightened people of New England, realizing the conditions resulting from abolition, would generally acquiesce."

In conclusion, Brown took a parting shot at Robert Toombs, the
most prominent supporter of Lawton. Toombs was still insisting that
the reconstruction amendments were null and void. All legislators
present, Brown explained, had taken the oath to support these amendments. Did they consider them null and void? Brown thought that
Toombs's trouble was that he failed to "learn wisdom by experience."
He always had "a turn for pulling down, and was never successful in
building up." As attorney for the state in numerous cases, Toombs had
run his own arm deep into the treasury and brought out handsome
fees, even though he considered himself "serving the commonwealth."
While he was charging others with dishonesty, Toombs should give an
accounting of his own fees. If men like Bullock and Blodgett were
thieves, why had not Toombs as servant of the Commonwealth convicted them. Toombs's course since the war, Brown concluded, could
best be illustrated by a little story: An old man and his wife started
for a visit with friends across the river. A strap on the harness broke,
the buggy ran down on the horse's heels, and the horse kicked himself
free and set out for home. The old man sat down by the river and began
cursing, but the old lady picked up the pieces, followed the horse
home, and sent a servant for the old man. The servant returned an
hour later. "'Where is the old man?'" the woman asked. "'He wouldn't
come,'" was the reply. Then, "'What is he doing?'" "'He is still sittin'
down on the river bank, cussin'.'" Old man Toombs had refused to
gather up the pieces resulting from defeat and make the most of the
situation. Even though a horse was sent back for him "he still refused
to come, and the report is that he is still sitting on the river bank a
cussin." The country must move forward, so "we are obliged to leave
him there and let him cuss."[54]

The election of a senator by the General Assembly was no contest.

54 Fielder, *Brown*, 531 ff; Atlanta *Daily Constitution*, November 16, 1880.

Brown won 146 to 64—a majority of 82 votes.[55] With "a pang at heart" Georgia had said "nay" to the aristocrat and "yes" to the plebeian who pointed his finger to the future, observed a contemporary. "The people loved Lawton's purity and shining character. They trusted Brown's sagacity and his wonderful management. . . . It was the last close struggle for supremacy between the spirit that ruled the old South and the spirit of the new South. The old South was a South of tradition, of sentiment, chivalric memories, of heroic impulses. The new is a South of conservative tendencies, of practical ambition, of democratic ideas."[56] It was at least unusual for the one with the long white beard to point toward the future. But Joseph E. Brown never shared the romance and ideals of the Old South. B. W. Frobel reasoned well when he wrote Alexander Stephens: "The election of Gov. Brown is an evidence of what the people want, and it is just this—they want material prosperity and whatever makes that—The old man sitting by the river and 'cussin' will get no more sympathy here. That day is all past and I am glad of it."[57] "We wished it otherwise," commented the Athens *Banner*, yet the editor recognized the senator's "remarkable ability." "He has won a great deal for himself . . . and he will doubtless bring his acquisitiveness to bear in behalf of his section . . . he is the very prince of plausibility, and is as capable as any man living, of making his side appear to be right one."[58]

Gordon's resignation from the Senate and acceptance of a position with the Louisville and Nashville Railroad plus Brown's leaving full-time supervision of the Western and Atlantic to become a senator gave further strength to the rumor that persons and companies outside the state were taking over control of the state road. The General Assembly ordered another investigation to determine whether, contrary to the terms of the lease, a majority of the shares in the leasing company were now held by nonresidents or certain railroad combinations resulting in discrimination against roads "having business connections with or relations to said Western and Atlantic Railroad." Brown testified at length. He did not know the identity of all the shareholders for the transfers from time to time had totaled well over one hundred. Many shares had

---

55 *House Journal*, 1880, pp. 120–21; *Senate Journal*, 1880, p. 83.
56 Quoted in Avery, *History of Georgia*, 603.
57 December 4, 1880, in Stephens Papers, Library of Congress.
58 November 23, 1880.

been subdivided into fractional shares. When asked if a majority of the shareholders were now residents of Georgia, Brown replied "I know nothing to the contrary."

When questioned about the interests held by the Louisville and Nashville Railroad, Brown revealed some interesting facts. In a conference prior to Gordon's resignation, Victor Newcomb of the Louisville and Nashville had intimated that he and his friends controlled a majority of the shares in the Western and Atlantic, and they were interested in discrimination against the newly opened Cincinnati Southern by making it more expensive to ship from Cincinnati to Chattanooga to Atlanta than from Louisville to Chattanooga to Atlanta. This could be done only if the Western and Atlantic would make rate concessions to the Louisville and Nashville. Although Newcomb "did not use language to indicate any control over the matter," Brown related, "his manner and everything connected with it satisfied my mind that he felt that he was in some condition to dictate." Brown declined to be a party to any discrimination, and some nonresident shareholders prepared to seek a writ of mandamus to compel a meeting of the Board of Directors. This plan was dropped, however, after Brown made his trip from Washington to New York to attend a meeting of the Louisville and Nashville board, and made it quite clear that the original lessees only had a vote in company matters. Those who had purchased shares from the original lessees had acquired rights to profits only. E. W. Cole also testified before the legislative committee, but he and Brown either could not or would not say for certain whether the Louisville and Nashville owned shares in the Western and Atlantic. Cole did say that while he was in charge of the Nashville and Chattanooga, before the Louisville took control, his company purchased seven and one-half shares, all from nonresidents of Georgia. He, however, never attempted to vote those shares. Cole further revealed that before he was forced out of control of the Nashville and Chattanooga he had arranged for through traffic from St. Louis to Savannah, yet in doing so he had not received any special concessions from the Western and Atlantic. William M. Wadley, president of the Central Railroad, testified that he too had purchased eleven fractional shares in the Western and Atlantic hoping to gain control, only to find out that original lessees alone could vote.

The investigating committee also called Henry W. Grady and

asked him if he knew whether or not the Louisville and Nashville controlled the Western and Atlantic. He did not. When asked who did control the road, he replied: "My general impression from knowledge of the man's character is that Joe Brown is the boss."[59] Clearly the Louisville and Nashville did not have nor could it acquire direct control of the Western and Atlantic, yet there was no answer as to how much indirect control it might be able to exercise as original lessees sold their shares and lost interest.

59 *Report of Committee . . . to investigate the Lease of the Western and Atlantic Railroad.*

Chapter XXIII

End of the Line

BROWN WAS BACK in Washington for the opening of the final session of the Forty-sixth Congress on December 6, 1880. The Senate immediately became involved in debate on public education. Brown, knowing this subject was soon to be discussed in Washington, had definitely committed himself in his Atlanta opera house speech. The bill before the Senate proposed to set aside for public education the proceeds from the sale of public lands and the net receipts from the Patent Office. These funds were to be invested in United States bonds and the interest thereon apportioned among the states. During the first ten years the apportionment would be based on that portion of the population ten years of age or above who could not read and write. After that period apportionment was to be on the basis of the number of persons between five and twenty-five years of age.

Brown spoke on December 15. If republican form of government was to be perpetuated and society improved, he declared, illiteracy must be eliminated. Intellectual superiority was not limited to children of the wealthy or aristocratic; many children in humble homes had the ability. What they needed was the opportunity to develop that ability. Since society in general would profit by this development, it was the duty of government to provide educational opportunities for the masses. It was the educated who exerted influence. As settlement moved westward it was the New England educated who became leaders. Thus had New England influence been strongly felt throughout the nation.

On the international level, Brown used Prussia and France as examples. When Napoleon swept over central Europe, Prussia was a third-rate power. A half century later the situation had changed. Through compulsory public education, Prussia had developed her greatest talents. France, on the other hand, had failed to keep pace; only the favored few had been educated. Thus by the 1870s Prussia was able to sweep over France, dethrone Napoleon III, and dictate terms of peace on French soil. "Without the education of the mass of the people, of the whole people, you cannot have the benefit of the whole intellect of the country brought to bear in the building up of society and the development of the resources and power of the state."

With much regret, Brown admitted that the proportion of illiteracy was greatest in his home section. There were several reasons for this unfortunate condition. In the past the "ruling class" had been educated in private schools; the masses had no schools. Further, it had been thought "unsafe" to educate the slave population. This later proved to be a very hazardous practice when illiterate slaves became free men. This was not to say that the welfare of the blacks had been totally neglected during their bondage. Traders from Britain and New England had taken heathen blacks from their African state of "wildest ignorance and most savage barbarity," where tribal warfare often resulted in "indiscriminate slaughter," and brought them to America. This practice was sanctioned by the governing classes in both Britain and New England. These traders believed in the right to sell slaves and the South in the right to buy them; all considered the Negro unfit for any status other than slavery.

In early days, Brown continued, Georgia forbade slavery within her borders. It was not until great pressure was applied, even from the great Methodist leader George Whitefield, that slaves were admitted. Thus it happened that while Britain and New England were insisting upon slave trade Georgia was resisting it. Here Brown injected the old argument that the South had carried out Divine plans in civilizing and Christianizing the black man. But he then added that Providence had not decreed that the black man should forever remain a slave. Slavery had to be eradicated, and probably the only way to accomplish this was "to tear it out by the roots." This the late war had done. The process of eradication, however, had cost the South $2 billion in slave property plus a like sum in war costs and destruction. Further, 4 million illiterate blacks had been given legal and political rights and citizenship. If the South was to progress, these blacks must be educated through public schools. This the South alone could not finance. Brown wished to thank the senators from wealthier states, particularly New England, for their support of the bill under consideration. They exhibited a "sense of justice," for the bill provided that during the first ten years special advantage would be given to those states in which illiteracy was highest.

His hope for the future of the black race had increased greatly since the day of emancipation, Brown explained. Over the past fifteen years blacks had shown capacity for education and "a disposition to elevate themselves." He thought this largely a result of association with whites. He admitted that at times blacks had been cheated at the ballot box and elsewhere, but he would add that "Ignorance may be cheated anywhere." The best safeguard against future abuse of the blacks would be to "educate them; teach them to know their rights and, knowing them, they will maintain them."

In conclusion, Brown expressed appreciation for the Morrill Act of 1862, which granted to the states considerable portions of public lands for the establishment of agricultural and mechanical colleges. Georgia had sold her land script and applied a portion of the proceeds toward establishing the College of Agricultural and Mechanical Arts in connection with the University of Georgia. A similar college had also been established at Dahlonega in the building which formerly housed the United States Mint, and junior branches had been established at Cuthbert and Thomasville. Brown's only objection to the bill under consideration was that it would not supply sufficient funds to do the job required, but he trusted "this is the entering-wedge," opening the way for further action in the future.[1] The junior senator from Georgia would be disappointed by the failure of this bill, yet he had definitely taken a place among the foremost advocates of public education.

The Browns did not return to Atlanta for the Christmas holidays in 1880, although they longed to be present at the family dinner at Julius' house. Mrs. Brown sent fifty cents each for four servants. She knew this was not much, she wrote her son Joe, but it would buy some tobacco

1 *Cong. Record*, 46th Cong., 3rd Sess., Pt. 1, pp. 151 ff.

for the men and "some little notion or trifle for the women." Senator
Brown's health was no worse than while in Atlanta, and they had a
number of invitations to dinner. In preparation for social occasions,
Brown had had "a thick dress coat" made and hired a carriage. Only
the Feltons were unfriendly. They were "very hostile, say a great many
hard things; but we say nothing, they have the field to themselves."[2]

The Felton hostility had developed as a result of the congressional
campaign of 1880. Prior to that time, although Brown had opposed the
Independent movement in North Georgia led by Dr. Felton, the two had
not been on bad terms. Early in the year, before Brown's appointment
to the Senate, he and Congressman Felton had corresponded relative
to a proposal to build a railroad connecting the coal mines with the
Western and Atlantic, and Brown also gave Felton his views on the
subject of the tariff. Felton was so impressed that he requested permission to make use of these views in Washington. Even during the summer campaign, Brown corresponded with Mrs. Felton soliciting support
in getting the right men elected to the legislature.[3] But before the
close of the 1880 campaign, in which Felton was defeated by Judson
Clements, Brown was accused of meddling in Seventh District politics.
In her *Memoirs*, Mrs. Felton would record that her husband was
"hounded over fourteen counties . . . as a 'dishonest' politician, as 'allied
with Republicans,' etc., and the pack that pursued and the gang that
yelped from the Chattahoochee to the Tennessee line" all "bent the
knee in homage to ex-Governor Brown. . . . We never failed to find
that Governor Brown had either his hand over or under Dr. Felton's
political opponents." To Alexander Stephens, Mrs. Felton confided that
almost daily she acquired additional knowledge of Brown's "fiendish
hate and mockery . . . . I hope God will grant us the privilege of seeing
that arch traitor well unmasked before the country. . . . Let him go
until God settles with him."[4]

Back in session after the 1880 Christmas recess, the Senate took
up a bill to allot lands "in severalty" to certain reservation Indians and
to extend to them the rights of citizenship. Although Brown grew up

2 Mrs. Brown to Joe Mackey Brown, December 19, 1880, in Hargrett Collection.
3 See Felton Papers under dates February 21, 26, September 29, October 11,
1880.
4 January 1, 1882, in Stephens Papers, College of Sacred Heart.

in a region from which the Cherokee had recently been forcibly removed, he had never expressed publicly his views relative to the Indian
question. However, he immediately gave support to this Indian bill,
although it was his contention that Indians were already citizens under
the provisions of the Fourteenth Amendment. He expressed admiration
for Indians in general for their failure to exterminate the early white
settlers while they possessed the power. Instead, they had treated
settlers with tolerance and for the most part kindness, permitting them
to acquire lands. Then when the whites became numerous they began
to dictate to the Indians as the stronger to the weak. "The whole history
of our dealings with them has, I think, been a history of wrong, mostly
on our part," Brown charged. As settlers moved west they took from
the Indians such lands as they desired; they made treaties but never
observed them. Now fifty million whites had complete power over a
quarter million Indians.

Brown favored permitting Indians to take separate lands and
establish private homes; they should have the same rights as whites.
They should be encouraged to become tillers of the soil and be protected
in the improvements they made. In their present condition they had
little protection; they were being robbed and then prevented from re-
covering their property. When they made attempts at recovery, war
and bloodshed followed. The establishment of homesteads would
change this condition, contributing to the advancement of civilization
and perhaps Christianity. "Instead of roving bands without fixed habi-
tations, goaded to desperation by injustice and wrong, spreading death
and destruction in their pathway, we shall find them in the homes of
civilized man, not only Christian people, but many of them cultivated
and honorable citizens."

On the question of whether or not the Indians were or should be
citizens, Brown quoted the Fourteenth Amendment: "All persons born
or naturalized in the United States, and subject to the jurisdiction thereof, are citizens of the United States, and of State wherein they reside.
No state shall make or enforce any law which shall abridge the privileges or immunities of citizens of the United States; nor shall any State
deprive any person of life, liberty, or property without due process of
law, nor deny any person within its jurisdiction equal protection of the

law." The first step in determining citizenship, Brown explained, was to determine if an Indian was a person. In view of the feats of King Phillip, Tecumseh, and Sequoyah, it was "absurd to deny that the Indian is a person." If they were persons, then were they born within the United States. To deny this would also be absurd. The government had decreed long ago that Indians were subject to laws made by the white man; therefore, there could be no question of their being subject to the jurisdiction of the United States. These facts being established, Indians could not be deprived of life, liberty, or property without due process of law. Neither could they be denied equal protection of the law.

There was another provision in the Constitution which referred to the Indian directly, Brown explained. In determining population for the purpose of apportioning representation, all persons were to be counted "excluding Indians not taxed." But Brown contended that Indians *were* taxed. Only authorized government agents could trade with them; therefore, Indians must buy and sell at prices determined by the agents. Many items sold to Indians were imported and subject to the tariff, the amount of the tariff being added to the price. Was this not a tax? Further, Brown wished to inquire, why give the rights of citizenship "to every person of every race and every color on the face of the earth who will come here and comply with our laws and not give it to the original inhabitants of our own country?"

The white man, being the stronger, might treat the Indian as he pleased, Brown observed. "But there is a Being stronger and much more powerful than we are." A nation, as well as an individual, must eventually answer for wrongdoing. He would not venture to predict the punishment awaiting the United States for the massacre of the Poncas or Cheyenne, yet he would say that "Our course is condemned by the civilization of the age. It is condemned by humanity, and it is condemned by Christian men and women everywhere who understand the facts." The Indians had, of course, engaged in some cruel wars, but these wars had usually been "provoked by bad white men or by agents of the government." Like the rattlesnake, the Indian was generally peaceful until trampled upon. Give the Indians the same opportunity as the whites and they could be civilized like the whites.[5] Congress was

5 *Cong. Record*, 46th Cong., 3rd Sess., Pt. 1, pp. 878 ff.

not yet ready to pass reasonable and needed legislation on the Indian question. Not until the Dawes Act of 1887, would provisions be made to divide tribal lands among individual Indians.

As was often the case, the short session of Congress did little while awaiting the inauguration of a new president. James A. Garfield took office on March 4, 1881, and immediately called the Senate into special session, which would continue until May 20. This would be a stormy session. Not including David Davis of Illinois, who had been elected by Independents and Democrats, and William Mahone of Virginia, who had been elected as a "Readjuster,"[6] the Senate was equally divided between Democrats and Republicans. Davis soon let it be known he would vote Democratic; Mahone delayed public commitment. Filibustering Republicans delayed selection of Senate officers until Mahone could be induced to join them. Rumor soon spread that Mahone was about to sell out to the Republicans. On March 14, Ben Hill addressed the Senate for the purpose of "smoking out" Mahone. He thought the Senate should proceed with the election of officers since with Davis' vote they had a majority, for no Democrat ever proved "faithless to his trust!" Of course this would be true only if the Republicans were unable to purchase some Democrat.[7]

In reply to these and other remarks, Mahone insisted that he had not been elected as a Democrat. He then referred to alleged inconsistencies of some Democrats, especially Brown. This gave Brown the opportunity he enjoyed most; he liked tracing his stormy career and pointing out how he emerged a winner. He launched a long discussion of his prewar, war, and reconstruction records, admitting many inconsistencies as if proud of them. Mahone had accused him of seizing private property in the "arms case." This he denied and then gave a review of the whole affair, which he was able to insert into the *Record*.[8] Mahone had also charged that Governor Brown withdrew Georgia troops from "the starry cross" just when the Confederacy needed them most. Instead of withdrawing troops, Brown replied, he had joined them in the field. He then retold the story of his relations with Presi-

6 This title referred to the position he took on paying Virginia's bonded indebtedness.
7 *Cong. Record*, 47th Cong., Special Sess., 21 ff.
8 *Ibid.*, 106 ff.

dent Davis, and again insisted that he offered no barrier to Confederate success.

Brown admitted that after the war he had acted with the Republicans for a time and sought to justify his having done so. But by 1872, he had rejoined the Democrats, or rather they had rejoined him, and since that date he had given the party his loyal support. Mahone had further accused him of accepting appointment as chief justice by a carpetbag governor. Brown denied that Bullock was a carpetbagger. He admitted resigning his judgeship to become president of a railroad company, which he made to pay its stockholders very well. Here, he explained, his career differed from that of the gentleman from Virginia; Mahone too had been president of a railroad, but his went into bankruptcy.

Brown further admitted that there was a charge of "bargain" when Governor Colquitt appointed him to the Senate, yet he thought the people, by reelecting the governor and choosing a legislature that would overwhelmingly return him to the Senate, had proved their disbelief in the bargain charge. But he had heard rumors that the gentleman from Virgina was himself connected with a "bargain." He did not wish to make such a charge himself, but wished only to say that the air was full of rumors. It was indeed strange that Republicans would filibuster against the selection of officers until a certain Democrat came over to their side. It was a "peculiar coincidence" that a man who had long been a Democrat should decide to become a Republican only after two of his friends were assured election as secretary and sergeant-at-arms. But still he did not wish to charge "bargain"; it was just a coincidence—"just one of those things that happen sometimes in life!"[9] A special session of the Senate, called to approve federal appointments, had been held inactive for weeks over the election of officers.

More weeks passed, and the Senate was still discussing resolutions relating to election of its officers. Little was said on the subject, but talking members availed themselves of the opportunity to hurl charges both personal and sectional. On April 14, Brown took the floor to defend himself and the South against what he considered slurs and falsehoods emanating from New England. The reconstruction measures, he asserted, had disenfranchised and driven from the ballot box "probably

9 *Ibid.*

two hundred thousand of the most intelligent, cultivated, and educated people of the South. . . . I fell in that class, and I stood by and saw my negroes, or those that had been mine," vote in the election of delegates to a convention under which the disfranchised must live. He did not charge that the count was not fair, but the ballot was certainly not free. Subsequently, amendments to the United States Constitution were proposed to guarantee the vote to the Negro. He thought the measures harsh yet advised acquiescence rather than make an issue. By making an issue the carpetbaggers were given an opportunity to influence the blacks.

But things had now changed in Georgia. The Democrats were now in control and standing firmly for "a free ballot and a fair count." Yet Senator Joseph R. Hawley of Connecticut had recently stated that the Solid South had declared the Fifteenth Amendment a failure and non-enforceable in letter and spirit. This Brown denied; nowhere in the world was there "a freer ballot" than in the South. Hawley had also said that every man must henceforth accept the fact that "universal suffrage" was now the law of the world and "the irreversible law of this Republic." This Brown also denied. The South did grant suffrage to all males over twenty-one years of age, yet neither Massachusetts, Connecticut, nor Rhode Island did. He would admit that these states had a right to set qualifications for voting; so did others. He greatly admired New England education and enterprise, Brown explained. "I admit that you are a great people, and that you are a powerful people; but while that is true, and you have ample time to attend to your own business and do it well, I think you appropriate too much of your time in attending to other peoples business." If New England would just be content to let other people exercise the same powers they themselves claim, "probably we should all get along better."

Brown then quoted from the Massachusetts Constitution the passages which required voters to be able to write and to read their constitution. He further cited other provisions and laws which denied the suffrage of six different categories of citizens. He would not say that these six categories should not be disfranchised; he would point out, however, that if Massachusetts laws were applied in Georgia, they would disfranchise eight-tenths of the blacks. If Georgia Negroes over twenty-one migrated to Massachusetts, which they had a legal right to do, would that state permit them to vote? Addressing the Chair, Brown declared: "Mr. President. All this ado about suffrage has but one object: it is to try to republicanize the South by the use of the negro."

Brown next proposed to examine the Negro question. The late war was not begun to free the Negro, he asserted. According to Union aims stated at that time, the war was for the preservation of the Union. Shortly after Bull Run, Congress stated that the war was not to make conquests nor to interfere with southern institutions. A declaration of this nature was necessary to hold the border states in the Union. And Lincoln's Emancipation Proclamation was purely a war measure, not a Negro measure. Even as late as the Hampton Roads conference, Lincoln himself had expressed doubt that his proclamation had set free any Negroes other than those within Union lines. He even went so far as to suggest that slaveholders might be compensated for the loss of their slaves. "Providence set the colored man free and not the Government of the United States," Brown asserted. "You did not expect it, and we did not expect it when we entered the contest; but God in his mercy and in his benign providence interfered and struck the shackles from the hands of the race and made them free, and I am glad to-day that it is so; I was not then." In short, God freed the slaves, yet the Republicans had claimed the credit and so informed the Negro.

Senators George F. Hoar and Henry L. Dawes of Massachusetts attempted to interrupt; Brown would not tolerate it. He was driving toward his main point and would not be sidetracked. After the war, what did the conquerors do? asked Brown. Laws such as those in force in Massachusetts were not applied in Georgia. Instead, southern intelligence was disfranchised "and you turned all the negro males of twenty-one years upward loose to the polls." He would not say that Massachusetts laws were unwise, but he would say that if they were wise in Massachusetts they would also have been wise in Georgia. He admitted that there had been outrages in Georgia during the reconstruction period; the wonder was that there were not more when a proud people, brought to ruin and bowed in grief, were driven from the polls and their places taken by ignorant former slaves.

Since a free ballot had been established in the South, Brown inquired what had the Republican party done for the Negro. He estimated that on the national level black votes constituted about one-fourth of the Republican party. How many public offices did they hold? Neither had the Republicans done well by their white members in the South. He had checked the *Official Register* and found almost unbelievable statistics. Discrimination was great in all departments, but that in the Treasury Department was probably the worst. Of 10,099 appointees only 157 were from Georgia and 81 of that number were *not* Georgia born.

Dawes interrupted to say that Senator Ben Hill had said there were not any Republicans in Georgia; so why reward something that did not exist. Brown replied that if there were no Republicans in Georgia, it was because they had been driven out of the party by injustices. He would suggest that in the civil service reforms being discussed that competitive examinations be provided so a Democrat might be "let in once in a while." He doubted that in coming elections Negroes would be found solidly within Republican ranks. He would welcome the day when there would be no color line in politics, but he would add that as long as "the moral, intelligent, upright property-holders" were suppressed and "the more idle, the more illiterate, and the more vicious" placed on top, there would be a Solid South. But this Solid South was a new South of limitless opportunities for investment and great capacity for production. "We invite you to our houses, to our parties, to our bosom."[10]

Argument was plentiful but the special session accomplished little. By the time Congress assembled in regular session on December 4, 1881, President Garfield had been assassinated, and Chester A. Arthur had succeeded to the presidency. The more important measures to be written into law during the Arthur administration would be the Pendleton Civil Service Act and the Chinese Exclusion Act. The report that Garfield had been continuously harassed by officeseekers and finally assassinated by one who had been disappointed brought to the attention of Congress the need for reform of the civil service and the introduction of the Pendleton bill. Brown was no advocate of civil service reform, especially when the Republicans held all the offices. In the case of the state-owned Western and Atlantic he had not sanctioned taking control out of the hands of the governor until pressured by evidence of mismanagement by Bullock and Blodgett and lured by the possibility of

10 *Ibid.*, 298 ff.

gaining control himself. On the national level he suspected Republican aims to entrench themselves in the better positions, leaving the crumbs for the Democrats. The Pendleton bill, according to its advocates, was designed "to regulate and improve" the civil service. Brown admitted there was need for improvement, yet he doubted that this bill would meet that need. He feared that it would merely "excite popular expectations" that would not be realized. He had heard it argued that our system should be modeled after the British system, for it was the best in the world. He would like to stress, however, that the part played by heredity in the British system made the two systems quite different. In the American system, heredity played no part, and in theory the highest positions were open to men of even the lowest origin, and both appointment and promotion were reward for "merit and qualifications." Still this system left changes in officeholding "to the frequent mutations of parties."

Brown questioned the statement that permanence in office would remove the officeholder from active politics. He thought the reverse might well be true. With no fear of dismissal as a result of political activities, officeholders would prove to be even more active in behalf of their favorite candidates. Brown even professed to see a permanent civil service as a threat to the American system of government. Citing the case of the Roman Praetorian guard as an example, he expressed fear that those who were charged with guarding our government might become its master. By creating lifetime civil tenure, we might create a lifetime aristocracy that would imitate the Praetorian guard.

Brown noted Pendleton's[11] statement that the bill did not contain a clause preventing removal from office. He agreed that there was no specific prohibition, yet Senator Hoar[12] had stated this was the spirit of the proposal and that it was unlikely a president "would venture to make removals" except for misconduct. Here Senator Hawley[13] interrupted to say that those who favored the bill *did* maintain that the president still would have the power of removal. He could not see how a Praetorian guard could "hurt" the president "if he can still take the Praetorian guard by the ear and lead them out any morning he pleases."

11 George H. Pendleton of Ohio, sponsor of the bill.
12 George F. Hoar of Massachusetts.
13 John R. Hawley of Connecticut.

If that be true, retorted Brown, of what value would the bill be. If the people were clamoring for civil service reform why give them this fraud. He thought the number of citizens demanding reform was small, but even they would consider this bill "a trick, a sham, a delusion."

Brown further noted that the bill applied to lower-level offices only. True, there were to be competitive examinations, but they would not apply to those incompetents already in office. The Democrats, now out of office, would have a chance for appointment as a result of competitive examination but to minor positions only. He wished to "talk plainly to Democrats," Brown announced, for there was no need to mince words. For the past twenty-two years the Republicans had controlled public offices. The avalanche of protest now sweeping the country was against Republican mismanagement. The time for change was near and the Democrats would win the next presidential election if they made "no great blunders," were "guilty of no great folly." It would be a blunder for Democrats to aid in passing the Pendleton bill and thus go before the public with no promise of reward for state and local party workers. Even if Pendleton himself should be the party nominee, what inducement would there be for party members to exert themselves when all of the more important offices would remain under control of the Republicans?

A civil service law had been passed during the Grant administration, and even Brown's good friend Judge Dawson A. Walker had been named one of the commission to implement it, yet it proved to be a farce. Congress soon refused to appropriate money for the salaries of the commissioners. William L. Marcy's famous statement that "to the victor belong the spoils" sounded rather coarse, yet the spoils had gone to the victor. And under the proposed bill the president would still find a way to reward his friends. Senator George[14] interrupted to say that he could see no reason for Brown's objections if even a Democratic president could find a way. That was just why this bill was a fraud and a humbug, Brown replied.

By this point, Brown's apparent contradictions had made his argument unimpressive. The truth was that he himself had always been a true spoilsman. While governor he was unyielding in his demand for loyalty regardless of an officeholder's efficiency. After returning to the

14 James Z. George of Mississippi.

Democratic party he continuously denounced Republicans for their complete control of public offices. Now that he saw a chance of Democratic victory, he meant for Democrats to enjoy the spoils. He did not believe there was any great demand for the type of reform being proposed, but he did recognize loud protest against Republican solicitation of campaign contributions from officeholders. He urged legislation that would make this "infamous practice a high misdemeanor, if not a felony." He thought the public further demanded that "unfaithful public servants be hurled from power" and "their places be filled with honest, capable men," who would eliminate unnecessary jobs and put an end to extravagance and waste. Brown did not specifically state whether or not there should be removals from office for political reasons, but he did assert that there could be no real civil service reform until heads of the departments turned out those "shrewd, sharp managing fellows" who had controlled public offices for the past twenty years. "You will never purify the service until you drive these old rats from the malt."[15] Brown argued in vain; the Pendleton bill became law.[16]

Coming from Georgia where there were no serious problems involving foreign immigrants, Brown met with a new experience when a Chinese immigration bill came before the Senate early in 1882. But being a stickler for points of law, he was soon in the field and fighting. So great was the need for laborers to work the gold mines and build railroads during the years immediately following the war, the United States wrote the Burlingame Treaty with China in 1868, granting to Chinese laborers the privilege of coming and going as they pleased and most favored nation treatment. But serious racial problems developed as floods of immigrants arrived and need for construction workers greatly decreased. West coast states, particularly California, began demanding restriction on immigration of laborers even to the point of exclusion. A new treaty was made with China in 1880 under which the United States might "regulate, limit, or suspend, but not absolutely prohibit" the immigration of Chinese laborers.

The bill under discussion in the Senate did not apply to laborers,

15 *Cong. Record*, 47th Cong., 2nd Sess., Pt. 1, pp. 1276 ff.
16 It created a civil service commission and charged it with administration of competitive examinations for such positions that the president and Congress might place on the classified list. Before the close of his term President Arthur had placed some 16,000 public employees on permanent tenure.

for they were already excluded, but it required others to secure Chinese passports and have them viséed by the American consul before leaving for America. Before landing, their papers must be approved by port authorities. Then they must register with the Treasury Department, giving their complete personal and family history. Brown opposed this bill as being in violation of the Chinese treaty, and that at a time when we could ill afford to irritate or offend the Chinese. They had only recently begun truly to open their country to American trade and missionary activities, both of which Brown stressed as of tremendous importance. Brown belonged to the Missionary Baptist Church and also to that New South group which looked toward great developments in production and manufacturing. He could see no need to offend 400 million potential users of southern cotton cloth.

Brown saw in the new proposal an attempt to discourage all Chinese from coming to America. Even those who did come would be subject to fine and imprisonment if caught without their papers. Yet in the treaty of 1880 Chinese were guaranteed most favored nation treatment. Senators James T. Farley and John F. Miller of California frequently interrupted to insist that Brown was misinterpreting the bill. The purpose was not to place limitations upon other classes but to distinguish them from laborers. Was such distinction required of the nationals of any other country? Brown inquired. "No," Farley replied, but the United States had no such treaty limiting immigrants from other countries. Quite true, Brown agreed, and we were threatening to violate this treaty with China. How else could it be determined who was or was not a laborer? Miller asked. Unless some such method was used, interrupted Farley, "You might as well undertake to discriminate between the flies on a bee-gum on a summer day."

The truth was, Brown asserted, that in making the treaty the Chinese diplomats had been too shrewd for the Americans. We had just as well face the fact, and if we could not abide by the treaty, we should seek to get it changed. It must be changed, not violated. If we placed great obstacles in the way of Chinese entering this country, might they not retaliate against our merchants and missionaries? As for the work of missionaries, Brown wished to encourage it. He thought, however, that it had already been demonstrated that heathen people were more easily Christianized within our own borders than in their native land. Missionaries had not been very successful among the blacks in Africa, yet observe what they had been able to do among the blacks in America. He did not profess to know the Divine plan; still he thought it quite possible that blacks and Chinese might be guided to our shores so that they might become Christians.

Brown would not accept the prediction that Chinese in America might sometime become sufficiently numerous to overrun the country. Within the past thirty years only 150,000 had arrived; during the past year not more than 20,000. This was but a small fraction of the total of three-quarters million immigrants who arrived during that year. "The Chinese empire is in a great deal more danger to-day of being overrun and subverted by Yankee energy and Yankee enterprise on the one side, and the Empire of Russia on the other, and England on the ocean, than this country is of being overrun by Chinamen." He saw in China a vast field opening to commerce, manufacturers, railroads, steamships, and all the inventions of the age. "It is a wide open field for us."

In conclusion, Brown touched upon the claim that Chinese laborers in competition with Americans were lowering the standard of living. This he definitely did not wish to happen, for he had always had the welfare of the laboring class at heart. But he was not so sure about the validity of this claim. Senator Hoar had recently submitted figures to show that California, where a majority of the Chinese laborers lived, paid better wages to those persons willing to work than any other state in the Union. Brown said he had also heard the suggestion that the Chinese did not intend to make America their permanent home. They merely intended to accumulate money and then return to China. Brown thought this theory scarcely in line with the one that had them eventually overrunning the country. But even if they did return to China after they had worked here for half what Americans would, doing work we could not get Americans to do, they would leave behind two dollars for each one they carried away.[17] Again Senator Brown had argued in vain; the Chinese exclusion bill became law.

Brown's opposition to discrimination against those unable to protect their own interests was also reflected in the Senate debate on bigamy and the privilege of voting. Before the Senate in February, 1882, was

17 *Cong. Record*, 47th Cong., 1st Sess., Pt. 1, pp. 1639 ff.

a proposed statutory amendment which would deny to bigamist or polygamist the privilege of voting in the Territory of Utah. Brown saw in this measure an attempt at rigorous suppression of Mormonism. He began his remarks with a definite statement of opposition to polygamy in any form "as one of the greatest social evils." Yet he recognized that it was sanctioned, even if not practiced, by three-fourths of the world's population. Britain had found it sanctioned in India and had not dared to make a strong effort to eliminate it. All the religions there approved of it. And when Christianity moved in, it too permitted converts to keep all of their wives. It was tolerated in the Old Testament and some believed it not forbidden in the New Testament, except in the case of certain churchmen. With this last interpretation, Brown said he did not agree. Yet he would not deny to others the right to think as they pleased.

This privilege he would also extend to the Mormons. They believed that Joseph Smith received a Divine revelation that superseded a portion of the Bible. This revelation sanctioned polygamy. Brown did not believe the Morman doctrine, but recognized Mormans as just as "earnest and honest" in their belief as the Baptists, Methodists, or Presbyterians. George F. Edmunds of Vermont interrupted to say that the bill would not disfranchise persons because of their beliefs. Brown disagreed and read from the bill: "That no polygamist, bigamist, or any persons cohabitating with more than one woman" should be eligible to vote or to hold office. He then read from *Webster's Unabridged Dictionary* the definition of a polygamist—"a person who practices polygamy or maintains its lawfulness." Brown declared that there was scarcely a person in the Territory of Utah who did not maintain the lawfulness of polygamy, although only a few practiced it. Edmunds again interrupted to submit figures that about 7,000 in Utah did not so believe. Brown was not convinced; even if there were 7,000, that was a very small percentage of the population. He knew that the Mormons dominated Utah, and polygamy was sanctioned by their religion. He then added that "In my opinion the people of Utah have at least one good quality and that is that an overwhelming majority of them are Democrats." But the purpose of this bill was a sweeping disfranchisement of the Mormons, Brown charged, and eventually the making of a Republican state out of a Democratic territory. And the agency for implementing this disfranchisement was to be a returning board. He had already witnessed "a returning-board" cheat the people "out of a election for President. . . . It stinks in the nostrils of honest men."[18]

Edmunds interrupted to read from a legal dictionary definitions of bigamist and polygamist which classified persons as to what they *did*, not what they *sanctioned*. Brown was not convinced; he preferred Webster's definition, and he feared that the returning board would also prefer Webster, thus disfranchising all Mormons. He further charged that the proposed measure was a violation of religious freedom. If Mormons could be punished for their belief in polygamy why could not Catholics be punished for their belief in transubstantiation and Baptist for close communion? Brown stressed that he believed polygamy to be immoral and he favored laws to punish immorality, but they must not be retroactive. One should not be punished for what he did before the law was passed, and he was unwilling to put such a power in the hands of a returning board dominated by Republicans, who were not interested in religion but in using religious beliefs to accomplish their political ends. Brown then offered an amendment that would specifically prevent disfranchisement because of one's belief.[19]

Perennial topics of discussion during the 1880s were the silver question and the tariff. Brown had pronounced views on both. Under acts of 1834 and 1837 the United States had adopted a double monetary standard. Those who held either gold or silver could have it minted at a fixed ratio. But by the mid-1850s the price of silver had changed to the extent that the amount of silver in a dollar was worth more than a dollar. Minting ceased and silver passed out of commercial use. After the war, with the opening of great silver deposits in the western states, silver owners and cheaper money advocates demanded a return to silver. But they found there was no longer such a thing as a legal silver dollar. A monetary act of 1873 had quietly and unnoticed "demonetized" silver by omitting the silver dollar from the list of coins. Pressure largely from the South and West resulted in the restoration of the silver dollar and the passage of the Bland-Allison Act of 1878, which obligated the government to purchase $2 million to $4 million

18 Brown proposed and secured approval of an amendment that would guarantee the Democrats two of the five seats on the board.
19 *Cong. Record*, 47th Cong., 1st Sess., Pt. 2, pp. 1202 ff.

worth of silver monthly. Silver certificates based upon this purchase were to be placed in circulation. But still the price of silver declined. Neither side to the controversy was satisfied. One side demanded contraction of silver and silver certificates; the other demanded unlimited coinage of silver. This was the situation when Brown entered the Senate.

On January 18, 1882, Brown introduced resolutions stating that it would be "inexpedient and unwise to contract the currency by the withdrawal from circulation what are known as silver certificates, or to discontinue or further restrict the coinage of silver. That gold and silver coins, based upon a proper ratio of equivalence between the two metals, and issues of paper, predicated upon and convertible into coin on demand, constitute the proper circulating medium of this country."

In speaking to his resolutions, Brown began with an elementary discussion of the interdependence of civilized man upon the production and services of one another and the need for a medium of exchange acceptable to all. Thousands of years earlier gold and silver had become acceptable, and the value of these metals depended to a considerable extent upon their use as coins. But in recent years Great Britain and Germany had demonetized silver and a few smaller Europeans nations had followed. Even though the United States had remonetized silver, its coinage was limited, and the price of silver continued to decline.

This decline, Brown contended, was not due to overproduction but to underuse. If there were unlimited coinage of silver into legal tender, "*with full debt-paying and purchasing capacity*," there would be "no more destruction of the equilibrium as heretofore established between gold and silver." Brown noted that with the remonetization of silver there had been gloomy predictions that commercial nations would ship large quantities of silver to the United States and carry away our gold. In other words, foreign nations would use their silver to purchase our gold, leaving us with a local silver circulation, and placing within the hands of Britain and Germany sufficient gold to force other nations to follow them in establishing monometalism. Brown thought the secretary of the Treasury had attempted to add to the gloom when he stated in his last report that to continue with the present rate of silver coinage would reduce the United States to the status of a minor nation—that we could not maintain position by selling on a silver standard and buying on a gold standard. The secretary also recommended the repeal of required coinage and the coinage of just so much as was necessary.

Brown disagreed with the gloomy predictions and the secretary's proposal. With the two Americas, most of Europe, and the Far East using both metals, why could they not hold silver in the position it had occupied for centuries. Since the United States and Mexico produced three-fourths of the world's silver and one-half its gold, why should they give up either metal and pass advantage to other countries? Further, the claim that other countries would flood the United States with silver and drain off our gold just was not sound. Brown then cited Treasury figures to show that during the previous fiscal year the United States had imported ten times as much gold as silver and exported seven times as much silver as gold. If these proportions should continue a few more years, Brown predicted that instead of being flooded with silver the United States would have "an almost exclusive gold currency." The secretary's theory might look well on paper, but "One practical fact is worth half a dozen theories that will not work in practice."

Brown next turned to the effects of the silver question upon the creditors of the United States. He explained that the United States had guaranteed the payment of bonds plus the interest thereon in gold or silver. This was even true of those sold during the war for depreciated paper. When silver was demonetized in 1873 it was no longer legal tender for debts above five dollars. This made gold alone legal for retiring bonds. Then when silver was remonetized in 1878 the secretary of the Treasury ruled that bond holders still had a right to demand gold. This Brown denied. The bondholder was due what was promised. To give him more was a "flagrant injustice" to the taxpayer.

The president had recently recommended not only further restriction of silver but also that the $66 million in silver certificates now in circulation be replaced with bank notes. Brown objected. Certificates backed by silver in the Treasury were much more convenient to handle in course of trade. If lost, the Treasury was the gainer. Bank notes were also backed by the government, but if lost or destroyed the bank was the winner, not the Treasury and the people. Further, the banks would issue just so many notes as they pleased. To adopt the president's proposal, Brown concluded, would be but to exchange a good currency for a worse one.[20] Brown's resolutions merely produced debate and tested sentiment; the next important silver legislation would be the Sherman Act of 1890.

The tariff was another subject of almost constant discussion during the 1880s. The Republican platform of 1880 had promised some tariff revision, but it had not promised substantial damage to protection. This was a subject on which Brown had said very little before going to Washington. His most complete statement was in a letter to Congressman Felton on February 21, 1880: "In reference to the tariff on ores, I would state that the common grades of ore are abundant in this country; & we probably need but little protection upon them. The quality of ore, however, out of which steel is made, is not so abundant; & it might be proper that there be some protection on that." He further stated that, since Felton represented a district where there was considerable mineral wealth, "you owe it to your constituents to see that there is no unjust legislation unfriendly to this interest."[21] Brown's mines were in Felton's district.

There were some who professed to believe it possible to propose such a tariff as would take the tariff out of politics. Accordingly, in the spring of 1882, a bill was introduced in Congress to authorize the president to appoint a commission to study tariff needs and report to Congress. Brown had no objection to the appointment of such a commission but, although complaining of a serious throat difficulty, he used the occasion to express his views on both the tariff and internal revenue. He thought the discussion on free trade or protection "more a war of words than ideas." He stated that he was neither for free trade nor for a tariff for revenue only. The import duties collected during the past year amounted to about $200 million. If these duties were abolished, how else could that amount of money be raised? There seemed to be no reasonable plan under which expenses could be substantially reduced; therefore, the amount would have to be raised from internal taxes. If this amount were apportioned among the states, Georgia would be required to pay about $5 million. This would increase Georgia's tax burden by fourfold. When this became known to taxpayers, Brown

20 *Ibid.*, 472 ff.
21 Felton Papers.

predicted it "would knock all the poetry out of the able free-trade speeches."

There was already a federal tax on a few items such as tobacco and whiskey. These taxes Brown opposed. He condemned "the present internal-revenue system as an excrescence upon the body-politic. . . . I wish to see the present internal-revenue system gotten rid of, so we may return to the old rule of the fathers," collecting from a tariff all funds needed to run the government. This was the policy advocated by the great statesmen of the days of Washington, Jefferson, and Jackson. "The sooner we return to the old beaten track trod by them the better."

He occupied a middle position, Brown explained. He favored neither free trade nor a tariff simply for protection, if the government did not need the money. His idea was to revise the tariff so as to supply all money needed and as far as possible provide "incidental protection to home industries and to American productions." He thought the South at present more in need of incidental protection than northern manufacturers. "We are now in our infancy; they have reached nearly to mature manhood. . . . They have skilled labor and the most improved machines; we have little skilled labor and much of our machinery is not of the best." Brown noted that some free-trade senators had pointed out to farmers how much they would save if there were no tariff on what they had to purchase. Yet they did not point out how much in additional direct taxes farmers would be required to pay if the tariff was removed. As a rule, farmers bought sparingly of dutiable items; therefore, they paid little of the $200 million collected from imports.

If a tariff for revenue only was the desire, Brown explained, then duties should be placed where they would yield the greatest income. Coffee and tea were not on the dutiable list, yet during 1881, $56 million in coffee and $21 million in tea had been imported. These items needed no protection, but a duty on them would bring in large sums of money. Money could also be had by a tariff on products made from cotton and flax and incidental protection given at the same time. The chief difference between these two cases was that the former would be more expensive to the poor taxpayer. If they could just rid themselves entirely of the Internal Revenue Bureau, Brown would favor expanding the tariff to other items. As now situated, the bureau was "an immense empire of political power" in the hands of the dominant party. He wished to see only one corps of tax collectors and that located in the port cities. He did not wish at present to recommend the raising, lowering, or expanding of duties; neither was he saying that the existing tariff was just. He favored appointment of the proposed commission to make a thorough study. Although he did not know what position the Democrats would take in the next election, Brown concluded, he would say that there were districts in the South that could not be carried on a plank for "revenue only."[22]

The commission, stacked with protectionists, made its study and reported, but the bill that would become the tariff act of 1883 was framed by a conference committee of the two houses of Congress. This committee was also dominated by protectionists. Brown again had his say, and he was clearly more interested in abolishing internal taxes than in the tariff per se. As to the internal revenue, he exclaimed, "I would abolish it absolutely. I would do away with this army of collectors and these illegal raiders. I would destroy the power and monopoly of the great whiskey ring, and I would collect the revenue at the ports of this country, as our fathers collected it, and as it was always done except when the exigencies of war required extreme measures." Brown was particularly irritated by stories of revenue agents chasing over the upland regions of the South, seizing stills and all property nearby, and even murdering innocent citizens. The actions of these revenue agents, Brown exclaimed, was in violation of both the English common law, upon which our legal system was based, and the constitutional protection of life, liberty, and property. (This was language North Georgia wildcatters could understand.)

Of the estimated $400 million that would be needed to meet appropriations for the coming year Brown proposed to raise at least $250 million by a tariff. He again expressed opposition to a tariff for protection only; he favored incidental protection while raising needed revenue. The only item for which he expressed a special interest was iron ore. Admitting that he had a personal interest in ore, he still insisted that the tariff must be sufficient to protect the livelihood of the thousands of miners as well as to assure reasonable profits to owners.[23]

22 *Cong. Record*, 47th Cong., 1st Sess., Pt. 3, pp. 2286 ff.
23 *Ibid.*, 1486 ff.

(He made no mention of the fact that his mines were worked by convicts.) As passed, the tariff bill of 1883 did increase the duty on iron ore. There were some reductions on other items, but no serious damage was done to the principle of protection.

Brown's Senate term would end with the close of the Arthur administration. He had not been a great influence in Washington, yet he had been heard on the more important topics of national interest, and what he said was generally acceptable to the people of Georgia. He would get some hostile feedback on the tariff, but even those who were not connected with wildcatting liked his position on internal taxes.[24] The Browns were not extensive participants in the Washington social whirl, although on one occasion Brown did write his daughter Mary that her mother was "primping up today to take dinner with the President at the Executive Mansion," where a state dinner was to be held that evening.[25] The Browns were a home-loving family, and they often expressed a desire to get back to Atlanta. Although frequently referring to his long hours of labor, Brown never expressed any pleasure from his work. He was constantly ill. His throat showed some improvement, but he developed a "nervous trouble" in his left leg. His doctor first thought it a form of paralysis but later pronounced it sciatica. Months later, there was still no improvement, and he was requesting his son-in-law, Dr. E. L. Connally, to send some strychnine pills. He was feeling the effects of forty years of labor, he explained, much of it "hard mental labor without very much physical exercise." Yet, in spite of all the years of labor and "serious difficulties," he had no "right to complain." He was thankful for his success and the service he had been able to render his generation. He was now content "to abide by the will of God whatever it may be, and try to be ready for the summons when it comes."[26]

The loss of associates and friends also cast its gloom over Senator Brown. His colleague Ben Hill went home to die with cancer of the tongue in the summer of 1882. Ironically, Brown had often accused him of having diarrhea of the tongue. Former Governor Alfred H. Colquitt was elected to complete Hill's unexpired term. Alexander H.

24 H. H. Carlton (Athens) to Brown, May 8, 1884, in Hargrett Collection.
25 March 12, 1884, in Spalding Collection.
26 Brown to Mary Brown Connally, December 27, 1882, April 1, 1884; Brown to E. L. Connally, April 15, 1884, in Spalding Collection.

Stephens had left Washington to become governor of Georgia in November, 1882, only to die in office the following March. His candidacy for governor was a bit pathetic. Many thought him senile and often under the influence of medication. It is not known whether Brown wished his physically unfit friend to make the race, but he gave him strong support. After toying with Dr. Felton's Independents and later denying that he had made them any promise, Stephens accepted a Democratic nomination. Lucius Gartrell, who for thirty years had wanted to be governor, was his Independent-Republican opponent.[27] Stephens won an easy victory, but there was much bitterness. The Feltons, who had been his close friends for several years, turned on him viciously and scratched him from their list forever. Mrs. Felton, no doubt referring to Brown, declared, "The same crowd that runs the Convict Ring in Georgia, got around Mr. Stephens to induce and flatter him into their control that they might profit . . . on convict labor."[28] Old wartime hostility was also in evidence. "Mr. Stephens imagines, or was led to imagine, that the people were crazy to make him Governor, without distinction of age sex or previous condition," confided William M. Browne to Jefferson Davis. "This is a very great mistake. The old soldiers have not forgot 1861–65." Joe Brown was supporting Stephens, yet Browne thought the people were "impatient of Joe Brown's role of Warwick in Ga. But he has millions of money, controls the W & Atlantic R. R., is in the Senate, commands patronage and appropriations, and is not as much controlled by scruples as may be thought desirable."[29]

During Brown's first year in the Senate, his son Charles McDonald died at the age of twenty-two. As a memorial to his son and to facilitate the education of deserving Georgia boys, he decided to establish the Charles McDonald Brown Scholarship Fund at the University of Georgia. His proposal was set forth in a letter to the Board of Trustees, of which he himself had been a member since 1857, dated July 15, 1882. He proposed to pay into the state Treasury the sum of $50,000 in cash to be used for any purpose the state might wish. In return for this deposit the state would issue to the university a like amount of fifty-

27 Rudolph Von Abele, *Alexander H. Stephens: A Biography*, (New York, 1946), 306 ff.
28 Undated manuscript in Felton Papers.
29 July 1, 1882, Rowland (ed.), *Jefferson Davis*, IX, 175–76.

year 7 percent bonds. These bonds would constitute an endowment, the income from which was to be used for scholarships, Brown's sons designating the recipients.

The trustees submitted the proposal to a committee of five, headed by Alexander Stephens, which quickly recommended its acceptance. The trustees approved, but Robert Toombs seems to have been absent when the vote was taken. Ever unwilling to abandon personal hostilities, Toombs attacked the proposal on constitutional grounds, and many of Brown's enemies flocked to his support. In order to implement the proposal, it would be necessary for the legislature to authorize the issuance of the bonds. This Toombs denied the legislature had the authority to do. The Constitution of 1877, in the framing of which Toombs had exerted so much influence, stated: "The bonded debt of the State shall never be increased except to repulse invasion, suppress insurrection, or defend the State in time of war." Since the bonds requested did not fit either of these categories, Toombs contended that they could not be issued.

All depended upon the interpretation of the constitutional clause. Did it mean that no new bonds could be issued even after existing ones had been retired? Or might new ones be issued provided the total did not exceed that of 1877? Toombs insisted upon the former interpretation and was a bit embarrassed when Brown produced a private letter written by him to L. N. Whittle the previous year taking the latter position.[30] Never one to surrender, by the time the legislature met, Toombs had his opposition forces well marshaled; Brown's proposal was rejected. In addition to the alleged constitutional prohibition, two other objections were raised. Since the state could sell its bonds at 4 percent, why pay 7? And some persons obviously thought that by reserving to his sons the power to designate recipients of the scholarship loans, Brown was attempting to gain control of the university.

Brown, now in Washington, was irritated and puzzled. Was there on record another case where a state legislature had rejected such a private donation for public education? Correspondents from South Carolina and Alabama assured Senator Brown that their states would

30 Thompson, *Toombs*, 254. For the Whittle correspondence with several prominent lawyers relative to the Elam Alexander bequest for educational purposes see Hargrett Collection under dates February 2, 23, 24, 1881; July 26, August 8, 1882.

be pleased to accept such a gift, and there is evidence that he seriously considered making the gift to the University of South Carolina. But wishing to keep his money in Georgia, he changed his proposal. There was a provision in the constitution which authorized the trustees of the University of Georgia to accept donations, bequests, grants of land, or other property. Therefore, he would purchase $50,000 of state bonds and present them to the trustees directly. The trustees accepted the donation, and Robert Toombs walked out of the meeting never to attend another session.[31] No figures are available as to how many young men have been educated under loans of the Charles McDonald Brown Scholarship Fund, but as of December, 1973, the principal had increased to $1,022,954.[32]

Although in Washington most of the time, Senator Brown kept a tight rein on his business enterprises, and his wealth continued to increase. The Louisville and Nashville Railroad purchased William Wadley's 7⅝ shares in the Western and Atlantic Company. When added to the 7½ shares already owned by its affiliate, the Nashville, Chattanooga and St. Louis, this gave the Louisville and Nashville ⅔ of the 23 shares. To conform to the Western and Atlantic charter requirements, some of these shares were transferred to "friends" in Georgia, yet the Louisville and Nashville did not gain control. Remaining firm in his ruling that only original shareholders had votes, Brown gave the majority shareholders only so much influence and information as he pleased. In 1881 the company paid a dividend of $5,000 per share; in 1882 the amount was reduced to $2,500 without explanation; and soon it would cease paying any dividends at all. Brown was said to be making improvements, yet the majority stockholder received no report as to their nature or cost. "The Governor is an astute politician," commented Milton H. Smith, vice-president in charge of Louisville and Nashville operations, "fully competent to wield this property in a manner to promote his own personal interests, and does not hesitate to do so. It adds greatly to his political power in the State and, in ways,

31 Thompson, *Toombs*, 354; Brown to L. N. Whittle, August 8, 1882, in Hargrett Collection. The correspondence relating to Brown's proposal is printed in Fielder, *Brown*, 570 ff. See also Trustees minutes of the University of Georgia, 1878–1886, pp. 366, 398, 401.
32 Brown also made a gift of $50,000 to the Southern Baptist Theological Seminary.

adds to his fortune." Smith charged that Brown's friend E. W. Cole (no longer connected with the Nashville, Chattanooga and St. Louis) was being paid a vice-president's salary by the Western and Atlantic, yet performed no services, and that Brown was also bestowing liberal favors upon members of his own family. "Nothing, however, can be done as long as Gov. Brown has absolute control of the property."[33]

Smith was correct in his charge that Brown had bestowed favors upon members of his own family; his son Julius was attorney for the Western and Atlantic and Joseph M. was passenger agent. Their appointments, however, did not give Brown as much relief from responsibility as might have been expected; the boys were a bit too visionary for the "Old Man." Brown kept a firm grasp on the controls. In the late summer of 1882, Julius took his wife to New York for medical treatment. While there he was invited to a conference aboard William P. Clyde's yacht. Clyde was a major stockholder in the Richmond and Danville Railroad and in a fleet of freight steamers out of New York. He related to Julius Brown plans to extend his influence into the southeast by working in close harmony with the East Tennessee Railroad and the North and South Carolina lines through Charlotte and Greenville to Atlanta. He was also considering acquiring control of the Central of Georgia connecting Atlanta with Savannah. He wanted the Browns in on the plan. But first the "wings" of the Georgia Railroad Commission must be "clipped." For legislative campaign purposes in 1884, Clyde and his associates would furnish $50,000 to be used by the Browns as they saw fit. After that, the same group would furnish $150,000 to "change the State Constitution, and alter the whole Commission business." (And "you know what money will do in Georgia," Julius reminded his father.) Commission members J. M. Smith and L. N. Trammell could be given some positions on the railroads if Brown so advised, Clyde suggested.

The plan was clearly to bypass the Western and Atlantic and the Louisville and Nashville system. Julius was apparently agreeable. The freight trains in the Atlanta yard, he explained to his father, were becoming such a nuisance they were "*bound to go*." As the work progressed on the new Capitol, the legislators were forced to cross the

33 Maury Klein, *The History of the Louisville & Nashville Railroad* (New York, 1972), 192–94.

tracks, and as the business section of the city developed, "the demand for them to go will be absolute." Senator Brown's immediate task, according to Julius, would be to control William G. Raoul of the Central. "I think you can do it."

In order to "break down the feeling between the roads and the people." Clyde further proposed that they open up an emigration office in Georgia, advertise the resources of the state, register land for sale, and haul prospective buyers over the railroads at half price. Julius Brown was completely taken in by the whole scheme. He thought arrangements could be made whereby the Browns, with New York money, could control the railroad system of the Southeast. "If we can get *all* the roads to go into it," he explained to his father, "I had rather own that belt line road than all our coal and iron investments."[34]

We have no record of Brown's immediate reaction to Julius' scheme, but the plan was not implemented. Brown opposed the very idea of strict control of railroads either by the state or the federal government, yet there is no evidence that he approved the use of money to influence either the commissioners or legislators. He was conscious of the protest against freight trains in Atlanta, yet he also realized that with the expiration of the Western and Atlantic lease he would be out of the railroad business.

Joseph M. Brown, passenger agent for the Western and Atlantic, also had his dreams. He wanted to make Marietta a resort area and then reap great profits for the Western and Atlantic from hauling passengers, even to putting on an extra train from Atlanta. Brown himself was not enthusiastic. The lease had only a few more years to run; Marietta business prospects did not appear very bright; and many of the people there had been very "ungrateful." Joe M. agreed that many people in Marietta had been ungrateful, but what about the people of Cartersville and Bartow County? They had been "vindictive, malicious, active and energetic in vituperation," fiercely attacking both the Western and Atlantic Company and Brown personally. Yet Brown had ignored it all and spent tens of thousands in developing mines in that county, greatly enriching the people, all in order to make money for himself and his company.

Joe M. compared Marietta to New Orleans and Florida and found

34 Julius Brown to Pa, September 23, 1883, in Hargrett Collection.

the Georgia town most attractive. He had recently circulated a brochure with what he considered very promising results. Apparently he had previously proposed other schemes which his father had not approved, for he now complained of always being vetoed by the "upper circle." "I really feel a little somewhat hurt at being always compelled to almost fight my way forward, even in our own railroad family, in the securing of the adoption of any new plan. I am getting tired of spending thought, labor and time for the road with the continuance of the old ways. . . . I have preferred to stay here and protect your interests and business reputation and expect to continue to do so; but I wish the time would come when I would be considered as something else than a twelve year old boy when I advance ideas as well as when I demonstrate its [sic] correctness and practicability."[35] We have no copies of Brown's replies to his aggressive sons. Perhaps he made them in person; he would remain at the throttle.

Brown had no interest in developing Marietta or in expanding the services of the Western and Atlantic. According to an article in the Atlanta *Constitution* on December 5, 1886, no doubt prepared by Henry W. Grady in consultation with Brown, the Louisville and Nashville and the Central of Georgia had spent $1 million in the purchase of shares in the Western and Atlantic, which no longer paid dividends and therefore were worthless. However, each share had paid its owner or owners a total of $115,000 over the years. The original owners of the shares, which had cost nothing, were still in control. Since the shares no longer paid dividends, all that was left to the owners was a hope for compensation for the improvements made on the road, which were referred to as "betterments." Eventually the company would present the state with a bill for $1,500,000, but a commission appointed by the legislature finally awarded slightly less than $100,000.[36] By the early 1880s, Brown had concluded that in view of the popular outcry against high freight rates and railroad practices, threats of federal and state regulation, and the great increase in competition, railroad stocks did not have a bright future. When Mrs. W. H. Felton of Cartersville, tempo-

35 Joseph M. Brown to Pa, March 19, 1886, *ibid.*
36 Atlanta *Daily Constitution*, February 12, May 14, 1891; *Letter from Joseph E. Brown on the Subject of the Settlement Between the State and the Lessees on the Question of Betterments, Taxes, etc., Discussed, Arbitration Proposed* (Atlanta, 1887).

rarily putting aside her hostility, offered to trade him six shares of Marietta and North Georgia Railroad stock for land, he declined the offer, replying that he had not purchased railroad stocks for several years. "I have my own view under the laws of the State & the present current of popular opinion as to the future value of railroad property as a dividend paying investment."[37]

Brown exchanged his stock in the Texas and Pacific for 28,000 acres of Texas land. When construction was resumed, the line ran through his property and "Joe Brown's Town" of Colorado City, Texas, sprang up at the intersection of the Texas and Pacific and the Colorado River. By 1884 the town was reported to have hotels, banks, a booming business, newspaper, and a population of six thousand. Brown donated lots for public buildings and churches, and made others available for residences and businesses at a price.[38]

Why a man in declining health, who had received the highest honors from his state, and had accumulated a fortune, would want another term in the United States Senate is a bit difficult to comprehend. There was one honor, however, that Senator Brown had never had—he had never been elected unanimously. It would be toward this goal that he and Henry W. Grady would labor throughout 1884. Grady would manage the campaign. Beginning in mid-February and continuing until Brown returned from Washington for the summer, he made regular reports on politics throughout the state, especially as to candidates for the legislature. The senator and the journalist planned their strategy well. The campaign would be a quiet one, conducted through private conferences and correspondence. Grady began with a conference with Governor Henry D. McDaniel, who was serving out Stephens' unexpired term and wished reelection. They agreed that those incumbents who wished reelection had "a *common cause* in a quiet race & in keeping down opposition." The governor promised full cooperation. "You have no idea how effectively I can use even his *quiet* influence between now & the senatorial election," Grady wrote Brown. "It is a *great point*."[39]

37 Brown to Mrs. Felton, July 23, 1883, in Felton Papers.
38 Colorado (Tex.) *Clipper*, February 23, 1884. Copy in Spalding Collection. This article was probably written by I. W. Avery.
39 February 17, 1884, in Hargrett Collection.

Grady analyzed almost the entire state, county by county, as to prospective candidates for the legislature and their attitude toward Brown. He often advised the senator to write key men and flatter them by requesting that they take over political affairs in his interest. Frequently using the expression "he is all right" or "he is anti-Brown," Grady compiled lists of those whose candidacy was to be encouraged or opposed by Brown's friends. Candidates and friends made frequent reports to Grady that "Joey B" was solid in their counties. "I think you & McD. both have a walk-over," Grady reported to Brown. "Mark this prediction—but *don't quit working.*" On another occasion Grady explained: "*Things look well* but 'eternal vigilance.' I don't want to fight another legislature that is packed against us."[40]

Grady rarely mentioned money, but his partner in the *Constitution*, Evan P. Howell, occasionally tossed in a bit of advice. In one letter he suggested that Brown send two hundred dollars for the "editor of the *Henry County Weekly*, who you know is a rampant opponent of yours," and a candidate for the state Senate. "I can fix him." Howell specifically warned Brown against trusting certain persons who might pose as his friend. The senator should be careful what he said to or about P. W. "Pete" Alexander, former law partner of former governor James M. Smith but no longer his friend, and chairman of the committee that ran Norwood against Colquitt in 1880. "There never was a more perfect son of a bitch in this world. He would sell his mother for gain." Pete was reported to be cooperating with those who planned to attack Brown as not being a true Democrat. Howell thought it would not "amount to a row of beans." He had also heard from Joe Cummings, "the only man who would have the courage to run against you," and he would not make the race. The only prominent newspaper that Howell warned against was the Macon *Telegraph and Messenger.* Although Macon was a long way from Dr. William H. Felton's home district, this newspaper was urging him to be a candidate for the legislature. "Felton is an open avowed enemy of yours—he is bitter and unrelenting," Howell added. He thought former senator H. V. M. Miller largely responsible for this encouragement of Felton, for he himself wanted to

40 Grady to Brown, February 25, March 5, 6, 8, 1884, *ibid.*

return to the Senate. Felton could help Miller's cause in the legislature by consolidating Brown's opposition. However, Howell thought the whole affair "a small cloud of dust."[41]

In a very quiet way Grady advised those who wished to be elected or appointed to office that they could greatly promote their cause by mounting the Brown bandwagon. "I saw Frank Haralson, the State Librarian, today," he wrote Brown. "He is running for Solicitor General before the next Legislature. I told him he could expect nothing unless he saw that a solid Brown delegation was brought down from the mountains. He says it needs no looking after."[42] In closing his report to Brown on April 17, Grady reaffirmed his own loyalty. He thought neither McDaniel nor Brown would have any trouble. "Let me say to you, in all frankness, Governor, that you *ought not to have any*. You have made a good Senator & have represented Georgia with distinguished honor, and outside of my personal preference & affiliation, I should esteem it a public calamity to see you beaten, or disturbed."[43]

Grady's secret campaign worked well; Brown's was the only name placed in nomination before the legislature for United States senator. Not even his known enemies voted against him in the Senate, but the House failed to make it unanimous; two die-hards voted for Robert Toombs.[44] Upon returning to Washington, the Brown family moved from the Metropolitan Hotel to the National. They found their new quarters comfortable and convenient but Brown disliked the hotel fare.[45] He was now suffering a great deal from dyspepsia. He found some temporary relief, however, when a friend from Baltimore sent him "two pones of cornbread." These he ate for breakfast on successive days, and complained to his daughter; "It is a great hardship that there is no chance to get a piece of corn-bread here under any circumstances."[46]

---

41 Howell to Brown, March 24, 25, 1884, *ibid*. Felton was elected to the legislature, and he spent the next six years defending the railroad commission. He apparently did not vote against Brown.
42 March 6, 1884, in Hargrett Collection.
43 Hargrett Collection.
44 *Senate Journal*, 1884, p. 209; Atlanta *Daily Constitution*, November 19, 1884.
45 Mrs. Brown reported on July 26, 1885, that it was doubtful whether the senator would be able to attend General U. S. Grant's funeral. Mrs. Brown to Mary Brown Connally, in Spalding Collection.
46 Brown to Mary Brown Connally, December 19, 1885, *ibid*.

A few months later he was still complaining. "I am getting very tired of this business for the present and should like greatly to come home," he wrote his daughter Mary.[47]

Despite physical difficulties, Brown continued active in senatorial affairs. Public demand for the regulation of railroads had become so great that a large portion of the final session of the Forty-eighth Congress would be devoted to discussion of that subject. Early in 1885, the House again passed its Reagan bill, first passed in 1878, forbidding discriminatory rates, rebates and drawbacks, and the formation of pools. The Senate now felt compelled to take some action. Thus began the debate that would result in the creation of the Cullom Committee to conduct public hearings on the subject. Although Brown had disposed of most of his railroad interests, he still had definite views on the subject of government regulation. Addressing the Senate on January 16, 1885, he asserted that the railroads had suffered "enormous loss" while "immensely" increasing the "wealth and power of the whole country." He estimated that the 125,000 miles of railroads constructed during the past half century represented an investment of $3,125,000,000. These roads had greatly enhanced the land values in the areas traversed by them. Using Atlanta as an example, he pointed out that, in 1830, 202.5 acres of land in the heart of the present city sold for "a horse, bridle, and saddle." At present, on that same plot of land were improvements worth probably $15 million. "Railroads have made Atlanta what she is." He did not advocate leaving the gigantic railroad systems "entirely unbridled," but he thought regulations should be done "wisely and constitutionally if at all." It was the railroads that had made possible the great boom and expansion enjoyed by America; the manner in which they had tied the country together to promote production and marketing was little short of a miracle.

Brown explained that it was easy to "excite popular prejudice against corporations and monopolies, as they are called," by proposing to take charge of and operate them "for our own benefit without having cost us anything." He also noted that when there was a proposal to build a new railroad, the people who hoped to benefit supported it with great enthusiasm. Yet when it was completed with the use of other people's

47 June 7, 1886, *ibid.*

money, many of these same people joined in a crusade to confiscate the road by reducing rates to where they would yield no profit on the investment, driving the company into bankruptcy.

Brown saw in railroad consolidation the only hope for survival. As an example, the Central Railroad had secured control of the Georgia Railroad through lease and the two lines were being operated as one. While they were prospering, several North Georgia railroads had gone into bankruptcy. Of the estimated $60 million that had been invested in Georgia railroads, Brown thought more than one-half had been lost to the investors, "and much of this has been the result of the popular clamor for reduced rates." He was opposed to any attempt to establish uniform rates. Rates must to a great extent depend upon the amount of traffic. Light traffic, although very important, must be subjected to higher rates. This was the only way that all sections of the country could be adequately served and railroads yield profits to those who invested. Only through a guarantee of adequate rates could new and badly needed railroads be constructed; uniform regulations would kill developments. He thought the Reagan bill, as passed by the House, would "result most disastrously to the whole internal commerce and carrying business of the country." He would, however, "vote for a commission with proper powers of investigation and report, leaving true regulation . . . where the common law leaves it." Or "arm the commission with power to lay down and enforce some general and just rules. . . . We can never regulate all the details of our internal transportation by legal enactments." To attempt to do so would disastrously cripple our internal commerce.[48]

The Cullom Committee created by the Senate carried on an extensive investigation during the latter part of 1885 and found public opinion overwhelmingly in favor of government regulation of interstate commerce. Another year of debate followed before the Interstate Commerce Commission was created early in 1887. The powers of this commission went considerably beyond what Brown advocated; he never changed his views.

Brown had actively supported the candidacy of Grover Cleveland and was delighted that the Democrats had finally recaptured the presidency, yet he never became a true administration man. He could not

48 *Cong. Record*, 48th Cong., 2nd Sess., Pt. 1, pp. 799 ff.

agree with Cleveland on either the tariff or the silver question. Cleveland urged reduction of the tariff of 1883 as a means of reducing the surplus in the Treasury. Several such measures were introduced and beaten down by protectionists. Finally, in December, 1887, in a speech devoted entirely to the tariff, President Cleveland "cracked the party whip" and made it a party measure in the campaign of 1888. On March 14, 1888, Brown delivered another tariff speech in the Senate, the length of which was exceeded only by its dullness. He had not changed his views. He denied being a protectionist per se. "I believe in a tariff for revenue, so adjusted as to afford incidental protection to American capital and American labor." In adjusting the tariff, he would put the heaviest burdens on luxuries "used mostly by the rich . . . and the lightest burdens upon articles of prime necessity which are used by the poor." He, however, was still more interested in eliminating internal taxes than in the tariff itself. He saw income from a tariff as the only means of accomplishing this end; therefore, he opposed general tariff repeal. Repeal would ruin capital investments and throw millions out of work.[49]

President Cleveland was a "gold" man, but during his first administration he did not push for legislation decreasing the use of silver. Neither was the silver question considered a party question. Brown stressed this fact when he spoke on the Beck resolution in January, 1886. On December 18, 1885, James B. Beck of Kentucky had introduced a resolution relating to the payment of custom duties in coin. Brown talked at length, but he had nothing new to say on the silver question. He reiterated his earlier argument against paying bondholders in gold and laborers in cheaper money. It was the bondholders, he contended, who were leading the fight against extensive use of silver. He advocated using the silver in the Treasury to pay off bondholders and stop the payment of interest. To pay bondholders in gold was "neither fair dealing nor common honesty."

As on a previous occasion, Brown cited the Treasury report, which revealed that of the amount of hard money in the country, two-thirds was gold and one-third silver. The favorable balance of trade with the outside world continued to pour gold into the Treasury, yet it was still being argued that silver should be decreased in order to prevent the

49 *Ibid.*, 2045 ff.

draining off of gold. There was nothing to the argument that labor would suffer from an increase in silver, Brown charged. Labor would not suffer while paid in legal tender silver. But strike down silver and down would go the price of labor.[50]

Apparently of more immediate concern to Senator Brown than either the tariff or silver question were the woman suffrage activities of Susan B. Anthony. Early in 1887 the Senate debated a proposed amendment to the Constitution offered by Henry W. Blair of New Hampshire, which would deny to the states the power to deprive persons of the right to vote because of sex. Brown became much aroused. This was a very serious matter, he informed the Senate. It seriously affected "the very pillars of our social fabric, which involve peace and harmony of society, the unity of the family, and much of the future success of our Government." This was a question that must be "met fairly and discussed with firmness." It was in no sense a party matter. He was convinced that God intended the male and female to be different and had endowed each with qualifications to perform their important role. To man was assigned the duty of protecting the family and providing for its needs. For this task he was given superior strength and ability "to combat the sterner realities and difficulties of life." It was man who must perform the services due the state, assist in governing, and protect society. He too must develop the means of production and transportation, performing his duties anywhere and at any time.

The Creator also assigned to women a definite position. Woman was "a queen" who alone was fitted to discharge the sacred trust of wife and "the endearing relations of mother." She must be in the doorway to welcome the husband and father returning from the day's toil to "find in the good wife solace and consolation, which is nowhere else afforded." Should his burdens be onerous, "she divides their weight by the exercise of her love and her sympathy." Yet more important still were the woman's duties as a mother in training and educating her children. "She trains the twig as the tree should be inclined." She molded character and intellect and inculcated "lessons of patriotism, manliness, religion, and virtue."

Should women be given the suffrage, Brown feared that only the "baser class of females"—the more ignorant and least refined—would

50 *Ibid.*, 648 ff.

wish to cast aside delicacy, disregard sacred duties, and rush to the polls. But to offset the influence of this baser element, the "intelligent, virtuous, and refined females would be forced to leave their sacred duties to perform the unpleasant act of voting." Ignorance among male voters was already bad enough; why add an additional burden of baser females?

Brown rejected the argument that the exercise of suffrage was necessary for women to find employment and receive just compensation for their labor. The argument might appear plausible, yet he saw in it "little real force." Employment and compensation would always be determined by supply and demand, and those with superior strength would be employed. The ballot could not supply women with the strength and abilities they lacked. Neither could it protect them from "the tyranny of bad husbands." If the husband dictated in other matters he would also determine his wife's use of the ballot. Most likely, woman suffrage would "promote unhappiness and dissension in the family circle." In the "rougher, coarser duties of life," man represented the family, but should the suffrage be extended to women and their individuality thrust into prominence, they would be expected to "answer for themselves." As voters, they would become politicians, and be expected to align themselves with political parties. Much political antagonism between husbands and wives would surely develop. "We can neither reverse the physical nor the moral laws of our nature," Brown concluded, "and as this movement is an attempt to reverse these laws, as to devolve upon the female sex important and laborious duties for which they are not by nature physically competent, I am not prepared to support this bill."[51] Senator Brown was unduly concerned; woman suffrage in his state of Georgia was decades in the future.

Measured by accomplishments, the Cleveland administration had not been a great success. The Democrats were divided on national issues and were certain to lose the Mugwump support received in 1884, yet they had no choice but to renominate Cleveland in 1888. These were Brown's views. He would not be present at the meeting of the Georgia Democratic convention called to select delegates to the national convention, but he sent to B. H. Bigham, chairman of the state executive committee, a detailed explanation of his views. He thought Georgia

51 *Ibid.*, 980 ff.

should give general endorsement to Cleveland's administration and select delegates who would vote for his renomination. If his administration had been such as to entitle his party to public confidence, then Cleveland should be renominated. He himself was among those Democrats who disapproved of the president's recommendation to "suspend the coinage of silver and adopt gold as the only legal money," for he believed it would "create great stringency in the money market, and we would soon reach a point where it would take a third more and probably twice as much property to raise money to pay a debt as it now takes." He was also among those who disapproved of the president's recommendation to reduce the surplus by reducing revenue from the tariff rather than by repealing internal taxes. However, he did not consider these differences within the party sufficient reason to deny the president a renomination. "We must tolerate the differences of opinion and act together for the accomplishment of objects greater than those upon which we differ. . . . We must agree to disagree, and must live and let live. Honest men will differ. After all, in politics a great deal has to be done by way of compromise."[52]

The Georgia Democratic Convention, meeting on May 9, 1888, went further than Brown suggested. Under the leadership of A. H. Colquitt, Brown's colleague in the Senate, it gave specific endorsement to Cleveland's demand for a reduction of the tariff. It was reported that most delegates came with instructions not to vote for any representative to the national convention who did not approve of the Mills bill, then pending in Congress, which provided for a reduction in the tariff. It was further reported that federal internal revenue officials throughout the state had been working hard in favor of tariff reduction instead of repeal of internal taxes. When General Phil Cook, addressing the convention, mentioned Brown and his tariff views, he was greeted with hisses.[53]

In thanking Cook for his kind remarks, Brown gave his reaction to the stand taken by the Georgia convention. He thought the Democrats could carry the South regardless of their platform. It was the strong manufacturing states outside the South that posed a problem. Why irritate the voters of those states by demanding drastic tariff

52 Brown to Bigham, March 10, 1888, in Hargrett Collection.
53 Evan P. Howell to Brown, May 10, 1888, *ibid.*

reduction when a majority of Congress had already spoken in opposition to such reduction? On the silver question there was also great diversity of opinion. Why take a definite stand on either question and thus irritate many members of the party?

Brown also noted that he disagreed with the president's ideas relating to civil service. "I am so old fashioned as to believe that when we elect a Democratic President the Democrats are entitled to the offices." The president and many Democrats thought otherwise. They would keep a strong Republican in office if he was faithful in discharge of his duties. However, since the Georgia convention had endorsed the president's views, Brown would acquiesce.[54]

The part taken by Colquitt in the Democratic convention so irritated Evan P. Howell of the *Constitution* that he solicited Brown's support in a movement to elect Henry Grady to succeed Colquitt in the Senate.[55] Brown was agreeable and no doubt Grady was also. To further add to the wrath of Howell and Grady, Colquitt refused to be a party to bringing William McKinley to Atlanta for a public address. Through the efforts of Grady and a few others, a Chautauqua had been organized at Salt Springs (Powder Springs) near Atlanta. In addition to a regular program Grady planned to bring Congressmen William McKinley of Ohio and Roger Q. Mills of Texas to the Chautauqua platform to present opposing views on the tariff. Colquitt would not join Brown in extending an invitation to McKinley; he wanted no high-tariff speeches in Georgia.[56] The rumor spread that McKinley, sensing considerable opposition in Georgia, would not accept the invitation. In much distress, Grady wired Brown, "Make him come."[57] McKinley came and spoke to a large crowd on August 21.

Grady did not make the race for the Senate. Finding himself opposed by John B. Gordon and Hoke Smith of the Atlanta *Journal*, he refused to permit his name to be placed before the legislature. (He died the following year.) Brown actively supported Cleveland and attributed the president's defeat to his stand on the tariff.

Brown's final two years in the Senate were not pleasant ones. He

54 Brown to Cook, May 12, 1888, *ibid.*
55 Howell to Brown, May 10, 1888, *ibid.*
56 Raymond B. Nixon, *Henry W. Grady: Spokesman of the New South* (New York, 1943), 280.
57 July 27, 1888, in Hargrett Collection.

would again speak on the subjects of tariff, internal revenue, and silver, even though he had nothing new to offer. Living expenses in Washington far exceeded his salary as a senator.[58] His physical condition continued to worsen. In walking he was now assisted by a stick of "hickory, with a walnut head" presented to him by Wade Hampton of South Carolina.[59] The only truly bright spot was his continued success in the business world. He was no longer interested in railroad stocks and had also grown sour on further investment in Atlanta real estate. "It is not my purpose to put money into Atlanta real estate, or in building houses while the present unjust rate of taxation is maintained in the city," he wrote Dr. E. L. Connally. He thought 4 percent nontaxable Georgia bonds a better investment.[60]

Senator Brown wrote a will in August, 1886, in which he gave the scope, but not the value, of his vast holdings. His Atlanta property consisted of buildings on Alabama Street, at the corner of Pryor and Wall streets, the Kiser Building, the Brown block and Pittman building on Wall Street, several city lots, and fifty-six acres near the Old Fair Grounds. He held an unspecified number of state, city, and business corporation bonds. He was major stockholder in the Dade Coal Company, Castle Rock Coal Company, Walker Iron and Coal Company, and Chattanooga Iron Company. He owned a plantation near Canton and a number of lots within the town, a plantation in Gordon County, almost thirty thousand acres in Texas, and a number of lots in Colorado City. The only railroad stock mentioned in the will was his share in the Western and Atlantic Company, which he directed should not be sold during the term of the lease.[61]

Senator Brown continued to keep close check on his mining interests, but actual management was gradually transferred to his sons. In December, 1887, the Dade and Castle Rock coal companies in their entirety were offered for sale. The only stockholders other than the Brown family were Jacob W. Seaver and Ellen A. Morrill, widow of W. C. Morrill. The minimum price was set at $1,200,000. J. W. Hoff-

---

58 Sixteen and one-half days' board at the National Hotel in January, 1889, cost Brown $485.84. See bill in Spalding Collection.
59 Brown to E. L. Connally, April 27, 1888, *ibid*.
60 Brown to Connally, June 7, 1886, *ibid*.
61 Copy in Hargrett Collection under date August 19, 1886.

man was to handle the sale for a minimum commission of $50,000.[62] There were no takers.

The few extant papers fail to reveal even a reasonably clear picture of the corporate maneuverings of the Brown-controlled coal and iron companies. In the spring of 1889 Joseph E. and Julius Brown incorporated the Bartow Iron and Manganese Company with a capital of $25,000. The capital was immediately increased to $50,000, and the entire increase was subscribed by the Dade Coal Company. In the same year there appeared the Georgia Mining, Manufacturing and Investment Company only to be immediately leased by another new company, the Georgia Iron and Coal Company, which in turn was owned by the Dade Coal Company. From all this corporate confusion one fact emerges very clearly—all of these companies were controlled by Dade Coal, and the Brown family controlled Dade Coal. In the election of officers on February 23, 1892, this company chose Julius Brown, president; Joseph M. Brown, vice-president; and Elijah Brown, secretary-treasurer. Joseph E. was listed as a director.[63]

The fact that Brown worked convict labor subjected him to constant attack. Pressure from public protest against the lease system resulted in no fewer than four investigations of convict camps. The investigating committees consistently gave Brown the best report, even though critical of the system in general. He did not hurt his cause by passing investigators along the Western and Atlantic without charge or having his friend E. W. Cole give a dinner for them at the Stanton House in Chattanooga.[64] Even favorable reports, however, did not protect Brown against the charge that while receiving public acclaim for his donations to churches and education he was acquiring his money through the sweat of convicts.[65]

After his retirement from the Senate in 1890 Brown spent most of his time at home. He wrote few letters and in all of his extant ones he

---

62 See contract in Brown Papers, Atlanta Historical Society.

63 See papers relating to the several companies *ibid.*

64 Atlanta *Daily Constitution,* July 15, 16, 1881; *Senate Journal,* 1882, p. 318; *House Journal,* 1886, pp. 426 ff; 1890, pp. 721 ff.

65 John C. Klein, reporting in New York *World,* April 21, 1890; Elizabeth Taylor, "The Abolition of the Convict Lease System," *Georgia Historical Quarterly,* XXVI, 273 ff.

comments on the poor condition of his health. To an old friend, who was approaching his one hundreth birthday, he stated that his own health was "in a very precarious condition," in fact, he had no "health that amounts to anything." Since neither of the two had much longer to live he sincerely trusted "we may have grace sufficient to our needs during the little balance of our pilgrimage here on earth." He was thankful for the "many blessings and kindnesses of Providence during my sufferings, physical and mental. The more I suffer, however, the more I am satisfied that it is God's will, and that it is my duty to be obedient and resigned to my fate, whatever may seem to Him most agreeable."[66]

Brown died at his home on Washington Street on November 30, 1894. "Just as a great proud ship lifts anchor and sails away to sea, did the strong soul of Hon. Joseph E. Brown glide away from the shores of life out upon the unknown waters whose harbor is Eternal Rest," exclaimed the *Constitution*. "It was in the evening of a life rich with honors and achievements—a life that left its impress on history. . . . The energy of a master mind was stopped forever."[67]

The body lay in state in the rotunda of the Capitol on December 2; services were held at the Second Baptist Church on the following day, the Reverend Henry D. McDonald officiating; burial was in Oakland Cemetery by the side of his sons, Franklin Pierce and Charles McDonald.

"A literal account of the life of Joseph Emerson Brown would read more like romance than reality," observed the Atlanta *Journal*. "At his death the last of a grand coterie of Georgians passed away. Stephens, Jenkins, Johnson, Toombs, Hill, Brown—all gone now."[68] "It will be many a year before Georgia will look upon his equal," lamented the Atlanta *Constitution*. "[It will be] many a year before she will have a son worthy to rival him in all those high and shining qualities which make a great statesman, a leader of men, a patriot and a Christian."[69] Indeed, it would be many a year before Georgia would ever see another Joseph E. Brown; the day has not yet arrived.

Brown was not a lovable person. His close friends were few; but

66 Brown to Wesley Shopshire, June 30, 1893, in Hargrett Collection.
67 Atlanta *Daily Constitution*, December 1, 1894.
68 December 1, 1894.
69 December 1, 1894.

his followers were many. Even those who disliked him secretly admired him. A Ben Hill, a Cobb, and a Toombs might bitterly denounce him, yet they respected, even feared, his ability and determination. Frustrated at their inability to control or even influence him, they often attempted to destroy him. Yet Joe Brown, pushed under at one point, always bobbed up at another. Again and again, his opponents thought him checkmated, only to see him come back in a manner that even surprised his supporters. He could adjust to a situation, but he preferred to create the situation instead, and he often did. His actions sometimes defied public explanation, yet he knew what he was doing, and rarely did he fail to emerge a winner. He possessed an uncanny ability to convert apparent failure into success.

Brown's enemies were bitter and persistent; the silent majority of voters supported him. He was not one to espouse a cause because it was popular; he often took a stand with the intention of making it popular. He was never the equal of Toombs or Ben Hill in fiery eloquence, yet as a cool, calculating master at maneuvering, he kept them in check. When they openly opposed him, they eventually experienced defeat.

Although a consistent winner, Brown lost the big one—the fight for southern independence. Like most leaders within the Confederacy, he misjudged northern willingness to fight to the bitter end. His active opposition to the Davis administration was unfortunate both for the Confederate cause and his place in history. This is not to say that Davis was always right or even an efficient leader in time of crisis. Brown definitely advocated peace in 1864, although not at any price. A victory under Davis' leadership, with a loss of what he considered state and individual rights, was not one of his desires. He did not consider himself a traitor, for he had never espoused the cause as represented by President Davis. Nonetheless, by word and deed, he weakened the Confederate effort and encouraged the violation of the law, even to the extent of threatening to use Georgia troops to prevent enforcement of Confederate authority. Yet to the end of his life, Brown insisted that he never placed barriers in the way of Confederate success, that he opposed Davis only when the president was in the wrong. The Georgia governor liked to pose as the champion of the constitutional rights of the people, he himself interpreting the Constitution. Whether in politics or in the business world, Brown was ever a leader; he could never follow.

When the war ended, the former governor accepted the verdict, turned his back upon the past, pointed toward the future, and became a very active part of what was often referred to as the "New South." Although the extent of his fortune was greatly exaggerated, there was no doubt of his financial success. Those less successful often accused him of being unscrupulous and dishonest, yet no action of his was ever proved illegal. He took advantage of opportunities and had the ability to detect the path leading to prosperity. When the path turned, he turned. In his late years, he became something of a patriarch, presiding over family and fortune. Enemies were fewer and less annoying, and he was content with his accomplishments and contributions.

Without doubt, Brown was the most influential man in Georgia from the time he became governor in 1857 until illness forced his retirement in the late 1880s; yet his contemporaries and succeeding generations have failed to award him proper recognition. No county, city, lake, highway, or other public facility bears his name; no public statue perpetuates his memory.[70]

70 The statue on the Georgia Capitol grounds was placed there by the Brown family.

Bibliographical Essay

ON JANUARY 5, 1878, Joseph E. Brown wrote Robert Toombs: "Our much beloved friend Linton Stephens is no more. You & Alec & I have each but a short time to remain here. . . . We four had more to do with maintaining the line of policy upholding self-government & the principles upon which we entered the conflict of 1861 than any other four men. We acted together in harmonious concert; each believed that our action was wise & just." It was known that Jefferson Davis was writing a history of the war, and Brown suspected that he was delaying publication "to see as many of us pass away as possible." When the work did appear, he had no doubt Davis would "assail us with a good deal of bitterness & stab with a Joab blade whenever he can." No doubt the president would "attribute much of the failure to what he will term the hostile movement in Georgia & elsewhere & . . . blacken as far as he can our reputation."

In view of these probable developments, Brown appealed to Toombs to join with him in sponsoring a publication that would record "a correct history of Georgia & Georgia policy . . . in which we would preserve all the facts of history necessary to our vindication." Brown reasoned that neither he nor Toombs had the time or physical strength to perform the task. Neither did Stephens, who had already published a general work which did not serve the purpose in mind. Brown's idea was to "employ some judicious man who has talent" and "let him frequently submit his work to us for inspections & suggestions."[1]

Toombs did not fully appreciate Brown's concern; he had less to justify than did the former governor. As for himself, he stated, he had no materials to furnish the person who should undertake the task; the Yankees stole all his papers shortly after he "ran away." He had reliable information that

1 Hargrett Collection.

Davis would publish within the next six months. He agreed that "no governor in the Confederate States was more earnest in the Confederate cause or efficient in sustaining it than yourself & the true history of your conduct during the war will fully vindicate you from all aspersions of Mr. Davis." He thought it best, however, to wait for Davis' publication. "I do not think he will assail you & I am sure he will never assail me while I live."[2]

Davis' work did not appear until 1881. Meanwhile, Brown grew weary with waiting and set out on his own. Late in 1879 he made a contract with an old friend, Herbert Fielder, a financially embarrassed third-rate lawyer whom both erroneously thought possessed literary talent. For the sum of three thousand dollars, Fielder would take leave from his nonexistent law practice and spend a year writing a biography of Joseph E. Brown. Fielder had already brought together some material on the period before the war, so it was agreed that the book might be of the "life and times" type.

Ahead lay little but frustration, disappointment, and hard feelings. Within the year Fielder put together a volume of pure eulogy of Brown. Brown read at least a portion of the manuscript and opened negotiations with possible publishers. No commercial publisher was interested; publication must be subsidized. When Brown learned that Fielder, pleading complete poverty, either could not or would not bear the expense of even placing the manuscript in the hands of a publisher, he lost interest. Meanwhile, having learned that Isaac W. Avery was preparing a history of Georgia since 1850, he left Fielder to complain and charge bad faith. Avery's *The History of Georgia From 1850 to 1881* appeared in 1881. A veritable storehouse of information, it immediately became and remained the most important work covering that period of Georgia history. But even Avery was such an admirer of Brown that he could not avoid a great amount of eulogy. Small wonder that after reading Avery's book, Brown was not enthusiastic about paying the total cost of printing and distributing Fielder's volume.

In the meantime, in spite of his pecuniary embarrassment, Fielder had moved to Texas, from which point he carried on an increasingly bitter correspondence with Brown, even to the point of threatening suit for the breach of a contract that was never made. Finally, Brown purchased the manuscript, deleted irrelevant chapters on slavery and states' rights, added a concluding chapter and an appendix of his Senate speeches, and through I. W. Avery published in 1883 *A Sketch of the Life and Times and Speeches of Joseph E. Brown.*[3]

A more modest man than Brown would have revised the manuscript before publishing, eliminating the extravagant eulogy, but he apparently liked it. Since he had reentered public life and would soon be seeking re-

2 Toombs to Brown, January 23, 1878, *ibid.*
3 For the extensive correspondence between Brown and Fielder see *ibid.* under dates November, 1879–October 1883.

election to the Senate, he promoted his cause by giving away more copies than he sold. Indeed, there is no record of his having sold any. The interpretations in this volume are of little value, but since Brown approved the manuscript it must be considered as factually correct as he wished it.

There are a few shorter sketches of Brown, some contemporary, others more recent, that are of value. Two are found in Lucian Lamar Knight, *Reminiscences of Famous Georgians* (Atlanta, 1907), and William J. Northern (ed.), *Men of Mark in Georgia*, 7 vols. (Atlanta, 1907–12), III. Others: Emory Speers, *Joseph E. Brown of Georgia* (Atlanta, 1905); John C. Reed, "Joseph E. Brown," in Julian A. C. Chandler *et al.* (eds.), *The South in the Building of the Nation* (Richmond, 1909–13), XI; Thomas R. Hay, "Joseph E. Brown, Governor of Georgia, 1857–1865," *Georgia Historical Quarterly*, XIII.

In 1939 Louise Biles Hill published a very good study, *Joseph E. Brown and the Confederacy* (Chapel Hill, 1939). By including chapters before and after the Civil War, she made her volume the best biography of Brown that had yet been published. Elizabeth Studley Nathans' *Losing the Peace: Georgia Republicans and Reconstruction, 1865–1871* (Baton Rouge) appeared in 1968. Although limited to a brief period, its penetrating analysis of the former governor's activities as a Republican merits a high position among studies on Brown. The thoroughness of Ms. Nathans' research has made the path easier for those who follow.

The most recent writing on Brown is Darrell C. Roberts, *Joseph E. Brown and the Politics of Reconstruction* (Tuscaloosa, 1973). This thin volume is an abridgement of his "Joseph E. Brown and the New South" (Ph.D. dissertation, University of Georgia, 1958), which was written before the larger collections of Brown papers were available. From this dissertation Roberts has also published a number of short articles in *Georgia Historical Quarterly*, XLIV, LII; *Georgia Review*, XIX; *Florida Historical Quarterly*, XL; and *Atlanta Historical Society Bulletin*, XIII, XV.

MANUSCRIPT COLLECTIONS

The papers of Joseph E. Brown suffered no fewer than three major acts of willful destruction. Although there was ample warning that Sherman's army on its march to the sea would move by way of Milledgeville, the General Assembly, governor, and other state officials failed to make adequate preparations to save public papers. Neither did Sherman exercise sufficient control over his troops to prevent unnecessary destruction. The result was that Union soldiers destroyed large quantities of documents, records, and public and private correspondence during their brief stay in the Georgia capital.

The Union officer sent to arrest Brown at the Mansion in May, 1865, was instructed to "seize his papers."[4] This the officer did not do, but after the governor had been taken away, Mrs. Brown and her son Julius, fearing the return of Union soldiers, "destroyed a great portion" of the governor's papers at the Mansion. Brown later stated that these papers contained many valuable letters from such men as Towns, McDonald, Warner, and Lumpkin.[5]

On October 23, 1935, Brown's son George wrote the state librarian, Ruth Blair: "The old letters to my father prior to and during the Civil War were destroyed when the Yankee army occupied Milledgeville. The letters since that date were largely considered business matters and we do not feel that it would be proper to turn these letters over to any one, and therefore my sister and myself have both decided that they should be burned."[6] Thus did most of Brown's business papers go up in smoke.

In spite of wanton destruction, a considerable quantity of Brown material did survive and has been made available during the past few years. The major portion of these papers are at the University of Georgia. Since they are preserved as separate collections, they will be referred to by the names of donors.

Hargrett Collection. Donated by Felix Hargrett. About 1,500 items. This is the most important collection of Brown letters, covering the entire period of his public life. The collection also contains legal papers, speeches, correspondence relating to the Western and Atlantic and the Texas and Pacific railroads, letterbooks, broadsides, Confederate imprints, and a short diary kept by Franklin Pierce Brown.

McLeod Collection. Donated by Cora Brown McLeod. About 1,000 items. Here are papers of Brown and his sons Julius and Joseph M. There is also a "collection of autograph letters, miscellaneous Brown family papers, printed material, pictures, a scrapbook, and newspaper clippings." The correspondence is with several men of state and national prominence.

Spalding Collection. Donated by Mary Connally and Elizabeth Grisham Spalding. About 1,300 items. This collection contains "correspondence, notes, pictures, indentures, and genealogical notes and records," and forty-six scrapbooks covering the years 1853–1891. The scrapbooks are mostly newspaper clippings, many from small-town papers, the files of which are no longer extant. Unfortunately, many clippings are not identified.

Still in private possession is the very important Charles Brockman, Jr., Collection of Brown and Grisham family papers, consisting of uncataloged correspondence, genealogy, records, and letterbooks, and a diary kept by Mrs. Brown, 1853–57.

4 *O.R.*, Ser. I, Vol. XLIX, Pt. 2, p. 680.
5 Brown to Mrs. W. H. Felton, February 4, 1887, in Felton Papers.
6 Brown Papers, Georgia State Archives.

The holdings of the Georgia State Archives, Atlanta, include one separate Brown folder. The great mass of Brown material is in the Civil War Collection:

Governor's letterbooks, 1861–65. Mostly correspondence with Confederate authorities. Much overlapping with the *War of Rebellion Records* and the *Confederate Records of Georgia*.

Executive secretary letterbooks. Sixteen volumes of replies to letters of all types.

Letters received. Numerous boxes. Very few of importance.

Executive minutes. One volume, consisting of correspondence, proclamations, and speeches.

Other small Brown collections are in the manuscript divisions of the Atlanta Historical Society (mostly business papers); Emory University (mostly miscellaneous items, particularly commissions issued by Brown; very few letters); Duke University (a few letters, mostly to Brown; some originals of letters of importance); University of North Carolina (mostly family material).

Of much importance to the study of Brown are the papers of Alexander H. Stephens. The Library of Congress holds a Stephens collection of about 14,000 items, including much correspondence with and relating to Brown. Manhattanville College of the Sacred Heart has about 3,000 items, mostly intimate correspondence between Stephens and his half-brother Linton. They contain a considerable amount of Brown material. Smaller collections of Stephens papers are at Duke University and Emory University. The Emory collection is of considerable value. Selections from this collection were published by Ulrich B. Phillips.

The Cobb family papers (about 50,000 items) at the University of Georgia contain several Brown letters and much material relating to him, mostly hostile. Phillips also published selections from these papers. Other valuable manuscript collections at the University of Georgia are the papers of Rebecca Latimer Felton and Henry P. Farrow and the Keith Read and Telamon Cuyler collections.

A few, in some cases very important, items are found in the following depositories:

Atlanta Historical Society: Papers of Benjamin F. Conley.

Duke University: Papers of John E. Bryant, Herschel V. Johnson, Edward Harden, Oze R. Broyles, Francis W. Pickens, and Iverson L. Harris.

Emory University: Papers of L. N. Trammell.

Georgia State Archives: Papers of Charles J. Jenkins, Herschel V. Johnson, Iverson L. Harris, Dawson A. Walker, Amos T. Akerman, Josiah R. Parrott, Joshua Hill, Rufus B. Bullock, and Alfred H. Colquitt.

Major General Meade's Report on the Ashburn Murder. Atlanta, 1868.

Majority and Minority Report of the Joint Committee Appointed to Investigate the Fairness or Unfairness of the Contract Known as the Lease of the Western & Atlantic Railroad. Atlanta, 1872.

Phillips, Ulrich B., ed. *Correspondence of Robert Toombs, Alexander H. Stephens, and Howell Cobb.* American Historical Association *Annual Report* for 1911. Vol. II. Washington, 1913.

Remarks and Statements on the Condition of the Western & Atlantic Before the Finance Committee of the House of Representatives, September 23, 1870. N.p.; n.d.

Report of the Joint Committee to Investigate the Condition of the Western & Atlantic Railroad, Submitted to the Two Houses of the General Assembly, Thursday, February 25, 1869. N.p.; n.d.

Report of the Joint Committee of the General Assembly of Georgia Appointed to Investigate the Lease of the Western & Atlantic Railroad, 1880–81. Atlanta, 1881.

Report of the Committee Appointed Under Resolution of the Convention, on the Financial Operations of the State of Georgia During the War. Milledgeville, 1866.

Report of Major General Meade's Military Operations and Administration of Civil Affairs in the Third Military District and Dep't of the South for the Year 1868, with Accompanying Documents. Atlanta, 1868.

Secession Convention. *Journal of the Public and Secret Proceedings of the Convention of the People of Georgia Held in Milledgeville and Savannah, in 1861. Together with the Ordinances Adopted.* Milledgeville, 1861.

Testimony [of Joint Committee to Investigate the Western and Atlantic Railroad]. [Atlanta, 1872]. Bound without title page.

Testimony Taken by the Joint Select Committee to Inquire into the Condition of Affairs in the Late Insurrectionary States, 13 vols. Washington, 1872, VI, VII.

United States Statutes at Large.

War of the Rebellion: A Compilation of the Official Records of the Union and Confederate Armies, 130 vols. Washington, D.C.: 1880–1901.

NEWSPAPERS

Long runs: Athens *Southern Banner*
            Atlanta *Daily Constitution*
            Daily Herald
            Daily Intelligencer
            Daily New Era
            Daily Sun

Journal
Southern Confederacy
Augusta *Chronicle and Sentinel*
Daily Constitutionalist
Macon *Journal and Messenger*
Telegraph
Milledgeville *Federal Union*
Southern Recorder
Savannah *Daily Morning News*
Republican

Short runs and scattered issues:

Albany *News*
Athens *Georgian*
Atlanta *Daily Examiner*
Augusta *Daily Press*
Evening Dispatch
Carrollton *Southern Democrat*
Cassville *Standard*
Cincinnati (Ohio) *Commercial*
Columbus *Sun*
Times
Covington *Star*
Gainesville *Advertiser*
Eagle
Griffin *Empire State*
Semi-Weekly Star
Macon (Ga.) *Citizen*
Madison *Madisonian*
News
Marietta *Advocate*
Monroe *Advertiser*
New York *Daily Tribune*
Herald
Sun
World
Pendleton (S.C.) *Messenger*
Quitman *Reporter*
Rome *Courier*
Even News
Savannah *Record*
Thomasville *Times*

MEMOIRS, REMINISCENCES, DIARIES, AND CONTEMPORARY WRITINGS

Andrews, Eliza Frances. *The War-time Diary of a Georgia Girl, 1864–65.* New York, 1908.

Andrews, Sidney. *The South Since the War: As Shown by Fourteen Weeks of Travel and Observation in Georgia and the Carolinas.* Boston, 1866.

Avary, Myrta Lockett, ed. *Recollections of Alexander H. Stephens: His Diary when a Prisoner at Fort Warren, Boston Harbour, 1865.* New York, 1910.

Davis, Jefferson. *The Rise and Fall of the Confederate Government,* 2 vols. New York, 1881.

Felton, Mrs. William H. *My Memoirs of Georgia Politics.* Atlanta, 1811.

Jones, John B. *A Rebel War Clerk's Diary.* 2 vols. New York, 1866.

Richardson, James D., ed. *A Compilation of the Messages and Papers of the Presidents.* 20 vols. (New York, 1897).

Sherman, William T. *Memoirs of William T. Sherman.* 2 vols. New York, 1875.

Stephens, Alexander H. *A Constitutional View of the Late War Between the States.* 2 vols. Philadelphia, 1868, 1870.

Wilson, James H. *Under the Old Flag.* 2 vols. New York, 1912.

PAMPHLETS

Address of Senator Joseph E. Brown Before the Joint Committee of the Georgia Legislature on Internal Improvements and Railroads, August 13, 1881. Atlanta, 1881.

Address of Rufus B. Bullock to the People of Georgia. N.p.; n.d.

Argument of Joseph E. Brown Before the Joint Committee of the Georgia Legislature on the Lease of the Western & Atlantic R.R. and the Sufficiency of the Bond Given by Said Company. Atlanta, 1881.

Argument of Joseph E. Brown, President Western & Atlantic Railroad on the Question: 1st, Who are the Lessees of Said Road? 2d, Does the Law Require that a Majority of the Lessees or Shareholders Continue to Reside in the State of Georgia? 3, Has There Been Discrimination? Atlanta, 1881.

Argument of Ex-Gov. Joseph E. Brown on the Unconstitutionality of the Test Oath as Applied to Attorneys-at-Law in the United States District Court, on the Motion of Hon. William Law, Who Applied to be Permitted to Resume His Practice in the Court Without Taking the Oath. Savannah, 1866.

By-Laws of the Western & Atlantic Railroad Together with Copies of the Charter and Lease. Atlanta, 1881.

Comments on Governor Joseph E. Brown's Gift to the University of Georgia. Atlanta, 1883.

Governor Brown and the Columbus Prisoners. N.p.; n.d.

Letter from Joseph E. Brown on the Subject of the Settlement Between the State and the Lessees on the Question of Betterments, Taxes, etc., Discussed, Arbitration Proposed. Atlanta, 1887.

Letter from Joseph E. Brown, President of the Western & Atlantic R.R. Co., to the General Assembly on the Subject of the Settlement Between the State and Lessees. Atlanta, 1888.

Letter from Hon. Jos. E. Brown to Gov. John B. Gordon, in Reference to the State Road, in Which the Rights and Liabilities of the Lessee and the Question of Betterments are Discussed. Atlanta, 1887.

Letter to Hon. Charles Sumner, of the United States Senate, Exposing the Bullock-Blodgett Ring in Their Attempt to Defeat the Bingham Amendment. Washington, 1870.

Letter from Rufus B. Bullock, of Georgia, to the Republican Senators and Representatives in Congress Who Sustain the Reconstruction Acts. Washington, 1870.

Opinion of Honorable John Erskine, United States District Judge, for the District of Georgia. In Ex parte William Law, Decided May Term, 1866. Savannah, 1866.

Proceedings of the Conservative Convention Held in Macon, Georgia, 5 December, 1867. Macon, 1868.

Radical Rule: Military Outrage in Georgia. Arrest of the Columbus Prisoners: With Facts Connected with Their Imprisonment and Release. Louisville, 1868.

Speech of Ex-Governor Brown of Georgia, Delivered in the National Republican Convention at Chicago, May 20, 1868.

Statement of Facts Connected with the Compromise Between the State and the Heirs of Samuel Mitchell, for the Park Property in Atlanta. By Joseph E. Brown. Atlanta, 1872.

Most of Brown's Senate speeches were published in pamphlet form. A bound volume of these speeches is in the rare book collection of the University of Georgia.

ARTICLES IN PERIODICALS

Bass, James H. "Civil War Finance in Georgia," *Georgia Historical Quarterly*, XXVI.

———. "The Georgia Gubernatorial Elections of 1861 and 1863." *Georgia Historical Quarterly*, XVII.

Black, Robert C. "The Railroads of Georgia in the Confederate War Effort," *Journal of Southern History*, XIII.

Bryan, T. Conn. "The Secession Movement in Georgia." *Georgia Historical Quarterly*, XXXI.

Coddington, Edwin B. "The Activities of a Confederate Business Man: Gazaway B. Lamar." *Journal of Southern History*, IX.

Johnson, Herschel V. "From the Autobiography of Herschel V. Johnson, 1856–1867." *American Historical Review*, XXX.

McGuire, Peter S. "The Railroads of Georgia, 1860–1880." *Georgia Historical Quarterly*, XVI.

Mitchell, Eugene Muse. "H. I. Kimball: His Career and Defense." *Atlanta Historical Bulletin*, III.

Phillips, Ulrich B. "An American State-Owned Railroad." *Yale Review*, XV.

Rabun, J. Z. "Alexander H. Stephens and Jefferson Davis." *American Historical Review*, LVIII.

Range, Willard. "Hannibal I. Kimball." *Georgia Historical Quarterly*, XXIX.

Russ, William A., Jr. "Radical Disfranchisement in Georgia, 1867–1871." *Georgia Historical Quarterly*, XIX.

Scroggs, Jack B. "Southern Reconstruction: A Radical View." *Journal of Southern History*, XXIV.

Shadgett, Olive Hall. "James Johnson, Provisional Governor." *Georgia Historical Quarterly*, XXXVI.

Stover, John F. "Northern Financial Interests in Southern Railroads, 1865–1900." *Georgia Historical Quarterly*, XXXIX.

Talmadge, John E. "Peace-Movement Activities in Civil War Georgia." *Georgia Review*, VII.

Tankersly, Allen P. "Basil Hallman Overby, Champion of Prohibition in Ante-Bellum Georgia." *Georgia Historical Quarterly*, XXXI.

Taylor, Elizabeth. "Origins of the Convict Lease System in Georgia." *Georgia Historical Quarterly*, XXVI.

———. "The Abolition of the Convict Lease System." *Georgia Historical Quarterly*, XXVI.

Thompson, C. Mildred. "The Freedmen's Bureau in Georgia in 1865–66." *Georgia Historical Quarterly*, V.

Ward, Judson C., Jr. "The New Departure Democrats of Georgia: An Interpretation." *Georgia Historical Quarterly*, XLI.

Wooster, Ralph A. "The Georgia Secession Convention." *Georgia Historical Quarterly*, XL.

———. "Notes on the Georgia Legislature of 1860." *Georgia Historical Quarterly*. XLV.

UNPUBLISHED DISSERTATIONS AND THESES

Bloom, Charles G. "The Georgia Election of April, 1868: A Re-examination of the Politics of Reconstruction." M.A., University of Chicago, 1963.

Coleman, Kenneth. "The Administration of Alfred H. Colquitt as Governor of Georgia." M.A., University of Georgia, 1940.

Cooper, Fleeta. "The Triumvirate of Colquitt, Gordon, and Brown." M.A., Emory University, 1931.

Freeman, Henri H. "Some Aspects of Debtor Relief in Georgia During Reconstruction." M.A., Emory University, 1951.

McDaniel, Ruth Douglas Currie. "Georgia Carpetbagger: John Emory Bryant." Ph.D., Duke University, 1973.

McCash, William B. "Thomas R. R. Cobb: A Biography." Ph.D., University of Georgia, 1968.

Mathis, Robert Neil. "Gazaway Bugg Lamar: A Southern Entrepreneur." Ph.D., University of Georgia, 1968.

Simpson, John Eddins. "A Biography of Howell Cobb, 1815–1861." Ph.D., University of Georgia, 1971.

Smith, Wallace Calvin. "Rufus Bullock and the Third Reconstruction of Georgia." M.A., University of North Carolina, 1964.

Ward, Judson C. "Georgia Under the Bourbon Democrats, 1872–1890." Ph.D., University of North Carolina, 1947.

BIOGRAPHIES

Cleveland, Henry. *Alexander H. Stephens*. Atlanta, 1866.

Coulter, E. Merton. *William Montague Browne, Versatile Anglo-Irish American, 1823–1883*. Athens, 1967.

———. *Negro Legislators in Georgia During the Reconstruction Period*. Athens, 1968.

Flippin, Percy Scott. *Herschel V. Johnson of Georgia: State Rights Unionist*. Richmond, 1931.

Hamilton, Holman. *Zachary Taylor: Soldier in the White House*. Indianapolis, 1951.

Hill, Benjamin H., Jr. *Senator Benjamin H. Hill of Georgia: His Life Speeches and Writings*. Atlanta, 1891.

Johannson, Robert W. *Stephen A. Douglas*. New York, 1973.

Johnson, Richard M., and William M. Browne. *Life of Alexander H. Stephens*. Philadelphia, 1878.

Klein, Philip S. *President James Buchanan*. University Park, Pa., 1962.

McKitrick, Eric L. *Andrew Johnson and Reconstruction*. Chicago, 1960.

Montgomery, Horace. *Howell Cobb's Confederate Career*. Tuscaloosa, 1959.

Nixon, Raymond B. *Henry W. Grady: Spokesman of the New South.* New York, 1943.

Northen, William J. *Men of Mark in Georgia.* 6 vols. Atlanta, 1907–1912.

Pearce, Haywood J., Jr. *Benjamin H. Hill: Secession and Reconstruction.* Chicago, 1928.

Phillips, Ulrich B. *The Life of Robert Toombs.* New York, 1913.

Rowland, Dunbar, ed. *Jefferson Davis Constitutionalist: His Letters, Papers, and Speeches.* 10 vols. Jackson, Miss., 1923.

Smith, William E. *The Francis Preston Blair Family in Politics.* New York, 1933.

Steele, Edward M., Jr. *T. Butler King of Georgia.* Athens, 1964.

Stovall, Pleasant A. *Robert Toombs: Statesman, Speaker, Soldier, Sage.* New York, 1892.

Talmadge, John E. *Rebecca Latimer Felton: Nine Stormy Decades.* Athens, 1960.

Tankersly, Allen P. *John B. Gordon: A Study in Gallantry.* Atlanta, 1955.

Thompson, William Y. *Robert Toombs of Georgia.* Baton Rouge, 1966.

Von Abele, Rudolph. *Alexander H. Stephens: A Biography.* New York, 1946.

Waddell, James D. *Biographical Sketch of Linton Stephens.* Atlanta, 1877.

GEORGIA MONOGRAPHS AND HISTORY

Arnett, Alex Mathews. *The Populist Movement in Georgia.* New York, 1922.

Avery, Isaac W. *The History of the State of Georgia from 1850 to 1881.* New York, 1881.

Bell, Earl, and Kenneth Crabbe. *The Augusta Chronicle, Indomitable Voice of Dixie.* Athens, 1960.

Bryan, T. Conn. *Confederate Georgia.* Athens, 1953.

Conway, Alan. *The Reconstruction of Georgia.* Minneapolis, 1966.

Corley, Florence Fleming. *Confederate City, Augusta, Georgia, 1860–1865.* Columbia, S.C., 1960.

Garrett, Franklin M. *Atlanta and Environs: A Chronicle of Its People and Events.* New York, 1954.

Griffith, Louis F., and John E. Talmadge. *Georgia Journalism.* Athens, 1951.

Johnston, James Houston. *The Western and Atlantic Railroad of the State of Georgia.* Atlanta, 1931.

Knight, Lucian Lamar. *A Standard History of Georgia.* New York, 1917.

Marlin, Lloyd G. *The History of Cherokee County.* Atlanta, 1932.

Montgomery, Horace. *Cracker Parties.* Baton Rouge, 1950.

Nathans, Elizabeth Studley. *Losing the Peace: Georgia Republicans and Reconstruction, 1865–1871.* Baton Rouge, 1968.

Phillips, Ulrich B. *Georgia and State Rights.* American Historical Association *Annual Report* for 1901, II. Washington, 1902.

Shadgett, Olive Hall. *The Republican Party in Georgia from Reconstruction Through 1900.* Athens, 1964.

Thompson, C. Mildred. *Reconstruction in Georgia.* New York, 1915.

Wooley, Edwin C. *The Reconstruction of Georgia.* New York, 1901.

OTHER MONOGRAPHS AND GENERAL HISTORY

Black, Robert C., III. *The Railroads of the Confederacy.* Chapel Hill, 1952.

Chandler, Julian A. C., et al., eds. *The South in the Building of the Nation.* Richmond, 1909–1913.

Coulter, E. Merton. *The Confederate States of America, 1861–1865.* Baton Rouge, 1950.

———. *The South During Reconstruction, 1865–1877.* Baton Rouge, 1947.

Craven, Avery O. *The Growth of Southern Nationalism, 1848–1861.* Baton Rouge, 1953.

Davis, William W. *The Civil War and Reconstruction in Florida.* Facsimile of 1913 edition; Gainesville, 1964.

Dorris, Johnathan T. *Pardon and Amnesty under Lincoln and Johnson.* Chapel Hill, 1953.

Kirkland, Edward C. *The Peacemakers of 1864.* New York, 1927.

Klein, Maury. *The History of the Louisville & Nashville Railroad.* New York, 1972.

Lonn, Ella. *Salt as a Factor in the Confederacy.* New York, 1933.

———. *Desertion During the Civil War.* New York, 1928.

Milton, George Fort. *Eve of Conflict: Stephen A. Douglas and the Needless War.* Boston, 1934.

Moore, Albert B. *Conscription and Conflict in the Confederacy.* New York, 1924.

Nevins, Allen. *The War for the Union.* 4 vols. New York, 1959–1971.

Nichols, Roy F. *The Disruption of American Democracy.* New York, 1948.

Overdyke, W. Darrell. *The Know-Nothing Party in the South.* Baton Rouge, 1950.

Owsley, Frank L. *State Rights in the Confederacy.* Chicago, 1931.

Phillips, Ulrich B. *A History of Transportation in the Eastern Cotton Belt.* New York, 1908.

Prince, Richard E. *The Nashville, Chattanooga and Saint Louis Railway.* Green River, Wyo., 1967.

Robinson, William M., Jr. *Justice in Grey: A History of the Judicial System of the Confederate States of America.* Cambridge, 1941.

Sefton, James E. *The United States Army and Reconstruction, 1865–1877.* Baton Rouge, 1967.

Stover, John F. *The Railroads of the South, 1865–1900: A Study in Finance and Control.* Chapel Hill, 1955.

Tatum, Georgia Lee. *Disloyalty in the Confederacy.* Chapel Hill, 1934.

Todd, Richard C. *Confederate Finance.* Athens, 1954.

Turner, George E. *Victory Rode the Rails.* Indianapolis, 1953.

Woodward, C. Vann. *Reunion and Reaction: The Compromise of 1877 and the End of Reconstruction.* Boston, 1951.

———. *Origins of the New South, 1877–1913.* Baton Rouge, 1951.

Index

Abrams, Alexander St. Clair, 478
Adair, G. W., 474
Adams, F. W., 185
Adjuster, 131, 132
Advertiser (Monroe), 519
Advertiser (Gainesville), 484–85
Advocate (Marietta), 89
Akerman, Amos T., 444; and debtor
 relief, 401–402; in 1868 campaign,
 415; and election laws, 445, 446, 447
Akin, Warren, 107, 175; and 1859
 election, 87, 88, 89
Alabama secession, 127
Alabama and Florida Railroad, 67
Albany and Gulf Railroad, 357
Alexander, P. W. "Pete," 565
Alston, Robert A.: and Atlanta *Herald*,
 478–79, and controversy with
 Brown, 494
American (Atlanta), 88
Anderson, A., 516
Anderson, G. T., 281
Andrews, Garnett, 14
Angier, Nedom L., 44
Anthony, D. C., 357
Anthony, Susan B., 570
Argus (Bainbridge), 31
Arthur, Chester A., 544
Ashburn, George W., 378; murder case
 of, 412, 413, 415–17
Atkins, Joseph, 439
Atlanta: threatened with martial law,
 210; destruction of, 294, 310

Atlanta and West Point Railroad, 67
Atlanta Hotel, 18
Atwater, E. D., 472n
Augusta, 186
Augusta Arsenal, 129–30, 381
"Augusta Ring," 400, 407
Augur, General Christopher C., 329
Avery, Isaac W., 370, 406, 441; and
 1863 election, 238; on Hill's new
 position, 448; observations on
 Colquitt-Gordon-Brown "deal," 513

Baker, Alfred, 355, 356, 400n
Baldwin County: in 1859 election, 88;
 in 1867 election, 393
Baltimore and Ohio Railroad, 451, 500
Baltimore Convention (1860), 105
Banks and banking (Georgia), 43, 45,
 46–49, 51, 69, 92, 122, 226, 356, 400
Banner (Newnan), 51
Bard, Samuel, 388, 413, 446, 459, 479
Bartow, Francis S., 342: addresses
 Atlanta meeting, 119; tenders troops
 to Davis, 147; controversy with
 Brown, 147; killed at Manassas, 148
Bateman, John, Neal, and Ellen
 (freedmen), 358
Bayard, William, 330
Beauregard, P. G. T., 192, 194, 321,
 322
Beck, James B., 569
Beckley, L. E., 472, 472n
Bedford County (Tenn.), 2

Bell, John, 106, 109, 342
Bell, William, 16
Benjamin, Judah P.: as secretary of war, 166, 169, 182, 193; orders Georgia troops to Virginia, 167; and coastal defense, 167; opposes scattering troops, 168
Bigham, B. H., 571
Billups, John, 211
Black, John, 52
Black, J. C. C., 525
Blade (Newnan): on bank bill and veto, 51; attacks *Constitutionalist*, 61
Blair, Francis P., Jr., 426
Bland-Allison Act, 551
Blodgett, Foster, 400, 404, 415, 442, 430; and Senate seat, 422, 423, 443: is defeated for mayor, 431; and Western and Atlantic, 449–57 *passim*, 499; seeks job as lobbyist, 497–99
Bonds (Georgia): endorsement of investigated, 463; are repudiated, 480–81
Boyd, W. W., 168
Boynton, Henry, 365
Bradley, Aaron Alpeoria, 393
Bragg, Braxton, 142, 217, 241, 244, 247, 248, 250, 259; at Chattanooga, 208, 246; invades Kentucky, 211; threatens martial law, 219; at Murfreesboro, 230
Breckinridge, John C., 105, 106, 109
Brewster, Patrick H., 15n, 88
Broadhead, James, 426
Brown, Aaron T., 142
Brown, Aaron V., 56, 57
Brown, Anna Broyles, 2
Brown, B. Gratz, 475, 476
Brown, Charles McDonald, 13, 558–60
Brown, Elijah, 485
Brown, Elizabeth Grisham (Mrs. Joseph E.): marriage of, 4–5; on status of women, 11; characteristics of, 11; secret wishes of, 11–12; on Know-Nothings, 14; and family matters, 15; and slaves, 16n; visits Milledgeville, 18; diary of, 55; reports on Mansion party, 73, 75–76; reports on governor's health, 84; records conditions at Mansion, 312; destroys personal papers, 330; re-

ports on situation at Milledgeville, 333
Brown, Franklin Pierce, 12, 378, 415, 423, 576
Brown, Hugh, 2
Brown, James, 3, 15, 101
Brown, Jemima Broyles (grandmother), 2
Brown, John Young, 492, 493
Brown, Joseph (great-grandfather), 1, 2
Brown, Joseph, Jr. (grandfather), 1, 2, 2n
Brown, Joseph Emerson: birth of, 2; attends school in South Carolina, 3; teaches at "old field" school, 3; admitted to Georgia bar, 3; studies law at Yale, 4; begins practice of law, 4; marries Elizabeth Grisham, 4–5; establishes home in Canton, 5; acquires property, 5, 6, 16, 259; elected to state senate, 6; supports slavery resolutions, 8; debates with Miller, 9; offers King resolution, 9–10; and women's rights, 10–11, 570–71; and 1853 election, 13; as attorney for state, 15; and treatment of slaves, 16n; speculates in copper, 16; as judge of Blue Ridge circuit, 17–19; is nominated for governor, 22–24, 25; and 1857 campaign, 25 ff.; is elected governor, 39; personal characteristics of, 40, 278, 385; takes oath as governor, 42; and life at Mansion, 42, 73; and Western and Atlantic Railroad, 44–58 *passim*, 67–68, 71–72, 74, 91, 449, 450 ff., 465, 466; and public education, 44, 72; and banks, 45, 47–49, 69, 70–71, 92, 122, 174; and patronage, 53, 54, 55; relations with Dr. John Lewis, 3, 55, 164; views on pardoning power, 51, 52; and relations with John H. Lumpkin, 63–65; and views on Kansas question, 66, 67; delivers annual message, 70 ff.; opposes change in divorce law, 73; vetoes local bills, 73; and reelection (1859), 75, 76–81, 83–89; and the press, 76, 283–84, 385–86, 465, 478, 479; and Alexander Stephens, 79, 101; and offensive-defensive alliance,

79; loses his dog, 88, 89; second inauguration and annual message, 90–92; proposes reduction in size of legislature, 91; defends use of veto power, 91; proposes military reorganization, 92; and Choice case, 93–94; and Charleston convention (1860), 97, 101, 102–103, 104; and Baltimore and Richmond conventions, 103; on disruption of Democratic party, 106; health of, 106, 491–92, 566–67; endorses Breckinridge, 107; and private business of, 107, 357–59; advises governor of South Carolina, 108; delivers annual message (1860), 110–11; delivers special message, 111–13; views on secession crisis, 114–17; and upcountry Georgia, 116, 134–35; urges South Carolina to secede, 118; advises Governor Pickens, 119–20; is authorized to raise Georgia troops, 123; denounces Georgia house of representatives, 123; lists Georgia arms, 124n; orders seizure of Fort Pulaski, 125; urges Gulf states and North Carolina to seize forts, 125; proposes seizure of works at Pensacola, 126; replies to Kentucky slavery proposal, 127; at secession convention, 127; demands surrender of Augusta Arsenal, 129–30; and Georgia arms, 130–32, 143, 144, 152; purchases arms, 134; seizure of Dahlonega Mint, 135; begins controversy with Confederacy, 136, 137; recruits volunteer companies, 137; addresses troops at Macon muster, 138–39; congratulates Virginia on secession, 139; argues with Secretary of War Walker over organization of troops, 140, 141; loses argument on generals and surgeons, 141–42; and coastal defense, 142, 143, 182–84; relations with President Davis, 144, 148, 153, 218, 290–92, 320; and raising troops, 145, 146; denounces and forbids removal of arms from Georgia, 147–48; urges nonpayment of northern debts, 149; calls for donation of money and supplies,

150–51; requests Confederate commissions for Georgians, 151–52, 153, 154; refuses to disband Phillips brigade, 154; offers thanks for Manassas, 155; appeals for soldier supplies, 156; and 1861 election, 156–59, 161–63; praises Wilson Lumpkin, 163–64; and coastal defense, 165–66; protests transfer of troops, 167; reorganizes state troops, 167–68; requests guns, 168; urges return of Georgia troops, 168, 169; inaugurated for third term as governor, 170; delivers annual message, 171–75; traces decline of states' rights in Union, 171–72; fears Confederate militarism, 172; favors treasury notes over bonds, 173; proposes tax increase, 173; urges fight against speculation, 174; on state and Confederate impressments, 174, 256, 258; vetoes salary increases, 175; proposes state collection of Confederate tax, 175; opposes transfer of troops to Confederacy, 176, 177; his language criticized, 179; and sale of bonds, 180; and Georgia pledge to support Confederacy, 181, 182; attempts to provide salt, 182, 191, 211–12, 224, 231; calls for day of fasting and prayer, 186; orders manufacture of pikes, 186–87; on production of clothing and provisions, 187–89, 232; attempts to regulate distilleries, 188, 189, 190, 191, 214, 234, 256–57, 261, 267–68; comments on Union tax burden, 188; tenders more regiments, 192; calls for more volunteers, 194–95; more controversy on election of officers, 195, 196, 258; and controversy over Confederate conscription, 196–passim, 221, 223–24, 264, 269, 284–89; urges offensive in Tennessee and Kentucky, 207–208; opposes martial law, 210; and Senate seat, 211, 422, 423–24; and deserters, 212, 229; reports on state finances, 214; reports on arms, 214; proposes increases in salaries and soldiers' pay, 214–15, 235; requests authority to seize

supplies, 215; proposes restrictions
on cotton production, 216, 234,
255, 267; urges state conscription
for local defense, 216; delivers
message on war and Confederate
relations, 217–19; and habeas corpus,
219, 266, 269–70; reports on activities of Federal Negro soldiers,
220–21; seeks Confederate commissions for friends, 228–29; opposes
state endorsement of Confederate
bonds, 234–35; and 1863 election,
236–37, 238, 239, 240, 241, 252;
favors Linton Stephens for governor,
237; suggests Robert Toombs for
governor, 237, 238; urges volunteering for local defense, 243–44; and
controversy with consul Fullarton,
245–46; more controversy over appointment of officers, 248, 250;
opposes reconstruction of Union,
249, 254; inaugurated for fourth
term as governor (1863), 253; delivers annual address, 253–56; on
relief measures, 255; on hiring substitutes, 255; opposes "tax in kind,"
257; removes personal property
from Canton, 259, 265; favors
Toombs for Senate, 259; and Home
Guard, 262; and "peace movement,"
265–66, 269, 271–72, 273–74, 278–
79, 280, 281; and war finance, 268;
and disloyalty, 268; and emancipation, 271; and Confederate office,
277–78; personal finances of, 281–
82, 288; controversy with Cobb over
conscription, 286–89; orders up all
able-bodied men, 290, 292; family
flees Milledgeville, 293–94; Canton
home burned, 293; promises cooperation to General Hood, 293; orders
removal of public property from
Milledgeville, 293n–94n; places
militia under Confederate command,
294; withdraws and militia furloughs, 294–95; and Sherman's
peace overtures, 295–99; favors
Josh Hill for legislature, 299; controversy over militia, 301–306; and
militia under Beauregard, 305, 321;
denounces Confederate tyranny,
306; urges convention of states, 307;
frees penitentiary inmates, 310;

flees Milledgeville, 311; attempts to
raise more state troops, 312; moves
headquarters to Macon, 312; orders
return of stolen state property, 312;
orders levy en masse, 312, 313;
receives advice from Governor
Vance, 317; blames Confederacy
for Georgia plight, 317–18, 319;
gives views on arming slaves, 318;
proposes revision of penal laws, 318;
urges abolition of conscription, 320;
favors revision of Confederate currency laws, 320; urges limit on Confederate impressments, 320; popular
image of, 322–23; and General
Wilson, 324–28; issues call for
session of Assembly, 325; arrest
and imprisonment of, 329–33; issues
farewell message to people, 334–
35; and President Johnson, 335–37,
338, 339, 347; confers with General
Steedman, 339; receives pardon,
339–40; and Wirtz trial, 340; relations with General Croxton, 341;
and constitutional convention
(1865), 342; and election of governor, 343, 344; gives views on
Toombs, 345–46; moves to Atlanta,
345; and Hill pardon case, 346; and
freedmen, 347–48, 358; and U.S.
senatorship, 348–49; business and
finances of, 350, 351–52, 353, 477–
78, 505, 506, 574; reports on Georgia
war finances, 351; reports on Federal destruction at Milledgeville,
353; as bank attorney, 355, 400;
views on repudiation of private
debts, 356; relations with Judge
Erskine, 359, 363–64; and William
Law case, 360–61; as informer for
Treasury Department, 364, 375; and
acceptance of congressional reconstruction, 367–70, 371–72, 378–
80, 382–85; and relations with
General Pope, 378, 399–400, 413–
14; and Ben Hill, 386–87, 390, 392;
corresponds with William Kelley,
387–88; advises Henry M. Turner,
389–90; and 1867 convention, 393,
394, 395–99; and debtor relief, 401–
403, 421–22; views of suffrage, 401;
and 1868 election, 406–13, *passim*;
and Ashburn murder case, 412,

413, 415–17; at National Republican convention, 418–20; and Rufus Bullock, 420, 433, 465, 496, 500–503; denounced at "Bush Arbor" meeting, 422; congratulated by John Erskine, 424; appointed to state supreme court, 424; and 1868 presidential election, 425–28; and Martin charge, 428–30; seeks Grant's political assistance, 430, 431, 437–38; views on status of Republican party, 431–33; on conditions in Georgia, 435; as judge in *White* v *Clements*, 437; encounter with students, 439; and test oath provisions, 441; reports on corruption rumors, 442; and Akerman Act, 445, 446, 447; resigns judgeship, 454; and Seago group, 458; replies to "ring" charge, 460; and party reorganization, 461; supports Smith for governor, 462; and "illegal bonds" question, 463; is urged to return to Democratic party, 463; and "duel" with Toombs, 467–70; and Mitchell heirs case, 467, 470, 472, 473, 474; and 1872 presidential election, 475, 476, 477; views on Negro rights, 481–83; travels west for health, 485; and 1876 presidential election, 485–91; supports Hill for Senate, 491; attacks Hayes "bargain", 492–95; clashes with Bob Alston, 494; and Texas and Pacific Railroad, 498–99; visits Hot Springs, 502, 503; and 1877 constitutional convention, 503–504; at Hayes banquet, 504–505; and use of convict labor, 506, 575; and alleged railroad agreement, 508; and appointment to Senate, 509 ff.; seeks "pork barrel" legislation for Georgia, 520; and pension bill, 521–23; defends own Civil War activities, 521–23; and 1880 election, 523–25; speaks at De Gives Opera House, 526–30; and election to Senate (1880), 525–31; at investigation of Western and Atlantic Company, 531–32; favors public education, 534–36; spends Christmas in Washington, 536–37; speaks on Indian affairs, 538–40; replies to Mahone, 540–41; on "free ballot and fair count," 541–43; defends self and South, 541–44; remarks on Negro question, 543; speaks on civil service reform, 545–47; opposes Chinese exclusion bill, 548–49; disapproves of Morman suffrage bill, 549–51; views on monetary policy, 552–54, 569–70; gives views on tariff, 554–57, 569–70; opposes internal revenue system, 555, 556, 559; remarks on Washington social life, 557; makes gift to University of Georgia, 558–60; and control of Western and Atlantic Company, 560–61; turns sour on railroad investments, 563–64; reelected to Senate, 564–66; and development of Colorado City, Tex., 564; and railroad regulations, 567–68; and 1888 Cleveland campaign, 571–73; and McKinley's Georgia visit, 573; prepares last will, 574; and Atlanta real estate, 574; death of, 576; tributes to, 576; career of evaluated, 576–78

Brown, Joseph Mackey, 12; and Western and Atlantic Company, 561; plan for development of Marietta, 562–63

Brown, Julius, 11, 108, 330, 333, 359, 503; railroad interests of, 561; and Western and Atlantic Company, 561

Brown, Mackey (father), 2, *2n*

Brown, Margaret Fleming (great-great-grandmother), 1

Brown, Mary Porter (great-grandmother), 1

Brown, Mary Virginia, 11

Brown, Sally Rice (mother), 2

Brown, William (great-great-grandfather), 1

Brown, William Carroll, 15

Brown-Bullock "ring," 460

Brown Hotel (Macon), 324

Browne, William M., 293; as Davis agent, 227–28; and opinion of Brown, 558

Brownlow, William G. "Parson," 375

Broyles, Aaron, 3

Broyles, Adam, 2

Broyles, O. R., 3

Brunswick and Florida Railroad, 357

Bryant, John E., 400, 401, 441, 442,
    444–45, 461
Buchanan, James, 20–36 passim, 57,
    63, 64, 65, 67, 81, 87, 96, 102, 113,
    119, 120
Buckner, Simon B., 247, 248
Buell, Don Carlos, 192, 207, 208
Bullock, Rufus, 530, 541, 544;
    characteristics of, 407; as governor,
    406 ff.; and lease of Western and
    Atlantic, 450–64 passim; and Bard
    loan, 459, 479, 480; resigns and
    flees state, 461; conduct of investi-
    gated, 463; and Mitchell heirs case,
    467, 471, 473; in exile, 480; and
    repudiated bonds, 480; seeks
    employment, 496, 500–503
Burlingame Treaty, 547
Burney, S. W., 96n, 98
Burton, W. H., 37
"Bush Arbor" meeting (Atlanta), 422
"Bushwhackers," 314
Butler, Benjamin, 445

Cabaniss, C. G., 222
Cabel, S. G., 190, 191
Calhoun Academy, 3
Calhoun, E. N., 82, 83
Calhoun, John C., 111
"Calico quilt", 29
Camden, N.J., 55
Cameron, Simon; and Western and
    Atlantic lease, 451, 453, 457; and
    Bullock employment, 496, 500
Camp Harrison, 178
Camp McDonald, 152, 153, 155, 166,
    167, 230
Camp Stephens, 155, 167
Campbell, D. C., 96n
Campbell, Tunis G., 393
Capers, Francis W., 168, 197, 206, 207
Carlisle, H., 259
Carroll Prison (Washington), 330
Carroll, William, 2
Cass County: selects anti-Brown
    delegates, 83; endorses Gardner for
    governor, 83; in 1859 and 1861
    elections, 88, 163
Cass, Lewis, 105
Castle Rock Coal Company, 574
Central Railroad and Banking
    Company, 458, 532, 568
Chandler, William W., 425, 487

Charleston Convention (1860), 96–102
Charleston fire, 180
Chase, Salmon P., 445
Chastain, Elijah W., 55, 134, 155,
    178, 189
Chattanooga, 71, 207
Chattanooga Iron Company, 574
"Cherokee Baptist Railroad," 59
Cherokee circuit, 59, 80
Cherokee County, 3, 6; wrangling in,
    68, 69; and 1860 convention dele-
    gates, 100, 101; Brown gives
    counsel to, 338
Cherokee Democracy, 54
Cherokee region, 27, 42, 73, 75
Chesnut, James, 247
Chinese exclusion bill, 547–49
Choice, William A., 93–94
Choice Hotel (Dahlonega), 5
Chronicle and Sentinel (Augusta), 447;
    supports Brown's reelection, 240;
    controlled by Brown, 284; comments
    of Davis, 300, is favorable to Brown,
    309; prints Hill's "Notes," 390–92;
    and Martin charge, 430; and Brown's
    resignation, 454; and Kimball House
    dinner, 455; charges Brown-Bullock
    "ring," 460
Cincinnati Platform (1856), 102, 104
Cincinnati Southern Railroad, 507,
    508, 532
Citizen (Macon), 87
City Bank (Atlanta), 478, 479
City Bank (Augusta), 355
Clark, Richard H., 23, 24
Clarke, James O., 138
Clements, Judson, 537
Cleveland, Grover, 568, 569, 571–73
Cleveland, Henry, 283, 284
Clyde, William P., 561–62
Coastal defense, 193–94
Cobb County, 6
Cobb, Howell, 6, 22, 42, 61, 62, 67, 77,
    78, 86, 133, 145, 228, 247, 248, 278,
    326, 342, 388, 406, 424; elected
    governor, 13; and 1856 election, 20;
    and Kansas controversy, 21; and
    1857 campaign, 26, 27, 28, 32, 34;
    reports to Stephens on Brown, 41;
    congratulates Brown, 40–41; on
    Western and Atlantic appointments,
    54, 56, 58; and the presidency, 60;
    interest in Lumpkin-Brown relations,

64, 65; and "offensive-defensive" alliance, 79–80; and selection of 1860 convention delegates, 94–101 *passim*; views on Charleston convention, 103–104; addresses Georgia convention, 105; supports Breckinridge, 107; visits South Carolina secession convention, 118; urges immediate secession, 120; at secession convention, 127; and coastal defense, 144; reports on Davis-Brown relations, 144; and Brown's reelection (1861), 163; with Georgia Home Guard, 248–49, 250, 251, 262, 264; confers with Davis in Georgia, 251; addresses legislature, 275–77; denounces Brown as "traitor," 281; controversy with Brown over conscription, 286–89; with state reserves, 293, 305, 310, 312; greets Davis at Macon, 299; confers with Wilson, 327–28; at "Bush Arbor" meeting, 422; and 1868 presidential campaign, 426, 427

Cobb, Mrs. Howell, 27, 138, 163, 241
Cobb, Howell, Jr., 372
Cobb, Lucy Barrow, 294n
Cobb, Thomas R. R., 67, 80; reports to Howell Cobb on Brown, 41; proposes disunion, 107; urges immediate secession, 127; appeals for arms for legion, 148
Cocke, William A., 489
Cohen, Solomon, 99, 100
Cole, E. W., 507–508, 532, 561, 575
Colfax, Schuyler, 421
Colorado City, Tex., 564
Colquitt, Alfred H., 80, 504, 572; and 1857 convention, 23, 24; as governor, 505; and Gordon-Brown "deal," 508 ff.; and 1880 election, 523, 524, 525; elected to Senate, 557
Columbus, Ky., 185
Commercial (Cincinnati), 385–86
"Condition of Affairs" in Georgia, 434–35
Confederacy (Atlanta), 78
Confederate peace commission, 139
Confederate Union (Milledgeville), 281
Conklin, Roscoe, 521
Conley, Benjamin, 400, 442, 461
Connally, E. L., 557, 574

Conscription, Confederate: proposed, 193; adopted, 195; controversy over, 198–206, 212–13, 284–85; court decisions on, 220; legislative ruling on, 226; expanded, 264; abolition urged by Brown, 320
Constitution (Atlanta), 446, 470, 487, 492, 503, 508; and Martin charge, 430; and Brown's test oath interpretation, 441; urges fair treatment of Brown, 484; on death of Brown, 576
Constitutional conventions (Georgia): (1865), 341–43; (1877), 392–93, 503, 504, 507
Constitutional Union party: (1851), 13; (1860), 106, 107
Constitutionalist (Augusta), 22, 73, 76, 283, 284, 459, 491; on Western and Atlantic management, 68; and 1859 election, 85, 88; on bank regulation, 92; and 1860 convention, 95; reports surrender of arsenal, 130; supports Brown for reelection, 240; opposes convention of states, 309; attacks Brown's position, 371
Convention of states, 320–21
Convict labor, 506, 557, 575
Cook, Phil, 572
Cooper, Mark A., 124
Cooper, Samuel, 250, 289
Cotton, 225, 232, 255, 267
Cotton cards, 282
Courier (Rome): and 1859 election, 80; and 1867 convention, 395; on purge of legislature, 442
Cowan Tunnel (Tennessee), 292
Cowart, Robert J., 16, 459
Cowgill, G. A., 489
Crawford, Martin J., 157
Crawford, Robert A., 78
Crook, L. W., 80
Croxton, John T., 340, 341, 365, 366
Cullom Commission, 568
Cumberland Gap, 207
Cumberland River, 182
Cummings, Alfred, 134
Cummings, Joe, 565
Cummings, J. F., 247, 261

Dade Coal Company, 506, 574
Dahlonega Mint, 135, 381
Davis, David, 540
Davis, Jefferson, 144, 145, 148, 151,

166, 169, 173, 192, 209, 217, 222, 230, 240, 247, 250, 258, 260, 278, 280, 296, 307, 308, 322, 323, 365, 528; declines Georgia brigade, 154; accepts Phillips' legion, 155; urges reenforcements for Beauregard, 194; and conscription, 200–205; requests further aid from governors, 227; relations with Stephens, 209; and seizure of Western and Atlantic, 231; furloughs Georgia legislators, 233; urges local defense units, 243; urges Stephens-Brown conference, 248; visits Georgia, 209, 251, 300; commended by Georgia Assembly, 283, 309; and defense of north Georgia, 290–92; and L. Stephens peace plan, 308; flight and arrest of, 323, 330

Dawes, Henry L., 543, 544
Dawes Act, 540
D. C. Hodgkins and Son, 124, 130
Debtor relief, 356, 401–402, 421–22
De Graffenried, William K., 96
Delano, Columbus, 453–61 *passim*, 497
Delano, John S., 451
Democrat (Carrolton), 37
Democratic executive committee (Georgia), 94
Democratic party: platform of (1856), 20; divisions of, 63, 102; in convention, 20–21, 22–26, 84–86, 406; victory of (1870), 448
Deserters, 212, 229, 230, 314
Devereaux Jarrett's Inn, 5
Dexter, H., 132
Dinsmore, W. B., 453, 455, 457
Distilleries, 188, 189, 190, 191, 214, 225, 234, 236, 256–57, 261, 267–68
Dobbins, Miles G., 464
Douglas, Stephens A., 63, 67, 96, 99, 102, 104, 105, 106, 109, 342, 349, 426
Dred Scott Decision, 10, 104
Duck River valley, 187
Duncan, J. W., 83
Dunwody, John, 208, 209

Early, Jubal, 301
East Tennessee and Georgia Railroad, 71
East Tennessee and Virginia Railroad, 67

East Tennessee railroads, 192
Edwards, George F., 550, 551
Elzey, Arnold, 129–30
Emancipation, 271, 543
Empire State (Griffin), 72, 76, 78
English Bill, 66, 67
Erie Railroad, 497
Erskine, Judge John, 365, 378, 420, 457; wartime activities of, 359; appointed to judgeship, 359–60; and Law case, 360–61; gives Brown political advice, 363–64; congratulates Brown on appointment, 424–25
Etawah Manufacturing and Mining Company, 110
Evening Dispatch (Augusta): 1857 election, 29; commends Brown, 133
Evening News (Rome), 490

Farley, James T., 548
Farrow, Henry P., attorney general, 238, 443, 448; rules on test oath provisions, 441
Federal Union (Milledgeville): and 1857 election, 29, 30, 35–36; on Western and Atlantic appointments, 59; on 1859 election, 76; defends governor, 81; reports on governor's health, 84; and renomination of Brown, 85; on Opposition convention, 87; on governor's levee, 89; on 1860 convention, 95; supports President Johnson, 336; could not defend Brown, 371
Felton, Rebecca Lattimer (Mrs. William H.), 524, 563; observations on Colquitt-Gordon-Brown controversy, 513, 514; denounces Brown, 537, 558
Felton, William H., 493, 537, 554, 565, 566
Fielder, Herbert, 228, 348, 406
Fields, E. M., 191
Fields, Jefferson, 62
Fifteenth Amendment, Georgia, 436, 443
First National Bank of Macon, 357
First Regiment Georgia Volunteers, 125
Fitch, Henry S., 359, 361
Florida secession, 127
Florida and Western Railroad, 520
Floyd County, 88, 163

Floyd, Henry H., 220
Floyd, John B., 124, 125
Floyd Sharpshooters, 152
Food production and transportation, 233, 247, 255, 267
Forrest, Nathan B., 242, 291, 292, 301
Fort Donelson, 185
Fort Henry, 185
Fort Pulaski, 124–25, 140, 192, 194, 207, 381, 416
Fort Sumter, 139
Foster, Charles, 492
Foster, Ira R., 75, 238; and Western and Atlantic appointments, 56, 57; represents Brown, 63, 64; and Georgia arms, 143–44; and evacuation of Milledgeville, 310–11, 353
Fourteenth Amendment, 364, 419, 420
Freedmen, 347–48
Freedmen's Bureau, 348, 359, 395
Frobel, B. W., 531
Fullarton, A., 245–46
Fulton County: convention in (1859), 82–83; in 1859 election, 88
Fulton, M. C., 239
Furlow, Timothy, 251, 252

Gaddistown, Ga., 2
Gardner, James, 30, 80, 283; and 1857 election, 22, 23, 26; attitude toward Brown, 61, 62; and 1860 election, 105; and Western and Atlantic Company, 459; and Brown-Toombs "duel," 468, 469
Gardner, Martha G. S., 459
Garfield, James A., 365, 540, 544
Gartrell, Lucius J., 76, 264; and relations with Brown, 63; and governorship, 240, 241, 558; defeated for Senate, 348, 349
Gaskill, V. A., 189
Gazette (Atlanta), 251
George, James Z., 546
Georgia secession, 128
Georgia coast: defense of, 182–83
Georgia Forester (Alapaha), 483–84
Georgia Military Institute, 72, 110, 184
Georgia Platform, 12–13, 66
Georgia Railroad, 451, 459
Georgia State Troops, 292
Georgia Telegraph (Macon): urges support of Brown, 81
Georgia upcountry: opposition in, 134;

troops from, 135; disloyalty in, 268; and 1868 election, 412–13
Georgia, University of, 72, 110, 536, 558, 560
Georgian (Clarksville), 50
Georgian (Savannah), 49
Gettysburg, battle of, 244
Golden Lead, 131
Golden Murray, 131
Gordon, George A., 237, 238
Gordon, John B., 532, 573; and 1868 election, 411, 414–15; attacked by Brown, 492–95; and Hayes "bargain," 492, 495; resignation from Senate, 508 ff.; and 1880 election, 525
Grady, Henry W.: on Hill "Notes," 392; reflections on Brown-Toombs "duel," 469; and Atlanta Herald, 478–79; reports on Brown in Florida, 487, 488; and Gordon-Brown resignation and appointment, 509, 514, 515–17; at investigation of Western and Atlantic Company, 532–33, 563; and Senate election of Brown, 564–66; death of, 573
Grant, Ulysses S., 192, 253, 323, 325, 381, 529; and Brown's arrest, 330; as candidate for president, 421; Brown seeks assistance of, 430, 431, 437–38
"Great Ratification Meeting" (Atlanta, 1868), 408
Greeley, Horace, 475, 476, 477
Greer, A. G., 57, 78
Grisham, Joseph, 4, 6
Grisham, Susan Melinda, 15
Grisham, William, 5, 118

Habeas corpus, suspension of, 219, 264, 266, 269–70, 282, 283
Hampton, Wade, 574
Hanks, J. A. R., 59
Haralson, Frank, 566
Hardee, William J.: and seizure of Fort Pulaski, 125; resigns from U.S. army, 134; appointed brigadier, 152; in Carolina, 314
Harden, Edward R., 55, 63, 134, 189
Harris, Judge Iverson, 220
Harrison, George P., 168, 197, 206, 207
Hawkins, N. S., 52
Hawley, Joseph R., 542, 545
Hayes, Rutherford B.: and election of

1876, pp. 486, 489; Brown's views on, 495, 496; visits Atlanta, 504
Henry County Weekly, 565
Herald (Atlanta), 478–79, 487
Herald (New York), 394, 487
Hewitt, Abrams S., 486
Hill, Benjamin H., 86, 114, 242, 388, 424, 432, 449, 463–64, 493, 544, 576; and campaign of 1857, 30 ff.; and Choice case, 93; supports Bell, 107; opposes immediate secession, 127; is suggested for governor, 157; is elected Confederate senator, 180; and exemption of overseers, 184; in defense of Davis, 222–23; denounces Brown's views on conscription, 223; is suggested for governor, 271; and observation on Brown's speech (1863), 279; greets Davis at Macon, 299; applies for pardon, 346; denounces Brown's stand on reconstruction, 386–87; publishes "Notes on the Situation," 390–92; and election of 1868, pp. 411, 414; at "Bush Arbor" meeting, 422; and presidential campaign of 1868, pp. 426, 427; expresses new views, 448; and lease of Western and Atlantic, 451, 452, 454, 455, 457, 463–64; and Mitchell heirs case, 470; elected to Senate, 491; escorts Brown, 520; "smoking out" Mahone, 540; death of, 557
Hill, Joshua, 299, 334, 431, 433; and governorship, 251, 252; and Sherman's peace overtures, 295, 298, 299; and Senate seat, 349, 423, 424, 435, 443, 448
Hill, Thomas J. W., 82, 83
Hillyers, George, 74, 75, 156
Hindman, Thomas C., 217
Hoar, George F., 543, 545, 549
Hoffman, J. W., 574
Holt, Joseph, 121, 125, 129
Home Guard (Georgia), 262; Cobb appointed to command of, 248; Brown reports on, 250; appointment of officers in, 251; service of, 256, 259; is dismissed by Brown, 264
Hood, John B., 293, 305, 309
Hook, J. S., 222
Hooks, C. H., 460
Hopkins, John L., 470

Howard, T. C., 82
Howard, W. P., 191
Howell, Evan P.: and senatorial election of Brown, 565; proposes Grady for Senate, 573
Hull, Hope, 23
Hull, John L., 476
Hunnicut, G. W., 209

Impressment, 256, 257–58, 268
Independent Regiment of Georgia Volunteers, 138
Indian affairs, 538–40
Inman, John H., 486
Inman, S. M., 486
Intelligencer (Atlanta), 76, 159, 361; and 1857 campaign, 35; supports Brown in 1861, pp. 161, 162: supports President Johnson, 336; advises caution, 371
Internal revenue system opposed by Brown, 555, 556, 569
Interstate Commerce Commission, 568
Irwin, David, 17, 410, 411
Irwin, Isaiah T., 24, 100
Iverson, Alfred, 21, 95, 99, 157, 180

Jackson, Andrew, 54
Jackson, Henry P., 141, 151, 190, 207, 226, 248, 250; addresses convention, 105; and Augusta arsenal, 129; and arms seizure, 130, 131; exchanges Confederate for Georgia commission, 168
Jackson, James, 64, 65, 80, 180, 352, 405; relations with Brown, 62; suggested for governor, 157; and Senate seat, 224
Jackson, Jesse W., 356
Jasper (Ga.), 135
Jefferson County, 393
Jenkins, Charles J., 390, 576; at secession convention, 127; and constitutional convention (1865), 342; and governorship, 344, 345, 346; vetoes stay law, 356; removed from office, 378, 395; appeals to U.S. Supreme Court, 381; and election of 1868, p. 411
Johnson, Andrew, 328, 336, 346; shows Brown no sympathy, 328; orders Brown arrested, 329; grants Brown interview and then city parole, 330,

332; orders Brown released, 332; appoints provisional governor, 333; pardons Brown, 340; swings around the circle, 363; and reconstruction, 418, 419
Johnson, E. V., 78
Johnson, Herschel V., 21, 22, 42, 54, 68, 114, 210, 390, 576; as governor, 13, 14, 43; and Brown administration, 62; and convention of 1860, pp. 104, 105: supports Douglas, 107; calls for convention of states, 127; and Confederate Senate seat, 180, 224, 258; disapproves Stephens' position, 278–80; and constitutional convention (1865), 342; elected U.S. senator, 349; and views on reconstruction, 388–89; and National Union convention, 383
Johnson, James: as provisional governor, 333–34, 336, 337, 342, 343, 346; defeated for senator, 349
Johnson, Sebastian K., 456
Johnston, Albert Sidney, 169, 185, 192, 194
Johnston, Joseph E., 305, 322, 326, 347, 516, 528; and defense of north Georgia, 259, 260, 261, 289–90; is replaced by Hood, 293; is reappointed to command, 321; surrender of, 323
Johnston, Richard M., 277
Jones, Charles C., 145
Jones, Edward, 259
Jones, John, 134, 293n, 352, 395
Jordan, Pleasant, 3
Journal (Atlanta), 573, 576
Journal (Macon), 430
Julia, 131, 132

Kansas-Nebraska Act, 14, 20
Kansas Territory, 20, 26, 27, 31, 35, 66, 67
Kelley, William D., 365, 366, 387, 388; and southern disabilities, 403–404
Kenan, Augustus H., 238, 275, 343
Kimball, Hannibal I., 466, 470; and lease of Western and Atlantic, 451, 453, 455, 457, 464; and Bard loan, 459, 479; flees state, 467; and Mitchell heirs case, 470, 471, 472, 473, 474; relations with Alston, 479; and repudiated Georgia bonds, 480–81; relations with Blodgett, 499

Kimball House (Atlanta), 453, 455, 493
King, John P., 451, 459
King, Thomas Butler: in California, 7, 9; and mission of to Florida, 126
King, William, 296–99
Kirby Smith, Edmund, 192, 207, 211, 228
Kirby, 131
Kiser Building (Atlanta), 574
Kneeland, G. K., 329
Know-Knothing party, 14, 18, 30 ff., 36, 86
Knox, Martha J., 5
Knox, Samuel, 5
Ku Klux Klan, 412, 434, 439, 461

Lamar, A. R., 524–25
Lamar, C. A. R., 133
Lamar, Gazaway B.: and New York arms seizure, 130, 131, 133
Lamar, Henry, 22, 23
Lamar, John B., 27, 101
Lamar, L. Q. C., 275
Lanier House (Macon), 138, 325
Law, William, 180; test case of, 360–61
Lawton, Alexander R., 99, 140, 143, 167, 196, 197, 260; and New York arms seizure, 131; at Fort Pulaski, 125; as candidate for Senate, 524, 525, 526, 531
Lawton, Mrs. Alexander R., 525
Le Compton plan, 66, 67
Lee, Robert E., 169, 182, 241, 247, 265, 308, 322, 528; urges Brown to send arms, 148; surrender of, 323
Letcher, John, 142
Leverett, Wesley, 3
Lewis, Hariett, 15
Lewis, John W., 3, 6, 58, 64, 74, 75, 84, 108; as official of Western and Atlantic, 54, 55, 68, 71, 164; relations with Brown, 55; supervises salt production, 192; and Confederate Senate seat, 181, 192, 211, 224
Liberal Republican party, 475, 476
Lincoln, Abraham, 106, 108, 114, 118, 119, 121, 139, 141, 142, 217, 296, 299, 301, 307, 308; denounced by Brown, 271
Locke, J. F., 257
Lockrane, A. O.: and Brown-Toombs "duel," 467–68, 469–70; and Mitch-

ell heirs case, 467, 470, 471, 472, 472n, 473
Logan, John A., 404
Lomax, Tenant, 20
Long Creek (S.C.), 2, 4
Longstreet, J. C., 59
Loyal Georgian (Augusta), 401
Lumpkin, James, 367
Lumpkin, John H., 77, 78, 82, 163; and 1857 election, 22, 23, 25, 26, 27, 28, 41; and Western and Atlantic appointments, 54, 56; and coolness of toward Brown, 59, 60; property interests of, 60; and relations with Brown, 62, 63, 64, 65, 66; reports to Cobb, 64; and offensive defensive alliance, 78–80; death of, 163n
Lumpkin, Joseph H., 80, 364: declines Senate seat, 181; sees gloomy future, 367
Lumpkin, Wilson: favors secession, 121; supports Brown for reelection, 163

McComb, M. D., 54
McDaniel, Henry D.: as governor, 564, 565, 566
McDonald, Charles J., 15, 62, 99; and elections of 1851 and 1857, pp. 13, 26
McDonald, Henry D., 576
McGehee, E. J., 96n
McIntosh County: in election of 1867, p. 393
McKay, H. K.: in *White v Clements*, 437
McKinley, William, Baldwin County planter, 294
McKinley, William, congressman, visits Georgia, 573
McLaw, Lafayette W., 134
McLin, Samuel B., 489
McNaughton, William, 464
Macon and Augusta Railroad, 407
Macon and Western Railroad, 107, 452, 458, 467
McWhorter, Robert L., 442, 443
Madisonian (Madison), 519
Mahone, William, 540
Manassas, battle of, 130, 155, 502
Marcy, William L., 546
Marietta (Ga.), 562–63
Marietta Paper Manufacturing Company, 506

Markham House, 504
Martial law, in Atlanta, 219
Martin, James H., 428
Maulden, B. F., 4
May, Andrew J., 16
Meade, George; and Georgia Reconstruction, 395, 399–400, 402, 403, 411, 420; and Ashburn case, 412, 413, 415–17
Mechanics Bank of Augusta, 355, 400
Memphis and Charleston Railroad, 67, 71
Mercer, Hugh W., 230
Mercer University, 439
Metropolitan Hotel (Washington), 566
Milledgeville, Ga., 310, 312
Milledgeville arsenal, 168
Milledgeville convention (1861), 159, 160
Milledgeville Manufacturing Company, 351
Miller, Andrew J.: as Whig leader, 7; debates with Brown, 9; on slavery resolutions, 9; proposes "Woman Bill," 10
Miller, Homer V. W., 433; and Senate seat, 423, 443, 448, 565–66
Miller, John F., 548
Mills, Roger Q., 573
Mirror (Fort Valley): defends "triumvirate," 519–20
Missionary Ridge, battle of, 259
Mississippi secession, 127
Mitchell heirs case, 467, 470–74, 499
Mitchell, John H., 470
Mitchell, Samuel, 469
Monetary policy, 569–70
Monticello, 130
Moore, Albert B., 124n, 126
Moore, Henry, 390–91
Morgan, E. D., 130, 131
Morgan, John H., 291, 292, 301
Morgan County "Clique," 413
Morning News (Savannah), 120; and campaign of 1857, p. 29; on Brown's resignation, 454
Morrill Act, 536
Morrill, Ellen A., 574
Morrill, William C., 574: and lease of Western and Atlantic, 453; interest in Dade Coal Company, 506
Morse, Nathan S., 284, 390

Nash Hotel (Clarksville), 5
Nashville, 185
Nashville and Chattanooga Railroad, 67, 71, 107, 451, 477, 507, 508; as a supply line, 230, 292
Nathans, Elizabeth S., 393
National Democrats, 414, 415
National Hotel (Atlanta), 377
National Hotel (Washington), 566
National Union convention (1866), 363
National Union Republican convention (1868), 418–20
Negro legislators, 428, 442
Negro preachers, 10
Negro soldiers, 220
Negroes: treatment of, 434
Newcomb, Victor: railroad interests of, 508; and Gordon-Brown deal, 515, 516, 517; attempts to control Western and Atlantic Company, 532
New Era (Atlanta), 388, 413, 446, 459; defends Brown, 371; and Martin charge, 429
New Orleans, battle of, 2
News (Atlanta), 484
News (Albany), 483, 519
News (Augusta), 518
News (Griffin), 467
News (Savannah): on Brown and the banks, 45, 49; supports Brown, 162; on Opposition convention (1859), 87; on selection of delegates, 97
Nicholls, John C., 468–69
Nisbet, Eugenius A., 105, 164, 170, 342; views on convention, 104; supports Douglas, 107; and secession, 127; in 1861 campaign, 160, 162
Nisbet, James T., 61
Noble Brothers and Company, 189
Northrop, L. B., 190
Norwood, Thomas M., 491, 523; opposes Brown, 221–22; and governorship, 525
Nunnally, A. D., 465

O'Connor, Charles, 476, 477
Oglethorp Infantry, 407
Opposition party, 86, 87
Overby, Basil H., 14

Panther Creek, Ga., 2
Pardoning power, 51, 52
Parrott, Josiah R., 331, 404; in 1867 convention, 394
Patterson, Andrew, 2
Patterson, David, 331, 340, 368, 365
Patton, Robert W., 381, 388
Peace movement in Georgia, 265–66, 271–72, 273–74, 275, 278, 282, 308, 314, 315
Phillips, George D., 55, 464, 465
Phillips, R. W., 466
Phillips, William, 141, 208, 378, 417; Brown urges commission for, 152, 153; commands legion, 155
Pickens, Francis, 119
Pierce, Franklin, 13, 30, 113
Pike, Zebulon M., 242
Pikes: manufacture of, 186; Brown defends use of, 242
Pillow, Gideon, 246
Pittman, D. E., 472, 472n
Pittman, W. H., 514
Pittman Building (Atlanta), 574
Plant, I. C., 357
Polk, James K., 30
Polk, Leonidas, 185
Polk County, 83
Pope, John, 434; and Georgia reconstruction, 377, 381, 391, 394, 395, 399–400, 413–14
Pope, John D., 359; and Mitchell heirs case, 467, 471, 472, 472n
Pope, Wiley, 54
Porter, Horace, 444, 445
Porter, Reese, 1
Porter, Violet Mackey, 1
Powell, Robert J., 471, 472, 473
Price, W. P., 525
Printup, Daniel S.: and Choice case, 93; on selection of delegates, 99; proposes to raise troops, 145

Radical party: takes control of Congress, 362
Railroads: state aid to, 507; regulations of, 507, 561, 567–68
Ramsey, James M., 138
Randolph, George W., secretary of war, 193, 195, 196, 207, 209; and deserters, 212
Raoul, William C., 562
Reagan bill, 568

Reconstruction acts, 377
Reconstruction sentiment in wartime: opposed by Brown, 249
Record (Savannah): attacks Brown and Gordon, 510, 518
Reed, J. P., 3
Reese, Anderson, 54
Reese, Augustus: in campaign of 1868, 410, 411; and Western and Atlantic investigation, 465
Regular Democrats (1852), 13
Reporter (LaGrange): and Martin charge, 428
Reporter (Quitman): defends "triumvirate," 519–520
Republican (Americus): attacks "triumvirate," 518
Republican (Savannah): and 1857 campaign, 38; criticizes Brown, 74, 75, 80–81; continues opposition to Brown (1859), 84; on Brown's 1859 inauguration, 90; praises Brown's handling of Choice case, 94
Rice, Dangerfield, 2, 2n
Rice, Margaret Looney, 2
Rice, Wilson, 459
Riley, "General" Harrison W.: and upcountry opposition, 135
Rising Fawn Company, 506
Roberts, J. E., 23
Rockwell, Charles F., 395
Rome "Regency," 56, 77
Rosecrans, William S., 230, 241, 247
Rowland, John S., 106; and Western and Atlantic, 165, 231
Ruger, Thomas H., 395
Russell, Phillip, 281

Safford, Thomas P., 96n, 98, 402
Salt, 191, 192, 224, 231–32
Sanford, John W. A., 126
Savannah, Albany and Gulf Railroad, 67
Schofield, John M., 328, 415
Schurz, Carl, 475
Scott, Dunlap, 450
Scott, Thomas A.: and lease of Western and Atlantic, 451; railroad interests of, 477; and Bullock employment, 497, 500; and Texas and Pacific, 498; and Blodgett employment, 498

Scott, Winfield, 13
Scott, Zerega and Company (N.Y.), 400
Seago, A. K., 191, 456, 464
Seago-Blodgett-Dobbins Company, 452, 455, 464
Seaver, Jacob W., 506, 572
Secessionist convention (Georgia), 120–21, 127–28
Secessionist meeting (Atlanta), 119
Seddon, James A., 244, 245, 258; calls for troops, 248, 262; and Georgia Home Guard, 250–51, 263; refuses to furlough Georgia legislators, 265; on conscription, 285; and Georgia militia, 301–306
Semmes, Paul J., 124, 141
Seward, James L., 238
Seward, William H., 340, 381
Seymour, Horatio, 426
Sharp Rifle Manufacturing Company, 134
Sherman, John, 381
Sherman, William T., 253, 318, 323, 325, 326; invades north Georgia, 289–90, 290–92, 308; peace overtures of, 295–99; orders evacuation of Atlanta, 309; and seizure of Georgia Capital, 309–310, 311; on toward the sea, 311
Sherman Act, 554
Shiloh, battle of, 194
Shorter, John Gill, 126
Silver question, 551–54, 569
Slavery resolutions on, 8
Smith, B. M., 82
Smith, Gustavus W.: appointed to command Georgia troops, 290; with troops, 302, 310, 313, 314
Smith, Hoke, 573
Smith, James A., 99
Smith, James M., 462, 561
Smith, Joseph, 550
Smith, J. Condit, 357
Smith, J. G., 259
Smith, J. Henley, 460, 461
Smith, Milton H., 560–61
Smith, Sumner J.: and 1857 election, 22, 23; as assistant quartermaster, 134
Snead, Thomas L., 480
Sons of Temperance, 10, 14

South Carolina secession, 117
South Western Railroad, 67, 107, 458
Southern Banner (Athens): and
election of 1859, p. 77; on election of
delegates, 98, 99, 100; praises Cobb,
101; on Brown's election (1880),
531
Southern Confederacy (Atlanta): and
election of 1861, p. 159
Southern Democrat (Carrolton): and
1857 campaign, 36
Southern Express Company, 407, 453
Southern Federal Union (Milledgeville): commends Brown, 133; supports Brown (1861), 161, 162; and
election of 1861, pp. 159, 160
Southern governors conference, 298
Southern Recorder (Milledgeville),
251
Southerner (Rome), 34
Spullock, James M., 53, 63, 64, 68, 74;
and Western and Atlantic, 43, 54,
56; opposes Brown, 59, 60; as federal
marshal, 77, 78; and 1860 election,
98, 99
Standard (Cassville), 26: and 1857
campaign, 33–34; on Western and
Atlantic appointments, 59; is critical
of Brown, 72
Stanton, Edwin M., 328, 329, 331
Stanton House (Chattanooga), 575
Star (Griffin), 371, 476
Star (Covington), 518
Stay law, enactment of, 356
Steedman, James B., 338, 339
Steele, J. H., 76
Stephens, Alexander H., 6, 22, 62, 78,
80, 86, 105, 138, 153–64 *passim*,
185, 189, 210, 236, 246, 248, 259,
260, 278, 279, 281, 283, 324, 331,
351, 378, 388, 390, 433, 438, 442,
443, 460, 461, 493, 498, 528,
531, 537, 559; and Constitutional
Union party, 13; in campaign of
1853, p. 13; in election of 1857, pp.
25, 32, 34; congratulates Brown on
victory, 41; and Western and Atlantic agents, 58; and Kansas
question, 66; decides to retire from
Congress, 79; and rumors of presidential support, 79; and 1860 convention, 95–102 *passim*; views on

convention, 104; supports Douglas,
107; addresses legislature on secession, 113–14; opposes immediate
secession, 127; and coastal defense,
144; and election of 1861, pp. 157,
158; relations with Davis, 209; and
"peace movement", 265–66, 274–81
passim, 299; defends views, 280; on
Brown's speech, 280; and Sherman's
peace overtures, 297–98; observations on Brown's release from
prison, 335–36; and governorship
(1865), 344; elected to Senate, 349;
as delegate to National Union convention, 363; and Brown's stand on
reconstruction, 373–75; and Ashburn case, 416–17; and Senate seat,
423, 431; views on Grant's administration, 430, 431; on Hill's change
of position, 448; and lease of
Western and Atlantic, 451, 456,
457; refuses to sell *Sun*, 465; continues to denounce lease, 465; commends Brown on Senate speech, 523;
and election of 1880, p. 524; and
governorship, 558; death of, 558
Stephens, Linton, 62, 80, 106, 187, 280,
283; and 1857 election, 24, 25;
presents portrait of brother, 79;
sends wine to governor, 84; and 1860
convention, 98; and 1861 election,
157; defends Brown, 222; and governorship, 237, 238; and "peace
movement," 265–66, 274, 278–79,
282, 308, 309; and habeas corpus,
274; works for brother's release from
prison, 339; and election of governor
(1865), 344; as delegate to National Union convention, 363; views
debtor relief, 402, 403; views
Brown's reconstruction policy, 403;
and Hill's change of position, 448;
denounces lease of Western and
Atlantic, 456, 457–58; urges Brown
to return to party, 462–63
Stevens, Thaddeus, 421, 445
Stewart, James D., 524
Stiles, William H., 22, 61
Stone Mountain, 410
Stone River, battle of, 230
Stovall, Marcellus, 167, 168
Sumner, Charles, 424

Sun (Atlanta), 460
Sun (Columbus), 393, 476–77
Swayne, Wagoner, 395

Tallulah Falls, 5
Tariff, 554–57
Tax in kind, 257
Taylor, Richard, 314
Taylor, Zachary, 7
Telegraph (Macon): analyzes Stephens' speech, 283; disapproves of convention of states, 309; supports President Johnson, 336
Telegraph and Messenger (Macon), 563
Temple, M. S., 232
Temperance Crusade, 32
Temperance party, 14
Tennessee Car Company, 499
Tennessee River, 182
Terry, Alfred H., 440, 441, 442, 443
Test oath, 440, 442
Texas and Pacific Railroad, 477, 564; Blodgett seeks to be lobbyist for, 497–98; seeks aid from Congress, 494
Thirteenth Amendment, 346–47
Thomas, George, 330, 338
Thomas, James, 60, 99
Thomas, John, 222
Thomas, Thomas W., 80, 139; and Democratic convention of 1857, pp. 20, 21, 34, 57; and Kansas, 21, 22; favored by Brown, 60; and election of 1861, p. 164; and distilleries, 189; and decision on conscription, 217, 219
Thompson, George H., 138
Thompson, Mildred, 393, 420
Thweatt, Jonas, 281
Thweatt, Peterson, 238, 378, 443
Tift, Nelson, 435
Tilden, Samuel J., 486, 489
Tilden "Victory Celebration" (Atlanta), 490
Times (Columbus), 50
Times (Dalton), 61
Times (Thomasville), 520
Toombs, Gabriel, 345–46
Toombs, Robert, 6, 21, 22, 66, 77, 80, 86, 134, 138, 155, 278, 280, 282, 324, 342, 406, 424, 432, 461, 463,

499, 528, 530, 576; and Constitutional Union party, 13; and election of 1855, p. 14; and campaign of 1857, pp. 25, 26, 32, 41; and Western and Atlantic agents, 57, 58; on convention of 1860, pp. 95, 104; supports Breckinridge, 107; addresses legislature on secession, 113; urges immediate secession, 120, 121, 127; reports to Walker, 137; confers with Brown, 137; and Confederate Senate seat, 180, 181, 258; denounces Brown's financial recommendations, 217; is suggested for governor, 237, 238; and Sherman's peace overtures, 297; with state reserves, 302; in exile, 345–46; denounces Brown and the Johnsons, 345, 422; and 1868 presidential campaign, 426, 427; at "Bush Arbor" meeting, 422; rejoices over Brown's defeat for Senate, 423–24; on organization of Bullock legislature, 442–43; denounces lease of Western and Atlantic, 456; as counsel for Seago group, 458; as attorney for Western and Atlantic investigation, 463, 465, 466–67; and Mitchell heirs case, 467, 470, 477; and threatened "duel" with Brown, 467–70; and presidential election of 1872, pp. 475, 476; supports Lawton for Senate, 524, 525; in 1877 constitutional convention, 507; opposes Brown's gift to University of Georgia, 559; receives two votes for senator, 566
Toombs, Mrs. Robert, 266
Towns, George W., governor's message of, 7–8; issues call for convention, 42
Trammell, Leander N., 229, 489; and 1857 campaign, 22, 23; is chosen president of state senate, 461; and railroad commission, 561
Tredegar Iron Works, 134
Tribune (N.Y.), 375–76, 475
Trice, Thomas C., 156
"Triumvirate" (Colquitt-Gordon-Brown), 518–20
Trout House (Atlanta), 93
True Democrat (Augusta), 121

True Georgian (Atlanta), 459, 479
Tucker, H. H., 439
Tucker, John A., 74
Turner, Henry M., 389, 393
Tyler, John, 35

Underwood, John W. H., 77, 78; and
1857 convention, 24; as speaker of
Georgia house, 57, 70; relations
with Brown, 57; and election of
1859, pp. 78, 79; and 1860 Georgia
convention, 95; suggested for governor, 157
Union Bank (Augusta), 355
Utah Territory, 549–51

Vance, Z. B., 316–17
Vicksburg, 224
Virginia and Tennessee Railroad, 231

Wadley, William M., 532, 560
Waitzfelder, Ezekeil, 351, 354, 451,
467, 470, 474
Waitzfelder, Leopold, 281, 333
Waitzfelder, Solomon, 281
Waldo, William, Jr., 133n
Walker, Dawson A., 378, 546; visits
Washington, 364; disability of, 404;
and 1868 election, 406, 408
Walker, Leroy Pope, 139, 206, 207;
on supplying troops, 136–43 *passim*
Walker, Robert J., 20–21, 26–37
passim
Walker, William H. T., 134, 141, 152
Walker Coal and Iron Company, 506,
574
Wallace, Campbell, 417
Walsh, Patrick, 524
Walters, Walter T., 497, 500–503
Ward, John E., 30, 65, 76; and 1857
convention, 25; denounces Brown's
bank veto, 48–49; as president of
Georgia senate, 60–61, 70; is appointed minister to China, 61; and
relations with Brown, 61
Warner, Hiram, 30, 61, 80, 99, 315,
378, 436, 454, 504; and convention
of 1857, pp. 22, 23; views conventions, 104; is delegate to Baltimore,
105; supports Douglas, 107; in
White v *Clements* decision, 437

Watkins, William, 191
Wayne, Henry C., 123, 126, 142, 184,
238, 289, 290
Waynes, James M., 365
Webb, Calvin, 93
Weil, Samuel, 25
Wellborn, C. B., 211
Western and Atlantic Company, 453,
457, 458, 464, 496, 560–62, 574;
Bullock seeks employment with,
500–503; and "betterments," 563
Western and Atlantic Railroad, 67–68,
78, 88, 110, 134, 259; construction
of, 37; as campaign issue (1857),
37–38; report on by governor, 43;
and patronage, 53–59 *passim*, 418;
lease of proposed, 53, 74; discon-
tinuance of trains on, 58; mail ser-
vice on, 59; ordered seized by Bragg,
230; as supply line, 260; is wrecked
by Sherman, 309; under Bullock-
Blodgett management, 449; private
lease of, 450 ff.; management of
investigated, 463; lease of investi-
gated, 465
Westmoreland, James G., 388
Westmoreland, John G., 82
Wheeler, Joe, 309
Whitaker, Jared I., 157, 212
White, A. J., 452, 458, 463
White v *Clements*, 437
Whitefield, George, 535
Whiteley, Richard H., 443, 448
Whittle, L. N., 559
Wilcox County, 314–15
Wilkes Republican, 38
Williams, Charles, 134
Wilmot Proviso, 7
Wilson, James, 341, 421; moves into
Georgia, 323; and Western and
Atlantic, 324; confers with Brown,
324–28; orders surrender of Georgia
troops, 325; forbids meeting of
Georgia Assembly, 328; and Brown's
arrest, 329; continues check on
Brown, 338, 339
Windsor, T. T., 232
Winslow, General Edward, 330
Wirtz, Henry, 340–41
Wofford, William T., 168, 378, 524
Woman suffrage, 570–71
World (N.Y.), 395

Wright, Ambrose "Ranse," 390; and
    state troops, 145, 313; requests
    advice from Davis, 308
Wright, Augustus R., 15, 62, 76, 233,
    237; admits Brown to bar, 3; and

Kansas resolution, 22; and 1857
convention, 24, 28; and Western
and Atlantic, 56, 57; in Congress,
57, 79–80; and Sherman peace overtures, 296, 298, 299